BOWETT'S LAW OF INTERNATIONAL INSTITUTIONS

AUSTRALIA
LBC Information Services
Sydney

CANADA AND USA
The Carswell Company
Toronto

NEW ZEALAND
Brooker's
Auckland

SINGAPORE AND MALAYSIA
Sweet & Maxwell Asia
Singapore and Kuala Lumpur

BOWETT'S LAW OF INTERNATIONAL INSTITUTIONS

By

PHILIPPE SANDS

Professor of International Law, University of London, (School of Oriental and African Studies); Global Professor of Law, New York University; Barrister, Matrix Chambers, London

and

PIERRE KLEIN

Professor of International Law, Université Libre de Bruxelles, Belgium

LONDON
SWEET & MAXWELL
2001

First Edition 1964
Second Edition 1970
Third Edition 1975
Fourth Edition 1982
Reprinted 1990
Reprinted 1995
Fifth Edition 2001

Published in 2001 by
Sweet & Maxwell Limited of
100 Avenue Road
Swiss Cottage
London NW3 3PF

(http://www.sweetandmaxwell.co.uk)

Typeset by LBJ Typesetting Ltd of Kingsclere

Printed in Great Britain by
Clays Ltd, St Ives plc

ISBN 0–421–53690 X

ACKNOWLEDGEMENTS

The arrival of a fifth edition of this book would not have been possible without the support and assistance of a number of colleagues and friends. First and foremost I would like to thank Derek Bowett for entrusting to us the task of bringing to date this pioneering book, and having the confidence in us to do so in accordance with our own vision of a fifth edition's structure and content. My academic colleagues at London University and New York University have been constantly encouraging and supportive, in particular Matt Craven in London and Dick Stewart and Ben Kingsbury at New York, as has James Crawford in Cambridge. I am deeply grateful to NYU Law School for providing me with an environment (and funds to cover the cost of research assistance) within which to undertake and complete my part of this project, and in particular to Norman Dorsen for his collegiality over many years, and Jennifer Larmour for her unstinting administrative support. Thanks are also due to colleagues at the Foundation for International Environmental Law and in the Project on International Courts and Tribunals, in particular Louise Rands, Ruth Mackenzie and Annette Guerda-Fischer; to a number of outstanding young scholars who have been willing to work for me as research assistants in London and New York, in particular Jackie Peel and Nicolas Burniat; to Radu Popa at the NYU Law School Library, who must be every academic's dream of what a reference librarian might be; and to my doctoral students, for their insight and patience, in particular Yuval Shany. Thanks also to Jon Klein at Getty Images and I also wish to express our appreciation to everyone at Sweet & Maxwell.

Finally, the biggest "thank you" is reserved for Natalia Schiffrin, for everything.

Philippe Sands
London
March 1, 2001.

I wish first of all to express my deep gratitude to the Wiener-Anspach Foundation (Brussels) for its generous financial support, which enabled me to complete the writing of this book during a stay in Cambridge in 1999–2000. I had the opportunity to spend most of that academic year at the Lauterpracht Research Centre for International Law of the University of Cambridge, which provided me with an environment that was both enjoyable and stimulating. I wish to thank the Centre's Director, Professor James Crawford, and Deputy-Director, Mr Daniel Bethlehem, for welcoming me to the LRCIL. I am also grateful to the Law Faculty of the Université Libre de Bruxelles which, by releasing me from most of my teaching obligations for one year, allowed me to concentrate on this project. I am indebted to my colleague Olivier Corten, who accepted part of the burden which resulted from the necessary reallocation of courses, in addition to his significant workload. Finally, I would like to express my heartfelt gratitude to Johanne, for her continued support and appreciation, and for convincing me that it would be possible to spend that year in England. It proved to be a fantastic and most rewarding experience, on all counts.

Pierre Klein
Brussels
March 1, 2001.

PREFACE

It gives me great satisfaction to see the publication of this new, fifth edition, prepared by Professors Philippe Sands and Pierre Klein. So much has changed since the last edition in 1982, that it needed both enthusiasm and knowledge of a high order to up-date a general textbook on this vast, rapidly growing topic: and, happily, the two new editors possess both qualities.

When I prepared the first edition in 1962, I noted the lack of textbooks on the subject to guide the student. That position no longer holds, but the need for a clear exposition of the many, many new developments remains, for without knowledge of these any attempt to analyse the legal problems encountered in these institutions is virtually impossible. I believe the new editors have met that need.

The importance of the subject can scarcely be doubted today, although the emphasis may change. In Europe, for example, the international institutions through which the European States promote the well-being of their people have a direct impact on their lives. This has more than offset the relative decline in interest in the United Nations.

The driving-force behind the growth of these many institutions, whether global or regional, remains what it always has been: the actual need for States to co-operate through permanent, organised structures. It is not idealism. It is the practical need for co-operation in an age when communications, trade, the environment and security demand continuing, close co-operation between States.

Derek W. Bowett
Cambridge
February 2001.

CONTENTS

TABLE OF CASES—
INTERNATIONAL, EUROPEAN AND
NATIONAL

PERMANENT COURT OF INTERNATIONAL JUSTICE

INTERNATIONAL COURT OF JUSTICE

EUROPEAN COURT OF JUSTICE

EUROPEAN COURT OF HUMAN RIGHTS

NATIONAL CASES

ITALY

MALAYSIA

SWITZERLAND

THE NETHERLANDS

ABBREVIATIONS

AB	Appellate Body (WTO)
AC	Appeal Cases
ACABQ	Advisory Committee on Administrative and Budgetary Questions
A.C.C.	Administrative Committee on Co-ordination
ACCT	Agency of Cultural and Technical Co-operation
ACP	African, Caribbean and Pacific Group
AD	Annual Digest
AEC	African Economic Community
AECA	American Economic Cooperation Administration
AEM	ASEAN Economic Ministers
AfDB	African Development Bank
AfDBAT	AfDB Administrative Tribunal
AFDI	Annuaire Français de Droit International
Afr.J.Int'l & Comp.L.	African Journal of International and Comparative Law
African HR Charter	African Human Rights Charter
AFTA	ASEAN Free Trade Area
AJIL	American Journal of International Law
ALADI	Latin-American Integration Association
Am.J.Comp.L.	American Journal of Comparative Law
Am.Pol.Sci.Rev.	The American Political Science Review
Am.U.J.Int'l.L.& Pol'y	American University Journal of International Law and Politics
American HR Convention	American Convention on Human Rights
AMM	ASEAN Ministerial Meeting
AMU	Arab Maghreb Union
Ann.IDI	Annuaire de l'Institut de Droit International
ANZUS	Tripartite Pact between Australia, New Zealand and the United States
AO	Advisory Opinion
AOI	Arab Organisation for Industrialisation
APEC	Asia-Pacific Economic Co-operation
APSR	American Political Science Review
ARABSAT	Arab Satellite Telecommunication
ASC	ASEAN Standing Committee

AsDB	Asian Development Bank
AsDBAT	AsDB Administrative Tribunal
ASEAN	Association of Southeast Asian Nations
ASIL	American Society of International Law
Australian L.J.	Australian Law Journal
Austrian J. of Pub.& Int'l.L.	Austrian Journal of Public and International Law
AYIL	African Yearbook of International Law
BCEAO	Central Bank of West African States
BEAC	Bank of Central African States
Benelux	Belgium, the Netherlands and Luxembourg Economic Union
BISD	GATT Basic Instruments and Selected Documents Series
BOAD	West African Development Bank
BYIL	British Yearbook of International Law
CACM	Central American Common Market
Cal.W.Int'l.L.J.	California Western International Law Journal
Can.B.R.	Canadian Bar Review
CARICOM	Caribbean Community
CARIFTA	Caribbean Free Trade Area
Case W.Res.L.Rev.	Case Western Reserve Law Review
CAT	Convention Against Torture and Other Cruel, Inhuman or Degrading Treatment or Punishment (1984)
CCAMLR	Commission for the Conservation of Antarctic Marine Living Resources
CCFF	Compensatory and Contingency Financing Facility
CDM	Clean Development Mechanism
CEDAW	Convention on the Elimination of Discrimination Against Women
CEEAC	Central African States Economic Community
CEMAC	Central African Economic and Monetary Community
CEPT	Common Effective Preferential Tariff
CERD	International Convention on the Elimination of All Forms of Racial Discrimination
CERN	European Organisation for Nuclear Research
CFC	Common Fund for Commodities
CFI	Court of First Instance
CICAD	Inter-American Drug Abuse Control Commission
CIE	Committee of Independent Experts (European Social Charter)

CILSA	The Comparative and International Law Journal of Southern Africa
CINCHAN	Allied Commander-in-Chief Channel
CIS	Commonwealth of Independent States
CITES	Convention on International Trade in Endangered Species of Wild Fauna and Flora
CLCS	Commission on the Limits of the Continental Shelf
CLRAE	Congress of Local and Regional Authorities of Europe
Cmd.	UK Command Papers
CMC	Common Market Council
CMEA	Council for Mutual Economic Assistance
CMF	Ministerial Conference of the Francophonie
CMG	Common Market Group
C.M.L.R.	Common Market Law Report
CMLRev.	Common Market Law Review
CMS	Convention on Migratory Species (1979)
Colo.J.Int'l.Envtl.L.& Pol'y.	Colorado Journal of International Environmental Law and Policy
Colum.J.Transnat'l L.	Columbia Journal of Transnational Law
Comecon	Council for Mutual Economic Assistance
COMESA	Common Market for Eastern and Southern Africa
Cong.	Congress
COREPER	Committee of Permanent Representatives of the European Council
Cornell Int'l.L.J.	Cornell International Law Journal
CPC	Committee for Programme and Coordination (UN)
CRC	Convention on the Rights of the Child (1989)
CSCE	Conference on Security and Cooperation in Europe
CSD	UN Commission on Sustainable Development
CTBT	Comprehensive Test Ban Treaty
CTS	Consolidated Treaty Series
CWC	Chemical Weapons Convention
CYIL	Canadian Yearbook of International Law
Dec.	Decision
Denv.J.Int'l.L.& Pol'y.	Denver Journal of International Law and Policy
Dep't. St. Bull.	Department of State Bulletin
Dick.J.Int'l.L.	Dickinson Journal of International Law
doc.	document

DOMREP	Mission of the Representative of the Secretary-General in the Dominican Republic
DSB	Dispute Settlement Body
DSU	Understanding on Rules and Procedures Governing the Settlement of Disputes (WTO)
Duke J.Comp. & Int'l L.	Duke Journal of Comparative and International Law
EAC	Commission for East African Cooperation
EAPC	Euro-Atlantic Partnership Council
EBRD	European Bank for Reconstruction and Development
EC	European Community
ECA	Economic Commission for Africa
ECAFE	Economic Commission for Asia and the Far East
ECB	European Central Bank
ECE	Economic Commission for Europe
ECE	Evaluation Committee of Experts (NAFTA)
ECEA	Economic Community of East Africa
ECHR	European Convention for the Protection of Human Rights and Fundamental Freedoms (1950)
ECtHR	European Court of Human Rights
ECJ	European Court of Justice
ECLAC	Economic Commission for Latin America and the Carribean
ECOMOG	ECOWAS Cease-Fire Monitoring Group
ECOSOC	Economic & Social Council of the United Nations
ECOSOC	Economic & Social Committee of the European Union
ECOWAS	Economic Community of West African States
ECR	European Court Reports
ECSC	European Coal and Steel Community
ECU	European Currency Unit
ECWA	Economic Commission for Western Asia
EDC	European Defence Community
EEA	European Economic Area
EEC	European Economic Community
EFTA	European Free Trade Association
EHHR	European Human Rights Reports
EHR Convention	See ECHR
EJIL	European Journal of International Law

ELDO	European Organisation for the Development and Construction of Space Vehicle Launchers
Emory Int'l.L.Rev.	Emory International Law Review
EMU	European Monetary Union
ENMOD Convention	Environmental Modification Convention
EP	European Parliament
EPIL	Encyclopedia of Public International Law
EPTA	Expended Program of Technical Assistance
ESA	European Space Agency
ESAF	Enhanced Structural Adjustment Facility
ESCAP	Economic and Social Commission for Asia and the Pacific
ESOC	European Space Operations Center
ESRO	European Space Research Organisation
ESTEC	European Space research and Technology Center
ETS	European Treaty Series
E.U.	European Union
EUMETSAT	European Meteorological Satellite Organisation
Eur. Yb.	European Yearbook
EURATOM	European Atomic Energy Community
EUTELSAT	European Telecommunication Satellite Organisation
FAO	Food and Agriculture Organisation
For.Inv.L.J.	Foreign Investment Law Journal
FRY	Federal Republic of Yugoslavia
FTAA	Free Trade Area of the Americas
FTC	Free Trade Commission
G.A.	General Assembly
Ga. J.Int'l & Comp.L.	Georgia Journal of International and Comparative Law
GAB	General Agreement to Borrow
GAOR	General Assembly Official Report
GATS	General Agreement on Trade in Services
GATT	General Agreement on Tariffs and Trade
GCC	Gulf Cooperation Council
GEF	Global Environment Facility
Geo. L.J.	Georgetown Law Journal
Geo.Wash. J. Int'l L.& Econ.	The George Washington Journal of International Law and Economics
GNP	Gross National Product
GTC	Grains Trade Convention
GYIL	German Yearbook of International Law

Harv.Int'l L.J.	Harvard International Law Journal
HIPC	Heavily Indebted Poor Countries
Hous.J.Int'l.L.	Houston Journal of International Law
How.L.J.	Howard Law Journal
HRC	Human Right Committee
Hum.Rts.Q.	Human Rights Quarterly
IACHR	Inter-American Court of Human Rights
IADB	Inter-American Development Bank
IADBAT	IADB Administrative Tribunal
IAEA	International Atomic Energy Agency
IA-ECOSOC	Inter-American Economic and Social Council
IBRD	International Bank for Reconstruction and Development
ICAC	International Cotton Advisory Committee
ICAO	International Civil Aviation Organisation
ICC	International Criminal Court
ICCO	International Cocoa Organisation
ICCPR	International Covenant on Civil and Political Rights
I.C.J.	International Court of Justice
I.C.J. Rep.	Reports of Judgments and Advisory Opinions of the International Court of Justice
ICLQ	International and Comparative Law Quarterly
ICO	International Coffee Organisation
ICOs	International Commodity Organisations
ICSID	International Centre for the Settlement of Investment Disputes
ICTR	International Criminal Tribunal for Rwanda
ICTY	International Criminal Tribunal for the Former Yugoslavia
IDA	International Development Association
IDB	Inter-American Defensive Board
IDB	International Development Bank
IEA	International Energy Agency
IEL MT	International Environment Legal Materials and Treaties
IFAD	International Fund for Agricultural Development
IFC	International Finance Corporation
IFOR	NATO Implementation Force in Bosnia and Herzegovina
IGA	International Grains Agreement
IGC	International Grains Council
IGO	International Governmental Organization
IIC	Inter-American Investment Corporation

IJIL	Indian Journal of International Law
IJRL	International Journal of Refugee Law
ILM	International Legal Materials
ILO	International Labour Organisation
ILOAT	ILO Administrative Tribunal
ILR	International Law Reports
IMCO	International Maritime Consultative Organisation
IMF	International Monetary Fund
IMFAT	IMF Administrative Tribunal
IMO	International Maritime Organisation
Ind.J.Global Legal Stud.	Indiana Journal of Global Legal Studies
INFCIRC	IAEA-Democratic People's Republic of Korea Safeguards Agreement
INMARSAT	International Maritime Satellite Organisation
INRO	International Natural Rubber Organisation
INSTRAW	International Research and Training Institute for the Advacement of Women
Int.J.Mar.&Coastal L.	International Journal of Maritime and Coastal Law
Int'l Conc.	International Conciliation
Int'l J.Legal Info.	International Journal of Legal Information
Int'l Labour Rev.	International Labour Review
Int'l Law.	International Lawyer
Int'l Org.	International Organisations
Int'l Rel.	International Relations
Int'l Rev. of the Red Cross	International Review of the Red Cross
INTELSAT	International Telecommunications Satellite Organisation
IOOC	International Olive Oil Council
IOPC Fund	International Oil Pollution Compensation Fund
IOPCW	International Organisation for the Prohibition of Chemical Weapons
IPCC	International Panel on Climate Change
IRO	International Refugee Organisation
ISBA	International Sea-Bed Authority
ITC	International Tin Council
ITLOS	International Tribunal for the Law of the Sea
ITO	International Trade Organization
ITTO	International Tropical Timber Organisation
ITU	International Telecommunication Union
ItYIL	Italian Yearbook of International Law
IWC	International Whaling Commission

J. Space L.	Journal of Space Law
JDI	Journal du Droit International
JWTL	Journal of World Trade Law
LAFTA	Latin-American Free Trade Association
LDC	London Dumping Convention (1972)
LJIL	Leiden Journal of International Law
LNTS	League of Nations Treaty Series
LoN	League of Nations
LoNAT	League of Nations Administrative Tribunal
Loy.L.A. Int'l & Comp.L.Rev.	Loyola of Los Angeles International and Comparative Law Review
LQR	The Law Quarterly Review
MARPOL	1973 International Convention for the Prevention of Pollution of the Sea from Ships
Max Planck Y.U.N.L.	Max Planck Yearbook of United Nations Law
MEPs	Members of the European Parliament
MERCOSUR	Southern Cone Common Market
Mich.J.Int'l L.	Michigan Journal of International Law
Mich.L.Rev.	Michigan Law Review
MIF	Multilateral Investment Fund
MIGA	Multilateral Investment Guarantee Agency
MINUGUA	United Nations Verification Mission in Guatemala
MINURCA	United Nations Mission in the Central African Republic
MINURSO	United Nations Mission for the Referendum in Western Sahara
MIPONUH	United Nations Civilian Police Mission in Haiti
Misc.	Miscellaneous
MONUA	United Nations Observer Mission in Angola
MONUC	United Nations Organisation Mission in the Democratic Republic of the Congo
NAB	New Agreement to Borrow
NAFTA	North American Free Trade Agreement
NAOs	National Administrative Offices (NAFTA)
NATO	North Atlantic Treaty Organisation
NEA	Nuclear Energy Agency
NGO	non-governmental organisation
NILR	Netherlands International Law Review
Nordic JIL	Nordic Journal of International Law
NPT	Treaty on the Non-Proliferation of Nuclear Weapons

Nw.J.Int'l L.& Bus.	Northwestern Journal of International Law and Business
NYIL	Netherlands Yearbook of International Law
N.Y.L.Sch.J.Int'l & Comp.L.	New York Law School Journal of International and Comparative Law
N.Y.U. J.Int'l L.& Pol.	New York University Journal of International Law and Politics
NZLJ	New Zealand Law Journal
OAS	Organisation of American States
OASAT	OAS Administrative Tribunal
OASTS	OAS Treaty Series
OAU	Organisation of African Unity
OCT	Overseas Country and Territory (EC)
ODECA	Organisation of Central American States
OECD	Organisation for Economic Co-operation & Development
OECDAT	OECD Administrative Tribunal
OEEC	Organisation for European Economic Co-operation
OERS	See ESRO
Off. Rec.	Official Record
OJ(EC)	Official Journal of the European Communities
OJLN	Official Journal of the League of Nations
ONUC	United Nations Operation in the Congo
ONUCA	United Nations Observer Group in Central America
ONUMOZ	United Nations Operation in Mozambique
ONUSAL	United Nations Observer Mission in El Salvador
ONUVEH	United Nations Observer Group for the Verification of the Elections in Haiti
ONUVEN	United Nations Observer Mission for the Verification of the Elections in Nicaragua
OPCW	Organisation for the Prohibition of Chemical Weapons
OPEC	Organisation of the Petroleum Exporting Countries
Osaka U. Law Rev.	Osaka University Law Review
OSCE	Organisation on Security and Cooperation in Europe
O.J.L.S.	Oxford Journal of Legal Studies
PARLACEN	Central American Parliament
PCA	Permanent Court of Arbitration
P.C.I.J.	Permanent Court of International Justice
PCOB	Permanent Central Opium Board

PEP	Political and Economic Planning
Philippine L.	Philippine Law
PLA	Palestinian Liberation Army
Plen. Mtgs	Plenary Meetings
PLO	Palestinian Liberation Organisation
PRC	People's Republic of China
Proc. ASIL	Proceedings of the American Society of International Law
PTA	Preferential Trade Area for East and Southern Africa
PYIL	Polish Yearbook of International Law
RADIC	Revue Africaine de Droit International et Comparé (See Afr. J.Int'l L.& Comp. L.)
RBDI	Revue Belge de Droit International
RCADI	Recueil des Cours de l'Académie de Droit International
RDI	Revue de Droit International
RECIEL	Review of European Community and International Environmental Law
REDI	Revue égyptienne de droit international
Res.	Resolution
RGDIP	Revue Générale de Droit International Public
RIIA Survey	Survey of the Royal Institute for International Affairs
RMC	Revue du Marché Commun
RPF	Rwandese Patriotic Front
SAARC	South Asian Association for Regional Co-operation
SACEUR	Supreme Allied Commander in Europe
SACLANT	Supreme Allied Commander Atlantic
SADCC	Southern African Development Coordination Conference
SADR	Sahrawi Arab Democratic Republic
SAFTA	SAARC Preferential Trading Agreement
SAYIL	South-African Yearbook of International Law
SBDC	Sea-Bed Disputes Chamber
SC	Security Council
SDR	Special Drawing Rights
SEATO	South-East Asian Treaty Organisation
SELA	Latin-American Economic System
Ser.	Série
Sess.	Session
SFDI	Société Française pour le Droit International
SFOR	NATO Stabilisation Force in Bosnia and Herzegovina

SG	Secretary-General
SHAPE	Supreme Headquarters of the Allied Powers in Europe
SICA	Central American Integration System
SOFA	Status of Force Agreement
SOM	Senior Officials Meeting (APEC)
Soviet YbIL	Soviet Yearbook of International Law
SPREP	South Pacific Regional Environment Programme
SRF	Supplemental Reserve Facility
STABEX	Système de stabilisation des recettes d'exportation
STF	Systemic Transformation Facility
Supp.	Supplement
SWAPO	South West African People's Organisation
SYSMIN	Système d'aide aux produits miniers
TAB	Technical Assistance Board
TAC	Technical Assistance Committee
TEU	Treaty on the European Union
TPRB	Trade Policy Review Board (WTO)
TPRM	Trade Policy Review Mechanism (WTO)
Trans. Grotius Soc.	Transactions of the Grotius Society
Transnat'l.L.&Contemp. Probs	Transnational Law and Contemporary Problems
TRIPS	Agreement on Trade-Related Aspects of Intellectual Property Rights
U. Ill. L.R.	University of Illinois Law Review
U.Pen.L.R.	University of Pennsylvania Law Review
U.Rich.L.Rev.	University of Richmond Law review
UAR	United Arab Republic
UDEAC	Central African Economic and Customs Union
UDHR	Universal Declaration of Human Rights
UEMOA	West African Economic and Monetary Union
UK	United Kingdom
UMOA	West African Monetary Union
UN	United Nations
UNAMIC	United Nations Advanced Mission in Cambodia
UNAMIR	United Nations Assistance Mission in Rwanda
UNAMSIL	United Nations Mission in Sierra Leone
UNASOG	United Nations Aouzou Strip Observer Group
UNAT	United Nations Administrative Tribunal
UNAVEM	United Nations Angola Verification Mission
UNCDF	United Nations Capital Development Fund

UNCIO	United Nations Conference on International Organisation
UNCITRAL	United Nations Commission on International Trade Law
UNCLOS	United Nations Convention on the Law of the Sea
UNCOK	United Nations Commission on Korea
UNCRO	United Nations Confidence Restoration Operation in Croatia
UNCTAD	United Nations Conference on Trade and Development
UNDCP	United Nations International Drug Control Programme
UNDOF	United Nations Disengagement Observer Force
UNDP	United Nations Development Programme
UNEF	United Nations Emergency Force
UNEP	United Nations Environment Programme
UNFICYP	United Nations Force in Cyprus
UNGA	United Nations General Assembly
UNGOMAP	United Nations Good Offices Mission in Afghanistan and Pakistan
UNHCR	United Nations High Commissioner for Refugees
UNICEF	United Nations Children's Fund
UNICRI	United Nations Interregional Crime and Justice Research Institute
UNIDIR	United Nations Institute for Disarmament Research
UNIDO	United Nations Industrial Development Organisation
UNIFEM	United Nations Development Fund for Women
UNIFIL	United Nations Interim Force in Lebanon
UNIIMOG	United Nations Iran and Iraq Military Observer Group
UNIKOM	United Nations Iraq-Kuwait Observation Mission
UNIPEDE	International Union of Producers and Distributors of Electrical Energy
UNIPOM	United Nations India-Pakistan Observation Mission
UNITAR	United Nations Institute for Training and Research
UNJY	United Nations Juridical Yearbook

UNMIBH	United Nations Mission in Bosnia and Herzegovina
UNMIH	United Nations Mission in Haiti
UNMIK	United Nations Interim Administration in Kosovo
UNMOGIP	United Nations Military Observer Group in India and Pakistan
UNMOP	United Nations Mission of Observers in Prevlaka
UNMOT	United Nations Mission of Observers in Tajikistan
UNMOVIC	United Nations Monitoring, Verification and Inspection Commission
UNOGIL	United Nations Observer Group in Lebanon
UNOMIG	United Nations Observation Mission in Georgia
UNOMIL	United Nations Observation Mission in Liberia
UNOMOZ	United Nations Operation in Mozambique
UNOMSA	United Nations Observation Mission in South Africa
UNOMSIL	United Nations Mission of Observers in Sierra Leone
UNOMUR	United Nations Observer Mission Uganda-Rwanda
UNOSOM	United Nations Operation in Somalia
UNOVER	United Nations Observer Mission to Verify the Referendum in Eritrea
UNPREDEP	United Nations Preventive Deployment Force
UNPROFOR	United Nations Protection Force
UNPSG	United Nations Civilian Police Support Group
UNRRA	United Nations Relief and Rehabilitation Administration
UNRWA	United Nations Relief and Work Agency for Palestine Refugees in the Near East
UNSCEAR	United Nations Scientific Committee on the Effects of Atomic Radiation
UNSCOM	United Nations Special Commission to oversee elimination of Iraq's Weapons of mass destruction and production facilities
UNSF	United Nations Security Force in West New Guinea (West Irian)
UNSMIH	United Nations Support Mission for Haiti
UNSSOD	United Nations Special Session on Disarmament

UNTAC	United Nations Transitional Authority in Cambodia
UNTAES	United Nations Transitional Administration for Eastern Slavonia, Baranja and Western Sirmuim
UNTAET	United Nations Transitional Administration in East Timor
UNTAG	United Nations Transition Assistance Group
UNTMIH	United Nations Transition Mission in Haiti
UNTS	United Nations Treaty Series
UNTSO	United Nations Truce Supervision Organisation
UNYB	United Nations Yearbook
UNYOM	United Nations Yemen Observation Mission
UPU	Universal Postal Union
U.S.	United States of America
USSR	Union of Soviet Socialist Republics
Va.J.Int'l .L	Virginia Journal of International Law
Vand.J.Transnat'l L.	Vanderbilt Journal of Transnational Law
VAT	value added tax
WBAT Reports	World Bank Administrative Tribunal Reports
WEU	Western European Union
WFP	World Food Programme
WHO	World Health Agency
WIPO	World Intellectual Property Organisation
WMO	World Meteorological Organisation
WTO	World Trade Organisation
WW	World War
WWW	World Weather Watch Programme
Yale J. of World Pub. Ord.	Yale Journal of World Public Order
Yale J.Int'l.L.	Yale Journal of International Law
Yale L.J.	Yale Law Journal
Yb ICJ	Yearbook of the International Court of Justice
YbWA	Yearbook of World Affairs
YEL	Yearbook of European Law
YILC	Yearbook of the International Law Commission
YUN	Yearbook of the United Nations
Z.a.ö.r.V.	Zeitschrift fur auslandisches offentliches Recht und Volkerrecht

THE UNITED NATIONS SYSTEM

The UNITED NATIONS system

UNITED NATIONS

PRINCIPAL ORGANS OF THE UNITED NATIONS

INTERNATIONAL COURT OF JUSTICE	SECURITY COUNCIL	GENERAL ASSEMBLY	ECONOMIC AND SOCIAL COUNCIL	TRUSTEESHIP COUNCIL	SECRETARIAT

SECURITY COUNCIL

- Military Staff Committee
- Standing Committee and ad hoc bodies
- International Criminal Tribunal for the Former Yugoslavia
- International Criminal Tribunal for Rwanda
- UN Monitoring, Verification and Inspection Commission (Iraq)
- Peacekeeping Operations and Missions

GENERAL ASSEMBLY

- Main committees
- Other sessional committees
- Standing committees and ad hoc bodies
- Other subsidiary organs

PROGRAMMES AND FUNDS

UNCTAD United Nations Conference on Trade and Development
  - **ITC** International Trade Centre (UNCTAD/WTO)

UNDCP United Nations Drug Control Programme

UNEP United Nations Environment Programme

UNDP United Nations Development Programme
  - **UNIFEM** United Nations Development Fund for Women
  - **UNV** United Nations Volunteers

UNFPA United Nations Population Fund

UNHCR Office of the United Nations High Commissioner for Refugees

UNICEF United Nations Children's Fund

WFP World Food Programme

UNRWA United Nations Relief and Works Agency for Palestine Refugees in the Near East

UNU United Nations University

OTHER UN ENTITIES

OHCHR Office of the United Nations High Commissioner for Human Rights

UNCHS United Nations Centre for Human Settlements (Habitat)

UNOPS United Nations Office for Project Services

RESEARCH AND TRAINING INSTITUTES

INSTRAW International Research and Training Institute for the Advancement of Women

UNICRI United Nations Interregional Crime and Justice Research Institute

UNITAR United Nations Institute for Training and Research

UNRISD United Nations Research Institute for Social Development

UNIDIR ** United Nations Institute for Disarmament Research

ECONOMIC AND SOCIAL COUNCIL

FUNCTIONAL COMMISSIONS

- Commission for Social Development
- Commission on Human Rights
- Commission on Narcotic Drugs
- Commission on Crime Prevention and Criminal Justice
- Commission on Science and Technology for Development
- Commission on Sustainable Development
- Commission on the Status of Women
- Commission on Population and Development
- Statistical Commission

REGIONAL COMMISSIONS

- Economic Commission for Africa (ECA)
- Economic Commission for Europe (ECE)
- Economic Commission for Latin America and the Caribbean (ECLAC)
- Economic and Social Commission for Asia and the Pacific (ESCAP)
- Economic and Social Commission for Western Asia (ESCWA)
- Sessional and Standing Committees
- Expert, ad hoc and related bodies

RELATED ORGANIZATIONS

IAEA International Atomic Energy Agency

WTO World Trade Organization

SPECIALIZED AGENCIES *

ILO International Labour Organization

FAO Food and Agriculture Organization of the United Nations

UNESCO United Nations Educational, Scientific and Cultural Organization

WHO World Health Organization

WORLD BANK GROUP
  - **IBRD** International Bank for Reconstruction and Development
  - **IDA** International Development Association
  - **IFC** International Finance Corporation
  - **MIGA** Multilateral Investment Guarantee Agency
  - **ICSID** International Centre for Settlement of Investment Disputes

IMF International Monetary Fund

ICAO International Civil Aviation Organization

IMO International Maritime Organization

ITU International Telecommunication Union

UPU Universal Postal Union

WMO World Meteorological Organization

WIPO World Intellectual Property Organization

IFAD International Fund for Agricultural Development

UNIDO United Nations Industrial Development Organization

SECRETARIAT

OSG Office of the Secretary-General

OIOS Office of Internal Oversight Services

OLA Office of Legal Affairs

DPA Department of Political Affairs

DDA Department for Disarmament Affairs

DPKO Department of Peacekeeping Operations

OCHA Office for the Coordination of Humanitarian Affairs

DESA Department of Economic and Social Affairs

DGAACS Department of General Assembly Affairs and Conference Services

DPI Department of Public Information

DM Department of Management

OIP Office of the Iraq Programme

UNSECOORD Office of the United Nations Security Coordinator

ODCCP Office for Drug Control and Crime Prevention

UNOG UN Office at Geneva

UNOV UN Office at Vienna

UNON UN Office at Nairobi

* Autonomous organizations working with the United Nations and each other through the coordinating machinery of the Economic and Social Council.
** Report only to the General Assembly.

Published by the United Nations Department of Public Information
DPI/2079 — March 2000

CHAPTER 1

GENERAL INTRODUCTION

A. HISTORICAL SURVEY

Bibliography: Reinsch, *Public International Unions* (1911); Woolf, *International Government* (1916); Sayre, *Experiments in International Administration* (1919); Hill, *The Public International Conference* (1929); Hill, *International Administration* (1931); Eagleton, *International Government* (3rd ed., 1948), Chap. 7; Potter, *An Introduction to the Study of International Organisation* (5th ed., 1948); Leonard, *International Organisation* (1951), Chap. 2; Mangone, *A Short History of International Organisation* (1954), Chap. 3; P. Reuter, *International Institutions* (trans. 1958), Pt. III, Chap. 1; Sereni, *Le organizzazioni internazionali* (1959); Chaumont, *Les organisations internationales* (1963); Monaco, *Lezioni di organizzazione internazionale* (2 Vol., 1965), pol. 1, Chap. 1; Kirgis, *International Organisations in Their Legal Setting* (2nd ed., 1993); Colliard and Dubouis, *Institutions internationales* (10th ed., 1995); Schermers and Blokker, *International Institutional Law* (3rd ed., 1995); Amerasinghe, *Principles of the Institutional Law of International Organisations* (1996).

The development of international organisations has been, in the main, a **1–001** response to the evident need arising from international intercourse rather than to the philosophical or ideological appeal of the notion of world or global government. The growth of international intercourse, in the sense of the development of relations between different actors—both private and public, natural and legal—has been a constant feature of maturing societies; advances in the mechanics of transport and communications combined with the desire for trade and commerce have produced a degree of intercourse which ultimately called for international regulation by institutional means. Historically, such regulation has taken different forms.

The institution of the consul, an official of the state whose essential task **1–002** was to watch over the interests of the citizens of his state engaged in commerce in a foreign port, was known to the Greeks and the Romans. It survives to this day as one of the less spectacular, but important, institutions of international law. The consul was not, however, concerned with representing his state as such, and for this purpose ambassadors were used, being dispatched for the purpose of a specific negotiation. By the fifteenth century this intermittent diplomacy had been replaced in the relations of certain of the Italian states by the institution of a permanent diplomatic

1

ambassador in the capital of the receiving state; the practice of exchanging ambassadors, complete with staff and embassy premises, is now a normal (albeit not compulsory) feature of relations between states. It is not the purpose of this book to survey the development of consular and diplomatic relations[1]; suffice it to say that in these two institutions can be found the distant origins of the subsequent and more complex institutions addressed in this book.

1–003 Situations soon arose in which the essentially bilateral relationships established by diplomatic embassies or missions proved inadequate. For example, a problem would arise that concerned not two, but three or more states. Whether what was proposed was a series of negotiations or even a formal treaty, there had to be found a means for representing the interests of all the states concerned. The means was the international conference, a gathering of representatives from several states; simply diplomacy writ large.[2]

1–004 The Peace of Westphalia in 1648 emanated from such a conference,[3] as did the settlement after the Napoleonic Wars in 1815 through the Congress of Vienna[4] and, even later, the post-1918 settlement negotiated at the Paris Conference of 1919 and embodied in the Treaty of Versailles.[5] Clearly, any general post-war settlement demanded a more general participation in the negotiations than could easily be achieved via the traditional methods of diplomatic intercourse. Bilateral negotiation also proved inadequate for other problems of a general nature involving more than two states. The Congress of Berlin of 1871[6] was convened to consider the Russian repudiation of the regime for the Black Sea which had earlier been established at the Paris Conference of 1856;[7] conferences met in Berlin in 1884 and 1885 to attempt to regulate the "scramble for Africa" which was leading to commercial rivalry and political antagonism between the European Powers.[8] The Hague Conferences of 1899 and 1907 constituted an

---

[1] Eagleton, *International Government* (3rd ed., 1948), pp. 137–144; Reuter, *International Institutions* (trans. 1958), pp. 160–167.

[2] Potter, *An Introduction to the Study of International Organisation* (5th ed., 1948), pp. 115–130.

[3] 1 CTS 1 (1648); "Westphalia, Peace of (1648)", EPIL, Vol. 7, pp. 536–539.

[4] Hill, *The International Conference* (1929), pp. 98–101; Mangone, *A Short History of International Organisation* (1954), pp. 35–39; "Vienna, Congress of (1815)", EPIL, Vol. 7, pp. 522–525.

[5] 225 CTS 188 (1919); Hill, *The Public International Conference*, pp. 104–109; C. Eagleton, *International Government*, pp. 248–250; "Versailles Peace Treaty (1919)", EPIL, Vol. 4, 276–282.

[6] Mangone, *A Short History of International Organisation*, pp. 55–57.

[7] Hill, *The International Conference*, pp. 101–103; Mangone, *A Short History of International Organisation*, pp. 53–54; "Paris Peace Treaty (1856)", EPIL, Vol. 3, pp. 890–892.

[8] Mangone, *A Short History of International Organisation*, pp. 135–136; "Berlin West Africa Conference (1884/1885)", EPIL, Vol. 1, pp. 389–391.

effort to secure, on a multilateral basis, agreement on different aspects of the law relating to the conduct of warfare on land and on the sea, and on the duties of neutral states.[9] These are but a few examples of the many earlier conferences that were called to solve problems on a multilateral basis, an approach which continues to be used to this day.[10]

The Congress of Vienna of 1815 initiated the "concert system" which, for **1–005** the purposes of any study of international organisation, constituted a significant development. As sponsored by the Czar Alexander I, what was envisaged was an alliance of the victorious powers pledged to conduct diplomacy according to ethical standards, which would convene at congresses held at regular intervals (the "Holy Alliance"). Four congresses were held between 1818 and 1822[11] but the idea of regular congresses was abandoned and meetings took place as occasion required.[12] The attempt to secure regular meetings was, however, a significant recognition that the "pace" of international relations demanded some institution for regular multilateral negotiations. The "Concert of Europe" remained a quasi-institutionalised system even after the Holy Alliance had broken up, until the First World War destroyed the balance of power on which it rested (or rather confirmed its demise); the London Conferences of 1912–13, at the end of the Balkan Wars, were the last conferences or congresses convened within the framework of the "concert system."[13] The conclusion of a conference would often be accompanied by a formal treaty or convention, or, where no such binding agreement was desired or obtainable, by a memorandum or minutes of the conference.

The disadvantages of this system of ad hoc conferences were numerous. **1–006** First, for each new problem which arose a new conference had to be convened, generally upon the initiative of one of the states concerned. The necessity of convening each conference anew complicated and delayed co-operation in dealing with the problem. Secondly, the conferences were not debating forums in the same way as the later assemblies of the League of Nations and the United Nations; delegations attended very much for the

---

[9] "Hague Peace Conferences of 1899 and 1907", EPIL, Vol. 2, pp. 671–677.
[10] See, *e.g.* UN Conference on Environment and Development, Rio Declaration on Environment and Development, 31 ILM 874 (1992); UN World Conference on Human Rights, Vienna Declaration and Programme of Action, 32 ILM 1661 (1993); UN International Conference on Population and Development [Cairo], Report of International Conference on Population and Development, UN Doc. A/CONF.171/13 (1994); UN Fourth World Conference on Women [Beijing, 1995], Declaration and Platform for Action, 35 ILM 401 (1996). On the "legislative" function exercised by such conferences, see *infra*, Chap. 11.
[11] These conferences took place at Aix-la-Chapelle (1818), Troppau and Laibach (1820, 1821), and Verona (1822). Mangone, *A Short History of International Organisation* (1954), pp. 40–48. For a separate treatment of the first of these conferences, see "Aix-la-Chapelle, Congress of (1818)", EPIL, Vol. 1, pp. 94–95.
[12] Eagleton, *International Government*, p. 243.
[13] Eagleton, *International Government*, p. 245.

purposes of delivering statements of state policy and, though concessions were often made, the conferences had a rigidity which disappeared in the later "permanent" assemblies of the League and the United Nations. Thirdly, the conferences were held by invitation of the sponsoring or host state; there was no principle of membership which conferred an automatic right to representation or participation. Fourthly, the conferences adhered to the strict rule of state equality, with the consequence that all states had an equal vote and all decisions required unanimity. As will presently be shown,[14] it is now broadly accepted that there are a growing range of matters in which it is necessary to subjugate the will of the minority to that of the majority if progress is to be made: the dominance of the unanimity rule represented a serious restriction on the powers of the ad hoc conference.

1–007　However inadequate the system of ad hoc conferences was for the solution of the political problems arising from international intercourse, it was even more inadequate for the regulation of the relations between groups representing private concerns in different countries arising from their common interests. Representatives of states at these conferences frequently did not have the expertise to address technical issues in the developing areas of international trade, commerce, transport and communication. The nineteenth century saw, therefore, an impressive development of associations or unions, international in character, between groups other than governments. This was followed by similar developments between governments themselves in the administrative (rather than political) field. These developments of the private international unions and of the public international unions (the former non-governmental, the latter governmental) is briefly summarised, for they foreshadowed the development of international organisations at the intergovernmental level.

(a) PRIVATE INTERNATIONAL UNIONS

1–008　These unions or associations sprang from the realisation by non-governmental bodies, whether private individuals or corporate associations, that their interests had an international character which demanded the furtherance of those interests via a permanent international association with like bodies in other countries. The World Anti-Slavery Convention of 1840 was perhaps the first of these "private" conferences, many of which led to the establishment of some permanent machinery of association. Between 1840 and the beginning of the First World War something like 400 permanent associations or unions came into existence. The variety of interests thus organised can be seen from the following examples of unions of this kind: the International Committee of the Red Cross (1863), the

---

[14] Chapter 11, paras 11.005 *et seq.*

4

International Law Association (1873), the Institut de Droit International (1873), the International Literary and Artistic Association (1878), the International Ornithological Committee (1884), the Inter-Parliamentary Union (1889), the International Dental Federation (1900), the International Chamber of Commerce (1919).[15] So great was the growth of these private unions that in 1910 an association, the Union of International Associations, was formed to co-ordinate their activities and to lay down the conditions of membership.

These conditions are not without interest; they were (1) the possession of **1–009** a permanent organ, (2) that the association's object must be of interest to all or some nations and not one of profit, and (3) that membership should be open to individuals or groups from different countries. A glance at the latest edition of the *Yearbook of International Organisations* will give some indication of the continued proliferation of these private unions today, as well as their more modern manifestation in the form of NGOs.[16] From the constitutional standpoint these private unions had a number of interesting features. They emphasised the need for permanent, as opposed to ad hoc, association and for periodic, regular meetings. Many set up a small, permanent secretariat. Many demonstrated by their membership the artificiality of a rigid distinction between "public" and "private" unions based upon function; membership sometimes comprised states, municipal authorities, national groups and societies and private individuals. Today, bodies like the International Council of Scientific Unions, the International Union for the Conservation of Nature, the International Commission for the Scientific Exploration of the Mediterranean Sea, the International Statistical Institute, and the International Hospital Federation provide some examples of the co-operation of states and non-state actors within the same association.

The activities of these private unions underlined, in many cases, the need **1–010** for governmental and state action in many of the areas in which these private actors were active. In some cases this was brought about by treaty, and the work of the International Committee of the Red Cross in promoting the Geneva Conventions of 1864, 1906, 1929 and 1949,[17] or that

---

[15] Some of these organisations have achieved greater prominence than others. See, *e.g.* "International Law Association", EPIL, Vol. 2, pp. 1207–1208; "Institut de Droit International", EPIL, Vol. 2, pp. 997–1000; "International Chamber of Commerce", EPIL, Vol. 2, 1066–1069; "Red Cross", EPIL, Vol. 5, pp. 248–254.

[16] The book lists a total of 17,077 unique international non-governmental organisations, as compared to 1,839 intergovernmental organisations. The number of international NGOs balloons to 43,958 when one includes subsidiary and internal bodies, national organisations, religious orders and secular institutes, autonomous conference series, and currently or apparently inactive groups. *Yearbook of International Organisations* (36th ed., 1999/2000), Vol. 1B, p. 2356.

[17] 129 CTS 361 (1864); 202 CTS 144 (1906); 118 LNTS 303 (1929); 75 U.N.T.S. 31 (1949).

of the International Maritime Committee in promoting the Conventions on the Safety of Life at Sea of 1914 and 1929[18] are good illustrations of this. In other cases the success of the private unions led directly to the establishment of a public union in the same field; private activity led and state activity followed. In this sense the International Congress of Weights, Measures and Moneys in 1867 was the forerunner of the Metric Union, the International Association of the Legal Protection of Labour that of the ILO, and the International Literary and Artistic Association that of the International Bureau of Literary and Artistic Property. It is not the purpose of this book, with its emphasis on the organisations of the present day, to deal in detail with the history of the development of the private unions. Mention will be made, at a later stage, of their relationship (as non-governmental organisations) with the Economic and Social Council of the UN. This brief treatment is intended solely to indicate the manner in which the private unions anticipated the development of the public unions and to stress that the growth of international organisation came as a response to a demonstrated human need.

(b) PUBLIC INTERNATIONAL UNIONS

1–011 In those fields where co-operation between governments became imperative, there developed public international unions; these were the origins of international organisation in the administrative sphere. The transition from private to public organisations was gradual, and no generally accepted definition of the public international union has ever been reached.[19] In general, however, they were permanent associations of governments or administrations (i.e. postal or railway administrations), based upon a treaty of a multilateral rather than a bilateral type and with some definite criterion of purpose.

1–012 In the field of communications, the Congress of Vienna of 1815 established the Rhine Commission, invested with considerable powers, including standard-setting and a judicial power as a court of appeal from the local courts in each riparian state established for the purpose of implementing the Rhine Convention and its Règlements.[20] Each riparian state had one vote within the Commission, and whilst equality and unanimity were the normal rule, in certain administrative matters voting power varied with the length of the river bank of the member state. The European Commission on the Danube, established in 1856, similarly had administrative and legislative functions.[21] Its budget came from tolls levied

---

[18] 219 CTS 177 (1914); 136 LNTS 82 (1929).

[19] See Eagleton, *International Government*, pp. 177–179, and the literature there cited.

[20] 64 CTS 13 (1815); Eagleton, *International Government*, pp. 162–163; "Rhine River", EPIL, Vol. 12, pp. 310–316.

[21] 114 CTS 410 (1856); Eagleton, *International Government*, pp. 163–164; "Danube River", EPIL, Vol. 1, pp. 934–937.

on river traffic, it frequently resorted to a majority vote, and the members of the Commission enjoyed diplomatic immunities.[22] Other international commissions existed for the Elbe (1821), the Douro (1835), the Po (1849) and the Pruth (1866), though none of these compared in importance and power with the Rhine and the Danube Commissions.[23] Railways, another means of transport susceptible to international administration, gave rise to numerous international conferences and, subsequently, to more institutionalised forms of co-operation. The International Union of Railway Freight Transportation, set up in 1890, in effect abolished the complete independence of the national administrations.[24] Whilst it possessed an Administrative Bureau it had no legislative power other than via the conference of member states meeting at regular intervals. It is noteworthy that the Bureau had power to arbitrate over disputes. Other unions, dealing with various aspects of rail communications, have been established and, in the European Conference on Time Tables (1923), there assembled delegates of states, of railway and steamship administrations, and of Pullman and air companies.[25]

The advent of wireless telegraphy and postal communications similarly **1–013** brought forth problems which called for international control. In 1865 the International Telegraphic Union was established with a permanent bureau.[26] The Conference of the Union had power to set standards. In 1906 the Radiotelegraphic Union was established, modelled on the Telegraphic Union and using the same permanent bureau.[27] The Universal Postal Union, established in 1874, provided for a five-yearly congress of plenipotentiaries, a conference of delegates of administrations, and a permanent international bureau.[28] This combination of a diplomatic conference with a conference of postal administrations was not successful, and the latter ceased to meet. The conference of plenipotentiaries had power to set standards, frequently by majority vote. Moreover, in order to eliminate the need for a formal conference for any and every amendment, the practice developed whereby the Bureau would circulate proposals for amendment

---

[22] An "International Commission" with competence over the Upper Danube was established after 1919.

[23] 72 CTS 19 (1821); 85 CTS 255 (1835); 103 CTS 147 (1849); 133 CTS 365 (1866). For a discussion of these historic bodies and other minor river commissions established in the nineteenth century, see Mangone, *A Short History of International Organisation*, pp. 68–73; Reuter, *International Institutions*, p. 207. For a separate discussion of the Elbe Commission, see "Elbe River", EPIL, Vol. 2, pp. 50–52.

[24] 174 CTS 1 (1890); Eagleton, *International Government*, pp. 165–166; Woolf, *International Government*, pp. 216–219.

[25] Eagleton, *International Government*, p. 160.

[26] 130 CTS 198 (1865); Mangone, *A Short History of International Organisation*, pp. 73–77.

[27] 203 CTS 101 (1906); Eagleton, *International Government*, p. 168.

[28] 147 CTS 136 (1874); Hill, *The International Conference*, pp. 132–136; Mangone, *A Short History of International Organisation*, pp. 77–79; Woolf, *International Government* (1916), pp. 186–205; "Universal Postal Union", EPIL, Vol. 5, pp. 383–386.

by post and, depending on the amendment, a notification of acceptance by either two-thirds or a simple majority would make the amendment binding on all members; this was a marked departure from the requirement of specific consent in the traditional "political" conference of states, as expressed in the taking of decisions by unanimity. The postal administrations of colonies and dependencies acquired separate representation and, in the case of the British Empire, did not always vote with the colonial power. The financing of the permanent bureau was by a technique, now common, of dividing members into seven classes and varying the contribution according to the class.

1–014   In the field of health, since disease did not respect national boundaries, much began to be addressed by international co-operation. After a number of conferences, sanitary councils on which several states were represented were set up at Constantinople, Tangiers, Teheran and Alexandria. The last, with a staff of 87 international health officers, regulated shipping and enforced quarantine regulations, having power to fine for the breach of those regulations. In 1907 the International Office of Public Health was established in Paris, with a much wider competence, and can be regarded as the predecessor of the World Health Organisation.[29]

1–015   In the economic field the Metric Union (1875),[30] the International Copyright Union (1886),[31] the International Sugar Union (1902),[32] and the International Institute of Agriculture (1905)[33] illustrate the breadth of activities undertaken. The Sugar Union had a permanent commission that by majority vote could order a change in municipal legislation that, for example, granted unfair bounties or imposed unfair tariffs—a significant abandonment of traditional adherence to sovereign rights.

1–016   This brief survey of some of the earlier public unions does not purport to be exhaustive, but simply illustrative of their nature and variety. Moreover, the constitutional developments and innovations made by the public unions remain of interest, for they anticipated those made by present-day intergovernmental organisations. In the first case, the trend towards permanence of association is very marked, whether in the form of permanent deliberative or legislative organs working with administrative organs (as in the Telegraphic Union, Metric Union, UPU, etc.) or of periodic conferences working in conjunction with a permanent bureau (Industrial Property, Railway Freight Transportation). The departures from the unanimity rule

---

[29] 206 CTS 21 (1907); Eagleton, *International Government*, pp. 175–176; Mangone, *A Short History of International Organisation*, pp. 79–82. See *infra*, Chap. 3.
[30] 149 CTS 237 (1875); Mangone, *A Short History of International Organisation*, pp. 83–84.
[31] 168 CTS 185 (1886); Eagleton, *International Government*, p. 171.
[32] 191 CTS 56 (1902); Eagleton, *International Government*, pp. 174–175.
[33] 198 CTS 355 (1905); Eagleton, *International Government*, pp. 173–174.

are equally striking, particularly when coupled with the grant of legislative powers in the Rhine Commission. Useful, also, was the tendency to distinguish the Convention, embodying general rules, from the Règlement, which provided for the detailed implementation of those rules and permitted amendment by a much simpler process. The representation of interests other than those of states, whether they were dependent territories, private companies or associations, and with or without the right to vote, injected a realism and degree of practicality which was of the utmost significance for future development. The techniques of weighted voting and of proportionate budgetary contributions pointed the way to the solution of difficult problems to which the principle of the equality of states provided no effective answer.

The outstanding problem was one of co-ordination of the activities of the **1–017** many unions, and in this connection it is appropriate to turn now to the League of Nations. This represented a first effort to establish some form of overall direction and co-ordinating authority.[34] However, the League never became the effective co-ordinator of the activities of these many administrative unions, illustrating the potential difficulties of associating these administrative unions too closely with an organisation having an avowedly political and diplomatic function. In particular, political failures by the organisation were likely to extend to other matters associated with it. As will be shown subsequently, there also exist considerable—and increasing—difficulties in coordinating the activities of administrative bodies, particularly to avoid jurisdictional overlap.[35]

(c) LEAGUE OF NATIONS

Bibliography: Munch, *Les origines et l'oeuvre de la Société des Nations* (2 Vol., 1923–24); Redslob, *Théorie de la Société des Nations* (1927); Miller, *The Drafting of the Covenant* (2 Vol., 1928); Williams, *Some Aspects of the Covenant of the League of Nations* (1934); Aufricht, *Guide to League of Nations publications: A Bibliographical Survey of the Work of the League, 1920–1947* (1951); Eagleton, *International Government* (3rd ed., 1948), Chaps 10–11; Walters, *A History of the League of Nations* (2 Vol., 1952); Stone, *Legal Controls of International Conflict* (1954), Chap. 6; Mangone, *A Short History of*

---

[34] Art. 24 of the Covenant of the League of Nations provided that "[t]here shall be placed under the direction of the League all international bureaux already established by general treaties if the parties to such treaties consent. All such international bureaux and all commissions for the regulation of matters of international interest hereafter instituted shall be placed under the direction of the League." The "direction of the League" was conceived, not as absorption of the bureaux or unions, but as the giving of support and the prevention of overlapping or duplication of activities, or of an unreasonable refusal to co-operate with other unions or the League itself. Few of the older unions consented to this direction, partly due to their desire for independence and partly due to the fact that often their members were not all members of the League, and those that were not were reluctant to accept the League's direction. Of the newly created unions, only five were admitted.
[35] See *infra*, Chap. 3.

International Organisation (1954), Chap. 5; Oppenheim, *International Law* (8th ed., 2 Vol., 1954), Vol. II, pp. 380–400.

1–018   The creation of a league of states, dedicated to the maintenance of peace, had long been advocated in philosophical and juristic writings[36] and in the aims of private organisations. The immediate source of the League of Nations was, however, a proposal introduced at the Peace Conference of Paris in 1919. The League's objective was "to promote international co-operation and to achieve international peace and security." The system of collective security envisaged in the Covenant rested, essentially, on the related notions of disarmament (Article 8), pacific settlement of disputes and the outlawing of war (Articles 11–15), a collective guarantee of the independence of each member (Article 10), and sanctions (Articles 16 and 17). The League's disarmament programme failed dismally. As envisaged in the Covenant, the pacific settlement of disputes likely to lead to a rupture of the peace was obligatory; parties to the dispute could choose to go to arbitration, judicial settlement or to the Council of the League. It was obligatory to accept the award or a unanimous report of the Council and there was an obligation on all members not to go to war with any state so accepting as well as a "moratorium" forbidding recourse to war within three months of the award or the Council's decision. Further, the members agreed to respect and preserve the "territorial integrity and existing political independence" of all members against external aggression. War was not made illegal *per se* but only where begun without complying with the requirement of the Covenant with regard to prior resort to pacific settlement of the dispute. A state resorting to war in violation of its undertaking with regard to pacific settlement was deemed to have committed an act of war against all other members. Yet it was left to each member to decide whether a breach had occurred or an act of war had been committed, so that even the obligation to apply economic sanctions under Article 16(1) was dependent on the member's own view of the situation. Military sanctions could be recommended by the Council, but the decision on whether to apply them rested with each member. Such was the ambition of the system envisaged; in itself perhaps not necessarily an unworkable one. After an initial success in dealing with the Graeco-Bulgarian crisis of 1925, and a less spectacular achievement in the Chaco dispute of 1928, the League witnessed the invasion of Manchuria in 1931, the Italo-Abyssinian War of 1935, the German marches into the Rhineland (1936), Austria (1938) and Czechoslovakia (1939), the Soviet Union's invasion of Finland in 1939 and, finally, the German invasion of Poland in 1939. Apart from half-hearted economic sanctions against Italy in 1935, no sanctions were ever really applied by the League. To this extent the failure

---

[36] For a brief review of the growth of the idea, see Leonard, *International Organisation* (1951), Chap. 2; Eagleton, *International Government*, pp. 246–247.

of the League was due, not to the inadequacies of the Covenant, but to the apathy and reluctance of the member states to discharge their obligations. This being said, it is still worthwhile to examine briefly the structure of the League to indicate the extent to which it provided a basis for the approach taken subsequently in other international organisations.

The League had three principal organs: the Council, the Assembly and **1–019** the Secretariat.[37] The Council was designed as the organ of limited membership, comprising originally "representatives of the Principal Allied and Associated Powers together with representatives of four other Members . . . selected by the Assembly from time to time . . ." (Article 4(1)). It was enlarged by stages. Germany became a permanent member and the non-permanent membership was increased to six in 1922, then to nine in 1926 and finally to 11 in 1936. At no time were a majority of major powers within its membership. In practice the Council met four times a year and could be specially convened in an emergency. Its decisions were to be reached by unanimous vote, subject to the exclusion of the vote of a party to a dispute (Article 15), but were not, as such, binding on member states. The Assembly was the plenary organ, meeting annually and including states signatories of the Versailles Treaty, "neutral" states named in the annex to the covenant as states invited to accede, and "any fully self-governing State, Dominion or Colony" admitted to membership by a two-thirds vote of the Assembly. Its terms of reference were wide: it could address "any matter within the sphere of action of the League or affecting the peace of the world" (Article 3(3)). The Assembly met annually, working through six main committees, and acted as a deliberative organ; it had only the power to make "resolutions" or "recommendations" and could not bind member states. Each state had one vote and the voting procedure required unanimity, except for matters of procedure or for the appointment of committees to investigate particular matters which required a simple majority of members present. However, the main committees made recommendations to the plenary by simple majority vote and the Assembly itself adopted the practice of making a recommendation or "voeu" (wish) by simple majority,[38] thus minimising to some extent the difficulties of securing complete unanimity. The third organ, the Secretariat, was by far the most

---

[37] Auxiliary organs consisted of the technical organisations (Economic and Financial Organisation, Communication and Transit Organisation, Health Organisation); the permanent advisory commissions (Mandates Commission, Opium Committee, Advisory Committee of Experts on Slavery, Commission on Intellectual Co-operation, etc.); the temporary advisory commissions (Commission of Enquiry for European Union, Special Committee on Contributions in Arrears); and the administrative or executive organisations (High Commissioner for Refugees (advisory commission for refugees, commissioner for Bulgarian refugees)). There were also the autonomous organisations like the ILO and the P.C.I.J., and the special organisations brought into relationship under Art. XX, such as the International Institute of Intellectual Co-operation (Paris) and the Nansen International Office for Refugees.

[38] Williams, "The League of Nations and Unanimity" (1925) 19 AJIL 475–488.

ambitious international civil service, or "bureau," ever established in international organisation. It will be noted that, although the establishment of the Permanent Court of International Justice was anticipated in the Covenant (Article 14), the court was a separate institution and not, as in the UN, an organ of the League itself.

1–020   The League experienced considerable constitutional development. Reference has already been made to the enlargement of the Council and to the inroads made into the unanimity rule by the Assembly. More significant, perhaps, was the gradual extension of the Assembly's role at the expense of the Council, an extension which came with the gradual disillusionment in the effectiveness of the Council and parallels the shift of power later experienced in the UN for the same reason. The Assembly's technique of securing agreement via inquiry and general debate proved more effective than the narrower diplomatic negotiation favoured within the Council. It is noteworthy, also, that the Assembly gradually took over control of the budget from the Council, and control of the purse-strings carries considerable weight. From the constitutional standpoint the League had several defects. The inclusion of the covenant within the four Peace Treaties led to certain legal difficulties and to a certain identification of the League with the victor states, even though later it came to be recognised as a treaty independent of the Peace Treaties and the League admitted to membership former enemy states. The unanimity rule, inherited from the traditional diplomatic conference, proved a severe hindrance and the Assembly's move towards simple majority was a clear recognition of this. Certain matters were within the exclusive jurisdiction of the Council (expulsion of members, for example) others were within the exclusive jurisdiction of the Assembly (admission of new members, revision of treaties); there was, however, concurrent jurisdiction in the most important matter of maintaining peace and the lack of any clear separation of powers in this matter (or of any priority in the right to deal with them) might give rise to difficulty where the Council and the Assembly differed in their approaches to the solution of a given problem affecting international peace. The Council's functions were too wide, for they included not merely its "political" functions but also certain administrative functions such as supervision over the Mandates system and the economic and social activities of the League. It was realised, too late, that the political impasse within the Council too easily spread to these other activities; it is significant that in the UN they are handled by separate organs. Amendment of the Covenant was by a process both vague and difficult, requiring ratification by a majority of the Assembly and all members of the Council (Article 26); the process over-estimated the adequacy of the initial drafting and under-estimated the rate at which development must take place, and thus introduced a static element into an inherently dynamic organisation. The wisdom of allowing for withdrawal from membership (Articles 1, 26(2), 16(4)) can be questioned in an organisation aiming at universality and perpetuity. Finally, as history proved, a "decentralised" system of sanctions was ineffective; there had to be some delegation of authority to an executive organ and an acceptance of the principle that its decisions would bind all members.

No lengthy appraisal of the League is required here. It never acquired a **1–021** universal character; handicapped from the outset by the non-participation of the United States of America, it remained predominantly a European organisation with a maximum membership of 59. The "delinquent" states, such as Japan, Germany and Italy, simply withdrew to pursue their aggression unembarrassed by membership. The relative progress of the League in the field of economics, finance, public health, mandates, transport and communications, social and labour problems, was overshadowed by its failure to prevent the outbreak of the Second World War. Potter has said of the League that it "made a far greater contribution to the progress of international organisation than any other institution in history."[39] It did, however, fail to fulfil the hopes which it engendered by its formation; as Potter noted, it was in a certain sense "history's most colossal failure and disappointment."[40] But, at the expense of repetition, it is worthwhile reaffirming that its failure was not necessarily due to its constitutional defects; it failed because of lack of political will, its members not being prepared to fulfil their obligations and ensure its success. That, in conception, it showed the right approach to the problem of maintaining peace cannot be doubted. The determination to establish the UN as its successor indicated that only by such or similar measures was humankind to be protected from the catastrophe of world conflict.

The formal demise of the League came on April 18, 1946. The Assembly of the League chose to dissolve the League by simple resolution (so also with the Permanent Court of International Justice). The actual liquidation was handed over to a Board of Liquidation and is described in greater detail in the latter part of this book, in the section dealing with dissolution of international organisations.[41] It is against this historical background that we now turn to the scope of the fifth edition of this book.

B. SCOPE OF THE BOOK AND DEFINITIONAL AND RELATED ASPECTS

The last edition of this book was published in 1982. Since then significant **1–022** changes have occurred which justify a new edition. A number of new institutions, including courts, have been created, both at the regional and global level. Other important institutions, such as the General Agreement

---

[39] Potter, *Introduction to the Study of International Organisation*, p. 257.
[40] Potter, *Introduction to the Study of International Organisation*, p. 257.
[41] See Chap, 15, paras 15–110 *et seq.* See also Potter, *Introduction to the Study of International Organisation*, p. 255–256.

on Tariffs and Trade, have been radically transformed. And yet other institutions, such as COMECON, have disappeared altogether. Decisions and resolution and other normative or operational acts of international institutions feature increasingly in daily life, raising legal issues in national law, as the litigation over the collapse of the International Tin Council illustrated. And the question of states' participation in international organisations now raises lively national debate, as was seen for example in demonstrations and debate in India, the United States and various E.U. member states over, respectively, the WTO negotiations, NAFTA and the Maastricht Treaty establishing the European Union.

1–023   In summary, in recent years international organisations have played an ever more active role in international affairs, with implications at the international and national levels. Their activities address subjects previously not addressed by international co-operation—for example, the exploitation of the deep sea-bed, regional monetary union (in the context of the EU), international trade in services at the global level (as opposed to goods), and a wide range of environmental issues from climate change to biotechnology. Within the more traditional fields of activity the involvement of international organisations is increasingly significant: for example, there has been a marked increase in institutional efforts at peacekeeping both at the regional and global levels, there are more international courts and quasi-judicial bodies involved in dispute avoidance and settlement, and international commercial and economic relations are ever more subject to the scrutiny of international organisations.

1–024   These and other developments bear witness to the great changes which have occurred in this field over the past two decades. In particular, the advent of "globalisation" so-called has created the conditions for an increased role for international institutions, whether legislative, administrative, or judicial. Consequently, the role of international institutions in the international legal order has been enhanced. Virtually all existing international institutions find themselves with an increase in the breadth and nature of their activities, and new institutions have had to be established to address new challenges. Moreover, efforts by some jurists to personify the concept of the "international community" and attribute to it rights and obligations through specified international organisations—for example the approach of the Court of Arbitration in the *St Pierre and Miquelon Case* in the case of the International Sea-Bed Authority—indicate the direction that may be taken in the years ahead.[42]

---

[42] Court of Arbitration for the Delimitation of Maritime Areas Between Canada and France: Decision in Case Concerning Delimitation of Maritime Areas (*St Pierre and Miquelon*), (1992) 31 ILM 1145, 1172 (para. 78).

(a) SCOPE

The purpose of the fifth edition of *Bowett's Law of International Institutions* is not to document and assess all the changes exhaustively. Rather, we have sought to integrate into the work's original approach those developments which we consider to be most noteworthy. More comprehensive general accounts may be found elsewhere, for example in the encyclopedic *International Institutional Law* by Schermers and Blokker.[43] And more detailed accounts of critical aspects may be found, for example, in Dr Amerasinghe's *Principles of the Institutional Law of International Organisations*.[44]

Our purpose is to provide an introductory overview of the law of **1–025** international organisations, including international courts and tribunals as a whole. This book offers a basic framework, insights into some of the more essential issues, and indications of where to find more detail. As readers of earlier editions will see, we have maintained to a considerable extent the basic structure and approach adopted by Professor Bowett. Accordingly, this general introduction is followed by Part I, which sets out in descriptive mode the global institutions and then the regional institutions. We have introduced a number of changes from earlier editions (and indeed from most works on the subject) in Chapter 4, entitled "Other Autonomous Organisations." Beyond bodies such as the World Trade Organisation or the International Sea-Bed Authority (which are not specialised agencies of the United Nations), there are also, increasingly, institutions established by particular treaties to address a single issue or set of issues, such as the Conferences of the Parties of many environmental agreements. Although not expressly endowed with international personality or "institutional" status, these bodies nevertheless emerge in practice as international organisations.[45] We have decided to devote space to those having global competence. The regional equivalents are noted in the regional chapters. Our approach to the classification of organisations is explained in further detail below.

Part II of the book addresses the various functions of international **1–026** organisations: "legislative," "executive" or "administrative" and "judicial." This departs to a certain extent from Professor Bowett's earlier approach. In essence, we take the view that the international legal order reflects elements of the separation of powers—a theme to which we return in our conclusion. Accordingly, it is appropriate to distinguish between the different functions much as one would in the domestic context, admittedly recognising the very significant differences which still exist.

Part III considers four sets of common institutional problems: the law **1–027** applicable to the organisations, legal personality (and its consequences),

---

[43] Schermers and Blokker, *International Institutional Law* (3rd ed., 1995).
[44] Amerasinghe, *Principles of the Institutional Law of International Organisations* (1996).
[45] See Chap. 4, paras 4–014–4–034.

membership and the representation of member and other interests, and financial and budgetary matters. This follows the general approach of Professor Bowett, a testament to the perspicacity of his vision in identifying many of the principal legal issues well before they arose in practice.

(b) DEFINITIONAL ASPECTS

1–028 International organisations exist in a variety of forms, and the term is capable of reflecting different situations. Commentators are in general agreement that for an entity to qualify as an international organisation, it must have the following characteristics:

- its membership must be composed of states and/or other international organisations;[46]

- it must be established by treaty;[47]

- it must have an autonomous will distinct from that of its members and be vested with legal personality;[48] and

- it must be capable of adopting norms addressed to its members.[49]

1–029 This definition excludes from the scope of this book other entities which are sometimes referred to as international organisations, such as international non-governmental organisations (NGOs) and inter-state enterprises (*établissements publics internationaux*),[50] on the grounds that the status and functioning of these entities is, for the most part, regulated by one or more national laws. The definition adopted includes within its scope other autonomous organisations which are sometimes referred to as "treaty-based organisations", namely those which are established within the

---

[46] Morgenstern, *Legal Problems of International Organisations* (1986), p. 19; Amerasinghe, *Principles of the Institutional Law of International Organisations*, p. 9. See *infra*, Chap. 16.

[47] Barberis, "Nouvelles questions concernant la personnalité juridique internationale" (1983 I) 179 RdC I 145, 216; Morgenstern, *Legal Problems of International Organisations*, p. 19; Schermers and Blokker, *International Institutional Law*, p. 23 (para. 33); Amerasinghe, *Principles of the Institutional Law of International Organisations*, p. 9. On the Instrument for the Establishment of the Restructured Global Environment Facility, 33 ILM 1278 (1994), adopted by resolutions of the World Bank, UNEP and UNDP; in this regard note the conclusion by the UN Legal Counsel below, n. 51.

[48] Seidl-Hohenveldern, "The Legal Personality of International and Supranational Organizations" (1965) 21 REDI 36, p. 66; Schermers and Blokker, *International Institutional Law*, pp. 29–30 (para. 44); Amerasinghe, *Principles of the Institutional Law of International Organisations*, p. 9. See *infra*, Chap. 15.

[49] Reuter, *International Institutional Law*, pp. 215–218.

[50] A basic definition of the latter is found in Adam, *Les organismes internationaux spécialisés: contribution à la théorie générale des établissements publics internationaux* (1992), pp. 15–37. The inter-state enterprises discussed include, *inter alia*, Air Afrique and Scandinavian Airlines.

framework of agreements establishing institutional arrangements for the putting into effect of substantive norms. As the UN Office of Legal Affairs put it in relation to the institutions created by the UN Framework Convention on Climate Change: "[o]nce th[e] Convention enters into force it will establish an international entity/organisation with its own separate legal personality, statement of principles, organs and a supportive structure in the form of a secretariat."[51]

(c) NATURE OF INTERNATIONAL INSTITUTIONAL LAW

It follows from the definitional aspects indicated above that the law of **1–030** international organisations inscribes itself as part of general public international law, from which it both draws inspiration and makes its own contribution. Within the global framework of international law, each organisation of course has its own governing law deriving from its constituent instrument and decisions and resolutions it adopts, as well as its established practise.[52] Each organisation may therefore be considered as something of a sub-system. However, that plainly does not preclude the possibility that there may exist a common law of international organisations[53] and that a degree of cross-fertilisation of basic principles might occur. As the World Bank Administrative Tribunal put it in its very first decision in 1981:

> "The Tribunal does not overlook the fact that each international organisation has its own constituent instrument; its own membership; its own institutional structure; its own functions; its own measure of legal personality; its own personnel policy; and that the differences between one organisation and another are so obvious that the notion of a common law of international organisations must be subject to numerous and sometimes significant qualifications. But the fact that these differences exist does not exclude the possibility that similar conditions may affect the solution of comparable problems."[54]

Both aspects—the specificity and commonality of the principles and practise of international institutions—will be referred to in the chapters which follow, most notably in Parts II and III.

---

[51] Memorandum of Under Secretary General for Legal Affairs to the Executive Secretary of the Intergovernmental Negotiating Committee for a Framework Convention on Climate Change, 4 November 1993. On the reasoning behind this approach, see *infra*, Chap. 15.

[52] See *infra*, Chap. 14.

[53] See Reuter, *International Institutions*, pp. 216–218; Schermers and Blokker, *International Institutional Law*, pp. 824–825 (para. 1339); Amerasinghe, *Principles of the Institutional Law of International Organisations*, pp. 397–402.

[54] Decision *In the matter of de Merode et al. v. The World Bank, Decision No. 1*, WBAT Reports [1981], p. 13 (para. 28).

(d) CLASSIFICATION OF ORGANISATIONS

1–031 In concluding this introductory chapter, a word must be said of the classification of international organisations.[55] Quite apart from the intrinsic interest of the problem of classification, the reader is entitled to know the reason for the adoption of a particular scheme of presentation of these organisations in the present book. From the descriptions of many of the public international unions in this chapter it will be readily apparent that organisations of an administrative or technical character preceded those of a predominantly political character, like the League or the UN.

1–032 A distinction based on function automatically suggests itself. Indeed, it may be broadly possible to distinguish between the "political" organisations, concerned primarily with the preservation of international peace and security, and the administrative organisations with more specific technical aims in the economic and social fields. The distinction is perhaps more accurately stated as one between organisations of comprehensive competence and organisations of limited competence.

1–033 This translates also into a distinction between organisations of a "global" membership and those of a "regional" membership. Therefore, in this book a separate section is devoted to regional organisations and, within some of the regions at least (because of the diversity of the organisations involved), it has been possible to make the same broad division between organisations of general competence and those of limited competence. Even the notion of a "regional" organisation is convenient rather than accurate, for in some organisations the "region" is based upon a political rather than a geographical test (*i.e.* NATO, OECD, Commonwealth Secretariat). Moreover, a "global" organisation like the UN has within it many "regional" bodies such as the regional commissions of ECOSOC (the Economic Commissions for Asia, the Far East, Europe, Latin America, Africa).

1–034 Prima facie, one might also distinguish the institutions for the judicial or other settlement of disputes, such as the International Court of Justice or the European Court of Justice or, possibly, the WTO's Dispute Settlement Body. In fact this broad classification into global and regional organisations, organisations of general or specific competence, and organisations having political, administrative or judicial functions is generally the one adopted in this book. This is reflected, for example, in the fact that the United Nations, the specialised agencies, regional organisations and judicial institutions are each given their respective sections. Its justification is not, however, its scientific accuracy, but simply its convenience for purposes of presentation and description.

---

[55] For a detailed treatment of the classification of international organisations, see Schermers and Blokker, *International Institutional Law*, pp. 33–44.

As we shall see, no rigid distinction in function is made in practice, and **1–035** the classification should not be taken to mask the interplay of functions. The "political" organisation, the United Nations, has amongst its organs the Trusteeship Council, which had primarily administrative functions whilst it functioned, and subsidiary bodies such as the UN Environment Programme, with many technical functions, as well as the I.C.J., its "principal judicial organ". The co-ordination achieved by bringing the specialised agencies into relationship with the UN also makes any clear classification by function difficult. One distinction which should be made is between organisations with "supranational" powers (power to bind member states by their decisions), such as the European Union, and those without such powers. But this may often be the characteristic of a particular organ, rather than the organisation as a whole, and whilst the possession of such powers must be pointed out where they exist, it is not intended to classify in this book on the basis of a distinction between powers. The adequacy of the system of classification adopted in this book will be for the reader to judge; its purpose is to simplify presentation and, in the absence of an agreed, scientific classification, this purpose seems a satisfactory guide.

Part I

OVERVIEW OF EXISTING INTERNATIONAL INSTITUTIONS

CHAPTER 2

THE UNITED NATIONS

Bibliography: United Nations, Conference on International Organisation (UNCIO), 15 Vols. (1945) (these volumes constitute the travaux preparatoires); United Nations, Repertory of Practice of UN Organs, Vols 1–5 and Supplements; Yearbook of the United Nations (1945–present)

Goodrich and Hambro, *Charter of the United Nations: Commentary and Documents* (2nd ed., 1949); Sohn, *Basic Documents of the United Nations* (1956); Weissberg, *The International Status of the UN* (1961); Chaumont, *Les organisations internationales* (1963); Higgins, *Development of International Law through the Political Organs of the UN* (1963); Sohn, *Recent Cases on UN Law (Suppl.)* (1963); Bowett, *UN Forces* (1964); Gardiner, *In Pursuit of World Order* (1964); Kelsen, *The Law of the United Nations* (1964); Falk and Mendlovitz, *The Strategy of World Order*, Vol. 3 (1966); Halderman, *The UN and the Rule of Law* (1966); Tunkin, *"The UN"* (1966) 4 Soviet Law and Government (No. 4), 3–12; Goodspeed, *The Nature and Function of International Organisation* (1967); Waters, *The UN International Organisation and Administration* (1967); Gutteridge, *The UN in a changing world* (1969); Khan, *Implied Powers of the UN* (1970); Manin, *L'ONU et le maintien de la paix* (1971); Virally, *L'organisation mondiale* (1972); Dimitrov, *Documents of International Organisations: A Bibliographic Handbook* (1973); Goodrich, *The United Nations in a Changing World* (1974); Hill, *The United Nations System* (1978); Luard, *The United Nations. How it Works and What it Does* (1994); Cot & Pellet (eds.) *La Charte des Nations Unies*, commentaire article par article (2nd. ed., 1991); Chaumont, L'ONU (13th ed., 1992); Simma (ed), *The Charter of the UN: a Commentary* (1995); Millenium Report of the UN Secretary General: "We, the peoples: The role of the UN in the 21st century", A/52/850 (2000). Website: http://www.un.org.

A. INTRODUCTION

The failure of the League of Nations to avert a Second World War did **2–001** not destroy the conviction, shared by many, that only by some form of general organisation of states could a system of collective security be achieved which would protect the international community from the scourge of war. The Allies were, even in 1941, calling themselves "The United Nations" and by 1943 the Moscow declaration had recognised "the necessity of establishing at the earliest practicable date a general international organisation, based upon the principle of sovereign equality of all peace-loving states, large and small, for the maintenance of international peace and security."[1] The formulation of definite plans for such an organisation took shape in stages, at Teheran in 1943, at Dumbarton Oaks in 1944, at Yalta in 1945 and, finally, at the San Francisco Conference in 1945 where 50 governments, upon the basis of the Dumbarton Oaks proposals prepared by the four sponsoring states, together drafted the United Nations Charter.[2]

2–002   The Charter is a multilateral treaty establishing or restating the rights and duties of the signatory states; it is not, however, subject to reservation or denunciation, although, despite the absence of a "withdrawal" clause, it may be assumed that legally a state can withdraw subject to its fulfilment of any outstanding obligations, such as its budgetary commitments.[3] The Charter is also the basic constitutional document of the organisation— Article 1 identifies the purposes of the organisation as being to maintain peace and security; to develop friendly relations among nations based on equal rights and self-determination; and to achieve international co-operation in solving economic, social, cultural and humanitarian problems. And to that end, Article 2 of the Charter identifies principles to govern the activities of the organisation and its members. As such, the Charter has an inherently dynamic character (which can be seen in the various constitutional developments since 1945), unlike a normal multilateral treaty. The organisation created by the Charter is not a "super-state" or anything resembling a world government.[4] As we shall see, it was envisaged first and foremost as a collective security system far more centralised than the League. The Security Council can take decisions binding on the members, but, in the main, the Charter provides special forms of co-operation between states, supplementing the traditional methods of inter-state inter-course, and extending into fields of political, social and economic affairs that lie outside a system of collective security simpliciter. Thus, the United Nations has played an especially important role in generating co-operation between states to develop norms in areas such as human rights and the environment. It proceeds essentially on the basis of voluntary co-operation by the members and "commands" only in the limited field of enforcement action via the Security Council. This reliance on co-operation can be regarded as a limitation on the powers of the organisation but it is perhaps preferable to regard it as a characteristic of any organisation to which the exercise of sovereign power is not delegated by the members.

---

[1] *Declaration of the Four Nations on General Security* (1943), reprinted in 38 AJIL 5 (1944).
[2] Eagleton, "The Charter Adopted at San Francisco", *The American Political Science Review*, Vol. 39, no. 5 (October, 1945), pp. 934–942; Kirk and Chamberlain, The Organization of the San Francisco Conference, *Political Science Quarterly*, Vol. 60, no. 3 (September 1945), pp. 321–342; Whitton, The Chairmanship of the San Francisco Conference, 39 AJIL 535 (1945).
[3] See *infra*, Chap. 16, paras 16–029 *et seq.* and 17.
[4] As recognised by the I.C.J. in the 1949 Reparations case; see Chap. 15, paras 15–006, 15–009.

It follows, therefore, that, since each member remains sovereign, in **2–003** principle the organisation as such has no competence in matters within the domestic jurisdiction of a state.[5] Thus, Article 2(7) of the Charter provides:

"Nothing contained in the present Charter shall authorise the United Nations to intervene in matters which are essentially within the domestic jurisdiction of any State or shall require the Members to submit such matters to settlement under the present Charter; but this principle shall not prejudice the application of enforcement measures under Chapter VII."

A review of the practice under this Article gives some indication of the **2–004** bitter controversies that have arisen over this limitation on competence.[6] The Assembly's recommendation in December 1946 that Spain be debarred from membership of any international organisation or conference connected with the United Nations, the discussions on the treatment of Indians within the Union of South Africa, or on the policy of apartheid pursued by the government of the Union, the discussion of the Tunisian, Moroccan and Algerian questions, and eventually of the Cyprus and, more recently, of the Iraqi and Yugoslav questions, have brought forward strong protests from the governments concerned. Indeed, on some occasions the delegates of South Africa and France withdrew in protest: in 1962, the British delegate withdrew when the General Assembly called for a more liberal constitution for Southern Rhodesia. The Security Council's willingness to establish peacekeeping forces in Rwanda and former Yugoslavia in the early 1990s are recent rejections of the argument that a civil war is necessarily "essentially within the domestic jurisdiction" of states. Developments in international law, for example in fields such as human rights and the environment, indicate that the "domestic jurisdiction" exception is increasingly subject to challenge in a "globalising" world, with all this implies for the role of a body such as the UN.

During the 1960s it became clear that the Assembly would refuse to **2–005** regard any colonial situation as a matter of domestic jurisdiction. It may, of course, be argued that discussion as such can never constitute "intervention" and is therefore not prohibited by Article 2(7).[7] Certainly a matter that becomes serious enough to threaten international peace and security would, *ipso facto*, cease to be essentially "domestic;" that is sufficiently recognised by the proviso to Article 2(7) regarding enforcement measures.[8]

---

[5] See Rajan, *The United Nations and Domestic Jurisdiction* (1958): also Higgins, *The Development of International Law through the Political Organs of the United Nations*, (1963), Pt II; Goodrich, *The United Nations and Domestic Jurisdiction, International Organization*, Vol. 3, no. 1 (February 1949), pp. 14–28.

[6] See *Repertory*, Vol. 1, pp. 27, *et seq.*

[7] Lauterpacht, *International Law and Human Rights*, (1950), pp. 166, *et seq.*

[8] But note that where, as in the Congo, the Security Council orders "provisional measures" under Art. 40, since these do not have the character of "enforcement action" the proviso to Art. 2(7) does not apply and the principle of non-intervention constitutes a limit upon the powers of the Organisation (see *infra*, paras 2–044, *et seq.*).

In that regard the Security Council has more recently tended to broaden the category of matters that may threaten international peace and security.[9] Equally clearly, where a state has assumed treaty obligations with respect to a certain matter it can no longer maintain that the matter is exclusively within its domestic jurisdiction. But beyond this the application of the Article is more a matter for political judgment than strict legal interpretation, and one should not assume complete consistency in the practise of the UN. Political considerations clearly stood behind the swiftness with which the Russian Federation was permitted to succeed to the seat of the former USSR on the Security Council and in the organisation, following the dissolution of the Soviet Union in 1991.[10] Replacement of the Government of the Republic of China in 1971 with that of the People's Republic of China, as the representative of China in the UN, also presented difficult political questions, though these were largely avoided by labelling the question as one of "representation."

2–006   A second general limitation on the powers of the United Nations springs from the normal principle of the law of treaties, *pacta tertiis nec nocent nec prosunt*; the Charter, as a treaty, cannot bind non-members. In general, therefore, the Organisation must proceed on the basis that the Charter obligations, where these go beyond the obligations of general international law, do not bind non-members. However, in Article 2 (6) it is provided that:

> "The Organisation shall ensure that States which are not Members of the United Nations act in accordance with these Principles so far as may be necessary for the maintenance of international peace and security."

Although this represents a technical variation from the *pacta tertiis* maxim the political justification for asserting the primacy of the United Nation's interest in maintaining international peace and security is undeniable. It should also be noted that the provision imposes an obligation on the organisation itself (which "shall ensure that [non-members] act in accordance . . ."), and not upon the non-members, which are not formally bound by the Charter. Resolution 232 (1966) of the Security Council, which decided upon economic sanctions against Rhodesia, specifically invoked Article 2(6) in addressing itself to non-members and urging them to act in accordance with it.[11] In a similar fashion, embargoes authorised by the

---

[9] See UN Security Council Doc. S/23500, January 31, 1992—"The absence of war and military conflicts amongst States does not in itself ensure international peace and security. The non-military sources of instability in the economic, social, humanitarian and ecological fields have become threats to international peace and security".

[10] See Blum, *"Russia Takes over the Soviet Union's Seat at the United Nations"* (1992) 3 EJIL 354; *infra*, Chap. 16, para. 16–016.

[11] For the somewhat equivocal responses of Austria (a member) and Switzerland (a non-member), based upon their special position as "neutralised" states, see S/7795 and S/7781, p. 58. See generally Falk, "The authority of the UN to control non-members" (1965) Rutgers L.R. 591. And see Gold, "The Fund and Non-Member States" IMF Pamphlet Series No. 7 (1966).

Security Council against Iraq,[12] Somalia,[13] Rwanda[14] and the former Yugoslavia[15] have called on all states, including non-UN members, to comply.

B. PRINCIPAL ORGANS

The principal organs of the UN established to give effect to its purposes **2–007** are the General Assembly, the Security Council and the Economic and Social Council. The work of the Trusteeship Council has come to an end since 1994, and is only briefly described. The International Court of Justice is considered in Chapter 13, and the role of Secretary General and the UN secretariat in Chapter 12.

(a) THE GENERAL ASSEMBLY

Bibliography: United Nations, *Repertory of Practice of UN Organs*, Vol. I (1955) and Suppl. No. 1 (1960), Vol. II (1958). Kelsen, *Recent Trends in the Law of the UN* (1951), Chap. 4; Johnson, "The Effect of Resolutions of the General Assembly of the UN" (1955–56) 32 B.Y.B.I.L. 97; Andrassi, "Uniting for Peace, (1956) 50 A.J.I.L. 563; Vallat, "The Competence of the UN General Assembly," (1959) 97 R.C. 203; Bailey: The General Assembly (1960); Lauterpacht, *The United Nations Emergency Force: Basic Documents* (1960); Bindschedler, The Delimitation of Powers in the UN (1963) 108 R.C. 305; Stoessinger, *Financing the UN* (1964); Asamoah, *The Legal Significance of the Declarations of the General Assembly of the UN* (1966); Chaumont, "The Respective Roles of the UN General Assembly and the Security Council" (1966) 12 Review of Contemporary Law (No. 2) 23; Castaneda, Legal Effects of UN Resolutions (1969); Yemin, *Legislative powers in the U.N. and specialised agencies* (1969); Finley, *The Structure of the UN General Assembly* (1977), 3 Vols; Finley, *The Structure of the United Nations General Assembly: its committees, commissions and other organisms, 1974–1980s* (1988); Blaine, *United Nations General Assembly Resolutions in our Changing World* (1991); Abi-Saab, *The Changing Constitution of the United Nations* (1997).

The General Assembly is the plenary organ of the UN, consisting of all **2–008** 189 member states, each with one vote but entitled to five representatives. This organ reflects the extent to which the UN has become universal and a "world forum," an effective sounding-board for world opinion. For many years, however, the UN fell far short of universality, for admission to membership was dependant on the fulfilment of certain conditions, and was to be achieved via a certain process, as Article 4 makes clear.[16] The

---

[12] S/RES/661 of August 6, 1990.
[13] S/RES/733 of January 23, 1992.
[14] S/RES/918 of May 17, 1994.
[15] S/RES/713 of September 25, 1991.
[16] Art. 4 provides: "1. Membership in the United Nations is open to all other peace-loving states which accept the obligations contained in the present Charter and, in the judgment of the Organisation, are able and willing to carry out these obligations. 2. The admission of any such state to membership in the United Nations will be effected by a decision of the General Assembly upon the recommendation of the Security Council."

conditions of membership remain the same, indicating the extent to which the problems which arose concerned their interpretation and application in the context of the political considerations then pertaining, principally the Cold War.[17] The current membership stands at 189, a figure which offers a favourable comparison with the League so far as universality is concerned.

2–009 It would be unwise to assume universality, or rather the lack of it, was the only problem on membership. Changes in the character of members, for example those arising from secession or from union, can and do occur. In the case of the division of India (an existing member) into the two states of India and Pakistan in 1947, the course taken was to regard the new "India" as a continuation of the old for the purpose of membership and to admit Pakistan as a new member. When the union between Egypt and Syria occurred in 1958 the resulting United Arab Republic (UAR) was not admitted to membership as a new state; the Secretary-General simply informed all members of the change and the UAR henceforth sat in place of the two states with, of course, only one vote instead of two. The reverse process was applied when the union was subsequently dissolved. The two German states of the German Democratic Republic and the Federal Republic of Germany were originally only admitted to the UN after a treaty concluded between the two ('Grundlagenvertrag') clarified that under international law there were two German states.[18] Following the reunification of Germany in 1990, the unified state was considered to be the successor of the Federal Republic of Germany and entitled to membership of the UN as such. In the case of the two Koreas, the long-lasting conflict between the existence of two separate states and the demand for unification was resolved in favour of both the Democratic People's Republic of Korea and the Republic of Korea being admitted as members.

2–010 The dissolution of the former Yugoslavia represents a case of new members being admitted to the UN as a result of secessions, similarly to the admissions of Pakistan and Bangladesh. Despite the uncertain and disputed status of the frontiers of the applicant states, all the emerging states (Bosnia and Herzegovina, the former Yugoslav Republic of Macedonia, Slovenia and Croatia) were admitted to the UN. The claim of the Federal Republic of Yugoslavia (Serbia and Montenegro) to continue the membership of Yugoslavia in the UN was rejected[19] and it was instead required to reapply for membership under Article 4 of the Charter, which it did in October, 2000. In contrast, following the dissolution of the Soviet Union, Russia was not required to apply for membership under Article 4

---

[17] On membership see Chap. 16, paras 16–002 *et seq.*
[18] G.A. res 3050 (XXVIII) September 18, 1973.
[19] S/RES/777 (1992) September 19, 1992 and G.A. res. 47/1 September 22, 1992. The FRY was admitted to UN membership on November 1, 2000.

but succeeded to the membership of the Soviet Union and took up its permanent seat in the Security Council. All the remaining former Soviet Republics (Armenia, Azerbaijan, Kazakhstan, Kyrgzstan, Moldova, Tajikistan, Turkmenistan and Uzbekistan), except for Georgia, were admitted to the UN on March 2, 1992.[20] The Security Council recommended Georgia for admission to the UN on July 6, 1992, with eventual admission on July 31, 1992.[21]

Functions and powers

The Assembly is a deliberative organ which proceeds via recommendation rather than binding decision; any attempt to draw analogies with a national assembly, parliament or legislature, is misleading unless this fundamental difference in powers is grasped—the Assembly cannot directly legislate for the member states. Although as a general rule its resolutions can have no legally binding effect on the members, there are some circumstances in which a recommendation may create direct legal obligations for members, for example by the Assembly's approval of the budget which creates an obligation on a state to pay its contribution or by decisions on elections to various organs or admission to membership; such matters normally relate to the internal working of the organisation as distinct from a recommendation addressed to a member.[22] **2–011**

What is of significant interest is the way in which certain resolutions of the Assembly may assume a "quasi-legislative" role. While they cannot create direct legal obligations for member states they can embody a consensus of opinion about what the law is so that, indirectly, they become evidence of international law. For example, the repeated affirmations of the right of self-determination have probably given normative status to what was originally regarded as a political doctrine.[23] The celebrated resolution 1803 (XVII) on permanent sovereignty over natural resources,[24] or resolution 2131 (XX) on non-intervention,[25] or resolution 2312 (XXII) embody- **2–012**

---

[20] G.A. res. 46/223–46/230. Belarus and Ukraine were already members of the UN in their own right. See further Chap. 16, para. 16–004.

[21] See 1992 UNYB 133–136, 137–138.

[22] See Johnson, "The Effect of Resolutions of the General Assembly of the UN," *ibid.* 32 (1955–56), 97; Falk, "On the Quasi-legislative Competence of the General Assembly" (1966) 60 AJIL 782; Arangio-Ruiz, "The Normative Role of the General Assembly" (1972) 137 R.C., 431; Higgins, *op. cit.*, pp. 1–10; Schermers, *op. cit.*, (1980), 598–619; Schreuer, "Recommendations and the Traditional Sources of International Law" (1977) 20 German Y.I.L., 103–118; the views of Judge Lauterpacht in the AO on S.W. Africa-Voting Procedure, (1955) I.C.J. Rep. 118–119, AO of July 20, 1962, on Certain Expenses of the UN, the separate opinion of Fitzmaurice (pp. 208–211) and of the majority (p. 164), and more recently, Judgment of June 26, 1992, on Certain Phosphate Lands in Nauru (1992) I.C.J. Rep. 240.

[23] East Timor (*Portugal v. Australia*), 1995 I.C.J. Rep. 90.

[24] Permanent Sovereignty Over Natural Resources, UN Doc. A/RES/1803 (1962).

[25] Declaration on the Inadmissibility of Intervention in the Domestic Affairs of States and the Protection of their Independence and Sovereignty, UN Doc. A/RES/2131 (1966).

ing a declaration on territorial asylum, [26] or resolution 3281 (XXIX) on the Economic Rights and Duties of States, are examples of resolutions which cannot be ignored in any contemporary evaluation of what is the relevant rule of international law. [27] Of course, where the resolution has not gained the support of many of the states principally concerned—as is the case with resolution 1653 (XVI) on the illegality of nuclear weapons—its evidential quality is correspondingly weakened. [28]

2–013   A quite distinct "legislative" role is played by the Assembly in formulating treaties open for accession by members, such as the Treaty on Principles governing the exploration and use of Outer Space (annexed to res. 2222 (XXI),[29] and the Covenants on Economic, Social and Cultural Rights and on Civil and Political Rights (annexed to resolution 2200A (XXI).[30] Here, of course, the normative character will arise not from this resolution but from the accessions of member states under the ordinary principles of treaty law. The Assembly also adopts resolutions establishing negotiating committees for the elaboration of agreements, such as the UN Convention on Climate Change,[31] the Law of the Sea Conventions,[32] and the Convention on the Law of the Non-Navigational Uses of International Watercourses.[33] The General Assembly regularly convenes conferences on various important topics, such as environment and development,[34] human rights[35] and social development.[36] These will often serve as fora for the subsequent development of new norms of international law.

2–014   However important though these "quasi-legislative" functions may be, the Assembly remains primarily a deliberative organ and not, at least directly, a legislative organ. The objection to conferring on resolutions of

---

[26] Declaration on Territorial Asylum, UN Doc. A/RES/2312 (1967).
[27] See the Award of Dupuy, making this point in relation to the 1974 Charter on Economic Rights and Duties of States in *Texaco v. Libya* (1977) 53 I.L.R. at 485 and also the Advisory Opinion of July 8, 1996 on the Legality of the Threat or Use of Nuclear Weapons, (1996) I.C.J. Rep. 226.
[28] See Chap. 11, para. 11–049.
[29] Treaty on Principles Governing the Activities of States in the Exploration and Use of Outer Space, Including the Moon and Other Celestial Bodies, UN Doc. A/RES/2222 (1966).
[30] International Covenant on Economic, Social and Cultural Rights, International Covenant on Civil and Political Rights and Optional Protocol, UN Doc. A/RES/2200 (1967).
[31] United Nations Framework Convention on Climate Change, UN Doc. A/48/49 (1993).
[32] See, for example, G.A. res. 2750C (December 17, 1970) convening the third comprehensive conference on the law of the sea in 1973.
[33] Adopted by G.A. res. 51/229 (May 21, 1997), UN Doc. A-51–869 (not yet in force). The elaboration of the framework convention was undertaken on the basis of G.A. res. 51/206 (January 16, 1997).
[34] G.A. res. 196 (December 20, 1988) convening the UN Conference on Environment and Development that took place in 1992.
[35] Such as the World Conference on Human Rights, held in Vienna from June 14–25 1993. See A/CONF.157/24 (Pt. I) for the Conference Report.
[36] Such as the World Summit for Social Development, held in Copenhagen from March 6–12, 1995. See A/CONF. 166/9 for the Conference Report.

the Assembly a direct, legislative effect so as to bind members stems from two separate considerations. First, there is the traditional objection to a simple or two-thirds majority binding the minority. Secondly, there is the objection that this circumvents the traditional treaty-making process, avoiding the need for ratification that, under the constitutions of some states, is regarded as essential if new international obligations are to be assumed.

The deliberative character of the plenary organ is reflected in Article 20, **2–015** which provides for "regular annual sessions" and for special sessions to be convened by the Secretary-General at the request of the Security Council or of a majority of the members of the UN. Since 1945 the Assembly has hosted 20 special sessions. This is to be contrasted with the capacity for continuous functioning of the Security Council. The powers of the Assembly are broadly stated in Chapter IV and include power "to discuss any questions or any matter within the scope of the present Charter or relating to the powers and functions of any organs provided in the present Charter" (Article 10). This provides the basis for the overall authority of the Assembly over the various organs of the UN although, clearly, in relation to the Security Council and the Court, this authority is limited. This "supervisory" role in relation to other organs is further specified in Chapters IX, X and XII of the UN Charter which give the Assembly a general power of supervision over the arrangements made by the Economic and Social Council (ECOSOC) with the specialised agencies, and an overall control over ECOSOC generally and also the Trusteeship Council. Further elements in this control are the Assembly's power to approve the budget (Article 17), which necessarily affects the scope of the activities of other organs, and the right to receive reports from these organs (Article 15). In practice, detailed examination and discussion does not take place on reports from the Security Council, but it may do on reports from ECOSOC and the Trusteeship Council; this emphasises what was said above, namely, that control over the Security Council is not of the same order as that exercised over other organs.

A further power of the Assembly is "to consider the general principles of **2–016** co-operation in the maintenance of international peace and security" (Article 11(1)) and "to discuss any questions relating to the maintenance of international peace and security" (Article 11(2)). In this lies the basis of the Assembly's political power of deliberation, and this power overlaps considerably with that of the Security Council. So also does the power to make recommendations with regard to "the peaceful adjustment of any situation regardless of origin, which it deems likely to impair the general welfare . . ." (Article 14); a glance at the Security Council's own powers in relation to pacific settlement under Chapter VI will demonstrate this. However, whilst a concurrent jurisdiction may exist in these spheres, a conflict is sought to be avoided by Article 11(2) which, in the last sentence, provides that: "Any such question on which action is necessary shall be referred to the Security Council by the General Assembly either before or after discussion." This stresses the fact that, so far as "action" may be required, it is the Council and not the Assembly that is competent; in other words it underlines the distinction between the executive and the deliberative organ. Further, under Article 12(1) (to which Articles 10 and 11(2) are subject) the Assembly may not make recommendations with regard to a dispute or situation in respect of which "the Security Council is exercising . . . the functions assigned to it . . .". Thus, the priority of the Council in such matters is maintained, and the Assembly is kept notified by the Secretary-General of the matters with which the Security Council is seised (Article 12(2)). Normally, when the Council wishes the Assembly to deal with a matter, it removes the item from its own agenda.[37] The difficult problem arises where this procedure is not followed and the Assembly places a matter on its agenda whilst it still remains on the agenda of the Council;[38] this occurred, for example, when the Assembly proceeded to discuss the Soviet Union's complaint that the USA had committed aggression against China by invading Formosa (now Taiwan), despite the fact that the Council had decided "to defer consideration" of this same question on September 29, 1950. And more recently this occurred when the Assembly discussed Bosnia whilst the matter remained on the agenda of the Security Council.[39] The justification for such action by the Assembly can be sought in part in the argument that the Council had ceased to, or was unable to, exercise the function assigned to it in this matter, or that discussion in the Assembly could not constitute "action"; the larger part of the justification is not, however, one of legal interpretation but of the necessity for the Assembly to promote the aims of the Charter when the Security Council cannot or will not do so.

2–017   The possibilities of a clash in competence between the Assembly and the Council have on occasion been sparked by the tendency of the Assembly to assume a larger role than that which the Charter would at first sight suggest. This larger role has sprung from the reaction of member states to the frustration of the Council consequent upon the East-West rivalry; there is a clearly apparent resolve to use the Assembly to achieve the aims of the Charter when the Council cannot or will not do so. This may be illustrated by two important and controversial early developments. The first resulted from the fact that added political responsibility was difficult for the Assembly to assume when it met in short annual sessions. In 1947,

---

[37] This procedure was followed, for example, on the Spanish question on November 4, 1946, on the Greek question on September 15, 1947, on the complaint of Chinese aggression against South Korea on January 31, 1951, and the *Lebanon* case (1958).
[38] See Memorandum on the Practice of the UN as regards the consideration of the same questions by the S.C. and the G.A. (1964) U.N.J.Y., 228.
[39] In 1993 and 1994.

therefore, the Assembly established, as a subsidiary organ under Article 22, an Interim Committee to function in between the sessions of the main Assembly; its purpose was to ensure continuity in the control the Assembly could exercise over major political problems. The Interim Committee was to have represented on it all the member states (though with only one delegate instead of five) and its competence was more restricted than that of the Assembly itself. It did, however, have power to discuss important disputes or situations submitted to the Assembly, to conduct investigations and to advise the summoning of a special session of the Assembly. This Committee was boycotted by the USSR on the ground that it was a perpetuation of the Assembly, contrary to Article 20, which provided for annual sessions, and a usurpation of the Council's role. The Committee was re-established only in 1948 and 1949. Since that time the Assembly has been able to exercise sufficient control by either convening a special session or else adjourning its regular session in December and continuing in the New Year.

The second development came after the Security Council authorised **2–018** member states to use force in order to help Korea to repel aggression, by resolutions of the Council of June 25 and 27, 1950.[40] These resolutions were passed only due to the fortuitous circumstance of the absence of the USSR from the Council, in protest at the refusal to recognise the communist government as the representative of China. The unlikelihood of a repetition of that circumstance led the Assembly, on November 3, 1950, to pass the Resolution on Uniting for Peace;[41] this was done in the face of the strongest opposition by the Soviet Union. The Assembly thereby assumed the power to determine a threat to the peace, breach of the peace or act of aggression and to recommend action by members including the use of armed force. This power is to be exercised only "if the Security Council, because of lack of unanimity, fails to exercise its primary responsibility for the maintenance of international peace and security"; it is virtually an assertion of a secondary responsibility. A Peace Observation Commission of 14 members is established which can be despatched to any "trouble-area" so as to advise the Assembly of any necessary action, and a Collective Measures Committee of 14 members is established to co-ordinate the action taken by members on the Assembly's recommendation. In the event of a breach of the peace or act of aggression the Assembly will, if not in session, meet within 24 hours of a request being made by nine members of the Security Council or a majority of the members of the Assembly. This procedure has in fact been rarely used. However, on October 31, 1956, when, after the United Kingdom and France had voted against the U.S. resolution in the Security Council proposing measures for the cessation of

---

[40] UN Doc. S/1501 (1950); UN Doc. S/1511 (1950).
[41] Res. 377 (V).

the military action against Egypt, the Suez question was transferred to the Assembly. Four days later, on November 4, following a Soviet veto, the Hungarian question was similarly referred to the Assembly. On September 17, 1960, and again following a Soviet veto, the Congo question was referred by the Council to the Assembly.[42]

2–019 The extent to which practice has demonstrated an acceptance within the Security Council of the Resolution on Uniting for Peace is not entirely clear. Two issues must be separated. The first is that of the appropriate procedure for convening an emergency session of the Assembly, for, whereas the resolution, as amended, provides for this by a vote of "any nine members of the Security Council" the Soviet Union contested the legality of this at the time of the adoption of the resolution on the ground that Article 20 governs the convening of emergency sessions and the vote of the Security Council is a non-procedural one to which, therefore, the veto applies.[43] However, the resolutions of the Council of October 31 and November 4, 1956, which both referred specifically to the Resolution on Uniting for Peace, were adopted against the votes of Britain and France in the first case and of the USSR in the second case. On neither occasion did the USSR raise the Article 20 argument and, indeed, it voted for the resolution of October 31. However, somewhat inconsistently, the USSR again raised this particular argument when on September 17, 1960, it opposed the convening of the emergency session of the Assembly to deal with the Congo. In 1971 the USSR abstained in the vote of the Council referring the Bangladesh issue to the Assembly under Uniting for Peace.[44] Again, in January 1980 the USSR's negative vote failed to stop the Assembly convening to discuss the Soviet invasion of Afghanistan, and calling for the withdrawal of all foreign troops. Similarly, vetoes by the US failed to prevent the convening of special sessions to deal with the Middle East/Palestine (1980), Namibia (1981) and Middle East/Golan Heights (1982) questions. Hence there now appears to be a rule that the convening of special sessions under the Uniting for Peace Resolution is a procedural matter not subject to the right of veto.[45]

2–020 The second issue is the more substantive one of the capacity of the Assembly to establish, even if only by recommendation, a UN Force. The USSR had constantly opposed this as being in breach of Articles 11(2) and 12 and the force monopoly of the Security Council envisaged under Chapter VII, and this became one of the principal Soviet contentions before the Court in the proceedings on the request for an advisory opinion

---

[42] UN Doc. S/P.V. 906, p. 116.
[43] For more on the veto, and on the voting procedure in the Security Council, see Chapter 11, paras 11–017 and 11–018.
[44] Res. 303 (1971), December 6, 1971.
[45] Simma, *The Charter of the United Nations* (1995), p. 346.

on Certain Expenses of the United Nations.[46] The USSR took the view that it was under no obligation to contribute towards the maintenance of UNEF since the force was illegal under the Charter. Although a number of states suggested to the Court that it was not necessary, in order to answer the actual question put to the Court, that the Court should consider the validity of the powers assumed by the General Assembly under the Resolution on Uniting for Peace, the Court did in fact examine the respective functions of the Assembly and the Security Council with respect to the maintenance of international peace and security.[47] Briefly summarised, the Court, in the majority opinion (nine votes to five), advised that the Security Council had "primary" and not exclusive authority, and that whilst the taking of enforcement action was the exclusive prerogative of the Council under Chapter VII, this did not prevent the Assembly from making recommendations under Articles 10 and 14; the limitation of Article 11(2) does not apply in such cases, since the "action" there referred to means only "enforcement action" which is in the nature of coercive action directed against a state. The UNEF "action" was not, in the Court's view, enforcement action, but rather "measures" recommended under Article 14.[48] It would therefore seem that, whilst the Court did not explicitly hold that the Resolution on Uniting for Peace was a lawful assumption of power by the Assembly, it implicitly did so, to the extent that the General Assembly may make recommendations that do not envisage "enforcement action" against states.

Hence, whatever be the arguments based on Articles 11 (2) and 12 of the **2–021** Charter and the absence of any specific power to determine a threat to the peace, breach of the peace or act of aggression,[49] the resolution may now be treated as justifiable, at least to the extent that it envisages a "peace-keeping" operation as opposed to "enforcement action," on the basis of the purposes and principles of the organisation. Naturally, the co-operation of members is entirely voluntary, for the Assembly has only the power to

---

[46] Advisory Opinion of July 20, 1962, 1962 I.C.J. Rep. 151; for the oral statement of Professor Tunkin on behalf of the USSR, see C.R. 62/32. He met the argument that, by voting for the resolution of October 31, 1956, the USSR had already accepted the legality of the resolution on Uniting for Peace by saying "but the S.C. did not ask the G.A. to take action for maintaining peace and security, which under the Charter the S.C. alone is competent to take" (*ibid.* p. 8). This is scarcely adequate, for the Resolution for Uniting on Peace clearly gives the Assembly such power, and the Resolution was specifically referred to in the resolution of October 31, 1956.
[47] (1962) I.C.J. Rep. 163, *et seq.*
[48] *ibid.* 172. Note that the validity of the Congo operations was not contested on the same grounds, because it was the S.C., not the G.A., which initiated them hence the Resolution on Uniting for Peace was not in question. The principal argument relating to the Congo was that the Secretary-General had exceeded and abused the powers conferred on him: this, too, was rejected by the Court.
[49] For a summary of the original arguments in 1950 on the legality of the resolution, see Repertory, Vol. 1, summary of practice under Art. 11, paras 5–167.

"recommend." The Assembly has used its powers under this resolution to condemn the Chinese intervention in Korea as aggression,[50] to recommend economic sanctions against China[51] and to bring about the withdrawal of British and French forces from Egypt in 1956.[52] However, since the Korean crisis the General Assembly has not used its powers under the Resolution to recommend the establishment of an armed force to act against an aggressor state. Instead, use of the Resolution has been limited to authorising peacekeeping operations or the convocation of special emergency sessions. It must be added that the future of the Assembly's peacekeeping powers insofar as these involve the use of military forces is in doubt. Part of the problem is budgetary, or financial,[53] but the larger part was the refusal of the Soviet bloc to concede such powers to the Assembly. It remains to be seen what the impact of recent political changes will be on this issue. After several years of search for a compromise, the Special Committee on Peacekeeping Operations (Committee of 33) failed to reach agreement on this central issue. Significantly, when UNEF was re-instated in the Middle East in 1973, it was done by resolution of the Security Council and not the Assembly.[54] So, too, UNDOF and UNIFIL were established in 1974 and 1978 (in the Golan Heights and the Lebanon) by the Council, not the Assembly.[55] And more recently, the forces established in Iraq (which was not a peacekeeping force), former Yugoslavia, Somalia, Rwanda and East Timor were all established by Security Council action.[56]

2–022   The additional and specific powers given to the Assembly under Chapter IV do not raise so acutely the problem of a conflict of jurisdiction with the Council. Article 13 lists a number of purposes for which the Assembly may make recommendations. Article 14 gives power of recommendation of measures for the peaceful adjustment of situations likely to impair the general welfare; under this Article the assembly put forward the famous and abortive Plan of Partition with Economic Union for Palestine in 1947, and UNEF must be regarded as established within this Article. Article 15, as has been previously mentioned, gives power to receive reports from other organs, and Article 16 refers to its functions relating to the Trusteeship system.[57] Article 17 confers on the Assembly the power to consider and approve the budget of the Organisation.

---

[50] Res. 498 (V) of December 14, 1950.

[51] Res. 500 (V) of May 18, 1951.

[52] Resolutions 997 (ES-I), 1002 (ES-I) and 1120 (XI) of November 2, 7 and 24, 1956.

[53] See Chap. 17, paras 17–014 and 17–015.

[54] UNEF was disbanded and its functions assumed by UNTSO on July 24, 1979, by decision of the Council.

[55] UN Doc. S/INF/30 (1974) established the United Nations Disengagement Observer Force; UN Doc. S/RES/425 (1978) and UN Doc S/RES/426 (1978) established the United Nations Interim Force in Lebanon.

[56] S/RES/678 (November 29, 1990) Iraq; S/RES/743 (February 21, 1992); S/RES/794 (December 3, 1992); S/RES/929 (June 22, 1994) Rwanda; S/RES/1264 (September 15, 1999) East Timor. On peacekeeping operations see *infra*, paras 2–052 *et seq.*

[57] See *infra*, paras 2–080 *et seq.*

This brief review of the functions and powers of the Assembly demon- **2–023** strates their complexity and variety. The Assembly addresses many questions each year (166 separate agenda items at the 51st (1996/7) session of the Assembly, for example). Accordingly, many matters are referred to the Assembly's elaborate system of committees (main, procedural and standing) and subsidiary bodies. The Assembly has six main committees:[58]

- First Committee—Disarmament and International Security;

- Second Committee—Economic and Financial;

- Third Committee—Social, Humanitarian and Cultural;

- Fourth Committee—Special Political and Decolonisation;

- Fifth Committee—Administrative and Budgetary;

- Sixth Committee—Legal.

There are two "procedural" committees: the General Committee (com- **2–024** posed of the President and 21 Vice-Presidents of the Assembly and the chairmen of the six main committees) and the Credentials Committee. At the beginning of each Assembly the General Committee, a kind of steering committee, allocates to each main committee those agenda items that, by reason of the subject-matter, fall within its competence. All main committees are plenary in composition and the bulk of the discussion takes place in the committees, the Assembly being called to meet towards the end of the session to vote on the reports from the main committees; discussion of the substance of an issue is rarely renewed in the Assembly.

There are also two standing committees that deal with essentially **2–025** "administrative" matters. The Committee on Contributions,[59] which addresses *inter alia* apportionment of contributions and the application of Article 19 of the Charter to cases of arrears; and the Advisory Committee on Administrative and Budgetary Questions (ACABQ) which provides administrative and financial advice to the Assembly and addresses budgets and accounts of the UN (regular and peacekeeping) and the administrative budgets of specialised agencies.[60]

---

[58] In 1993, by res. 47/233 the Assembly merged the Special Committee and Fourth Committee, reducing the number to six.
[59] Established by Ass. res. 14(I) (1946), amended most recently by Ass. res. 31/96 (1976).
[60] Established by Ass. res. 14A(I) (1946), amended most recently by Ass. res. 32/103 (1977).

2–026   In addition to these, the Assembly has power under Article 22 to establish "such subsidiary organs as it deems necessary for the performance of its functions."[61] It has, therefore, established a large number of subsidiary organs. Some work closely with the Assembly, and include a wide range of intergovernmental bodies,[62] including bodies established to consider matters of reform[63] and advisory bodies on specific issues,[64] as well as expert bodies.[65] Others, described in Chapter 4, have a greater degree of autonomy. These subsidiary organs differ in function, membership, duration and other respects. Most are established by a resolution of the Assembly itself, although in certain cases the Secretary-General has been requested to establish the organ. Membership is sometimes dealt with in the resolution, sometimes separately by the Assembly on its own or by the Assembly upon the recommendation of the President of the Assembly or of a Main Committee, and sometimes by election where the members of the committee or organ are individuals and not states. The latter is true, for example, of organs like the UN Administrative Tribunal[66] or the Inter-

---

[61] "Subsidiary organs" is a phrase apt to include any organ established by or under the authority of a principal organ of the UN in accordance with Art. 7 (2); such organs are an integral part of the Organisation. They must be distinguished from, on the one hand, the "specialised agencies" (as to which see Chap. 3), and on the other the "special bodies" such as the Permanent Central Opium Board (P.C.O.B.) or the Narcotic Drugs Supervisory Body, both of which were established by multilateral treaty prior to the establishment of the UN and have been given a special status within the UN. See generally the "Summary of internal Secretariat Studies of constitutional questions relating to agencies within the framework of the UN," Doc. A/C.1/758 (1954).

[62] These bodies include: UN Disarmament Commission (Ass. res. 502(VI) (1952) (as amended by UNSSOD-10/2 (1978)); UN Scientific Committee on the Effects of Atomic Radiation (UNSCEAR) (Ass. res. 10/913 (1955); Committee on Peaceful Uses of Outer Space (Ass. res. 14/1472 (1959) (as amended by Ass. res. 49/33 (1994); Special Committee on Peacekeeping Operations (Ass. res. 2006(XIX) (1965)); Special Committee on the Implementation of the Declaration on Decolonisation (Ass. res. 1654(XVI) (1961); Committee on Relations with the Host Country (Ass. res. 2819(XXVI) (1971); Conference on Disarmament (UNSSOD I, res. S-10/2, succeeding the Committee on Disarmament (Ass. res. 1772 (1961) and 2602 (1969)); ad hoc Committee on the Indian Ocean (Ass. res. 2992(XXVII) (1972); Committee on Conferences (Ass. res. 3351(XXIX) (1974); Committee on the Exercise of the Inalienable Rights of the Palestinian People (Ass. res. 3376(XXX) (1975); Special Committee on the Charter of the UN and on the Strengthening of the Role of the Organisation (Ass. res. 3499(XXX) (1975); Committee on Information (Ass. res. 33/115C (1978)); International Criminal Court Preparatory Committee (Ass. res. 50/46 (1995)).

[63] See, for example, Informal Open-Ended Working Group on an Agenda for Peace (Ass. res 47/120A and B) (1992)); Open-Ended Working Group on the Question of Equitable Representation and Increase in the Membership of the Security Council (Ass. res. 48/26 (1993)); High-Level Open-Ended Working Group on the Financial Situation of the UN (Ass. res. 49/143 (1994)); Open-Ended High-Level Working Group on the Strengthening of the UN System (Ass. res. 49/252 (1995)).

[64] See, *e.g.* Advisory Committee on the UN Programme of Assistance in the Teaching, Study, Dissemination and Wider Appreciation of International Law (Ass. res. 2099(XX) (1965)).

[65] Board of Auditors (Ass. res. 74(I) (1946)); International Law Commission (Ass. res. 174(II) (1947)); UN Administrative Tribunal (Ass. res. 351A(IV) (1949)); Investments Committee (Ass. res. 155(II) (1947)); UN Joint Staff Pension Fund (Ass. res. 248(III) (1948)); UNCITRAL (Ass. res. 21/2205 (1966)); International Civil Service Commission (Ass. res. 3042(XXVII) (1972)).

[66] See *infra* Chap. 13, at paras 13–159 to 13–183.

national Law Commission (I.L.C.),[67] although in the case of the 36 member UN Commission on International Trade Law (UNCITRAL), the elective process was also applied to an organ composed of states.

The question of the competence of the Assembly to establish a particular **2–027** organ has been raised on a number of occasions. In general, the Assembly can only establish organs with powers which fall within the scope of the Assembly's own powers; however, these must be ascertained not simply by reference to specific provisions of the Charter but by necessary implication from the powers and duties of the Assembly in general. Hence the I.C.J. did not doubt that the Assembly could establish the Administrative Tribunal with power to render judgments binding on the UN, even though no specific power to that effect was given in the Charter.[68] Moreover, in the same opinion, the Court expressed the view that the Assembly could establish a judicial organ with power to take decisions binding on the Assembly itself, even though it was not itself endowed with judicial powers.[69]

In concluding, therefore, the overall picture which the Assembly gives is **2–028** of an organ which has assumed extensive political power over a growing range of issues as the Security Council reflected an early inability to act so as to achieve the purposes and principles of the Charter. This *de facto* "amendment" of the Charter has posed questions of the constitutional validity of the various steps in this development, but, by and large, the Assembly has sought to regulate its actions by reference to those purposes and principles and has been undeterred by the narrower questions of the legal interpretation of specific articles of the Charter.

(b) SECURITY COUNCIL

Bibliography: United Nations, Repertoire of practice of the Security Council, 1946–51 (1954) and Suppl.1952–55 (ST.PSCA/1/Add.1) (1958); United Nations, Repertory of practice of UN Organs, Vol. II (1955) and Suppl. No. 1, Vol. I (1958)

Jimenez de Arechega, *Voting and the Handling of Disputes in the Security Council* (1951); Stone, *Legal Controls of International Conflict (1959)*, Chaps VII and VIII; Kerley, "The Powers of Investigation of the UN Security Council," (1961) 55 AJIL 892; Schachter, "Legal Aspects of the UN Action in the Congo, (1961) 55; Kahng, *Law, Politics and the Security Council* (1964); Higgins, *The Place of Law in the Settlement of Disputes by the Security Council*, (1970) 64 AJIL, 1–18; Bailey, *Voting in the Security Council* (1969); Berdal, *The Security Council, Peacekeeping and Internal Conflict after the Cold War*, (1996) 6 Duke J Comp. & Int'l L. 71; Bailey and Daws, *The Procedure of the UN Security*

---

[67] See *infra* Chap. 2, at para. 2–091.
[68] I.C.J. Rep. 1954, p. 47.
[69] *ibid.*

Council (1998); Osterdahl, *Threat to the Peace* (1998); Fassbender, *UN Security Council Reform and the Right of Veto: A Constitutional Perspective* (1998); Cox, "Beyond Self-Defence: United Nations Peacekeeping Operations and the Use of Force", (1999) 27 Denver J. Int'l L. & Pol'y 239.

2–029 The Dumbarton Oaks proposals had envisaged an executive organ of limited membership that would be entrusted with "primary responsibility for the maintenance of international peace and security." What was perceived to be needed was a small, executive organ, functioning continually and able to take decisions quickly and effectively so as to bring into operation the enforcement machinery of Chapter VII of the Charter whenever international peace and security was threatened. Proposals were therefore made for the creation of a Security Council within which procedures for the maintenance of international peace and security would be centralised, in contrast with the situation that had prevailed at the League of Nations. Indeed, the increased degree of centralisation, as contrasted with the League, made the Security Council even more essential than the Council of the League. Whilst it may be true that the Security Council has not generally met all the expectations of its creators, the present section should show that any failure has generally been due more to the attitude of its members, and the overall geo-political situation during the Cold War, than to any constitutional defects in the Charter provisions.

2–030 With the end of the Cold War, governments increasingly turned to the UN to deal with ethnic and nationalist conflicts that flared up in all regions of the world. The period between 1988 and 1994 saw the adoption of more resolutions by the Security Council than ever before, with the major upsurge occurring in August 1990 following the Iraqi invasion of Kuwait. The use of force pursuant to Chapter VII of the Charter was also authorised to deal with threats to international peace and security arising out of the conflicts in former Yugoslavia,[70] Somalia[71] and Rwanda.[72] In line with the broader concept of "threat to the peace" endorsed by the 1992 Heads of State and Government Declaration,[73] the Security Council took resolutions under Chapter VII dealing with matters such as international terrorism and the imposition of economic and other sanctions against aggressor states.[74] Beginning in 1995 there was a noticeable decline in Security Council activity, followed by a brief upsurge in activity in response to the situations in Kosovo and East Timor.[75] The Security Council's handling of the Kosovo crisis, however, revealed new divisions between the permanent members, leaving

---

[70] S/RES/743 (February 21, 1992).
[71] S/RES/794 (December 3, 1992).
[72] S/RES/929 (June 22, 1994).
[73] UN Security Council Doc. S/23500 of January 31, 1992.
[74] See, for example, SC res. 731, 748 and 883 (1992/1993) concerning the Lockerbie incident.
[75] See, for example, S/RES/1244 (June 10, 1999) and S/RES/1239 (May 14, 1999) on Kosovo and S/RES/1264 (September 15, 1999) establishing a multinational force for East Timor.

the initiative for authorisation of a multinational force to deal with the situation in the hands of NATO in June and July 1999.[76]

(i) Composition

Article 23, as amended,[77] provides that the Security Council shall consist **2–031** of 15 members of whom five are "permanent members," namely China, France, the Russian Federation,[78] the United Kingdom and the United States. These five permanent members have enjoyed an exceptional status not only by virtue of their permanency but also by reason of special voting rights amongst which, as we shall presently see, the most important is the power of "veto." The justification for granting this exceptional status to five members lies in the "inescapable fact of power differentials," to use Jessup's phrase. In other words, the basic premise was that upon these members would fall the brunt of the responsibility for maintaining international peace and security and, therefore, to them must be given the final or decisive vote in determining how that responsibility should be exercised. To this end, all the signatories of the Charter agreed to a system that would otherwise (*i.e.* without such agreement) have been contrary to "the principle of the sovereign equality of all its Members" upon which the organisation is based (Article 2(1)).

The assumption made in 1945 that these five named states were the **2–032** "great Powers" was, of course, a political judgment. The actual naming of them in the Charter introduces a static element into this instrument, for it cannot be assumed that these identical five will necessarily remain the five "great Powers," and indeed in the case of at least two it cannot realistically be said that they do so today. In an organisation intended to endure, problems may well arise when any marked shift of power does occur. Those problems will be rendered more acute by the cumbersome procedure for amendment of the Charter that, under Articles 107 and 108, requires the consent of the named five members to any amendment. Although it is difficult to imagine a permanent member voting itself out of that status,

---

[76] See Chap. 12, para. 12–074.

[77] See Amendments to Arts 23, 27 and 61 which entered into force on August 31, 1965: U.N.J.Y. (1965), 159.

[78] The Russian Federation informed the UN on December 24, 1991 that the membership of the Soviet Union in the Security Council and all other UN organs was being continued by it, and that the Russian Federation remains responsible in full for the rights and obligations of the former Soviet Union. This was accepted by the other members of the UN. The text of the Accords by Former Soviet Republics Establishing a Commonwealth of Independent States, including the declaration that the Russian Federation would assume the USSR's UN membership and its seat on the Security Council, was circulated as an official UN document, UN Doc. A/47/60 (1991) and UN Doc. S/23329 (1991). For a detailed discussion of how and why the Russian Federation was allowed to simply assume the USSR's UN membership and Security Council seat, see Scharf, "Musical Chairs: The Dissolution of States and Membership in the United Nations," 28 Cornell Int'l L.J. 29, 43–52 (1995).

since 1993 discussions have been underway to alter the balance of representation on the Security Council.[79]

2–033   The ten other members of the Security Council, the non-permanent members, are elected for two years by the General Assembly, and are not immediately eligible for re-election. In order to ensure a certain continuity, the elections are staggered, five states being elected each year, and by a two-thirds majority vote. Article 23 itself indicates certain criteria to be applied in these elections, namely, contribution to "the maintenance of international peace and security and to the other purposes of the organisation," and "equitable geographical distribution." The ten seats are now allocated according to the following formula: Afro-Asia (5), Eastern Europe (1), Latin-America and the Caribbean (2), Western Europe and others (2).[80] This allocation is based upon General Assembly resolution 1991 (XVIII)A and replaced the earlier "gentleman's agreement" of 1946.[81]

2–034   Beyond the Military Staff Committee envisaged by Articles 45 to 47 of the Charter, the Security Council has three standing committees to deal with administrative matters.[82] From time to time it has also established other bodies to address specific issues as they arise. These bodies include ad hoc sanctions committees, of which there are currently nine;[83] two International Criminal Tribunals (for the former Yugoslavia and Rwanda);[84] and Commissions charged with addressing particular matters.[85]

(ii) Functions and Powers

2–035   These are stated in Articles 24–26 of the Charter. In conferring on the Council "primary responsibility for the maintenance of international peace and security", the members of the Organisation agree that it "acts on their

---

[79] UN Doc. A/RES/47/62 (1993); UN Doc. A/RES/48/26 (1993) (establishing an Open-Ended Working Group "to consider all aspects of the question of an increase in the membership of the Security Council and other matters related to the Council."); UN Doc. A/48/47 (1994) (report of the Working Group); UN Doc. A/50/47 (1996) (report of the Working Group). For an exhaustive survey of the effort to reform the Security Council from 1991 to 1997, see Fassbender, UN Security Council Reform and the Right of Veto: A Constitutional Perspective, 221–275 (1998).

[80] For current composition, see the United Nations Website, http://www.un.org/Overview/Organs/sc.html#MEMBER.

[81] For the practice under this earlier agreement see Repertory, Vol. 11, paras 14, et seq.

[82] Committee of Experts on Rules of Procedure; Committee on Admission of New Members; Committee on Council Meetings away from Headquarters.

[83] Committees have been established on Iraq (S.C. res. 661(1990)); Yugoslavia (S.C. res. 724 (1991)); Libya (S.C. res. 748 (1992)); Somalia (S.C. res. 751 (1992)); Angola (S.C. res. 864 (1993)); Rwanda (S.C. res. 918 (1994)); Liberia (S.C. res. 985) (1995)); Sierra Leone (S.C. res. 1132 (1997)) and Kosovo (S.C. res. 1160) (1998). On the functioning of the sanctions committees see Chap. 12.

[84] See infra, Chap. 13, paras 13–088—13–090.

[85] See e.g. UN Special Commission (UNSCOM) to oversee elimination of Iraq's weapons of mass destruction and production facilities (S.C. res. 687 (1991)); UN Compensation Commission (S.C. res. 687 (1991)), infra, Chap. 13 paras 13–193 et seq.); International Commission of Inquiry in Burundi (S.C. res. 1012 (1995)); International Commission of Inquiry (Rwanda) (S.C. res. 1013 (1995)).

behalf." The Council thus acts as the agent of all the members and not independently of their wishes; it is, moreover, bound by the Purposes and Principles of the Organisation, so that it cannot, in principle, act arbitrarily and unfettered by any restraints. At the same time, when it does act *intra vires*, the members of the Organisation are bound by its actions and, under Article 25, they "agree to accept and carry out the decisions of the Security Council in accordance with the present Charter." This agreement would not extend to a mere "recommendation" as opposed to a "decision."[86]

Although Article 24(2) refers to "the specific powers granted . . . in **2–036** Chapters VI, VII, VIII and XII," practice has now confirmed the view that this enumeration is not exhaustive. There exist such other "implied" powers as may be required in the execution of its overall responsibility.[87]

(a) Maintenance of international peace and security

Bibliography: Damrosch (ed.) *Law and Force in the New International Order* (1991); Weckel, "Le Chapitre VII de la Charte et son application par le Conseil de sécurité" AFDI (1991) 165; Dupuy, *"Sécurité collective et organisation de la paix"* RGDIP (1993) 617; Damrosch, *"The Role of the Great Powers in United Nations Peace Keeping"*, 18 Yale J. Int'l L. 415 (1993); Durch, *The Evolution of UN Peacekeeping: Case Studies and Comparative Analysis* (1993); Woelckel "Quelques aspects de la conduite des opérations de maintien de la paix" AFDI (1993) 65; Corten & Klein, "Action humanitaire et chapitre VII—La redéfinition du mandat et des moyens d'action des Forces des Nations Unies", AFDI (1993) 105; SFDI, Colloque de Rennes 1994, *Le Chapitre VII de la Charte des Nations Unies et les nouveaux aspects de la sécurité collective*; Österdahl, *Threat to the Peace: an interpretation by the Security Council of Article 39 of the Charter* (1998); Sarooshi, *The UN and the Development of Collective Security: the Derogation by the UN Security Council of its Power under Chapter VII* (1999).

The Council's primary function, the maintenance of international peace **2–037** and security, is to be exercised by two means; the first is the pacific settlement of such international disputes as are likely to endanger international peace and security, and the second (which presupposes the failure or inapplicability of the first) is the taking of enforcement action.

(1) Pacific settlement of disputes. Chapter VI sets out the various means by which the Council may assist in the settlement of disputes. As Article 33 makes clear, the methods of Chapter VI are supplementary to those methods traditionally established in international law and which the parties must "first of all" utilise, as appropriate. Moreover, it is with disputes

---

[86] But "decisions" are not confined to decisions under Chapter VII of the Charter: see the *Namibia* case, (1971) I.C.J. Rep. para. 113; and see *infra*, Chap. 11.

[87] See *Repertory*, Vol. II, pp. 19–25; a good example is the responsibility the Security Council was to assume under the Statute of the Free Territory of Trieste, including a power to appoint a Governor.

"likely to endanger international peace and security" that the Council is concerned, and not with all disputes.

2–038   The following have a right to submit disputes to the Council: the Assembly (Articles 11 and 12), the Secretary-General (Article 99), member states (Article 35(1)), and non-member states (Article 35(2)). It will be noted that the non-member states are bound, in so doing, to accept in advance and for the purposes of the dispute "the obligations of pacific settlement provided in the present Charter" (Article 35(2)). There is also a duty imposed on parties to a dispute likely to endanger international peace and security to submit the dispute to the Council if they cannot settle it by the traditional means enumerated in Article 33; this is provided for in Article 37.

2–039   The dispute, once submitted, is not automatically incorporated on the Council's agenda. The Council itself decides, by a majority of nine (*i.e.* a procedural decision), whether or not to place the matter on the agenda and even this decision is without prejudice to the question of competence. It may well be that the Council, after considering the matter, decides that the dispute is not an "international" one—in other words a dispute in respect of which it is precluded from exercising any jurisdiction by virtue of the domestic jurisdiction clause of Article 2(7). Similarly, it is for the Council itself to decide whether and when a dispute shall be removed from its agenda, and again by a procedural vote.[88]

2–040   Once seised of a "dispute" the Council is bound under Article 32 to invite the parties to participate in the discussion (but without the right to vote); the Council may invite member states under Article 31 to participate in the discussion of "any question," whether or not a "dispute," when the Council considers that the interests of that state are specially affected. Naturally the Council is not limited by the statements of the parties. It may undertake its own investigations[89] of the matter by setting up an investigation under Article 34, using a subsidiary organ for that purpose. Under Article 29 the vote is procedural; under Article 34 it is non-procedural and the Council's decision to investigate a dispute should, as agreed at San Francisco, be made only with the concurrence (or at least non-opposition) of the five permanent members.[90] There is no legal obligation spelt out in the Charter to the effect that a state must comply with the decision of the Council in the sense of permitting a commission of investigation to have

---

[88] For details of the controversy which arose over this question in the Iranian dispute of 1946, see *Repertoire*, 1946–51, pp. 92–93.
[89] See Kerley, "The Powers of Investigation of the UN Security Council" (1961) 55 AJIL 892.
[90] See, as an example of controversy on this point, the discussion in the Czechoslovakian question in 1948: *Repertory*, Vol. II, pp. 231–233.

access to its territory. Yet, without such access, the value of a commission is much decreased and it can be argued that such an obligation exists by virtue of the general terms of Article 25.

In dealing with a dispute the Council has a number of alternative ways of **2–041** proceeding. It may, under Article 33(2), simply call upon the parties to utilise the traditional means of settlement, leaving the choice of any particular means to the parties. Or it may, under Article 36(1), recommend a particular means of settlement, but taking into consideration that "legal disputes should as a general rule be referred by the parties to the International Court of Justice . . ." (Article 36(3)).[91] The Council may even go further and, under Article 37(2), recommend the actual terms of a settlement in addition to the means or procedures for settlement; this is tantamount to assuming a quasi-judicial function where the dispute affects the legal rights of the parties. This way of proceeding is available only where the dispute is considered by the Council to endanger international peace and security; otherwise the Council could only so act, under Article 38, with the consent of all the parties. A final alternative is for the Council to set up a machinery for settlement within the United Nations—such as the Committee of Good Offices in Indonesia in 1947, or the Mediator between India and Pakistan over Kashmir, the Good Offices Mission in Afghanistan and Pakistan established as part of the peace arrangement achieved by the Geneva Agreement of April 14, 1988,[92] or the UN Assistance Mission in Rwanda given a mandate in April 1994 to act as an intermediary between the warring groups to seek a cease-fire[93]—or to refer the dispute to an existing organ, as was done by the Council in referring the Spanish case and the Palestine question to the General Assembly.

Whatever the course adopted under Chapter VI, it must be adopted by a **2–042** non-procedural decision. The original justification for this lay in the so-called "chain of events" theory. This provided that, it being granted that any permanent member could veto enforcement action, it was necessary to grant the same veto in matters of pacific settlement lest the permanent member should otherwise become committed to a course of action against its wishes that might ultimately lead to taking enforcement action. This reasoning does not really bear close examination. As we shall see, any permanent member can, whatever course has been adopted under Chapter VI, cast its veto to prevent the determination of a "threat to the peace, breach of the peace or act of aggression" under Article 39 without which none of the enforcement measures under Chapter VII can be applied.

---

[91] In the *Corfu Channel* case the Council made such a recommendation, although it recommended arbitration in the *Suez Canal Company* case, the India/Pakistan dispute in 1951 and the Indonesian dispute in 1947.

[92] See UN Doc. S/19835, p. 3, *et seq.*

[93] See S.C. res. 912 (April 21, 1994).

2–043   One final point must be noted in connection with Chapter VI, and that is that the powers of the Security Council are to make "recommendations." These are not binding on the states to whom they are addressed, for Article 25 relates only to "decisions." Hence, the recommendation by the Council to the parties in the Corfu Channel dispute, that they submit their dispute to the International Court of Justice, was not regarded by the majority of the Court as creating a legal obligation to submit to the Court's jurisdiction.[94]

2–044 **(2) Enforcement action.** A striking difference between the Covenant of the League of Nations and the Charter of the United Nations lies in the degree of centralisation accorded to the Council—the executive organ of limited membership. Under the League each member state reserved the right to determine for itself whether a particular state had resorted to war in breach of the Covenant, and also whether or not to comply with the recommendation of the Council with regard to the "sanctions" to be taken. In the UN the Security Council has the power, under Article 39, to determine, on behalf of the Organisation as a whole, whether or not there has been a "threat to the peace, breach of the peace or act of aggression," and its decisions with regard to any enforcement action to be taken are binding on the member states by virtue of Article 25.

2–045   The Security Council has two forms of enforcement action available to it; those described in Article 41 (not involving the use of armed force), and those described in Article 42 (involving action by air, sea or land forces). Before deciding upon either it is necessary for the Council to "determine the existence of any threat to the peace, breach of the peace, or act of aggression" under Article 39. This determination, as with all other decisions under Chapter VII, can only be made by a non-procedural vote. The unanimity (or abstention) of the permanent members is essential and it is most unlikely that any enforcement action could ever be taken under Chapter VII against any of the permanent members or any other state securing their support; the veto ensures that result. It is for this reason, above all others, that the measures envisaged in Chapter VII have been practically irrelevant in an age in which the threats to the peace, breaches of the peace or acts of aggression occured in situations in which there was a conflict of interests between, notably, the USA and the USSR and, consequently, no unanimity amongst the permanent members. That said, there is some evidence that since the political changes of 1990–91 the situation has evolved.

1945–90

2–046 As to the earlier period, after the Indonesian affair in 1947 (in which there was unanimity) and until the Congo crisis of July 1960, there had been only one occasion in which the Security Council effectively used its powers

---

[94] *Corfu Channel* case (*United Kingdom v. Albania*), Judgment of April 9, 1949, (1949) I.C.J. Rep., p. 4.

under Chapter VII. The exception was Korea in 1950, and this only due to the temporary absence of the former USSR.[95] The successive crises of Berlin, Palestine, Indo-China, Hungary and Suez, to pick random samples, all involved East-West conflict of interests and, therefore, the Council never used its enforcement powers. The Congo crisis of 1960 appeared, at the outset, to be a unique example of a situation that called for UN action but which did not involve the East-West conflict. Hence the three major resolutions of July 14 and 22 and August 9 came from the Security Council, enabling the Secretary-General to provide military assistance to the government of the Congo. Admittedly the action taken was not "enforcement action" under Articles 41 or 42, but rather the "provisional measures" envisaged in Article 40.[96] It nevertheless marked an unprecedented and initially successful use by the Security Council of its powers under Chapter VII. However, in due course the Cold War conflict re-emerged even here, and with the loss of unanimity effective control passed to the Assembly, convened in emergency session under the Resolution on Uniting for Peace procedure by the Security Council on September 17, 1960, against the votes of the USSR and Poland. Some semblance of unanimity—or at least the absence of a veto—returned during the Council's handling of the Rhodesian affair: the resolutions of April 9, 1966 (221 (1966)), December 16, 1966 (232 (1966)) and May 29, 1968 (253 (1968)) envisaged sanctions under Chapter VII, the later two resolutions in fact specifically invoking Articles 39 and 41. On November 4, 1977 the Council also unanimously imposed an arms embargo against South Africa under Chapter VII.[97] However, as a general rule the veto invariably frustrated the Council's enforcement powers. It is only more recent events that have made the following discussion of Chapter VII more necessary. It must be emphasised that by the end of the 1980s the only true coercive measures ordered by the Council, and made mandatory for all members, had been the economic sanctions against Rhodesia and the arms embargo against South Africa.[98]

1990–present

With the end of the Cold War and the dissolution of the USSR in 1991, **2–047** Security Council action in response to threats to international peace and security once again became a possibility. The revitalisation of the Security

---

[95] See *supra*, para. 2–018.
[96] See Schachter, "Legal Aspects of the UN Action in the Congo" (1961) 55 AJIL 1. The I.C.J., in its Advisory Opinion of July 20, 1962, on Certain Expenses of the UN, took the view that ONUC was not "enforcement action" against any state, and that the S.C. could "police a situation" (p.167) without agreements existing under Art. 43, and without characterising its actions as "enforcement action."
[97] S.C. res. 418 (November 4, 1977).
[98] The USA imported chrome-ore from Rhodesia under Act of Congress (the Byrd amendment) despite the mandatory sanctions. In *Diggs v. Shultz* U.S. Court of Appeals, D.C. Circuit, 1972 the Court accepted that this was a "blatant disregard of our treaty undertakings." (470 F.2d 461).

Council's role in maintaining international peace and security began with the series of resolutions made by the Council in response to Iraq's invasion of Kuwait. Pursuant to resolution 661 of August 6, 1990, the Security Council called on all states to freeze Iraqi assets and to take economic sanctions against the aggressor state. This resolution was amplified by resolution 670 of September 25, 1990 calling on all member states to impose embargoes on air and sea transportation to Iraq. In the face of Iraq's continued occupation of Kuwait and refusal to comply with previous Security Council resolutions, on November 29, 1990, the Security Council by resolution 678 authorised member states "to use all necessary means" to uphold and implement previous Security Council resolutions and to restore peace and security in the area. This formula ("all necessary means") has been used by the Council in a number of subsequent resolutions, and is well accepted as amounting to an authorisation to use force against the state upon which the coercive measures are imposed.

2–048 In 1991, in the face of the conflict between Croatia, which sought independence from Yugoslavia, and the Serb dominated central Yugoslavian authorities, the Security Council again exercised its powers under Chapter VII, calling on all states to implement an arms embargo against Yugoslavia.[99] With the secession of Bosnia and Herzegovina in April 1992, intense fighting again broke out between the Bosnian, Croat and Serb communities within Bosnia. The Security Council reacted by imposing comprehensive economic sanctions on Serbia and Montenegro.[1] Efforts to ensure the safety of the delivery of humanitarian assistance in Bosnia-Herzegovina led to the Security Council's authorisation of a ban on military flights in the country's airspace.[2] This ban was strengthened by a further resolution authorising member states, acting nationally or through regional organisations or arrangements, to take all necessary measures to ensure compliance with the ban.[3] Later the Security Council authorised member states, acting nationally or through regional arrangements, to use air power to support the UN Protection Force (UNPROFOR) in performance of its mandate to keep the peace in "safe areas" established in Bosnia and to protect the delivery of humanitarian aid to those areas.[4] This mandate was eventually acted on some two years later when NATO forces attacked Bosnian Serbs, bringing to an end the siege of Sarajevo.

2–049 When tensions again flared up in the region, this time in Kosovo in 1998/1999, the Security Council was unable to take decisive enforcement action in the face of likely vetoes by Russia and China. Military action was

[99] S.C. res. 713 (September 25, 1991).
[1] S.C. res. 757 (May 30, 1992).
[2] S.C. res. 781 (October 9, 1992).
[3] S.C. res. 816 (March 31, 1993).
[4] S.C. res. 836 (June 4, 1993).

thus taken unilaterally by NATO, with the Security Council relegated to a more peripheral role of calling upon the parties to cease hostilities,[5] making provision for relief assistance to refugees[6] and taking action for the deployment of an international civil and security presence in Kosovo following the withdrawal of Yugoslavian forces.[7] With the conclusion of the NATO actions matters returned to the Security Council for the purposes of ratifying the terms of the conclusion of the conflict.

There are other cases in which coercive measures have been authorised, **2–050** on the basis of a broad interpretation of the notion of a threat to international peace and security which is not limited to inter-state conflicts. UN members were authorised to use force in Somalia in 1992, by resolution 794, and the UN peacekeeping operation in Somalia—UNOSOM II—was itself authorised to resort to force. Arms embargoes and related economic measures have been authorised in relation to situations *inter alia* in Liberia Sierra Leone, and Yugoslavia, and coercive measures have been aimed also at particular groups, such as UNITA in Angola and the Khmer rouge in Cambodia.[8] In the case of Haiti, in 1993, the Security Council determined that the failure to reinstate the democratically elected President, Jean-Bertrand Aristide, was a threat to international peace and security. The Council considered that the persistence of the situation gave rise to a "climate of fear of persecution and economic dislocation which could increase the number of Haitians seeking refuge in neighbouring Member States",[9] destabilising the area. Following the initial imposition of an embargo on the supply of arms or petroleum products to Haiti,[10] and its expansion to comprehensive economic sanctions a year later,[11] in July 1994 the Security Council went one step further, authorising the formation of a multinational force under unified command and control to restore the legitimately elected authorities in Haiti.[12]

The most recent example of the Security Council's use of the enforce- **2–051** ment powers under Chapter VII has been in respect of the situation in East Timor. By S.C. res. 1264 of September 15, 1999, the Council determined that the deteriorating security situation in East Timor, and the widespread, displacement of, and violence against, the East Timorese constituted a threat to international peace and security. The Resolution authorised the establishment of a multinational force to restore peace and security in East Timor.

---

[5] See S.C. res. 1199 (September 23, 1998).
[6] See S.C. res. 1239 (May 14, 1999).
[7] S.C. res. 1244 (June 10, 1999).
[8] See Chap. 12, paras 12–071 *et seq.*
[9] S.C. res. 841 (June 16, 1993), para. 11.
[10] *ibid.*
[11] S.C. res. 917 (May 6, 1994).
[12] S.C. res. 940 (July 31, 1994).

(b) Peacekeeping Operations

2–052 Since 1945 the UN has been involved in 53 peacekeeping and observation operations. These have involved the deployment of international military and civilian personnel to a conflict area, with the consent of the parties to the conflict, with a view to limiting hostilities or supervising the carrying out of a peace agreement. These actions do not constitute enforcement action within the meaning of Chapter VII, but they operate under the direction of the UN organ that established them, subject to the oversight of the Secretary-General.

2–053 In the first 45 years of the UN, only 13 peacekeeping operations were established, whereas in the years since 1990 some 40 operations have been deployed throughout the world. Accompanying this explosion in the number of UN peacekeeping operations has been an increase in their scope from missions merely carrying out military peacekeeping tasks to complex missions involving political, military and humanitarian activities. Between 1945 and 1960 three peacekeeping operations were undertaken;[13] from 1961 to 1989 there were ten operations;[14] from 1990 to 1999 23 operations were completed.[15] And at the time of writing 17 operations are underway.[16]

---

[13] Middle East (UNEF I) (Nov. 1956–June 1967); Lebanon (UNOGIL) (June–December 1958); Congo (ONUC) (July 1960–July 1964).

[14] West New Guinea (UNSF) (October 1962–April 1963); Yemen (UNYOM) (July 1963–September 1964); India/Pakistan (UNIPOM) (September 1965–March 1966); Dominican Republic (DOMREP) (May 1965–October 1966); Middle East (UNEF II) (October 1973–July 1979); Afghanistan/Pakistan (UNGOMAP) (April 1988–March 1990); Iran/Iraq (UNIIMOG) (August 1988–February 1991); Angola (UNAVEM I) (January 1989–June 1991); Namibia (UNTAG) (April 1989–March 1990); Central America (ONUCA) (November 1989–January 1992).

[15] Angola (UNAVEM II) (June 1991–February 1995); El Salvador (ONUSAL) (July 1991–April 1995); Cambodia (UNAMIC) (October 1991–March 1992); Guatemala (MINUGUA) (January–May 1992); Cambodia (UNTAC) (March 1992–September 1993); Former Yugoslavia (UNPROFOR) (March 1992–December 1995); Somalia (UNOSOM I) (April 1992–March 1993); Mozambique (ONUMOZ) (December 1992–December 1994); Somalia (UNOSOM II) (March 1993–March 1995); Liberia (UNOMIL) (September 1993–September 1997); Haiti (UNMIH) (September 1993–June 1996); Rwanda (UNAMIR) (October 1993–March 1996); Rwanda/Uganda (UNOMUR) (June 1993–September 1994); Chad/Libya (UNASOG) (May–June 1994); Angola (UNAVEM III) (February 1995–June 1997); Croatia (UNCRO) (March 1995–January 1996); Former Yugoslav Republic of Macedonia (UNPREDEP) (March 1995–February 1999); Croatia (UNTAES) (January 1996–January 1998); Haiti (UNSMIH) (July 1996–July 1997); Angola (MONUA) (July 1997–February 1999); Haiti (UNTMIH) (August–November 1997); Croatia (UNPSG) (January 1998–October 1998); Sierra Leone (UNOMSIL) (July 1998–October 1999).

[16] UN Military Observer Group in India and Pakistan (UNMOGIP) (S.C. res. 39 (1948)); UN Truce Supervision Organisation (Palestine) (UNTSO) (S.C. res. 50(1948)); UN Force in Cyprus (UNFICYP) (S.C. res. 186 (1964)); UN Disengagement Observer Force (UNDOF, Syria/Israel) (S.C. res. 350 (1974)); UN Interim Force in Lebanon (UNIFIL) (S.C. res. 425 (1978)); UN Iraq-Kuwait Observation Mission (UNIKOM) (S.C. res. 687 (1991)); UN Mission for the Referendum in Western Sahara (MINURSO) (S.C. res. 690 (1991)); UN Observer Mission in Georgia (UNOMIG) (S.C. res. 858 (1993)); UN Mission in Haiti (MIPONUH) (S.C. res. 867 (1993)); UN Mission of Observers in Tajikistan (UNMOT)

Discussion

The determination of a "threat to the peace, breach of the peace or act **2–054** of aggression" under Article 39 must precede the use of the Council's powers under Articles 41 and 42, whether or not that Article is specifically invoked or cited. With the exception of the resolutions 232 (1966) and 253 (1968) on Rhodesia, the practice of the Council has been to avoid specific reference to that Article[17] (a practice, incidentally, not limited to Article 39); even in determining that the armed attack upon the Republic of Korea constituted a "breach of the peace," no specific reference to Article 39 was made by the Council in its resolution of June 25, 1950.[18] Two difficulties in the making of this determination call for comment. The first is that the "peace" referred to must mean "international" peace. It would be contrary to the intention of the Charter to assume that the Council could forcibly intervene in any civil strife which did not threaten international peace, and both in the Korean question and in the earlier Indonesian question the argument was advanced that action by the Council was barred on the ground that it intervened in the purely domestic jurisdiction of the state concerned. However, that argument was in both cases implicitly rejected. In the Congo affair, although the Council probably acted under Article 40, and although there was there a specific request from the government for UN intervention, it may also be recalled that the principle of non-intervention guided the Secretary-General in instructing the UN Force not to intervene in the internal struggle for political power but to confine its activities to the maintenance of law and order, the protection of human life and the elimination of the foreign elements (originally Belgian troops and later mercenaries) which tended to create a threat to international peace.[19] The second difficulty arose from the lack of any definition in the Charter of the terms used, *i.e.* "threat to the peace, breach of the peace or act of aggression." This lack was intentional. At San Francisco an area of discretion was intentionally left to the Council and although, in resolution

---

(S.C. res. 968 (1994)); UN Mission in Bosnia and Herzegovina (UNMIBH) (S.C. res. 1035 (1995)); UN Mission of Observers in Prevlaka (UNMOP) (S.C. res. 1038 (1996)); UN Interim Administration in Kosovo (UNMIK) (S.C. res. 1244 (1999)); UN Mission in Sierra Leone (UNAMSIL) (S.C. res. 1270 (1999)); UN Mission in the Central African Republic (MINURCA) (S.C. res. 1271 (1999)); UN Transitional Administration in East Timor (UNTAET) (S.C. res. 1272 (1999)); UN Observer Mission in the Democratic Republic of the Congo (MONUC) (S.C. res. 1279 (1999)).

[17] See Repertory, Vol. II, pp. 334, *et seq.* More recent resolutions of the Security Council determining a threat to peace and security (*e.g.* for Iraq, Haiti, former Yugoslavia, East Timor, etc.) have similarly made reference to acting "under Chapter VII" rather than to Article 39 of the Charter.

[18] S/1501; similarly in the resolution of June 27, 1950 (S/1511). It may be noted that neither resolution, the latter of which recommended members to furnish assistance to the Republic of Korea, cited Arts 41 or 42. One construction of these resolutions is that they were in exercise of the power of "recommendation" under Art. 39.

[19] Schachter, *loc. cit.*, pp. 15–20, and see especially the Secretary-General's statement to the Security Council (UN doc. S/P.V 887).

3314 (XXIX) in 1974 the General Assembly succeeded in adopting a definition of aggression, this is only for the "guidance" of the Council and the list of aggressive acts is not exhaustive. In practice the problem may be one of acquiring accurate factual knowledge of events, rather than one of legal definition, and in Korea the Council relied heavily on the report of UNCOK (UN Commission on Korea), just as in considering the situation in Lebanon in 1958 it relied on the reports from UNOGIL (UN Observer Group in Lebanon). The presence of such groups "on the spot" is a tremendous advantage and, as has already been suggested, the Council has the power under Article 34 to send a committee or group where none already exists.

2–055 The practice of the Council suggests that the power under Article 40 to call upon the parties to comply with "provisional measures" does not depend upon a prior determination under Article 39. In relation to Palestine Article 40 was specifically invoked, in ordering a cease-fire and calling for a withdrawal behind provisional truce-lines; similar measures were ordered by the Council in Kashmir. In the Congo, whilst there was abundant evidence, both in the terms of the request for assistance by the government of the Congo and in statements by representatives in the Security Council, that a "threat to international peace" existed, no specific determination under Article 39 was made. The resolutions of the Council were, however, probably based upon Article 40. The question whether a resolution "calling upon" states or other bodies to comply with the provisional measures is mandatory cannot be answered in the abstract. It was, however, clear that the three resolutions of July 14 and 22 and August 9, were considered as mandatory, for the Secretary-General's conclusion[20] that Articles 25 and 49 applied was confirmed by the Security Council in the resolution of August 9. Both those articles refer to the decisions of the Security Council that are binding on all members.[21] The "provisional measures" ordered under Article 40 do not prejudice the rights of the parties; they are simply a means of preventing an aggravation of the situation and the Council may take account of a failure to comply with such provisional measures.

2–056 The crux of the scheme envisaged in Chapter VII lay in the provision to the Security Council of the armed forces necessary to enforce its decisions against recalcitrant states, and this was to be effected by agreements between the member states and the Council, for which provision is made in Article 43. No such agreements have ever been concluded, so that the

---

[20] Statement to the Security Council on August 8; doc. S/P.V 884, pp. 9–10.

[21] Note that the U.K. (Letter of December 12, 1979, S/13688) took it upon itself to decide that the obligations under Article 25 in relation to sanctions against Rhodesia were at an end. The Council, in its resolution of December 21, 1979 and the Assembly in res. 34/192 of December 18, took the view that this was for the Council to decide.

Council lacks the "teeth" with which to bite, and the Military Staff Committee for which provision is made in Articles 46 and 47 (although established since 1946) has no real function since its purpose was to make plans for the application of armed force and to advise and assist the Council in the use of forces placed at its disposal. The absence of agreements under Article 43 would not, however, prevent member states from agreeing ad hoc, and in relation to a particular situation, to permit members to commit their forces or to place forces at the disposal of the Council; in fact this is precisely how the United Nations Command was composed in Korea in 1950 and how the UN Force in the Congo was subsequently constituted. However, dependence on "voluntary contributions" cannot be said to be the surest guarantee of effectiveness.

The failure of the Security Council to fulfil its primary purpose of **2–057** maintaining international peace and security in the period prior to 1990 led to three major developments. The first was the assumption by the General Assembly of a role which was certainly never intended for it, namely that of determining a breach of the peace or an act of aggression and recommending action by members, including the use of armed forces.[22] The second was the development of powerful regional security systems or alliances outside the UN, such as NATO and the now defunct Warsaw Treaty Organisation, a development symptomatic of the breach of unity between the permanent members and the lack of confidence in the efficacy of the general collective security system based on the Security Council.[23] The third was the development of "peacekeeping" operations under either Chapter VI or Chapter VII of the Charter, using limited military forces, voluntarily contributed by member states, for observation and fact-finding (*e.g.* UNTSO, UNMOGIP (Kashmir), UNYOM (Yemen), UNIFIL (Lebanon), UNDOF (Golan Heights)) or maintaining law and order in a situation involving an actual or incipient threat to peace (*e.g.* ONUC (Congo), UNFICYP (Cyprus)), or monitoring cease-fires (*e.g.* UNEF). This role fell between Chapters VI and VII—some have advocated a new Chapter VIbis—and, since it is one shared by the Assembly, is discussed in the preceding section.

While the Security Council's use of enforcement powers under Chapter **2–058** VII has increased since 1990, the UN maintains a strong focus on peacekeeping operations, both to enforce peace accords (secured following action by a multinational UN force to restore peace and security), and to provide humanitarian and other assistance in the aftermath of civil war. For example, the UNIKOM Mission in Iraq-Kuwait was deployed, following the ceasefire, to monitor the Khor Abdullah and a demilitarised zone between

---

[22] See *supra*, para. 12–017 *et seq.*
[23] See Chap. 6, paras 6–003 and 6–064.

Iraq and Kuwait.[24] In Bosnia-Herzegovina, the UN Mission (UNMIBH) was entrusted with tasks under the Dayton Peace Agreement relating to deployment of a civilian police force and the co-ordination of the UN contribution to implementation of the peace agreement.[25] In Rwanda the UN Assistance Mission (UNAMIR) was initially established to assist in implementation of the peace agreement signed between the warring forces of the Government of Rwanda and the Rwandese Patriotic Front (RPF) in August 1993.[26] However, UNAMIR's mandate underwent several changes in response to the Civil War that again broke out following the death of the Rwandan President in an air crash on April 6, 1994. Initially UNAMIR was authorised to act as an intermediary between the warring parties to seek a cease-fire,[27] but later its mandate was expanded to contribute to the security and protection of the millions of Rwandan refugees fleeing to neighbouring Tanzania.[28] In June 1994 the Security Council authorised the deployment of a multinational operation for humanitarian purposes—Operation Turquoise.[29] Following RPF's unilateral declaration of cease-fire, ending the civil war, UNAMIR assumed responsibility for Operation Turquoise until the completion of its mission in March 1996.

2–059   In Somalia, peacekeeping forces were once again deployed to deal with the consequences of the Civil War. In December 1992, the Security Council authorised member states to intervene, using "all necessary means" to establish a secure environment for humanitarian related operations in Somalia.[30] The UNOSOM missions were established with the intention of taking over peacemaking and peacekeeping in Somalia after the initial intervention by a US-led multinational force.

2–060   One of the most recent peacekeeping operations, that in Kosovo (UNMIK), demonstrates the trend to broaden the scope of such operations from merely undertaking military tasks to more complex missions of civil reconstruction. On June 10, 1999, in the aftermath of NATO's suspension of air operations and the withdrawal of Yugoslav forces, the Security Council authorised the Secretary-General to establish an interim civilian administration in Kosovo.[31] The breadth of executive tasks vested in the mission is unprecedented, with the UNMIK being given authority over the territory and people of Kosovo, including over its legislature, administration and judiciary. The mission will involve a complex five stage process

---

[24] See S.C. res. 687 (1991).
[25] S.C. res. 1035 (1995).
[26] S.C. res. 872 (October 5, 1993).
[27] S.C. res. 912 (April 21, 1994).
[28] S.C. res. 918 (May 17, 1994).
[29] S.C. res. 929 (June 22, 1994).
[30] S.C. res. 794 (December 3, 1992).
[31] S.C. res. 1244 (June 10, 1999).

with four sectors (civil administration, humanitarian assistance, democratisation and institution building and economic reconstruction) involved in implementing the civilian aspects of rehabilitation and reformation in Kosovo. The same pattern was followed a few months later with the establishment of the UN Transitory Administration for East Timor (UNTAET).

(c) ECONOMIC AND SOCIAL COUNCIL (ECOSOC)

Bibliography: United Nations, *Repertory of Practice of UN Organs*, Vol. III (1955) and Suppl. No. 1; Vol. II (1958)

Goodrich and Hambro, *Charter of the United Nations* (1949), 2nd ed., Chaps IX and X; Jenks, "Co-ordination in International Organisation: an Introductory Survey", (1951) 28 B.Y.B.I.L. 29; Cheever and Haviland, *Organising for Peace* (1954), Chaps 7 and 8; Goodspeed, "Political Considerations in the UN Economic and Social Council," (1961) Y.B.W.A. 135; Hadwen and Kaufmann, *How UN Decisions are Made* (1962); Falk and Mendlovitz, *The Strategy of World Order*, Vol. 4 (1966), Chap. 6; Kirdar, *The Structure of UN Economic Aid to Underdeveloped Countries* (1966); Mangone, *UN Administration of Economic and Social Programs* (1966); Gardner and Millikan, The Global Partnership: International Agencies and Economic development" (1968) 22 Int. Org. No. 1; Sharp, *The UN Economic and Social Council* (1969); Kaufmann, *The Economic and Social Council and the New International Economic Order,* in Forsyth (Ed), The UN in the World Political Economy 54 (1989).

Before dealing in any detail with the structure and functions of ECOSOC **2–061** it is appropriate to review, historically, the trend of governmental co-operation in the economic and social fields; only in this way can the present role of ECOSOC be really appreciated. In the first Chapter mention was made of the prolific growth of international public unions in these fields; the various river commissions, the UPU, the ITU, the Metric Union and the Sugar Union are but a few of the many instances of governmental co-operation which preceded the League of Nations. During the First World War co-operation between the Allies extended through various bodies such as the Wheat Executive (1916) and Allied Maritime Transport Council (1917), although this was based on the personal integration of the national administrations rather than on any formal delegation of executive power. The League of Nations, however, failed to make full use of this background of co-operation. Not only was the League's co-ordination of the work of the public unions superficial, but the Covenant did not reflect any real appreciation of the relationship of international economic and social stability to world peace;[32] these matters received the briefest of mention in the Preamble and Article 23(e) of the Covenant. No special responsibilities

---

[32] Pt XIII of the Versailles Treaty, the Constitution of the ILO, contained fuller recognition of this relationship.

were assigned to the Assembly or the Council and no special organ was created to undertake such responsibilities. There developed, instead, an elaborate structure of advisory committees, working under the Council, which together constituted the Economic and Financial Organisation of the League.[33]

2–062   Of these the two principal committees were the Economic Committee and the Financial Committee, composed of technical experts serving in their personal capacity rather than as governmental representatives; their work was purely advisory. There were, in addition, various subsidiary committees, also advisory.[34] As the years progressed the League was, almost against its own inclination, forced into ever more economic and social activity. Indeed, the trend of events, of which the general depression of 1928–31 is a singular example, made this inevitable. The League convened various conferences,[35] made reconstruction loans to various countries,[36] and established a number of institutions having an economic or social function.[37] By a curious irony of events, the League's economic and social activities, on which so little emphasis had originally been placed, became more impressive than its political activities. By 1939 the Bruce Committee, set up by the League to review these activities, recommended that the Council be relieved of them, or rather of responsibility for them, and that a separate Central Committee of 24 governmental representatives and eight experts should assume direct responsibility.

2–063   The Second World War, repeating the experience of the First World War, produced a strong record of inter-allied co-operation in the economic field. Combined boards were set up, allocating essential supplies and materials, pooling resources and sublimating national interests in the common aim of victory.[38] On a larger basis of participation, a United Nations Conference on Food and Agriculture in May 1943 laid the foundations for co-operation and in November 1943, 44 governments established the United Nations Relief and Rehabilitation Administration (UNRRA).[39] In July 1944 the Bretton Woods Conference established the

---

[33] See, generally, Hill, *The Economic and Financial Organization of the League of Nations* (1946). There was also the Organisation of Communications and Transit, which originated in Pt XII of the Treaty of Versailles and was founded on a Statute provided by the Barcelona Conference of 1926; this had a general conference (meeting four times yearly) which drafted treaties, an Advisory and Technical Committee (meeting twice yearly) and six permanent committees. Then there was the Health Organisation, which drafted treaties and provided assistance to states.

[34] *e.g.* the Fiscal Committee, the Committee of Statistical Experts, the Co-ordination Committee and the International Loan Contracts Committee.

[35] *e.g.* the Monetary Conference of 1933 and the World Economic Conference of 1927.

[36] *e.g.* Austria and Bulgaria.

[37] *e.g.* the International Relief Union, the Communications and Transit Organisation, and the Bank for International Settlements.

[38] See Schwarzenberger, *Power Politics* (1951), Chap. 21.

[39] See *infra*.

International Monetary Fund (IMF) and the International Bank for Reconstruction and Development.[40] In December 1944 at Chicago the Convention on Civil Aviation was signed, which provided for the new organisation ICAO.[41]

When, therefore, the San Francisco Conference met to sign the UN **2–064** Charter there existed an emerging framework of co-operation in the economic and social fields. The League's history suggested a need for greater emphasis on these fields and a separate organ to deal with responsibility for them. The existence of the older specialised organisations (unions), coupled with the creation of the new ones referred to in the previous paragraph, pointed to the necessity for co-ordination within the framework of the new, general organisation. This emphasis on economic and social issues is reflected in the fact that ECOSOC was established as a principal organ of the UN. In 1991, following a review of the functioning of the subsidiary bodies of the ECOSOC and the GA requested by the Assembly,[42] the Assembly charged the Secretary-General with implementing a programme for restructuring and revitalisation of the UN in the economic, social and related fields.[43] The objective of the restructuring was to enhance the efficient functioning of the subsidiary bodies to be more responsive to the needs of enhancing international economic co-operation and promoting development of developing countries. This has involved the restructuring of the composition of some bodies to ensure equitable geographic representation, the strengthening of the role of the regional commissions, the transformation of some of the subsidiary bodies and the creation of others.[44]

(i) Composition

As a principal organ of the UN, the Economic and Social Council now **2–065** has 54 members, elected by the General Assembly by "staggered" elections so as to ensure some continuity. There is no permanent membership as of right, as in the Security Council (though in practice the permanent members are always elected),[45] and, as we shall see, the principle of equality is also applied to voting power. In the elections an attempt is always made to represent a variety of social, economic, cultural and geographical interests. The amendment of Article 61 of the Charter, decided upon in resolution 2847 (XXVI), establishes five categories of members corres-

---

[40] See *infra*, Chap. 3.
[41] See *infra*, Chap. 3.
[42] G.A. res. 45/264 (May 13, 1991).
[43] G.A. res. 46/235 (April 13, 1992).
[44] *ibid.*
[45] Note that when the U.S. failed to get elected to the G.A. budget committee—ACABQ—a requirement was adopted for ACABQ to consult with the Committee for Programme and Co-ordination on which the U.S. is represented.

ponding to the following groups: Africa, Asia, Latin America, Western Europe and others, and Eastern Europe. Article 69 gives a right of participation to any member of the UN "on a matter of particular concern to that Member," but without a right to vote.

(ii) Functions and powers

2–066   The Council has been described as "the pivot of the economic and social organisation under the auspices of the UN". It operates "under the authority of the General Assembly" (Article 60) in assuming responsibility for the discharge of the functions of the Organisation set out in Chapter IX (Articles 55–60). These call for some comment. Article 55 sets out three heads of "aims" which the UN shall promote. From a reading of that Article it becomes apparent that these could touch upon matters that could be considered as normally falling essentially within the domestic jurisdiction of states. At San Franscisco Committee II/3, dealing with the articles on economic and social co-operation, took note of the general application of Article 2(7) and recognised that nothing in the new Chapters IX or X warranted intervention by the UN in a state's jurisdiction. The impact of these aims should not, therefore, be exaggerated and it will be noted that Article 56 contains a mere pledge to co-operate on the part of members in the promotion of those aims. Moreover, the Council has only the power to "recommend" to states, to the Assembly and to the specialised agencies (Articles 58 and 62); it has no sort of "legislative" power.

2–067   ECOSOC is, therefore, an organ of very wide terms of reference but of limited powers. Since much of the economic and social field falls directly within the competence of the specialised agencies, the Council is to a large extent a "residuary legatee" and, in order to avoid duplication, operates in those areas for which no agency exists. As outlined in Article 62, it may operate in various ways.

(a) Functions and powers under Article 62

2–068   **(i) Studies**. ECOSOC may make or initiate studies which, in practice, range from those of a very general character (such as the study requested by the Secretary-General on the economic development of under-developed countries),[46] to those which are quite specific and restricted (such as the study of the effects of chewing coca leaf undertaken by a commission of inquiry dispatched to Peru). The requests for studies are addressed to the Secretary-General, to the regional economic commissions, to ad hoc committees, bodies of experts or the specialised agencies. In most cases the recommendations of the Council are directly based upon such studies.

---

[46] Res. 416F (XIV).

(ii) Recommendations. The Council may make recommendations, either **2–069** under Article 62(1) or, without being related to any particular study, under Article 62(2). The word "recommendation" signifies the non-obligatory character of the resolution, for in practice many different terminologies are used such as "commends", "refers" and "calls upon". The recommendations are addressed to states, sometimes calling for specific legislative action by them as in resolution 368 (XIII) dealing with methods of financing development in under-developed countries; to the Assembly, especially where, as in budgetary matters, action is required by the Assembly pursuant to the Charter; or to the specialised agencies: Article 62 (2) places no limit on the possible addressees.

(iii) Draft Conventions. These may be prepared for submission to the **2–070** Assembly, which adopts them and opens them for signature; for example, the Convention on the Prevention and Punishment of the Crime of Genocide was dealt with in this way.[47] Or, where a draft calls for detailed discussion, it may be referred to a special international conference of states convened for that purpose; the Draft Protocol relating to the Status of Stateless Persons was thus referred to a special UN Conference in 1954.[48]

(iv) Calling of Conferences. Conferences may be called under Article **2–071** 62(4), quite apart from their function in relation to a draft convention prepared by the Council, where the work cannot be done by an organ of the UN. They may be of a universal or a regional character and, in fact, have already been called into being on matters such as health, trade and employment, transport, refugees and stateless persons. The conferences can also be non-governmental in character, such as the World Population Conference of 1954, or even conferences of experts, such as the UN Scientific Conference on the Conservation and Utilisation of Resources, 1949; there is no basis for construing "international" conferences as meaning solely conferences of states. More recently the trend has been to convene large scale "world conferences" involving both governmental and non-governmental participation, such as the Fourth World Conference on Women held in Beijing in September 1995 and the Second UN Conference on Human Settlements (Habitat II) held in Istanbul in June 1996.

(b) Assistance to other organs, states and specialised agencies

The Council also acts as an organ of assistance to two other main organs; **2–072** to the Security Council under Article 65, and to the General Assembly under Article 66(1) and (3). It may, also, with the approval of the Assembly, assist member states and specialised agencies. The most striking

---

[47] UNTS, Vol. 78, p. 277.
[48] Convention relating to the Status of Stateless Persons, UNTS, Vol. 360, p. 117.

example of assistance to states lay in the field of technical assistance that, until the end of 1965, flowed through three main channels. First, there was the "regular" programme carried on by ECOSOC independently of the specialised agencies. Secondly, there was the Expanded Programme of Technical Assistance (EPTA) carried out by ECOSOC together with 10 participating specialised agencies with a Technical Assistance Committee (T.A.C.) of the Council determining basic policy questions and the execution of the policy being entrusted to the Technical Assistance Board (T.A.B.) in which the specialised agencies participated. Thirdly, there was the Special Fund, first established in 1958 and based entirely on voluntary contributions from member states and controlled by its own Governing Council and Consultative Board. However, in 1965 the General Assembly fused the EPTA and the Special Fund into one programme, the UN Development Programme (UNDP).[49] In a further attempt to address economic development issues General Assembly resol. 2186 (XXI) established a new Capital Development Fund, equipped with its own Executive Board of 24 states elected by the Assembly, a Managing Director and staff. Moreover, a second Development Decade was begun in 1971.[50] In May 1974 the UN Special Fund was established to provide emergency economic relief.

(c) Co-ordination of work with and between the specialised agencies[51]

2–073   As has been stressed previously, one of the main tasks envisaged for the Council was the co-ordination of the work of the various specialised agencies that, to that end, were to be brought into relationship with the UN. That relationship was to be established by agreements, concluded under Articles 57 and 63, with organisations fulfilling the criteria of Article 57 (1), namely, establishment by intergovernmental agreement (thus excluding NGOs), having "wide international responsibilities," and in "economic, social, cultural, educational, health and related fields." The scheme of co-ordination is described in Chapter 3.

(d) Relations with other intergovernmental organisations and non-governmental organisations

2–074 As previously mentioned, the Preparatory Commission did not exclude the possibility that the Council should effect a relationship with inter-governmental organisations other than the "specialised agencies." No

---

[49] See infra.
[50] G.A. res. 2626 (XXV). This aims at a 6% annual growth rate, with the economically advanced countries giving 1% of their GNP. By 1980 its resources had reached $121.5 million. The 1979 Program of Action visualised a 14% growth rate annually, regarded sceptically by Western Powers.
[51] See, generally, Hill, The United Nations System (1978); also Jenks, "Co-ordination in International Organisation" (1951) 28 B.Y.B.I.L. 78, et seq. and (same author) "Co-ordination: a new problem of international organisation" R.C. 1950 (11), p. 156, especially Chap. III; Dupuy, "Le droit des relations entre les organisations internationales" R.C. Vol. 100 (1960), p. 461.

formal relationships comparable to those with the specialised agencies have been established, but both the Council and the Assembly have on occasions invited observers from *inter alia* the League of Arab States, the Organisation of African Unity, the Afro-Asian Legal Consultative Committee, the Latin American Economic System, the Organisation of the Islamic Conference and the Organisation of American States to attend their meetings. There are, moreover, informal arrangements for reciprocal representation, consultations, exchange of documents and information with various other organisations; the Council of Europe is one example.

Relations with non-governmental organisations (NGOs) are more for- **2–075** malised. Article 71 specifically provides for "suitable arrangements" and in practice the Council has established three categories in which NGOs, on their application, may be placed. Organisations with "general consultative status" includes NGOs which have a basic interest in most of the activities of ECOSOC; organisations with "special consultative status", those with a special competence in some of the aspects of the Council's work; and "The Roster"—a third category—has on it those which, by means of ad hoc consultation, are able to make occasional and useful contributions to the work of the Council in particular areas.[52] All NGOs applying for consultative status are required to have a democratically adopted constitution, the authority to speak for their members, a representative structure and accountability mechanisms, and funds derived from contributions of national affiliates or other components or from individual members.[53] In no case does an NGO have rights comparable to states under Article 69, or specialised agencies under Article 70; the difference between "participation" and "consultation" is fundamental. However, all three categories may send[54] observers to public meetings of the Council and its commissions; general and special consultative organisations may submit written statements for circulation to the members of the Council, and those in general consultative status may even present their views orally and propose agenda items. Organisations merely "on the Register" may be invited to submit written statements or, at the request of a commission, may be heard orally by the Council. The number and variety of NGOs is broad and over 1600 enjoy consultative status in one or other category.

(iii) The committee structure of ECOSOC

The diversity of the work of the Council makes it essential that it should **2–076** work through subsidiary bodies. There are three plenary "sessional" committees (economic, social, programme and co-operation) and, in addi-

---

[52] As of July 31, 1998, 103 NGOs were in general consultative status, 755 in special consultative status and 755 on the roster.

[53] See ECOSOC res. 1996/31 (July 25, 1996).

[54] Representatives of NGOs enjoy no privileges and immunities, and whilst section 11 of the Headquarters Agreement with the U.S. provides for freedom of access to the Headquarters District for representatives of NGOs recognised under Art. 71 of the Charter, the U.S. authorities have occasionally denied visas to particular persons. See Weissberg, *The International Status of the UN*, pp. 158–161. On privileges and immunities, see Chap. 15, paras 15–044 *et seq.*

tion, several "standing" committees. Article 68 gives specific power to set up commissions. These vary considerably in type, structure, functions and composition, but may be grouped into three classes:[55] functional, regional and standing.

(a) Functional commissions

2–077   These are established and defined by subject-matter. They are nine in number, with one sub-commission, and comprise a Statistical Commission[56] and Commissions: for Social Development;[57] on the Status of Women;[58] on Population and Development;[59] on Human Rights;[60] on Narcotic Drugs;[61] on Crime Prevention and Criminal Justice;[62] on Science and Technology for Development;[63] and on Sustainable Development.[64] Whilst varying in the number of states represented, these commissions are essentially composed of representatives of states, assisted by technical experts. The Council decided in 1946 against a proposal to have on these commissions independent experts who would consider these problems as experts and unfettered by governmental instructions.

(b) Regional commissions

2–078   These were not foreseen at San Francisco, but experience has shown that economic and social problems vary tremendously by region and can be better considered at a regional level. There now exist five such commissions: the Economic Commissions for Europe (ECE);[65] for Asia and the Pacific (ESCAP);[66] for Latin America and the Caribbean (ECLAC);[67] for Africa (ECA)[68] and for Western Asia (ECWA).[69] They are primarily operational commissions, as distinct from the functional commissions, and can deal directly with governments as well as reporting back to the Council. Non-UN members are associated with their work; ESCAP and ECLAC provide for associate membership and ECE for consultative status. The

---

[55] The G.A. res. 32/197 of January 9, 1978 accepted the recommendations of its ad hoc Committee on the Restructuring of the Economic and Social Sectors of the UN system and called for ECOSOC to take over the work of many of its subsidiary bodies.

[56] ECOSOC res. 8(I) (1946).

[57] ECOSOC res. 10(II) (1946).

[58] ECOSOC res. 11(II) (1946).

[59] ECOSOC res. 3(III) (1946); also Ass. res. 49/128 (1994).

[60] ECOSOC res. 9(II) (1946); see infra, Chap. 13.

[61] ECOSOC res. 9(I) (1946); also the Sub-Commission on Illicit Drug Traffic and Related Matters in the Near and Middle East, ECOSOC res. 1776(LIV) (1973).

[62] ECOSOC res. 1992/1 (replacing the Committee on Crime Prevention and Control).

[63] ECOSOC res. 1992/218 (1992).

[64] ECOSOC res. 1993/207 (1993).

[65] ECOSOC res. 36(IV) (1947).

[66] ECOSOC res. 37(IV) (1947).

[67] ECOSOC res. 106(VI) (1948).

[68] ECOSOC res. 671A(XXV) (1958).

[69] ECOSOC res. 1818(LV) (1973).

General Assembly has insisted upon decentralisation of the economic and social activities of the UN so that the regional commissions have assumed increasing importance over recent years. Their activities include policy work and the promotion of international law by the adoption of regional agreements.

(c) Standing committees and other bodies

Certain other bodies have been established to respond to a special need **2–079** which falls into neither of the above two categories. These include the Administrative Committee on Coordination[70] and Committees on Non-Governmental Organisations[71] and for Programme and Coordination,[72] and the Commission on Human Settlements (HABITAT).[73] Expert bodies have been established to address *inter alia* international co-operation on tax matters,[74] and include Committees for Development Planning,[75] on Transport of Dangerous Goods,[76] on Economic, Social and Cultural Rights,[77] on Natural Resources,[78] and on New and Renewable Sources of Energy and on Energy for Development.[79] Other bodies, such as UNDP and UNCTAD, are addressed in further detail below.

(d) TRUSTEESHIP COUNCIL

Bibliography: United Nations, *Repertory of Practice of UN Organs*, Vol. IV (1955) and Suppl. No. 1; Vol. II (1958); United Nations, *Yearbook of the United Nations*, 1946–1994.

League of Nations, The Mandate System: Origins-Principles- Application, L. of N. Doc., 1945, VI.A. I; Kunz, "Chapter XI of the United Nations Charter in Action," (1954) 48 AJIL 103; Parry, "The Legal Status of the Trusteeship Agreements," (1950) 27 B.Y.B.I.L. 164; Toussaint, *The Trusteeship System of the United Nations* (1956); Prince, "The United States, the United Nations, and Micronesia: questions of procedure, substance and faith", (1989) 11 Mich. J. Int'l L. 11; Reisman, "Reflections on State Responsibility for Violations of Explicit Protectorate, Mandate, and Trusteeship Obligations", (1989) 10 Mich. J. Int'l L. 231; Gordon, "Some Legal Problems with Trusteeship", (1995) 28 Cornell Int'l L.J. 301; Reyes, "Nauru v Australia: The International Fiduciary Duty and the Settlement of Nauru's Claims for Rehabilitation of its Phosphate Lands", (1996) 16 N.Y.L Sch. J. Int'l & Comp. L. 1; Lee, "Post Trusteeship Environmental Accountability: case of PCB contamination on the Marshall Islands", (1998) 26 Denv. J. Int'l L. & Pol'y 399.

---

[70] ECOSOC res. 13(III) (1946).
[71] ECOSOC res. 3(II) (1946).
[72] ECOSOC res. 920(XXXIV) (1962).
[73] Gen. Ass res. 32/162 (1977).
[74] ECOSOC res. 1273(XLIII) (1967).
[75] ECOSOC res. 1035(XXXVII) (1964).
[76] ECOSOC res. 468G(XV) (1953).
[77] ECOSOC res. 1988(LX) (1976); res. 1985/17 (1985).
[78] ECOSOC res. 1992/218 (1992).
[79] ECOSOC res. 1992/218 (1992) (replacing ECOSOC res. 1535(XLIX) (1970).

2–080   The work of the Trusteeship Council came to an end in 1994 with the termination of the Trusteeship Agreement for the last Trust Territory of the Pacific Islands.[80] Nevertheless, the trusteeship system has been of considerable historical interest, and it remains (at least theoretically) open for further use or transformation in the future, so a brief description of the system is justified. The trusteeship system was the successor to the Mandates system under the League of Nations; both rested, essentially, on the idea of an administering authority, normally a state, assuming responsibility for the government of a territory whose peoples had not developed to the stage necessary for independence or self-government, and being in some measure accountable internationally for the administration of the territory.

2–081   Under the League the territories placed under the Mandate system were those detached from Turkey and Germany at the conclusion of the First World War. They were placed in three categories (A, B, and C) according to the stage of development reached. No express provision for termination of the system was to be found in the League's Covenant, but for those territories in category A it was clearly implied that independence would eventually be granted; for those in category B the implication was less clear; and for those in category C the contrary implication arose by reason of the fact that such territories were to be administered as an "integral part" of the territory of the administering state.

2–082   The UN trusteeship system was potentially wider in scope, for Article 77 contemplates three categories to which it might apply:

   (a) territories held under mandate;

   (b) territories which may be detached from states as a result of the Second World War;

   (c) territories voluntarily placed under the system by states responsible for their administration.

2–083   Only territories within the first two categories were placed under trusteeship, and of the second category there was but one example, Somaliland, a territory which achieved independence. Thus, in practice, the scope of the system was actually narrower than that of the League. The third category, the real "innovation" of the Charter, has never been used, although trusteeship has often been suggested for "problem areas" such as Jerusalem, Trieste, Berlin, and even the Congo (always, however, with the UN as the possible administering authority). The trusteeship system therefore applied in practice to territories formerly under mandate, and all

---

[80] S.C. res. 956 (1994).

such territories, with one exception, were voluntarily placed under the system. The exception was the territory of South West Africa which the mandatory power, South Africa, refused to place under trusteeship and, instead, proposed to incorporate into its own territory. The I.C.J. gave four advisory opinions and one judgment on the matter.[81] In 1950 the Court, at the request of the General Assembly, gave an opinion[82] which *inter alia* determined that for a territory remaining under the League mandate, the supervisory functions previously exercised by the League subsequently rested in the General Assembly of the UN, provided that the degree of supervision exercised should not exceed that which applied in the Mandates system and should conform, as far as possible, to the procedure followed by the Council of the League. In 1956 the Court gave a further opinion[83] to the effect that the Assembly's Committee on South West Africa[84] could grant oral hearings to petitioners (a practice which the League had had the right to follow but which it had never exercised). Subsequently, Liberia and Ethiopia brought a complaint against South Africa alleging *inter alia* that the practice of apartheid breached Articles 2 and 22 of the Mandate; in its 1962 Judgment the Court rejected South Africa's claim that these two states had no locus standi to bring the case.[85] In 1966 the Court gave its main judgment which to the surprise of many, instead of dealing with the merits of the complaint, returned to the jurisdictional issue and found, contrary to its earlier judgment, that it had no jurisdiction.[86]

The dissatisfaction with this judgment within the General Assembly was **2–084** so great that by resolution 2145 (XXI) of October 27, 1966, the Assembly recorded its own conviction that there had been a breach of the mandate, of the UN Charter and of the Declaration on Human Rights and terminated the mandate. It also established an ad hoc Committee to consider means whereby the Territory might be administered and by resolution 2248 (S-V) of May 19, 1967 established an 11–Member UN Council for South West Africa and a UN Commissioner to administer the territory, which, by resolution 2372 (XXII), was to be called Namibia. By the end of 1968 the UN Council for Namibia had failed to secure admission to the Territory. The Territory was then considered by the Assembly to be no longer under mandate but held, illegally, by South Africa: legally, "sovereignty" must be regarded as in suspense but the right of administra-

---

[81] AO on International Status of S. W. Africa, (1950) I.C.J. Rep. 128; AO on S. W. Africa-Voting Procedure (1955) I.C.J. Rep. 67; AO on Admissibility of Hearings of Petitioners by the Committee on S.W. Africa, (1956) I.C.J. Rep. 23; Namibia AO, (1971) I.C.J. Rep. 16; South West Africa, (1966) I.C.J. Rep. 6.

[82] (1950) I.C.J. Rep. 128.

[83] (1956) I.C.J. Rep. 23.

[84] This is now dissolved.

[85] (1962) I.C.J. Rep. 319: by a majority of eight to seven.

[86] (1966) I.C.J. Rep. 6. Professor Bowett expressed support for the Dissenting Judgment of Judge Jessup, an expression with which the present authors associate themselves.

tion was vested directly in the UN. In 1970, by resolution 284 (1970), the Security Council requested a further advisory opinion from the Court, posing the question "What are the legal consequences for states of the continued presence of South Africa, notwithstanding Security Council resolution 276 (1970)?"[87] The Court advised that all member states were bound to recognise the illegality of the South African presence and to refrain from any acts or dealings which might imply the legality of that presence.[88] The matter was only brought to an end with the independence of the territory, now known as Namibia, in 1990.

The Trusteeship Agreements

2–085 A territory could only come under trusteeship when an agreement to that effect was concluded. An initial question, therefore, was at whose initiative this agreement was reached, and who were the parties to it? In practice the initiative came from the state administering the territory, the former mandatory power;[89] the "agreement" was contemplated by Article 79 as being between "the states directly concerned." Yet no criteria are stipulated for determining which these states are, and in practice the various administering authorities reached their own decisions on this, submitting the draft agreement to certain states and to others "for information purposes only." The role of the Assembly, or the Security Council in the case of "strategic areas," was limited to the mere "approval" of the agreement reached; it may well be that the UN was not a "party."[90] However, under Article 81 the administering authority may be "one or more states or the Organisation itself," so that if the UN ever did assume the administration of a territory it would be in the curious situation of having to give its "approval," via the Assembly or Security Council, to an agreement already reached between itself and any "states directly concerned."

2–086 The Agreements formed the legal basis for the supervision by the UN and the administration by the administering authority and, in the main, repeated and supplemented the relative Charter provisions to which, by Article 103, they had to be subject. Some provisions in the Agreements went beyond the Charter provisions, either by according additional rights or

---

[87] This resolution re-affirmed the General Assembly's termination of the mandate and declared the continued presence of South Africa in Namibia to be illegal.

[88] See, generally, Dugard, *S.W. Africa Namibia Dispute* (1973).

[89] Except in the case of Somaliland when the agreement was drafted by the Trusteeship Council, and Italy, the chosen administering authority, had no vote in the drafting committee the case was exceptional because Italy was not at that time a UN member.

[90] Kelsen, *Law of the UN*, pp. 586, 608–609, and Toussaint, *The Trusteeship System of the UN*, p. 78, regard the agreements as embodying in reality two agreements, the first between states directly concerned and the second between the administering authority and the UN. Parry, "The Legal Nature of the Trusteeship Agreements" (1950) 27 B.Y.B.I.L. 166, and Schachter, *ibid.* 25 (1948) 130–131 deny that the UN is a party.

obligations to the administering authority or by giving additional guarantees to the inhabitants of the territory. The Agreements could be altered or
amended, under Article 79, by agreement between the "states directly
concerned," subject to the approval of the Assembly or Security Council.
Termination was, however, another matter, for the Charter says nothing of
this and only the Agreement for Somaliland included a termination date
(ten years from the signing of the Agreement).

The objectives of the system are set out principally in Article 76, as **2–087**
supplemented by Articles 73 and 84, which emphasises the contribution of
the Trusteeship system to international peace and security. The system
distinguished between territories (or parts of territories) which were
"strategic areas" and those which are not (Article 82), and in the case of
the former it is the Security Council rather than the General Assembly
which approved the trusteeship agreement and exercised supervisory functions. The trusteeship system therefore aimed at removing territories from
possible competition between states and ensuring that they played a part in
the collective security system envisaged by the Charter. Article 76 (b)
provides for the goal of "self-government or independence," as may be
appropriate in the circumstances and according to the wishes of the persons
concerned. No trust agreement omitted "independence" as the goal.
Undoubtedly the political sentiment of the majority of the UN members
was always in favour of early independence, and the administering authorities were under a fairly constant pressure within the UN to bring this
about. The majority in the General Assembly, in terminating trusteeship
agreements, appeared to abandon the original requirement that development purposes be attained before termination. For example, the resolutions
of the 16th session, terminating the trusteeships over Western Samoa,
Tanganyika and Rwanda-Urandi,[91] and those with respect to Nauru and
New Guinea,[92] did not contain any comment as to whether the administration of the trust territories had attained its purposes or not. However, the
assumption that independence was the proper goal for all trust territories
was difficult to justify on political and economic grounds. In relation to
Nauru, for example, with an indigenous population of 2,800 on an island of
5,263 acres, the independence achieved in January 1968 raised the crucial
question of whether the inhabitants were to be re-settled or, as eventually
decided, the land excavated for phosphates should be rehabilitated.[93]
Indeed, the Trusteeship Council appeared to set its face against any
alternative to independence. The people of the trust territory of the Pacific
Islands expressed a desire for integration with the USA, a wish simply

---

[91] G.A. res. 1626 (XVI) (October 18, 1961); 1642 (XVI) (November 6, 1961); 1646 (XVI)
(November 6, 1961).
[92] G.A. res. 2347 (XXII) (December 19, 1967); 3284 (XXIX) (December 13, 1974).
[93] See "Certain Phosphate Lands in Nauru" (1992) I.C.J. Rep. 240.

"noted" by the Trusteeship Council; its fulfilment would be neither independence nor self-government. In fact, the USA set 1981 as the date for termination of the trusteeship agreement and full self-government for "Micronesia." However, it was not until 1986 that the U.S. issued a proclamation that it had satisfied its obligations under the trusteeship agreement for the Trust Territory of the Pacific Islands, termination being held up by the need to obtain the approval of the Security Council that the strategic trust obligation had been properly fulfilled.[94]

The machinery of supervision

2–088 The UN's supervisory powers are based on the Charter and on the trusteeship agreements and, in the event of any conflict between the provisions of the two, the Charter prevails (Article 103). Beyond the Trusteeship Council, three other organs participated in the supervision. The General Assembly exercised the functions of the UN with regard to all areas not designated as "strategic", whereas the Security Council exercised UN functions for "strategic" areas. The Economic and Social Council was only involved subsidiarily.

C. SUBSIDIARY ORGANS, PROGRAMMES AND OTHER BODIES

2–089 A number of the subsidiaries bodies established by the General Assembly have emerged as having an especially important function, either politically or as a means of providing social and economic services, or carrying out research in fields related to the work of the UN.

(a) ADMINISTRATIVE COMMITTEE ON CO-ORDINATION[95]

2–090 The Administrative Committee on Co-ordination (A.C.C.) comprises the Secretary-General and the administrative heads of the specialised agencies.[96] Directly, and through its sub-committees, it reviews the whole field of operations of the various UN organisations in the light of the need for co-ordination, fixing priorities and enabling a concentration of efforts and resources.

---

[94] Prince, "The United States, the United Nations, and Micronesia: the questions of procedure, substance and faith" (1989) 11 Mich. J. Int'l L. 11.

[95] Hill in Luard (ed.), *The Evolution of International Organisations*, pp. 104–37 (1966); "Tassin, Administrative Coordination in the UN Family", in de Cooker (ed.), *International Administration*, Chap. I.2 (1990) Website: http//www.acc.vnsystem.org.

[96] Under Art. XI of the Agreement with the IAEA, the Agency agrees to participate in the work of the A.C.C., even though the Agency is not a specialised agency.

(b) INTERNATIONAL LAW COMMISSION[97]

The International Law Commission was established by G.A. res. 174 (II) in **2–091** 1947 with a membership of 15 persons of recognised competence in international law. The membership of the Commission has been increased several times, most recently by G.A. res. 36/39 (1981) and now stands at 34. The members of the Commission sit in their personal capacity as experts rather than as representatives of their respective governments. The function of the Commission is to undertake the codification and progressive development of international law. The Commission's work has given rise to a number of multilateral international legal instruments, such as the 1961 and 1963 convention on diplomatic and consular relations, the 1969 and 1986 Vienna Conventions on the Law of Treaties,[98] and more recently, the Convention on the Law of the Non-Navigational Uses of International Watercourses[99] and the Statute of the International Criminal Court.[1] Topics currently under consideration within the Commission include state responsibility, reservations to treaties, diplomatic protection and unilateral acts of states.

(c) UNICEF[2]

The UN International Children's Emergency Fund was originally estab- **2–092** lished as a temporary body to provide emergency assistance to children in countries ravaged by the Second World War.[3] G.A. res. 802 (VIII) (1953) placed the body on a permanent footing and changed its name to the UN Children's Fund (UNICEF). UNICEF's functions include advocating for the protection of children's rights, helping meet their basic needs and expanding their opportunities to reach their full potential. The organisation provides assistance, particularly to developing countries, in the development of permanent child health and welfare services.

G.A. res. 48/162 (1993) decided that the Executive Board of UNICEF **2–093** should be reconstituted to comprise 36 members (rather than the previous 41), and be responsible for the provision of intergovernmental support to,

---

[97] Website: http//www.un.org/law/ilc/index.htm. Briggs, *The International Law Commission* (1965); Ramcharan, *The I.L.C.—Its Approach to the Codification and Progressive Development of International Law* (1977); Goswami, *Politics in law making: a study of the I.L.C. of the UN* (1986); McRae, *The I.L.C.: Codification and Progressive Development after Forty Years*, 25 CYIL 355 (1987); Sinclair, *The International Law Commission* (1987); Sucharitkul, *The role of the I.L.C. in the decade of international law*, 3 LJIL 15 (1990); UN, *The Work of the I.L.C.*, 5th ed., 1996; UN, *Making Better International Law: the I.L.C. at 50* (1998); AJIL each year publishes the report of the Commission.

[98] 8 ILM 679 (1969).

[99] 36 ILM 700 (1997).

[1] 37 ILM 999 (1998).

[2] Website: http://www.unicef.org. Rios-Kohn, The Impact of the United Nations Convention on the Rights of the Child on UNICEF's Mission, 6 Transnat'l L. & Contemp. Probs 287 (1996).

[3] G.A. res. 57(I) (1946).

and supervision of, the activities of UNICEF. Membership of the Board is according to the principle of equitable geographical representation.

(d) UNRWA[4]

2–094   The UN Relief and Works Agency for Palestine Refugees in the Near East (UNRWA) was established by G.A. res. 4/302(1949) to carry out relief and works programmes for Palestine refugees in co-operation with local governments. Its three principal areas of activity are education, health and relief and social services. UNRWA began operation on May 1, 1950 and has had its mandate periodically renewed, most recently by G.A. res. 53/46 (1998).

(e) OFFICE OF THE UN HIGH COMMISSIONER FOR REFUGEES (UNHCR)[5]

2–095   A UN High Commissioner for Refugees was initially appointed by GA res. 319(IV) (1949) to continue the work of the International Refugee Organisation after it terminated its activities. The Statute of the Office of the UN High Commissioner for Refugees, detailing its functions and responsibilities, was contained in G.A. res. 428(V) (1950). The Office came into being on January 1, 1951 and has had its mandate periodically renewed, with the most current being until December 31, 2003. The UNHCR reports annually to the Assembly through ECOSOC.

(f) OFFICE OF THE UN HIGH COMMISSIONER FOR HUMAN RIGHTS[6]

2–096   The Office of the UN High Commissioner for Human Rights was established by G.A. res. 48/141 (1993) to promote and protect the effective enjoyment by all of civil, cultural, economic, political and social rights. The High Commissioner is the UN official with primary responsibility for UN human rights activities. The High Commissioner acts under the direction and authority of the Secretary-General and within the framework and

---

[4] Website: http://www.un.org/unrwa. Dale, UNRWA: A Subsidiary Organ of the UN, 23 ICLQ 576 (1974); Stebbing, UNRWA: An Instrument for Peace in the Middle East, 8 Int. Rel. 270 (1985).

[5] Maynard, "The legal competence of the UN High Commissioner for Refugees", 31 ICLQ 415 (1982); Singh, *The role and record of the UN High Commissioner for Refugees* (1984); Warner, "Forty years of the UNHCR Executive Committee: from the old to the new", 2 IJRL 238 (1990); Guest, "The UN, the UNHCR, and refugee protection: a non-specialist analysis", 3 IJRL 585 (1991).

[6] Website: http://www.unhchr.ch. Ayala-Lasso, "Making human rights a reality in the twenty-first century", 10 Emory Int'l L. Rev. 497 (1996); Cerna, "A small step forward for human rights: the creation of the post of UN High Commissioner for Human Rights", 10 Am. U. J. Int'l L. & Pol'y 1265 (1995); Lord, "The UN High Commissioner for Human Rights: challenges and opportunities", 17 Loyola LA Int'l & Comp. L.J. 329 (1995); Hannum, "Setting a new agenda for UN human rights activities", 15 Mich. J. Int'l L. 823 (1995).

authority of the General Assembly, ECOSOC and the Commission on Human Rights.

(g) UN INSTITUTE FOR TRAINING AND RESEARCH (UNITAR)[6a]

UNITAR was established by G.A. res. 1934 (XVIII) (1963) on recom- **2–097** mendation of ECOSOC. The Statute of UNITAR was promulgated by the Secretary-General in 1965 (annexed to Executive Director's Report in Document E/42000 of May 5, 1966) and describes the purpose of the institute as being to enhance the effectiveness of the UN in achieving its major objectives, particularly maintenance of international peace and security and the promotion of economic and social development. UNITAR provides training to persons, particularly those from developing countries, for assignments within the UN or specialised agencies and for assignments in their national services that are connected to the work of the UN.

In 1993 UNITAR underwent significant restructuring as a result of G.A. res. 47/227 (1993). The headquarters of the organisation were moved from New York to Geneva and its funding arrangements were changed to provide that, from January 1, 1994, all expenses would be covered by voluntary contributions, donations and special purpose grants.

(h) UN CONFERENCE ON TRADE AND DEVELOPMENT (UNCTAD)[7]

UNCTAD was established as one of the organs of the General Assembly by **2–098** G.A. res. 1995(XIX) (1964). The Conference meets every four years and held its most recent session (UNCTAD X) in February 2000. The primary function of UNCTAD is the promotion of international trade and develop- ment opportunities, particularly for developing countries. Its functions are continued between sessions of the Conference by its executive body, the Trade and Development Board. The Trade and Development Board has its own subsidiary bodies, known as Commissions, to perform integrated policy work with specified terms of reference. There are currently three Commis- sions: (1) the Commission on Investment, Technology and Related Finan- cial Issues, (2) the Commission on Trade in Goods and Services, and Commodities and (3) the Commission on Enterprise, Business Facilitation and Development.

(i) UN DEVELOPMENT PROGRAMME[7a]

The UN Development Programme emerged in 1966 following G.A. res. **2–099** 2029(XX), combining the pre-existing UN Expanded Programme of Tech- nical Assistance (EPTA) with the Special Fund. The Programme is the

---

[6a] Website: http://www.unitar.org.
[7] Website: http://www.unctad.org. Kohl, *The Legal Framework of UNCTAD in World Trade* (1977); Rohstein, *Global Bargaining: UNCTAD and the quest for a new international economic order* (1979); Zammit Cutajar, & Malinowski, (eds), *UNCTAD and the South- North Dialogue: the first 20 years* (1985).
[7a] Website: http//www.undp.org.

principal channel for multilateral technical and investment assistance to developing countries. By G.A. res. 48/162 (1993) it was decided to transform the Governing Council of the UNDP into an Executive Board, responsible for supervising and providing intergovernmental support to UNDP. The financial resources of UNDP are derived principally from voluntary contributions by governments. The Programme also has active co-financing arrangement with donor and recipient governments, as well as with the international financing institutions. In addition the UNDP is responsible for the—

(i) UN Capital Development Fund (UNCDF)—established by G.A. res. 2186(XXI) (1966). UNDP assumed management functions for the UNCDF by G.A. res. 2321(XXII) (1967); and

(ii) UN Development Fund for Women (UNIFEM)—established by G.A. res. 39/125 (1984) and administered by the UNDP Board.

(j) WORLD FOOD PROGRAMME (WFP)[8]

2–100   The World Food Programme (WFP) was established by parallel resolutions of the General Assembly (G.A. res. 1714(XVI) (1961)) and the FAO Conference in 1961.[9] The WFP provides food aid to low-income, food-deficit countries as well as assistance in the implementation of social and economic development projects and disaster relief.

(k) UN ENVIRONMENT PROGRAMME[10]

2–101   The UN Environment Programme (UNEP) was established in 1972 by G.A. res. 2997(XXVII) (1972) following the Stockholm Conference on the Human Environment. The Programme is based in Nairobi and comprises a Governing Council of 58 members elected by the General Assembly and an Environment Secretariat headed by the UNEP Executive Director. The Governing Council meets annually at its Nairobi headquarters and reports to the General Assembly through ECOSOC. At its nineteenth session, the Governing Council decided to strengthen its existing subsidiary organ, the Committee of Permanent Representatives, and to establish an additional subsidiary organ, the High-Level Committee of Ministers and Officials.

2–102   UNEP is the only UN body exclusively dedicated to international environmental matters. Its constituent instrument commits it to promote international environmental co-operation, to provide policy guidance for

---

[8] Website: http://www.wfp.org/index.htm. Charlton, "Innovation and inter-organizational politics: the case of the World Food Programme", 47 Int. J. 630 (1992).
[9] FAO res. 1/61.
[10] Website: http://www.unep.org. Lausche, *UNEP Environmental law in-depth Review 1981: a presentation by subject areas* (1982); Petsonk, "The role of the United Nations Environment Programme (UNEP) in the development of international environmental law", 5 Am. U. J. Int'l L. & Pol'y 351 (1990).

the direction and coordination of environmental programmes within the UN system, to receive and review reports from UNEP's Executive Director on the implementation of the UN's environment programmes, to review the world environment situation, to promote scientific knowledge and information and to contribute to technical aspects of environmental programmes and maintain under review the impact of national and international environmental policies on developing countries.

(l) UN COMMISSION ON SUSTAINABLE DEVELOPMENT (CSD)

In 1992, pursuant to its mandate emerging from the UNCED, the **2–103** General Assembly and ECOSOC established the UN Commission on Sustainable Development (CSD).[11] The CSD comprises representatives of 53 states elected by the ECOSOC with due regard to equitable geographic distribution, and on the basis of representation at a high level, including ministerial participation. Other member states of the UN and its specialised agencies are able to participate as observers, and international organisations participate to assist and advise the CSD in the performance of its functions. The CSD is assisted by a secretariat based in New York and meets in New York or Geneva, states having been unable to agree on a permanent location.

The CSD is the UN body primarily responsible for sustainable develop- **2–104** ment issues and has ten enumerated environmental functions including monitoring progress in the implementation of the UNCED's Agenda 21 and the integration of environmental and development goals, considering information provided by governments, considering the progress made in the implementation of environmental conventions and making recommendations to the General Assembly on the implementation of Agenda 21.

(m) OTHER ORGANS, PROGRAMMES AND BODIES

(i) *International Research and Training Institute for the Advancement of Women (INSTRAW)*[11a]

INSTRAW was established by ECOSOC res. 1998(LX) (1976) following a **2–105** recommendation made by the World Conference on the International Women's Year in Mexico in 1975. At its fourth session INSTRAW's Board of Trustees adopted a governing Statute, which was approved by ECOSOC res. 1984/124 (1984) and endorsed in G.A. res. 39/249 (1985).

(ii) *UN Institute for Disarmament Research (UNIDIR)*[11b]

The UNIDIR was established by G.A. res. 37/99K (1980) as an autonomous **2–106** institution for undertaking independent research on disarmament and related international security issues. Its Statute was approved by the

---

[11] G.A. res. 47/191 (1992) and ECOSOC res. 1993/207.
[11a] Website: http://www.un.org/instraw.
[11b] Website: http://www.vnog.ch/unidir.

General Assembly in G.A. res. 39/148H (1984). The Director of the UNIDIR reports annually to the General Assembly on the activities of the Institute.

(iii) *UN Interregional Crime and Justice Research Institute (UNICRI)*[11c]

2–107 UNICRI was established as the United Nations Social Defence Research Institute in 1968 pursuant to ECOSOC res. 1086B (XXXIX) (1965), with the task of conducting and promoting research into the prevention of crime and the treatment of offenders. Its competence was expanded by ECOSOC res. 1989/56 (1989) to include technical co-operation and training.

(iv) *UN Research Institute for Social Development*[11d]

2–108 The UN Research Institute for Social Development was founded in 1963 by a decision of the Secretary-General, with the aim of conducting multidisciplinary research on the social dimensions of contemporary development problems. The institute is an autonomous institution within the UN system, funded entirely by voluntary contributions.

(v) *UN University*[11e]

2–109 The UN University was established by G.A. res. 2951(XXVII) (1972) as an autonomous organ of the General Assembly. The UN University is intended to be an international community of scholars, forming a bridge between the UN and the international academic community, and serving as a think-tank for the UN system, as well as contributing to capacity building, particularly in developing countries. The UN University is based in Tokyo, Japan, though it has research and training centres and programmes in Finland, the Netherlands, Macau, Ghana and Zambia. It is governed by a Council consisting of 28 members, 24 of whom are elected in their individual capacity by the UN Secretary-General and the Director-General of UNESCO. The remaining four members are the Rector, the UN Secretary-General, the Director-General of UNESCO and the Executive Director of UNITAR.

(vi) *UN Volunteers*[11f]

2–110 The UN Volunteers Programme was created by G.A. res. 2659(XXV) (1970) to serve as an operational partner in international development. Volunteers must have the technical and personal qualifications necessary to contribute to the development of recipient countries. The Programme operates under the overall administration of UNDP.

[11c] Website: http://www.unicri.it.
[11d] Website: http://www.unrisd.org.
[11e] Website: http://www.unu.edu.
[11f] Website: http://www.unv.org.

(vii) *UN International Drug Control Programme (UNDCP)*[11g]

The UNDCP was established by G.A. res. 45/179 (1990) and became **2–111** operational in 1991. Its efforts are linked to various treaties: the 1961 Single Convention on Narcotic Drugs (and its 1972 amending Protocol),[12] *the 1971 Convention on Psychotropic Substances[13] and the 1988 United Nations Convention against Illicit Traffic in Narcotic Drugs and Psychotropic Substances.[14] The UNDCP is also an integral part of the Office for Drug Control and Crime Prevention, together with the Centre for International Crime Prevention.

(viii) *UN Population Fund*

The UN Population Fund dates back to G.A. res. 2211(XXI) (1966), which **2–112** called upon organisations of the UN system to provide assistance in the field of population. The Fund was placed under the authority of the General Assembly by G.A. res. 3019(XXVII) (1972), with the UNDP Governing Council as its governing body. The Fund's current name was established by G.A. res. 42/430 (1987). In 1993, the Governing Council of UNDP was replaced by UNDP's Executive Board as the governing body of the Fund.[15]

[11g] Website: http://www.undcp.org.
[12] 11 ILM 804 (1972).
[13] 10 ILM 261 (1971).
[14] 28 ILM 493 (1989).
[15] G.A. res. 48/162 (1993).

CHAPTER 3

UN SPECIALISED AGENCIES

A. INTRODUCTION

Bibliography: Mathieu, *Les institutions spécialisées des Nations Unies* (1977); Ameri, *Politics and Process in the specialized agencies of the United Nations* (1982); Williams, *The specialized agencies and the United Nations: the system in crisis* (1987); Harrod, "UN Specialized Agencies: From Functionalist Intervention to International Cooperation?" In Harrod and Schrijver (eds) *The UN Under Attack* (1988).

Specialised agencies are international organisations of limited competence **3–001** linked to the UN by special agreements.[1] Together with the UN, they constitute what is commonly called "the United Nations system." The specialised agencies are endowed with a separate legal personality and complement the action of the UN in more technical fields, while sharing the same overall objectives as the UN itself. Like the UN, they are universal organisations.

(a) ESTABLISHMENT OF THE SPECIALISED AGENCIES

The failure of the League of Nations, contrasted with the—relative— **3–002** success of organisations such as the International Labour Organisation or the International Office of Public Health, emphasised the need to (re)create such specialised organisations as entities legally distinct from, but at the same time closely tied to, the newly-born universal "political" organisation. The basic idea was to ensure the continued existence of these agencies, even in the event of the disappearance of the UN itself and to organise a division of work between a "political" organisation of general competence and more specialised institutions.[2] Some of these agencies are the continuation of pre-existing organisations (under the same name, as in the case of ILO or UPU, for instance, or under a different designation, as in the case of the International Telecommunications Union, which succeeded in 1947

---

[1] For a more complete definition, see *infra*, Relationship with the United Nations (paras 3–007 *et seq*).
[2] For more on this, see the commentary of Art. 57 of the UN Charter by Lemoine, in Cot and Pellet, *La Charte des Nations Unies—Commentaire article par article*, 2nd ed. (1991), pp. 897 *et seq.*

to the International Telegraphic Union established in 1865), whereas others (such as IBRD, IMF or IFAD) emerged as entirely new institutions.

3–003　　The establishment of specialised agencies has largely been inspired by the so-called "functionalist" theories.[3] It was hoped that, by decentralising the system the politicisation of economic and social co-operation might be avoided. The focus on the technical aspect of these organisations' tasks would avoid putting at risk their effectiveness and universality, which could have been threatened if political issues were given broad currency.[4] As many authors have noted however, the very idea that those organisations could avoid politicisation amounted to a myth that the evolution of international relations during the second part of the twentieth century would prove to be untenable.[5] Accusations of politicisation of agencies such as ILO, UNESCO, IBRD, IMF, WHO or UPU, amongst others, have multiplied since the beginning of the 1960s, and a few states have even withdrawn from some organisations in protest against politicisation.[6]

3–004　By way of recent example, arguments about politicisation have been put forward by some states opposing the WHO request for an advisory opinion on the legality of the use of nuclear weapons in armed conflict. France for instance considered that:

> "the World Health Assembly is not the appropriate forum to deal with such a subject, which has purely political connotations. [France] deeply regrets that the work of the Assembly, which has such important implications for the health of the world's peoples, should have been disturbed and delayed by political considerations which were quite out of place."[7]

3–005　　A review of the history of specialised agencies indicates the difficulties with this approach. As some authors have pointed out, the very use of the term "politicisation" (or related expressions) is "so loaded with pejorative connotations that serious questions arise about its analytical utility" that it is bound to raise suspicion, especially in view of the fact that states never use it to characterise their own actions.[8] Accusations of "politicisation"

---

[3] *ibid.*

[4] See *e.g.* Meng, Comment of Art. 57, in B. Simma (Ed.), *The Charter of the United Nations— A Commentary* (1995), p. 804.

[5] See *e.g.* Meng, *ibid.*; Lemoine, *loc. cit.*; Klein, Specialized Agencies, *Encyclopedia of Public International Law* 5, p. 366.

[6] See sp. Williams, *The specialized Agencies and the United Nations—The System in Crisis* (1987), 55 *et seq.* For more on this see also *infra,* Chap. 16, para. 16–030.

[7] WHA46/1993/REC/2: Forty-sixth World Health Assembly, 1993, *Verbatim Records of Plenary Meetings*, p. 277, quoted in Judge Oda's separate opinion, I.C.J. Rep., 1996, p. 94, para. 13. See also, in the same sense, the position taken by Russia, doc. A46/VR/13, p. 15, quoted in Judge Weeramantry's dissenting opinion, *ibid.*, p. 106.

[8] Lyons *et al.*, "The 'Politicization' Issue in the UN Specialized Agencies", in Kay (Ed.), *The Changing United Nations—Options for the United States* (1977), pp. 84–85.

appear closely related to situations where substantive differences arise about a given matter, since they assume that "the functional is by definition the non-political, and thus is synonymous with 'non-controversial' or 'technical' in terms of procedure."[9] The (non-) political character of a subject-matter dealt with by a specialised agency will inevitably be relative.

As one commentator pointed out:

> "[i]f everyone agrees that including the Palestinian Liberation Organisation (PLO) in the deliberations of a particular functional agency is appropriate, then such an act is routine and by definition nonpolitical. Organisations become 'politicized' to the degree that the issues that they deal with become controversial."[10]

The limit between "political" and "technical" matters thus appears less **3–006** capable of distinction than functionalist theories imply. It follows that a strict division of competences along functional lines between elements of the United Nations system may be somewhat utopian in aspiration. This, however, did not prevent the International Court of Justice from adopting a somewhat functionalist line of reasoning in its 1996 advisory opinion, and finding that it was not able to give the opinion requested by the WHO since it did not relate to an issue arising within this organisation's scope of activities.[11]

(b) RELATIONSHIP WITH THE UNITED NATIONS

The specialised agencies' relationships with the UN are established by **3–007** agreements concluded under Articles 57 and 63 of the UN Charter. Under Article 57 (1), such agreements may only be concluded with international organisations fulfilling certain criteria, namely those established by intergovernmental agreement (thus excluding NGOs) and having "wide international responsibilities" in "economic, social, cultural, educational, health and related fields." The second criterion has been interpreted in both a geographical and a functional sense, thus excluding regional organisations and those with a limited area of responsibility. The Preparatory Commission at San Francisco had not excluded the bringing into relationship of other intergovernmental agencies, but these were not to be termed "specialised agencies."[12]

---

[9] Sewell, *Functionalism and World Politics* (1966), pp. 43–44.

[10] Lyons *et al.*, The "Politicisation" Issue, p. 85.

[11] I.C.J. Rep., 1996, p. 84, para. 31–32. The Court acknowledged the WHO's competence to express concerns for the *effects* of nuclear weapons on human health and the environment, but not to consider the issue of the *legality* of the use of such weapons (*ibid.*, p. 81, para. 27). For critical comments, see Klein, "Reflections on the principle of speciality revisited and the "politicisation" of specialised agencies", in Boisson de Chazournes and Sands (Eds.), *International Law, the International Court of Justice and Nuclear Weapons*, (1999), pp. 78–91 and Leary, The WHO case: Implications for specialised agencies, in *ibid.*, pp. 112–127.

[12] See for instance the particular situation of the IAEA in that respect, *infra*, para. 3–072.

3–008   The agreements contemplated were negotiated at the initiative of the Economic and Social Council and through a Negotiating Committee which negotiated directly with the organisation concerned; they were then submitted to the Council and, finally, for approval by the General Assembly. At present there are agreements with 13 specialised agencies[13] and the International Finance Corporation (IFC).[14]

3–009   Whilst the agreements all follow a general pattern,[15] with a number of common features, certain differences do occur. Of particular note is the greater degree of autonomy possessed by the IMF, the IBRD and the IFC. The common features include the following:

- recognition of the status of the organisation as a "specialised agency," but in the case of the IMF, the IBRD and the IFC agreements stressing their independent character;[16]

- a clause linking membership in specialised agencies to membership in the United Nations[17] (hence UNESCO gives ECOSOC a right to recommend the rejection of applications and links loss of membership to suspension or expulsion from the UN);[18]

- a clause on reciprocal representation (but without the right to vote) at each other's meetings, but with a good deal of variation in the bodies to which this applies;

- a clause providing for reciprocal rights to propose agenda items, after necessary consultations, to the appropriate organ (in the UN,

---

[13] The International Labour Organisation (ILO; December 14, 1946, 1 U.N.T.S. 183), United Nations Educational, Scientific and Cultural Organisation (UNESCO; December 6–14, 1946, 1 U.N.T.S. 233), the Food and Agriculture Organisation (FAO; February 3, 1947, 1 U.N.T.S. 207), the International Civil Aviation Organisation (ICAO; December 16, 1946– May 13, 1947, 8 U.N.T.S. 325), the International Telecommunications Union (ITU; September 4–November 15, 1947, 26 U.N.T.S. 299), the International Monetary Fund (IMF; April 15, 1948, 16 U.N.T.S. 325), the International Bank for Reconstruction and Development (IBRD; April 15, 1948, 16 U.N.T.S. 341), the World Health Organisation (WHO; November 15, 1947–July 10, 1948, 19 U.N.T.S. 193), the International Maritime Organisation (IMO; November 18, 1948, 324 U.N.T.S. 273), the World Meteorological Organisation (WMO; December 20, 1951, 123 U.N.T.S. 245), the World Intellectual Property Organisation (WIPO; December 17, 1974, 956 U.N.T.S. 405), the International Fund for Agricultural Development (IFAD; December 14–15, 1977, 1080 U.N.T.S. 331) and the United Nations Industrial Development Organisation (UNIDO, December 17, 1985, 1412 U.N.T.S. 305).

[14] The UN-IFC Agreement was concluded by the Bank on behalf of the IFC and simply adopts the UN-Bank Agreement with a few amendments: 265 U.N.T.S. 314. Of the other agencies, the International Refugee Organisation (IRO) has been discontinued and the Charter of the International Trade Organisation (ITO) has never come into force (for more on this, see *infra*, Chap. 4 and the conclusion of the present Chapter). The International Development Association is an affiliate of the World Bank and is not, technically, a separate specialised agency (see *infra*).

[15] For details see Jenks, (1951) 28 B.Y.B.I.L. 67; Parry, *ibid.*, 26 (1949) 138–139; Weissberg, International Status of the UN (1961), pp. 41–50.

[16] See Art. 1, 2 of the respective agreements.

[17] See *infra*, Chap. 16, para. 16–002.

[18] See Art. II of the agreement.

this organ is not always the General Assembly; IMO, for example, has this right *vis-à-vis* ECOSOC and the Trusteeship Council,[19] whereas the IMF, the IBRD and the IFC undertake only to give "due consideration" to the inclusion of any item proposed by the UN);[20]

- another common clause allows the General Assembly or the Council to make recommendations to the agency, which body is then obliged to submit the recommendations to the appropriate organ (again, in the case of the IMF, the IBRD and the IFC, the obligation is weaker, for the Assembly can only make recommendations after prior consultation with the agency and there is also a "hands-off" clause whereby the UN undertakes to respect the autonomy of the agencies in matters affecting their loan and financing policy).[21]

Other clauses relate to the exchange of information and documents and **3–010** the transmission of regular (or annual) reports by the agency; requiring assistance to be rendered by the agency to the Security Council and, in some cases, other principal[22] and even subsidiary organs; providing for furnishing information to be provided to the I.C.J., and establishing the right of the agency (other than the UPU) to request an advisory opinion from the Court on questions falling within the agency's competence.[23] Some agreements contain undertakings by the agency to associate regional offices with those of the UN; there is, it should be noted, no evidence of any wish to combine the headquarters of all the agencies and the UN in one central location.

One standard clause (except for the UPU, ITU, IMF, IBRD and IFC) **3–011** recognises the desirability of a "single unified international civil service" and the agencies agree to develop "common personnel standards" and to consult regarding the establishment of an International Civil Service Commission, which was eventually established in 1974.[24] There is, in practice, no real unification of secretariats. There have been, however, frequent consultations and liaison on matters such as salaries and allowance scales and recruitment policies; and several agencies participate in the UN Joint Staff Pension Fund. The Staff Rules and Regulations of the various Secretariats follow a similar pattern and disputes between the respective

---

[19] Art. III of the agreement.
[20] Art. III of the respective agreements.
[21] Arts IV and VI of the respective agreements. On the controversy which arose between the UN and the World Bank in the 1960s, see *infra*, Chap. 14.
[22] In 1951, at the request of ECOSOC, the ILO, UNESCO, FAO, WHO and ICAO undertook to give assistance to the General Assembly, on request, in action taken by it under the Resolution on Uniting for Peace (Res. 377 (V)).
[23] See also *infra*, Chap. 14.
[24] UNGA Res. 3357 (XXIX) of December 18, 1974.

agencies and their agents are submitted either to the UN Administrative Tribunal, to the ILO Administrative Tribunal, to the World Bank Administrative Tribunal, or to the IMF Administrative Tribunal.[25]

3–012   Yet other clauses address the desirability of co-operation in statistical compilations, in making efficient use of administrative and technical services, provide for revision of the agreements and the adoption of supplementary agreements to be concluded by the Secretary-General and his counterpart in the various agencies and, for the agencies established after August 1947, the right to use the UN "laissez-passer."

3–013   The provisions on budgeting and financial arrangements are complex and varied. Most agreements recognise the desirability of close relationship on these matters, but there is no common or overall budget; the autonomy of the IMF, IBRD and IFC is particularly striking. The budgets of the agencies are, in practice, considered by the Assembly's Advisory Committee on Administrative and Budgetary Questions.

3–014   Clearly these agreements provide a useful framework for co-ordination. The submission of reports by the agencies, the examination of these reports by the Council and the power to make recommendations to the agencies are useful factors in securing co-ordination and avoiding duplication. There are, however, additional means of co-ordination. The first is the Administrative Committee on Co-ordination (A.C.C). Comprising the Secretary-General and the administrative heads of the agencies,[26] directly and through its sub-committees,[27] it can review the whole field of operations of the various organisations in the light of the need for coordination, fixing priorities and enabling a concentration of efforts and resources.[28] ECOSOC has itself established a Committee for Programme and Co-operation which holds joint meetings with the A.C.C.

3–015   Co-operation between specialised agencies and various UN organs is a common feature within the framework of various programs.[29] Co-operation in the field between UN programmes or organs and specialised agencies is

---

[25] On which see *infra*, Chap. 13, para. 13–163.

[26] Under Art. XI of the Agreement with the IAEA, the Agency agrees to participate in the work of the A.C.C., even though the Agency is not a specialised agency.

[27] Such as the Consultative Committee on Substantive Questions/Operational Activities or the Consultative Committee on Administrative Questions. More recently, the A.C.C. also established committees on more specific issues, such as the Inter-Agency Committee on Sustainable Development (established in October 1992; see (1992) YUN 681,941) or the Inter-Agency Group on New and Renewable Sources of Energy. Ad hoc inter-agency meetings are also regularly held on various topics (for examples, see (1992) YUN 941 and (1995) YUN 1433).

[28] For more details on A.C.C.'s recent activities, see (1995) YUN 1432; also Chapter 2; para. 2–090.

[29] See, *e.g.* the Joint FAO/WHO Codex Alimentarius Commission, vaccination campaigns undertaken by WHO and UNICEF, collaboration between UNDP, WHO, UNICEF and the World Bank in the area of water supply (1995) YUN 1478–79); see also the Memorandum of understanding signed by ILO, FAO, OECD, UNEP, UNIDO and WHO in March 1995, defining their co-operation in an Inter-Organisation Programme for the Sound Management of Chemicals (*ibid.*, p. 1467).

sometimes formalised in specific instruments, such as the "Executing Agency Agreements" concluded by UNDP with various specialised agencies, under which the latter agree, *e.g.* to carry out specific UNDP technical co-operation activities with governments "at the request of UNDP, as the Executing Agency may accept."[30] Specialised agencies have also concluded co-operation and co-ordination agreements with each others, which generally provide for consultation, reciprocal representation, exchange of information and documents and co-operation between secretariats.[31] These are framework agreements the effectiveness of which will depend on the will of the partners. Finally, there is an Inter-Organisation Agreement concerning transfer, secondment or loan of staff among the organisations applying the United Nations common system of salaries and allowances, which facilitates the movement of staff—and the transfer of expertise—between the various agencies.[32]

In spite of these various mechanisms, it is obvious that co-ordination problems persist within the UN system, as evidenced for instance by UNGA Resolution 50/130 of December 20, 1995, aiming at remedying the lack of communication for development programmes in the system.

Efforts are also made to ensure co-ordination between the agencies at **3–016** the national level. The membership of the UN and the specialised agencies is, whilst not identical, sufficiently close to enable each individual member to ensure that its own efforts in each organisation are co-ordinated; indeed the General Assembly, in a resolution of November 20, 1947,[33] stressed the need for this co-ordination at the national level; an obvious but apparently necessary admonition!

We turn now to a more detailed description of each of the specialised **3–017** agencies' institutional structure and functioning. As we shall see, their structure is broadly similar, comprising in most cases a plenary organ, an organ of limited composition (vested with some degree of normative and executive power) and a secretariat which constitutes the administrative backbone of each organisation. It is worth noting, however, that the plenary organ is often entrusted with significant powers, and that the organ of limited composition conversely finds itself in a situation of relative subordination. This important feature of these agencies merits the attention of those who, familiar with the UN, tend to think of the organ of limited composition as the executive, effective organ where real power lies.

---

[30] See, for instance, the Agreement between UNDP and IFC, signed at Washington, on February 8, 1988, 1492 U.N.T.S. 235, the Agreement between UNDP and IMF, signed at Noordwijk, on July 16, 1989, 1540 U.N.T.S. 369; the Agreement between UNDP and WHO, signed at New York and Geneva, on September 17 and October 19, 1992, *ibid.*, no II–1066.

[31] See for instance the Agreement for co-operation between UNESCO and UNIDO, signed at Paris and Vienna, April 22 and June 5, 1989, 1541 U.N.T.S. 367.

[32] Agreement of March 17, 1972, U.N.T.S., n. II-938.

[33] Res. 125 (III), para. 1.

B. THE AGENCIES

Food and Agriculture Organisation (FAO)[34]

Website: http://www.fao.org; Bibliography: Marchisio and Di Blase, *The Food and Agriculture Organisation (FAO),* (1991); Abbott, *Politics and Poverty—A Critique of the Food and Agriculture Organisation of the United Nations,* (1992).

3–018 The FAO was established by the United Nations Conference on Food and Agriculture, which met in May–June 1943,[35] and assumed the functions and assets of the former International Institute of Agriculture at Rome.[36] Its functions are to collect, analyse, interpret and disseminate information relating to nutrition, food and agriculture; to promote international action with respect to research, the improvement of education and administration relating to nutrition, food and agriculture, the conservation of natural resources, improvements of agricultural production, marketing and distribution, the adoption of policies for credit and agricultural commodity agreements; to furnish technical assistance; to organise expert missions; and generally to contribute to the raising of standards of nutrition and of living and ensuring humanity's freedom from hunger (Article I). Through its Office for Special Relief Operations the organisation provides emergency food assistance to countries affected by food shortages. Since 1975, it also runs a Global Information and Early Warning System which monitors crop and food outlooks to detect emergency food shortages and disasters.[37] More recently the emphasis of the organisation has been on sustainable agriculture and development.

3–019 The FAO has three main organs: the Conference, the Council and the Director-General. Each member is represented in the Conference by one delegate (Article III). The Conference determines the general policy of the organisation, approves its budget and is vested with the power to make recommendations to members concerning questions relating to food and agriculture; it may also review any decision taken by the Council or by any commission or committee of the Conference or the Council (Article IV). The Council has 49 members elected by the Conference, which also formulates the rules governing their tenure and other conditions of office. The Conference is the policy-making organ, and the powers of the Council are those which the Conference may delegate to it (Article V). The technical side of the FAO's work is the province of a number of technical

---

[34] The FAO had 179 member states and one member organisation in 1999.
[35] The Constitution has been amended in 1947, 1954, 1963, 1964 and 1991. The consolidated text of the Constitution is reproduced in Knipping (Ed.), *The United Nations System and its Predecessors*, Vol. I (1997) 1157.
[36] The Institute had been created by a Convention of June 7, 1905; see original text in Knipping (Ed.), *The United Nations System and its Predecessors*, Vol. II (1997) 135.
[37] (1995) YUN 1469.

committees (Program, Finance, Commodity Problems, Constitutional and Legal Matters) and the regional offices specifically provided for in the constitution (Article X), as well as regional conferences. The Director-General heads the staff and is responsible for directing the work of the organisation under the general supervision of the Conference and the Council (Article VII).

It should be noted that the FAO is the first—and up to now the only— **3–020** specialised agency to have admitted another international organisation— the European Community—as a full member. This was made possible by a 1991 Amendment to the Constitution.[38]

In order to improve and extend the organisation's work, a joint UN/FAO **3–021** programme—the World Food Programme (WFP)—was initiated in 1961,[39] with a view to facilitating the best possible use of food surpluses for developing countries and to establish "adequate and orderly procedures on a world basis for meeting emergency food needs," including by the establishment of food reserves.[40] The Programme is operated under the control of an Executive Board of 36 states elected half by ECOSOC and half by the FAO Council.[41]

International Civil Aviation Organisation (ICAO)[42]

Website: http://www.icao.org; Bibliography: ICAO, Memorandum on ICAO; The Story of International Civil Aviation Organisation (1951); Buergenthal, *Law-Making in ICAO*, (1969); Manin, *L'Organisation de l'Aviation Civile Internationale, (1970)* Abeyratne, "Law making and decision making power of the ICAO Council: a critical analysis" (1992) 41 Zeitschrift fur Luft-und Weltraumrecht 387; Al-Ghandi, *Towards globalization in the 21st century: trend analysis for civil aviation* (1994); J. Ducrest, "Legislative and quasi-legislative functions of ICAO: toward improved efficiency" (1995) 20 Annals of Air and Space Law 343.

The ICAO was established by the Chicago Convention of December 7, **3–022** 1944,[43] which replaced with a more comprehensive aviation institution the one originally set up by the Paris Convention of 1919.[44] ICAO's objectives

---

[38] See Art. II, 3 of the Constitution. For more details on this, see also *infra*, Chap. 16, A.
[39] See UNGA res. 1714 (XVI) of December 19, 1961.
[40] Part I of the resolution on the utilisation of food surpluses adopted by the Conference of the FAO on November 24, 1961.
[41] UNGA res. 50/8 of November 1, 1995. The Executive Board was preceded by the joint Intergovernmental Committee (1961–75) and the Committee on Food Aid Policies and Programmes (1975–95). Both were composed along the same lines as the Executive Board.
[42] The ICAO had 185 member states in 1999.
[43] 15 U.N.T.S. 295. The Constitution has been amended in 1954, 1961, 1962, 1968, 1971 and 1974. The consolidated text of the ICAO Constitution is reproduced in Knipping (Ed.), *The United Nations System and its Predecessors*, Vol. I (1997) 1264.
[44] October 13, 1919, 11 LNTS 173.

are to develop the principles and techniques of international air navigation and to foster the planning and development of international air transport so as to ensure the safe and orderly growth of international civil aviation, and encourage design and operation for peaceful purposes; to encourage the development of air navigation facilities, to prevent economic waste caused by unreasonable competition, to avoid discrimination and promote safety and the development of all aspects of international civil aeronautics (Article 44). In order to achieve these aims the ICAO has developed technical programs on communication, navigation and surveillance/air traffic management (CNS/ATM) system.[45]

3–023   The ICAO's main organs are the Assembly and the Council. The Assembly is the organisation's plenary organ. Its powers and duties include taking actions on the reports of the Council and decisions on matters referred to it by the Council as well as voting annual budgets (Article 49). The Council is a "permanent body responsible to the Assembly" (Article 50). It consists of 33 states elected by the Assembly every three years. The Assembly's discretion in holding these elections is limited by a constitutional formula designed to afford representation to the states most vitally affected by the ICAO's activities, although no precise criteria are provided to determine "chief importance" and "largest contribution." To that extent the formula is an elastic one. Article 50 (b) provides:

> "In electing the members of the Council, the Assembly shall give adequate representation to (1) the States of chief importance in air transport; (2) the States not otherwise included which make the largest contribution to the provision of facilities for international civil air navigation; and (3) the States not otherwise included whose designations will insure that all the major geographical areas of the world are represented on the Council [. . .]".

3–024   The Council is clearly subordinate to the Assembly. It "carries out the directions of the Assembly," reports to the Assembly, administers finances, appoints the Secretary-General, collects and publishes information, makes studies and conducts research (Article 54). Its more unusual functions include appointing and controlling the Air Transport Committee and the Air Navigation Commission (which advises the Council on the ways to favour the advancement of air navigation; Article 57), and reporting to states any violations of the Convention and to the Assembly when a state has failed to remedy such an infraction. It also adopts international standards and practices. Clearly it is to the latter more technical body that the Council will look for advice in pursuing this last function. The Council may also "investigate, at the request of any contracting State, any situation

---

[45] (1995) YbKUN 1491.

which may appear to present avoidable obstacles to the development of international air navigation, and, after such investigation, issue such reports as may appear to it desirable" (Article 55). This power of investigation extends to all situations where the application of the norms governing international civil aviation is in issue.[46] One may also note that the President of the Council is sometimes called upon to play a role in the resolution of disputes between member states.[47]

The World Bank Group

Website: http://www.worldbank.org; Bibliography: Morris, *La Banque mondiale* (1965); Shonfield, *"The World Bank"* in Luard: *The Evolution of International Organisations* (1966); R. Lavalle, *La Banque mondiale et ses filiales: aspects juridiques et fonictionnement* (1972); Shihata, *The World Bank in a Changing World*, 2 vols. (1991, 1995); Salda, *World Bank* (1995).

The group commonly referred to as "the World Bank Group" consists of **3–025** four organisations: the International Bank for Reconstruction and Development (IBRD), the International Finance Corporation (IFC), the International Development Association (IDA) and the Multilateral Investment Guarantee Agency (MIGA). The latter three were created under the auspices of the IBRD to supplement its activities in fields which did not originally fall within the sphere of competences of IBRD. The Group also includes the International Centre for the Settlement of Investment Disputes (ICSID),[48] the mandate of which is to provide facilities for conciliation and arbitration of investment disputes.[49] Due to its mainly adjudicatory functions, ICSID is considered later on.[50]

There is a strong insitutional relationship between the components of the **3–026** Group reflected in the fact that the President of IBRD is *ex officio* President of IDA,[51] Chairman of the Board of Directors of IFC[52] and MIGA[53] and of the Administrative Council of ICSID.[54] Moreover, Governors of the IBRD who are appointed by a member of the Bank which is also a member of IFC or IDA are *ex officio* Governors of the Corporation

---

[46] See, *e.g.* Resolution of June 27, 1996 on the shootdown of civil aircrafts off Cuba, and the attached report.
[47] See for instance the mediation by the President of the Council which settled a dispute between the United States and Cuba over the rights of Cuban-registered aircrafts to overfly the United States on flights to and from Canada (Press communiqué of June 19, 1998, available on http://www.icao.org/cgi/goto.pl?/en/updates.html).
[48] Internet address: http://www.worldbank.org/icsid.
[49] See Art. 1 of the Convention on the settlement of investment disputes between States and nationals of other States (February 18, 1965, 575 U.N.T.S. 159).
[50] See *infra*, Chap. 13, para. 13–057a.
[51] IDA, Art. VI, section 5(a).
[52] IFC, Art. IV, section 5(a).
[53] MIGA, Art. 32(b).
[54] See Art. 5 of the ICSID Convention.

or the Association, respectively.[55] Equally, the annual meeting of the IFC Board is held "in conjunction with the annual meeting of the Board of Govenors of the Bank."[56] Nevertheless, members of the Group enjoy legal and financial independence from each other.[57]

International Bank for Reconstruction and Development (IBRD)[58]

Website: http://www.worldbank.org.

3–027 The IBRD emerged from the Bretton Woods Conference in July 1944, and the constitution of the Organisation is to be found in Annex B to the Final Act there adopted.[59] Its purposes are to assist in the reconstruction and development of territories by facilitating the investment of capital,[60] to promote private foreign investment by means of guarantees or participation in loans and other investments made by private investors and otherwise to supplement private investment, to promote the long-range balanced growth of international trade and the maintenance of equilibrium in the balance of payments by encouraging investment designed to develop productivity, and generally to assist in bringing about a smooth transition from a wartime to a peacetime economy.[61] The Bank's loans are made mainly to governments or to agencies or corporations owned by governments. In order to finance its activities, the Bank borrows money on financial markets.[62]

3–028 The institutional structure of the Bank consists of three main organs. The Board of Governors is the plenary organ and is vested with "all the powers of the Bank," which include the admission of new members, changes to the capital stock, and the determination of the distribution of the net income of the Bank. The Board may also "adopt such rules and regulations as may be necessary or appropriate to conduct the business of the Bank."[63] The Executive Directors are responsible for the conduct of the general operations of the Bank and to exercise the powers delegated to them by the Board of Governors.[64] The President is the head of the operating staff and conducts the ordinary business of the Bank.[65]

---

[55] IFC, Art. IV, section 2(b); IDA, Art. VI, section 2(b).

[56] IFC, Art. IV, section 2(e).

[57] See, *e.g.* IFC, Art. IV, section 6; IDA, Art. VI, section 6. The situation of IDA is nonetheless particular in that respects; see *infra*, para. 3–033.

[58] The IBRD had 181 member states in 1999.

[59] December 27, 1945, 2 U.N.T.S. 134. The Articles of Agreement have been amended in 1965 and 1987. The consolidated text of the Articles of Agreement is reproduced in Knipping (Ed.), *The United Nations System and its Predecessors*, Vol. I (1997) 932.

[60] Regional Banks established under the auspices of the regional economic commissions of the UN coordinate their activities with the IBRD to that end. For more on those, see *infra*, Chapters 6 (European Bank for Reconstruction and Development), 7 (Inter-American Development Bank), 8 (Asian Development Bank) and 10 (African Development Bank).

[61] Art. I of the Articles of Agreement.

[62] Medium- and long-term borrowings totalled $9 billion in 1995 (1995) YUN 1483.

[63] *ibid.*, Art. V, section 2.

[64] *ibid.*, section 4(a).

[65] *ibid.*, section 5.

In 1998, the Bank's current loans totalled $19,232 million.[66] Its oper- **3–029** ations are of a highly technical character, which is reflected in the constitutional provisions. States participate by making subscriptions to the authorised capital of the Bank, standing at $184 billion in 1995, of which $176.4 billion has been subscribed.[67] These subscriptions vary greatly from state to state. This variation of "interest" is reflected in the constitution in various ways, such as weighted voting and membership of organs.[68]

Since the 1980s, the Bank has developed a policy of "conditionality", **3–030** requiring borrowing states to undertake significant economic—and sometimes financial—reforms in order to benefit from the Bank's loans. The social cost of these "Structural Adjustment Programs" has attracted wide attention, and this led the Bank to announce plans to increase social spending by 50 per cent over the 1995–98 period, including, *e.g.* the provision of $15 billion for basic social needs.[69] Since the beginning of the 1990s the Bank has also endeavoured to take greater account of environmental issues, as well as the impact of the projects it finances on indigenous people.[70] A new program, launched by the Bank in conjunction with the other international financial institutions and aimed at reducing the financial burden of the Heavily Indebted Poor Countries (HIPC), came into effect in 1998.[71]

International Finance Corporation (IFC)[72]

Website: http://www.ifc.org; Bibliography: Baker, *The International Finance Corporation: Origin, Operations and Evaluation* (1968).

The IFC was created as an "affiliate" of the Bank by the Washington **3–031** Agreement of May 25, 1955.[73] Its purpose is to further economic development by encouraging the growth of productive private enterprise in member countries, particularly in the less-developed areas, thus supplementing the activities of the Bank. To this end it aims to assist in the financing of private enterprises by making investments, without guarantee of repayment by the member government concerned, in cases where sufficient private capital is not available on reasonable terms. The IFC also

---

[66] World Bank, Annual Report, 1998.
[67] (1995) YUN 1483.
[68] For more on this, see *infra*, Chap. 11, A.
[69] (1995) YUN 1482.
[70] See, *e.g.*; Kingsbury, Operational Policies on International Institutions as Part of the Law-Making Process: The World Bank and Indigenous Peoples, in Goodwin-Gill and Talmon (Eds.), *The Reality of International Law—Essays in Honour of Ian Brownlie* (1999), p. 323.
[71] World Bank, Annual Report, 1998.
[72] The IFC had 174 member states in 1999.
[73] 264 U.N.T.S. 117. The Articles of Agreement have been amended in 1961, 1965 and 1992. The consolidated text of the Articles of Agreement is reproduced in Knipping (Ed.), *The United Nations System and its Predecessors*, Vol. I (1997) 962.

brings together investment opportunities, domestic and foreign private capital, and experienced management, and seeks to stimulate the flow of private capital into productive investment.[74] The IFC also provides technical assistance and advisory services to private businesses and governments.

3–032 Thus, whereas the Bank is limited in its ability to lend directly and for the most part acts as guarantor of loans by private foreign investors, the Corporation expressly aims at actually participating in private investments; it is an investing rather than a lending institution. A major development of the IFC's lending powers came in 1966 when, following amendments to the charters of both the Bank and IFC, the Bank was empowered to make loans up to $400 million to the IFC; this enabled the IFC to increase the scope and size of its investments. These investments may not cover more than half the cost of an enterprise and range from $1 million to $100 million; they carry the right to participate in the growth of the enterprise. In 1998, the IFC financed 255 projects in a broad range of sectors, for a total amount of $2.8 billion.[75] The Corporation's capital is divided into shares with a par value of $1,000. Members subscribe to a given number of shares, ranging from two in the case of Panama to 35,168 in the case of the U.S. This variation in the weight of interest is likewise reflected in the constitution, which is very much modelled on that of IBRD. Like the Bank, IFC's institutional structure consists of three main organs. The powers of the Corporation's Board of Governors are comparable to those of the Board of Governors of IBRD. The same goes for the Board of Directors (which is the equivalent of the Bank's Executive Directors), its voting procedure being "weighted" just as in the Bank, as well as for the Chairman of the Board of Directors and the President of the Corporation.[76]

International Development Association (IDA)

Website: http://www.worldbank.org/ida; Bibliography: Weaver, *The International Development Association, A new approach to foreign aid* (1966).

3–033 The IDA is the second of the "affiliates" of the Bank, created in 1960.[77] Having the same Executive Directors, officers and staff it is, for operational purposes, part of the Bank. The Association is not, therefore, a technically separate specialised agency. It should also be noted that "unlike the IBRD and the IFC, IDA does not have a share capital but has relied, after the initial subscriptions, on voluntary contributions which are periodically replenished by its donor members."[78] Whilst the high income countries paid

---

[74] *ibid.*, Art. I.
[75] IFC, Annual Report, 1999.
[76] *ibid.*, Art. IV, sections 2, 4 and 5, respectively.
[77] January 26, 1960, 439 U.N.T.S. 249.
[78] Shihata: *The World Bank in a Changing World* (1991) 11. IDA's Fund was replenished for the 12th time in 1999.

100 per cent of their initial subscription in convertible currencies, the developing countries pay only 10 per cent and the rest in their own currencies which may not be used without their consent.[79] The IDA's essential purpose is to raise standards of living in the less-developed areas of the world by providing finance to developing countries "on terms that are more flexible and bear less heavily on the balance of payments than those of conventional loans."[80] IDA's present policy aims, to a large extent, to attempt to reduce the debt burden of a number of severely indebted poor countries.[81] In order to reach this aim, the Association offers "soft" loans, that is to say loans which are long-term, have no interest other than a "service charge" and which require no governmental guarantees.

Multilateral Investment Guarantee Agency (MIGA)[82]

Website: http://www.miga.org; Bibliography: Shihata, *MIGA and Foreign Investment—The Origins, Operations, Policies and Basic Documents of the Multilateral Investment Guarantee Agency* (1988) ; Pettinato, Il contributo della MIGA all'evoluzione del regime giuridico degli investimenti stranieri, (1990) R.D.I. 320 ; P. Schaulfelberger, *La protection juridique des investissements internationaux dans les pays en développement: étude de la garantie contre les risques de l'investissement et en particulier de l'Agence multilatérale de garantie des investissements (AMGI)* (1993); Jos, L'Agence multilatérale de Garantie des Investissements: une contribution positive, mais insuffisante, pour pro- mouvoir les investissements utiles aux pays en développement, (1994) R.G.D.I.P. 387.

The Multilateral Investment Guarantee Agency was created in 1985 within **3–034** the framework of the World Bank.[83] Its objective is to encourage foreign investment, in particular in developing countries, mainly by issuing guaran- tees, including coinsurance and reinsurance, against non-commercial risks (*i.e.* risks such as expropriation, breach of contract or war and civil disturbance) in respect of investments in member countries which flow from other member countries (Articles 2 and 11). To this end, the Agency concludes contracts of guarantee with investors who are nationals of (in the case of natural persons) or are incorporated in (in the case of juridical persons) a member country other than the State in which the investment takes place. MIGA may also conclude contracts of reinsurance in respect of specific investments (Article 20). In addition to these functions, the Agency's mandate extends to the promotion of investment in developing countries, for example by the dissemination of information and the provision of technical assistance to improve the investment conditions in member states (Article 23).

---

[79] Art. II, section 2 of the Articles of agreement.
[80] *ibid.*, Art. I.
[81] (1995) YUN 1487.
[82] MIGA had 149 member states in 1999.
[83] October 11, 1985, ILM 24 (1985) 1605.

3–035 The three main organs of the Agency are the Council of Governors, the Board of Directors and the President. The Council is the organ of general competence; its powers include the admission and suspension of members, the decision to increase or decrease capital, and the amendment of the Constitution (Article 31). It is composed of one Governor and one Alternate designated by each member state, and holds annual meetings. The Board, composed of at least 12 Directors elected by the Governors, is responsible for the general operation of MIGA, while the President, as administrative head of the Agency, conducts the ordinary business of the organisation under the general control of the Board (Article 33).

3–036 MIGA's capital stock of one billion Special Drawing Rights is divided into 100,000 shares available for subscription by members (Article 5).[84] As with other financial institutions, each member of the Agency has a certain number of membership votes plus one subscription vote for each share of stock (Article 39). In 1999, MIGA guarantee-programme resulted in the execution of 72 guarantee contracts; the total amount of the coverage issued amounted to U.S. $1.3 billion.

International Monetary Fund (IMF)[85]

> Website: http://www.imf.int; Bibliography: Aufricht, *The IMF: Legal Bases, Structure, Functions* (1964); Fawcett, "The IMF and International Law" (1964) 40 B.Y.B.I.L. 32; Gold, *The IMF and International Law* (1966); Scammell, "The IMF" *in* Luard: *The Evolution of International Organisations* (1966); de Vries, Horsefield, *Twenty years of International Monetary Cooperation,* 3 vol. (1969); de Vries, *The System under Stress,* 2 vol. (1976); de Vries, *Cooperation on Trial,* 3 vol. (1989); Gianvitti, The International Monetary Fund and external Debt, R.C.A.D.I., 1989–III, vol. 215, 205; Salda, *The International Monetary Fund (Bibliography)* (1992); Johnson, *The International Monetary Fund 1944–1992—A Research Guide* (1993).

3–037 The IMF is very much the "partner" of the Bank, originating from the same 1944 Bretton Woods Conference.[86] Its purposes are to promote monetary co-operation through a permanent institution providing machinery for consultation and collaboration on monetary problems, to facilitate the expansion and balanced growth of international trade, to promote exchange stability and avoid competitive exchange depreciation, to assist in the establishment of a multilateral payments system and the elimination of foreign exchange restrictions hampering the growth of world trade, to make

---

[84] The division of shares between member states is to be found in Schedule A to the Convention. A resolution adopted by the Council of Governors on March 29, 1999 provides for a capital increase of SDR 850 million.

[85] The IMF had 182 member states in 1999.

[86] December 27, 1945, 2 U.N.T.S. 39. The Articles of Agreement have been amended in 1968, 1976 and 1990. The consolidated text of the Articles of Agreement is reproduced in Knipping (Ed.), *The United Nations System and its Predecessors,* Vol. I (1997) 859.

the Fund's resources available to members so as to enable them to correct maladjustments in their balance of payments and, generally, to shorten the duration of any disequilibrium in the international balance of payments of members.[87] To achieve those objectives the Fund concludes different types of agreements with member states: stand-by arrangements are short-term and focus on macroeconomic policies and aim at overcoming balance-of-payment difficulties; extended fund facility arrangements are used to make credit available for longer periods; enhanced structural adjustment facility (ESAF) arrangements provide low-income member states with loans to support macroeconomic adjustment policies and structural reforms.[88] In order to help members cope with specific difficulties, other special facilities have also been created for limited periods of time, such as the compensatory and contingency financing facility (CCFF), the systemic tranformation facility (STF) created in 1993 to meet the needs of economies in transition from centrally planned to market economies,[89] and the Supplemental Reserve Facility (SRF) established in 1997 to meet the supplementary demand for IMF resources resulting from the Asian crisis. In 1998, IMF disbursed a total of SDR 19.3 billion to member states.[90] That same year, the Fund agreed to a three-year plan to lend a total of $22.3 billion to Russia alone.[91] Since the 1970s, the IMF has developed a practice of conditionality similar to that of the World Bank.[92]

The preliminary comments made above in relation to the IBRD apply **3–038** equally to the IMF; in fact the two constitutions are remarkably similar. Each member has a quota, ranging from $2.5 million for Marshall Islands to $26,526 million for the USA. The total of the quotas exceeds $145 billion.[93] The quotas were originally paid as to 25 per cent in gold and the rest in the member's own currency. The member then has "drawing rights", enabling it to purchase other currencies of which it is in need through the Fund for a small service charge and provided, in general, its requests do not cause the Fund's holding of its own currency to exceed 25 per cent of its own quota. The "par value" of each currency is fixed for most Fund members and cannot be changed by a member without consultation with the Fund.[94] Drawing rights were increased by 50 per cent of the original

---

[87] *ibid.*, Art. I.
[88] (1995) YUN 1488.
[89] *ibid.* (1995) YUN 1488.
[90] IMF, Annual Report, 1998.
[91] *Le Monde*, July 15, 1998, pp. 1–2.
[92] For more on this, see *e.g.* Denters, "The IMF in the 1990s: Structural adjustment through co-operation", in Chowdury, Denters and de Waart (Eds.), *The right to development in international law* (1992), 366; Sorel, Sur quelques aspects juridiques de la conditionnalité du F.M.I. et de leurs conséquences, (1996) EJIL 42.
[93] See figures in Knipping (Ed.), *The United Nations System and its Predecessors*, Vol. I (1997) 930.
[94] Article III of the Articles of Agreement.

quota in 1959, and by a further 25 per cent in 1966. In June 1968, amendments to the IMF Articles of Agreement were adopted giving "Special Drawing Rights" (SDR) to enable members to meet balance of payments difficulties or falls in their reserves: these SDR's are additional to the normal drawing rights.[95] They may be used by the member states in their financial transactions.

3–039   The liquidity of the Fund has been greatly helped by the "General Arrangements to Borrow" (GAB), first concluded in 1962 and extended to 1970, whereby 10 industrial countries agreed to lend the Fund up to $6,000 million if required to forestall an impairment of trade. A New Agreement to Borrow (NAB) took effect in 1998, making a total of SDR 34 billion of credit available to the Fund. The GAB was used for the first time in 20 years to provide support for the Russian adjustment programme in 1998. In addition, in response to an UNCTAD recommendation, a system of compensatory export financing was introduced to permit larger drawing rights for the developing countries dependent upon the export of primary products.

3–040   The Fund's organs are the Board of Governors, the Executive Board and the Managing Director. The Board of Governors is the plenary organ and the body of general competence.[96] The Executive Directors of the Fund are "responsible for the conduct of the general operations of the Fund and for this purpose shall exercise all the powers delegated to them by the Board of Governors;"[97] in short, the Directors execute the policies and decisions of the plenary Board of Governors. They function in continuous session, necessary in view of the functions of the Fund, and the chairman is the Managing Director, the chief executive officer equivalent to the Secretary-General in the UN. Of the Directors,

> "(i) five shall be appointed by the five members having the largest quotas;
> (ii) fifteen shall be elected by the other members."[98]

The distinction made between "appointed" and "elected" directors is understandable, and the elections of the latter are governed by a complicated system set out in Schedule E to the Agreement, and are held every two years.

3–041   Each appointed director is entitled to cast the number of votes allotted to the member appointing him (250 + 1 for each $100,000 of its quota) and each elected director is entitled to cast the number of votes which counted

---

[95] See Gold, Special Drawing Rights: the Role of Language, IMF (1971).

[96] Art. XII, section 2 of the Articles of Agreement.

[97] *ibid.*, Art. XII, section 3.

[98] *ibid.*; the number of Directors elected under Art. XII, section 3, ii) may be increased or decreased by the Board of Governors (*ibid.*). There were 19 Directors of the second category in 1999.

towards his election, and the general voting rule is a simple majority.[99] This system of "weighted" voting, plus the fact that, in the event of a vacancy during a term the same members who elected the director elect his successor, suggests that the directors are representatives of the countries either appointing them or electing them, and not independent experts or international civil servants. The fact that they are paid a salary from the Fund and hold a contract of service, a quite unusual feature for an executive organ, does not really detract from this, and it is of interest to note that there is no provision comparable to that applying to the Administrative Council of ITU, or the Executive Board of UNESCO and of WHO, whereby functions are exercised on behalf of the entire body of members.[1]

United Nations Educational, Scientific and Cultural Organisation (UNESCO)[2]

Website: http://www.unesco.org; Bibliography: Hajnal, *Guide to UNESCO* (1983); Wells, *The UN, UNESCO, and the Politics of Knowledge* (1987).

The UNESCO constitution was drawn up at the London Conference and **3–042** signed on November 16, 1945.[3] The purpose of the Organisation is "to contribute to peace and security by promoting collaboration among the nations through education, science and culture ...". To this end the organisation is to collaborate in the work of advancing the mutual knowledge and understanding of persons, through all means of mass communication and to that end recommends such international agreements as may be necessary; it is to maintain, increase and diffuse knowledge by conserving the world's inheritance of books, works of art, etc., by encouraging co-operation among the nations in all branches of intellectual activity, and by initiating methods of international co-operation calculated to give to the people of all countries access to the printed and published materials produced by any of them.[4]

UNESCO's institutional structure consists of the General Conference, **3–043** the Executive Board and the Secretariat. The General Conference is to "determine the policies and the main lines of work of the Organisation" and is vested with recommendatory powers.[5] The Executive Board of 58

---

[99] *ibid.*, Art. XII, sections 3 and 5.
[1] See *infra*, paras 3–043, 3–046 and 3–062.
[2] UNESCO had 188 member states in 1999.
[3] 4 U.N.T.S. 275. It has been amended in 1947, 1968, 1972, 1976, 1978 and 1980. The consolidated text of the Constitution is reproduced in Knipping (Ed.), *The United Nations System and its Predecessors*, Vol. I (1997) 1105.
[4] Art. I of the Constitution.
[5] *ibid.*, Art. IV(2) and (4).

members is elected by the General Conference. It is to act "under the authority of the General Conference," being responsible for the "execution of the programme adopted by the Conference . . . ."[6] The members are state representatives, but there is a clear attempt to secure a Board of technical competence and to ensure that, in their capacity as members of the Board, they act as representatives of the Conference rather than of their states. This is seen in the provision that, in electing them, the Conference "shall endeavour to include persons competent in the arts, the humanities, the sciences, education and the diffusion of ideas, and qualified by their experience and capacity to fulfil the administrative and executive duties of the Board."[7] It is also provided that regard shall be had "to the diversity of cultures and a balanced geographical distribution." There is a further provision according to which the members "shall exercise the powers delegated to them by the General Conference on behalf of the Conference as a whole and not as representatives of their respective Governments."[8] This is something of a compromise between the traditional position of state representatives and that of international civil servants. The essential function of the Board is to undertake the execution of the programme adopted by the Conference, to which the Board is responsible. The voting procedure is not provided for in the constitution, but in the rules of procedure, and simple majority is the basic rule. Several subsidiary organs have also been established to manage the organisation's main programmes.

3–044   UNESCO went through a significant crisis in the 1980s when two influential members (United Kingdom and United States) withdrew from the organisation in protest against the increasing "politicisation" of its debates and actions, as well as against its poor management.[9] The U.K. has nevertheless reintegrated the organisation in 1997, and the U.S. announced its intention to do so in 1994.[10]

World Health Organisation (WHO)[11]

Website: http://www.who.int; Bibliography: Beigbeder, *L'Organisation mondiale de la Santé* (1995); Siddiqi, *World Health and World Politics—The World Health Organisation and the UN System* (1995); Lakin, "The legal powers of the World Health Organisation" (1997) 3 Medical Law International 23; Beigbeder, *The World Health Organisation* (1998).

---

[6] *ibid.*, Art. V(5), b).
[7] *ibid.*, Art. V(2).
[8] *ibid.*, Art. V(12).
[9] Singapore also withdrew from UNESCO at the same time, but the reasons for withdrawal were stated to be economic, rather than political in character.
[10] See 98 RGDIP (1994) 166. This, however, was not effective in 2000, the U.S. retaining observer status only.
[11] The WHO had 191 member states in 1999.

As pointed out in Chapter 1, international co-operation in the field of **3–045** health has a long history. The WHO was established by a Constitution dated July 22, 1946,[12] assuming the functions of the International Office of Public Health, which had operated under the League of Nations from Paris.[13] It also undertook some of the work of the Health Division of the temporary UN Relief and Rehabilitation Administration (established to provide assistance to European populations after the Second World War). The objective of the Organisation is "the attainment by all peoples of the highest possible level of health," and to this end there is a list of 22 functions, including rendering assistance to governments, furnishing technical assistance, proposing conventions and agreements, promoting research, developing international standards with respect to pharmaceutical products, and undertaking of studies and the provision of information.[14] The WHO has been instrumental in the eradication of several illnesses (smallpox being an example) and in the fight against infectious diseases.

WHO's organs are the World Health Assembly, the Executive Board and **3–046** the Secretariat. The functions of the Assembly include determining the policies of the organisation, reviewing and approving activities of the Board and of the Director-General, and instructing the Board in regard to matters upon which action, study, investigation or report may be considered desirable[15]; it is the Assembly which is entrusted with the "legislative" process.[16] The Executive Board's 32 members are elected by the Assembly, taking into account equitable geographical distribution, and should be "technically qualified" persons. They exercise their powers "on behalf of the whole Health Assembly," so the intention of avoiding a pure representation of state interests is the same as in UNESCO. Elections are for three years and are staggered. Voting is governed by the same procedure as in the Assembly.[17] The Executive Board's task, as executive organ, is essentially to carry out the decisions and policies of the Assembly although it has a certain independent power of action to deal with epidemics and sudden calamities. As for the FAO, there is considerable stress on regional co-operation, so that a quite separate strata of organs is provided for, necessarily of limited composition. There are in fact six regions, geographically defined by the Assembly under its powers in Chapter XI, each consisting of a separate regional "organisation" with a regional committee

---

[12] 14 U.N.T.S. 185. It has been amended in 1959, 1967, 1973, 1976, 1978 and 1986. The consolidated text of the Constitution is reproduced in Knipping (Ed.), *The United Nations System and its Predecessors*, Vol. I (1997) 1042.

[13] See original text in Knipping (Ed.), *The United Nations System and its Predecessors*, Vol. II (1997) 140.

[14] Arts 1 and 2 of the Constitution.

[15] *ibid.*, Art. 18.

[16] *ibid.*, Art. 21.

[17] *ibid.*, Art. 60.

and a regional office (Secretariat);[18] naturally, membership of regional committees is confined to members and associate members of that region.

International Labour Organisation (ILO)

Website: http://www.ilo.org; Bibliography: Johnson, *The ILO* (1970); *ILO, The Impact of International Labour Conventions and Recommendations* (1976); Tortora, *Institution spécialisée et organisation mondiale: Etudes des relations de l'OIT avec la SDN et l'ONU* (1980); Osieke, *Constitutional Law and Practice in the International Labour Organisation* (1985); Ghebali, *The International Labour Organisation. A Case Study on the Evolution of UN Specialised Agencies* (1989); Valticos, The ILO: A retrospective and future view, (1996), International Labour Rev. 135; Bartolomei de la Cruz and Euzeby, *L'Organisation internationale du travail* (1997).

3–047 The ILO originally formed part of the League of Nations system, and its constitution was to be found in Part XIII of the Treaty of Versailles;[19] it was, however, an autonomous institution, like the P.C.I.J., yet its links with the League made amendment of its constitution necessary when the League was dissolved. The constitution was amended by the International Labour Conference at Montreal in October 1946,[20] its aims being widened and a new relationship with the UN anticipated. The principal aim, as set forth in the Preamble, is the improvement of conditions of labour; this is to be achieved, for example, by the regulation of hours of work, regulation of the labour supply and the prevention of unemployment, protection of the worker against sickness and industrial injury, recognition of the principle of equal remuneration for work of equal value, recognition of the principle of freedom of association and the organisation of vocational and technical education. The fact that the Organisation is designed to promote the interests of part of the community within the state, as opposed to the interests of the state as such, has led to a form of representation of interests other than state interest. This was unique at the ILO's inception, since member states are represented by a tripartite delegation comprising representatives of the government, and of the national workers' and employers' associations, respectively.[21]

3–048 The most efficient tool devised by the ILO to achieve its aims have been the international labor conventions, 182 of which have been concluded to date.[22] Moreover, a Declaration on fundamental principles and rights at

---

[18] For more on the history and status of these (with emphasis on the Middle East Office), see, *e.g.* the I.C.J. Advisory Opinion on the Interpretation of the Agreement of March 25, 1951 between the WHO and Egypt, December 20, 1980, I.C.J. Rep. 1980, sp. pp. 76 *et seq.*

[19] See original text in Knipping (Ed.), *The United Nations System and its Predecessors*, Vol. II (1997) 709.

[20] October 9, 1946, 15 U.N.T.S. 35. The Constitution has been amended again in 1953, 1962 and 1972; for the text of this amendment, see 958 U.N.T.S. 167.

[21] For more on this, see *infra*, Chap. 16.

[22] For further details see Jenks, "Some characteristics of international labour conventions," (1935) 33 Can. B.R. 448–462; "The significance for international law of the tripartite character of the I.L.O.," (1936) 22 Trans. Grotius Soc. 45–86; "The revision of international labour conventions," (1933) 14 B.Y.B.I.L. 43–64; also Dillon, *International Labour Conventions,* (1941), especially Chaps III and IV.

work, aiming at ensuring respect by all member states of four fundamental rights (freedom of association, elimination of forced labour, abolition of child labour and elimination of discrimination in respect of employment) and establishing a follow-up mechanism was adopted by the Conference in June 1998 in an attempt to reinforce the organisation's normative framework.[23]

The ILO's institutional structure consists of three main organs: the **3–049** General Conference, the Governing Body and a Secretariat, the International Labour Office. The Conference is the plenary organ and is vested with "legislative" powers. The functions of the Governing Body are general supervision of the International Labour Office, formulation of policies and programmes, the adoption of the agenda for meetings of the Conference, drafting proposals for the budget, appointment of the Director-General, and an important role in situations where a complaint of non-observance of a Convention by a member is made.[24] Except when the constitution requires a two-thirds majority, voting is by simple majority of the representatives on the Governing Body; apart from their numerical superiority, there is no voting privilege for the governmental representatives or for those from the states "of chief industrial importance." The International Labour Office lends assistance to the Conference and Governing Body in the preparation of their work, provides legal and administrative assistance to governments in the field of labour and generally exercises "such other powers and duties as may be assigned to it by the Conference or by the Governing Body."[25]

Recent years have seen an expansion in size of these organs, largely in **3–050** recognition of the increase in total membership. In the ILO the Governing Body is, because of its tripartite character, unique amongst the organs of limited composition in the specialised agencies. Of the 56 representatives, 28 are representatives of governments, 14 of employers and 14 of workers. Of the 28 government representatives, 10 are to be appointed by the members "of chief industrial importance" (Article 7(2))[26] and the other 18 are elected by the Conference. The task of determining which are the members "of chief industrial importance" is now entrusted to the Governing Body, which is enjoined to make rules and to ensure that the question is considered by an impartial committee before being decided by the Governing Body. There is, further, a right of appeal by a member against the decision of the Governing Body to the Conference. The device is of interest in comparison with that used in the Security Council for determining which

---

[23] Text in 37 ILM (1998) 1237.

[24] Arts 24 *et seq.* of the Constitution. For more on this, see *infra*, Chap. 12, para. 12–035.

[25] *ibid.*, Art. 10.

[26] In 1999, these were Brazil, China, France, Germany, India, Italy, Japan, Russia, U.K. and USA.

states, because of their predominant interest in the matters with which the organisation is concerned, shall have security of tenure on the executive organ. The Charter's solution was to actually name the "Big Five," thus rendering the choice a final one, bearing in mind the fact that the veto applies to amendments of the Charter. In the ILO, the solution adopted allows for a change of membership; admittedly it may be far easier to adopt statistical criteria of industrial importance than of political power. The Governing Body as a whole enjoys a period of office of three years; there are no "staggered" elections. Ten committees have been established by the Governing Body to supplement its activities in various fields. The best known of these is probably the Committee on Freedom of Association, responsible for examining the complaints submitted to the Governing Body alleging violations of the freedom of association.[27]

As with other specialised agencies, the ILO had to face accusations of politicisation which led the United States to withdraw from the Organisation between 1977 and 1980.

World Meteorological Organisation (WMO)[28]

Website: http://www.wmo.ch; Bibliography: Ott, *L'organisation météorologique mondiale* (1976); Leese, "World Meteorological Organisation—demonstrated accomplishments and strong plans for the future in applying space technology" (1986) 14 Journal of Space Law 140; Davies (Ed.), *Forty Years of Progress and Achievement—A historical review of WMO* (1990).

3–051 The activities, resources and obligations of the International Meteorological Organisation, established in 1878, were transferred to the World Meteorological Organisation on April 4, 1951, although the Convention of WMO had been opened for signature in Washington on October 11, 1947.[29] The WMO's objectives are to facilitate worldwide co-operation in the establishment of networks of stations for making meteorological observations; to promote the establishment of systems for the rapid exchange of weather information; to further the application of meteorology to aviation, shipping, agriculture, and other human activities; to promote the standardisation of meteorological observations and to ensure the uniform publication of observations and statistics, as well as to encourage research and training in meteorology.[30] Its recent activities include action in support of sustainable development "in areas such as climate change, natural disaster mitigation, water resources management and environmental

---

[27] For more on this, see, *e.g.* Swepston, Human Rights Law and the Freedom of Association: Developments through ILO Supervision, (1998) International Labour Rev. 137, 169–194. See Chapter 12, paras 12–064, *et seq.*

[28] The WMO had 179 member states in 1999.

[29] 77 U.N.T.S. 143. It has been amended in 1963, 1967, 1975, 1979 and 1983. The consolidated text of the Constitution is reproduced in Knipping (Ed.), *The United Nations System and its Predecessors*, Vol. I (1997) 1323.

[30] *ibid.*, Art. 2.

monitoring."[31] The WMO has also developed the World Weather Watch (WWW) Programme, in order to "collect, analyse and disseminate meteorological data, and process products for national meteorological services."[32]

The WMO's organs are the World Meteorological Congress, the Executive **3–052** Council, the Regional meteorological associations, the technical commissions and the Secretariat. The Congress is the plenary organ and determines "general policies for the fulfilment of the purposes of the Organisation." It is vested with recommendatory power.[33] The functions of the Congress are, in addition to normal plenary functions such as elections and considering reports from the various organs, to adopt technical regulations covering meteorological practices and procedures, to determine general regulations prescribing the constitution and functions of the various other bodies of the Organisation; the congress is clearly "the supreme body of the Organisation."[34] Voting is normally by a two-thirds majority, except for election of individuals to serve in one capacity or another (*i.e.* expert commissions) which is by simple majority. The Congress is composed of representatives of members amongst which one "should be the director of its meteorological service, as its principal delegate."[35] The Executive Council consists of the President and Vice-Presidents, the Presidents of Regional Associations, and 26 Directors of Meteorological Services of members.[36] Its functions include the supervision of the execution of the resolutions of the Congress, the provision of technical information, the making of studies, the preparation of the agenda of Congress and the administration of finances. The Council is also "to consider and, where necessary, take action on behalf of the Organisation on resolutions and recommendations of regional associations and technical commissions."[37] It will be noted that the representatives are expected to be technically competent, and are elected in their personal capacities and not as representatives of governments. WMO also has a strong emphasis on regionalism, and Regional Meteorological Associations, which therefore qualify as organs of limited membership, are provided for in Article 18. These meet "as often as necessary," and so far six regional associations have been formed. Finally, the Congress has established eight technical commissions the mandate of which is to study and make recommendations to the Congress and the Council on "any subject within the purpose of the Organisation". These commissions consist of technical experts, but member states also have the right to be represented on them.[38]

---

[31] (1995) YUN 1499.
[32] *ibid.*
[33] Constitution, Art. 8.
[34] *ibid.*, Art. 7, (a).
[35] *ibid.*, Art. 7.
[36] *ibid.*, Art. 13.
[37] *ibid.*, Art. 14, (c).
[38] *ibid.*, Art. 19.

International Maritime Organisation (IMO)[39]

Website: http://www.imo.org; Bibliography: Mankabady (Ed.), *The International Maritime Organisation* (1984); Simmonds, *The International Maritime Organisation* (1994).

3–053 A Provisional Maritime Consultative Council was established in 1946, and a UN Maritime Conference in February–March 1948 drew up the Convention of the Intergovernmental Maritime Consultative Organisation (IMCO).[40] Delay in securing the necessary 21 ratifications, seven of which had to be nations with one million gross tons of shipping, meant that the Convention did not enter into force until 1957. In 1982, the name of the Organisation was changed to the International Maritime Organisation (IMO).[41]

3–054 The IMO's purposes are to provide machinery for co-operation among governments in the field of governmental regulation and practices relating to technical matters affecting shipping engaged in international trade and to encourage the adoption of the highest possible standards in matters of maritime safety and efficiency in navigation;[42] to encourage the removal of discriminatory action and unnecessary restrictions by governments affecting shipping engaged in international trade; to provide for the consideration by the organisation of matters concerning unfair restrictive practices by shipping concerns; to provide for the consideration by the organisation of any matters concerning shipping that may be referred to it by any organ or specialised agency of the UN; and to provide for the exchange of information among governments on matters under consideration by the organisation.[43]

3–055 The IMO's institutional structure consists of an Assembly, a Council and four specialised Committees. The Assembly meets every two years, although extraordinary sessions can be summoned by the Council or one-third of the members. Its functions include the voting of the budget and consideration of the reports of the Council.[44] But it is apparent that it does not enjoy, *vis-à-vis* the Council, the same dominant role as the plenary organs of some of the organisations reviewed above. Whilst it may establish

---

[39] The IMO had 157 member states in 1999.
[40] March 6, 1948, 289 U.N.T.S. 48. The convention has been amended in 1964, 1965, 1974, 1977, 1979. The consolidated text of the IMO Convention is reproduced in Knipping (Ed.), *The United Nations System and its Predecessors*, Vol. I (1997) 1301.
[41] Upon entry into force of the 1975 amendment to the 1948 Convention; see text in 1276 U.N.T.S. 468.
[42] It was via IMCO that in 1976 Inmarsat was established as a separate organisation to develop the use of satellites as an aid to marine navigation: see 1143 U.N.T.S. 105. For more on this organisation see *infra*, Chap. 4, paras 4–058 *et seq.*
[43] Art. 1 of the IMO Convention.
[44] *ibid.*, Art. 15.

temporary subsidiary bodies, it may only establish permanent subsidiary bodies "upon recommendation of the Council."[45] Its powers of election of members to the Council are carefully circumscribed by the provisions of Article 17 dealing with the composition of this organ. Whilst the Assembly is to "perform the functions of the Organisation" and has the power to address recommendations to member states, it is for the Council to take the effective action in matters connected with the essential purposes of the organisation, in the drafting of conventions, agreements or other instruments to be recommended to governments and inter-governmental organisations, or in the convening of conferences. Formally, it will be the Assembly which recommends to governments, but in practice these recommendations will be those of the Council, for the Assembly has no power to alter the Council's recommendations, only to refer them back to the Council with its comments.[46]

The evidence so far suggests that this relationship seems to work in **3–056** practice. Certainly a reading of the constitution conveys the impression that the major maritime powers which, as we shall see, are entitled to representation on the Council, have drafted the constitution so as to ensure that effective power remains in their hands in the organ of limited composition and does not stray into the unpredictable forum of the Assembly, in which each member has one vote. In fact one is reminded very much of the General Assembly/Security Council division of power.

IMO's Council of 32 members[47] is elected by the Assembly and is composed as follows:

"(a) Eight shall be States with the largest interest in providing international shipping services;

(b) Eight shall be other States with the largest interest in international seaborne trade;

(c) Sixteen shall be States not elected under (a) or (b) above, which have special interests in maritime transport or navigation and whose election to the Council will ensure the representation of all major geographic areas of the world."[48]

This formula differs from the formula which pertained under the original **3–057** 1948 Constitution. Whereas under the original formula it was for the Council to determine which states fell into certain categories (thereby

---

[45] *ibid.*, (c).
[46] *ibid.*, (h).
[47] An amendment to the constitution has been adopted in 1993, which will increase this number to 40 when it comes into force (upon ratification of two-thirds of the members).
[48] *ibid.*, Art. 17.

limiting the area of discretion left to the Assembly) the new formula merely prescribes the principles to be applied by the Assembly but otherwise leaves it to the Assembly to conduct the election process. This is symptomatic of the move away from the dominance of the Council over the Assembly which was a characteristic of the original constitution. It is also symptomatic of the tendency to place more emphasis on equitable geographical distribution of seats and less on "technical" criteria.

The Council meets at a month's notice "as often as may be necessary," upon the summons of the Chairman or upon the request of four or more members. Its functions are to receive the reports, proposals and recommendations of the various Committees for transmission to the Assembly with its own comments and recommendations, appointment of the Secretary-General, submission to the Assembly of a report on the organisation's activities and of the budget estimates, conclusion of agreements with other organisations subject to the approval of the Assembly, and, between sessions of the Assembly, to "perform all the functions of the Organisation . . ."[49] The voting procedure is the same as for the Assembly.

3–058   The four Committees all are plenary organs. They are the Maritime Safety Committee, the Legal Committee, the Marine Environment Protection Committee and the Technical Cooperation Committee.[50] The functions of the Maritime Safety Committee are to consider matters concerned with aids to navigation, construction and equipment of vessels, manning from a safety standpoint, rules for the prevention of collisions, etc., and generally matters directly affecting maritime safety.[51] Its proposals are submitted to the Assembly through the Council. It meets annually and votes according to the same procedure as the Assembly and Council. The Legal and Marine Environment Protection Committees were both established by the 1975 amendment to the IMO Convention.[52] The former's mandate is to consider legal matters within the scope of the organisation, and more precisely to submit to the Council drafts of internationals conventions and of amendments to internationals conventions which the Committee has developed.[53] The latter's function is to consider matters within the scope of the organisation concerned with marine pollution, and in particular to perform functions conferred upon the organisation by or under international conventions for the prevention and control of marine pollution from ships, to consider measures to facilitate the enforcement of such conventions and

---

[49] *ibid.*, Arts 21–26.
[50] The Convention had initially provided for one of them only, the Maritime Safety Committee. The interpretation of the provision governing this organ's composition gave rise to a serious controversy between the member states. The question was submitted to the I.C.J. (see Advisory Opinion of June 8, 1960, I.C.J. Rep. 1960, 150). For more on this, see *infra*, Chap. 11, paras 11–027 *et seq.*
[51] Art. 28 of the Convention.
[52] The amendment came into force in May 1982.
[53] *ibid.*, Arts 33–34.

to "provide for the acquisition of scientific, technical and any other practical information on the prevention and control of marine pollution from ships for dissemination to States [. . .] and, where appropriate, make recommendations and develop guidelines."[54] Recommendations, guidelines and proposals for regulations are submitted to the Council. Finally, there is the Technical Cooperation Committee established by the 1977 amendment to the Convention.[55] Its mandate is to consider "any matter within the scope of the Organisation concerned with the implementation of technical co-operation projects funded by the relevant United Nations programme for which the Organisation acts as the executing or cooperating agency or by funds-in-trust voluntarily provided to the Organisation. . . ."[56] It may also submit recommendations to the Council. As in all organisations, the Secretariat provides the IMO's administrative backbone.

Universal Postal Union (UPU)[57]

> Website: http://www.upu.int; Bibliography: Codding, *The UPU* (1964); Menon, "The UPU" (1965) Int. Council No. 552; Chaubert, *L'Union postale universelle* (1970); Omeorogbe, "Functionalism in the UPU and the ITU" (1987), 27 Indian Journal of International Law 50.

Like the WHO and ILO, the UPU has distinguished antecedents, and the **3–059** Constitution signed at Vienna on July 10, 1964[58] is a direct successor to the Postal Convention of 1874 establishing a General Postal Union,[59] which became known as the Universal Postal Union after the Congress at Paris in 1878. Its functions and powers are briefly stated in Article 1, which describes the members as "a single postal territory for the reciprocal exchange of letter-post items," and sets out the aim as being "to secure the organisation and improvement of the postal services and to promote in this sphere the development of international collaboration." The 1964 constitutional revision radically altered the legal structure of the Union. There are now four basic Acts: (a) the Constitution of the Union (designed to be of a more permanent character and not renewed with each Congress as are the other Acts); (b) the General Regulations, providing for the implementation of the Constitution; (c) the Universal Postal Convention, containing the general provisions relating to postal services; and (d) the Detailed Regulations of the Universal Postal Convention.[60]

---

[54] *ibid.*, Art. 38.
[55] The amendment came into force in November 1984.
[56] *ibid.*, Art. 43.
[57] UPU had 169 member states in 1999.
[58] 611 U.N.T.S. 7. It has been amended in 1969, 1974, 1984, 1989 and 1994. The consolidated text of the Constitution is reproduced in Knipping (Ed.), *The United Nations System and its Predecessors*, Vol. I (1997) 1339.
[59] See original text in Knipping (Ed.), *The United Nations System and its Predecessors*, Vol. II (1997) 84.
[60] Art. 22 of the Constitution.

3–060 UPU's organs are the Congress, the Council of Administration (formerly Executive Council), the Postal Operations Council (formerly Consultative Council for Postal Studies) and the International Bureau.[61] The Congress is the plenary organ and supreme body of the Union.[62] It meets every five years in order to revise or complete the Acts of the previous Congress. The Council of Administration, which is an organ of limited membership, ensures the continuity of the work of the Union between Congresses. Such an organ is almost essential when the plenary conferences meet but once in five years. The 40 member countries of the Council are appointed by Congress on the basis of equitable geographical distribution. The actual representatives of the members elected by the Congress "carry out their functions in the name and in the interests of the Union."[63] The Postal Operations Council is "entrusted with carrying out studies and giving opinions on technical, operational and economic questions concerning the postal service,"[64] whereas the International Bureau, placed under the authority of the Council of Administration, serves as "an organ of execution, support, liaison, information and consultation."[65]

International Telecommunications Union (ITU)[66]

Website: http://www.itu.int; Bibliography: Godding, *The International Telecommunications Union-An experiment in international co-operation* (1952); Godding and Rutkowski, *The International Telecommunication Union in a Changing World* (1982); Omeorogbe, "Functionalism in the UPU and the ITU" (1987), 27 Indian Journal of International Law 50; Savage, *The Politics of International Telecommunications Regulation* (1989); Harris, "The new telecommunications development: Bureau of the International Telecommunications Union," (1991) Am. U.J. Int'l L. & Pol'y 83.

3–061 An International Telegraphic Union had been established in 1865, and, after the Berlin Conference of 1906, it took radio under its wing; the Telecommunication Conference of Madrid in 1932 abrogated the previous conventions and established the International Telecommunications Union, which was revised in 1947. The ITU Convention has been subject to further amendments in 1952 and 1961, and was radically revised in 1965[67] and again in 1992.[68] The ITU's purposes are to maintain and extend international co-operation in the use of telecommunications of all kinds, and to

---

[61] Those changes in the designation of the organs were brought by the 1994 amendment to the Constitution, which came into force in January 1996.

[62] Art. 14 of the Constitution.

[63] *ibid.*, Art. 16(2).

[64] *ibid.*, Art. 17.

[65] *ibid.*, Art. 18.

[66] The ITU had 189 member states in 1999.

[67] Montreux Convention on Telecommunications, November 12, 1965, U.N.J.Y. (1965) 184

[68] The text of the new Constitution is reproduced in Knipping (Ed.), *The United Nations System and its Predecessors*, Vol. I (1997) 1357.

promote the development of technical facilities and the efficiency of telecommunications services. To do this, the Union allocates radio frequency spectrum and registers radio frequency assignments so as to avoid harmful interference between the radio stations of different countries. It also fosters collaboration with a view to establishing low rates for users and undertakes studies and publishes information.[69] It is remarkably similar to UPU. The ITU's constitutional foundations are threefold: its basic instrument is the Constitution, the provisions of which are complemented by those of the Convention of the International Telecommunications Union[70] and by those of the Administrative Regulations in the fields of international telecommunication and of radio.[71]

The institutional structure of the Union consists of the Plenipotentiary **3–062** Conference, the Council, world conferences on international telecommunications, three technical Sectors and the Secretariat. The functions of the Plenipotentiary Conference, which is the plenary organ and supreme body of the Union,[72] include the revision of the Convention, determining general policies, establishing the budget, considering the report of the Council on the activities of the Union, and entering into agreements with other international bodies.[73] The Council ensures continuity of administration in the interval of five years between Plenipotentiary Conferences. It meets yearly, or upon the request of a majority of its members, and has a total membership of 46 members of the Union, elected by the Plenipotentiary Conference.[74] Though representatives of members, the individuals must be "qualified in the field of telecommunication services," and the Council ensures the efficient co-ordination of the work of the Union, approves the annual budget, arranges for the convening of the plenipotentiary and administrative conferences and generally acts in the interval between Conferences "on behalf of the plenipotentiary conference within the limits of the powers delegated to it by the latter."[75] As for the World Conferences on International Telecommunications, they have the power to revise the International Telecommunication Regulations and "may deal with any question of a worldwide character within [their] competence and related to [their] agenda."[76]

---

[69] Art. 1 of the Constitution.
[70] The latest Convention has been adopted on December 22, 1992 and amended in October 1994. See text in Knipping (Ed.), *The United Nations System and its Predecessors*, Vol. I (1997) 1388.
[71] Art. 4 of the Constitution.
[72] Only members and associate members participate fully; telecommunications operating services of the UN, permanent organs of the Union, and observers from non-members may participate as advisers or observers.
[73] Art. 8 of the Constitution.
[74] Art. 4 of the Convention.
[75] Art. 10(3) of the Constitution.
[76] *ibid.*, Art. 25.

3–063   The three "technical" sectors carry out more specialised functions and each of them has its own institutional structure. The main function of the radiocommunication sector is to ensure "the rational, equitable, efficient and economical use of the radio-frequency spectrum by all radiocommunication services." The sector works through world and regional radiocommunication conferences, the Radio Regulations Board, radiocommunication assemblies and study groups as well as the Radiocommunication Bureau.[77] The World Radiocommunication Conference has the power to revise the radio regulations, whereas the Board has competence to assign radio frequencies. It should be noted that the latter's nine members are elected by the Plenipotentiary Conference, but are to perform their duties for the Union independently and serve "not as representing their respective Member State nor a region, but as custodians of an international public trust."[78] Members of the board cannot participate in any manner in any branch of telecommunications apart from the work of the board. They thus come very near to assimilation to international civil servants. The bureau performs administrative tasks necessary for the Sector's functioning.

3–064   The Telecommunication Standardisation Sector's mandate is to study "technical, operating and tariff questions and adopting recommendations on them with a view to standardising telecommunications on a worldwide basis."[79] The sector works through world telecommunication standardisation conferences and study groups (which prepare draft recommendations to the attention of the world conferences), and the Telecommunication Standardisation Bureau.

3–065   Finally, the Telecommunication Development Sector is to discharge the Union's responsibility "so as to facilitate and enhance telecommunications development by offering, organising and coordinating technical co-operation and assistance activities."[80] It works through world and regional telecommunication development conferences, telecommunication development study groups and the Telecommunication Development Bureau, which respectively carry out the same types of functions as described above for the two other sectors.[81]

---

[77] *ibid.*, Art. 12.
[78] *ibid.*, Art. 14.
[79] *ibid.*, Art. 17.
[80] *ibid.*, Art. 21.
[81] On the Sector's recent activities, see Tchikaya, "La première conférence mondiale pour le développement des télécommunications—La transcription juridique du développement au sein de l'UIT", (1995) R.G.D.I.P. 77.

The World Intellectual Property Organisation (WIPO)[82]

Website: http://www.wipo.int; Bibliography: Ekedi-Samnik, *L'organisation mondiale de la propriété intellectuelle (OMPI)* (1975); A. Bogsch, *Brief History of the First 25 Years of the World Intellectual Property Organisation* (1992); Gurry, "The WIPO arbitration center and its services" (1994) 5 American Review of International Arbitration 197.

Established by convention of July 14, 1967[83] this organisation became a **3–066** specialised agency of the UN by General Assembly resolution 3346 (XXIX) of December 17, 1974. Its purpose is to promote the protection of intellectual property throughout the world, *inter alia* by furthering the harmonisation of national legislation in that field, performing the administrative tasks originally assigned to the Paris Union (1883) and the Berne Union (1886),[84] and providing legal and technical assistance to states in the field of intellectual property.[85] Its present activities include the strengthening of intellectual property systems in developing countries and the facilitation of the acquisition of intellectual property protection through international registration.[86] The Organisation established an Arbitration Centre in 1994.

WIPO has a General Assembly, a Conference, a Co-ordination Com- **3–067** mittee and an International Bureau. The Assembly meets biennially and is composed of the states parties to the Conventions which are members of any of the pre-existing Unions. Its functions include the appointment of the Director General, the review of reports of the Director General, and the adoption of the Organisation's budget.[87] The Conference consists of the states party to the WIPO convention whether or not they are members of any of the pre-existing unions. It is vested with recommendatory powers in the field of intellectual property, and has the power to amend the WIPO Convention.[88] The functions of the Co-ordination Committee are mainly advisory, whilst the International Bureau performs administrative tasks for the day-to-day functioning of the Organisation.[89]

---

[82] WIPO had 171 member states in 1999.
[83] 828 U.N.T.S. 3. The Convention has been amended in 1979. The consolidated text of the WIPO Convention is reproduced in Knipping (Ed.), *The United Nations System and its Predecessors*, Vol. I (1997) 1141.
[84] See original text of the Bern Convention in Knipping (Ed.), *The United Nations System and its Predecessors*, Vol. II (1997) 118.
[85] Art. 4 of the Convention.
[86] (1995) YUN 1505. It is worth mentioning that the latter activity enables WIPO to cover 91% of its budget.
[87] Art. 6 of the Convention.
[88] *ibid.*, Art. 7.
[89] *ibid.*, Arts 8 and 9.

International Fund for Agricultural Development (IFAD)[90]

Website: http://www.ifad.org; Bibliography: Sauvignon, "Le Fonds international de développement agricole", 24 (1978) AFDI 660–677; Talbot, "The International Fund for Agricultural Development", 95 (1980) *Political Science Quarterly* 261–276.

3–068 The decision to establish the International Fund for Agricultural Development was taken by the World Food Conference in 1974, the Fund being created in 1976.[91] In December 1977 the General Assembly by resolution adopted the relationship agreement, making this a new specialised agency. Its principal task is to mobilise the agricultural production of food throughout the world, by financing agricultural development.[92] To this end, in 1977 members pledged resources of $1,022,100,000. The Fund's resources have been replenished four times since its creation; the fourth replenishment took place between 1995 and 1997. IFAD's resources are provided to developing states which are members of the Fund or to international organisations in which such members participate, priority being given to "the need to increase food production and to improve the nutritional level of the poorest populations in the poorest food deficit countries."[93] Financing by the Fund takes the form of loans and grants. IFAD's loans and grants total $5,670 million since its establishment.[94]

3–069 The organ of general competence and plenary body of the Fund is the Governing Council which, amongst other powers, addresses membership issues, and adopts regulations and by-laws to conduct the business of the Fund, laying down policies and criteria for the financing of projects.[95] The Executive Board of IFAD is responsible for the conduct of the general operations of the Fund, such as the selection and approval of projects and programmes for financing.[96] It consists of 18 members elected by the Governing Council by a voting arrangement unique in the United Nations. The members are placed in three Groups: Group I (OECD countries), Group II (OPEC countries) and Group III (developing countries). Each Group has 600 votes, and within each group there is a formula to allocate these votes between the members of the group. In Group III, the votes are distributed equally amongst all the members. In Groups I and II, a certain percentage of the 600 votes is allocated equally (17.5 per cent in Group I, 25 per cent in Group II), with the rest being allocated on the basis of financial contributions. The third main organ of IFAD is the President, who

---

[90] IFAD had 161 member states in 1999.
[91] June 13, 1976, 1059 U.N.T.S. 191.
[92] *ibid.*, Art. 2.
[93] *ibid.*, Art. 7, section 1.
[94] (1995) YUN 1505.
[95] Art. 6, section 2 and Art. 7, section 1 of the Agreement.
[96] *ibid.*, Art. 6, section 5 and Art. 7, section 1.

heads the staff and is responsible for conducting the business of the Fund under the control of the Governing Council and the Executive Board.[97]

The UN Industrial Development Organisation (UNIDO)[98]

Website: http://www.unido.org; Bibliography: Charvin, "L'Organisation des Nations Unies pour le Développement Industriel" (1969) 73 RGDIP 744; Phelps, "The United Nations Industrial Development Organisation, the consultation system, and health" (1984) 39 Food Drug Cosmetic Law Journal 469.

The constitution of UNIDO was adopted in April 1979[99] so as to permit **3–070** this hitherto subsidiary body of the UN General Assembly to become the most recent specialised agency of the UN.[1] Its original aim was the promotion of industrial development in developing countries, with a view to assisting in the establishment of a new international economic order, as well as the promotion of industrial development and co-operation on global, regional, national and sectoral levels.[2] To this end, UNIDO *inter alia* encourages and extends assistance to developing countries for the development, expansion and modernisation of their industries, provides a forum and acts as an instrument to serve the developing countries and the industrialised countries in their contacts, and assists the developing countries in the establishment and operation of industries.[3] The Constitution also provides for the constitution of an Industrial Development Fund financed through voluntary contributions to increase the resources of the organisation.[4] In order to "adjust to the new economic environment of the 1990s" UNIDO adopted a new mission statement in 1995, which emphasises its role as "a catalyst seeking to harness the joint forces of government and the private sector, with the overall aims to foster competitive industrial production, develop international industrial partnerships and promote socially equitable and environmentally sustainable industrial development," thus departing from the initial new international economic order rhetoric which inspired its establishment.[5]

UNIDO's organs are the General Conference, the Industrial Develop- **3–071** ment Board and the Secretariat. The Conference, as plenary body, determines the guiding principles and the policies of the organisation and is vested with recommendatory powers, while the Industrial Development Board of 53 members has responsibility for the general operation of the organisation.[6]

---

[97] *ibid.*, Art. 6, section 8.
[98] UNIDO had 168 member states in 1999.
[99] 1401 U.N.T.S. 3.
[1] UNIDO was originally created by UNGA res. 2152 (XXI) of November 17, 1966.
[2] Art. 1 of the Constitution.
[3] *ibid.*, Art. 2.
[4] *ibid.*, Art. 17.
[5] See (1995) YUN 1510.
[6] *ibid.*, Arts 8 and 9.

International Atomic Energy Agency (IAEA)[7]

Website: http://www.iaea.org/worldatom; Bibliography: Scheinman, *The International Atomic Energy Agency and World Nuclear Order* (1987); Szasz, *The Law and Practice of the IAEA* (1970); Lohmann, *Die Rechtliche Struktur der Sicherungsmassnahmen der Internationale Atomenergie-Organisation* (1993); Szasz and Rainer, *The Law and Practice of the IAEA* (1993); Hackel, *Tightening the reins: towards a strengthened international nuclear safeguards system* (2000).

3–072 The International Atomic Energy Agency (IAEA) was created in 1956.[8] This organisation is not a specialised agency, since the agreement which links it to the UN has been concluded with the G.A. and not with ECOSOC, as provided for in Articles 57 and 63 of the UN Charter. This agreement of November 14, 1957, is nevertheless modelled on the agency agreements except that the IAEA is more autonomous and, because of the implications for peace and security of the development of nuclear energy, the G.A. and S.C. are the organs with which the main relationship exists, and not ECOSOC.[9] The IAEA's objective is "to accelerate and to enlarge the contribution of atomic energy to peace, health and prosperity throughout the world," while ensuring that assistance provided by it "is not used in such a way as to further any military purpose."[10] To that end, the Agency, *e.g.* encourages and assists research on, and development and practical application of, atomic energy for peaceful uses, fosters the exchange of scientific and technical information on peaceful uses of atomic energy, establishes and administers safeguards designed to ensure that special fissionable and other materials, services, equipment, facilities and information made available by it are not used in such a way as to further any military purpose and establishes standards of safety for protection of health and minimalisation of danger to life and property and provides for the application of these standards.[11] It is to be noted that the Agency both promotes and regulates the peaceful uses of nuclear energy. Its recent activities include the assessment of the safety of nuclear power plants, mainly in eastern Europe and countries of the former USSR and the development of a programme on radioactive waste management; the IAEA also performs safeguards inspection at a steady pace (some 2500 such inspections were conducted in 1998, for instance). It should be noted as

---

[7] The IAEA had 131 member states in 1999.
[8] October 26, 1956, 276 U.N.T.S. 3. The Statute has been amended in 1961, 1970 and 1984. The consolidated text of the IAEA Statute is reproduced in Knipping (Ed.), *The United Nations System and its Predecessors*, Vol. I (1997) 1448.
[9] See text of the Agreement in 281 U.N.T.S. 369, and see Bechhofer, "Negotiating the Statute of the IAEA" (1959) 13 International Organisation 38.
[10] Art. II of the Statute.
[11] *ibid.*, Art. III.

well that the Agency played an important role in monitoring Iraq's nuclear capacities since the end of the Gulf War.[12]

The IAEA's organs are the General Conference, the Board of Governors **3–073** and the Secretariat. The General Conference is the plenary organ of the Agency. Its functions include the admission and suspension of members, the approval of reports to be submitted to the UN in compliance with the relationship agreement, and the amendment of the Statute.[13] The Board of governors consists of 35 members elected by the Conference according to a complex formula which is to ensure both an equitable representation of the various regions of the world and the presence on the Board of the states most advanced in the technology of atomic energy. The Board's main task is to carry out the functions of the Agency, subject to its responsibilities to the General Conference.[14]

Conclusions

UN specialised agencies thus cover large fields of human activities. **3–074** Proposals have been made to establish new agencies competent to deal with matters which until now have been managed by various departments of the United Nations Secretariat. Only a few of these proposals have taken a concrete form, but, contrary to earlier developments, these have taken place outside the UN institutional system. This is the case, for example, of the World Trade Organisation, established in 1994 as an autonomous institution.[15] This results to a large extent from the desire to set up an organisation whose effectiveness would not be hampered by certain (perceived) shortfalls of UN agencies (bureaucratic weight, role of extraneous political considerations, etc).[16] Similarly, the International Sea-bed Authority, the creation of which had been envisaged in the conferences on the law of the sea convened under the auspices of the United Nations, is not a specialised agency, but an autonomous institution.[17] Other factors seem to have prevented the creation of new specialised agencies. Hence, the proposed World Space Organisation, the functions of which would have included the promotion and supervision of space exploration and utilisation, never came into existence, principally for financial reasons.[18] It is

---

[12] See S/Res. 687 (1991), paras 12 and 13; S/Res. 699 (1991), para. 2; S/Res. 707 (1992). For recent developments on the Agency's role, see also Lefebvre, "Les garanties de l'Agence internationale de l'Energie atomique à l'épreuve des crises récentes du régime de la non-prolifération nucléaire", (1996) A.F.D.I. 137. See Chap. 12, paras 12–050 *et seq.*

[13] *ibid.*, Art. V.

[14] *ibid.*, Art. VI.

[15] For more on this, see *infra*, Chap. 4.

[16] See, *e.g.* Jackson, *The World Trade Organisation—Constitution and Jurisprudence*, (1998), 52.

[17] It is nevertheless linked to the UN by a Relationship Agreement, which has been submitted to the General Assembly (see A/RES/52/27 of November 26, 1997).

[18] The United States were unwilling to find themselves in the position of being the main contributor to the organisation's budget without being in a position to decide of its course of action. The proposal to create this organisation had been put forward by the Soviet Union, last in 1988 (Doc A/AC/105/L 171, June 13, 1988).

therefore difficult to predict what its institutional status would have been, but one may doubt, in view of the present tendency, that it would have become a new UN specialised agency. It seems, however, that the unwillingness of states to create new specialised agencies as a privileged form of interstate co-operation at the universal level is not to be seen as a desire to undermine the UN system. As has been seen, a number of subsidiary and quasi-autonomous bodies have been created within that framework over previous years, being often more closely related to the universal organisation than the specialised agencies.[19] In fact, the main reasons for the diminishing appeal of this latter form appear to be essentially practical (inadequacies of the present salary scales and exaggerated level of protection resulting from the privileges and immunities regimes are often mentioned in that respect). This suggests that a thorough reform and rationalisation of the overall UN system will at some point be required.[20]

---

[19] See *supra*, Chap. 2, paras 2–089 *et seq.*
[20] See generally, Szasz, "The Complexification of the United Nations System", 3 Max Planck UNYB (1999) 1.

CHAPTER 4

OTHER AUTONOMOUS ORGANISATIONS

A. INTRODUCTION

Beyond those institutions mentioned in Chapter 3, there is another **4–001** category of global organisations, which includes bodies that are created within the framework of a treaty intended to establish substantive rules regulating conduct within a specialised area, but that are not fully part of the United Nations system. In certain fields—such as trade, disarmament, human rights, environment, the Antarctic, commodities, maritime affairs and telecommunications—important treaties with broad membership have established institutional arrangements for the implementation, development and review of the treaties' substantive aims and objectives. These institutional arrangements take a variety of names and forms, ranging from "commissions" or "committees" or "authorities" to "ad hoc conferences (or meetings) of the parties to the treaty." These other autonomous organisations are sometimes referred to as "treaty organisations." Many have international legal personality and varying capacities and powers at international and national levels, rules of procedure and membership and enumerated powers relating to decision-making and adjudication and, occasionally, enforcement powers. Some enjoy privileges and immunities in the territory of their members. There are now a very large number of treaty organisations that are increasingly active and that contribute significantly to the development and application of international law and other international standards. Frequently their activities are not well documented.

The establishment of these organisations can scarcely be said to have **4–002** resulted from a systematic approach to substantive or institutional development. Rather, these organisations are products of the somewhat ad hoc character of international law-making. Moreover, whilst covering a broad range of subject matters, they are by no means comprehensive in their activities and numerous important gaps exist. The extent of membership varies widely and is generally less universal than that of the UN, although in some cases, for example, the institutions established under the Law of the Sea Convention and the Climate Change Convention, membership is approaching that of the UN itself. The Convention on the Rights of the Child already has more state parties than the UN.

4–003   The discussion that follows is not intended to be exhaustive. It aims rather to identify the principal treaty institutions active in the main areas, indicating the general institutional characteristics that prevail and such peculiarities meriting comment. It is worth noting that the character and function of the institutions differ markedly as between the various subject matters they address. Human rights bodies have an avowedly adjudicative character. Disarmament institutions, particularly in recent times, have been charged with verifying compliance, whereas in the environmental field the institutions assume more of a standard-setting (and development) function. From this survey it will be apparent that no general principles can readily be identified: each institution is to be taken on its own merits, with its powers, functions and personality being determined by its constituent instrument and in its particular context.

B. Overview of Institutions

(a) TRADE

Bibliography: Long, *Law and its Limitations in the GATT Multilateral Trade System* (1987); Krueger (ed.), *The WTO as an International Organisation* (1998); Jackson, *The World Trade Organisation: Constitution and Jurisprudence* (1998); Das, *The World Trade Organisation: A Guide to the New Framework for International Trade* (1999); Jackson, *The Jurisprudence of GATT and the WTO* (2000).

4–004   The pre-eminent agreement in the international trade arena, the General Agreement on Tariffs and Trade (GATT), was originally negotiated in 1947 among some 23 major trading countries. When initially drafted, the GATT was intended to be a provisional agreement, preceding the creation of the International Trade Organisation (ITO), which would provide an appropriate institutional mechanism for dealing with international trade matters. However, mainly due to U.S. opposition, the ITO never materialised so that in fact the provisional GATT became the permanent institutional basis for the multilateral trading system. It was left to the trade negotiations (or "rounds") held under the auspices of the GATT to devise a *de facto* institutional machinery of a GATT Council of Ministers, as well as various committees, subcommittees and working parties.

4–005   The latest round of negotiations, the Uruguay Round (1986–93) saw the creation in 1994 of the World Trade Organisation[1] (WTO) as the new principal institution of the multilateral trading system. The Uruguay Round WTO Agreement[2] is an umbrella agreement, establishing the WTO and

---

[1] Websites: http://www.wto.org; http://www.gatt.org.
[2] The three principal instruments are the Final Act, 33 ILM 1 (1994); the Agreement Establishing the World Trade Organisation, 33 ILM 13 (1994) and the General Agreement on Tariffs and Trade in Goods (GATT 1994), 33 ILM 28 (1994).

bringing within its structure the GATT and a number of other agreements to which all member states must, with a few exceptions, subscribe. The WTO itself is intended to "provide the common institutional framework for the conduct of trade relations among its Members."[3] The highest-level decision making body of the WTO is the Ministerial Conference, which meets, at least, once every two years. Below this body is the General Council (replacing the GATT Council of Ministers), which meets several times a year and consists for the most part of ambassadors and heads of delegations in Geneva. Both organs comprise representatives from all members and generally take decisions by consensus, though provision is made for majority and qualified majority voting when consensus cannot be achieved.[4] The General Council is responsible for governance issues not otherwise dealt with by the Ministerial Conference and also meets as the Trade Policy Review Body and the Dispute Settlement Body. In its latter role the General Council is responsible for the appointment of panels to investigate and make recommendations concerning complaints, the adoption of panel and Appellate Body reports, the surveillance of implementation of rulings and recommendations and the suspension of concessions or obligations under the covered agreements. The Dispute Settlement Understanding[5] negotiated during the Uruguay Round established a new appellate body with power to hear appeals from panel decisions on questions of law. The Appellate Body, unlike the panels, is a standing body of seven members, who are persons of recognised authority with demonstrated expertise in law, international trade and the covered agreements generally.[6]

Reporting to the General Council are the Goods Council, the Services **4–006** Council and the Trade-Related Aspects of Intellectual Property Rights (TRIPS) Council. Numerous specialised committees, working groups and working parties deal with the individual agreements[7] of the WTO, as well as other areas such as the environment, development, membership applications and regional trade agreements. The first Ministerial Conference, held in Singapore in 1996, added three new working groups to this structure in the areas of trade and investment, trade and competition policy and transparency in government procurement. At the second Ministerial Conference, held in Geneva in 1998, the Ministers decided that the WTO should study the area of electronic commerce, a task to be shared out among the existing councils and committees. The November 1999 Ministerial Conference in Seattle was marked by widespread protests led by citizens and consumers groups, as well as labour unions and agricultural

---

[3] Art. 2(1) of WTO Agreement.
[4] Art. 9 of WTO Agreement.
[5] 33 ILM 112 (1994).
[6] See Chap. 13, paras 13–078 et seq.
[7] Examples are the Committee on Antidumping, the Subsidies Committee, the Committee on Government Procurement and the Safeguards Committee.

groups. These demonstrations, together with the lack of agreement amongst the WTO members on the launching of a "Millennium Round," resulted in a collapse in the meeting. The protests also indicated the extent to which the activities of international institutions can now be subject to public and media scrutiny as non-state actors seek increasingly to participate in the affairs of international institutions which can affect daily lives across the globe.

4–007   Technical support for the various councils and committees and the ministerial conferences is provided by the WTO Secretariat, headed by a Director-General and based in Geneva. In addition to furnishing administrative support for the organs of the WTO, the Secretariat also provides technical assistance for developing countries, carries out analyses of world trade, offers some forms of legal assistance in the dispute settlement process, advises governments wishing to become members of the WTO and manages the organisation's relations with the public and the media.

(b) DISARMAMENT

Bibliography: Goldblat, *Arms Control: A Guide to Negotiations and Agreements* (1996).

4–008   The institutional arrangements established by global conventions relating to disarmament, arms control and arms limitation are varied. The earliest instruments, for example the 1963 Partial Test Ban Treaty,[8] made no provision for the establishment of permanent institutional structures. The 1968 Nuclear Non-Proliferation Treaty[9] (NPT) allocates a role for the IAEA in the application of its provisions on nuclear safeguards (Article 3). It also provides for the convening of an ad hoc conference to consider treaty amendments and for regular conferences to be held every five years to review the operation of the treaty "with a view to assuring that its purposes are being realised" (Article 8). The last review conference was held in 1995, and it determined by a majority of the participants that the NPT would continue in force indefinitely.[10] Other instruments have adopted similar arrangements for review conferences.[11]

Chemical weapons

Bibliography: *The Chemical weapons Convention: implementation issues* (1992, Center for Strategic and International Studies); Krutsch, *A Commentary on*

---

[8] 480 U.N.T.S. 3 (1963).

[9] 729 U.N.T.S. 161 (1968).

[10] See Decision 3 of the 1995 Review and Extension Conference of the Parties to the Treaty on Non-Proliferation of Nuclear Weapons, 34 ILM 959, 973 (1995). The decision was made in accordance with article 10(2) of the NPT.

[11] See, *e.g.* Seabed Treaty, Art. 7, 955 U.N.T.S. 115 (1971); Biological Weapons Convention, Art. 12, 1015 U.N.T.S. 163 (1972); ENMOD (Environmental Modification) Convention, Art. 8, 1108 U.N.T.S. 152 (1977).

the Chemical Weapons Convention (1996); Bothe, Ronzitti, Rosas (eds), *The New Chemical Weapons Convention: Implementation and Prospects* (1998); OPCW, *OPCW: the Legal Texts* (1999).

Recent arms control agreements have paid a greater degree of attention **4–009** to the issues of verification and compliance, which has led to the adoption of powerful institutional arrangements. The 1993 Chemical Weapons Convention[12] (CWC) provides for the establishment of the Organisation for the Prohibition of Chemical Weapons[13] (OPCW), with the task of achieving the object and purpose of the convention, ensuring implementation of its provisions and establishing a forum for consultation and co-operation amongst the parties (Article 8(1)). Based in The Hague, the OPCW comprises a Conference of State Parties, an Executive Council and a Technical Secretariat. The Conference is composed of all members of the organisation and meets annually unless agreed otherwise, or at special sessions. It is the OPCW's principal organ and has competence over any matter within the scope of the CWC. It makes recommendations and can take decisions on any questions raised by a party or brought to its attention by the Executive Council. Its powers include authorising necessary measures to ensure compliance with the CWC and to redress and remedy any situation that contravenes the convention's provisions (Article 8(21)(k)).

The Executive Council comprises 41 members with regard being paid to **4–010** "equitable geographic distribution, the importance of chemical industry, and political and security interests." The Executive Council is the executive organ of the OPCW and its acts are subject to the recommendations, decisions and guidelines of the Conference. Its overall task is to promote the effective implementation of, and compliance with, the CWC, and to supervise the activities of the Technical Secretariat, as well as to co-operate with the national authorities of each Party (Articles 8(30)–8(31)). The international personality of the organisation is reflected in the fact that the Executive Council is to have the power to conclude agreements or arrangements with states and international organisations, and in the extensive privileges and immunities with which the OPCW is endowed (Articles 8(48)–8(51)). The Technical Secretariat provides assistance to the Conference and the Executive Council, in particular in relation to the CWC's verification measures.

These elaborate institutional arrangements are no doubt premised on the **4–011** far-reaching powers available to parties and the OPCW under the convention itself. The CWC has potentially serious implications for international trade in those chemicals that might be used for chemical weapons;

---

[12] 32 ILM 800 (1993).
[13] Website: http://www.opcw.nl.

accordingly, "challenge inspections" are available at the instigation of any state party, with the involvement of the OPCW, when another party is not considered to be in compliance with the provisions of the convention (Article 9(8)).

Nuclear weapons

Bibliography: Dembinski and Pac, "The Comprehensive Test Ban Treaty: Legal and institutional issues", (1996) *International Geneva Yearbook 32–43*.

4–012   The model established by the CWC has since been taken up in similarly extensive institutional arrangements to be found in the regime created in the 1996 Comprehensive Test Ban Treaty[14] (CTBT). Although not yet in force, the Treaty commits parties to undertake not to carry out any nuclear weapons test, explosion or other nuclear explosion and to prohibit and prevent such explosions at any place under their jurisdiction or control. The CTBT establishes a Comprehensive Nuclear Test Ban Organisation, comprising a Conference of the State Parties, an Executive Council and a Technical Secretariat; the latter includes an International Data Centre. The powers of the organs are broadly similar to those established by the CWC; the CTBT establishes a Comprehensive Scheme for Verification, comprising an international monitoring system, consultation and clarification, on-site inspections and confidence-building measures (Article 4). To that end, the organisation is provided with extensive powers of investigation, including, in particular, the right to conduct on-site inspections (Articles 4(56)-4(57)). When a dispute arises between one or more state parties relating to the application and interpretation of the CTBT, by mutual consent the parties may have recourse to "referral to the International Court of Justice in conformity with the Statute of the Court" (Article 6(2)). The Conference is to take necessary measures to ensure compliance with the treaty and to redress and remedy any situation that contravenes its provisions (Article 2). The CTBT also endows the Organisation with privileges and immunities (Articles 2(54)–2(57)).

(c) HUMAN RIGHTS

4–013 Some international human rights conventions provide for limited forms of institutional arrangement, establishing quasi-adjudicative bodies that may receive, consider and comment upon reports submitted by parties, adopt recommendations and, in certain cases, receive petitions from individuals and issue general comments on points relating to the conventions. These treaty bodies are addressed in Chapter 13. A prime example is the Human Rights Committee established by the Optional Protocol to the 1966 Covenant on Civil and Political Rights, as well as the proposed equivalent

---

[14] 35 ILM 1439 (1996).

mechanism to be established under the 1966 Covenant on Civil and Political Rights. Other bodies include the Committee on the Elimination of Racial Discrimination, the Committee on the Elimination of Discrimination Against Women, the Committee Against Torture, the Committee on the Rights of the Child and the Committee on the Elimination of Discrimination Against Women.

(d) ENVIRONMENT

Bibliography: Sands, *Principles of International Environmental Law* (1995), Chap. 5; Werksman, *Greening International Institutions* (1996).

Over the past three decades a great number of treaty organisations have **4–014** been established in the environmental field, often attracting a broad (and in some cases virtually universal) membership. These treaty organisations have evolved considerably over the past two decades. Several have become particularly influential in the absence of a strong UN body dealing with environmental matters. Collectively, they comprise a far more extensive structure than the two UN bodies whose activities they supplement: UNEP,[15] which does not have the status of a specialised agency, and the Commission of Sustainable Development.

Biodiversity conservation

Many of the earliest environmental treaties had no formal institutional **4–015** arrangements to oversee their implementation.[16] One of the first to establish institutional arrangements was the 1971 Ramsar Convention on Wetlands,[17] whose Conferences on the Conservation of Wetlands and Waterfowl are charged with reviewing implementation of the convention. Originally, the conferences were to meet "as the necessity arises" (Article 6(1)); in fact, they now meet every three years. The Conferences have an essentially advisory character, with the power to consider problems of implementation, additions and changes to the list of protected wetland areas. They also may make recommendations to the parties on the conservation, management and wise use of wetlands and their flora and fauna (Article 6(3)). The structure of the conference has been followed in subsequent instruments. Each party has one vote at the Conference, and recommendations are adopted by simple majority of votes cast, provided that half the parties vote (Article 7(2)). The Conference has established a

---

[15] See *supra*, Chap. 3.
[16] See, *e.g.* the International Convention for the Protection of Birds, 638 U.N.T.S. 185 (1950), which replaces the 1902 convention on the same subject.
[17] 996 U.N.T.S. 245 (1971). The convention, which entered into force in 1975, has been amended twice: by the 1982 Paris Protocol, 22 ILM 698 (1982); and by the Regina Amendments of May 28, 1987, not in force 977 IEL MT 9/13. The Paris Protocol inserts a new Art. 10 *bis* to provide for amendment of the convention. Website: http://www.ramsar.org/index.htm/.

number of working groups to prepare for, and oversee implementation of, decisions of the conferences. The Conference is serviced by a standing secretariat, the services for which are provided by the International Union for the Conservation of Nature and Natural Resources (Article 8).

4–016 This loose arrangement has been taken as a model for other treaty institutions in the field of biodiversity conservation. In 1973, 21 countries adopted the Convention on International Trade in Endangered Species of Wild Fauna and Flora[18] (CITES), whose provisions are designed to prevent over-exploitation of animals and plants by regulating or prohibiting their international trade. It too has a Conference of the Parties, which meets at least every two years to consider and adopt binding amendments to Appendices I and II (the effect of which is to limit trade in listed species), to review the progress of restoration and conservation of listed species and to make recommendations for improving the convention's effectiveness (Article 11). Unlike the Wetlands Conference, the CITES Conference may take binding decisions to list endangered species, the effect of which is to limit trade. It has a permanent secretariat that oversees the application of the CITES system, although the day-to-day operation is a matter for the national authorities of the parties (Article 12). The Conference of the Parties has established committees, sub-committees and working groups; in 1987 these were consolidated into a Standing Committee of the Conference of the Parties, an Animals Committee, a Plants Committee, an Identification Manual Committee, and a Nomenclature Committee.

4–017 Migratory species of wild animals are governed by the 1979 Convention on Migratory Species[19] (CMS), which has similar institutional arrangements to CITES: the Conference of the Parties is the principal decision-making organ and is assisted by a Scientific Council and a Secretariat (Articles 8–9). Amendments to its appendices are adopted at meetings of the conference by a two-thirds majority of parties present and voting, and enter into force 90 days after the Conference of the Parties at which they were adopted for all parties, except for those entering a reservation within that 90–day period (Article 11).

4–018 More recently, the 1992 Convention on Biological Diversity[20] (adopted under the auspices of UNEP) has as its objectives conserving biological diversity and ensuring the sustainable use of its components and the fair and equitable sharing of the benefits arising out of the utilisation of genetic

---

[18] 993 U.N.T.S. 243. Amending Protocols were adopted in Bonn on June 22, 1979 (in force April 13, 1987) and in Gaborone on April 30, 1983 (not in force). For a detailed guide to the convention and its history, see Wijnstekers, *The Evolution of CITES* (4th ed., 1995). Website: http://www.wcmc.org.uk/CITES/eng/index.shtml.

[19] 19 ILM 15 (1980). Website: http://www.wcmc.org.uk.

[20] 31 ILM 822 (1992). Website: http://www.biodiv.org.

resources. It is served by a Conference of the Parties, which monitors implementation of the convention (Article 23); a Subsidiary Body on Scientific, Technical and Technological Advice, which provides advice to the Conference of the Parties (Article 25); and a permanent Secretariat (Article 24). The convention provides for settlement of disputes concerning its interpretation or application according to traditional means, including negotiation, the use of good offices and mediation (Article 27); an annex describes the procedures for submitting the dispute for arbitration and conciliation (annex 2).

Atmosphere

In the field of atmospheric protection, global regimes have been established **4–019** to protect the ozone layer and to address climate change. These are relatively sophisticated arrangements, with detailed mechanisms to address scientific and compliance issues. The treaties have spawned their own innovative institutional arrangements, building on the traditional approach outlined above.

The ozone regime comprises the 1985 Vienna Convention for the **4–020** Protection of the Ozone Layer[21] and its 1987 Montreal Protocol on Substances that Deplete the Ozone Layer,[22] negotiated under the auspices of UNEP. The 1985 convention has a Conference of the Parties and a Secretariat (Articles 6–7); the Conference of the Parties has been responsible for negotiations of the Montreal Protocol and its amendments. The protocol has its own Meeting of the Parties, which comprises a different membership than the convention's Conference of the Parties; however, the two bodies share the same secretariat.

The ozone regime has innovative provisions on law-making. The Con- **4–021** ference of the Parties may adopt amendments to Protocols by qualified majority voting. The Meeting of the Parties to the Protocol may adopt formal adjustments that are binding on all parties without possibility of objection by means of a two-thirds majority of the parties present and voting who represent at least 50 per cent of the total consumption of controlled substances (Protocol, Article 2(9)(c)–(d)). These are significant legislative powers for any institution, particularly given their economic consequences. Various subsidiary bodies have been established under the Conference and the Meeting of the Parties. Of particular note is the Implementation Committee established pursuant to Article 8 of the Montreal Protocol; the Committee is charged with determining non-compliance with the provisions of the Protocol and the subsequent treat-

---

[21] 26 ILM 1516 (1987). Website: http://www.unep.ch/ozone/home.html.
[22] 26 ILM 1541 (1987).

ment of parties found to be in non-compliance. This extremely innovative adjudicatory mechanism is addressed in Chapter 13.

In 1990 the Montreal Protocol was further amended to establish a mechanism to provide financial and technical co-operation to developing country parties to enable their compliance with the substantive provisions of the amended protocol. This mechanism is to meet all agreed incremental costs of developing country parties and establishes a multilateral fund to meet those costs.[23]

4–022   The 1992 Climate Change Convention[24] essentially builds on the arrangements developed by the ozone regime. It too has a Conference of the Parties and a Secretariat (Articles 7–11). There are also two subsidiary bodies established under the Convention: a Subsidiary Body for Scientific and Technological Advice and a Subsidiary Body for Implementation. Unlike the Montreal Protocol, the Climate Change Convention does not provide for its own financial mechanism. The Convention entrusted the Global Environment Facility (GEF) of the UNDP, UNEP and IBRD with the operation of the financial mechanism on an interim basis, calling for the GEF to be "appropriately restructured and its membership made universal" to enable it to fulfil the requirements of Article 11 of the Convention (Article 21). Following the restructuring of the GEF,[25] that body has continued to serve as the financial mechanism.

4–023   In 1997 the Kyoto Protocol[26] was adopted by the parties to the Climate Change Convention. Interestingly, the Protocol provides that it is the Conference of the Parties to the Convention that is to serve as the Meeting of the Parties to the Protocol, although decisions are only to be taken by the Parties to the Protocol itself (Article 13). The Convention Secretariat will also serve as the Protocol Secretariat, as will the subsidiary bodies of the Convention (Articles 14–15). The Kyoto Protocol provides for potentially far-reaching commitments on developed parties to reduce their emissions of greenhouse gases, and to that end provides for arrangements to allow these parties to meet their obligations with a degree of flexibility. Thus, the Protocol provides for trading of emissions in carbon dioxide, joint implementation of the parties' obligations, and a Clean Development Mechanism (CDM) to assist developing country parties "in achieving sustainable development and in contributing to the ultimate objective of the Convention" and to assist developed parties to achieve compliance with their emission limitations and reduction commitments under the Protocol (Article 12).

---

[23] 1990 amendment, Art. 10(2) and (3).
[24] 31 ILM 849 (1992). Website: http://www.unfccc.int.
[25] See *infra*.
[26] 37 ILM 22 (1998).

The institutional structure of the CDM is yet to be determined. However, **4–024** it is envisaged that the Conference of the Parties will designate operational entities to certify emissions reductions resulting from projects covered by these provisions. The establishment of the Clean Development Mechanism marks an interesting and innovative new structure in international institutional arrangements, including a formal role for non-state actors. It is to be noted that the preparatory work leading to the adoption of the Climate Change Convention was largely assisted, in the scientific field, by the Intergovernmental Panel on Climate Change (IPCC). The IPCC was created to assess available scientific information on climate change and formulate response strategies. It was established by the WMO and UNEP with the support of various other organisations.

Marine environment

In relation to the marine environment, a number of global institutions have **4–025** been established to address matters ranging from intervention to prevent oil pollution on the high seas, liability for damage and the development of ship standards. Some of the earliest instruments were essentially of a contractual nature, providing for no institutional mechanisms to oversee implementation. This was the case, for example, with the 1954 International Convention for the Prevention of Pollution of the Sea by Oil,[27] and the 1969 International Convention relating to Intervention on the High Seas in cases of Oil Pollution Casualties.[28] The same held true even for the 1990 Oil Pollution Preparedness Convention.[29]

The "conference of the parties" approach is reflected in other instru- **4–026** ments, such as the 1972 London Dumping Convention, which provides for the convention to be administered by Consultative Meetings of the Parties. These Consultative Meetings are responsible for keeping under review the implementation of the convention, amending it and its annexes, ensuring the availability of relevant scientific and technical information and developing and adopting procedures and criteria for determining exceptional and emergency situations (Article 14). The meetings take place each year in London at the IMO, which has provided secretariat functions for the convention since 1975. The Consultative Meetings have established a number of subsidiary bodies, including a scientific group on dumping and an ad hoc legal group of experts that has recently been discussing issues such as the relationship between the London Convention and the Antarctic Treaty regime, the development of a liability regime and further interpretations on the definitions of dumping. The Consultative Meetings have a

---

[27] 327 U.N.T.S. 3 (1954).
[28] 970 U.N.T.S. 211 (1969). This convention does, however, foresee a role for the IMO (Art. 4).
[29] 30 ILM 733 (1991).

quasi-legislative function; in 1993, for example, they adopted amendments to Annex 1 of the Convention prohibiting the disposal of all radioactive wastes at sea.[30] In 1996, a Protocol to the 1972 Convention was adopted, establishing further commitments and a separate meeting of the contracting parties, with a continuing role for the IMO in providing secretariat facilities.

4–027   Altogether more substantial are the institutional arrangements to give effect to a 1971 International Convention on the Establishment of an International Fund for Compensation of Oil Pollution Damage,[31] which was adopted to provide additional compensation for victims of oil pollution and to transfer some of the economic consequences of loss to the owners of the oil cargo, as well as to ship owners subject to liability under the 1969 Civil Liability Convention.[32] The 1971 Convention creates an International Oil Pollution Compensation Fund which has two main objectives: to provide compensation for pollution damage which is inadequately compensated by an earlier 1969 Convention and to relieve ship owners from additional financial burdens provided they complied with safety at sea and other conventions (Article 2(1)). The Fund has legal personality under the laws of each party (Article 2(2)) and comprises an Assembly, a Secretariat and an Executive Committee (Articles 16–30). The Assembly includes all parties to the Convention, and has overall responsibility for the administration of the Fund and the proper execution of the convention. Its functions include approving the settlement of claims, taking decisions in respect of the distribution of funds and provisional payments and electing the Executive Committee. Its decisions are generally taken on the basis of a simple majority of those present and voting, with special provision for certain decisions to be taken on the basis of the qualified majority vote of those present (Articles 32–33). There are 15 members of the Executive Committee, who are elected on the basis of equitable geographic distribution, including parties particularly exposed to the risks of oil pollution and having large tanker fleets (approximately one-half of those parties in whose territory the largest quantities of oil are received). The functions of the Executive Committee include approving the settlement of claims and giving instructions to the Director. A 1992 Protocol discontinues the Executive Committee (Articles 17–24) and provides that the Director is to be the Chief Administrative Officer of the Fund. He or she is to perform functions assigned to him or her by the Convention, the internal regulations of the Fund and the Assembly (Article 21 of 1992 Protocol).

4–028   To fulfil its first objective, the Fund pays compensation to any person suffering pollution damage if that person has been unable to recover full and adequate compensation under the 1969 Civil Liability Convention. To

---

[30] Resolution LDC 51 (16).
[31] 1110 U.N.T.S. 57 (1971).
[32] 973 U.N.T.S. 3 (1969).

fulfil its second objective the Fund indemnifies the owner and guarantor for that portion of the liability under the 1969 convention that remains, up to a ceiling. In certain circumstances the Fund may also assume the obligations of a guarantor, in which case it has a right of recovery from an owner if and to the extent it would have been exonerated under the relevant provisions of the Convention. The IOPC Fund is therefore actively involved in bringing and defending a large number claims in various courts around the world. It is based in London, together with its Secretariat.

Hazardous wastes and chemicals

The 1989 Basel Convention[33] establishes a global regime for the control of **4–029** international trade in hazardous and other wastes. The Convention is kept under review by a Conference of the Parties and a Secretariat (Articles 15–16). Compared to many other environmental agreements of this type, the Basel Convention sets out relatively detailed tasks for the Secretariat, including gathering and sharing information and examination of notifications made under its provisions and other aspects of transboundary movements. Secretariat services are provided by UNEP. A number of subsidiary and other bodies have been established under the Conference of the Parties to the Convention, including the expanded bureau of the Conference of the Parties and an open-ended ad hoc committee for the implementation of the Convention.

Global Environment Facility

The Global Environment Facility[34] (GEF) was established in 1990 as a **4–030** three-year "experiment" to provide grants for investment projects, technical assistance and research to developing countries to protect the global environment and transfer environmentally benign technologies.[35] It was established jointly by the World Bank, UNEP and UNDP. Originally, governance of the GEF was under the control of participating governments, namely those who had contributed to the GEF or announced their intention to do so. Governments were assisted by an Implementation Committee comprising the World Bank, UNEP and UNDP, a Scientific and Technical Advisory Panel, the GEF Chairman and an administrator of the GEF. The three implementing agencies were charged with translating the policies adopted by the participants' assembly into practice. UNDP assumed responsibility for technical assistance and training activities; UNEP for environmental expertise to the GEF process; and the World Bank for investment projects and acting as the repository for the Global Environmental Trust Fund.

---

[33] 28 ILM 649 (1989). Website: http://www.basel.int.
[34] Website: http://www.gefweb.org.
[35] See Resolution 91–5 of the Executive Directors of the World Bank, November 1991.

4–031   In April 1992, the participating governments reached broad agreement on the restructuring of the GEF, in line with the expectations that had been expressed in the negotiation of treaties in the context of the UN Conference on Environment and Development. In 1994 the participating states agreed on the adoption of an Instrument for the establishment of the restructured Global Environment Facility.[36] The Instrument entered into force through the subsequent adoption of resolutions by the governing bodies of UNDP, UNEP and the World Bank; thus, the GEF is not established by direct treaty, but rather is the progeny of three distinct institutions. The World Bank serves as trustee of the new GEF Trust Fund that receives and administers contributions.

4–032   Any member of the UN or its specialised agencies may become a participant in the restructured GEF, which has an Assembly, a Council and a Secretariat as well as a Scientific and Technical Advisory Panel (paras 7, 11 and 24 of Instrument). The Assembly comprises representatives of all participants, whereas the Council consists of representatives of 32 members representing constituency groups—16 from developing countries, 14 from developed countries and two from central and eastern Europe (paras 13 and 16 and annex E).

4–033   Of particular interest are the principles on decision-making (para. 25). These generally provide that decisions of the Assembly and Council are to be taken by consensus. However, decisions requiring a formal vote are to be taken by a double-weighted majority, comprising an affirmative vote that represents both a 60 per cent majority of the total number of participants and a 60 per cent majority of the total contributions. The Instrument provides that GEF participants are to be grouped into 32 constituencies, comprising 18 composed of recipient countries and 14 composed of non-recipient countries (annex E).

Other instruments

4–034   The 1994 Convention to Combat Desertification[37] similarly provides for the establishment of a Conference of the Parties and a Secretariat (Articles 23–24). These are assisted by a Committee on Science and Technology (Article 25). Similar arrangements are also reflected in the 1998 Rotterdam Convention on Harmful Chemicals and Pesticides.[38]

(e) COMMODITY AGREEMENTS

Bibliography: Fawcett, "The Function of Law in International Commodity Agreements", 44 B.Y.I.L. 157 (1970); Fisher, *The International Coffee Agree-*

---

[36] 33 ILM 1273 (1994).
[37] 33 ILM 1328 (1994). Website: http://www.unccd.int/main.php.
[38] 38 ILM 1 (1999). Website: http://www.pic.int.

ment: A Study in Coffee Diplomacy (1972); Khan, *The Law and Organisation of International Commodity Agreements* (1982); Kohona, *The Regulation of International Economic Relations through Law* (1985); Chimni, *International commodity agreements: a legal study* (1987); Araim, *Intergovernmental Commodity Organisations and the New International Economic Order* (1991); Eisemann, "L'épilogue de la crise du Conseil international de l'étain" (1990) 36 AFDI 678–703; Kestenbaum, *The Tin Men: A Chronicle of Crisis* (1991); Mann, "International Organisations as National Corporations" 107 LQR 357–362 (1991); Chandrasekhar, "Cartel in a Can: The Financial Collapse of the International Tin Council" (1989) 10 NW J. Int'l L. & Bus. 309–322; Sadurska and Chinkin, "The Collapse of the International Tin Council: A Case of State Responsibility" (1990) 30 Vir. J. Int'l L 845–890; Gramlich, "International Commodity Regimes in Disrepute: Lessons from the Tin Debacle" (1989) 40 Law & State 45–71; Colchester, "The International Tropical Timber Organisation: Kill or Cure for the Rainforests?" (1991) 43 Int'l Transnat'l Assoc. 226–234.

International law has long sought to regulate the production of, and trade **4–035** in, basic commodities. Sugar was regulated by international agreement as early as 1864, and the first rubber agreement was adopted in 1934. Chapter 6 of the Havana Charter for the proposed International Trade Organisation addressed international agreements on primary products, which are also addressed in Article 16(B) of the GATT. Various other organisations have addressed primary products: in 1947 the UN Economic and Social Council created an Interim Co-ordinating Committee on International Commodity Arrangements,[39] as well as a Commission of International Commodity Trade,[40] which were replaced in 1965 by the Committee on Commodities.[41] Efforts to address commodities are also undertaken within the activities of the FAO and the GATT/WTO, as well as regional arrangements such as the Asian Pacific Coconut Community and the Lomé accords between the European Community and African, Caribbean and Pacific States. In spite of these efforts at developing a systematic regime, commodities remain for the most part regulated by specialised, single commodity agreements that establish their own institutional regimes. These began to be adopted in the post Second World War period, and included agreements for wheat (1949), sugar (1953), tin (1954), olive oil (1956), coffee (1962), cocoa (1973), rubber (1979) and tropical timber (1986).

The high point for these institutions came, in the context of the "New **4–036** International Economic Order", with the adoption in 1980 of the Common Fund for Commodities,[42] which entered into force on June 19, 1989, more than seven years later than originally expected. The Common Fund is the

---

[39] ECOSOC res. 30 (IV) of March 28, 1947.
[40] ECOSOC res. 691 A (XXVI).
[41] G.A. res. 1995 (XIX).
[42] Agreement Establishing the Common Fund for Commodities of June 27, 1980, 19 ILM 896 (1980) (hereafter the Fund Agreement).

key instrument for attaining the objectives of the Integrated Programme for Commodities embodied in UNCTAD resolution 93(IV),[43] and is entrusted with the task of facilitating the conclusion and functioning of international commodity agreements. For that purpose, two separate accounts are established. The first is designed to support international buffer stocks and internationally co-ordinated national stocks, established by the International Commodity Organisations (ICOs) that have become associated with the Common Fund, provided that these agreements rest on joint financing by producers and consumers. The second account is for financing measures in the field of commodities other than stocking. The Common Fund is also to act as a centre for co-ordination of, and consultation on, commodity policies.

4–037 The financial resources of the Common Fund are comprised of direct government contributions (so-called Directly Contributed Capital), voluntary contributions, additional shares, guarantees from member states, stock warrants and borrowings, as well as resources of the associated ICOs in proportion to their borrowing entitlements, or maximum financial requirements for buffer stocking operations.[44] The Common Fund has three organs: a Governing Council, an Executive Board and a Managing Director. The Governing Council is the organisation's supreme body,[45] on which all members are represented by one governor and one alternate.[46] The Group of 77 and the Group B (the developed countries, mainly consumers) reached a compromise on the distribution of votes within the Fund. The Group of 77 developing countries were granted nearly half of the votes, although the developed countries were required to contribute to the greater part of the Fund's capital. This arrangement was designed to prevent any group of countries from having a simple majority. In practice, simple majorities were difficult to avoid because votes would then be weighted according to the size of the pledges of guarantee capital made by members of the ICOs associated with the Fund.[47]

4–038 The Executive Board is the executive body of the organisation, responsible for the conduct of the operations of the Common Fund. It consists of 28 executive directors and 28 alternates, elected by the Governing Council. The Managing Director is the chairman of the Executive Board and the chief executive officer of the Common Fund, in charge of all ordinary business, and head of the organisation's staff.

---

[43] Art. 2, Fund Agreement.
[44] Tait and Sfeir, "The Common Fund for Commodities" (1982) 16 G.W. J. Int'l L. & Eco. 483, 499.
[45] Art. 20(1) of the Fund Agreement: "All the powers of the Fund shall be vested in the Governing Council."
[46] Art. 20(2) of the Fund Agreement.
[47] Tait and Sfeir, "The Common Fund for Commodities" (1982) 16 G.W. J. Int'l L. & Eco. 483, 501.

The future impact of the Common Fund remains uncertain. At around **4–039** the same time as the Common Fund came into being, the election of market-oriented governments in Germany, the United Kingdom and the United States lessened the appetite for state-sponsored involvement in international markets, including artificial price maintenance. The financial collapse of the International Tin Council in 1985 heralded a diminished role for institutions established by the various commodity agreements and has called into question whether buffer stocks are an efficient means of stabilising prices and supplies. The principal institutional arrangement thus continues to be reflected in the international commodity agreements, of which eight main agreements remain in force.[48] The limited role of current arrangements is to a great degree influenced by the story of the International Tin Council.

Tin

Tin had been the subject of an international agreement dating back to **4–040** the 1954 First International Tin Agreement, which was entered into for five years. It was intended to address difficulties caused by differences between supply of, and demand for, tin by stabilising tin prices, ensuring adequate supplies at reasonable prices and generally promoting the economic production of tin. Participating states were divided into producers and consumers. The First Agreement contained the machinery for fulfilling these objects by establishing and operating a "buffer stock" of tin, which was to be under the control of a manager and to be financed by fixed contributions in cash or tin by the producing countries, although other countries could also make voluntary contributions (Articles 8–9). The manager's function, operating under the Agreement, was to use the buffer stock as a means of stabilising tin prices by buying or selling in accordance with a prior formula, devised by reference to the price of tin on the London Metal Exchange, in accordance with prices set under the Agreement. Broadly speaking, the manager would buy tin when the price fell below a certain level and sell it when it went above that level. This approach to a "buffer stock" was reflected in other commodity agreements. The Second Tin Agreement introduced a further power for the Council, namely to borrow for the purposes of operating the buffer stock. These provisions were broadly reflected in the Sixth Agreement (1981).[49] In October 1985 the Council announced that it was no longer able to meet its obligations, and that through borrowing and related activities designed to operate the buffer stock and maintain the price of tin, it had incurred debts of tens of millions of pounds that were in excess of members' contributions and that it

---

[48] Other arrangements include intergovernmental study groups, *e.g.* the International Nickel Study Group, 1566 U.N.T.S. 29 (1986) and the International Copper Study Group, 1662 U.N.T.S. 229 (1989).
[49] 1282 U.N.T.S. 205 (1981).

was therefore unable to meet. Proceedings were brought in the English courts, raising amongst other matters the question of whether the members of the Council could incur liability for the acts of the Council, including the debts it had incurred through the operation of the buffer stock system. This aspect of the personality of the organisation is considered elsewhere: in brief, the House of Lords ruled that under English law (and probably also under international law) the members of the Council could not be held liable for their acts in this case.[50] As a result of the Council's indebtedness, in June 1986 the members decided not to negotiate a successor to the Sixth Agreement, which was to be the last. For administrative purposes, in 1987 the Sixth Agreement was extended for two years until June 30, 1989, when it terminated. The Council ceased to exist in 1990, and with it a general commitment to operating (and financing) buffer stock agreements in other contexts (with the exception of that relating to natural rubber).

4–041   The agreements that remain in force today function with a more limited mandate than they previously had. The first such arrangement related to sugar, the regulation of which was intended to prevent practices which interfered with competition, for example by the grant of certain prohibited subsidies. The objective of this original approach was to liberalise international trade, an objective that was to be superseded from the 1950s onwards.[51] As described below, the objectives of the various agreements differ depending upon subject matter.

Grains

4–042   The International Grains Council[52] (IGC) dates back to 1949, when it was known as the International Wheat Council. With the entry into force of the International Grains Agreement (IGA) on July 1, 1995, the administration of the component conventions of the IGA, the Grains Trade Convention[53] and the Food Aid Convention[54] has been vested in the IGC. The Grains Trade Convention (GTC) applies to trade in wheat, coarse grains and their products and seeks to further international co-operation in all aspects of the grain trade, promote the expansion of openness and fairness in the grains sector, contribute to grain market stability and enhance world food security. These purposes are accomplished by information sharing, analysis and consultation. The organisation does not maintain buffer stocks.

---

[50] *Rayner (Mincing Lane) Ltd. v. Dept. of Trade and Industry,* [1990] 2 AC 418 (HL); see Chap. 15, paras 15–101–15–105.

[51] Colliard and Dubouis, *Institutions Internationales* (10th ed., 1995), pp. 413–414.

[52] Website: http://www.igc.org.uk.

[53] Grains Trade Convention 1995, December 7, 1994, Doc. International Wheat Council CL 122/5.

[54] Food Aid Convention 1995, December 5, 1994, Doc. Food Aid Committee FAC (95) 1. A new Food Aid Convention 1999 was concluded at London on April 13, 1999 (text at website: http://www.un.org/Depts/Treaty/collection/notpubl/nonpubl.htm).

The IGC, meeting biannually, includes representatives of all parties to the GTC. Members are designated as either importers or exporters on the basis of their average trade in grains. A chairman and vice-chairman of the IGC are elected annually, with the positions alternating between representatives of exporting and importing members. The Council is assisted by an Executive Committee and a Market Conditions Committee, with a Secretariat providing administrative services.

Sugar

The current International Sugar Agreement[55] (1992) dates back to the **4–043** 1953 agreement, which was intended to balance economic objectives (an organised and stable market) with social objectives. The 1992 agreement replaced a 1977 agreement, which was designed to stabilise the price of sugar within a certain range, through a system of export quotas and nationally held, but internationally controlled, stocks. The 1977 agreement failed in this objective, in part because it failed to attract the necessary membership of producer and consumer countries.[56] The 1992 agreement does away with a role for the organisation in the functioning of the market, and seeks instead to provide a forum for consultation, monitoring activities (price and production) and encouragement of increased demand for sugar. The International Sugar Council consists of all members of the organisation, with an Administrative Committee composed of elected representatives.

Olive oil

The International Olive Oil Council (IOOC), headquartered in Madrid **4–044** and dating back to 1956, is subject to the 1986 International Agreement on Olive Oil.[57] The council plays an essentially co-operative function, promoting research and study, seeking to reduce the handicaps of fluctuating markets, addressing unfair competition practices and enhancing market access. Each contracting party is a member of the IOOC, although the number of votes it has depends upon the size of its production and imports. The Olive Oil Agreement provides for a joint promotion fund set up every year with compulsory contributions from the main producing countries. The contribution of each member determines the weight of its vote.

---

[55] International Sugar Agreement concluded in March 20, 1992, in Geneva, UN Doc TD/SUGAR.12/6; website: www.isasugar.org/abron.html.

[56] Smith, "Prospects for a New Sugar Agreement" (1983) 17 JWTL 308.

[57] Art. 1 of the International Agreement on Olive Oil and Table Oils, concluded on July 1, 1986, in Geneva, 1219 U.N.T.S. 135; Misc. 10 (1987), Cm 203; website: www.internationaloliveoil.org.

Coffee

4–045 The International Coffee Organisation[58] (ICO) was first established in 1962 and is now governed by a 1994 agreement.[59] Its function is to secure co-operation between coffee producing and coffee consuming countries to achieve a balance between supply and demand, to keep prices at fair levels, and to encourage increased consumption. Based in London, the ICO is composed of 44 exporting members and 18 importing members, and comprises a Council and an Executive Board with eight exporting members and eight importing members. The ICO previously administered a scheme to stabilise coffee prices by means of export quotas linked to an agreed price range, and a Diversification Fund to finance projects to rationalise coffee production on a country-by-country basis. A Promotion Fund to finance programmes designed to increase coffee consumption does continue to operate.

Cocoa

4–046 The London-based International Cocoa Organisation[60] (ICCO) was established in 1973 to administer the first International Cocoa Agreement (1972) and its successor agreements (1975, 1980, 1986 and 1993). The agreements were concluded among the governments of cocoa-producing and cocoa-consuming countries, under the auspices of the United Nations. Membership of the 1993 agreement comprises 41 countries, representing over 91 per cent of world cocoa production and over 62 per cent of world cocoa consumption. Non-member countries often participate in meetings as observers. Under the 1993 agreement the ICCO performs a co-operative function, seeking also to contribute to a balance between the supply of, and the demand for, cocoa in the world market, to promote transparency in the world cocoa economy through the collection and dissemination of statistics and other data on cocoa, to promote scientific research and development in the field of cocoa, and to develop its role as an International Commodity Organisation (ICO) in relation to the Common Fund for Commodities (CFC).[61] One of the principal aims of the first International Cocoa Agreement in 1972 had been to stabilise the cocoa market on the basis of an agreed price range of a minimum and a maximum price per pound. This stabilisation was to be achieved by an export quota scheme and a buffer stock (with a maximum capacity of 250,000 tonnes of cocoa beans), which was designed to absorb production in excess of quotas. Levies were placed on exports and imports of cocoa beans by member countries to provide funds for the buffer stock. The quota system was abandoned in the 1980

---

[58] Website: http://www.ico.org.
[59] 1827 U.N.T.S. 3 (1962).
[60] Website: http://www.icco.org.
[61] UN Doc. TD/COCOA.8/17 (1993).

agreement and price regulation was based directly on the buffer stock, which was maintained up to 1993. No provision was made for a buffer stock in the 1993 agreement.

Rubber

The International Natural Rubber Organisation[62] (INRO), first estab- **4–047** lished in 1979 and located in Kuala Lumpur, is now governed by a 1995 agreement.[63] It is composed of six exporting members and 18 importing members. Its objects are principally to achieve balanced growth in supply of, and demand for, natural rubber, to avoid excessive fluctuations in prices, to stabilise export earnings of producers, to expand international trade, to improve competitiveness and, generally, to further international co-operation through research, assistance and other programs. INRO comprises a Council, which is responsible for the operation of the buffer stock. There are 2,000 votes in the Council, divided equally between exporting and importing countries. The size of each member's vote turns on its production or imports. The Council delegates functions to four committees, dealing with administration, buffer stock operations, statistics and other measures. The Council appoints the executive director and a buffer stock manager. The members' financial contribution is broadly proportionate to their voting strength. To achieve its price stabilisation objectives, the Rubber Agreement provides for the operation of an international "buffer stock" of natural rubber, with a total capacity of 550,000 metric tons. This buffer stock is the only instrument of market intervention in the Rubber Agreement and, apparently, the only such buffer stock still in operation today.

Tropical timber

The International Tropical Timber Organisation[64] (ITTO) is concerned **4–048** with the conservation and sustainable development of the world's tropical forests. It commenced operations in 1986 under the 1983 International Tropical Timber Agreement. In 1994, a successor agreement was adopted and is due to enter into force shortly.[65] The ITTO comprises a Secretariat based in Yokohama, Japan, and a Council made up of its 49 member governments, which between them account for over 80 per cent of the world's tropical rainforests and more than 95 per cent of the trade in tropical timber. The Council has met every six months since 1987 to determine the ITTO's policy and project work. The agreement establishes two categories of membership in the Organisation—producers and

---

[62] Website: http://www.inro.com.my/inro.
[63] International Natural Rubber Agreement, in force on February 14, 1997, UN Doc TD/ RUBBER 3/10.
[64] Website: http://www.transport.com/leje/itto.html.
[65] 33 ILM 1014 (1994).

consumers—and defines the tropical timber products governed by the Agreement—logs, sawn wood, veneer and plywood. The ITTO has several objectives. It aims to provide an effective framework for co-operation between its members, to promote the expansion and diversification of international trade in tropical timber and to promote research and development. It seeks to encourage processing of tropical timber in producing member countries in an effort to promote their industrialisation, to support reforestation and forestry management activities, to improve marketing and distribution of tropical timber exports of producing members and to encourage the development of national policies for sustainable development of tropical forests.

Cotton

4–049   The International Cotton Advisory Committee[66] (ICAC) is an association of governments having an interest in the production, export, import and consumption of cotton. The functions of the Committee, as set out in its Rules and Regulations,[67] include obtaining statistics on world cotton production, trade, consumption, stocks and prices; suggesting measures the Advisory Committee considers suitable and practicable for the furtherance of international collaboration; and providing a forum for international discussions on matters related to cotton prices. The organisation evolved out of an International Cotton Meeting held in Washington D.C. in 1939. At first its membership was limited to cotton producers but the organisation is now open to any United Nations or FAO member expressing an interest in cotton. Plenary meetings of the Advisory Committee are held each year, with a Standing Committee, composed of representatives of all member governments, carrying out the activities of the ICAC between plenary meetings. Administrative support is provided by a Secretariat located in Washington D.C. Member governments are required to establish permanent national co-ordinating agencies to provide the Secretariat with statistics on the cotton situation and to distribute publications and reports received from the Secretariat.

(f) MARITIME AFFAIRS

Bibliography: Churchill and Lowe, *The Law of the Sea* (3rd ed., 1999).

4–050   Beyond the activities of the United Nations and specialised agencies in law of the sea matters, the 1982 United Nations Convention on the Law of the Sea (UNCLOS) established three new international institutions to

---

[66] Website: http://www.icac.org.
[67] Rules and Regulations of the International Cotton Advisory Committee as adopted by the 31st Plenary Meeting, June 16, 1972 (available at website: http://www.icac.org/icac/misc/information/rules.html).

address specific aspects of the law of the sea. These are the International Tribunal for the Law of the Sea, which is addressed in Chapter 13, the Commission on the Limits of the Continental Shelf[68] and the International Seabed Authority.[69] The Commission on the Limits of the Continental Shelf is established under Article 76 and Annex 2 of the 1982 Convention. Although it does not have separate personality, it is nevertheless worth considering given the potential significance of its functions. Moreover, the UN legal counsel has recently concluded that members of the Commission can be considered to be experts on mission and therefore entitled to privileges and immunities under the 1946 Convention, on the grounds that the Commission is an organ of the UN.[70] It is charged with making recommendations to coastal states concerning the outer limits of the continental shelf in areas where those limits extend beyond 200 nautical miles, and providing scientific and technical advice to coastal states with regard to the preparation of materials relating to those recommendations. The limits of the shelf established by a coastal state on the basis of the recommendation of the Commission are to be binding *vis-à-vis* third states (Article 76(8)). The Commission comprises 21 members with expertise in the fields of geology, geophysics or hydrography, who serve in their personal capacity. They are elected by state parties, having due regard to the need to ensure equitable geographical representation (annex 2, Article 2). Members serve five-year terms and function by way of sub-commissions composed of seven members. The UN's Division for Ocean Affairs and the Law of the Sea serves as the Secretariat to the Commission.

Rather more significant is the International Sea-bed Authority, which **4–051** was first established under Part XI of the 1982 Convention but whose functions were significantly altered by a 1994 agreement.[71] It establishes the regulatory regime for the Area (defined in the Convention as the sea-bed and ocean floor and sub-soil beyond the limits of national jurisdiction). By Article 136 the Area and its resources are stated to be "the common heritage of mankind," within which no state is entitled to claim or exercise sovereignty or sovereign rights, and whereby all rights in resources in the Area are vested in mankind as a whole, on whose behalf the Authority is to act (Article 137). The Authority's principal organs are the Assembly, the Council and the Secretariat (Article 158), and there is also established the Enterprise. The principal function of the Authority is to organise and control activities in the Area, with a view to administering resources there

---

[68] Website: http://www.un.org/Depts/los/tempclcs/clcs.htm.
[69] Website: http://www.isa.org.jm.
[70] See letter dated March 11, 1998 from the Legal Counsel, CLCS/5 (citing the previous opinion that the Committee on the Elimination of Racial Discrimination is an organ of the UN: *UN Juridical Yearbook*, 1969, pp. 207–210: *infra*, Chap. 13). As a UN organ the Commission could properly be addressed in Chap. 3.
[71] 33 ILM 1309 (1994).

located. However, the United Kingdom, the United States and Germany declined to sign the 1982 Convention on the grounds that the regime established by Part XI was unacceptable, principally because it failed sufficiently to promote market forces and incentives for private sector involvement. Consequently, negotiations began to amend the regime proposed by the 1982 Convention. In 1994 an Agreement relating to the implementation of Part XI of the 1982 Convention was adopted under the auspices of UN General Assembly Resolution 48/263. The 1994 Agreement, which has been brought into force provisionally (Article 7), has significantly modified the functions, management, membership and decision-making of the Authority, in particular the Council and the Enterprise. The original intention was that the Assembly, which consists of all members of the Authority, would be the supreme organ of the Authority, to which the other principal organs would be accountable. The Assembly would set general policies in accordance with UNCLOS; make elections; establish subsidiary organs as it considered necessary; consider and approve, on the recommendation of the Council, the rules, regulations and procedures on the equitable sharing of financial and other economic benefits derived from activities in the Area; decide upon the equitable sharing of financial and other economic benefits derived from activities in the Area; suspend the exercise of rights and privileges of membership (Article 185); and discuss various other matters (Article 160). The 1994 Agreement significantly amends principles governing decision-making and the production policy of the Authority. Changes have also been adopted in relation to the policies for assisting developing countries, and ensure that the functions of the Enterprise are generally to be carried out by the Secretariat of the Authority. Further changes include the transfer of the functions of the Economic Planning Commission to an expanded Legal and Technical Commission until the Council decides otherwise, or until the approval of the first plan of work for exploitation of a mine site in the deep sea-bed Area. In relation to decision-making, the 1994 Agreement stresses that the rule of consensus is generally to apply and establishes new provisions on decision-making.[72]

4–052   The Council is the smaller, executive body, with a limited membership of 36 members elected by the Assembly in accordance with the criteria set out in the convention (Article 161(1)). As the executive organ of the Authority, the Council is charged with establishing specific policies to be pursued by the Authority and, *inter alia*, supervising and co-ordinating the implementation of the provisions of Part XI; making recommendations on appointments, including that of the Secretary-General; entering into agreements with the UN or other international organisations on behalf of the Authority; considering the reports of the Enterprise and issuing directives to the

---

[72] See Chap. 11.

Enterprise; approving plans of work in the Area; making selections for production authorisations; instituting proceedings on behalf of the Authority before the Sea-bed Disputes Chamber of ITLOS in cases of non-compliance and disapproving areas for exploitation by contractors or enterprises in cases where substantial evidence indicates the risk of serious harm to the marine environment. The Council is to be assisted by two subsidiary organs, namely a Legal and Technical Commission, and an Economic Planning Commission.

The third organ is the Secretariat headed by a Secretary-General. Finally, **4–053** Article 170 and Annex 4 of the Convention provide for the establishment of an Enterprise, which was originally charged with carrying out activities in the area, as well as the transporting, processing and marketing of minerals recovered from the area (Article 170(1)). The 1994 Agreement substantially modified this proposed structure so that the Enterprise's functions will be far more limited. It has been transformed into an entity primarily entrusted with monitoring and assessment functions. Moreover, any "initial deep sea-bed mining operations" which it might conduct must be conducted through joint ventures. Further, the original requirement that the Enterprise be provided with funds to explore and exploit will no longer apply, and the state parties have no obligation to finance any of the operations in any mine site of the Enterprise, even under its joint venture arrangements.

Although the Authority has not yet become operational in relation to **4–054** activities within the Area, its implications for future activities, and for an enhanced role for international organisations more generally, are beginning to be felt. By way of example, the Court of Arbitration in the *St Pierre and Miquelon* case between Canada and France, which concerned the delimitation of the maritime area between the two states, ruled that it could not delimit the area over the continental shelf beyond 200 nautical miles because to pronounce a delimitation would involve a delimitation "not 'between the Parties' but between each one of them and the international community, represented by organs entrusted with the administration and protection of the international sea-bed area (the sea-bed beyond national jurisdiction) that has been declared to be the common heritage of mankind. This Court is not competent to carry out a delimitation which affects the rights of a party which is not before it."[73]

(g) THE ANTARCTIC

Bibliography: Auburn, *Antarctic Law and Politics* (1982); Joyner and Chopra, *The Antarctic Legal Regime* (1988); Viogradov, *Verification machinery in the Antarctic Treaty System* in Butler (Ed.), *Control over Compliance with Inter-*

---

[73] Award of June 10, 1992, 95 ILR 545 at 674. It remains to be seen what the impact of the 1994 Agreement will be for the approach taken by the Court of Arbitration.

national Law (1991); Wolfrum, *The Convention on the Regulation of Antarctic Mineral Resources* (1991); Watts, *International law and the Antarctic Treaty System* (1992); Gautier, *Institutional Developments in the Antarctic Treaty System*, in Francioni and Scovazzi, *International law for Antarctica* (1996).

4–055   The Antarctic region is subject to a number of specific international agreements establishing their own institutional arrangements. The principal instrument is the 1959 Antarctic Treaty,[74] which dedicates the Antarctic to peaceful purposes and prohibits military activities. The 1959 Treaty does not establish a Secretariat, but rather provides for regular Consultative Meetings of the Parties to ensure consultation on matters of common interest, to exchange information, and recommend measures to the parties. Some 26 parties have consultative status under the Treaty, which allows them to vote, while 15 do not have such status.[75] The Consultative Parties adopt recommendations and measures on a range of subject matters.

4–056   The Commission for the Conservation of Antarctic Marine Living Resources[76] (CCAMLR) is established by the 1980 Convention,[77] which has as its object the conservation (including rational use) of the marine living resources in the Antarctic area, and the surrounding area. Membership is open to parties with full decision-making rights. Its function is to give effect to the object and principles of the Convention, including the adoption of conservation measures (Articles 7–13). The CCAMLR has legal personality and wide-ranging powers, particularly to acquire and disseminate information and notify parties of activities that are contrary to the Convention. The CCAMLR has a limited compliance role, being able to draw the attention of all parties to any activity that, in its opinion, affects the implementation by a party of obligations, as well as activities undertaken by nationals or vessels of non-parties. The commission is assisted by a Consultative Scientific Committee for the Conservation of Antarctic Marine Living Resources.

In 1988, the Antarctic Mineral Resources Convention[78] was adopted. It was intended to be an integral part of the Antarctic Treaty System, to provide the framework for determining whether Antarctic mineral resource activities were acceptable, and if so under what conditions they could be carried out. The Convention has not entered into force, and is unlikely to do so following its veto by France and Australia. Nevertheless, the Convention remains noteworthy for the interesting range of new institutions that would have been created. Primary amongst them would be the

---

[74] 402 U.N.T.S. 71 (1959).
[75] Parties achieve consultative status by "conducting substantial scientific research activity" in the region (Art. 9(2)).
[76] Website: http://www.ccamlr.org.
[77] 19 ILM 841 (1980).
[78] 27 ILM 868 (1988).

Antarctic Minerals Resource Commission, which would have been granted broad powers to designate areas in which mineral activities could be carried out, and to determine the conditions of such activities. The 1988 convention was superseded by the 1991 Antarctic Environmental Protocol, together with its annexes, which establishes a 50–year moratorium on Antarctic mineral resources activities. The operation of the protocol is premised upon the supervision of the Antarctic Treaty Consultative Meetings and a newly created Committee for Environmental Protection.

(h) FISHERIES

Bibliography: Mirvahabi, *The International Legal Regime for Conservation and Management of the World Fisheries* (1978); Yturriaga, *The International Regime of Fisheries: from UNCLOS 1982 to the Presential Sea* (1997); W. Burke, *The New International Law of Fisheries: UNCLOS 1982 and Beyond* (1994); Orrego Vicuna, *The Changing International law of High Seas Fisheries* (1999); Hey (Ed.), *Developments in International Fisheries Law* (1999).

Beyond the arrangements established under the auspices of the Food and **4–057** Agricultural Organisation, there is no global institution with general competence over fisheries matters. The 1995 Agreement Regarding Conservation and Management of Straddling Fish Stocks and Highly Migratory Fish Stocks[79] did not establish institutional arrangements to give effect to its provisions. Despite this there are a growing number of regional fisheries organisations established to affect particular types of fisheries activity within given regions.

The only institution of potentially global competence is the Commission established under the 1946 International Whaling Convention.[80] The 1946 Convention began as a whaling club established to "provide for the proper conservation of whale stocks and thus make possible the orderly development of the whaling industry," while taking into account the need to safeguard whale resources from over-fishing and achieve optimum levels of whale stocks without causing widespread economic and other distress (Preamble). The International Whaling Commission (IWC)[81] is the principal institutional organ established by the Convention, assisted by a Secretariat. Subsidiary organs include a Finance and Administrative Committee, a Scientific Committee and a Technical Committee, and other subcommittees established on an ad hoc basis. Decisions of the IWC are taken by simple majority of those members voting, except that a three-quarter majority of those voting is required for action under Article 5 of the Convention.[82] The Commission's functions include studies and investigations, collecting and analysing statistical information, and identifying

---

[79] UN Doc. A/CONF.164/38/ (1995).
[80] 161 U.N.T.S. 72 (1946).
[81] Website: http://ourworld.compuserve.com/homepages/iwcoffice.
[82] For more on the Commission's powers under Art. 5 see *infra*.

methods of maintaining and increasing populations of whale stocks. More specifically, it has the power under Article 5(1) to amend the provisions of the Schedule to the Convention by adopting "regulations" for the conservation and utilisation of whale resources (under Article 6 it may also make non-binding recommendations on any matter relating to whales or whaling). The powers under Article 5 are extensive: the Commission may fix protected and unprotected species, open and closed seasons and waters and catch limits. Under this provision, the Commission has taken binding decisions on whaling, although the Convention establishes strict criteria for the adoption of amendments to the Schedule. Amendments must be necessary to carry out the objectives of the Convention; they must be based on scientific findings; they must take into consideration the interests of the consumers of whale products and the whaling industry (Article 5(2)). Interestingly, an amendment adopted by the IWC is binding on all parties unless one or more object to the amendment, in which case it is binding on all parties except those which object to it within a specified period of time. The significance of this power is reflected in the amendment adopted in 1982, once the requisite three-quarters majority existed, for the adoption of an outright prohibition on commercial whaling (see 1992 IWC Schedule, paragraph 10(e)).

(i) TELECOMMUNICATION

INMARSAT

Bibliography: Aukenthaler, "Recent developments at INMARSAT," 20 Annals of Air and Space Law 53 (1995); Majid, *Legal Status of International Institutions: SITA, INMARSAT and EUROCONTROL Examined* (1996); Sagar, "Recent developments at INMARSAT", 23 Annals of Air and Space Law 343 (1998); 53 Sagar, "INMARSAT and the mariner", 14 Int.J.Mar.&Coastal.L 423 (1999)."

4–058   The International Maritime Satellite Organisation[83] (INMARSAT) was established in a 1979 convention[84] with the aim of serving the maritime industry by developing satellite communication for ship management, distress and safety applications. The organisation grew out of the initiative of the then Intergovernmental Maritime Consultative Organisation (now the International Maritime Organisation (IMO)), which recognised the potential for satellite communications to assist in maritime distress situations. The organisation began operation in 1981 and has since diversified its operations into a range of telecommunications areas, including services for land-based vehicles, mobile and aeronautical communications. INMARSAT's global satellite system is now used by a range of people in transit or

---

[83] Website: http://www.inmarsat.org/.
[84] 1143 U.N.T.S. 105 (1976). The INMARSAT Operating Agreement is included in an annex to the convention.

in remote areas, including journalists, broadcasters, health teams and disaster relief workers, land transport fleet operators, airlines, airline passengers and air traffic controllers, government workers, national emergency and civil defence agencies and heads of state. INMARSAT is financed by contributions of its signatories. Each signatory is given a financial interest in the organisation, in proportion to its investment share, determined in accordance with the convention's Operating Agreement (Article 5(1)).

The organs of INMARSAT are the Assembly, the Council and the **4–059** Directorate, headed by the Director-General. The Assembly is the plenary body of the organisation, composed of representatives from all of the parties meeting biannually. Decisions of the Assembly on matters of substance require the votes of a two-thirds majority of the parties present and voting. For procedural matters a simple majority only is necessary. Each party represented in the Assembly is entitled to one vote (Article 11). The Council carries out the executive functions of the organisation. It consists of 22 representatives, made up of 18 representatives from signatories or groups of signatories who have the largest investment shares in the organisation and four representatives from signatories not otherwise represented on the Council who are elected by the Assembly, irrespective of their respective investment shares. In the election of the latter group of representatives the "principle of just geographical representation is [to be] taken into account, with due regard to the interests of developing countries" (Article 13(1)(b)). The Council meets at least three times a year and seeks to take decisions on a unanimous basis, failing which the same pattern of voting as in the Assembly applies (Article 14). The Directorate is headed by the Director-General, the chief executive and legal representative of the organisation.

INMARSAT was originally designed as a joint co-operative venture **4–060** between governments, with their signatories—nominee organisations, in most cases the country's post and telecommunications providers—contributing capital and bearing the risk of the venture. Some 20 years on the organisation has diversified into a range of telecommunications sectors and is providing not only public services but also services to independent service providers. In recognition of the organisation's change of focus, the Assembly agreed in September 1998 to privatise the organisation[85] making it the first "treaty organisation" to do so. The restructured organisation will compromise two entities; a private company that will seek initial public offering within approximately two years of formation and an intergovernmental body to ensure that the organisation continues to meet its public service obligations, such as the Global Maritime Distress and Safety System.

---

[85] See INMARSAT Member Countries Elect Director of Secretariat, February 5, 1999, available at website: http://www.inmarsat.org/newsroom/index.html.

INTELSAT

Bibliography: Cheng, "INTELSAT, the definitive arrangements", in Krishan Rao and Nawaz, *Essays on International law in Honour of Krishna Rao* (1976); Snow, *INTELSAT: Economic and institutional Challenges Facing an International Organisation* (1987); Field, INTELSAT at a crossroads, 25 Law and policy in International Business 1335 (1994).

4–061   The International Telecommunications Satellite Organisation[86] (INTELSAT) was the product of a multilateral agreement[87] and operating agreement[88] that were concluded in Washington in 1971 and entered into force in February 1973. INTELSAT owns and operates a global communications satellite system providing capacity for voice, video, corporate or private networks and Internet communications in more than 200 countries and territories. While INTELSAT is the owner of the INTELSAT space segment and all other property acquired by the organisation, each signatory[89] has an investment share, determined in accordance with the Operating Agreement, corresponding to its percentage of all utilisation of the INTELSAT space segment by all signatories. Each signatory is also obliged to contribute to the capital requirements of the organisation and users pay utilisation charges determined in accordance with the provisions of the Agreement (Article 5).

4–062   The organs of INTELSAT are the Assembly of Parties, the Meeting of Signatories, the Board of Governors and an executive organ responsible to the Board. The Assembly is composed of representatives of all the parties and is the principal organ of INTELSAT. Decisions on matters of substance are to be taken by a two-thirds majority of parties' representatives who are present and voting, whereas procedural matters require a simple majority only (Article 7). The Meeting of Signatories is composed of representatives from all signatories. The meeting considers and expresses views to the Board on the annual report and the annual financial statements, considers amendments and future programmes, establishes general rules for the guidance of the Board, and makes decisions concerning the withdrawal of signatories. The meeting also serves as a forum for the consideration and expression of views on complaints referred to it by the Board or the parties. The meeting oversees the policies and programmes of the organisation and prepares reports on their implementation (Article 8).

4–063   The Board of Governors is the organ responsible for the design, development, construction, establishment, operation and maintenance of the INTELSAT space segment (Article 10). The Board is composed of

---

[86] Website: http://www.intelsat.int.
[87] 1220 U.N.T.S. 21 (1971).
[88] 1220 U.N.T.S. 149 (1971).
[89] According to Art. 1(g) of the Agreement, "signatories" are either parties to the Convention, or more commonly, telecommunications entities designated by each party. Signatories have signed the Operating Agreement and it has entered into force for them.

Governors representing signatories, with one governor representing each signatory whose investment share is not less than the minimum investment share,[90] one governor representing each group of signatories whose combined investment share is not less than the minimum investment share, one governor representing any group of at least five signatories not otherwise represented from any one of the regions defined by the Plenipotentiary Conference of the International Telecommunication Union held in Montreux in 1965, regardless of their investment shares, providing there are no more than two such governors from any region or more than five governors for all such regions (Article 9(a)). The governors have voting participation equal to that part of the investment share of the signatory or group of signatories represented derived from utilisation of the INTELSAT space segment for specified services (Article 9(f)).

The executive organ of INTELSAT is headed by a Director-General, **4–064** who is its chief executive and legal representative. The Director-General is directly responsible to the Board of Governors for performance of all management functions (Article 11). Like INMARSAT, INTELSAT's Assembly of Parties has recently agreed to privatise the organisation.[91] The organisation was due to develop final restructuring recommendations during 2001 for future consideration.

(j) OTHER

Commonwealth Secretariat

> Bibliography: Dale, "Is the Commonwealth an International Organisation?" 31 ICLQ 451 (1982); Dale, *The Modern Commonwealth* (1983). Website: http://www.thecommonwealth.org.

The Commonwealth is a voluntary association of 54 independent sov- **4–065** ereign states, all of which have experienced direct or indirect British rule or are linked administratively to another Commonwealth country.[92] The association has no constitution or charter, but members commit themselves to the statements of beliefs set out by the heads of government in the 1971 Singapore Declaration of Commonwealth Principles.[93] The Commonwealth Secretariat was established in 1965 as the main inter-governmental agency of the Commonwealth. Its role is to facilitate co-operation among member

---

[90] Under Art. 9(b)(i), this minimum share was originally equal to the investment share of the thirteenth largest investor, but it has been revised annually since the first meeting of the Meeting of Signatories.

[91] The decision to privatise was taken at the Assembly's meeting in Penang, October 26–29, 1999. See INTELSAT Members Decide to Privatise, Washington D.C., November 1, 1999, available at website: http://www.intelsat.int/news/press/99–30e.htm.

[92] The one exception is Mozambique, a former Portuguese colony, which was admitted to the Commonwealth in 1995.

[93] Reaffirmed in the Harare (Zimbabwe) Declaration of 1991.

countries, to organise the Commonwealth Heads of Government meetings and to execute the organisation's developmental programmes. The Secretariat is headed by the Commonwealth Secretary-General, elected by the Heads of Government, who is assisted by three deputies in the areas of Political Affairs, Economic and Social Affairs and Development Co-operation respectively. Thirteen divisions carry out the work and projects of the Secretariat.

4–066   The core functions of the Secretariat (organisation of Commonwealth Summits and Ministerial meetings and promotion of consultation on political, economic and social matters) are supported by the assessed contributions of full members of the Commonwealth. Since July 1993, the Secretariat has adopted a programme-driven approach to its work, with the Divisions collaborating to implement programmes developed to reflect the priorities of the 1991 Harare Declaration.[94] More recently, the Commonwealth has made headlines by taking a more active interest in the human rights performance of its members, leading to the suspensions of Nigeria in November 1995 (following the execution of Ken Saro-Wiwa and other activists) and of Pakistan in November 1999 (following a military coup).

Organisation Internationale de la Francophonie

4–067   The Agence de la Francophonie,[95] an organisation of French speaking nations, was established on March 30, 1970 in Niamey, Niger. The original organisation was known as the Agency of Cultural and Technical Co-operation (ACCT) and its membership was limited to three French-speaking African states—Senegal, Tunisia and Niger. By 1996 the ACCT had a membership of 21 states and governments. In 1996 the ACCT became the Agence de la Francophonie. Today the organisation has 47 members and two associate members, spanning five continents and all sharing French as a common language. The organisation is based in Paris. The Conference of the Heads of State or Government is the principal institution of the organisation. Since 1986 the Conference has held Summits biannually. Following a decision of the Summit of Chaillot in 1991, a Ministerial Conference of the Francophonie (CMF) was created. The CMF consists of the Ministers of Foreign Affairs and/or Francophonie of each of the member states. The CMF allows for political continuity between the Summits, meeting both as a preparatory and follow-up conference for the Summits, and as a general conference and a board of directors of the Agency. The country hosting the summit in the previous or following year provides a chair. The permanent political body of the organisation is the Permanent Council of the Francophonie, with 18

---

[94] These are (i) advancing fundamental political values, (ii) promoting sustainable development, (iii) gender equality, and (iv) Secretariat governance and management.
[95] Website: http://www.francophonie.org/oif.cfm.

permanent members representing heads of state or government. The members of the Council are chosen at each Summit on the basis of equitable regional distribution. Representatives of other states not elected to the Council can still take part in the Council's meetings, which take place four times a year. As for the CMF, the Council is chaired by the representative of the state or government hosting the Summit in the previous or following year. In addition to its main institutions, the Agency maintains associations with two permanent Ministerial Conferences of the Francophonie—the Conference of the Ministers of Education (with 33 members) and the Conference of the Ministers for Youth and Sports (with 32 members).

African, Caribbean and Pacific Group

The African, Caribbean and Pacific Group[96] (ACP) consists of former **4–068** colonies of the European powers that have signed the 1974 Lomé Convention.[97] The ACP was established by the 1975 Georgetown Agreement[98] to ensure the realisation of the objectives of the Lomé Convention, as well as contribute to the regional development and co-operation of its member countries. The original 1975 Lomé Convention between the then nine member states of the European Community and the 46 countries of the African, Caribbean and Pacific area, sought a partnership between the contracting parties to promote and expedite the economic, social and cultural development of the ACP members. The 1975 Lomé Convention was followed by three other conventions, each of which ran for a five-year period, with the exception of Lomé IV, which ran for ten years and expired in the year 2000.[99] A new ACP-EC Convention has been adopted in Cotonon, in 2000.

The institutional structure of the ACP is relatively simple, consisting of a **4–069** Council of Ministers, with representatives from each state, assisted by the Committee of Ambassadors, an executive body. An additional body is the ACP-EC Joint Assembly, which brings together representatives of the European Parliament and representatives from ACP states, with the aim of promoting greater interdependence of the North and South.

Organization of the Islamic Conference

Bibliography: Moinuddin, The Charter of the Islamic Conference and Legal Framework of Economic Co-operation among its Member States (1987) Website:http://www.oic-oci.org.

---

[96] Website: http://www.acpsec.org.
[97] 14 ILM 595 (1975).
[98] 1247 U.N.T.S. 147.
[99] Lomé II, 1277 U.N.T.S. 3 (1979); Lomé III, 24 ILM 571 (1985); Lomé IV, 29 ILM 783 (1990).

4–070   The Organisation of the Islamic Conference (OIC) was established by Charter adopted in 1972 by 30 states, following the first meeting of Islamic leaders held in Morocco in September 1969. Membership is open to every Muslim State. The objectives of the OIC, which is based in Jeddah, Saudi Arabia, include the promotion of Islamic solidarity among the member states; co-operation among members in economic, social, cultural, scientific and other fields; the elimination of racial segregation, discrimination and colonialism; and the co-ordination of efforts for the safeguarding of the "Holy Places" and support the people of Palestine (Charter, Art. 2A). To those ends the members are guided by a number of principles, including "total equality" between themselves; respect of the right of self-determination and non-interference in the domestic affairs of member states; respect for the sovereignty, independence and territorial integrity of each member states; and abstention from the threat or use of force against the territorial integrity, national unity or political independence of any member states.

4–071   The Organisation's principal organ is the Conference of Kings and Heads of State and Government, which is the "supreme authority" of the Organisation and meets every three years (Art. 4). There is also a Conference of Foreign Ministers, which generally meets annually and is charged with overseeing implementation of the OIC's general policy and adopting resolutions to achieve the OIC's aims and objectives (Art. 5(2)). These resolutions are adopted by a two-thirds majority (Art. 5(3)). The OIC's day-to-day activities are entrusted to the General Secretariat—headed by the Secretary-General—and which is charged amongst other matters with "consolidating" relations between the OIC and Islamic organisations of an international character (Art. 9). A number of standing, permanent and specialised committees are also established. The OIC has a seven subsidiary organs[1] and four specialised institutions and organs,[2] as well as a number of "affiliated institutions".

---

[1] Including training and research centres, Islamic universities in Niger and Uganda, an Institute for Technology, and a Centre for the Development of Trade.

[2] The Islamic Development Bank and the Islamic States Broadcasting Organisation, both in Jeddah; the Islamic Educational, Scientific and Cultural Organisation, in Rabat; and the International Islamic News Agency. These bodies have their own statutes and independent budgets.

CHAPTER 5

REGIONAL INSTITUTIONS: INTRODUCTION

Bibliography: Bebr, "Regional Organisations: a United Nations Problem" (1955) 49 A.J.I.L. 166; Saba, "Les Accords régionaux dans Charte de L'O.N.U." (1952 I) 80 R.d.C. 635; Wilcox: "Regionalism and the UN" (1965) 18 Int. Org. 789; R. Yakemtchouk, "Le régionalisme et l'ONU" (1955) R.G.D.I.P. 406; Yalem, *Regionalism and World Order* (1965).

Even prior to the League of Nations, "regionalism," in the sense of a **5–001** grouping of states by a common bond of policy, existed; the Holy Alliance or the International Union of American Republics are obvious examples. Article 21 of the League Covenant recognised that the new global organisation had to co-exist with such regional groupings by providing that "Nothing in this Covenant shall be deemed to affect the validity of international engagements such as treaties of arbitration or regional understandings like the Monroe doctrine for securing the maintenance of peace." The League therefore saw the creation of the Balkan Entente, the Locarno Agreements, and the Briand proposal for a European Union. When, at San Francisco, the same problem of reconciling the new global organisation with regional understanding arose, there was already in existence a fairly comprehensive Inter-American system (Pan-American Union), which in 1948 was to become the "Organisation of American States"[1] and also the newly-formed League of Arab States, inaugurated by the Pact of March 22, 1945.[2] As a consequence of the predominantly "regionalist" approach of the states which took part to the San Francisco Conference, provision was expressly made to ensure that the new arrangements for collective security in the Charter, operating under the Security Council, should not stultify the arrangements already in being on a regional basis.[3] Article 52(1) of the UN Charter therefore provides that:

"Nothing in the present Charter precludes the existence of regional arrangements or agencies for dealing with such matters relating to the

---

[1] See *infra*, Chap. 7.
[2] See *infra*, Chap. 9.
[3] See Kodjo, "Accords régionaux—Article 52" in *La Charte des Nations Unies* (Cot and Pellet (eds), 2nd ed., 1991), p. 800.

maintenance of international peace and security as are appropriate for regional action provided that such arrangements or agencies and their activities are consistent with the Purposes and Principles of the United Nations."

5–002   Clearly, the concern here is to avoid a conflict between the respective security systems of the United Nations and the "regional arrangements." However, the attempt at San Francisco to reconcile the conflicting claims of regionalism and universalism produced a compromise which had within it two areas of latent difficulty. The first area of difficulty was that of pacific settlement of disputes.[4] Article 33 of the Charter includes resort to regional arrangements as a method which the parties must use "first of all," before having recourse to the Security Council. Article 52(2) imposes upon the parties the obligation to utilise regional procedures for settlement. However, Article 52(4) specifically states that "this Article in no way impairs the application of Articles 34 and 35," so that the Council's own right to investigate a dispute or situation, and the member state's right to appeal to the Council seems to be preserved: the inherent contradictions appear obvious.

5–003   Thus, in the practice of the OAS, the Arab League and the OAU there has been advanced the thesis that regional procedures have a "priority" over the Security Council's procedures for settlement and even, in its extreme form in the U.S. argument in the Guatemalan case in 1954, an "exclusive" competence over inter-regional disputes so as to deny a state the right to appeal to the Security Council.[5] This argument over jurisdictional competence was politically motivated, especially in an OAS practice where the USA feared that reference to the Security Council would bring a Soviet veto and where the Soviet Union feared that the OAS procedures would be dominated by U.S. influence.

5–004   The Security Council, after a somewhat questionable abdication of jurisdiction in the Guatemalan case, has later shifted towards a more pragmatic approach in which, whilst supporting the use of regional procedures, it nevertheless retains a "supervisory" jurisdiction by maintain-

---

[4] See, generally, Acevedo, "Disputes under Consideration by the UN Security Council or Regional Bodies" in *The International Court of Justice at Crossroads* (Damrosch ed, 1987) p. 42; Rivlin, "Regional Arrangements and the UN System for Collective Security and Conflict Resolution: A New Road Ahead?" (1992) 11 *Foreign Relations* 95.

[5] See, on the OAS practice, Claude Jr., "The OAS, the UN and the United States" (1964) *International Conciliation* (No. 547); Ann Thomas and A.J. Thomas, *The Organisation of American States* (1963), Chaps 16–17; Macdonald, "The Developing Relationship between Superior and Subordinate Political Bodies at the International Level—A Note on the Experience of the United Nations and the Organisation of the American States" (1964) 2 Can. Y.B.I.L. 21, 41. On the Arab League see Macdonald, *The League of Arab States* (1965), Chap. X.

ing the question on its own agenda (as in the Haitian and Panama Cases in 1963 and 1964) and even, in the case of the Dominican Republic in 1965, despatching its own observer mission.[6]

Any attempt to rationalise the competing claims to jurisdiction over a **5–005** dispute must take account of three basically different categories of "disputes."

(a) Disputes involving no actual or potential threat to international peace: here the priority of the regional procedures is undisputed, and the matter ought not to be referred to the Security Council.

(b) Disputes involving a potential threat to international peace: here, the matter seems to fall squarely under Chapter VI of the Charter, so that the rights of the Council under Article 34, and of states under Article 35, are clear. Reference to a regional organisation's procedures becomes a matter of convenience, not of obligation, and much depends on the willingness of the parties to accept such a reference.

(c) "Disputes" which involve an actual threat to peace: here the situation properly belongs in Chapter VII, not Chapter VI, and the "primary responsibility" of the Security Council to deal with the matter is clear; there can be no question of "priority" for regional procedures. Equally clearly, there is nothing to prevent the Security Council utilising regional procedures to assist in any measures taken under Chapter VII, but they do this subject to the Council's primary responsibility.

This last category brings us into the second area of difficulty, namely that **5–006** of "enforcement" action which, under Article 53, cannot be taken except under the authorisation of the Security Council.[7] The practice of the OAS has shown a tendency to minimise this restriction on the scope of regional collective action of a coercive character in three ways. First, the OAS (and the U.S. in particular) has argued that the concept of "enforcement action" subject to prior authorisation by the Security Council does not embrace measures falling short of the use of armed force[8] or taken pursuant to a

---

[6] For later practice of the Security Council in relation to regional conflicts in Africa and Europe, see Chap. 2, paras 2–047 *et seq.*

[7] See, generally, Ress, "Comment of Article 53" in *The Charter of the United Nations—A Commentary* (Simma ed., 1994), pp. 730 *et seq.*

[8] Hence the partial economic sanctions against the Dominican Republic (1960), Cuba (1962) and full economic sanctions against Cuba (1964) would not require Security Council authorisation. See the U.S. and U.K. arguments in the Security Council in the *Dominican* case, 1960. It is difficult to reconcile this view with the concept of intervention embodied in the G.A. res. 2131 (XX), or Art. 15 of the OAS Charter, or the I.C.J.'s definition of enforcement action in the Expenses Case ("Certain expenses of the United Nations (Art. 17, para. 2, of the Charter), Advisory Opinion of July 20, 1962" (1962) I.C.J. Rep. 151, 170–177).

recommendation as opposed to a decision[9] and, moreover, that the Security Council's "authorisation" can lie in an *ex post facto* approval or even failure to disapprove the action.[10] Secondly, the OAS has taken a broad definition of the notion of "collective self-defence" which, under Article 51 of the Charter, is clearly distinct from enforcement action and does not require prior authorisation.[11] Thus, the view that has been taken would not confine self-defence to "armed attack" but would embrace indirect aggression or subversion: this view is reflected in the 1962 Punte del Este Declaration. This view was long criticised by the Soviet Union, although the intervention by Warsaw Pact countries in Czechoslovakia in 1968 seems to have marked a reversal of policy. Thirdly, the OAS in the Dominican case in 1965, and the Arab League in Kuwait in 1961 and in Lebanon in 1976, have developed a concept of "regional peace-keeping" involving the use of armed forces but not for "enforcement action."[12]

5–007 The difficulty with these developments is that they expand the role of regional arrangements in the vital area of the regulation of coercion without necessarily offering any real guarantee that this role will be subject to the safeguards of world opinion which, whatever the weaknesses of the UN, do find reflection in UN organs. Nor can one region develop a role which can be denied to another region, so that whatever the OAS can do under the UN Charter, so can the OAU and others. It is not therefore desirable for regional autonomy to develop too far in this area.

5–008 Not all organisations with membership limited to states in a given area are regarded as "regional arrangements" within the sense of Chapter VIII. The relative subordination of the regional arrangement to the Security Council became politically embarrassing once the "Cold War" developed; the Western powers wished to create an organisation for security against the Soviet Union, yet any "regional arrangement" they contrived would be virtually under the control of an organ of the United Nations in which the Soviet Union held a veto. Hence the North Atlantic Treaty Organisation, formed in 1949, made no mention of any relationship to the Security Council as a "regional arrangement," nor did it contain any provision providing for action only upon the authorisation of the Council or for reporting activities "in contemplation." Instead, the treaty expressed the organisation to be one for "collective self-defence," under Article 51 of the

---

[9] Meeker, "Defensive Quarantine and the Law" (1963) 57 AJIL 521: this is a misunderstanding of the I.C.J. opinion in the *Expenses* Case, *supra* at n. 8.

[10] Chayes, "Law and the Quarantine of Cuba" (1963) 41 *Foreign Affairs* 550. This must be nonsense both in terms of the plain meaning of "authorisation" and the fact that a U.S. veto would thus always ensure "authorisation" of OAS action. Nor does the Security Council practice in the *Dominican* case support it.

[11] See Inter-American Institute of International Legal Studies, *The Inter-American System: Its Development and Strengthening* (1966), pp. 105–154.

[12] For later developments in that respect, see *infra*.

Charter, and, correspondingly, embodied only the obligation to report "measures taken" to the Council. Several aspects of its evolution and the re-definition of its mandate since the beginning of the 1990s, may, however, lead one to consider that NATO can also be regarded now as a regional organisation within the meaning of Chapter VIII.[13] The question whether all regional security arrangements must necessarily be "regional arrangements" under the Charter is complicated by the fact that no definition of a regional arrangement is given in the Charter; various attempts to insert one at San Francisco were rejected on the ground of incompleteness.[14]

It has been suggested that, in this form, the problem posed is in fact a **5–009** sterile one.[15] The question is not whether a given organisation is a regional arrangement or not, but rather whether particular action is taken as a regional arrangement or not. No one doubts the capacity of the Organisation of American States, which is expressly stated to be a "regional arrangement" in Article 1 of the Treaty of Bogota, 1948, to take collective self-defence, and in so doing it would be subject to the obligations of Article 51; Chapter VIII would be irrelevant to that situation. But assume a situation where the action contemplated is coercive action directed against a state and authorised by a competent UN organ (here we accept the Expenses Case definition of "enforcement action") and, clearly, the regional organisation can act only under the authority of that organ.

In any event, the relations between the UN and regional organisations **5–010** the mandate of which touches upon security matters has evolved significantly since the end of the Cold War.[16] Hence, on several occasions since the beginning of the 1990s, the Security Council has authorised or called upon UN member states to take either "nationally or through regional agencies or arrangements" coercive measures under Chapter VII of the Charter in order to restore international peace and security.[17] Joint UN-regional organisation peace-keeping operations have even been established.[18] The United Nations' willingness to cooperate with regional organ-

---

[13] See e.g. on that question Higgins, "Some Thoughts on the Evolving Relationship between the Security Council and NATO" in *Essays in Honour of Boutros-Ghali* (1998), Vol. 1, p. 512 *et seq.* and 522.

[14] See the arguments developed by Sir W. Eric Beckett (*The North Atlantic Treaty, the Brussels Treaty and the Charter of the United Nations* (1950)) and Kelsen ("Is the North Atlantic Treaty a Regional Arrangement?" 45 AJIL (1951) 162; and *Recent Trends in the Law of the United Nations* (1951), p. 918 *et seq.*), respectively.

[15] Bowett, *Self-defence in International Law* (1957), p. 222 *et seq.*

[16] See generally Walter, "Security Council Control over Regional Action" (1997) 1 *Max Planck Yearbook of United Nations Law* 129.

[17] See, for example, res. 770 (1992) of August 13, 1992, para. 2; 816 (1993), March 31, 1993, para. 4 (ex-Yugoslavia). In some cases, it is only action "through or in co-operation with" a regional organisation (NATO, as it was) which was authorised (see res. 1031 (1995) of December 15, 1995, paras 14 *et seq.*).

[18] See res. 866 (1993) of September 22, 1993, preambular para. 5 (Liberia; joint UNOMIL-ECOMOG Force).

isations in order to maintain international peace and security within the framework of Chapter VIII has also been expressed in more general terms by the UN Secretary General in the Agenda for Peace[19] and by the General Assembly in its 1994 Declaration on the Enhancement of Cooperation Between the United Nations and Regional Arrangements or Agencies in the Maintenance of International Peace and Security.[20] As the military operations undertaken by NATO against Yugoslavia in 1999 have shown however, the subordination of regional organisations to the Security Council remains illusory in some cases.

5–011   Irrespective of the emphasis laid on these in the UN Charter, we shall, however, see that the scope of regional organisations is much wider than either that of "regional arrangements" or even regional collective security organisations. Whilst it is true that, because of the outbreak of the "Cold War" and the consequent breakdown of the UN collective security system, regionalism has developed mostly in the form of organisations for collective security, it has never been contended that collective security was the only domain in which the principle of regionalism could operate. It was self-evident that, in the political and economic fields, greater progress might be made on a regional basis, between states whose fundamental similarity of political and economic institutions lessened the barriers to progress and co-operation. The United Nations itself recognised this fact by establishing the regional economic commissions, like ECA, ECE, ESCAP, ECLA. Hence, nothing in the UN Charter has, equally, prevented the growth of regional organisations in these other fields, and many of the organisations to be dealt with will be seen to have no connection with the "regional arrangements" mentioned in Article 52, or, indeed, with collective security as such. It is worth mentioning, however, that whereas the main emphasis is indeed put on economic co-operation in most regional organisations established since the Second World War, considerations for peace and regional stability as a precondition for economic development and prosperity have led many of these groupings to extend their activities to the field of defence and security.[21]

5–012   It will be seen also that very few regional organisations have a membership that extends to all the states of the continent on which they are located. Most of them are actually "sub-regional" groupings, the members of which often have significant political or ideological affinities. In fact, a

---

[19] Doc. A/47/277–S/24111, of June 17, 1992, paras 60–65; Supplement, Doc. A/50/60–S/1995/1 of January 3, 1995, paras 85–88.

[20] Res. 49/57 of December 9, 1994.

[21] This can be observed in Europe, as well as in Africa or in the Middle East, for instance. As to the status of some of these organisations in relation to the provisions of Chapter VIII, see Hummer and Schweitzer, "Comment of Article 52" in *The Charter of the United Nations—A Commentary* (Simma ed., 1994), pp. 706–707.

number of regional organisations appear to have been established as a substitute for a greater degree of integration, which was envisaged at some point—quite often in the shape of a federation of states—but ultimately never put in concrete form. Debates have thus been frequent, in almost every region, between states advocating a more "federalist" approach of institutional integration, and others favouring much looser forms of co-operation.

Finally, it must be noted too that some of the organisation dealt with in **5–013** the following chapters actually cover more than one region or continent. The Organisation for Economic Cooperation and Development (OECD), the North Atlantic Treaty Organisation (NATO) and the Organisation for Security and Cooperation in Europe (OSCE) are clear examples of this phenomenon. Such organisations may nevertheless be considered as "regional" due to the fact that they do not have any claim of universality as far as their membership is concerned. On the contrary, they are generally strictly limited to states which, once again, share common values and have strong common interests in those organisations' area(s) of competence. These will be addressed in the chapter covering the continent with which their ties—often for historical reasons—are the most prominent.

By and large, and setting aside the development of the regional blocs for **5–014** military purposes, the development of these strong regional tendencies has been a beneficial one in terms of the co-operation achieved between states. There is, however, a certain danger which is most obvious in the collective security field but which is also of a general character, namely that states may so concentrate on their regional associations as to minimise their efforts to co-operate on a global or universal basis through the United Nations and the specialised agencies. Trygve Lie once said that "regional arrangements can never be a substitute for world organisation;" indeed, these developments should be regarded as complementary to, and not in substitution for, those embraced by the UN and its agencies.

The organisations treated in the following chapters are dealt with by **5–015** regions, and then grouped according to whether their competence is general or limited. It has been thought preferable to adopt this method of presentation, rather than to attempt a classification according to function which cuts right across any regional grouping. The fact is that within one region the different organisations may form part of one comprehensive system, and become explicable only by reference to that system.

CHAPTER 6

EUROPEAN ORGANISATIONS

Bibliography: Political and Economic Planning (PEP), *European Organisations* (1959); Pinto, *Les organisations européennes* (1965); Reuter, *Organisations européennes* (2nd ed., 1970); Robertson, *European Institutions: Co-operation, Integration, Unification* (3rd ed., 1973); Cartou, *Organisations européennes* (10th ed., 1991); Yearbook of European Law (annually).

THE European scene has been remarkable for the growth and develop- **6–001** ment of international institutions since the end of the Second World War; indeed, it has been in Europe, the traditional centre of nationalism and state sovereignty, that experiments in co-operation have been set afoot which involve limitations on the exercise of national sovereignty unparalleled elsewhere in the world. The sources of this dynamism are complex, but, at the risk of over-simplification, they may be said to be four: first, the need for co-operation on the practical level brought about by the fact of increased inter-relationships; secondly, the feeling that the rapid economic reconstruction necessary to make European economies viable and competitive once more after the Second World War could only be achieved by concerted action; thirdly, the ideological appeal of "European Unity," a kind of "United States of Europe" which would emerge to replace the independent, sovereign states (although this factor may be said to have lost some weight since the mid-1990s); and fourthly, until the end of the 1980s, the fear of Soviet aggression against Western Europe which manifested itself in the formation of Western military alliances. The order in which these sources are put should not be taken as indicating the relative importance which they have had in promoting co-operation; neither would we suggest that they are exhaustive. In particular, the relative practical success of many of the early institutions has indicated the viability of the approach.

The institutional landscape in Europe has evolved significantly since the **6–002** end of the Cold War. Some organisations set up mainly by socialist Central and Eastern European countries have disappeared altogether, while other European organisations, whose membership was traditionally limited to Western European states, are expanding Eastwards. Many Central and Eastern European states have indeed turned to the latter institutions and either joined them as members (as in the case of the Council of Europe and, in much smaller numbers, NATO) or applied for membership (in the case of the European Union and, again, NATO). A few words should nevertheless be said of the former Eastern European organisations, if only "for the record." The most important of these were active in the field of defence (Warsaw Treaty Organisation) and economics (Council for Mutual Economic Aid), respectively.[1]

6–003 The Warsaw Treaty Organisation was established by a Treaty of Friendship, Co-operation and Mutual Assistance at Warsaw on May 14, 1955.[2] The Organisation was a direct counterpart of NATO,[3] and, as the Treaty's preamble recited, was prompted by the re-armament of Western Germany and its inclusion in NATO. Membership was open to all other states "irrespective of their social and state systems" ready to assist in preserving peace. It was, therefore, in practice only and not by its terms confined to Eastern Europe; this was consistent with the repeated invitation by the USSR to the Western Powers to join in a general European security treaty.[4] The crux of the security system was found in Article 4 whereby, on the basis of Article 51 of the UN Charter, an armed attack in Europe on any member gave rise to the individual and collective obligation to render "immediate assistance . . . by all the means it may consider necessary, including the use of armed force." Originally, the Treaty was interpreted to apply only to aggression by an external Power. However, the Soviet intervention in Hungary in 1956 and the combined invasion of Czechoslovakia by the Soviet Union and other Warsaw Pact members in 1968, which were justified on the basis of the Treaty, clearly demonstrated that the Treaty was not so limited in practice. The armed forces of the members were under a joint command and were in effect treated as an organic whole.[5] The Warsaw Treaty Organisation was essentially a defensive alliance, with organs for consultation and co-operation, and did not purport to attain the wider economic and political aims of NATO, nor did it have the very comprehensive structure of organs which NATO possesses. Due to

---

[1] For more on the former international institutions of Eastern Europe, see Ginsburgs, "The Constitutional Foundations of the 'Socialist Commonwealth'" (1973) 27 Y.B.W.A. 173; Szawlowski, *The System of International Organisations of the Communist Countries* (1976); Butler (ed.), *A Source Book on Socialist International Organisations* (1978).

[2] 219 U.N.T.S. 25. See Lachs, "The Warsaw Agreement and the question of collective security in Europe" (1955) *International Affairs*; Skubiszewski, "L'Organisation du Traité de Varsovie" [1967] Revue Belge de D. Int. 69. Members were Albania (which withdrew in 1968), Bulgaria, Czechoslovakia, German Democratic Republic (which withdrew in 1990), Hungary, Poland, Romania and Soviet Union.

[3] For more on this organisation, see *infra* at para. 6–064. See also http://www.nato.int.

[4] This is one of the main factors that later led to the establishment of the CSCE; for more on this, see *infra* at para. 6–084.

[5] Art. 5. The status of Soviet forces on the territory of other members was governed by a series of bilateral agreements, according to principles broadly similar to the NATO Status of Forces Agreement; see USSR/German Democratic Republic Agreement of March 12, 1957, USSR/Hungary, May 27, 1957, USSR/Poland, December 17, 1956; texts in (1958) 52 AJIL 210–221.

the political changes in the Pact's member states and to the overall evolution of Europe's geopolitical landscape, the alliance was dissolved in July 1991.[6] The Council for Mutual Economic Aid (COMECON or CMEA) was established at an economic conference in Moscow in January 1949, obviously as a counterpart to the OEEC which had been established in western Europe in the previous year.[7] The Council was, in principle, simply an organ for consultation between governments in the economic field. Until 1956 it operated largely on the technical level but from 1956 onwards it drew up more comprehensive five-year plans for economic co-ordination. In 1962 the Council was opened up to non-European states.[8] In close liaison with COMECON were several organisations amongst which the International Investment Bank, an Organisation for Space Communication called Intersputnik and the International Bank for Economic Co-operation.[9] For reasons similar to those which brought the Warsaw Pact's existence to an end, the COMECON was dissolved in June 1991.[10] Intersputnik is the only organisation of the former Soviet bloc which remains active at present.[11]

It should also be noted that the states which emerged from the breakup **6–004** of the Soviet Union agreed in 1991 on the creation of a new institution, the Commonwealth of Independent States (CIS), which comprises all the former Soviet republics except the Baltic states.[12] The Charter of the CIS was adopted in 1993.[13] The purposes of the institution are generally to "serve further development and enhancement of the relations, good neighbourhood, inter-ethnic accord, confidence, mutual understanding and mutually beneficial co-operation among member states" (Charter, Article 1); these are to be accomplished through co-operation in political, economic, ecologic, humanitarian and other spheres, and co-operation in the field of security (Article 2). The Charter also defines in broad terms the spheres of joint activity of the member states, which have to be "realised by common coordinating institutes;" these run from the co-ordination of

---

[6] (1991) Keesing's 38365.

[7] For a general description of the Council see Agoston, *Le marché commun communiste* (2nd ed., 1965); Grzybowski, *The Socialist Commonwealth of Nations* (1964), Chaps 3, 4.

[8] Cuba, Mongolia and Vietnam were the non-European members of the organisation. The European members were Albania (which however withdrew from the organisation), Bulgaria, Czechoslovakia, German Democratic Republic, Hungary, Poland, Romania and Soviet Union.

[9] On this, see Focsaneanu, "La Banque Internationale de Coopération Économique" (1965) 92 Journal du D.I. 591.

[10] (1991) Keesing's 38315.

[11] It had 24 member states as of July, 2000, and has formed a joint venture in 1997 with the American company Lockheed Martin to become a global satellite operator. For more information see http://www.intersputnik.com.

[12] December 8, 1991 (Minsk) and December 21, 1991 (Alma Ata); texts in (1992) 31 ILM 138. Georgia joined the CIS in 1993.

[13] June 22, 1993, (1995) 34 ILM 1279.

foreign political activities and the co-operation in formation and development of common economic space to the struggle against organised criminality and the co-operation in the field of defence policy and protection of external frontiers (Article 4). The emphasis is nevertheless put on co-ordination, the Charter itself insisting on the fact that the CIS "shall not be supranational" (Article 1). The CIS institutional structure is complex and includes a Council of Heads of States, a Council of Heads of Government, a Council of Foreign Ministers, a Coordination and Consultative Committee, a Council of Defence Ministers, a Council of the Frontier Troops Chief Commanders, an Economic Court, a Commission on Human Rights and an Interparliamentary Assembly. It should finally be noted that none of those texts provides explicitly for the legal personality of the CIS, which can therefore only be implicit.[14] A Treaty on Creation of Economic Union was adopted within the framework of CIS in 1993, and provides legal guidelines for the formation of the common economic space envisaged in the Charter.[15] The CIS thus appear to provide for a degree of reintegration within significant parts of the borders of the former Soviet Union.[16]

6–005   Beyond the CIS the institutions which have developed in Europe, and which remain active today, can be broadly grouped according to whether the primary aims are of a general political character, or are limited to matters of economics, defence, security or others areas still. The first group covers the Council of Europe and institutions under its aegis; the second the OECD, the European Communities, NATO, Western European Union, OSCE and ESA amongst others. As will soon be apparent, these organisations can only be said to be political, economic or military by reference to their principal competence or purpose; many of their activities overlap into other fields, thus making the classification one of convenience for the purposes of presentation rather than one which is descriptively or normatively accurate.

A. Organisations of General Competence

(a) THE COUNCIL OF EUROPE

Bibliography: Robertson, *The Council of Europe. Its Structure, Functions and Achievements*, (2nd ed., 1961); Vasak, *Le Conseil de l'Europe* (1965); Bartsch, "Council of Europe—legal co-operation", 10 YEL 493 (1990); Burban, *Le Conseil de l'Europe* (1993) (2nd ed.). Website: http://www.coe.int.

---

[14] For more on this, see *infra*, Chap. 15. The CIS legal personality may be said to result, *e.g.* from the conclusion of an agreement with Czechoslovakia in 1992 (see David, *Droit des organisations internationales*, Vol. I (1998) 16; teaching materials for the Université Libre de Bruxelles).

[15] September 24, 1993; text in (1995) 34 ILM 1301.

[16] See, *e.g.* the introductory note to the Treaty on Creation of Economic Union by Khabarov in (1995) 34 ILM 1298.

The idea of the political unification of Europe is by no means of recent **6–006** origin, but in the recent past it has manifested itself in numerous national and international organisations sponsoring European unity, such as the United Europe Movement, the European Union of Federalists and the Economic League for European Co-operation. These combined in 1947 to form the "International Committee of the Movements for European Unity" which then organised a "Congress of Europe" at The Hague in May 1948. This whole development was non-governmental; that is to say, whilst many prominent statesmen participated in it, they did so as private individuals, not as state representatives. However, the resolution of the Hague Congress, expressing a desire for a "united Europe," stimulated governments into action. The Consultative Council of the Brussels Treaty Organisation, an organisation for collective self-defence set up in March 1948,[17] established a committee to study proposals for European unity. It was here that the basic features of the new political organisation were worked out before being submitted to a conference of ambassadors which included not only representatives of the Brussels Treaty Powers but also representatives from Ireland, Italy, Denmark, Norway and Sweden. A draft Statute of the Council of Europe emerged, to be signed by 10 countries on May 5, 1949.[18] The Statute represented a victory for those states which favoured a "functional" approach to unity as opposed to outright federation, namely, an approach based upon voluntary co-operation between states retaining their full, sovereign powers. Such co-operation would, however, extend into various sectors of their economy and of their social and cultural policies.

The membership of the organisation, which originally comprised 10 **6–007** countries, gradually extended to the whole of western Europe with the demise of the last southern European dictatorial regimes in the 1970s and later on to eastern Europe with the end of the Cold War at the end of the 1980s. Forty-one european countries are now members of the Council of Europe, and only a small number of states of the continent remain outside the system.[19] Adhesion to the European Convention on Human Rights and its supervisory mechanism, as well as the commitment to abolish the death penalty have more recently been set as express prerequisites for admission to the organisation.[20]

The aims of the Council, as set out in Article 1 of the Statute, are to **6–008** achieve a "greater unity between its members for the purposes of safeguarding and realising the ideals and principles which are their common

---

[17] See further *infra*, para. 6–064.
[18] 87 U.N.T.S. 103.
[19] The last member to be admitted was Georgia, in April 1999. In December 1999, the Federal Republic of Yugoslavia was still not a member of the Organisation.
[20] See the Vienna Declaration of October 9, 1993; text available at http://www.coe.fr/eng/std/viennad.htm.

heritage and facilitating their economic and social progress." This aim is to be pursued through the organs of the Council "by discussion of questions of common concern and by agreements and common action in economic, social, cultural, scientific, legal and administrative matters and in the maintenance and further realisation of human rights and fundamental freedoms." The aims are thus very broadly phrased, but it will be noted that the medium for achieving them is discussion and agreement; as we shall see when the organs are examined, the powers for the achievement of these aims are extremely limited. There is one broad exclusion from these aims: Article 1 (d) provides that "matters relating to National Defence do not fall within the scope of the Council of Europe." The exclusion is accounted for partly by the pre-existence of NATO, and partly by the fact that some "neutral" members like Ireland, Austria[21] and Sweden were not willing to participate in any military bloc.

6–009   The Organs of the Council are the Committee of Ministers and the Consultative Assembly. The latter introduced a quite novel form at the time whereby representation was of the parliaments of the members. Provision is made for a Secretariat to serve both organs, and this is very much modelled on the UN Secretariat, although the Council's Secretariat is not a "principal organ" and, surprisingly, the Statute says nothing of the powers of the Secretary-General. A Congress of Local and Regional Authorities of Europe subsequently added to this institutional structure.

(a) The Committee of Ministers

6–010   According to Article 14 of the Statute, the Committee of Ministers is composed of the Ministers for Foreign Affairs of the member states or alternates who shall be, wherever possible, members of their governments. From 1952 onwards the practice has developed, without any express authority in the Statute, of appointing "deputies" who are able to take decisions of the same force and effect as the Ministers themselves except on important questions of policy.[22] The scope of the functions of the Committee is very wide. Under Article 15:

"(a) On the recommendation of the Consultative Assembly or on its own initiative, the Committee of Ministers shall consider the action required to further the aim of the Council of Europe, including the conclusion of conventions or agreements and the adoption by Governments of a common policy with regard to particular matters. [. . .]

---

[21] Austria was merely an "observer" from 1952–56 and only thereafter became a full member following the Austrian State Treaty.

[22] These "deputies" are often the Permanent Representatives which members have accredited to the Council of Europe, similar to those accredited to the UN and fulfilling the role of an ambassador accredited to a foreign state in so far as they maintain permanent contact and liaison.

(b) In appropriate cases, the conclusions of the Committee may take the form of recommendations to the Governments of Members, and the Committee shall request the Governments of Members to inform it of the action taken by them with regard to such recommendations."

It is readily apparent that the Committee cannot take decisions binding **6–011** upon governments; its only power is to recommend matters to governments, so that it is in no sense an executive organ. Wide functions are combined here with extremely limited powers and the only power to take binding decisions relates solely to questions of internal organisation (Article 16). It is also true that in practice the initiative for such action as has been taken has come from the Assembly rather than from the Committee, indicating a lack of common political will amongst the members. Nevertheless, the Committee of Ministers plays an important role in the conclusion of conventions and agreements as well as, *inter alia*, in the supervision of the judgments of the European Court of Human Rights.[23] The Committee has an elaborate and well-developed structure of committees and subsidiary bodies of governmental experts, mostly established on a permanent basis and meeting regularly.

(b) The Consultative Assembly

The Assembly consists of 286 representatives, each member being repres- **6–012** ented by a number corresponding to its population size.[24] These representatives are generally elected by parliaments of members or otherwise appointed from among the members thereof (Article 25(a)). Representatives must be nationals of the member they represent, though not necessarily parliamentarians. In practice, however, they invariably are, and it is the intention that a given national delegation should represent the political balance of the parties within the national parliament. Representatives sit in personal alphabetical order, not in country delegations, and European political groups have formed which bring representatives together on a political rather than national basis.

The function of the Assembly is deliberative; Article 22 describes it as **6–013** the "deliberative" organ, with power to make recommendations to the Committee of Ministers upon any matter within the aim and scope of the organisation (see also Article 23(a)). The conclusions of the Assembly are presented to the Committee in the form of "recommendations," requiring a two-thirds majority vote, or of "resolutions" or "opinions" requiring a simple majority; "resolutions" can also be addressed directly to governments. The difference is largely one of terminology, although in general

---

[23] For more on this, see Art. 46 of the 1950 ECHR (as modified by Protocol 11).
[24] The number of representatives each member state is entitled to is given in Art. 26 of the Statute.

recommendations call for action by the Committee and resolutions do not, and opinions are given on questions referred to it by the Committee. The essential point is that they are all of a purely persuasive character; the Assembly cannot bind the Committee or any state by its actions, and thus, whilst its composition is reminiscent of a parliamentary body, it is very far indeed from being a true European Parliament with real legislative power.

6–014   Under Article 32 the Assembly is to meet annually, normally for not more than a month at a time; it presently holds four plenary sessions a year. The Assembly has its own elastic committee structure. The Standing Committee meets in between and during sessions, preparing the agenda and co-ordinating the work of other committees. There are also general (or permanent) committees covering matters such as Political Affairs, Economic Affairs and Development, Social and Health Questions, Legal Affairs, Culture and Education, Science and Technology, etc.; then there are ad hoc committees for special problems. These may all meet between sessions and thus provide continuity and preparation for the work of the Assembly.

6–015   The Statute contained little formal procedure for liaison between the Assembly and the Committee of Ministers: Article 19 demanded only an annual written report from the Committee to the Assembly containing a statement of its activities. This was supplemented in 1951 by the creation of a Joint Committee of up to 14 members, seven of them from the Assembly, in order to examine problems common to both organs[25]; it is essentially a liaison committee. The Joint Committee works most effectively at the "deputy" level, with the Assembly putting written questions to the deputies for answer.

6–016   The same Committee of Ministers' resolution of May 1951 also envisaged the creation of European specialised authorities with competence in the economic, social, cultural, legal, administrative and other related fields. These were to be linked to the Council of Europe in the same fashion as the specialised agencies are linked to the UN. Even though such European specialised authorities never came into being—the development of co-operation between European states in more specialised fields materialising within other institutional frameworks with the creation of the ECSC in 1951 and of the EEC and Euratom in 1957[26]—five "conferences" directly under the aegis of the Council of Europe have been established: the Conference of Local and Regional Authorities, the European Parliamentary and Scientific Conference, the Conference of Ministers of Education,

---

[25] See the resolution adopted by the Committee of Ministers at its 8th session in May 1951; text available on the Council of Europe's Website (http://www.coe.fr/eng/legaltxt/1e.htm).

[26] On these, see *infra*, paras 6–030, *et seq.*

the Conference of European Ministers of Justice and the Ministerial Conference on the Environment. The first of these has been turned into a full-fledged organ of the Council of Europe by a resolution adopted in 1994 by the Committee of Ministers.[27]

(c) The Congress of Local and Regional Authorities of Europe (CLRAE)

The CLRAE[28] is a consultative body representing local and regional **6–017** authorities. Its creation stems from the consideration that "one of the bases of a democratic society is the existence of a solid and effective local and regional democracy" and from the will to give those sub-state entities a voice in the institutional structure of the Council of Europe.[29] To that purpose, the CLRAE may "submit proposals to the Committee of Ministers in order to promote local and regional self-government" (Article 2, para. 1, b) and has to be consulted by the Committee and the Assembly "on issues which are likely to affect the responsibilities and essential interests of the local and regional authorities which the CLRAE represents" (Article 2, para. 2). Along the same lines as the Assembly, the Congress is composed of "representatives holding a local or regional authority electoral mandate or a mandate as a person directly responsible to an elected local or regional body," each member state having the same number of seats as it has in the Parliamentary Assembly (Article 3, para. 2). It comprises two Chambers: the Chamber of Local Authorities and the Chamber of Regions (Article 4, para. 2). Here too, a Standing Committee is responsible for ensuring the continuity of the work of the organ and for acting on its behalf between sessions, which are held once a year.

It should finally be noted that another institutional development took **6–018** place on an informal basis (*i.e.* without any modification of the Statute) during the 1990s with the organisation of summits of heads of states and governments of the participating countries. Two such summits were held in 1993 and 1997, fixing the general lines of action of the Council of Europe, giving it thereby a new political impetus.

(d) The European Conventions

Quite apart from engendering a habit of co-operation and greater mutual **6–019** understanding between the member states, work of a more tangible nature has been accomplished by the Council of Europe. This work is seen particularly in the conclusion of various conventions. Since its inception, the Council of Europe has produced an important number of conventions,

---

[27] Statutory resolution (94) 3 of January 14, 1994; see now resolution (2000)1 of March 15, 2000.
[28] See http://www.coe.fr/cplre.
[29] See the preamble of the resolution.

agreements and protocols.[30] The most important is the European Convention for the Protection of Human Rights and Fundamental Freedoms, concluded on November 4, 1950, which has been supplemented by 11 Protocols. This really attempts to amplify the conditions of membership set out in Article 3 of the Statute. It sets out a number of individual rights and establishes a Court, to which there is a right of individual petition.[31] Other instruments worthy of mention include the 1961 European Social Charter, the 1955 Convention on Establishment,[32] the 1957 Convention on Extradition,[33] the 1977 Convention on the Suppression of Terrorism,[34] the 1985 Charter of Local Self-Government,[35] the 1987 Convention for the Prevention of Torture,[36] the 1989 Convention on Transfrontier Television [37] or the 1995 Framework-Convention for the Protection of National Minorities.[38] There are also conventions dealing with the exchange of blood plasma, television films, compulsory insurance against civil liability in respect of motor vehicles, mutual assistance in crime detection, insider trading and the abolition of visas for refugees, for example. The broad character of the issues dealt with in these instruments reflects the fact that the Council of Europe is an organisation of general competence.

(e) Relationships with other bodies

6–020   The Council of Europe has relationships with other international organisations with a view to co-ordination of their activities. Agreements have been concluded with the UN, the ILO, WHO, UNESCO, FAO and several European organisations, providing for reciprocal communication of matters of common interest, consultation, and attendance at meetings by observers; certain of the specialised agencies transmit their annual reports to the Council. Not surprisingly, relationships with the European organisations tend to be closer. With OECD the arrangements provided for permanent liaison committees and the economic reports of OECD provide the basis for the Council's debates on economic affairs. With Western European Union, the Council has virtually taken over much of its cultural work and the Assembly of the Union is, by the treaty establishing the Union, to be composed of two-thirds of the members of the Consultative Assembly; thus the principle of identity of membership is adhered to and provides an effective safeguard against unnecessary overlapping. The Council of Europe also works in close co-operation with the European Union and the OSCE.[39]

---

[30] As of November 1999, 174 Conventions had been adopted under the Organisation's auspices.

[31] For more on this, see *infra*, Chap. 13, paras 13–062 *et seq.*

[32] *European Treaty Series*, no. 19.

[33] *ibid.*, no. 24

[34] *ibid.*, no. 90

[35] *ibid.*, no. 122.

[36] *ibid.*, no. 126.

[37] *ibid.*, no. 132.

[38] *ibid.*, no. 157.

[39] On these organisations see *infra*, at paras 6–030 *et seq.* and 6–084 *et seq.*, respectively.

B. Organisations of Limited Competence

(a) ECONOMIC

1. The Organisation for Economic Co-operation and Development (OECD)

Bibliography: Hahn, "Die Organisation für wirtschaftliche Zusammenarbeit und Entwicklung (OECD)," (1962) 22 Z.f.a.ö.r.u.v. 49; Miller, "The OECD" (1963) Y.B.W.A. 80–95; J. Szuldrzynski, "Legal Aspects of OEEC" (1953) 2 ICLQ 579. Website: http://www.oecd.org.

It may be recalled that by a Convention of April 16, 1948,[40] the OEEC **6–021** was established to administer, in conjunction with the American Economic Co-operation Administration (ECA), the aid provided by the United States to European countries within the framework of the Marshal Plan as part of the efforts towards the reconstruction of Europe after the Second World War. The organisation was open to "any signatory European country" (Article 25), although in fact it became very much a Western European Organisation since the USSR, Poland and Czechoslovakia declined to participate. Twelve years later, with the economic recovery of Europe virtually completed, the decision was taken to reconstitute the organisation as the Organisation for Economic Co-operation and Development. This reconstitution was accomplished by the treaty of December 14, 1960.[41] The membership of OECD is wider than in OEEC; according to Article 16 it is open to "any Government" by unanimous invitation of the Council; the OECD now has 29 members, including countries such as Australia, New Zealand, Canada, Japan, the USA, Mexico and Korea.[42] To this extent it becomes somewhat artificial to treat OECD within the "European Organisations," but its links with OEEC and its predominantly European character justify this course.

The aims of the new organisation were necessarily changed to reflect the **6–022** change in purpose from one of restoration of the European economy to maintenance of economic growth and the promotion of economic development both within and beyond the territories of the members themselves. OECD's purposes are "to achieve the highest sustainable economic growth and employment and a rising standard of living in Member countries . . . and thus to contribute to the development of the world economy;" to "contribute to sound economic expansion in Member as well as non-member countries . . .;" and "to contribute to the expansion of world trade

---

[40] 888 U.N.T.S. 141.

[41] 888 U.N.T.S. 179. For an excellent general commentary see Hahn, "Die Organisation für wirtschaftliche Zusammenarbeit und Entwicklung" (1962) 22 Z.a.ö.R.V. 49.

[42] It should also be mentioned that a group of Eastern European states became members of the organisation in 1995–96 (Hungary, Poland, the Czech Republic).

on a multilateral, non-discriminatory basis" (Article 1). The aims are therefore no longer European, but global. To this end the members undertake obligations with regard to efficient use of economic resources, development of these resources and research, the pursuit of policies to achieve growth and stability without endangering the economy of others, the pursuit of efforts to minimise trade barriers and payments difficulties, and contribution to general economic development in member and non-member countries (Article 2). The OECD emerges mostly, as we shall see, as a forum for discussion and consultation, as well as collection and exchange of information between member states in the economic field. Negotiations within the framework of the organisation have also led to the adoption of a number of multilateral conventions dealing with various economic topics.[43] Over the years, the OECD has become one of the strongest advocates of market economy on the world stage.[44] The organisational structure established for these purposes is essentially a medium for co-operation between members; the French desire in 1948 for a "stronger" institution was opposed by the United Kingdom and, thus, there was, and still is, nothing of a "supra-national" element and action rests with the members on a voluntary basis. The organs of the OECD are the Council, the Committees and the Secretariat.

(a) The Council

6–023 This, the principal organ, comprises all the members and is "the body from which all acts of the Organisation derive" (Article 7). The Council develops directives on the work to be undertaken and sets priorities for the activities of the organisation. Representatives meet at the level of Ministers (once a year) or of Permanent Representatives. Under Article 6, decisions and recommendations are by unanimity, unless otherwise agreed for special cases, and it is expressly provided that the abstention of any member will not invalidate decisions or prevent them from becoming binding on other members; for this reason the unanimity rule has never developed into a "veto," for states in opposition to a resolution have simply abstained. Decisions are therefore binding only upon the members which have voted for them, once they have complied with their own constitutional procedures (Article 6, para. 3). Each state has one vote. The OECD may thus influence in a significant way the options taken by the member states in the economic field but it must be

---

[43] See, *e.g.* the 1997 Convention on Combating Bribery of Foreign Public Officials in International Business Transactions, (1998) 37 ILM 1. and the much debated project of Multilateral Investments Agreement.

[44] Attempts to promote strong liberal policies amongst other groups of countries have nevertheless not always proved very successful, as shows particularly the demise of the Multilateral Agreements on Investment originally drafted by the Organisation in 1995. For more on this, see, *e.g.* the 1998 special issue (No. 3) of the *Cornell International Law Journal* (Vol. 31) and Baumgartner, "The Demise of the Multilateral Agreement on Investment" (1999) Col. J. Int'l Envt'l. L. & Pol'y 1998 Y.B. 40.

noted that this is at least as much the result of group dynamics ("peer pressure") resulting from the adoption of recommendations or even expert reports concerning the economic situation of one particular member [45] as the effect of legally binding decisions taken by the Council.

(b) The Committees

The OECD has in fact over 200 specialised committees and working **6–024** groups which are competent in particular areas coming under the general competence of the organisation. The Development Assistance Committee, for example, is amongst the better known, setting a number of objectives to be reached by member states as far as development co-operation is concerned.[46] These committees are composed of experts and specialists representing member states (such as administration officials) and provide fora for consultation between members on the topics dealt with by the committees, which in turn contributes to the shaping of policies of member states in those fields. The role of committees further illustrates the role of the OECD as a pre-eminently functional organisation which collects and collates data and studies questions of common concern to the members which, by and large, adhere to systems reflecting similar economic and social values.

(c) The Secretariat

The OECD's Secretariat is essentially similar to the UN Secretariat. **6–025** Because of the rather specialised, economic character of the work, it tends nevertheless to employ more personnel on secondment from industry, the universities and government departments. One of its main task is indeed to research, compile and analyse information in the economic field, which will in turn be fed to the committees and made available to the member states. It is headed by a Secretary-General with somewhat lesser powers than those of the UN Secretary-General, but with the important power of being able to submit his or her own proposals to the Council or any other body of the organisation (Article 10, para. 2). The OECD also has its own administrative tribunal for disputes between the staff of the Secretariat and the organisation.

(d) De-centralisation of the functions of the organisation

The variety of economic problems with which OEEC, and later the OECD, **6–026** concerned itself meant that considerable de-centralisation was essential, involving the creation of a number of operating agencies. These agencies

---

[45] On this, see *infra*, at para. 6–029.

[46] One may also mention, for example, the Economic Policy Committee, the Economic and Development Review Committee, the Technical Co-operation Committee, Trade Committee, Payments Committee, Committee on Agriculture and Fisheries, Committee for Invisible Transactions, and other committees dealing with Insurance, Energy and Industry, Tourism, Maritime Transport, Manpower, Fiscal Matters, Scientific and Technical Personnel and Scientific Research, Consumer Policies, Environment, Restrictive Business Practices, and Multinational Enterprises.

are distinct from the organisation's own organs, as each is endowed with its own institutional structure, but related to them in varying degrees. Three of these agencies are still active, and even if they are linked to the OECD their resepctive membership differs. The Nuclear Energy Agency,[47] first established in December 1957 by the Council of OEEC and equipped with similar functions to Euratom which had been set up shortly before.[48] The Agency is operated by the Council's own Steering Committee for Nuclear Energy, created in 1956.[49] In the same field, the OECD Council also approved a Convention on the Establishment of a Security Control in the Field of Nuclear Energy, which was signed on December 20, 1957,[50] to ensure the restriction of the joint enterprises envisaged, and their products, to non-military purposes. The Convention gives considerable powers of inspection and control to a Control Bureau, composed of one representative from each state. It also establishes a Tribunal to adjudicate on questions of default, which has never been utilised. Another unusual venture in this field, which is worthy of mention, was the formation under a treaty and as a "joint undertaking" of the European Nuclear Agency of an international company, Eurochemic, by 12 OEEC countries in the same month;[51] this company built and operated a plant processing irradiated fuel until it ceased operations in 1974.[52]

6–027　A further offshoot from OEEC, in the sense that it began from the initiative of the OEEC Council, is the European Conference of Ministers of Transport, created by a Protocol signed at Brussels on October 17, 1953. This body kept on functioning within the framework of OECD. Its chief aim is the rationalisation and integration of the enlarged European transport system.

6–028　The third autonomous body still active today is the International Energy Agency (IEA) which was set up by the Council in 1974 to develop co-operation on energy questions following the oil crisis of 1973.[53] Its programme includes the promotion of rational energy policies and the improvement of the world's energy supply by the development of alternative energy sources.

---

[47] Not to be confused with the European Organisation for Nuclear Research (CERN), established by treaty of July 1, 1953, for the purpose of collaboration in research and consisting of a Council and Director; CERN is linked very loosely with UNESCO. The statute of the Nuclear Energy Agency can be found in V European Yearbook 273.

[48] For more on this, see *infra* at section 2. The 1957 Treaty was replaced by a Treaty of 1972 on the adhesion of Japan.

[49] See Arts 12 *et seq.* of the NEA Statute.

[50] V *European Yearbook* 283.

[51] Treaty of December 20, 1957, *ibid.*, 303.

[52] Eurochemic was finally wound up in 1990; for more on this, see Strohl, "Les aspects internationaux de la liquidation de la Société Eurochemic" (1990) 36 AFDI 727.

[53] Agreement of November 18, 1974, (1975) 14 ILM 1.

An assessment of the work of OECD, and even a proper description of **6–029** its activities, is probably more a task for the economist than for the lawyer. It is nevertheless apparent, as far as the legal approach is concerned, that certain institutional techniques have developed which have made the organisation a more effective body than a literal reading of its powers might suggest. It is an organisation based wholly on voluntary co-operation by states, with little if any enforcement or "sanctioning" power. However, by a variety of techniques, including the use of small groups of technical experts, the use of questionnaire, analysis of the replies of states and "confrontation" within the committees, that is to say cross-examination of state representatives on those replies, the organisation has been able to impose a general standard of concurrence in its activities which is not without its impressive qualities.

2. The European Union and the European Communities: the European Coal and Steel Community (ECSC), the European Community (EC) and the European Atomic Energy Community (Euratom)

Bibliography: Reuter, *La Communauté européenne du charbon et de l'acier* (1953); Efron and Nanes, "The Common Market and Euratom Treaties: Supranationality and the Integration of Europe" (1957) 6 ICLQ 670; Polach, *Euratom: Its Background, Issues and Economic Implications* (1964); Lasok and Bridge, *Law and Institutions of the European Communities* (5th ed., 1991); Schermers and Waelbroeck, *Judicial Protection in the European Communities* (5th ed., 1992); Louis, *The Community Legal Order* (3rd ed., 1995); Kapteyn and Verloren Van Themaat, *Introduction to the Law of the European Communities* (3rd ed., Gormley ed., 1998); Steiner and Woods, *Textbook on EC Law* (6th ed., 1998); T. Hartley, *The Foundations of European Community Law* (1998, 4th ed); Hartley, *Constitutional Problems of the European Union* (1999). Website: http://www.europa.eu.int.

(a) The Aims of the Communities

For six states of Europe—France, Germany, Italy, the Netherlands, **6–030** Belgium and Luxembourg—the Council of Europe and OEEC were insufficiently ambitious. They accordingly sought means to achieve a closer economic (and possibly, at a later stage, political) integration. The first step was the creation of the European Coal and Steel Community (ECSC) by the Treaty of April 18, 1951.[54] Coal and steel were considered strategically important products since they constituted an essential basis of war industries at the time. Hence, the creation of European institutions vested with substantial regulatory powers in that field was seen as another guarantee for the preservation of peace in post Second World War Europe by integrating coal and steel industries. ECSC had as its objective the creation of a single market for coal, iron and steel, involving the elimination of all barriers to free, competitive trading such as tariff barriers, quota systems,

---

[54] 261 U.N.T.S. 141.

all forms of price discrimination (including those in transport), restrictive agreements and cartels. ECSC has virtually achieved its objective of creating a single market; nevertheless, the diminishing use of coal as a source of energy is one of the factors that will lead to the disappearance of this organisation at the beginning of the new millennium.[55] A second, but abortive, step was the attempt in 1954 to create a European Defence Community (EDC), which failed because of the French opposition to the transfer of the exercise of sovereign powers to an international organisation in that field. A third step was successfully taken, however, by the conclusion of the Rome Treaties in March 1957. These created two new institutions: the European Economic Community (EEC)[56] and the European Atomic Energy Community (Euratom).[57] The six initial member states of the three Communities were joined by Denmark, Ireland and the United Kingdom in 1973,[58] by Greece in 1981,[59] by Portugal and Spain in 1986[60] and by Austria, Finland and Sweden in 1995.[61] Further enlargement of the organisation is considered, talks being under way in that perspective with several countries of the Mediterranean basin and of central and eastern Europe.[62]

6–031   The essential aim of the EEC was to establish in three stages, over a transitional 12 to 15-year period, a "common market" in which all internal tariffs, quota restrictions, etc., would be eliminated and a uniform external tariff created.[63] Incidental to this main aim was the promotion of the free movement of labour and capital, the adoption of a common transport policy, control of cartels, the establishment of a European Investment Bank[64] and a European Social Fund. The latter was to contribute to the raising of the standard of living of workers and to assist in the retraining and resettlement of workers facing unemployment due to the conversion of their industries. Agricultural commodities were included in the scheme, albeit under a special regime envisaging price control and the gradual evolution of a common agricultural policy.[65] The approximation of national

---

[55] The Treaty of Paris expires in 2002; coal and steel will by then become two of the many areas covered by the Treaty of Rome.

[56] 298 U.N.T.S. 11.

[57] 298 U.N.T.S. 167.

[58] See Treaty of Accession of January 22, 1972, [1972] O.J. L73/5.

[59] See Treaty of Accession of May 28, 1979, [1979] O.J. L291.

[60] See Treaty of Accession of June 12, 1985, [1985] O.J. L302.

[61] See Treaty of Accession of January 1, 1995, [1995] O.J. L1.

[62] On this, and on the previous enlargements, see, *e.g.* Preston, *Enlargement and Integration in the European Union* (1997) and Curzon Price, Landau and Whitman (eds.), *The Enlargement of the European Union* (1999).

[63] For the legal aspects, see, *e.g.* Lasok, *The Trade and Customs Law of the European Union*, (3rd ed., 1998).

[64] This has a capital of $2,025 million, its own Board of Governors, Board of Directors and Management Committee; it gives or guarantees loans to members or to public or private enterprises to assist investment projects.

[65] For more on this, see *e.g.* Barents, *The Agricultural Law of the EC* (1994).

laws in various fields where such harmonisation was considered necessary in order to establish a common market (taxation being a classical illustration) also constituted one of the objectives of the EEC.

The Treaty of Rome has been significantly amended on three occasions. **6–032** Changes were introduced to the institutional structure of the community, but also to the definition of its scope of activities and competences, which underwent a deep evolution.[66] The 1986 Single European Act provided for new powers for the EEC, *e.g.* in the fields of environment or of research and development, and attempted to create a framework for a common foreign policy of the member states. The 1992 Maastricht Treaty on the European Union, which came into force in 1993 after approval by the national parliaments or through national referendums, introduced even more significant changes.[67] First of all, it amends the Treaty of Rome, which is re-named "Treaty establishing the European Community", confirming thereby the fact that the organisation's activities formally extend far beyond economics.[68] The Community is, amongst others, given competence—although not exclusive competence—in the fields of education (Article 126), culture (Article 128), public health (Article 129), consumer protection (Article 129a) and development co-operation (Article 130u). This extension of powers is balanced by the introduction of the principle of subsidiarity as a general principle of Community law,[69] according to which

"In areas which do not fall within its exclusive competence, the Community shall take action [. . .] only if and in so far as the objectives of the proposed action cannot be sufficiently achieved by the Member States and can therefore, by reason of the scale or effects of the proposed action, be better achieved by the Community"
(Article 5 of the consolidated version of the Treaty establishing the European Community).

Some kind of "efficiency principle"—which is at the same time protective **6–033** of the member states' sovereignty—is hereby introduced. Action by the community in fields of shared competences will not be the rule and will only take place when it is shown to be more effective than individual or collective action by member states due to the scale of the action to be undertaken.[70]

---

[66] See generally Pinder, *The Building of the European Union* (3rd ed., 1998).

[67] Text in (1992) 31 ILM 247.

[68] The Treaty of Maastricht also amends, although in a less significant way, the Treaties establishing ECSC and Euratom.

[69] Previously the subsidiarity principle had applied only in the environmental field.

[70] The subsidiarity principle being enshrined in the revised Treaty of Rome, its application is subject to judiciary review, and the forthcoming jurisprudence of the Court of Justice will certainly help to ascertain its scope and meaning with greater precision. For more on subsidiarity, see *e.g.* Vause, "The Subsidiarity Principle in European Union Law—American Federalism Compared" (1995) 27 Case W. Res. J.I L.61.

6–034   Beyond these amendments to the 1951 and 1957 Treaties,[71] the Treaty of Maastricht provides for the creation of a new entity—the European Union—which is superimposed over the existing structure. The Union is "founded on the European Communities, supplemented by the policies and forms of co-operation established by this Treaty. Its task shall be to organise, in a manner demonstrating consistency and solidarity, relations between the Member States and between their peoples" (Article A). It is based on three "pillars": the *first* one relates to co-operation in the economic, social and monetary fields, which remain the task of the European Community; the *second* relates to co-operation on justice and home affairs; and the *third* relates to the development and implementation of a common foreign and security policy, which may eventually lead to a common defence.[72] These last two are independent from the original Treaty of Rome framework and do not therefore constitute Community law, one of the consequences being that actions taken in those areas are not subject to judicial review by the Court of Justice.[73] The Maastricht Treaty is supplemented by a Protocol and an Agreement on Social Policy to which all the member states are now parties.[74] The Agreement states that "the Community and the Member States shall have as their objectives the promotion of employment, improved living and working conditions [. . .] and the combating of exclusion" (Article 1) and gives further powers to the Community in the field of social protection (Article 2). The Community remains the core organisation of the Union, which is not (up to now, at least) endowed with a separate legal personality.[75] This whole corpus was further amended in 1997 by the Treaty of Amsterdam which provides for new substantive and procedural evolutions, and incidentally also completely renumbers the articles of the previous Treaties. This came into force in 1999.[76] The three pillar structure is maintained and their respective contents strengthened. Hence, Community competence is to be extended to the field of visa, asylum and immigration policies (Title IV), while a new title on employment is included in the Treaty, laying new responsibilities

---

[71] Other innovations yet could be mentioned, such as the creation of a citizenship of the European Union (Art. 8 of the revised Treaty of Rome); on this, see *e.g.* O'Leary, *The Evolving Concept of Community Citizenship* (1996).

[72] On this, see, *e.g.* Part One of Koskenniemi (ed.), *International Law Aspects of the European Union* (1998).

[73] For more on this, see *infra*, Chap. 13.

[74] The U.K. did not originally sign up. It became a party to those instruments in 1997.

[75] On this, see, *e.g.* Klabbers, "Presumptive Personality: The European Union in International Law" in *International Law Aspects of the European Union* (Koskenniemi ed., 1998), pp. 231–253. The Community's legal personality, on the other hand, is provided for by Art. 281 of the revised Treaty of Rome. On the inferences that may be drawn from the limited treaty-making power attributed to the E.U. by Article 24 of the Amsterdam Treaty, see also the prudent conclusions of Hafner, "The Amsterdam Treaty and the Treaty-Making Power of the European Union: Some Critical Comments", in *Liber Amicorum Professor Seidl-Hohenveldern in Honour of His 80th Birthday* (1998), 283–4.

[76] Text in (1998) 37 I.L.M. 56.

upon the community (Title VII). A stronger emphasis is also put on rights and freedoms, and on democratic principles.[77]

Most of the aims set by the treaties have gradually been achieved. A **6–035** customs union for all industrial products, and therefore a common external tariff, came into effect on July 1, 1968. On the same date free trade for nearly all agricultural products came into effect. The disappearance of internal borders and the creation of the internal market have been completed to a large extent. Free movement of persons, and freedom of establishment, have also been achieved.[78] The next step in the integration process will be the establishment of a European monetary union which will be completed in 2002 with the introduction in 12 of the 15 members of the new European single currency, the Euro.[79] Progress has, up to now, been significantly slower, though, in fields such as social policy, foreign policy and defence. Attempts by the European Union to play a role in the settlement of local or regional crises, such as in ex-Yugoslavia, have up to now not proven successful.[80] Overseas territories were associated with EEC by decision of the Council, thus enabling any member to invest in and trade in such territories on the same conditions as the parent country. With the advent of independence for many of these overseas territories a more formal Association Agreement was concluded at Yaounde with 18 African states—mostly of West Africa—in 1963 and revised in 1969. The Arusha Agreement was concluded in 1969 in order to extend the co-operation to East African states. The Yaounde Convention and the Arusha Agreement were then replaced by the Lome Convention of 1975 between the European Communities and 46 African, Caribbean and Pacific States (the ACP States). It accommodates the states newly-associated with the Communities as a result of the United Kingdom's accession in 1973 and has since been further extended and now applies to 70 developing countries. A new Lome II Convention of October 31, 1979[81] provide for tariff-free entry into the Community of ACP exports, without reciprocity, and a scheme to stabilise

---

[77] See, *e.g.* Arts 6, 7 and 49 of the consolidated version of the Treaty establishing the E.U.

[78] A separate international agreement which is not part of Community law, the Schengen Accord was concluded in 1990 between all member states, except Denmark, Ireland and the U.K., providing for the modalities of control over movements of persons through internal and external borders. It came into force in 1994 and was integrated in the European Union legal framework by the second Protocol to the Treaty of Amsterdam.

[79] See Title VII of the consolidated version of the Treaty establishing the European Community. Denmark and the U.K. have decided not to participate in the monetary union for the time being; Greece, which had initially not met the criteria set for being part of the monetary union, joined in 2000. For more on the monetary union, see, *e.g.* Andenas *et al.* (eds.), *European Economic and Monetary Union: The Institutional Framework* (1997); Temperton (ed.), *The Euro* (2nd ed., 1998); Beaumont and Walker (eds.), *Legal Framework of the Single European Currency* (1999).

[80] On the implication of the Union in the follow-up of some aspects of the Yugoslavian crisis, see, however, Pagani, "L'administration de Mostar par l'Union Européenne" (1996) 42 AFDI 234.

[81] Text in 1278 U.N.T.S. 3.

export earnings from commodities produced by the ACP states called STABEX.[82] Associated territories and states also benefit from Development Funds set up by the successive Lome Conventions. The Funds are the main financial tool for co-operation; the sums made available within the framework of the eighth Development Fund (the endowment of which was agreed upon in 1995) amounted to 13,3 billion ECUs.[83] The co-operation between ACP states and the community was continued through the extension of the Lome Convention, up to this day.[84] A new ACP-EC Convention has been concluded in Cotonon in 2000, and keeps the same features, during an initial five-year transitional period at least.[85] The future of the elements which make the originality and interest of the system (STABEX and SYSMIN) nevertheless appears uncertain, since their compatibility with the rules of international trade has lately been called into question on several occasions.[86] The community also concluded association agreements with various countries of the Mediterranean basin, Asia and Latin America (including, in this case, "block-to-block" co-operation, as is evidenced by the EC-Mercosur agreement of 1995,[87]) as well as, more recently, of eastern and central Europe.[88]

6–036   Although the creation of a customs union lay at the root of the ideas behind the Rome Treaty, it was apparent that, in the first stages, it did not create such a union. France, particularly, regarded it as premature to take that step at an early stage. However, the treaty did not prevent particular members from establishing a customs union *inter se*, and this has in fact been done in the treaty by which Belgium, Netherlands and Luxembourg instituted the Benelux Economic Union of February 3, 1958.[89] The Benelux Treaty also set up a Committee of Ministers, a Consultative Interparliamentary Council, a Council of the Economic Union, a College of Arbitra-

---

[82] See Simmonds, "The Lome Convention and the New International Economic Order" (1976) 13 C.M.L. Rev. 315–334; Simmonds, "The Second Lome Convention: the Innovative Features" (1980) 17 C.M.L. Rev. 415–436.

[83] (1995) 99 RGDIP. 965; on the Fund, see, generally, Ndoung, *L'évolution du Fonds européen de développement prévu par les Conventions de Yaoundé et Lomé* (1994).

[84] Lome III (1985) and Lome IV (1990, revised in 1995); see generally Maganza, "La Convention de Lomé" in *Le Droit de la Communauté Économique Européenne: vol. 13* (Megret ed., 1990).

[85] See (1998) 102 RGDIP 1059. See also McMahon, "Negotiating in a Time of Turbulent Transition: The Future of Lomé" (1999) 36 C.M.L.R. 599.

[86] See, *e.g.* the "banana war" which put the USA against the Community and the report of the World Trade Organisation's Appellate Body in this matter (Doc. WT/DS27/AB/R of September 9, 1997).

[87] [1996] O.J. L69/13. For more on the Mercosur, see *infra*, Chap. 7.

[88] See, *e.g.* the Agreements concluded with Hungary in 1991 (O.J. L347/1 of December 31, 1991), or with Latvia (COM (92) 176 final), Estonia (COM (92) 177 final) and Lithuania (COM (92) 179 final) in 1992. On the E.C. and E.U. external relations generally, see for instance Piening, *Global Europe: The European Union in World Affairs* (1997) and Koskenniemi (ed.), *International Law Aspects of the European Union* (1998).

[89] V European Yearbook 167. A description of Benelux can be found in Van der Meersch, *Organisations Européennes* (1966), pp. 419–451.

tors, an Economic and Social Advisory Council and various committees. A Benelux Court of Justice was added in 1965, consisting of nine judges, whose task is to promote uniformity in the application of legal rules specified either in conventions or in decisions of the Committee of Ministers. The Court has both a contentious and an advisory jurisdiction. The College of Arbitrators must suspend its own function of settling differences in any case where a matter of interpretation of such rules arises, pending a decision of the Court.[90]

The European Atomic Energy Community (EURATOM) is very much **6–037** the twin of the EEC, although confined to a narrower field of operation. The aim of the community, as defined in Article 1 of the 1957 constitutive Treaty,[91] is to contribute to the raising of the standard of living in the member states and to the development of commercial exchanges with other countries by creating the conditions necessary for the speedy establishment and growth of nuclear industries. Its functions (Article 2) include the creation of a common market for specialised materials and equipment, investment, development of research and dissemination of information, establishing standards for the protection of public health, the supply of ores and nuclear fuels, ownership of special fissionable materials, co-operation with other countries and organisations for the peaceful use of nuclear energy and security control.

Certain of the powers may be mentioned by way of illustration of the **6–038** extent to which the community has gone beyond mere co-operation and adopted measures unknown in international organisations outside the European Communities. The community has a right of access to nuclear installations in member states (Article 81), it may discuss investment programmes directly with individuals or firms (Article 43), it has the exclusive right to purchase nuclear materials from outside the community (Article 64), the option to purchase all materials produced within it (Articles 57 *et seq.*), and an exclusive right to export such materials (Articles 59 and 62). The Council of EURATOM may, by unanimous vote, fix prices (Article 69). Special fissile materials, whether produced in or imported by member states, automatically become the property of the community (Article 86). The control system, designed to ensure that nuclear materials are used for the intended purpose and not, for example, for military purposes, includes a right in the Commission to demand the production of operating records and the deposit of any excess of special fissionable materials with the Agency (the supply organ of Euratom) (Article 79). The

---

[90] *XIII European Yearbook* 259.
[91] 298 U.N.T.S. 172. The original treaty was amended in 1992 by Title IV of the Maastricht Treaty. The amendments mostly bring changes to the institutional structure of Euratom, parallel to those brought to the EEC's.

Commission may also, after consultations, send inspectors into the territories of the member states, and these shall have access at all times "to all places and data and to any person who by reason of his occupation deals with materials, equipment or facilities. . ." (Article 81).

6–039 EURATOM is, therefore, entrusted with far wider powers than the European Nuclear Energy Agency established by the Council of OEEC in December 1957;[92] the latter is, true to the OECD pattern, essentially an organisation of voluntary co-operation with no "supra-national" element. EURATOM is also to be distinguished from CERN, the European Organisation for Nuclear Research which originated from UNESCO's initiative and is based on a treaty of July 1, 1953.[93] This is, equally, an organisation through which a number of European states have collaborated to conduct research of a kind which is too costly for individual states to contemplate.

(b) The Institutions of the Communities

6–040 Although the three communities were established as separate organisations, based upon separate treaties, their institutional structure was almost uniform. This, together with the obvious need to co-ordinate the overall economic planning of the three, suggested the desirability of common organs, namely the Council, Commission and Parliament originally established by each treaty. Accordingly, simultaneously with the conclusion of the Rome Treaties establishing EEC and Euratom, a "Convention relating to certain institutions common to the European Communities" was concluded providing for a single Court to replace the ECSC Court.[94] The same Convention also provided for one Assembly for all three organisations, to be called the European Parliamentary Assembly. However, it was not until July 1, 1967 that it became possible to merge the executive organs of the three communities, namely the three councils into one council and the three commissions (actually called "High Authority" in ECSC) into one commission.[95] In addition to introducing the abovementioned developments in substantive community law, the 1992 Maastricht Treaty also provided for the creation of a new institution, the European Central Bank, the task of which is to implement the new European monetary policy.[96] The main

---

[92] See *supra*, para. 6–026.
[93] 200 U.N.T.S. 149.
[94] 298 U.N.T.S. 267.
[95] See Treaty Establishing a Single Council and a Single Commission of the European Communities, XIII European Yearbook 461: the Treaty is dated April 8, 1965, but came into force in 1967. For commentary see Houben, "The Merger of the Executives of the European Communities" (1965–66) 3 C.M.L. Rev. 37; Weil, "The Merger of the Institutions of the European Communities" (1967) 61 A.J.I.L. 57.
[96] For more on this, see *e.g.* Brentford, "Constitutional Aspects of the Independence of the European Central Bank" (1998) 47 ICLQ 75.

features of today's institutions—the Council, the Commission, the European Parliament, the Court of Justice and the Court of Auditors—will be presented in the following pages. It is important to note that as these various institutions are technically organs of different international organisations, their powers and competences will vary according to the treaty from which those derive and under which the institutions act in each specific situation. However, whether they act as organs of the ECSC, Euratom or the E.C., a common feature of their "executive" organ is the substantive degree of normative power with which they are entrusted, as described below.[97]

The Council. The Council consists of representatives of each member state, **6–041** with equality of representation—one representative each: the Minister attending depends on the subject-matter being discussed in the meeting (fisheries, agriculture, industry, etc.). Meetings, to be held on the initiative of the President (an office rotating among the member states at six-monthly intervals) or upon the request of a member or of the Commission, will normally be preceded by a preparatory meeting of the Committee of Permanent Representatives (COREPER) to prepare the work of the Council.[98] The main function of the Council under the E.C. Treaty is "to ensure the co-ordination of the general economic policies of the Member States" and it has power to take decisions to that end (Article 202). According to the Treaty, decisions taken by the Council are generally based upon proposals or recommendations made by the Commission and are, in some instances, to be approved by the Parliament.[99] The voting procedure of the Council depends upon the Treaty under which it acts and on the specific procedure required for the specific action taken. The general rule under the current Treaty establishing the European Community is majority voting (Article 205).[1] The Treaty nevertheless provides for decision-making by a qualified majority—for the calculation of which votes of the members are weighted, the largest states having 10 votes each and the smallest having two votes each[2]—in a number of areas (agriculture, competition, environ-

---

[97] See *infra*, Chap. 11. On this issue, see generally Craig and Harlow (eds.), *Lawmaking in the European Union* (1998).

[98] See Arts 203–207.

[99] See *infra.*, para. 6–050.

[1] It must be noted that, under the EEC Treaty, as part of the transition from the second to the third stage on January 1, 1966 the changes in voting in the Council gave rise to serious disputes between France and the other five members. A French six-months boycott of the Council ended after a compromise was reached, which provided that "Where, in the case of decisions which may be taken by majority vote on a proposal of the Commission, very important interests of one or more partners are at stake, the members of the Council will endeavor, within a reasonable time, to reach solutions which can be adopted by all the members of the Council while respecting their mutual interests and those of the Community . . ." (text in (1965–66) 3 C.M.L.R. 469). The whole controversy was symptomatic of the growing French emphasis on sovereignty and a distrust of a powerful Commission.

[2] The number of votes for each member state is specified in Art. 205.

ment, amongst others) and by unanimity in others areas (*e.g.* taxation, finances, appointments, admission of new members). A "qualified majority" is constituted by 62 votes (out of a total of 87), and, in the case of a decision on a proposal by the Commission, any 62 will suffice. In other cases the 62 votes must include those of at least ten members. A decision which constitutes an amendment of a proposal by the Commission must be taken unanimously, otherwise the proposal must be referred back to the Commission (Article 250). It is in this provision that considerable power is given to the Commission, as indicated below, for its views will prevail unless there is unanimity in the Council, or the Council is prepared to leave the problem unsolved.

6–042 So far as the actual powers of the Council are concerned, these of course vary with each Treaty, but in effect the Council expresses the political will of the members and exercises a legislative or regulatory function. In general terms, the Council has lesser powers (and the Commission correspondingly more) under the ECSC Treaty.[3] However, even under this Treaty certain decisions of the Commission require the concurrence of the Council, for example the restriction of exports when a serious shortage of certain products occurs[4]; the Council is itself empowered to take decisions on a number of matters.[5] It is also the Council which instructs the Commission on negotiations with third states relating to economic relations with the community.

6–043 The strengthening of the communities, their enlargement and the extension of political co-operation made the reinforcing of existing structures imperative. The personal intervention of the heads of government in the community process has constituted a major development. Their so-called summit meetings, held in addition to ordinary meetings of the Council, were often required to take decisions which came to be regarded as the major guidelines for the development of the community. In answer to the evident need for more frequent consultation at the highest level, it was decided at the summit meeting in Paris in December 1974 to institutionalise the meetings, under the appellation of "European Council," as distinct from the Council of Ministers.[6] The European Council brings together heads of state or government, the foreign ministers and the president and a vice-president of the Commission. They meet twice a year, generally in the capital of the member state which currently exercises the

---

[3] But see the suggestion by Reuter that in practice the powers of the High Authority proved less, and those of the Council of Ministers more, than the treaty envisaged: Law and Contemporary Problems: European Regional Communities (1961) 26, No. 3, "Juridical and Institutional Aspects of the European Regional Communities" 381 at 387.
[4] Art. 59(5); see further examples in Arts 55(2), 56(1), 58(1) and 74.
[5] See for instance Arts 9, 29, 32, 58(3) and 81.
[6] See Lauwaars, "The European Council" (1977) 14 C.M.L. Rev. 25.

presidency of the Council of Ministers. They provide an opportunity for dialogue in an informal atmosphere. The European Council's existence and functions have been confirmed by the TEU, which states that it "shall provide the Union with the necessary impetus for its development and shall define the general political guidelines thereof" (Article 4 of the consolidated version of the TEU). It is therefore not an organ of the community, but of the European Union, within which it plays a role, *e.g.* in the orientation of the common foreign and security policy (Article 13).

The Commission.[7] The Commission is composed of 20 members "chosen **6–044** on the grounds of their general competence and whose independence is beyond doubt" (there are no more than two members from any one state) (Article 213 EC). Though nationals of the members, they retain their essential character as individuals acting only in the interest of the Community as such. They are to be chosen "by mutual agreement" between the members and hold office for four years; this period is renewable. The Commission acts by simple majority vote. Its functions and powers vary from treaty to treaty.

Under the ECSC Treaty the Commission takes three kinds of normative **6–045** acts: "decisions" which are binding in all their details; "recommendations" which are binding so far as the objectives they specify are concerned, but which leave the states or enterprises to which they are directed free to choose the appropriate means for attaining these objectives; and "opinions" which are merely persuasive. It is in the decision-making powers, which directly bind the enterprises without any need for intervention by governments, that the core of the Commission's so-called "supra-national" character is to be found.[8] Moreover, the Commission has power to enforce its decisions by the imposition of fines and penalties on enterprises (Articles 50, 54 and 59) and, if these are not paid, the Commission may withhold sums which it is itself due to pay to the enterprises; this power has been used frequently. Apart from this right of withholding sums, the Commission must rely on enforcement of its decisions via the executive agencies of the member states, for it possesses no executive arm of its own. Hence, under Article 92, "[d]ecisions of the Commission which impose a pecuniary obligation shall be enforceable. Enforcement in the territory of member states shall be carried out by means of the legal procedure in force in each state. . . ." The member states are themselves bound "to take all appropriate measures, whether general or particular, to ensure fulfilment of the obligations resulting from decisions and recommendations of the institutions of the community . . ." (Article 86). The Commission is,

---

[7] See, *e.g.* Edwards and Spence (eds.), *The European Commission* (2nd ed., 1997).
[8] This term, used in the ECSC Treaty, no longer figures in any subsequent text, presumably due to some member states' sensitivity on this point.

therefore, not a federal authority equipped with its own powers of direct enforcement; but the ability to take decisions binding on states, and on enterprises within these states without the intervention of the states, is evidence of the extent of powers the exercise of which member states have transferred to this organ.

6–046   Under the E.C. and Euratom treaties the powers of the Commission are more limited, and responsibility for achieving the aims of the treaty is shared with other organs of the Community, particularly the Council. The Commission will more frequently be called upon to "formulate recommendations or deliver opinions" and "participate in the shaping of measures taken by the Council and by the European Parliament" (Article 211), being thereby given an important role in initiating Community legislation. The Commission does have a limited power of decision, by simple majority, in certain matters delegated to it by the treaty; but, all in all, the more important decisions rest with the Council and it is for the Commission to assist in carrying them out. Yet, the Commission plays an important role in ensuring "that the provisions of [the Treaties] and the measures taken by the institutions pursuant thereto are applied" (Article 211); this organ is therefore often pictured as the "guardian of the treaties."[9] It is in virtue of this provision that the Commission controls the compliance of member governments' actions with Community law. To this end, the Commission may—and regularly does—institute proceedings against defaulting member states before the European Court of Justice (actions for infringement of the Treaty—Article 226).[10] Finally, it should also be noted that the Maastricht Treaty entrusted the Commission with the monitoring of the budgetary situation and of the stock of government debt in the member states and the examination of compliance with budgetary discipline in the framework of the economic and monetary union (Article 104).

6–047   Under the three treaties there exists an advisory body to the Commission, called Consultative Committee (ECSC)[11] or Economic and Social Committee (E.C. and Euratom). These are consultative committees which are to represent professional, trade union and similar interests. The 156 members of ECOSOC are appointed by the Council, acting unanimously and after consultation with the Commission. Consultation with the Com-

---

[9] On this aspect of the Commission's task, see, *e.g.* Gil Ibanez, *The Administrative Supervision and Enforcement of EC Law: Powers, Procedures and Limits* (1999).

[10] See *infra*, Chap. 13.

[11] This is not a main organ or "institution," but an advisory body designated to assist the Commission. The members, which number between 84 and 156, are appointed by the Council and must include producers, workers, consumers and dealers in equal numbers. They act in a purely individual capacity and are intended to present the Commission with a sounding-board of general opinion through the Community. It appears, however, that the experiment is not very successful and only the trade unionists meet systematically in a group which cuts across national loyalties.

mittee is obligatory in certain matters, such as formulating rules for the free movement of workers (Article 49), otherwise optional. The Commission also has under its direction some 23 General Directorates, covering all the functions of the three executives, and embracing a common administration or civil service. This has required uniform staff regulations and uniformity of privileges and immunities: the latter has been provided for in a protocol annexed to the Merger Treaty.

Not surprisingly, checks have been provided against a misuse or abuse of **6–048** these considerable powers by the Commission. As we shall see, the Commission is answerable for its actions to the Parliament which, in the last resort, can bring about the collective resignation of the Commission by a vote of censure. There is also the European Court of Justice, which has power to adjudicate on the legality of the action of the Commission under the treaty.[12] Less stringent, but more often used in practice, are the checks involved in the role of the Council as a "harmoniser" of the action of the Commission and of the member governments.

A final point, worth mentioning because it is a feature rarely seen in international organisations, is that the financing of the ECSC is not by subscriptions to a budget by the governments, but by the Commission, which has the power to borrow or to place a levy on the production of coal and steel which is paid by enterprises direct to the Commission (Articles 49 ff). By contrast, the revenues of the E.C. and Euratom stem from national contributions although in 1970 the Council decided that as from 1975 the budget should be financed entirely from the Communities' own resources. These resources consist of import levies on agricultural produce and customs duties and, in addition, a fraction of the VAT charged in each member state. The Merger Treaty has rationalised the financial provisions of the three treaties.[13] There is now a common budget, but excluding the operational expenditures (and the corresponding revenues from levies) of ECSC because of this "self-financing" feature.

The European Parliament

Bibliography: Cot, "Le Parlement européen: fausse perspective et vrai paradoxe" *Mélanges Dupuy* 121

The European Parliament is the parliamentary organ of the European **6–049** Community. It meets in ordinary sessions several times a year in Strasbourg, Luxembourg or Brussels and consists of 626 representatives of the peoples of the member states.[14] In the same fashion as in the

---

[12] For more on this, see *infra*, Chap. 13.

[13] Note, in particular, that the E.C. budget procedure now applies to all three communities. It is the Council which adopts the budget after consultation with the Assembly (for more on this, see *infra*, para. 6–052).

[14] The number of representatives elected in each member state is listed in Art. 190 of the consolidated version of the treaty establishing the European Community.

Parliamentary Assembly of the Council of Europe, alignments of the representatives are less on a national basis than along political lines.[15] There are several officially recognised political groups in the E.P.: the Socialists (Party of European Socialists), Christian Democrats (European People's Party), Liberals (European Liberal, Democrat and Reform Party), Conservatives, (Union for Europe), Communists (European United Left), Ecologists (Green Group), Radicals (European Radical Alliance) and Nationalists (Independents for a Europe of Nations). Since 1979, the representatives (now Members of the European Parliament—MEPs) are elected by direct universal suffrage for a five-year term.[16] According to Article 19 of the (revised) treaty, a citizen of the union residing in a member state of which he or she is not a national shall have the right to vote and stand as a candidate in elections to the E.P. in the member state in which he or she resides under the same conditions as nationals of that state. In addition to the plenary sessions, the parliament also works through 20 commissions dealing with matters such as agriculture, fisheries, external relations, research, development, co-operation, etc.

6–050   Paradoxically, the parliament had for a long period few, if any, normative powers—these being vested in the Council and the Commission. The 1986 Single European Act and the 1992 Maastricht Treaty brought an end to this situation. In response to numerous calls to fight the "democratic deficit" in the Community,[17] the E.P. has become increasingly involved in the community decision-making process in various fields. Currently, a "co-operation" procedure is used for decision-making in various fields, which enables the parliament to amend or reject a "common position" taken by the Council on a proposal from the Commission (Article 252 of the consolidated version of the treaty establishing the European Community). In such cases, the parliament's vote may nevertheless be by-passed by a unanimous decision of the Council. The E.P. is also endowed with a power of "co-decision" with the Commission and the Council in other matters, such as culture, education and environment (Article 251). This goes further than the co-operation procedure, since it gives the E.P. the power to oppose the adoption of a normative act when a consultation procedure between the parliament and the Council has failed. Finally, the parliament now also has to approve international agreements concluded by the Community in co-decisions areas or entailing institutional or budgetary implications (Article 300(3)).

6–051   In addition to those normative powers, the parliament possesses a power of control over the Commission which is unique in international organisations and is reminiscent of the power of a national parliament to force the

---

[15] The existence of political parties at the European level is acknowledged in Art. 191 of the consolidated version of the treaty establishing the European Community.
[16] See Art. 190.
[17] For more on this, see *infra*, para. 6–053.

resignation of a government. This lies in the right of the Parliament to force the resignation of the entire Commission by a vote of censure, passed in open ballot by two-thirds of the members voting and a simple majority of the total membership of the parliament (Article 201). Several votes of censure have been taken against the Commission, but the motions have never obtained the majority necessary to unseat the Commission. In March 1999, it is on its own initiative that the Commission collectively resigned following widespread allegations of fraud.[18] Threats of tabling a motion of censure at the parliament nevertheless seems to have played an important role in the Commission's decision to resign. In any event, the fact that the Commission is answerable to parliament is important, for it helps to maintain the independence of the Commission from the Council. The Commission's obligation to reply to written or oral questions from members of parliament is also part of the technique of control.

The parliament's powers also extend to other matters. When it was **6–052** decided to give the Community financial resources of its own, the member states agreed to increase the parliament's budgetary powers.[19] It has the right to amend the draft budget submitted by the Council and may propose modifications "relating to expenditure necessarily resulting from th[e] treaty or from acts adopted in accordance therewith" (Article 272). Basically, this is expenditure on the Common Agricultural Policy, most of it for price support. These modifications nevertheless have to be approved by the Council. The parliament may also reject the draft budget as a whole, as it has in 1979 and 1984. Its control also extends to the implementation of the budget, for which it has to give a discharge to the Commission at the end of each fiscal year (Article 276).[20] Far from being exclusively technical, the power to give discharge quickly acquired a strong political content. It enables the European Parliament to pronounce—if only *a posteriori*—on the policies followed and options taken by the "executive" institutions, to criticize their action and thereby to influence the shaping of future policies. Finally, it must be noted that Article 230(3) entitles the parliament to bring actions before the ECJ against the Council, the Commission and the European Central Bank for the purpose of protecting its prerogatives.

The shift to direct elections has reinforced the Assembly's claim to **6–053** enhanced legitimacy and wider powers. The argument is, however, more complex. It lies, essentially, in the proposition that, as the communities exercise more power, so the national governments necessarily exercise less: there occurs a "transfer" of the exercise of powers. From this it would follow that the democratically-elected representatives of the people should

---

[18] See newspapers/Keesing's, March 16, 1999.
[19] See, *e.g.* the changes brought by the 1975 Treaty of Brussels (*infra*, n. 24).
[20] Up to now, the Parliament refused to do so only once, in 1982.

exercise the same control over these governmental powers via the European Parliament as they did in national parliaments when the powers lay with national governments. Even though the parliament has been relatively successful in asserting its authority and powers in various fields, the so-called "democratic deficit" often denounced in the administration of European affairs at the community level remains to a certain extent a reality. This may be evidence of the fact that, as within states, democracy in international organisations does not boil down to parliamentary action or control only.

6–054 The Court of Justice. This is addressed in Chapter 13.[21] It may be noted at this juncture, however, that rather than have separate courts for each of the three organisations of the Community, it was decided to have a single court to replace the ECSC Court and also serve the EC and Euratom.[22] A Court of First Instance was established in 1989 in order to re-inforce the judicial mechanism in the Communities (Article 225).

6–055 The Court of Auditors.[23] The Court of Auditors was set up by the second Budget Treaty of July 22, 1975[24] and held its constituent meeting in Luxembourg in October 1977. The Court took over from the EEC and Euratom Audit Board and from the ECSC Auditor as the body in charge of external auditing of the Community's budget and the ECSC's operational budget; the internal audit is still a matter for the financial controller of each institution. The members of the Court, one from each state, are appointed for a term of six years by the Council acting unanimously after consulting parliament (Article 247 E.C.). The Court examines the accounts of all revenue and expenditure of the community and any body created by the community, and draws up a report on its work at the end of each financial year. The court has the right to submit observations on specific questions on its own initiative, and may deliver opinions at the request of an institution.

6–056 The court has more authority than its predecessors. Not only is it a permanent institution with its own staff, but parliament has shown its intent to make the most of the opportunities offered by the court in order to re-inforce its own control over the community budget. The Treaty of Maastricht confirmed the Court of Auditors' importance by making it the fifth institution of the Communities, on equal footing with the Council, Commission, European Parliament and Court of Justice (Article 7). Its independence is thereby reinforced.

---

[21] See *infra*, Chap. 13.
[22] See the Convention relating to certain Institutions common to the European Communities.
[23] See, generally, de Crouy-Chanel and Perron, *La Cour des comptes européenne* (1998).
[24] Treaty amending certain financial provisions of the treaties establishing the EEC and of the treaty establishing a single council and a single commission of the E.C., Brussels, July 22, 1975, Art. 28.

The European Central Bank. While it is not, properly speaking, an **6–057** institution of the Community,[25] the European Central Bank (ECB), established in June 1998, has a very important role to play in the implementation and management of the European Monetary Union. It will have the exclusive right to authorise the issue of banknotes within the community (Article 106), and has to be consulted by the Council in order to determine exchange-rate policies in relation to non-community currencies (Article 111). The decision-making bodies of the ECB are the Executive Board (comprising the President, Vice-President and four other members appointed by common accord of the member states) and the Governing Council (comprising the members of the Executive Board and the Governors of the national central banks) (Article 112).

3. EUROPEAN BANK FOR RECONSTRUCTION AND DEVELOPMENT (EBRD)

Bibliography: Shihata, *The European Bank for Reconstruction and Development—A Comparative Analysis of the Constituent Agreement* (1990); Sands, "The European Bank for Reconstruction and Development" (1991) 40 ICLQ 730; Dunnett, "The EBRD: a legal survey", 28 CMLRev 571 (1991). Website: http://www.ebrd.com.

The end of the Cold War and the evolution of Eastern European **6–058** countries towards market economies brought about the creation of the European Bank for Reconstruction and Development in 1990.[26] Based in London, the EBRD is a multilateral lending institution similar to those created after the Second World War at the universal (IBRD) or regional (Inter-American, African and Asian Development Banks) levels. Its purpose is "to foster the transition towards open market-oriented economies and to promote private and entrepreneurial initiative in the Central and Eastern European countries committed to and applying the principles of multiparty democracy, pluralism and market economy" (Article 1). It is worth noting that, contrary to the World Bank and IMF, the EBRD is thus authorised—one may even say obliged—by its constitution to take into account in its lending policy the political situation prevailing in the borrowing state. In this respect, its constitution expressly requires it to have regard to non-economic matters, including human rights and the environment. The abovementioned aims are to be achieved through the same means as used by other international development banks, *i.e.* the mobilisation of capital and the provision of technical assistance (Article 2). The EBRD is open to European and non-European countries which are members of the IMF, and to selected international organisations (Article

---

[25] The ECB is not listed in Art. 7, which describes the Community's institutions, and is endowed with a separate legal personality (Art. 107, para. 2).
[26] May 29, 1990; text in 1646 U.N.T.S. 97.

3). All of the E.C.'s member states, the European Community and the European Investment Bank, most of the Central and Eastern European countries, other European countries as well as non-European countries such as Australia, Mexico, Morocco and the United States were original members.[27] Its capital is divided into paid-in and callable shares, available for subscription by members (Article 4).

6–059   The Bank's organs are the Board of Governors, the Board of Directors and the President. The Board of Governors is composed of representatives of member states, one Governor being appointed by each member (Article 23). Its powers include the admission and suspension of members, the decision to increase or decrease the Bank's authorised capital and the amendment of the Bank's articles of agreement (Article 24). The Board of Directors is composed of 23 members which are elected by the different groups of member states, each group being assigned a fraction of the total number of positions (Article 26). It is responsible for the direction of the general operations of the Bank and takes decisions, *e.g.* concerning loans, guarantees, investments and borrowing by the Bank (Article 27). As in other financial institutions, the votes at EBRD are weighed, the voting power of each member being equal to the number of its subscribed shares in the capital stock (Article 29). Finally, the President heads the Bank's staff and is the legal representative of the organisation; he or she conducts the current business of the Bank, under the supervision of the Board of Directors (Article 30).

By 1998, the EBRD had been active in all countries of eastern and central Europe, and had lent a total of ECU 13.9 bn.

4. THE EUROPEAN FREE TRADE ASSOCIATION (EFTA)

Bibliography: Meyer, *The EFTA* (1960); Figgures, "Legal Aspects of the European Free Trade Association" (1965) 14 I.C.L.Q. 1079; Lambrinidis, *The Structure, Function and Law of a Free Trade Area* (1965); Doswald, "The Future of EFTA" (1994) 37 G.Y.I.L. 40. Website: http://www.efta.int.

6–060   The essential characteristic of a free trade area is that, whilst it aims at a gradual elimination of protective customs duties and quota restrictions between the members, it permits each member to fix its own external tariff *vis-à-vis* non-member states: the degree of sovereignty surrendered is therefore minimised. In contrast, a customs union—or "common market"—envisages a common external tariff and, correspondingly, a need to develop a common commercial policy towards the outside world. This difference produces many consequences, for a customs union will tend to induce by regulation free movement of goods, labour and capital and to attempt a harmonisation of social and economic policies so as to bring

---

[27] 58 states are members of the Bank.

about an equalisation of the cost elements in production. The customs union is therefore moving towards complete economic integration, involving a far more substantial transfer of the exercise of sovereignty.

The European Free Trade Association is a clear example of the first **6–061** model. It was established by the Convention of January 4, 1960[28] as a counterpart to the EEC.[29] Of the seven original member states of the Association, five have acceded to the European Community at different times,[30] whereas two new members joined EFTA over the same period.[31] Its essential objective is the promotion of a sustained expansion of economic activity, fair competition in trade and the avoidance of significant disparity between members in the conditions of supply of raw materials within the Area (Article 2). Tariff and quota restrictions in practice apply largely to manufactured goods. Agricultural goods, fish and other marine products are largely excluded and, in these spheres, it was anticipated that the countries exporting these products would find compensation in bilateral agreements on agricultural products (Article 27) or that an expansion of trade in fish and other marine products would occur so as to offset the loss of tariffs on imported manufactures (Article 28).

The bilateral free trade agreements which each EFTA member had **6–062** concluded with the E.C. and the free trade system for industrial products between the E.C. and EFTA, achieved in 1972, have been replaced in 1992 by a more comprehensive agreement by which the members of both organisations and the European Communities themselves created the European Economic Area (EEA).[32] The aim of this agreement is to extend to EFTA countries the four fundamental freedoms enshrined in the Treaty of Rome (free movement of goods, persons, services and capital) (Article 1).[33] It also provides for co-operation between the two partners in the field of education, environment, social policy and for the creation of new institutions to control the implementation of the agreement. These include a Council, composed of ministers of the participating countries, the role of which is essentially of a political nature (giving impetus for the implementation of the agreement) (Article 89), a joint committee consisting of

---

[28] 370 U.N.T.S. 3.

[29] A good, non-technical, account is given in *The European Free Trade Association* (2nd ed., 1980) published by the EFTA Secretariat.

[30] Austria, Denmark, Portugal, Sweden and the U.K.

[31] Present members are Iceland, Liechstenstein, Norway and Switzerland.

[32] Agreement signed in Oporto on May 2, 1992; the text of the Agreement is available on the organisation's website (http://www.efta.int/docs/EFTA/LegalTexts). On the EFTA side, Switzerland has declined to join the EEA. The conclusion of the agreement raised complex institutional questions on the EEC side; see especially the two opinions delivered by the European Court of Justice on the draft agreement (Opinions 1/91, December 14, 1991, (1991) *Rep.* I-6084 and 1/92, April 10, 1992, (1992) *Rep.* I-2825).

[33] On the material and institutional aspects of the agreement, see, *e.g.* Evans, *The Law of the European Community, including the EEA Agreement* (1994).

representatives of states and the European Commission, which is entrusted with monitoring functions regarding the implementation of the agreement and with the settlement of disputes concerning the EEA agreement (Articles 92 and 111), a Joint Parliamentary Committee and a Consultative Committee (Articles 95 and 96). EFTA also concluded a number of free trade agreements with Eastern European states and countries of the Mediterranean basin since the beginning of the 1990s. These aim mainly at ensuring to products originating from EFTA countries the same treatment as is given in the partner countries to products from the E.U. The organisational structure of EFTA is relatively simple. The Council is the plenary supreme organ on which all the four members have one vote: discussions or recommendations generally require unanimity although an abstention does not act as a veto. Decisions are usually adopted by consensus. The Council may "legislate" to the extent that it can by decision amend the Convention in many particulars or enact new treaty-law in furtherance of EFTA's objectives. The Council can, by a majority vote, regulate in detail such matters as are provided for in general terms by the Convention. Thus, any member can veto new, substantive obligations but not mere decisions implementing the existing obligations. The Council also adjudicates on disputes between members, but may (and, if a state requests, must) refer the matter to the Examining Committees provided for in Article 33: these are "ad hoc" and lend a certain objectivity to proceedings in which some members of the Council will be interested parties. The Council adopts a recommendation by majority and, if not accepted and the Council finds there is a breach of obligation, may ultimately authorise any member state to suspend obligations under the Convention owed to the recalcitrant member.[34] In broad outline, the procedure follows the original GATT procedure.

6–063   The Council has set up various subsidiary committees under its general power to establish subsidiary organs (Article 32(3)): there are committees on Customs, Budget, Economics, and Technical Barriers to Trade, among others and also a Committee of Trade Experts and a Consultative Committee. There is also a permanent Secretariat, based on the Council's power "to make arrangements for the secretariat services" (Article 34(b)), but consisting of persons on loan from governments rather than career international civil servants. It has three "branches": one—the headquarters—in Geneva, dealing with matters related to the tasks of the Council, one in Brussels (EEA matters) and one in Luxembourg (office of the statistical advisor). The establishment of the EEA rendered necessary the creation of new organs to monitor the implementation of the 1992 agreement on the EFTA side. The most important of these are the Surveillance Authority, which plays for

---

[34] For detailed discussion of the complaints procedure see Lambrinidis, *The Structure, Function, and Law of a Free Trade Area* (1965) Chap. 11.

EFTA member states which are also members of the EEA a role similar to that of the Commission for the EC, and the EFTA Court. The court is composed of three judges and has jurisdiction over EFTA states parties to the EEA agreement; its powers are tantamount to those of the European Court of Justice under the Treaty of Rome.[35]

(b) POLITICS AND SECURITY

1. The North Atlantic Treaty Organisation (NATO)

Bibliography: Salvin, "The North Atlantic Pact" (1949) International Conciliation 373; Ball, NATO and the European Union Movement (1959); Buchan, "The Reform of NATO" (1962) 40 *Foreign Affairs* 165; North Atlantic Treaty Organisation, NATO: Facts and Figures; Guérin, "L'ONU, l'OTAN et le maintien de la paix" (1994) 40 AFDI 171. Website: http://www.nato.int.

By 1948 there was growing concern in the West over the security of **6–064** Western Europe. It was increasingly feared that the Brussels Treaty Organisation, established on March 17, 1948, by the United Kingdom, France, Belgium, Netherlands and Luxembourg, and purporting to be an organisation for collective self-defence under Article 51 of the Charter, was inadequate for the defence of Western Europe almost as soon as it was formed. Moreover its purpose of preventing a "renewal by Germany of an aggressive policy" was not the purpose for which effective defence was now seen to be needed; eyes were on the Soviet Union, not Germany. The Berlin blockade and the Communist coup in Czechoslovakia in February 1948 increased the alarm and by June 1948 the Vandenberg Resolution was adopted by the U.S. Senate, authorising the government to associate the USA with alliances for defensive purposes. It had been clear for some time that, under the conditions then prevailing, security could not be guaranteed by the collective security machinery of the UN Security Council. Thus, in signing the North Atlantic Treaty on April 4, 1949,[36] the Western powers determined to create a regional security organisation capable of defending Western Europe and North America. Essentially a Western military alliance against the Soviet block, the organisation has undergone a significant evolution since the end of the cold war. Since the beginning of the 1990s, its mandate has been extended to fostering peace and stability in the Euro-Atlantic area through crisis management and involvement in peace-keeping operations, for instance.[37] NATO has thus been particularly active in ex-Yugoslavia, where it has been entrusted by the UN Security Council with the follow-up and implementation of the Dayton Peace Agreements

---

[35] See Arts 31 *et seq.* of the Agreement between the EFTA States on the establishment of a Surveillance Authority and a Court of Justice.

[36] 34 U.N.T.S. 243.

[37] For more on this, see *e.g.* Woodlife, "The Evolution of a New NATO for a New Europe" (1998) 47 ICLQ 174.

for Bosnia-Herzegovina.[38] On this occasion the organisation set up the first field operation in its history and established an Implementation Force (IFOR) in 1995, which was replaced by a Stabilisation Force (SFOR) one year later.[39] Those forces have generally succeeded in maintaining peace in Bosnia up to this day. However, in March 1999, NATO became further embroiled in the former Yugoslavia when it launched air raids against the Federal Republic of Yugoslavia (FRY) to force a settlement on the status of the province of Kosovo. In contrast with the abovementioned operations in Bosnia, however, the latter raised serious concerns of legality.[40]

6–065 As a result of the above-mentioned geo-political changes NATO also opened up to Eastern European countries and new fora were established for dialogue and consultation between NATO members and other European countries.[41] Similarly, a dialogue with Mediterranean states in order to contribute to security and stability in the Mediterranean was initiated in 1997, as a result of the NATO Madrid Summit.

6–066 The NATO Treaty was originally signed by 12 states, including the USA, Canada and Iceland; it was open to other European states by invitation, and in 1952 Greece and Turkey also joined. The number was brought up to 15 in 1955 with the accession of Western Germany and to 16 in 1982 with the accession of Spain. The organisation now has 19 members, Hungary, Poland and the Czech Republic having joined in March 1999.[42] NATO is not, therefore, strictly European; but it is so much the organisation for the security of Western—and, gradually, the whole of—Europe that the only sensible course is to treat it as being part of the family of European institutions. Following a period of substantial disagreement between France and the remaining members, particularly over the United States/United Kingdom control of the nuclear deterrent capacity of NATO, in March 1966 General de Gaulle notified the NATO members of France's decision to withdraw all French military personnel from the integrated commands, to require the removal from French territory of these commands and to refuse the common use of joint infrastructure undertakings on its territory. France has never, however, ceased to be a party to the NATO Treaty,[43] and reintegrated itself into the military structure of the organisation in 1995.[44]

---

[38] Previous NATO actions in the conflict include air strikes launched to support UNPROFOR's operations on the ground.

[39] See the authorisation given in Security Council Resolutions 1031 of December 15, 1995 (IFOR) and 1088 of December 12, 1996 (SFOR). It should be noted that both forces included elements from states other than NATO members.

[40] For more on this, see, para. 6–067.

[41] For more on these, see, para. 6–072.

[42] See Lippman, "NATO Embraces 3 From Warsaw Pact; Poland, Hungary, Czech Republic Join" in *The Washington Post*, March 13, 1999, A1 and, more generally, Müllerson, "NATO Enlargement and the NATO-Russian Founding Act: The Interplay of Law and Politics" (1998) 47 ICLQ 192.

[43] See Stein and Carreau, "Law and Peaceful Change in a Subsystem: 'Withdrawal' of France from the North Atlantic Treaty Organisation" (1968) 62 AJIL 577.

[44] See (1997) 101 RGDIP 213.

Under the treaty the parties agree to "consult together, whenever, in the **6–067** opinion of any of them, the territorial integrity, political independence or security of any of the Parties is threatened" (Article IV); as we shall see, the institutional forms are designed to bring about almost continuous consultation. The heart of the treaty lies in Article V, in which the parties agree that "an armed attack against one or more of them in Europe or North America shall be considered an attack against them all. . . ."; Europe and North America are more closely specified in Article VI, so that a geographical area is defined and, after the accession of Turkey and Greece, this was extended by a Protocol of October 17, 1951, to cover their territories. The obligation of each Party in the event of an armed attack on a member within the area is to take forthwith, individually and in concert with the other Parties, "such action as it deems necessary." Technically, therefore, the commitment is a weak one,[45] as it is for each party to decide on the form of assistance it will give. In practice however, as we shall see, the system is far more centralised. As Articles 1 and 7 of the 1949 Treaty itself indicate, all actions undertaken within the framework of the organisation must be in compliance with the rules of international law governing the use of force in international relations. More specifically, NATO constitutes a regional organisation whose actions, when they involve the use of force in circumstances other than collective self-defence, must be authorised by the United Nations Security Council under Chapter VIII of the UN Charter. The conditions under which the abovementioned operations in Bosnia-Herzegovina took place offer clear evidence of this.[46] It is, on the other hand, for this reason that the air strikes conducted by NATO against the FRY in 1999 raised grave concern of legality under international law since they did not amount to self-defence nor were authorised by the Security Council.[47]

The brevity of the treaty on its institutional forms is extraordinary, for it **6–068** mentions only a Council and a Defence Committee. Considerable constitutional changes nevertheless occurred in 1951–52 and again since the beginning of the 1990s.

---

[45] The absence of a more concrete obligation is due to the difficulty of obligating the USA to take armed action when, constitutionally, a declaration of war is a matter for the Senate.

[46] See in particular the above-mentioned enabling Security Council Resolutions.

[47] See, *e.g.* the preoccupations expressed by the International Court of Justice in its order rejecting the Yugoslav request for the indication of provisional measures in the case concerning the *Legality of use of force (Yugoslavia v. United Kingdom et al.)*, June 2, 1999, para. 16. See also, *e.g.* Simma, "NATO, the UN and the Use of Force: Legal Aspects" (1999) 10 EJIL 1–22; for a somewhat different overall view (but not on the question of legality), see Cassese, "*Ex iniuria ius oritur*: Are We Moving towards International Legitimation of Forcible Humanitarian Countermeasures in the World Community?" *ibid.* 23–30.

(a) The Council

6–069 The Council is the supreme organ, a political organ on which each member is represented; it is to be so organised as to be able to meet "promptly at any time" (Article 9). In fact the task in hand called for almost continuous session and now members appoint permanent representatives to the NATO Council who have the same powers as Foreign Ministers. The Council also meets "at the summit", with the heads of states and governments gathering on more solemn occasions.[48] The procedures of the Council are somewhat unusual. It has no voting procedure and in fact never takes a decision by a vote. Its aim is to secure unanimous agreement, and this illustrates the essential character of the Council as a forum for negotiation. Its meetings also bring out this same character, for they can be either "normal" or "restricted" (with only one or two advisers present besides the representative) or "informal" (only the permanent representatives, and with no agenda or records). Another unusual feature is that the Secretary-General is the permanent Chairman of the Council. The entirety of the other bodies are subject to the Council. These other bodies are part of either the "civil" organisation or the "military" organisation. It is best to treat the two separately, taking into account the reorganisation and relocation consequent upon the French partial withdrawal.

(b) The "Civil" Organisation

6–070 The Defence Committee, intended as a Committee of Defence Ministers to advise the Council on the implementation of Articles 3 and 5 of the Treaty (see Article 9), was absorbed into the Council itself in 1951. There being no other committees named in the treaty, the Council simply uses the general power to create committees in Article 9; some of these are highly technical, but others are of wider competence and cover problems which are adequately indicated by their titles, such as the Committee of Political Advisers, the Committee of Economic Advisers, the Defence Planning Committee, the Defence Production Committee, the Civil Defence Committee, the Nuclear Defence Affairs Committee and, under it, the Nuclear Planning Group. All committees are advisory.

6–071 The Secretariat may also be included on the "civil" side of the organisation. There is, moreover, the development of the North Atlantic Assembly (initially under the appellation of "NATO Parliamentary Conference"), which first met in 1955 and now meets annually. This is a conference of parliamentarians from NATO countries, which makes recommendations to the Council; but it is quite "unofficial" and is nowhere mentioned in the constitutional texts. The Assembly is nevertheless now well established as a

---

[48] See for instance the 1994 Brussels Summit Meeting and the 1997 Madrid Summit Meeting, where the decisions on the enlargement of NATO were taken.

consultative assembly and clearly indicates that NATO is something more than a military alliance.

The change in mandate and the overall evolution of the political **6–072** landscape in Europe has also led to institutional evolution. New co-operation structures and fora for dialogue between traditional NATO members and other European states have been established, which sometimes parallel OSCE's institutions.[49] Hence, the Euro-Atlantic Partnership Council (EAPC) (which succeeded in 1997 to the North Atlantic Co-operation Council) offers a framework for political consultation and co-operation in the military, but also economic, scientific and environmental fields between NATO members and close to thirty Central and Eastern European or neutral states. The EAPC thus gives an institutional structure to the Enhanced Partnership for Peace (in 1997 this replaced the Partnership for Peace originally launched in 1991), which aims at developing peaceful and stable relations between all states of the Euro-Atlantic area through a series of more specific objectives.

The co-operation of NATO with other organisations active in the same **6–073** fields is also evidenced by joint meetings of organs, such as the joint meetings of the NATO Council and the Council of the Western European Union[50] or annual joint meetings of the Assemblies of NATO and the WEU.

(c) The "Military" Organisation

This, too, operates under the authority of the Council. It is headed by the **6–074** Military Committee, as the supreme military authority of NATO and containing the Chiefs of Staff of all the members. It is actually a Military Committee which meets almost continuously in Washington on their behalf. The Military Committee's primary task is to give strategic direction to NATO.

Beneath the Military Committee, and responsible to it, is the Supreme **6–075** Allied Commander in Europe (SACEUR), with his headquarters known as SHAPE. Under his own immediate command is a vast network of air, sea and land commands, split into different regions for Northern, Central and Southern Europe, plus the separate naval commands of SACLANT (Atlantic) and CINCHAN (the English Channel).[51] The extent to which co-operation has progressed, with joint training staff colleges, standardisation of weapons, the construction of NATO installations, pipelines, depots, airfields (the infrastructure programme) and the like now means that a

---

[49] For more on this organisation, see *infra*, paras 6–084 *et seq.*
[50] For more on this organisation, see *infra*, paras 6–076 *et seq.*
[51] For more details on this network, see *The NATO Handbook* (1996).

party is much more involved than the rather loose obligation in Article 5 suggests. Its defence programme and expenditure are examined yearly in the Annual Review, based on a searching questionnaire, and the Supreme Allied Commander makes recommendations directly to governments. Admittedly, there is no legal hindrance to a party cutting down its defence programme or even withdrawing its forces from their NATO commitments, and this has been done by France; but it is now difficult for one party to act in a way to which the rest are opposed. The "sanction" is political, not legal, and the forum for its application is the Council, not an international court.

2. Western European Union (WEU)[52]

Bibliography: Imbert, *L'Union de l'Europe occidentale* (1968); Bloed and Wessel (eds.) *The Changing Functions of the Western European Union (WEU)* (1994); Dumoulin and Remacle, *L'Union de l'Europe occidentale* (1998). Website: http://www.weu.int.

6–076   The inadequacy of the Brussels Treaty Organisation for the defence of Western Europe has already been referred to; with the development of NATO the Brussels Treaty Organisation became virtually redundant. During the years 1949–54 it did attempt to develop activities in the social and cultural fields, although even these could have been handled by the Council of Europe. In 1954, however, events transpired which brought the Brussels Treaty Organisation a new lease of life, albeit with an enlarged membership and a different title—the Western European Union.

6–077   The French refusal to ratify the treaty creating the European Defence Community, combined with the NATO Council's decision that West Germany should be re-armed and take her place in the Western system of collective security, brought about a need for some machinery to permit, but at the same time control, that participation. Thus a series of Protocols to the Brussels Treaty were signed in Paris on October 23, 1954,[53] transforming the Brussels Treaty Organisation so as to meet that need. According to the first Protocol, WEU's aim is to promote the unity and encourage the progressive integration of Europe. It is, like NATO, an organisation for collective self-defence, based on the idea that an attack on one is an attack on all. However, the obligation to assist the immediate victim is, under Article 5, much stronger, for it contains no clause such as "such action as it deems necessary."

6–078   The first Protocol also provided for close co-operation with NATO, for a Council of WEU and an Assembly. The second Protocol set upper limits to the sizes of the forces which WEU members can maintain on the Continent

---

[52] Members are Belgium, France, Germany, Greece, Italy, Luxembourg, Netherlands, Portugal, Spain and the U.K.; associated members are Iceland, Norway and Turkey.
[53] II *European Yearbook* 313, *et seq.*

and provided for their command by the Supreme Allied Commander (SACEUR); in this lay the limitation on German re-armament. The third Protocol and its four Annexes bound West Germany—and now Germany—not to undertake the manufacture of certain weapons (atomic, chemical or biological, warships and strategic bombers, etc.). The fourth Protocol set up an Agency for the Control of Armaments to ensure that the commitments in the third Protocol were observed.[54]

In spite of this reform, the WEU did not play any significant role in the **6–079** shaping of European defence during most of the cold war. After a rather long period of inactivity, attempts to revive it were made in 1984 (Declaration of Rome), and consultation between its members was extended from mostly technical to more political co-operation. From then on, it aimed at promoting a stronger and more autonomous European identity in the field of security, without calling into question the existence and role of NATO. This evolution took a new orientation with the end of the cold war. The Maastricht Treaty established close ties between WEU and the European Union by requesting the former "which is an integral part of the development of the [European] Union, to elaborate and implement decisions and actions of the Union which have defence implications" (Article J.4, 2), thereby giving WEU the status of "defence pillar" of the new European construction.[55] A further step in that direction was taken in the Treaty of Amsterdam of 1997, according to which the WEU is to provide the European Union with access to an operational capacity in the context of humanitarian and rescue tasks or peacekeeping and peacemaking operations (Article 17). In order to further this co-operation between the two organisations, the headquarters of WEU were transferred from London to Brussels in January 1993. In 1992 a Eurocorps was created, consisting of about 50,000 troops from five member states (initially France and Germany, joined later by Belgium, Spain and Luxembourg) and is intended to constitute the backbone of a future European army.[56] The WEU played a role in a few field operations since the beginning of the 1990s (enforcement of the UN embargoes against Iraq in the Persian Gulf in 1990 and against Yugoslavia in the Adriatic and on the Danube between 1992 and 1996, to mention the most significant of these).[57] All in all, however, it appears difficult for the organisation to assert its role so long as NATO dominates both European and transatlantic defence architectures.

---

[54] This was dissolved in 1989.

[55] This was confirmed by the WEU Council meeting of Petersberg in June 1992.

[56] The Euro-corps has a naval equivalent of smaller proportions, the Euromarforce (on this, see (1995) 99 RGDIP 672).

[57] On the Organisation's involvement in the Adriatic, see *e.g.* (1994) 98 R.G.D.I.P. 201. Members of the Euro-corps were also part of the NATO-led SFOR in Bosnia.

(a) The Council

6–080   This consists of the Foreign Ministers of the member states and is the executive body of the organisation; it is to be "so organised as to be able to exercise its functions continuously," hence it meets more frequently as a meeting of ambassadors resident in Brussels under the chairmanship of the Secretary-General and is then called the "Permanent Council." Its basic voting rule is unanimity, although for certain matters specified in the Protocols either a qualified or even a simple majority may suffice. It reports annually to the Assembly but is not in any way controlled by it.

(b) The Assembly

6–081   This was established by Article 5 of Protocol I, providing merely that the Council shall report to it annually and that it shall consist of the representatives of the members to the Consultative Assembly of the Council of Europe. Thus the "identity of membership" principle is established. Otherwise the treaty is silent, and it has been left to the Assembly itself to deal with practical matters like finance, privileges and immunities, procedure, committee structure, etc. It has adopted a Charter and Rules of Procedure; the former provides:

> "Article I(a) The Assembly carries out the parliamentary functions arising from the application of the Brussels Treaty. In particular, the Assembly may proceed on any matters arising out of the Brussels Treaty and upon any matter submitted to the Assembly for an opinion by the Council.
>
> (b) The Assembly shall determine its own Agenda in conformity with the provisions of paragraph (a) above and having due regard to the activities of other European organisations."

6–082   The Assembly meets twice yearly, mostly takes decisions by majority vote, and has its own committee structure;[58] it also holds ad hoc joint meetings with the Council to promote co-operation between the two bodies. It possesses its own Secretariat, distinct from that of the Council, and has a separate budget which can, however, be amended by the Council.[59]

6–083   Essentially this is a consultative organ, with no control over the executive organ equivalent to that which the European Parliament possesses over the Commission. Yet it can record its disagreement with the substance of the

---

[58] Committees include those on Defence Questions and Armaments; General Affairs; Budgetary Affairs and Administration; Rules of Procedure and Privileges.

[59] If an amendment is more than 20% of any one subhead there is a provision for a joint meeting between the two organs.

annual report by the Council. Moreover it can transmit resolutions directly to governments and it has an independent power of investigation.

3. Organisation for Security and Cooperation in Europe (OSCE)

Bibliography: Bloed (ed.), *From Helsinki to Vienna: Basic Documents of the Helsinki Process* (1990); Bloed (ed.), *The Conference on Security and Cooperation in Europe—Basic Documents—1972–1993*, (1993); Bloed (ed.), *The Conference on Security and Cooperation in Europe—Basic Documents—1993–1995*, (1997); Nesi, "Dalla CSCE all'OSCE: La Conferenza di riesame di Budapest" (1994) Communita Internazionale 736; Ghebali, *L'OSCE dans l'Europe post-communiste—1990–1996: Vers une identité paneuropéenne de sécurité* (1996). Website: http://www.osce.org.

The roots of the Organisation for Security and Cooperation in Europe **6–084** are to be found in the Conference on Security and Cooperation in Europe (CSCE), which was aiming at establishing a collective security system in Europe by providing a forum for discussion between Eastern and Western European countries. The first stage of the Conference started in 1973, its third and final stage witnessing the adoption of the Final Act of Helsinki by the 35 participating states (33 European states, Canada and the USA) in 1975.[60] The Final Act consists of four "baskets" corresponding to the various fields of co-operation ascertained during the Conference: questions relating to security, co-operation in the field of economics, of science and technology and of the environment, co-operation in humanitarian and other fields, and follow-up to the Conference. Several follow-up meetings have taken place since 1975, sometimes resulting in the adoption of substantive concluding documents.[61] The 1990 Charter of Paris for a New Europe, which contributed to reshaping the European political landscape after the end of the cold war, was also adopted within the framework of the CSCE.[62] Originally, the CSCE was not endowed with any permanent institutional structure. In addition to the periodic follow-up meetings, though, specialised conferences and experts meetings have been organised since 1978 and have increased both in number and scope.[63] As of 1990, the institutional structure of the CSCE was redefined as follows[64]: the Council, consisting of Ministers for Foreign Affairs of the participating states,

---

[60] August 1, 1975, (1975) 14 ILM 1292; on this see, *e.g.* van Dijk, "The Final Act of Helsinki— Basis for a Pan-European System?" (1980) XI NYIL 97.

[61] On the concluding document of the Vienna follow-up meeting (1986–1989), see in particular Bloed and van Dijk (eds.), *The Human Dimension of the Helsinki Process—The Vienna Follow-up Meeting and its Aftermath* (1991).

[62] (1991) 30 ILM 190.

[63] One could for instance mention in that regard the 1990 Copenhagen Meeting of the Conference on the Human Dimension of the CSCE or the 1991 Valletta Meeting of Experts on Peaceful Settlement of Disputes (see resulting documents in (1990) 29 I.L.M. 1305 and (1991) 30 ILM 382, respectively).

[64] See the Supplementary Document to Give Effect to Certain Provisions Contained in the Charter of Paris for a New Europe, (1991) 30 ILM 209.

provided the central forum for regular political consultations and was to meet at least once a year; the Committee of Senior Officials was to "prepare the work of the Council, carry out its decisions, review current issues and consider future work of the CSCE including its relations with other international fora;" the Secretariat was to provide administrative support to the Council and to the Committee of Senior Officials; the Conflict Prevention Centre's mandate was to assist the Council in reducing the risk of conflict and to give support to the implementation of Confidence and Security Building Measures; the Office for Free Elections was to facilitate contacts and the exchange of information on elections within participating states. Specialised conferences and experts meetings kept on being provided for. The will of participating states to maintain the CSCE as cost-efficient as possible is evidenced, *e.g.* by the provisions relating to staffing arrangements, according to which the directors and officials were to be seconded by their government and appointed for short and non-renewable terms.[65] A Parliamentary Assembly was created in 1991. It consists of representatives of national parliaments of each participating state (from two for Liechtenstein to 17 for the USA, the total number of seats being 312) and its mandate includes the assessment of the implementation of the objectives of the CSCE, the promotion of initiatives in favour of co-operation and security in Europe and the information of national parliaments on its activities.[66] Further changes were introduced to the CSCE's institutional structure by the 1992 Helsinki Decision on the strengthening of CSCE institutions and structures.[67] The Council became the CSCE Council, a Chairman-in-Office responsible for the co-ordination of current CSCE affairs was appointed, as well as a High Commissioner on National Minorities.

6–085   The outbreak of regional conflicts in different parts of Europe in the first half of the 1990s led the CSCE to play—or attempt to play—a more active role in the field. The institution thus became involved at an early stage in the Yugoslav conflict—before stepping aside owing to the increasing involvement of the E.C. and of the UN—and engaged in diplomatic missions, monitoring activities or peacekeeping operations in Nagorno-Karabakh, Georgia, Moldova and Tadjikistan.[68] Of course, CSCE (and now OSCE) peacekeeping operations may only take place within the framework of Chapter VIII of the Charter of the United Nations.[69] The CSCE also

---

[65] *ibid.*, 215–216.
[66] See Ghebali, *L'OSCE dans L'Europe post-communiste, 1990–1996* (1996) pp. 76–77.
[67] July 10, 1992, (1992) 31 ILM 1394.
[68] For a general framework, see, *e.g.* the 1992 Helsinki Decision on Early Warning, Conflict Prevention and Crisis Management (Including Fact-Finding and Rapporteur Missions and CSCE Peacekeeping), Peaceful Settlement of Disputes, (1992) 31 ILM 1399 and, for an update, the 1999 Istanbul Charter on European Security; for an account of those specific activities, see, *e.g.* Ghebali, *L'OSCE dans L'Europe post-communiste, 1990–1996* (1996) pp. 88–90.
[69] *ibid.*, para. 19. This was reaffirmed in the Charter on European Security, paras 7 and 11.

engaged into longer term preventive diplomacy activities, in the Baltic states amongst others.

The participating states decided to change the name CSCE to OSCE in **6–086** 1994, principally to emphasize the importance of the institution and to reflect the growth in its role in shaping the participating states' common security area.[70] Even though the Budapest Decision makes it clear that "[t]he change in name from CSCE to OSCE alters neither the character of [the participating states'] CSCE commitments nor the status of the CSCE and its institutions,"[71] one may take the view that the OSCE now qualifies as a full-fledged international organisation.[72] It has been endowed with legal capacity in the various states hosting CSCE/OSCE institutions and has been vested—together with its officials—with some privileges and immunities; it also has permanent organs and is obviously able to undertake legal international commitments in its own name on the international plane.[73] As far as the institutional structure is concerned, the Ministerial Council replaces the CSCE Council as the central decision-making and governing body of the organisation, the Senior Council replaces the Committee of Senior Officials, and the Permanent Council takes over the responsibilities of the Permanent Committee as the regular body for political consultation and decision-making.[74] The overall responsibility for executive action remains with the Chairman-in-Office, supported by the Secretary-General.[75] The other institutions or organs are not affected. Here again, the requirement for a "flexible and dynamic" organisation is put forward.[76] In 1998, the OSCE had 55 member states.

(c) OTHER

The other European organisations described hereafter are mainly active **6–087** in the field of space activities, in which Europe's role has grown significantly over the last decades.

ESA.[77] The will to compete with the two "superpowers" in the field of **6–088** space exploration and exploitation led European states to pool their resources and technical expertise. Three different institutions were set up to

---

[70] See the Budapest Summit Declaration of December 6, 1994, and the Decision on the Strengthening of the CSCE, (1995) 34 ILM 767 and 773, respectively. The change was effective as of January 1, 1995.

[71] Decision on the Strengthening of the CSCE, para. 29.

[72] See, *e.g.* Bertrand, "La nature juridique de l'Organisation pour la sécurité et la coopération en Europe (OSCE)" (1998) 102 R.G.D.I.P. 365 *et seq.*; *contra*, see Sapiro, "Changing the CSCE into the OSCE: Legal Aspects of a Political Transformation" (1995) 89 A.J.I.L. 631–637.

[73] It should be noted, however, that the 1999 Charter for European Security refers to the difficulties arising "from the absence of a legal personality of the Organisation," admittedly referring to personality on the international plane (para. 18).

[74] Decision on the Strengthening of the CSCE, paras 16–18.

[75] *ibid.*, paras 19–20.

[76] *ibid.*, para. 29.

[77] For more information on the ESA, see http://www.esa.int.

that end in the 1960s: the European Organisation for the Development and Construction of Space Vehicle Launchers (ELDO),[78] the European Space Research Organisation (ESRO)[79] and the European Conference for Satellite Telecommunications. Technical and financial motives led in 1975 to their merge into a single organisation, the European Space Agency (ESA).[80] The purpose of the Agency is "to provide for and to promote, for exclusively peaceful purposes, co-operation among European States in space research and technology and their space applications, with a view to their being used for scientific purposes and for operational space applications systems."[81] To that end, ESA is *e.g.* to elaborate and promote: (i) a long-term European space policy; (ii) activities and programmes in the space field; (iii) the industrial policy appropriate to its programme.[82] As of November 2000, the Agency had 15 member states;[83] one non-European country (Canada) enjoys a special status and takes part in several ESA programmes. It should be noted that the activities of the Agency include mandatory activities (such as technological research work or the elaboration and execution of scientific programmes), in which all member states participate, and optional activities (such as the "design, development, construction, launching, placing in orbit and control of satellites and other space systems" or the "design, development, construction, and operation of launch facilities and space transport systems"), in which all states participate apart from those that formally declare themselves not interested in participating therein.[84] The system is thus—at least partly—"à la carte".

6–089   The Agency's organs are but two: the Council and the Director General. The Council, composed of representatives of the member states, constitutes the "executive" organ; its functions include the approval of activities and programmes, the election of the Director General, the adoption of budgets and, more generally, the definition of "the policy to be followed by the Agency in pursuit of its purpose."[85] The Director-General is the "chief executive officer" of the Agency and its legal representative; heading the Agency's staff, he or she is responsible for the management of the Agency, the execution of its programmes and the implementation of its policy.[86] He or she has authority over all of the establishments of the Agency (such as Estec, the European Space Research and Technology Centre, or Esoc, the European Space Operations Centre, for instance).

---

[78] March 29, 1962, 507 U.N.T.S. 177.
[79] June 14, 1962, 528 U.N.T.S. 33.
[80] May 30, 1975, 1297 U.N.T.S. 161.
[81] *ibid.*, Art. II.
[82] *ibid.*
[83] Austria, Belgium, Denmark, Finland, France, Germany, Ireland, Italy, Netherlands, Norway, Portugal, Spain, Sweden, Switzerland and the U.K.
[84] 1297 U.N.T.S. 161, Art. V.
[85] *ibid.*, Art. XI.
[86] *ibid.*, Art. XII.

ESA is the only organisation of general competence in the field of space **6–090** activities. It has proved much more efficient than its predecessors and has been—and still is—involved in all European projects in that field (Ariane, Spacelab, Meteosat, Marecs are among the best known of these). The Agency also is an important partner in the international space station. In order to operate these projects, new entities have sometimes been created, that enjoy various status: private companies, such as Arianespace, or IGOs, such as EUTELSAT and EUMETSAT, of which a little bit more shall now be said.

EUTELSAT. The European Telecommunication Satellite Organisation **6–091** was established in 1982. It had 47 member states, of Western and Eastern Europe, in 1998. EUTELSAT carries out the same type of functions as INTELSAT (*i.e.* the conception, building and operation of a satellite network),[87] but on a regional, European, level. It operates a fleet of 14 satellites. Its organs are the Conference of the Parties, the Board of Signatories, which is vested with the power to take decisions on commercial, financial, legal, technical and operational matters, and the Executive Organ, which performs administrative functions. EUTELSAT has decided to follow the same path as the global organisations active in that field (INTELSAT and INMARSAT) and is to become a private company in 2001. It is envisaged that the current members will be the initial shareholders and, as in the case of the organisations just mentioned, a small intergovernmental supervisory structure will remain, ensuring that the new company continues to apply basic public service principles.[88]

EUMETSAT. The European Meteorological Satellite Organisation was **6–092** created in 1986.[89] This took over the Meteosat programme, which had been launched under the aegis of ESRO in 1972. Its main objective is to establish and operate a European system of meteorological satellites, contributing thereby to the monitoring of the global climate (Article 2, para. 1 of the original Convention and revised Convention). Seventeen European states were members of the organisation in 1998. The main organs of Eumetsat are the Council which, as plenary organ, determines the general policy of the organisation and the Secretariat, acting under the authority of the Director, who is the legal representative of the organisation. Eumetsat presently operates three satellites and provides data to national meteorological administrations as well as to various other users, ranging from universities to airlines.

---

[87] See *supra*, Chap. 4.
[88] See the press communiqué released by the organisation on May 21, 1999; text available in adobe acrobat format at http://www.eutelsat.org.
[89] Its constitution has been adopted on May 23, 1983, but did not come into force before 1986. For more information see http://www.eumetsat.de.

CHAPTER 7

THE AMERICAS AND THE CARIBBEAN

Bibliography: Inter-American Institute of International Legal Studies, *The Inter-American System, its Development and Strengthening* (1966); Connell-Smith, *The Inter-American System* (1966); Instituto Interamericano de Estudios Jurídicos Internacionales, *Problemática Jurídica e Institucional de la Integración de América Latina* (1967); García-Amador, "Institutional Developments in Central American Integration" (1967) 61 Proc. ASIL 167; Shaw, *Central America, Regional Integration and National Political Development* (1978); Bond, "Regionalism in Latin America: Prospects for the Latin American Economic System (SELA)" (1978) 32 International Organisation 401; Bawa, *Latin American Integration* (1980); Bulmer-Thomas, *The Political Economy of Central America Since 1920* (1987); Lipsey and Meller (eds.), *Western Hemisphere Trade Integration* (1997).

The Americas and the Caribbean have a well-established history of **7–001** institutional development, dating back to the nineteenth century and including the first permanent international court.[1] The main regional organisation is the Organisation of American States which, together with the Inter-American Commission and Court of Human Rights and the Inter-American Development Bank, provide region-wide institutional structures. In recent years there have been particularly significant strides in promoting economic integration and regional free trade, and even beyond the organisations described below there are numerous regional conventions establishing technical institutions—for example in the field of telecommunications, fisheries and the environment—which are not addressed here, such as the 1978 Treaty for Amazonian Cooperation.[2]

A. ORGANISATIONS OF GENERAL COMPETENCE

(a) THE ORGANISATION OF AMERICAN STATES (OAS)

Bibliography: Canyes, *The Organisation of American States and the United Nations* (6th ed., 1963); Dreier, *The Organisation of American States and the Hemisphere Crisis* (1962); Ball, *The OAS in Transition* (1969); Scheman, "The OAS and the quest for international co-operation: American vision or mirage" (1981) 13 *Case Western Reserve Journal of International Law* 83;

---

[1] See Chap. 13, paras 13–105 and 13-154.
[2] (1978) 17 ILM 1045. The treaty entered into force on August 2, 1980.

Baena Soares, "The Organisation of American States and International Law" (1986) 80 Proc. ASIL 1; Caminos, "The Question of Competence in Intra-regional Conflicts and Disputes: the United Nations and the OAS Charters" (1986) *Canadian Council on International Law. Proceedings of the Annual Conference* 245; Pirrone, "The use of force in the framework of the OAS" in Cassese (ed.), *The Current Legal Regulation of the Use of Force: Legal Restraints on the Use of Force 40 Years after the UN Charter* (1986) 223; Dolzer, "Enforcement of International Obligations through Regional Arrangements: Structures and Experiences of the OAS" (1986) 46 Z.f.a.ö.r.u.v. 113; Caminos, "The OAS Charter After Forty Years" (1988) 82 Proc. ASIL 101; Acevedo, "Relationship between the Organisation of American States and the United Nations with regard to settlement of regional disputes" (1991) 18 Thesaurus Acroasium 61; Perret (ed.): *The OAS in the Centennial of the Inter-American System* (1992); Stoetzer, *The Organisation of American States* (2nd ed., 1993). Vaky and Munoz (eds.), *The Future of the Organisation of American States* (1993); D. Sheinin, *The Organisation of American States* (1995). Website: http://www.oas.org.

7–002 The historical development of the OAS provides a good illustration of varying kinds of co-operation between states, and is worth considering in its historical context. The International Union of American Republics, formed in 1890, was not an organisation in the modern sense of the term, but rather a series of conferences designed to promote commerce and peaceful settlement of disputes; it was assisted by a Commercial Bureau which came to be called the "Pan-American Union." By 1906 wider aims were accepted, and policies were determined by a plenary governing board, but these aims still remained non-military and largely non-political. Even after the First World War, whilst the series of Inter-American Conferences continued, the unilateral character of the Monroe Doctrine, by which the United States had established a hegemony over the Western Hemisphere, prevented any real political co-operation from developing. With the change to a "good neighbour policy," the USA at the Montevideo Conference of 1933 accepted the principle of non-intervention in the affairs of other American States and at Buenos Aires in 1936[3] accepted the principle of consultation between the American states as an alternative to unilateral United States action on matters affecting the peace of the continent.[4] Thus the principle of equality, and consequently, prospects for co-operation, began to emerge. In 1938, at the Lima Conference, a Meeting of Foreign Ministers was established as a procedure for such consultation, and use was made of this organ to make various affirmations of common policy during the early stages of the Second World War.

7–003 After the Second World War, at the Mexico City Conference in 1945, the Act of Chapultepec reaffirmed the basic postulate upon which the security system had developed, namely, that an attack against any one of the

---

[3] Convention on Rights and Duties of States, Art. 8; (1934) 28 AJIL Supp. 75, 76.
[4] Convention for the Maintenance, Preservation and Reestablishment of Peace; (1937) 31 AJIL Supp. 53.

American states constituted aggression against all, and resolved to give the Inter-American system a permanent charter or constitution. Since the Act of Chapultepec was in the form of a "declaration," it was subsequently incorporated in treaty form (so far as the security system was concerned) in the Rio Treaty of 1947, properly termed the Inter-American Treaty of Reciprocal Assistance,[5] a treaty which gave definitive form to the security system and established an Organ of Consultation, a consultative organ of Foreign Ministers. The charter or constitution came in the following year, in 1948 (with the Pact of Bogota),[6] establishing the Organisation of American States. Meanwhile, at the San Francisco Conference the American states had combined to introduce alterations to the Dumbarton Oaks proposals, so that the UN Charter as it finally emerged contained not only the present Article 51, which was designed to ensure that the security system envisaged in the Act of Chapultepec could operate, but also a comprehensive Chapter VIII on regional arrangements which catered for the regional pacific settlement procedures which had for long been an essential part of the Inter-American system.

Recent decades have seen significant development of the OAS. Indeed, **7–004** general dissatisfaction with the structure and functioning of the OAS led to a series of Special Inter-American Conferences in 1964, 1965 and 1967 which produced significant amendments to the OAS charter.[7] Dissatisfaction continued and, in 1973, the Assembly called for a complete re-structuring of the organisation. A further revision of the charter resulted from the protocol of Cartagena de Indias of 1985, which entered into force in 1988.[8] In the 1980s and 1990s significant change occurred within the organisation with a range of new roles and priorities being established. Principal amongst these has been the initiation of the Free Trade Area of the Americas (FTAA) process stemming from the Summit of the Americas held in Miami in 1994, which aims to establish a FTAA spanning the Western Hemisphere by 2005. Other initiatives included the creation of the Inter-American Drug Abuse Control Commission in 1986 to deal with the growing problem of the consumption, production and trafficking of illicit drugs in the Americas;[9] and the establishment of the Inter-American Council for Integral Development in 1996 to promote co-operation among member states in fostering development and combating poverty. Further changes to the OAS charter occurred in 1997 with the ratification of the Protocol of Washington.[10] The reforms to the OAS charter include the conferral of power on the OAS to suspend a member state whose

---

[5] (1949) 43 AJIL Supp. 53 and see 1975 amendments in (1975) 14 ILM 1122.
[6] (1952) 46 AJIL Supp. 43. It came into effect on December 13, 1951.
[7] (1967) 6 ILM 310: Protocol of Buenos Aires, February 27, 1967.
[8] OAS Treaty Series, No.66.
[9] This Commission is known by its Spanish acronym, CICAD.
[10] I-E Rev. OEA Documentos Officiales OEA/Ser. A/2 Add. 3 (SEPF).

democratically elected government is overthrown by force (Article 9). In 1998, the Second Summit of the Americas took place in Santiago, Chile. The member states assigned new mandates to the OAS in a number of areas, including human rights, trade, education, anti-drug co-operation and summit follow-up.[11]

Aims and purposes

7–005 The Bogota charter describes the Organisation of American States as a "regional agency" within the United Nations (Article 1), membership of which is open to all American states.[12] However, the Act of Washington of 1964 established a procedure for admission requiring a two-thirds vote of the Council and excluding from membership any political entity whose territory is subject to litigation with an extracontinental country until the dispute is ended: this procedure was subsequently embodied in the 1967 Protocol of Amendment. The Protocol of Cartagena de Indias inserted a new and controversial Article 8, which provides that:

> "Membership in the Organisation shall be confined to independent states of the hemisphere that were members of the United Nations as of December 10, 1985, and the autonomous territories mentioned in document OEA/Ser. P, AG/Doc.1939/85, of November 5, 1985 when they become independent."

This article opened the way to Belize and Guyana joining the OAS in 1991, but closed it for the Malvinas/Falklands, if, in the future, it gains independence. Whilst members can withdraw from the OAS, there is no provision for expulsion under the charter. However, on January 31, 1962, the Conference of Foreign Ministers resolved by a two-thirds majority to expel Cuba from the organisation on the ground that the Castro regime was incompatible with the principles and objectives of the OAS; it is understood that the six abstaining members abstained because of their doubts on the legality of expulsion.

7–006 The purposes of the organisation, stated in Article 2, include not only common action for the peace and security of the continent, and ensuring the pacific settlement of disputes between members, but also the wider ones

---

[11] See Second Summit of the Americas: Santiago Declaration and Plan of Action (1998) 37 ILM 947.

[12] All 35 countries of the Americas have now ratified the OAS Charter and belong to the Organisation. The 21 original members were Argentina, Bolivia, Brazil, Chile, Colombia, Costa Rica, Cuba, Dominican Republic, Ecuador, El Salvador, Guatemala, Haiti, Honduras, Mexico, Nicaragua, Panama, Paraguay, Peru, United States, Uruguay and Venezuela. The other 14 countries subsequently became members at the following times; Barbados, Trinidad and Tobago (1967), Jamaica (1969), Grenada (1975), Suriname (1977), Dominica, Saint Lucia (1979), Antigua and Barbuda, Saint Vincent and the Grenadines (1981), The Bahamas (1982), St. Kitts and Nevis (1984), Canada (1990) and Belize, Guyana (1991).

of solving common political, juridical and economic problems and promoting, by co-operative action, their economic, social and cultural development. New purposes were added by the 1985 Protocol of Amendment including promoting and consolidating representative democracy and achieving an effective limitation of conventional weapons so as to devote the largest amount of resources to the economic and social development of member states. There is, therefore, no doubt of the "comprehensiveness" of the organisation. Chapter II sets out the basic principles which govern relations between members, and Chapter IV sets out the fundamental rights and duties of states.[13] Chapter V relates to procedures for pacific settlement of disputes, which do not, however, impair the rights and obligations of the member states under Articles 34 and 35 of the UN charter; the actual procedures are contained in the separate American Treaty of Pacific Settlement of 1948.[14] This provides for good offices and mediation, investigation and conciliation, arbitration and judicial settlement by the I.C.J. However, this treaty has never entered into force and the council in practice developed its own techniques of peaceful settlement, using the Inter-American Peace Committee. Significantly, under the 1967 amendments to the OAS charter, a considerable emphasis was placed on pacific settlement and this was made a major function of the Permanent Council (Articles 85–90).

Chapter VI, on collective security, consists of but two brief articles which **7–007** virtually incorporate the Rio Treaty, so it is to that treaty that one must turn for a more detailed appreciation of the system of collective security. The treaty is based upon the premise that "an act of aggression against one American state is an act of aggression against all the other American states,"[15] thus giving rise to the right of collective self-defence under Article 51 of the UN charter. When such an attack occurs either within the region described in Article 4 or within the territory of an American state, the obligation on all members to assist the victim arises automatically; in all other cases, as where the attack is outside that area or the aggression does not take the form of an armed attack, the obligation is merely one of consultation. For characterising action as aggression and for consultation and agreement on measures to be taken an Organ of Consultation was established, a consultative body of all the foreign ministers; these functions are now formally assumed under the Bogota charter by the Meeting of

---

[13] To some extent a re-statement of principles embodied in previous inter-American agreements such as the Convention on the Duties and Rights of States in the Event of Civil Strife, 1928; the Convention on the Rights and Duties of States, 1933; and the Protocol on Non-Intervention 1936. A later Protocol to the Convention on Civil Strife was signed in 1957.

[14] Text in Sohn, *World Law* (1950), p. 1059.

[15] Charter of the Organisation of American States Art. 3. For further details see J. Kunz, "The Inter-American Treaty of Reciprocal Assistance" (1948) 42 AJIL 111, 117.

Consultation of foreign ministers. Chapters VI, VII and VIII of the charter originally dealt respectively with economic, social and cultural standards, but were consolidated in 1985 into a single Chapter VII dealing with "Integral Development."

Organs

7–008 The OAS has a number of organs. The General Assembly is nominally the "supreme organ," a plenary body on which each state has one vote and which meets each year at the time stipulated in its Rules of Procedure. It decides "the general action and policy of the organisation" and determines "the structure and function of its organs;" it also has the authority to "consider any matter relating to friendly relations among the American states" (Article 54(a)). Its terms of reference could, therefore, scarcely be wider. The Meeting of Consultation of Ministers of Foreign Affairs serves as the Organ of Consultation under the Rio Treaty, its task being to "consider problems of an urgent nature" (Article 61). But, in addition, it has tended to serve as the "supreme organ," exercising broad powers ascribed to the General Assembly. A meeting can be convened by a majority of the Council (see below) at the request of any one member (Article 62). However, a meeting is obligatory, and without delay, in the event of an armed attack within the territory of an American state or the region defined in Article 4. The convening of the Meeting of Consultation in its capacity as the Organ of Consultation has occurred less frequently than might be supposed, due to the way in which the Permanent Council (see below) has solved most of the disputes without finding it necessary to convene the Organ of Consultation. However, when in 1960 the foreign ministers were convened by the Council to deal with a Venezuelan complaint against the Dominican Republic, this was the sixth time it had been so convened; it was also the first time sanctions had ever been decided on, in this case taking the form of a call for a severance of diplomatic relations with the Dominican Republic by all OAS members, the imposition of an arms embargo and further economic sanctions as necessary. A seventh meeting in 1960 virtually condemned Cuba for accepting the promise of soviet military protection against a possible U.S. attack, and, as already mentioned, in January 1962 the meeting voted to suspend Cuba from membership and to both establish an arms embargo and consider the desirability of extending the embargo to other items of strategic importance. In 1964 these sanctions against Cuba were extended to cover a severance of diplomatic and consular relations, a general boycott of trade and sea transportation; in June 1967 the twelfth meeting of Ministers of Foreign Affairs recommended members to blackball vessels trading with Cuba.[16] The fifteenth meeting attempted to discontinue the 1964 sanctions

---

[16] As discussed earlier, these "sanctions" raise a difficult problem of relationship with the Security Council. However, the new Art. 8 as revised in 1975 explicitly allows the Organ of Consultation to adopt sanctions, including the use of armed force.

against Cuba, however, the resolution did not obtain the necessary two-thirds majority for effectiveness. Finally, in 1975, at the sixteenth meeting it was resolved that every member could decide independently on the resumption of relations with Cuba, removing this issue from the agenda of future meetings. Subsequently, the Meeting of Consultation dealt with several inter-American conflicts in an attempt to maintain peace and security in the region. These included the 1969 "Soccer War" between Honduras and El Salvador, the 1971 dispute between the United States and Ecuador over fishing jurisdiction, the Nicaraguan Revolution resulting in the fall of the Somoza regime, the Peruvian-Ecuadorian confrontation in the El Condor Mountain Range in 1991, and the Falklands/Malvinas conflict. The OAS also attempted to intervene and broker a peaceful settlement (though without success) in the civil wars in Nicaragua and elsewhere in the region in the late 1980s.

An Advisory Defence Committee advises on problems of military co- **7–009** operation, meeting concurrently with the Meetings of Foreign Ministers when defence against aggression is involved, or at other times when requested by the General Assembly or the Meeting of Foreign Ministers or two-thirds of the member governments. The only permanent defence organ is the Inter-American Defence Board, established in 1942, which has been continued and acts as the organ of preparation for collective self-defence and also serves as the secretariat for the committee. There is no kind of joint command and, compared with the NATO system, the collective defence machinery is rudimentary. One suspects that the Latin-American members are not so far convinced of the necessity for development of this military side of the OAS. Indeed, whilst an Inter-American Peace Force was created in 1965 during the Dominican crisis, the discussion on constitutional amendment between 1965 and 1967 saw strong opposition to the idea of giving any permanence to such an institution, and none was established. In more recent times procedures established by resolution 1080/91 of the OAS General Assembly have been used to address threats to democracy in member states such as Haiti (1991), Peru (1992), Guatemala (1993) and Paraguay (1996). In line with the emphasis on representative democracy found in the revised charter, one of the newest roles assumed by the OAS has been in the monitoring of national elections in member states.[17]

The Permanent Council is a plenary body, meeting at ambassadorial **7–010** level, which is subordinate to the previous two organs. It is, in effect, the continuation of the old governing board. It supervises the General-Secretariat, co-ordinates the activities of the American specialised con-

---

[17] For example, the OAS was involved in monitoring elections during 1990 and 1991 in the following member states: Nicaragua, Haiti, Guatemala and Suriname.

ferences and organisations and concludes agreements with them, and promotes collaboration with the UN and other international organisations. The Council has the power to create its own committees, which include the following permanent committees: Committee on Juridical and Political Affairs, Committee on Administrative and Budgetary Affairs, Committee on Hemispheric Security, Committee on Civil Society Participation in OAS Activities and Special Committee on Inter-American Summits Management. The Council also has important political functions assigned to it under the Rio Treaty, whereby it "serves provisionally as the Organ of Consultation" (Article 83, Bogota charter). In practice this gives it considerable powers except in those situations where the Meeting of Foreign Ministers is obligatory; in all other situations it may virtually constitute itself the provisional Organ of Consultation when a request for consultation is made (under Article 6 of the Rio Treaty, for example). In practice it has often been able to settle disputes itself without even summoning the actual Meeting of Foreign Ministers; for example, during the Dominican crisis in 1965 it was the council which assumed a continuing responsibility, with the Meeting of Ministers of Foreign Affairs convening only intermittently, and in 1964 the council dealt with the Panama/U.S. dispute exclusively. The council's work in the area of political settlement is of great importance. In matters of fact-finding and investigation it has frequently relied upon the Inter-American Peace Committee, first established in 1940, with the same composition as the council. Under its earlier statutes the powers of investigation of this committee did not even require the consent of both parties. However, an amendment in 1956 introduced the requirement of consent and much reduced the committee's powers.[18] On occasions the council has set up ad hoc conciliation missions, such as the peace mission sent to the Dominican Republic in 1965. Since the 1960s the council placed increasing importance on its economic work, and an Inter-American Economic and Social Council (IA-ECOSOC) was established as a subsidiary organ of the Council. The IDB, the OAS and ECLAC all participated in a Tripartite Committee on Co-ordination. This complex of economic institutions under, or related to, the OAS failed to satisfy the economic aspiration of the OAS, spurring the decision of the Chiefs of State at the Punta del Este meeting in April 1967 to establish a Latin-American Common Market.[19]

---

[18] For a survey of the Inter-American Peace Committee's activities see Cornell-Smith, *The Inter-American System* (1966), pp. 82–104.
[19] Text in Dept. State Bull. No. 1453, May 1967, 712. In 1969, in a meeting in Venezuela, it was decided to postpone the target date of a future Latin American Common Market to 1980. These events have been overtaken by new initiatives to develop a FTAA by 2005.

The Inter-American Council for Integral Development was established in **7–011** 1996 pursuant to the 1993 Protocol,[20] and is similar in organisational structure to the permanent council and of equivalent status to the former council. Each member state may appoint to the council one representative of ministerial or equivalent rank, which members are to meet at least once a year. The purpose of the Council is "to promote co-operation among the American states for the purpose of achieving integral development and, in particular, helping to eliminate extreme poverty, in accordance with the standards of the charter" (OAS Charter, Article 94). Its functions include:

(a) the formulation and recommendation to the General Assembly of a Strategic Plan for co-operation for integral development;

(b) the formulation of guidelines for the preparation of the programme-budget for technical co-operation and other activities of the Council;

(c) the promotion, co-operation and assignment of responsibilities for the execution of development programmes and projects to subsidise relevant organisations in areas such as economic and social development, education and strengthening the civic conscience of the American people;

(d) the establishment of co-operative relations with the UN and other national or international agencies; and

(e) the periodic evaluation of co-operative activities for integral development to be reported on to the General Assembly.

Like the permanent council, the Inter-American council for integral development may establish specialised committees to assist it in the performance of its functions.

The General-Secretariat is described as "the central and permanent **7–012** organ of the Organisation of American States" (Article 107). It is located in Washington and headed by a Secretary-General who is elected by the General Assembly and who may participate in any of the organs, but without the right to vote. The role of the General-Secretariat is the customary role of any international secretariat, and Articles 118 and 119 safeguard its independence by imposing obligations on personnel not to seek or receive outside instructions and on states not to give them.

The OAS also sponsors Specialised Conferences to address "special **7–013** technical matters or to develop specific aspects of inter-American co-operation" (Article 122); they can be convened by the General Assembly or the

---

[20] The Council was established by the Protocol of Managua (1994) 33 ILM 1009, replacing the Inter-American Economic and Social Council and the Inter-American Council for Education, Science and Culture.

Meeting of Consultation, on its own initiative or at the request of one of the Councils or "specialised organisations" (see below). The programme and regulations for the conferences will be prepared either by the councils or by the specialised organisations. They have been held on a variety of matters, including copyright, travel, cartography and highways, education, ports and harbours, statistics, agriculture and private international law. Finally, it is appropriate to mention that in an attempt to co-ordinate the activities of the various intergovernmental, technical organisations operating in the Western hemisphere, the Bogota charter envisaged a kind of relationship between the Organisation of American States and these "specialised organisations" roughly comparable to that between the UN and the specialised agencies. The specialised organisations enjoy the fullest technical autonomy (Article 126), but submit to the General Assembly annual reports on their work and on their budgets.[21]

7–014 The OAS is the most comprehensive of the regional organisations outside Europe. It is perhaps more impressive structurally than in practice, for its achievements do not really compare with those in the European sphere. The frequent internal conflicts between the members of the organisation have done little to demonstrate the political unity necessary for further political integration, and, whilst most of these conflicts have been satisfactorily dealt with under the settlement procedures of the Meeting of Consultation of Foreign Ministers and the Permanent Council, the Guatemalan and Cuban cases show a far less satisfactory outcome.

(b) THE ORGANISATION OF CENTRAL AMERICAN STATES (ODECA)

7–015 This is, in a sense, a regional organisation within a regional organisation. Established under a charter signed in 1951,[22] the organisation embraced Costa Rica, El Salvador, Guatemala, Honduras and Nicaragua. Its early history was not impressive but in December 1962 the new San Salvador charter was signed, entering into effect in March 1965. This attempted to revitalise the organisation and, whilst in no real sense a "supra-national" organisation,[23] it was re-structured to give increased effectiveness. In December 1991 a further restructuring of the ODECA took place as a result of the reforms to the charter introduced by the Protocol of Tegucigalpa.

---

[21] The organisations now brought into relationship with the OAS are: the Pan-American Institute of Geography and History; the Pan-American Health Organisation (whose bureau is the regional office for WHO); the Inter-American Indian Institute; the Inter-American Institution for Co-operation on Agriculture; the Inter-American Children's Institute; the Inter-American Commission of Women; the Inter-American Nuclear Energy Commission; the Inter-American Music Council and the Inter-American Development Bank.

[22] (1952) 4 Annals of the OAS, 352–355.

[23] Although certain provisions give the Executive Council and the Economic Council limited law-making and "decision-taking" powers reminiscent of the European communities.

The 1991 Protocol established the Central American Integration System **7–016** (SICA), comprising the original members of the ODECA together with Panama.[24] SICA is to be the institutional framework of the Central American Regional Integration, the main objective of which is to achieve the integration of Central America as a region of peace, freedom, democracy and development (Article 3). A series of governing principles are set out in Article 4. The Protocol modifies the institutional structure pre-existing in Central America and regulated before by the ODECA. By its Article 12 the Protocol establishes an institutional framework of four main organs: the Meeting of Presidents, the Council of Ministers, the Executive Council and the Secretary-General. The protocol also provides for a Central American Parliament (PARLACEN),[25] a Central American Court of Justice[26] and a Consultative Committee. The "supreme organ" of the ODECA is the meeting of presidents, which meets regularly and takes decisions by consensus. The Council of Ministers is responsible for setting the agenda and executing decisions of the meeting of presidents. Representation at the council is by the relevant minister. The Foreign Affairs Ministers' Council is the "principal organ" of co-ordination. Substantive decisions are taken on the basis of consensus. The Executive Council is composed of a representative of each member state. The President of the Council is the representative of that state where the last ordinary Meeting of Presidents took place. The Executive Council is charged with the implementation of decisions of Meeting of Presidents (Article 24). The structure of the Council and its functions replicates, to a certain extent, some other models present in other regions of the world (*i.e.* Council of the European Community). Finally, the Secretary General is the legal representative of the SICA (Article 26). The SICA has legal personality and within the framework of its competencies it may enter into treaties or agreements subject to the previous institutional control according to the functions established (Article 31).

(c) THE CARIBBEAN COMMUNITY (CARICOM)

Bibliography: Simmonds, "The Caribbean Economic Community: A New Venture in Regional Integration" (1974) 23 ICLQ 453; H. Geiser *et al.*, *Legal Problems of Caribbean Integration* (1976); Meijers, "New International Persons in the Caribbean" (1977) 24 Netherlands International Law Review 160; Axline, *Caribbean Integration* (1979); Carnegie, "Commonwealth Caribbean Regionalism: Legal Aspects" (1979) 33 Yearbook of World Affairs 180; Payne, *The Politics of the Caribbean Community* (1980); Menon, "Regional

---

[24] The 1991 Protocol also encourages Belize to join: Art. 36.
[25] PARLACEN was created by the "Esquipulas Agreements I" adopted in Esquipulas (Guatemala) on May 25, 1986, These Agreements led to the Constitutional Treaty which was adopted in 1987 in Guatamala initially ratified by Guatamala, Honduras, El Salvador and Nicaragua and ratified by Panama in 1994. The PARLACEN was finally settled in Guatamala on October 28, 1991. For more information see http://parlacen.org.gt.
[26] See Chap. 13, para. 13–154.

integration: a case study of the Caribbean community (CARICOM)" (1995) 5 Caribbean Law Review 81. Website: http://www.caricom.org.

7–017 The Treaty of Chaguaramas establishing CARICOM, which was signed by Barbados, Jamaica, Guyana and Trindad and Tobago, came into effect on August 1, 1973.[27] The organisation replaced CARIFTA, the Caribbean Free Trade Area, and currently has 14 full members; the original four members, together with Antigua and Barbuda, the Bahamas, Belize, Dominica, Grenada, Montserrat, St. Kitts and Nevis, Saint Lucia, St. Vincent and the Grenadines and Suriname.[28] The principal organs of the community are the conference of heads of government and the community council of ministers. The conference is the supreme organ with the primary responsibility for the determination and provision of policy direction for the community. In October 1992, at the special meeting of heads of government, a decision was taken to create a Bureau of the Conference. Its responsibilities are to initiate proposals, update consensus and mobilise and secure implementation of CARICOM decisions. Subordinate to the Conference is the Council, consisting of ministers responsible for community affairs, as well as any other minister designated by member states in their absolute discretion. The Council's functions are to develop strategic planning of CARICOM and co-ordination in the areas of economic integration, functional co-operation and external relations. In addition to the principal organs there are a number of Ministerial Councils established to streamline the functioning of the community. These include the Council for Trade and Economic Development, the Council for Foreign and Community Relations, the Council for Finance and Planning and the Council for Human and Social Development.

7–018 Presently the CARICOM is undergoing change with a large number of Protocols of Amendment to the Treaty of Chaguaramas proposed to achieve the creation of a Caribbean Common Market.[29] Chief among the proposals are those for a CARICOM Single Market, with free trade in goods, services, people and capital throughout the community, and a

---

[27] See Inter-American Institute of International Legal Studies, *Instruments of Economic Integration in Latin-America and the Caribbean* (1975), p. 645.

[28] The Republic of Haiti has satisfied all the terms and conditions for membership of the community, except the deposit with the Secretary-General of an appropriate instrument of accession. Once this formality is completed, Haiti will assume full membership of the community.

[29] There are nine Protocols proposed; Protocol I addresses organs, institutions and procedures of the community; Protocol II addresses the right of establishment, right to provide services and the right to move capital; Protocol III addresses the community industrial policy; protocol IV addresses trade liberalisation; protocol V addresses the community agricultural policy; protocol VI addresses the community transport policy; Protocol VII addresses disadvantaged countries, regions and sectors; Protocol VIII addresses Rules of Competition and Protocol IX addresses Dispute Settlement. The text of these Protocols can be found at the CARICOM website (http://www.caricom.org).

CARICOM single economy aiming to harmonise further economic, monetary and fiscal policies and measures across all member states to underpin sustainable development of the region. In 1999 CARICOM states also began work on a Caribbean Court of Justice, with jurisdiction on criminal appeals and to replace the London-based Privy Council, a relic of the colonial period.

B. ORGANISATIONS OF LIMITED COMPETENCE

The region is characterised by a surprisingly large number of organisations **7–019** and arrangements dedicated to the promotion of economic integration and free trade. As will be seen, their institutional structures vary widely.

(a) THE CENTRAL AMERICAN COMMON MARKET (CACM)

The 1960 Treaty of Managua—the General Treaty for Central American **7–020** Economic Integration—was to a large extent born out of frustration with ODECA and the belief that by concentrating on the economic sphere more impressive progress could be made.[30] The experience is not uncommon: the emergence of the European communities out of frustration with the Council of Europe and OEEC, or of the African regional "Common Markets" out of frustration with the OAU are comparable developments. The CACM aimed at a fully established Common Market in five years as well as a customs union. The Organisation was, however, virtually wrecked by the 1969 hostilities between El Salvador and Honduras, with Honduras withdrawing from the CACM in December 1970. The signing of the Central American Peace Agreement (Esquipulas II) in August 1987[31] made possible renewed efforts for economic integration in the region. In June 1990, at the 8th Summit of Central American Presidents held in Antigua, Guatemala, an Economic Action Plan for Central America was approved that envisioned insertion of the region's economy into the global economy. In July 1991, at the San Salvador 10th Summit, it was agreed to include Panama in certain aspects of the economic community. The 11th Summit in Tegucigalpa, Honduras saw the modification of several CACM institutions and their incorporation into the System of Central American Integration (SICA).[32] In 1992 Honduras rejoined the integration process, signing the Transitional Multilateral Free Trade Agreement with the other Central American countries. Although numerous impediments to integration, from military to economic issues, remain in the region, the CACM may

---

[30] Text in Inter-American Institute of International Legal Studies, *Instruments Relating to the Economic Integration of Latin-America* (1968), p. 23.

[31] Costa-Rica—El Salvador—Guatemala—Honduras—Nicaragua: Agreement on Procedure for Establishing Firm and Lasting Peace in Central America (1987) 26 ILM 1164.

[32] For further information concerning this organisation refer to its website at http://www.sicanet.org.sv (Spanish only).

nevertheless be revived by the recent surge of interest in economic integration triggered by the North-American Free Trade Agreement (NAFTA).

(b) THE LATIN-AMERICAN ECONOMIC SYSTEM (SELA)[33]

7–021 SELA was established by the Agreement of Panama of October 1975, as a regional entity for joint consultation in economic and social matters.[34] It has a permanent Secretariat and two other organs. One is the Latin-American Council, meeting annually at Ministerial level and voting either by consensus or by two-thirds majority, according to the nature of the matter in question. The other organ, or set of organs, are the Action Committees, designed to carry out specific studies or programs. There are currently two permanent bodies; the Latin American Technological Information Network and the Latin American Fisheries Development Organisation, as well as numerous co-operation mechanisms.[35] Since its inception SELA has promoted regional co-ordination on economic issues of common interest, focusing on inserting the region into the world's economic globalisation process.

(c) THE ANDEAN PACT

Bibliography: García-Amador, *The Andean Legal Order* (1978); Vargas-Hidalgo, "An Evaluation of the Andean Pact" (1978) 10 Lawyer of the Americas 401; Middlebrook, "Regional Organisations and Andean Economic Integration, 1969–75" (1978) 17 Journal of Common Market Studies 62; García-Amador, "Some Legal Aspects of the Andean Economic Integration" in: *Jus et Societas, Essays in Tribute to Wolfgang Friedmann* (1979), p. 96; Esquirol, "Foreign Investment: Revision of the Andean Foreign Investment Code" (1988) 29 Harvard ILJ 169; S. Arteta, "Andean Pact Developments" (1992) 7 Florida Journal of International Law 113. Website: http://www.comunidadandina.org.

7–022 This organisation began as a sub-regional agreement within the Latin America Free Trade Association. Under the Treaty of Bogota of May 26, 1969,[36] the states of Bolivia, Chile, Colombia, Ecuador and Peru[37] moved towards closer integration than was possible within LAFTA itself, and the sub-regional grouping was approved by the LAFTA Permanent Executive Committee. Significant policy and institutional reforms to the organisation

---

[33] An English version of the website for this organisation can be found at http://lanic.utexas.edu/sela/english.htm.

[34] The organisation embraces countries from both Central and South America, as well as Caribbean states: text in (1976) 15 ILM 1081.

[35] These co-operation mechanisms include the Latin American Commission for Science and Technology, the Latin American and Caribbean Handicrafts Co-operation Programme, and the Latin American and Caribbean Trade and Foreign Trade Information Programme.

[36] (1969) 8 ILM 910.

[37] Venezuela adhered by a separate instrument: *ibid.,* 939. Chile subsequently withdrew in 1976.

were accomplished by the protocols of Trujillo and Sucre, which established the Andean Community and the Andean Integration System. The Andean Community commenced operation on August 1, 1997 with a General Secretariat as its executive body. There are three principal organs of the organisation: the Andean Presidential Council, the Andean Council of Foreign Ministers and the Commission of the Andean Community. The Presidential Council is the supreme organ of the Andean Integration System. It is responsible for issuing guidelines concerning sub-regional integration, which are then implemented by other bodies and institutions of the system. The Council of Foreign Ministers provides political leadership for the organisation, ensuring the attainment of objectives for sub-regional integration and carrying out the Andean Community's foreign policy. The Council may adopt non-binding statements, referred to as Declarations, or legally binding "decisions." Consensus is required for both types of statements. The Commission is the primary policy-making body of the Andean Integration System. The Commission may also assume a legislative role, adopting decisions with the Council of Foreign Ministers.

The judicial body of the Andean Community is the Court of Justice, **7–023** comprising of five judges, each representing one of the member states.[38] The Protocol Modifying the Charter of the Court of Justice of the Andean Community, approved on May 28, 1996, confers new functions on the court relating to labour actions and actions concerning an omission to act.[39] An Andean Parliament was established in 1979, which functions as the deliberative body of the Andean Integration System.[40] Currently each member sends five representatives from its National Parliament to make up the body, however, it is intended that its members will be elected by direct and universal vote after the entry into force of the 1997 Additional Protocol on Direct and Universal Elections. The Andean Development Corporation was established as a separate institution, with a mission to support the integration and sustainable development of the shareholder countries by raising funds for the delivery of financial services.[41] The current objectives of the Andean Community include facilitating participation in the regional integration process with the aim of creating a Latin-American Common Market.

(d) REGIONAL DEVELOPMENT BANKS

The Inter-American Development Bank (IDB) is headquartered in Wash- **7–024** ington D.C., and was established in December 1959 under the auspices of the Economic Conference of the OAS with the aim of contributing "to the

---

[38] (1979) 18 ILM 1203.
[39] The instrument entered into force on August 25, 1999.
[40] (1980) 19 ILM 269.
[41] For the Agreement of 1968 see *ibid.* 940.

acceleration of the process of economic and social development of the regional developing member countries."[42] The financial resources of the bank come partly from contributions made by member states, together with reserves and borrowings. Currently 46 nations are members of the bank, including both regional and non-regional countries.[43] The highest authority of the IDB is the Board of Governors, with one representative from each member state.[44] The majority of the board's operational powers are delegated to the Board of Executive Directors. In addition to the bank, the IDB Group includes the Inter-American Investment Corporation (IIC) and the Multilateral Investment Fund (MIF). The IIC is an affiliate of the bank, established to promote economic development of the region by financing small and medium scale private enterprises. The MIF was created in 1992 in order to promote investment reforms and stimulate private sector development.

The IDB's functions under its Charter are to:

(a) utilise its own capital, funds raised by it in financial markets and other available resources for financing the development of borrowing member countries;

(b) supplement private investment when private capital is not available on reasonable terms and conditions; and

(c) provide technical assistance for the preparation, financing and implementation of development plans and projects.

7–025 During the 1960s and 1970s the Bank's lending emphasised the productive sectors of agriculture and industry, the physical infrastructure sectors of energy and transportation and the social sectors of environmental and public health, education and urban development. Its current lending priorities have shifted, and the focus is now on poverty reduction and social equity, modernisation and integration and the environment.

7–026 The Carribean Development Bank was established in 1969, and is based in Barbados.[45] By Article 1 of its Charter its purpose is "to contribute to the harmonious economic growth and development of the member countries in the Caribbean and to promote economic cooperation and integration

---

[42] Washington D.C., April 8, 1959, in force December 30, 1959, (1961) 389 U.N.T.S. 69. Website: http://www.iadb.org.

[43] The bank's original membership included 19 Latin-American and Caribbean countries together with the U.S. Subsequently, eight other western hemisphere nations, including Canada, joined the bank. Between 1976 and 1993, 18 non-regional countries joined the bank, their entry being authorised by the 1974 Declaration of Madrid.

[44] Usually the ministers of finance, presidents of central banks, or other comparable officers of member states.

[45] Website: http://www.caribank.org.

among them, having special and urgent regard to the needs of the less developed members of the region." Its functions include assisting regional members in the co-ordination of their development programmes with a view to achieving better utilisation of their resources, making their economies more complementary, and promoting the orderly expansion of their international trade, in particular intra-regional trade; mobilising additional financial resources for the development of the region; financing projects and programmes contributing to the development of the region or any of the regional members; providing technical assistance to its regional members; promoting public and private investment in development projects; and stimulating the development of capital markets within the region (Article 2). It currently has 20 regional and six non-regional members. The bank's institutional structure comprises a board of governors and a board of directors, as well as a president and secretariat. The bank's lending activities are divided into two major categories: ordinary operations and special operations, and the bank's operations provide principally for the financing of specific projects, whether forming part of national, sub-regional or regional development programmes in such fields as agriculture, livestock, fisheries, forestry, marketing, manufacturing, mining, refining, tourism, export services, transportation, housing, education, power, water, sewerage, infrastructure and related services, waste management, environment protection and poverty reduction. Special attention is given to ensure that the intervention by the bank promotes social equity and environment protection. By Article 13 of its charter the bank may also make equity investments, but there are strict limitations placed on its exercise of this power.

(e) MERCOSUR (SOUTHERN CONE COMMON MARKET)

Haines-Ferrari, "Mercosur: A New Model of Latin American Economic Integration?" (1993) 25 Case Western Res. J. of Int. Law 413; Rosselli "MERCOSUR and the Free Trade Area of the Americas" (1996) 27 *Revue Generale de* Droit/Universite dé Ottawa 83; Borba Casella, "From dispute settlement to jurisdiction? Perspectives for the Mercosur" (1997) 11 Studies in Transnational Economic Law 553; Etcheverry, "Settlement of disputes in the South American Common Market (Mercosur)" (1997) 11 Studies in Transnational Economic Law 543; Guira, "MERCOSUR as an Instrument for Development" (1997) 3–3 NAFTA: Law and Business Review of the Americas 53; Lopez, "Dispute Resolution Under MERCOSUR from 1991 to 1996: Implications for the Formation of a Free Trade Area of the Americas" (1997) 3–2 NAFTA: Law and Business Review of the Americas 3. Website: http://www.mercosur.org.

The MERCOSUR group, consisting of Argentina, Brazil, Paraguay and **7–027** Uruguay,[46] was formed by the Treaty of Asuncion in 1991.[47] The main objective of the group was the creation of free trade zones, leading to

---

[46] Chile and Bolivia initially were associate members, and joined MERCOSUR in 1996.
[47] Treaty Establishing a Common Market, March 26, 1991, UN Doc. A/46/155 (1991).

customs unification and finally to a Common Market. A target date of December 31, 1994 was set for the lifting of import duties by all members of the group, though this was subject to a list of exceptions for particular products of the different member states. Currently, 95 per cent of the bloc's trade is duty free and the remaining barriers are set to be abolished no later than December 31, 1999.[48] The two primary institutions of MERCOSUR are the Common Market Council (CMC) and the Common Market Group (CMG). The CMC consists of Ministers of Foreign Relations and Economics for each of the member states. The CMC is the highest level agency in the organisation, providing political leadership and responsible for policy development. Meetings of the CMC are held at least annually, with all decision-making by consensus. The CMG is the executive agency of the organisation, in charge of overseeing and implementing the treaty and enforcing decisions of the CMC. The CMG also devises and oversees a schedule for movement of the member states towards a common market. The CMG consists of four permanent members and four alternate members representing each state, who meet at least annually. The CMG may establish work subgroups to carry out studies on special areas of concern to the organisation. Representation for the parliaments of the member states is provided by the MERCOSUR Joint Parliamentary Commission,[49] which has responsibility for accelerating the internal procedures of member states so that the norms of the Common Market are made effective. In addition to these institutions, there is a Trade Commission created to oversee the implementation of common trade rules and policies. The original dispute resolution mechanism provided for under the Treaty of Asuncion involved three stages; direct negotiations between the parties, failing which the dispute could be referred to the CMG, which had to render a decision within 60 days, or referral of the dispute to the CMC for analysis. The Brasilia Protocol for Dispute Settlement, adopted in late 1991, significantly expanded the scope of issues that can be subject to dispute settlement and introduced an arbitral mechanism whereby parties can refer the dispute to an ad hoc tribunal of three judges. To date, MERCOSUR may be Latin-America's most successful attempt at regional integration, the organisation representing the second largest trading group in the region.[50] Recent negotiations between MERCOSUR and the Andean Pact countries foreshadow a future trade area spanning South America and providing a powerful counterpart to NAFTA.

(f) NORTH AMERICAN FREE TRADE AGREEMENT (NAFTA)

Bibliography: Abbott, "Integration without Institutions: The NAFTA Mutation of the EC Model and the Future of the GATT Regime" (1992) 4

---

[48] Anderson, "The Future of Hemispheric Free Trade: Towards a Unified Hemisphere?" (1998) 20 Houston J. of International Law 635, 654.
[49] Provision for this new institution was made in the protocol of Ouro Preto concluded in Brazil on December 31, 1994.
[50] The largest regional trading group being the North American Free Trade Agreement (NAFTA).

American Journal of Comparative Law 917; Appleton, *Navigating NAFTA: A Concise User's Guide to the North American Free Trade Agreement* (1994); Garcia, "NAFTA and the Creation of the FTAA: A Critique of Piecemeal Accession" (1995) 35 Virginia Journal of International Law 539; de Mestral, "The Significance of the NAFTA Side Agreements on Environmental and Labour Cooperation" (1998) 15 Arizona Journal of International and Comparative Law 169. Website of the NAFTA Secretariat: http://www.nafta-sec-alena.org.

The North American Free Trade Agreement (NAFTA), between the United States, Canada and Mexico, came into effect on January 1, 1994.[51] NAFTA aims to reduce tariffs and other trade restrictions within the three member states over a 15 year period. The free trade zone established by NAFTA comprises more than 360 million people, and while not designed to operate as a fully fledged Common Market, is intended to liberalise treatment of investment, intellectual property and services across North America by providing a free trade zone in goods and services. **7–028**

NAFTA builds upon the framework of the Canada-United States Free Trade Agreement,[52] incorporating many of the latter's provisions. In addition to the text of NAFTA itself, there are Supplementary Agreements on Labour[53] and Environmental Co-operation.[54] The institutional structure of NAFTA is limited, and in this sense it is not an international organisation in the sense of many others identified in this part of the book. Nevertheless, it is substantively important and those organs which have been established justify its consideration in these pages. **7–029**

The principal organ and political structure of NAFTA is the Free Trade Commission (FTC), composed of cabinet-level representatives from the respective parties. The FTC supervises the work of all NAFTA committees and work groups (Article 2001). Domestic judicial or administrative tribunals of the parties may refer interpretation questions in any case to the FTC, a rough equivalent to the system of preliminary references provided for in the E.C. system. The Commission has the power to make interpretative rulings on NAFTA that are binding on dispute resolution panels.[55] The FTC is assisted by a secretariat, established pursuant to Article 2002 of NAFTA. In addition to providing assistance to the FTC and supporting the work of other NAFTA committees and groups, the Secretariat is charged with providing assistance to dispute resolution panels established under Chapters 11, 14, 19 or 20 of the agreement. **7–030**

NAFTA contains 22 chapters of provisions dealing with various aspects of the liberalisation of trade and investment in North America. Unlike the Canada-United States Free Trade Agreement on which it was based, the **7–031**

---

[51] (1993) 32 ILM 289.
[52] (1988) 27 ILM 281.
[53] North American Agreement on Labor Co-operation, (1993) 32 ILM 1499.
[54] North American Agreement on Environmental Co-operation, (1993) 32 ILM 1480.
[55] Chap. 13, paras 13–157 *et seq.*

NAFTA adopts a negative listing process such that the inclusion of a subject in NAFTA means that all matters falling within that subject are included unless specifically exempted from the provisions of the agreement. By virtue of Article 105 of the agreement, the parties are to ensure that "all necessary measures are taken" to give effect to the provisions of NAFTA, "including their observance, except as otherwise provided in this Agreement, by state, provincial and local governments." In Article 103 of NAFTA, each party affirms its rights and obligations under the GATT and other international agreements though it is provided that NAFTA takes priority over other international agreements unless otherwise stated. The objectives and scope of the NAFTA are set out in Chapter 1 of the agreement. These objectives include eliminating barriers to trade promoting fair competition, expanding foreign investment, protecting intellectual property rights, and establishing a framework for further trilateral, regional and multilateral co-operation to expand and enhance the benefits of the agreement.

7–032 NAFTA has supplementary agreements dealing with labour and environmental co-operation, seeking to address concerns over domestic enforcement by member states of environmental and labour laws. The agreements establish a general obligation on the parties to provide fair treatment under, and enforcement of, their labour and environmental laws. The agreements, however, do not establish any specific levels of required environmental or labour protection and there are no requirements for harmonisation of laws in an upward fashion. The objectives of the environmental co-operation agreement include the promotion of sustainable development, co-operation on the conservation, protection and enhancement of the environment and the effective enforcement of and compliance with domestic environmental laws. The parties are to ensure that their laws provide for high levels of environmental protection and are to strive for continuous improvement of those laws, though each party retains the right to establish its own levels of protection, policies and priorities. A Commission for Environmental Co-operation was created to oversee the implementation of the agreement. It is headed by a Council of Ministers and assisted by a Secretariat and a Joint Public Advisory Committee. The Council has limited powers to adopt non-binding recommendations concerning environmental impact assessment, public access to information, appropriate limits for specific pollutants and reciprocal access to rights and remedies for damage or injuries resulting from transboundary pollution. In respect of the enforcement process for the agreement, the Council has a more prominent role, being able to accept complaints of failures by a party to enforce its environmental laws effectively and to establish arbitral panels. Panel reports are intended to form the basis of an agreement between the disputing parties on a mutually satisfactory action plan.

In a similar manner, the Labour Co-operation Agreement obliges parties **7–033** to ensure that their labour laws and regulations provide for high labour standards, consistent with high quality and productive workplaces, and to strive to improve those standards in that light. Parties are to ensure effective enforcement of their labour laws, including the assurance of access by persons with a legally recognised interest to administrative, judicial and related tribunals through which labour rights can be enforced in a binding fashion. A trinational Labour Commission is created by the agreement, headed by a Ministerial Council and assisted by a secretariat and National Administrative Offices (NAOs) established by each party. Provision is made for co-operative consultations and evaluation of questions concerning the enforcement of labour laws at the level of NAOs or the Ministerial Council. The Ministerial Council may also create an ad hoc Evaluation Committee of Experts (ECE) to conduct analyses and make recommendations to the Council. Where a dispute concerning a party's persistent failure to enforce labour laws cannot be resolved through the mechanism of an ECE report and consultations, any party may request the establishment of an arbitral panel to resolve the dispute. Once again, the panel's report is intended to lead an agreement between the parties on a mutually satisfactory action plan.

(g) THE LATIN-AMERICAN INTEGRATION ASSOCIATION (ALADI)[56]

This organisation, created by Treaty of August 12, 1980, replaced LAFTA, **7–034** the Latin-American Free Trade Association, with the long-range objective of establishing a Latin-American Common Market.[57] Its novel feature is that it envisages differential treatment amongst the members to accommodate their differing levels of economic development. It has a Council of Foreign Ministers as a supreme organ, taking decisions on broad policy. Yet, since the crucial commitments of members will derive from the agreements to be freely negotiated between members, the Council is not a "supra-national" body. There is a conference, meeting every three years, and a permanent body in the form of a Committee of Representatives, plus a Secretariat. The council, conference and committee take decisions by a two-thirds majority vote provided no member country casts a negative vote on certain defined, important questions (Article 43).

---

[56] This organisation maintains its own website at http://www.aladi.org.
[57] (1981) 20 ILM 672. Many of the members are also members of SELA. LAFTA had aimed at the elimination of tariff barriers between all members by 1972, and in this it failed, in part due to the differences in economic development of the members. ALADI classifies members into three groups, according to development, and provides for tariff concessions to be granted individually rather than collectively, but with preferences being given to the poorer countries.

CHAPTER 8

ASIA

Bibliography: Haas, *Basic Documents of Asian Regional Organisations* (1974–85) Vols 1–9.

Asia is characterised by a singular lack of regional organisations as **8–001** compared with Europe, the Americas and Africa. The reasons for this are not entirely clear, although it may not be unrelated to the broad range of geopolitical interests and cultural groupings within the region. For many years the principal regional organisations were the two established for collective self-defence, namely the South-East Asian Treaty Organisation (SEATO) and the tripartite pact between Australia, New Zealand and the United States (ANZUS). With the dissolution of SEATO in June 1977, ANZUS remains as the only notable defence pact and there is still no comprehensive military organisation embracing the majority of states within the region. Beyond the organisations which are part of the UN—such as the Economic Commission for Asia—the most significant regional organisations concerned with political and economic matters are the Association of Southeast Asian Nations (ASEAN), formed in August 1967 between Indonesia, Malaysia, Thailand, Philippines and Singapore, and the South Asian Association for Regional Co-operation (SAARC) established by seven South Asian countries in August 1983. In the economic field the Colombo Plan, established in 1950, was initially the most important regional forum for consultation, supplementing the work of the UN agencies such as the World Bank, UNDP and ECAFE.[1] At the meeting of the Plan's Consultative Committee in November 1980, the member countries reaffirmed the objectives of the Plan and agreed to extend its life indefinitely. However, both the Consultative Committee, which is concerned with economic development in general, and the Council for Technical Co-operation, which is concerned with the narrower field of technical assistance, are consultative conferences of governments: the

---

[1] Basch, "The Colombo Plan: A Case of Regional Economic Cooperation" (1955) 9 International Organization, 1–18; Waugh, "The Colombo Plan: Origins and Progress" (1954) Dept. State Bull., 640, 644. The Colombo Plan for Co-operative Economic Development in South and South-East Asia: Report by the Commonwealth Consultative Committee, London, September–October 1950, British Command paper, Cmd. 8080 (1950); Burns, "The Colombo Plan," (1960) Y.B.W.A. 176.

organs are simply a forum for discussion of common problems and even the aid supplied is by means of bilateral agreements. The plan therefore represents an example of governmental co-operation at the most elementary level from the organisational point of view.[2]

8–002 In 1965 the Asian Development Bank was established[3] and, more recently, the Asia-Pacific Economic Co-operation (APEC) established in 1989 with members from both within and outside the region has assumed growing significance, although its institutional structure remains rudimentary and it has, as yet, no legal personality of its own. There are a number of other inter-governmental organisations in this region which space will not permit to be treated: the Asian-African Legal Consultative Committee (a kind of regional International Law Commission); the Asian-Pacific Coconut Community, the Asian Productivity Organisation and the South Pacific Forum, a consultative body made up of the governments of independent and self-governing Pacific Island countries together with Australia and New Zealand. For historical reasons it is also worth mentioning the Conference of Afro-Asian States, held at Bandung in 1955, which was an ad hoc conference for the discussion of common problems which, in its final communiqué, put forward resolutions on matters such as economic co-operation, cultural co-operation, human rights and self-determination, problems of dependent peoples and world peace.[4] Twenty-nine governments were represented at that conference. Subsequently, at Cairo in 1958, the second Afro-Asian Solidarity Conference was held and set up a Permanent Council, to meet annually and composed of one representative from each national committee, and a permanent Secretariat headed by a Secretary-General. It is financed by the governments, but at the Cairo Conference "peoples" rather than states were represented, there being 400 representatives from 46 peoples of Asia and Africa. The organisation thus appears to be something of a hybrid, for it cannot be regarded as a strictly inter-governmental organisation since 1958.

(a) THE ASSOCIATION OF SOUTH EAST ASIAN NATIONS (ASEAN)

Bibliography: ASEAN, The Asean Report (1979), 2 Vols; Garnut (ed.), *ASEAN in a Changing Pacific and World Economy* (1980); Broinowski (ed.), *Understanding ASEAN* (1982); ASEAN Secretariat (ed.), *ASEAN: The First Twenty Years* (1987); Kenevan and Winden, "Flexible Free Trade: The ASEAN Free Trade Area" (1993) 34 Harvard International Law Journal 224;

---

[2] The participating governments are now no longer confined to members of the Commonwealth, but include the USA, Philippines, Japan and Indonesia. Following the expansion of participation in the Plan to non-Commonwealth countries its name was officially changed to the "Colombo Plan for Economic and Social Development in Asia and the Pacific."

[3] (1966) 5 ILM 262: and see (1965) 4 Philippine L.1. Spec. Supp.

[4] See RIIA Survey, 1955–56, and Documents, 1955, Part IV; the text of the final communiqué is given in the latter at p. 429.

Davidson, ASEAN: the legal framework for its trade relations", 49 Int.Jnl 588 (1993–4); Chew, "A Primer on the ASEAN Free Trade Area" 11 Bulletin for International Fiscal Documentation 594 (1994); Stephenson, "ASEAN and the multilateral trading system (1994) 25 Law and Policy in International Business 439; Goyer, "ASEAN Free Trade Area: making the region more investment competitive" (1996) 18 East Asian Executive Reports 9. Website: http://www.aseansec.org.

ASEAN developed from the Declaration of August 8, 1967 of the foreign **8–003** ministers of Indonesia, Thailand, Malaysia, Singapore and the Philippines, which made ASEAN open for participation by other nations in the South-East Asian region.[5] In the late 1960s and 1970s, Cambodia, Laos and South Vietnam attended some of ASEAN's meetings as observers. However, regional instability thwarted any further development of regional co-operation until the 1980s. In January 1984 Brunei Darussalem was admitted as the sixth member of ASEAN. More admissions did not follow until ten years later when Vietnam was admitted in July 1995. The admissions of Laos and Myanmar followed in 1997, and with the admission of Cambodia in 1999 ASEAN attained its goal of securing the participation of all ten South-East Asian nations in the organisation.

The aims of ASEAN, as expressed in the 1967 Declaration, are both **8–004** economic and political, for they include not only the promotion of economic collaboration but also the promotion of regional peace and stability. The parties' aspirations to peace, friendship and co-operation were reaffirmed in the 1976 Treaty of Amity and Co-operation in South-East Asia,[6] which was endorsed by the UN General Assembly in 1992. Chapter IV of the treaty provides for the peaceful settlement of disputes between the parties. A High Council consisting of ministerial representatives is established to take cognisance of the existence of disputes or situations likely to disturb peace and harmony in the region. The High Council may recommend appropriate means of settlement to the disputing parties or itself provide good offices, mediation, inquiry or conciliation with the consent of the parties. The provisions of the Chapter do not preclude recourse to modes of peaceful settlement under Article 33(1) of the UN Charter. Other ASEAN initiatives in the field of promotion of regional peace and security are the 1971 Zone of Peace, Freedom and Neutrality Declaration and the 1995 Treaty on the Southeast Asia Nuclear Weapon-Free Zone.[7]

The declaration of ASEAN Concord,[8] signed at Bali in February 1976, **8–005** set out more detailed objectives in the fields of economic co-operation, social development and regional security in amplification of the 1967

---

[5] (1967) 6 ILM 1233.
[6] (1976) 1025 U.N.T.S. 297.
[7] 35 ILM 635 (1996).
[8] See *supra*. n. 6.

Declaration. The economic objectives of the ASEAN Concord embraced co-operation in the field of commodities, ASEAN industrial projects and joint efforts towards achieving preferential trading arrangements and improving access to markets outside ASEAN. Its social objectives related principally to the acceleration of development of low-income groups and rural populations, and dealing with traffic in narcotics between the member states. In the area of regional security the Concord endorsed the continuation of co-operation on a non-ASEAN basis between the member states in accordance with their mutual needs and interests. The 1990s have seen attempts to further ASEAN economic co-operation with agreement at the Fourth ASEAN Summit in 1992 to establish an ASEAN Free Trade Area (AFTA) by 2008. In September 1994 the Parties agreed to accelerate the AFTA process, reducing the target date by five years. The main mechanism for realisation of the AFTA is the Common Effective Preferential Tariff scheme (CEPT) launched on January 1, 1993. The CEPT covers both manufactured and agricultural products and requires the reduction of tariffs on all included products, as well as the elimination of quantitative and non-tariff barriers. In terms of social development, ASEAN has initiated co-operative mechanisms in the field of science and technology, the environment, culture and information, social development, drugs and narcotics control and the civil service. The majority of these co-operative mechanisms take the form of ASEAN Committees.[9]

8–006   The highest authority of ASEAN is the meeting of the heads of government. At the fourth ASEAN summit, held in Singapore in 1992, it was decided that the heads of government would meet formally every three years, rather than annually, with informal summits in between. The ASEAN ministerial meeting (AMM) has replaced the heads of government meeting as the primary method for regularly reviewing the work and policies of ASEAN. This body is composed of ASEAN foreign ministers and meets annually. The AMM is responsible for the formulation of policy guidelines and the co-ordination of ASEAN activities. In addition to the AMM, the ASEAN Economic Ministers (AEM) meets annually to direct ASEAN economic co-operation.[10] At the Fourth Summit the AFTA Council was established within the AEM to supervise, co-ordinate and review the implementation of the CEPT scheme.

8–007   The Agreement of Establishment of the Permanent Secretary of ASEAN, signed at Bali in February 1976,[11] provided for the appointment of a full time Secretary-General of ASEAN who co-ordinates (but does not

---

[9] Some examples are the ASEAN Committee on Science and Technology, ASEAN Senior Officials on the Environment, the ASEAN Committee on Culture and Information and the Committee on Social Development.
[10] This body was institutionalised at the 1997 Kuala Lumpur Summit.
[11] (1983) 1331 U.N.T.S. 243.

replace) the national Secretaries-General in the member states. The 1992 Protocol amending the 1976 Agreement provides that the secretary-general is responsible to the heads of government meeting, to all meetings of ASEAN Ministers when in session and to the chairman of the ASEAN Standing Committee (ASC). The ASC is the policy arm and organ of co-ordination of ASEAN between the AMM's. It consists of a chairman (the foreign minister of the country hosting the AMM), the secretary-general and the director-generals of the national secretariats. In addition to these organs, ASEAN has established various committees to handle ASEAN's external relations with each of its "Dialogue Partner" countries.[12]

(b) ASIAN DEVELOPMENT BANK

Bibliography: Website: http://www.adb.org.

The Asian Development Bank (ADB) is a multilateral finance institution **8–008** established in 1966. In the early 1960s, the Economic Commission for Asia and the Far East estimated that Asia and the Pacific faced an annual deficit of $1 billion in external assistance and conceived the ADB as a means of filling that gap. Following an inaugural meeting in Tokyo in November 1966, the ADB was installed in Manila, Philippines.[13] The ADB originally had 31 member countries, but that number has now grown to 57, 41 of whom are from the region and 16 of whom are non-regional countries. The ADB is headed by a board of governors, which delegates functions to the executive body—the board of directors. The President of the ADB oversees its overall operation and is assisted by three vice-presidents with respon-sibility for western programmes, eastern programmes and finance and administration respectively. The primary functions of the ADB are:

(a) extending loans and equity investments for economic and social development of its developing member countries;

(b) providing technical assistance for the preparation and execution of development projects and programmes and for advisory services;

(c) promoting and facilitating investment of public and private capital for development purposes; and

(d) responding to requests for assistance in co-ordinating development policies and plans of its developing member countries.

In 1995 the ADB adopted a medium term strategic framework which emphasises five strategic development objectives as part of the Bank's

---

[12] Australia, China, Russia, India, Canada, Korea, Japan, New Zealand, Pakistan and U.S., UNDP and the E.U. are also dialogue partners of ASEAN.

[13] In addition to its headquarters in Manila, the Bank maintains representative offices in donor countries: Europe (Frankfurt), Japan (Tokyo) and North America (Washington DC).

mandate to contribute to sustainable development of the region's countries: economic growth; reducing poverty; supporting human development; improving the status of women and protecting the environment.

(c) SOUTH ASIAN ASSOCIATION FOR REGIONAL CO-OPERATION

Bibliography: Website: http://www.south-asia.com/saarc.

8–009   The South Asian Association for Regional Co-operation (SAARC) consists of seven member countries: Bangladesh, Bhutan, India, Maldives, Nepal, Pakistan and Sri Lanka. The member countries issued the Declaration on South Asian Regional Co-operation in August 1983 and, at the first Summit held in Dahaka in 1985, the charter formally establishing the organisation was signed.[14] The objectives of SAARC include the promotion of welfare in its member countries; acceleration of their economic growth and development; strengthening of collective self-reliance; co-operation on a variety of functional and social issues and co-operation with similar regional and international organisations. An Integrated Programme of Action, launched contemporaneously with the 1983 declaration, provided the basis for co-operation in five areas; agriculture, rural development, telecommunications, meteorology and health and pollution activities. Later further areas of co-operation were designated as transport, postal services, scientific and technical co-operation, sports, arts and culture. One of the newest SAARC co-operative initiatives is the SAARC Preferential Trading Agreement (SAFTA) that came into force in December 1995. The agreement seeks to develop an institutional framework for furthering trade liberalisation in the region, with the aim of achieving a free trade area by 2001.

8–010   The institutional structure of SAARC is relatively simple. The highest authority is the heads of state or government, meeting annually at Summit level. Policy formulation and development is the responsibility of a council of ministers, consisting of the foreign ministers from the member states meeting twice annually or in extraordinary session with the agreement of the parties. A Standing Committee composed of the foreign secretaries of the member states is responsible for overall monitoring and co-ordination of programmes, determining priorities and modalities of financing, mobilising resources and identifying new areas for co-operation. The formulation and preparation of joint projects is overseen by various technical committees composed of representatives of member states. Finally there is a secretariat, headquartered in Kathmandu, with responsibilities for co-ordinating and monitoring the implementation of activities, servicing

---

[14] Charter of the South Asian Association for Regional Cooperation, December 8, 1985. The Charter is reproduced on the organisation's website: http://www.south-asia.com/saarc/charter.html.

meetings and providing a channel of communication between SAARC and other international organisations.

(d) ASIA-PACIFIC ECONOMIC CO-OPERATION (APEC)

Bibliography: Kodama, "Asia-Pacific Region: APEC and ASEAN" (1996) 30 International Lawyer 367; Website: http://www.apecsec.org.sg.

APEC was established in 1989 in response to the growing interdepen- **8–011** dence among economies of the Asia-Pacific region. It began as an informal dialogue group between its 12 founding members; Australia, Brunei Darussalam, Canada, Indonesia, Japan, Korea, Malaysia, New Zealand, the Philippines, Singapore, Thailand and the United States, but has developed into the primary vehicle for promoting open trade and economic co-operation in the region. With its growth APEC has added new members; China, Hong Kong and Taipei in 1991, Mexico and Papua New Guinea in 1993, Chile in 1994 and Peru, Russia and Vietnam in 1998. At this time APEC lacks any formal institutional structure. Decision-making is by consensus within the framework of annual meetings of the foreign and economic ministers of its parties. Regular Senior Official Meetings (SOM) are held prior to the ministerial meetings to devise recommendations and carry out decisions of the ministers. The SOM also oversees and co-ordinates the budgets and work programmes of APEC fora. An APEC secretariat was created as a result of the fourth APEC ministerial meeting. The secretariat is based in Singapore and provides advisory, operational, logistical and technical services for the organisation. In addition to these bodies a large number of advisory groups and committees have been established with competence in particular areas of concern to the APEC members.[15]

In the early years of APEC its member countries concerns were simply to **8–012** advance Asia-Pacific economic co-operation and promote a positive conclusion to the Uruguay Round of GATT negotiations. At the 1994 APEC Meeting in Bogor, Indonesia a goal was set of establishing free and open trade and investment in the Asia-Pacific by 2010 for developed member economies and 2020 for developing member economies.[16] The following year the parties agreed upon the Osaka Action Agenda that set out three areas of primary APEC activity:

---

[15] These advisory groups include the APEC Business Advisory Council, the Committee on Trade and Investment, the Economic Committee, the Budget and Management Committee, the SOM Sub-Committee on Economic and Technical Co-operation, the Policy Level Group on Small and Medium Enterprises, the Energy Working Group, the Fisheries Working Group, the Human Resource Development Working Group, the Industry, Science and Technology Working Group, the Marine Resource Conservation Working Group, the Telecommunications Working Group, the Tourism Working Group, the Trade Promotion Working Group, the Transport Working Group and the Agriculture and Technical Cooperation Experts Group.

[16] Bogor Declaration of Common Resolve, Bogor, Indonesia, November 1994.

(a) trade and investment liberalisation;

(b) business facilitation; and

(c) economic and technical co-operation.

8–013　The Manila Action Plan for APEC, endorsed by the APEC Ministers at the 1996 meeting, compiled the members' initial individual action plans to achieve the objectives outlined in the Bogor Declaration. At the 1997 meeting in Vancouver a plan of early sector liberalisation in 15 sectors was agreed to, with implementation to begin in 1999. The ministers also agreed to a Blueprint for APEC Customs Modernisation envisioning harmonisation and simplification of customs controls in the region by 2002. The Asian financial crisis has slowed efforts to achieve regional free trade and investment and recent meetings have focused on ways to assist rebuilding of the economies in the region.

(e) SOUTH PACIFIC FORUM

Bibliography: Website: http://www.forumsec.org.fj.

8–014　The South Pacific Forum is a regional organisation representing the heads of government of all of the independent and self-governing Pacific Island countries,[17] together with Australia and New Zealand. It is essentially a forum for expression of the joint political views of its member countries and for facilitating co-operation in areas of common political and economic concern. The first meeting of the Forum was held in 1971 in Wellington, New Zealand. Since then annual meetings have been held at the Head of Government level. Immediately following these meetings, post-Forum dialogue takes place at the Ministerial level with the Forum dialogue partners.[18] The administrative arm of the Forum is the South Pacific Forum Secretariat,[19] based in Suva, Fiji. The secretariat is headed by an executive, consisting of the Secretary-General and the Deputy Secretary-General. It oversees the implementation of programmes and activities of the organisation under guidelines decided by the Forum leaders.[20] The Secretary-General also chairs the South Pacific Organisation Co-ordinating Committee that supervises the activities of a number of regional organisa-

---

[17] Cook Islands, Federated States of Micronesia, Fiji, Kiribati, Nauru, Niue, Palau, Papua New Guinea, Republic of the Marshall Islands, Samoa, Solomon Islands, Tonga, Tuvalu, Vanuatu.

[18] Canada, European Union, France, Japan, Korea, Malaysia, China, U.K., U.S. and the Philippines.

[19] Originally the "Trade Bureau" and later the "South Pacific Bureau for Economic Cooperation;" the Secretariat's current name was adopted in 1988.

[20] There are currently four divisions within the Secretariat: Development and Economic Policy, Trade and Investment, Political and International Affairs and Corporate Services. Each division oversees a range of programmes designed to improve the capacity of member countries and to co-ordinate action on matters of common interest.

tions, including the South Pacific Regional Environment Programme (SPREP).[21]

The aims of SPREP are to promote co-operation in the South Pacific **8–015** region and to provide assistance in order to protect and improve its environment, and to ensure sustainable development for present and future generations. The organisation has 26 members, the 22 Pacific Island countries together with Australia, New Zealand, France and the U.S. SPREP grew out of a joint venture, established in 1982, between regional organisations (the South Pacific Bureau for Economic Co-operation—now the Forum Secretariat—and the South Pacific Commission) and the international organisations of the UN Environment Programme and the UN Economic and Social Commission for Asia. In 1991 the governing body of SPREP agreed that it should become an autonomous regional organisation. The Agreement Establishing the SPREP came into force with ratification by its tenth party on August 31, 1995. A large number of its projects receive input from the international community and it is actively involved in a range of environmental issues affecting the region, such as biodiversity conservation and climate change. The activities of SPREP are currently guided by the Action Plan for Managing the Environment of the South Pacific Region, which specifies the areas in which programmes are to be undertaken up to the year 2000.

(f) ANZUS COUNCIL

Bibliography: Starke, *The ANZUS Treaty Alliance* (1965); Spender, *Exercises in Diplomacy, the ANZUS Treaty and the Colombo Plan* (1969); McLachlan, "ANZUS: the treaty reappraised", NZLJ 271–9 (1985).

By Article VII of the tripartite security pact between Australia, New **8–016** Zealand and the United States (whose initials give rise to the term "ANZUS") a council was established "to consider matters concerning the implementation of this Treaty;" the treaty entered into force in April 1952.[22] This organisation is, as SEATO was, on the NATO pattern as an organisation for collective self-defence. It pre-dated SEATO and, with the establishment of SEATO, lost a good deal of its *raison d'etre*. However, the two differed in the areas covered and in their definition of the *casus foederis*. The obligations of assistance in the event of aggression are not automatic, as in NATO, but of the much weaker kind which was in due course adopted for SEATO. Apart from the council, a consultative organ of foreign ministers meeting annually, there has been established a council of

---

[21] The other organisations supervised by the Committee are the Forum Fisheries Agency, the Pacific Islands Development Programme, the South Pacific Applied Geoscience Commission, the South Pacific Commission, the South Pacific Tourism Organisation and the University of the South Pacific.

[22] Security Treaty between Australia, New Zealand and USA (1952) 131 U.N.T.S. 83–89.

deputies to meet in between sessions of the main council,[23] and a military committee of military representatives meeting as the governments decide. Any decisions are by unanimity. ANZUS has no formal or informal relationship with NATO, and the treaty makes no provision for other states to become parties. In August 1986, following the 1984–1985 dispute over the visit to New Zealand of U.S. nuclear "capable" warships,[24] the USA "suspended" its security obligations in favour of New Zealand under the treaty. Since that time, the alliance has operated as, in effect, two separate and quite different bilateral relationships between, on the one hand, the U.S. and Australia, and on the other, Australia and New Zealand. Annual bilateral Australia/U.S. meetings have continued to be held, with Australia and the U.S. recently reaffirming their commitment to the defence alliance in the Sydney declaration issued at the 1996 Australia–U.S. ministerial meeting.

---

[23] Though no formal meeting has ever taken place.

[24] The dispute arose as New Zealand refused to allow U.S. warships to visit its ports without express guarantees as to their nuclear-free status, guarantees that would have violated the "neither confirm or deny" policy of the U.S. and which the U.S. thus refused to give. Subsequent introduction of legislation in New Zealand to ban nuclear powered or armed ships in its waters has ensured that the dispute has lingered into the 1990s.

CHAPTER 9

THE MIDDLE EAST

Flory and Agate (eds.), *Le systéme régionalé arabe* (1989).

A. ORGANISATIONS OF GENERAL COMPETENCE

(a) THE LEAGUE OF ARAB STATES

Bibliography: Macdonald, *The League of Arab States* (1965); Saab, "The League of Arab States: An Innovation in Arab Institutional History" (1966) 7 World Justice 449; Beyssada, *La Ligue Arabe* (1968); Boutros-Ghali, "La Ligue des Etats Arabes" (1972 III) 137 R.d.C. 1; Hassouna, *The League of Arab States and Regional Disputes: A Study of Middle East Conflicts* (1975); Ben Achour, La réintégration de l'Egypte au sein de la ligue des Etats Arabes (1990) 94 R.G.D.I.P. 743. Website: http://www.leagueofarabstates.org.

The League of Arab States (also known as the Arab League) is a **9–001** regional, political organisation of comprehensive aims. Although, in the exploratory discussions in September 1944 between delegates of Arab States, the possibility of federal union was discussed, the organisation which eventually emerged in the pact signed on March 22, 1945[1] is one for co-operation between sovereign states and nothing more.

Membership, under Article I of the Pact, is open to independent Arab **9–002** states which "shall have the right to adhere to the League." However, the subsequent membership of Libya, Sudan, Morocco, Tunisia, Bahrein, Qatar, Oman, Mauritania and the United Arab Emirates was by application, and "acceptance" of the application by the Council of the League, so that membership does not in practice seem to be as of right. Withdrawal is provided for in Article XVIII, and so is expulsion on the ground that the state is not fulfilling its obligations under the Pact. No other form of membership is provided for, but in practice there is an "observer" status, and in 1959 representatives of the Algerian Nationalists were admitted in this capacity.

---

[1] Text in (1945) 39 AJIL Supp. 266.

9–003   The aims of the League are broad. The main aim is to co-ordinate the
political programme of members "in such a way as to effect real collaboration between them, to preserve their independence and sovereignty. . .".
Incidentally to this main aim, co-operation is envisaged specifically in
economic and financial affairs, commercial relations, customs, currency,
agriculture and industry, communications, cultural affairs, nationality questions, social and health affairs (Article III). The removal of all customs and
trade restrictions has been attempted since the 1960s, and still remains the
main objective of the Greater Arab Free Trade Area, the creation of which
has been called for by the member states in 1996.[2]

9–004   Under Article V the League members renounce recourse to force to
resolve disputes between them and, whilst they do not accept the jurisdiction of the Council of the League to mediate or arbitrate as compulsory
over such disputes, if they do have recourse to the Council its decision is
binding. In practice the League Council has used the more informal
processes of conciliation on many occasions in dealing with inter-regional
disputes, without any formal acceptance of the Council's jurisdiction under
Article V. Indeed, in the Kuwait crisis in 1961, the Council established an
Inter-Arab Force as a "peace-keeping" operation in view of the dispute
between Kuwait and Iraq.[3] The Council did the same from 1976 to 1982 in
Lebanon.[4] Further initiatives of the organisation in the field of the
settlement of disputes include the projected creation of an Arab Court of
Justice and establishment of a mechanism for the prevention, management
and resolution of conflicts among Arab states.[5]

9–005   Under Article VI each member has a right to summon the Council
immediately in the event of aggression, whether by another League
member or an outside state. The Council may then, by unanimous vote
(excepting the aggressor state), decide upon measures to check the
aggression. This collective security function is further specified in a separate
collective security pact, based upon Article 51 of the UN Charter and on
the notion that aggression against any League member is aggression against
all; the pact entered into force on August 23, 1952, and established a
Permanent Joint Defence Council and Permanent Military Commission.
On the occasion of the Anglo-French aggression against Egypt in 1956,
involving the landing of troops in Suez, the collective security machinery

---

[2] Decision taken at the June 1996 Arab Summit Conference; text in (1996) 35 ILM 1290.
[3] For more on this, see Hassouna, *The League of Arab States and Regional Disputes: A Study of Middle East Conflicts* (1975) sp. 122 *et seq.*
[4] See Feuer, "La Force arabe de sécurité au Liban" (1976) 22 AFDI 51; I. Pogany, "The Arab League and Regional Peacekeeping" (1987) 34 NILR 54; K. Boustany, *Le conflit intraétatique au Liban—Problèmes de maintien de la paix* (1994).
[5] See the resolution adopted at the June 1996 Arab Summit Conference; text in (1996) 35 ILM 1289.

failed to bring assistance to Egypt. Prior to the Arab/Israeli war of June 1967, Egypt, Jordan and the PLA (Palestine Liberation Army) instituted a joint military command, although it is clear that no integration of armed forces comparable to that which has occurred in NATO and the Warsaw Pact had then happened.

The Arab League thus qualifies as a "regional arrangement" within the **9–006** meaning of Chapter VIII of the UN Charter.[6] It also plans to operate as an organisation for collective self-defence, akin to NATO. The organisational structure established to carry out these aims and functions is comparatively simple. The Council is the supreme organ, meeting twice yearly and composed of representatives of each participating state, each with one vote. Under Article VII unanimity is the basic rule and decisions taken unanimously are obligatory on all the participating states, which are bound to execute these decisions in accordance with their own constitutions; decisions on measures to check aggression require unanimity under Article VI. Other decisions, such as decisions consequent upon arbitration or mediation under Article V or on the matters specified in Article XVI (personnel, budget, decisions to adjourn), can be taken by majority vote.

Apart from the Council, Article IV calls for committees of plenary **9–007** composition on each of the matters specially mentioned in Article II (economic affairs, communications, cultural affairs, etc.). The voting rule is simple majority and they meet annually. The Secretary-General of the League has developed a political role similar to the UN Secretary-General and is far more than a mere administrative head.

Following the pattern of the UN system, the League has also set up a **9–008** number of specialised agencies, among which the Arab Educational, Cultural, Scientific Organisation (1964), the Arab Labour Organisation (1965), the Arab Organisation for Agricultural Development (1970), the Arab Monetary Fund (1975), the Arab Atomic Energy Agency (1982) and the Arab Industrial Development and Mining Organisation (1990). The functions of these various agencies are widely similar, at the regional level, to those of their equivalents in the UN system. Other institutions linked to the League of Arab States include The Organisation of Arab Petroleum Exporting Countries (1968), the Arab Bank for Economic Development in Africa (1973) and the Arab Satellite Telecommunication Organisation (ARABSAT) created in 1976.

The overall impression is, therefore, of an organisation which is of a **9–009** rather rudimentary form. The area in which the co-operation has been most effective is that of co-ordinating policies in relation to third states. On

---

[6] See Khadduri, "The Arab League as a Regional Arrangement" (1946) 40 AJIL 756; also Boutros-Ghali, "The Arab League 1945–1955," 498, International Conciliation.

issues such as the complaints against France over the Tunisian, Moroccan and Algerian questions, or against the United Kingdom over the Yemen and Oman, or in relation to the blockade against Israel, the League acts as a forum in which common policy can be formulated. The effectiveness of this can also be seen in the United Nations, for there it is quite evident that, via the League, the Arab states have unified their policies well in advance of the UN meetings and act as a "bloc." Above all, on the Israeli question the League maintained a general unity which was effective until President Sadat's independent peace initiative with Israel in 1978. In March 1979 the Baghdad Conference of the League suspended Egypt's membership of the League with effect from the date of Egypt's signature of the peace treaty with Israel and transferred the League's headquarters from Cairo to Tunis. Following the evolution of the League's position on the Arab-Israeli conflict, Egypt reintegrated the organisation in 1990, and the latter's headquarters were subsequently transferred back to Cairo, Tunis retaining the headquarters of several of the League's specialised agencies.

B. Organisations of limited competence

9–010 A number of regional organisations have been established which are of more limited competence. One of the most effective has been the Gulf Cooperation Council, although mention must also be made of the, Islamic Development Bank which is headquartered in the Middle East (although this institution has a membership which extends beyond the region).

(a) THE GULF COOPERATION COUNCIL

Bibliography: Al-Muslemani, *The Legal Aspects of the Gulf Cooperation Council* (1989); Van Orden Gnichtel, "The Arab States' Gulf Cooperation Council: Unified Rules for Trade and Industry" (1986) 20 Int'l Lawyer 309; Farajallah, "Le Conseil de Coopération des Etats arabes du Golfe" RCADI., 1991–III, Vol. 228, 9.

9–011 The Gulf Cooperation Council (GCC) has been established in 1981 by six states of the Arabo-Persian Gulf region.[7] Its objectives are far-reaching, since it aims to "effect coordination, integration and interconnection between member states in all fields in order to achieve unity between them;" this is to be achieved by the formulation of similar regulations in various fields, including economic and financial affairs, commerce, customs and communications, education and culture, social and health affairs, information and tourism, and legislation and administrative affairs as well as by the implementation of common projects (Article 4). The GCC also

---

[7] The Charter was signed on May 25, 1981; text in 1288 U.N.T.S. 131. Member states are Bahrain, Kuwait, Oman, Qatar, Saudi Arabia and the United Arab Emirates.

aims at ensuring the collective security of the region by promoting military co-operation between its members.[8] A common defence force, numbering 4,000 troops, has been established in that framework.[9] The principles for economic co-operation within the framework of the GCC are outlined in the Unified Economic Agreement concluded shortly after the Charter.[10] Beyond those proclaimed objectives, one may also note that the GCC was instrumental in attempts to settle some conflicts between its members, as in the maritime boundary dispute between Qatar and Bahrain, for instance.[11]

Its organs are the Supreme Council, which is formed of heads of member **9–012** states and constitutes the highest authority of the organisation (Article 7), the Ministerial Council, which comprises the foreign ministers of the member states or other delegated ministers (Article 11), and the Secretariat-General (Article 14). The Supreme Council is to lay down the higher policy for the organisation (Article 8), whereas the Ministerial Council is to propose policies, prepare and adopt recommendations, studies and projects aimed at developing co-operation between member states (Article 12). There is also, attached to the Supreme Council, a Commission for the Settlement of Disputes, the mandate of which is to resolve disputes over interpretation or implementation of the Charter which have not been settled within the Ministerial Council or the Supreme Council (Article 10), and an Advisory Commission for the Supreme Council has been established in 1998. Other agencies have been set up later on under the auspices of the Organisation: the Gulf Standards Organisation (1982), the Gulf Investment Corporation (1984), the GCC Patent Office (1992) and the GCC Commercial Arbitration Centre (1993).

(b) ISLAMIC DEVELOPMENT BANK

Bibliography: Meenai, *The Islamic Development bank: a case study of Islamic co-operation (1989); Website at http://www.idb.org.*

The Islamic Development bank was established in 1973 with the purpose **9–013** of fostering economic development and social progress of member countries and Muslim communities individually as well as jointly in accordance with the principles of Shari'ah (Islamic) law. It now has 53 members, and provides equity capital and grants loans for projects, as well as providing financial assistance to member countries and establishing and operating

---

[8] An agreement on a common security strategy has been concluded by four of the GCC members in 1994; Kuwait and Qatar have not signed the document ((1995) 99 RGDIP 107).
[9] See (1995) 99 RGDIP 665.
[10] The Agreement was signed in November 1982; text in (1987) 26 ILM 1160.
[11] See the *Case Concerning Maritime Delimitation and Territorial Questions between Qatar and Bahrain*, Judgment of July 1, 1994, [1994] I.C.J. Rep. at 118, para. 19.

special funds to assist Muslim communities in non-member countries. It is only permitted to accept deposits and to obtain financial resources through Shari'ah compatible modes. The bank is based in Jeddah, Saudi Arabia, and also has offices in Morocco and Malaysia.

CHAPTER 10

AFRICA

Bibliography: Sohn,. *Basic Documents of African Regional Organisations (1971–72);* Akintar,. *The Law of International Economic Institutions in Africa* (1977); Mazzeo, Domeniaco, Ed., *African Regional Organisations* (1984); Glele-Ahanhanzo, *Introduction à l'Organisation de l'Unité africaine et aux organisations régionales africaines,* Paris, LDGJ, (1986); Elias, *Africa and the Development of International Law* (1988); Fredland, *A Guide to African International Organisations* (1990); Mahiou, "Le cadre juridique de la coopération Sud-Sud", 241 R.C.A.D.I. (1993); Thompson, "Economic Integration Efforts in Africa," African Journal of International and Comparative Law, 747–767 (1994); Soderbaum, *Handbook of Regional Organisations in Africa* (1996); Malawu, Tiyanjana, *International Law in Post-Colonial Africa* (1999).

Regional organisations have blossomed in Africa over the last two decades. **10–001** Besides the Organisation of African Unity, created in 1963, dozens of what many termed "sub-regional" organisations have been established through the continent. These are mainly active in the economic field even if an extension of their competence into other areas such as defence and security has been seen more recently. This chapter deals with (A) the African organisation of general competence and (B) organisations of limited competence.

A. ORGANISATION OF GENERAL COMPETENCE

(a) THE ORGANISATION OF AFRICAN UNITY

Bibliography: Boutros-Ghali, L'OUA durant un quart de siècle, *Mélanges Dupuy* 53 (1991); Cervenka: *The OAU and its Charter* (1968); Addona, *The Organisation of African Unity* (1969); Boutros-Ghali, Boutros, *L'Organisation de l'unité africaine* (1969); Osmanczyk, Edmund Jan OAU, *What is it? How it Works? What it Does?* Addis Ababa, 1973 ; El-Ayouty (Ed.): *The OAU after Thirty Years,* Westport, Praeger, 1994; Elias: "The Charter of the OAU" 59 AJIL 243 (1965); Amate, *Inside the OAU: Pan Africanism in Practice* (1986); Krafona, Kwesi, (Ed.), *Organisation of African Unity 25 Years On: Essays in Honour of Kwame Nkrumah* (1988); Gonidec, *L'OUA trente ans après,* Paris, Kartala, (1993); Harris, *Organisation of African Unity (a bibliography);* Oxford, Clio, (1993); Kamto *et al.,* L'OUA: *rétrospective et perspectives africaines,* Paris, Economica, (1990); Naldi (Ed.), *Documents of the Organisation of African Unity,* London, Mansell, (1992); Harris, Gordon, Comp., *Organisation of African Unity* (1994); Naldi, Gino, *The Organisation of African Unity: An*

Analysis of Its Role (1999); Bello, Emmanuel, *Organisation of African Unity*, (addendum by Juliane Hilf), *Encyclopedia of Public International Law*. Vol. III, pp. 802–10. Website: http://www.oau-aia.org.

10–002   As far as co-operation at the continental level was concerned, two main trends emerged among the African states which had achieved independance at the beginning of the 1960s. The first, led by Ghana President Nkrumah, advocated a strong "federalist" view according to which Africa had to "unite or perish". A fully integrated organisation, responsible for managing common defence, currency, foreign relations and diplomacy, etc., was needed to achieve that aim. The majority of leaders, on the contrary, favoured a more classical, "confederal" approach where, far from aiming at the integration of African states, sovereignty would be preserved in the framework of a much looser arrangement.[1] This option was clearly consecrated at the May 1963 Addis Ababa Summit Conference of Heads of State and Governments. From this summit emerged the Charter of the Organisation of African Unity.[2] The purposes of the Organisation and the basic principles upon which its action is founded shall hereafter be detailed (a), before presenting its institutional structure (b) and appraising the results of its actions (c).

(a) Purposes and principles

10–003   These are set out in the Preamble and in Articles II and III of the Charter. Being based on the "sovereign equality of all Member States" (Article III (1)) it is clear that the OAU falls far short of the federal union for which Nkrumah had argued. Rather, it is a loose organisation for co-operation with no kind of supra-national element. The intended scope of activity is very wide, embracing "political and diplomatic co-operation," "economic co-operation, including transport and communications," "health, sanitation and nutritional co-operation," "scientific and technical co-operation," and "co-operation for defence and security" (Article II (2)). The principles established to guide these activities correspond in their language to that of the UN Charter, except possibly in two respects. The first is the emphasis on "absolute dedication to the total emancipation of the African territories which are still dependent" (Article III (6)): the elimination of colonialism and the struggle against *apartheid* (which for African states constituted simply another aspect of colonialism) were thus given primary emphasis. Indeed, as we shall see, this aspect of the organisation's work has attracted more effort on the part of member states than any other. The second is the "affirmation of a policy of non-alignment with regard to all blocs" (Article III (7)). In none of the other regional organisations has there been this express, constitutional dedication to the policy of non-alignment.

---

[1] On these debates, see *e.g.* GLELE, 21–22.
[2] May 25, 1963, 479 U.N.T.S. 39.

As far as basic principles are concerned, it may also be observed that the **10–004** Organisation's adherence to the principle of "non-interference in the internal affairs of states" (Article III (2)) has not prevented it from taking into account the growing importance of the concept of democratic legitimacy since the end of the cold war. Hence, in a 1990 resolution, the OAU's heads of state and government committed themselves "to the further democratisation of [their] societies and to the consolidation of democratic institutions in [their] countries," while the same organ stated in 1997 that future coups on the continent would not be tolerated.[3]

It may safely be said that, on the whole, the OAU has maintained a **10–005** harmonious relationship with the UN, which had been prompt to recognise it as a "regional organisation" within the meaning of Chapter VIII of the UN Charter, and which followed the OAU's position by granting observer's status to "representative" African national liberation movements.[4] One recent episode nevertheless appears worthy of mention in that respect. In a move unprecedented by any other regional organisation, the OAU's Assembly decided in June 1998 that it would disregard certain sanctions imposed by the UN Security Council against Libya in 1992 as a consequence of this country's alleged involvement in the 1989 bombing of Pan Am flight 103 over Lockerbie.[5] It may prove to be difficult to assess the precise influence of this decision on the lifting of sanctions by the Council later that year.[6] Nevertheless, it cannot be excluded that such a course of conduct might influence the practise of other regional organisations which may be concerned about the legality of some of the decisions taken by the UN Security Council, particularly in the absence of any system of checks and balances or of judicial review of its acts.

(b) Institutions

The principal institutions named in Article VII are the following: **10–006**
   (i) Assembly of Heads of State and Government. This is the "supreme" organ, a plenary body where each state has one vote. The organisation meets annually or in extraordinary session with the approval of a two-thirds majority. It discusses "matters of common concern to Africa with a view to co-ordinating and harmonising the general policy of the organisation." The organisation's resolutions are passed by a two-thirds majority, except on questions of procedure, which require a simple majority. Apart from

---

[3] See extracts of the 1990 resolution in XXIII African Contemporary Records (1990–92) 122.
[4] On the recognition of OAU as a regional organisation by the UN Security Council, see *e.g.* Hummer/Schweitzer, Comment of Article 52 in Simma (Ed.), *The Charter of the United Nations—A Commentary,* Oxford, 1994, p. 700, para. 68.
[5] See 102 RGDIP (1998) 815. For a detailed discussion, see Kalala, "La decision de l'OUA de ne plus respecter les sanctions décrétées par l'ONU contre la Libye: désobéissance civile des Etats africains à l'égard de l'ONU?" (1999) R.B.D.I.
[6] Resolution 1192 (1998), August 27, 1998.

resolutions or decisions having an effect internal to the organisation, such as the adoption of the budget or appointment of committees, the Assembly's decisions are in effect no more than recommendations to member states. The Assembly is empowered by Article XX to establish "such Specialised Commissions as it may deem necessary", including the following:

(1) Economic and Social Commission.

(2) Educational, Scientific, Cultural and Health Commission.

(3) Defence Commission.

10–007　The Commissions are plenary and are intended to be composed of the appropriate ministers from each government. For this reason they have taken the view that while they are clearly subordinate to the assembly, they are not subordinate to their equals and counterparts in the council.

10–008　Ideological divisions within the Assembly, and a growing unwillingness of the heads of state and governments to attend the meetings have made it relatively uneffective; this in turn has impaired the good functioning of the organisation over a long period of time.[7] An example of the deep divisions affecting the Assembly can be found in the crisis triggered by the admission to the Organisation of the Sahrawi Arab Democratic Republic (SADR) in 1982. This issue split the organisation in two: "progressive" states supporting admission and "conservative" states backing Morocco and opposing the admission. Morocco withdrew from the OAU as a result of the decision to admit the SADR.[8]

10–009　(ii) Council of Ministers. This body consists of Ministers (normally foreign ministers) of the member states and meets twice-yearly or in extraordinary session. It meets immediately prior to the Assembly and is "entrusted with the responsibility of preparing conferences of the Assembly" (Article XIII). It also implements the decisions of the Assembly and has a general responsibility for co-ordinating inter-African co-operation. Finally, it considers and approves the Regulations of the Specialised Commissions and the budget of the organisation. Its voting procedures are the same as those of the Assembly and it is, as a body, responsible to the Assembly. The Council emerges as the most dynamic organ of the OAU, but, subordinated as it is to the Assembly, it enjoys only rather limited

---

[7] Kamto, 19 et seq.

[8] The membership of the SADR was questioned on various occasions since, the last one being at the 1998 OAU Summit, where the SADR's exclusion from the organisation was debated (see 102 RGDIP (1998) 815). This would raise further legal problems in view of the fact that the 1963 Charter does not provide for exclusion other than as a sanction for non-compliance with the member's statutory obligations. For more on this, see infra, Chap. 16.

decisional powers. The Rules of Procedure of the Council (adopted in August 1963) provide that meetings shall be held in private, but leave it possible for the Council to decide, by simple majority, upon public meetings.

(iii) General-Secretariat. This is headed by a Secretary-General **10–010** appointed by the Assembly. The initial title of "Administrative Secretary-General" indicated the determination not to create an office with independent political powers comparable to those of the Secretary-General of the United Nations. A 1979 reform, aimed at giving more weight to the Secretary-General, led to the deletion of the word "administrative;" it proved, however, of little practical effect, since it did not simultaneously provide for any extension of the Secretary-General's powers. The latter therefore remains dependent on the Organisation's "sovereign" political organs. This limited political role has been partly compensated by a factual development which, over the years, has seen OAU's Acting President ("Président en exercice") increasingly representing the Organisation in relations with third parties.[9]

Article XVIII is almost identical to Article 100 of the UN Charter and attempts to ensure the complete independence of the staff. Also, the Protocol on Privileges and Immunities, adopted in 1964,[10] follows closely the 1946 Convention on the Privileges and Immunities of the United Nations.

A number of specialised agencies have also been established to supple- **10–011** ment the action of the Organisation in more technical fields. These include the African Bureau for Educational Sciences, the African Civil Aviation Commission, the Pan-African News Agency, the Pan-African Postal Union, the Pan-African Railways Union and the Pan-African Telecommunications Union. Even though they are not properly speaking organs—not even subsidiary organs—of the OAU, the African Commission and the forthcoming African Court of Human and Peoples' Rights must also be mentioned in this context.[11] In the same fashion as the UN Human Rights Committee, the Commission is a treaty monitoring organ which has been set up "within the OAU to promote human and peoples' rights and ensure their protection," and its expenses are supported by the organisation's regular budget.[12] While not subject to the authority of OAU's political organs it therefore has clear institutional links with the Organisation.

---

[9] For more on this, see Kamto, 25 *et seq*.

[10] 1000 U.N.T.S. 393.

[11] See the draft protocol to the African Charter on Human and People's Rights on the establishment of an African Court of Human and People's Rights, doc. OAU/LEG/EXP/AFCHPR/PROT (III), December 12–13, 1997; text in 9 R.A.D.I.C. (1997).

[12] See the African Charter of Human and People's Rights of June 17, 1981, Arts 30 and 44, respectively; text in 21 ILM (1982) 58.

(c) The Organisation's achievements

10–012 An appraisal of OAU's achievements leads to contrasted results. There is wide agreement on the fact that the Organisation's record in the field of decolonisation is by far its most impressive contribution. It has legitimised the action of national liberation movements and been successful in maintaining the question on the international agenda for a long period of time.[13] The common positions taken by OAU members within the UN have even made it possible for the African organisation to exercise a significant influence on the evolution of international law in that field.[14] In that respect, it should also be noted that several important conventions have been adopted under the auspices of the Organisation.[15]

10–013 The OAU's involvement in the settlement of disputes within the region has been much less significant. The Commission of Mediation, Conciliation and Arbitration, provided for in the 1963 Charter (Article XIX) was undoubtedly indicative of the decision to treat inter-African disputes as exclusively African affairs and to exclude, so far as possible, the over-riding authority of the UN Security Council.[16] But this organ quickly fell into abeyance and was never seised of any of the numerous conflicts that erupted in various parts of the continent.[17] The fact that the Charter did not provide for any role for the Organisation in the resolution of *internal* disputes (which proved to be much more frequent in Africa than interstate conflicts during the relevant period), as well as the growing personal involvement of heads of states and governments in the settlement of disputes, may be some of the obsolescent factors of the Organisation. A recent attempt to revive the OAU's role in that field has not proven much more successful. The Mechanism for Conflict Prevention, Management and Resolution established by the Organisation's supreme organ in 1993 has rather ill-defined competences and is endowed with limited and imprecise means of action;[18] it does not seem to have been involved in the resolution of any African conflict, with the exception of the severe crisis that followed the 1993 coup in Burundi.[19]

---

[13] The same may be said of the fight against *apartheid*, even though results in that respect have taken much longer to achieve. As a result of the elimination of *apartheid* in South Africa, this country was admitted as the 53rd member of OAU in May 1994.

[14] See Kodjo, in El-Ayouty (Ed.): *The OAU after Twenty Years*, 1984, 7; Gonidec, 71 *et seq.*

[15] See for instance the 1969 Convention governing the specific aspects of refugee problems in Africa, the 1977 Convention for the elimination of mercenaries in Africa, or the aforementioned 1981 African Charter on Human and People's Rights; texts in Naldi, *op. cit.*.

[16] See Elias, "The Commission of Meditation, Conciliation and Arbitrationi of the OAU", 40 B.Y.B.I.L. (1964) 336.

[17] KAMTO, 36; GONIDEC, 99.

[18] See the Declaration of the Assembly of Heads of State and Government on the establishment within the OAU of a mechanism for conflict prevention, management and resolution, June 28–30, 1993; text in 6 R.A.D.I.C. (1994) 158. For more on this, see Djiena-Wambou, "A propos du nouveau mecanisme de l'OUA sur les conflits", 5 RADIC (1993) 725.

[19] See *e.g.* RGDIP (1994) 190.

Finally, the Organisation's action in the field of economic co-operation is **10–014** still offering the image of a work in progress. In order to give effect to the provisions of the Charter, which make economic co-operation one of the main purposes of the Organisation, the heads of state and government committed themselves, in the final act of the 1980 Lagos Summit, to endow Africa with an African Economic Community (AEC) by the year 2000. The treaty on the creation of the AEC was signed on June 3, 1991 in Abuja.[20] According to Article 6 of the Treaty, the Community shall be established in six stages, over a 34-year transitional period (from May 1994, the date the Treaty went into effect). These include the creation or strengthening of regional economic communities,[21] the strengthening of sectoral integration at the continental and regional levels, the establishment of a customs union, and finally the establishment of a Common Market and an African monetary union. The AEC shares—at least in part—the OAU's institutional structure and it is not endowed with a legal personality distinct from that of its parent organisation, of which it "shall form an integral part" (Article 98, para. 1);[22] similarly, its budget shall constitute "an integral part of the OAU regular budget" (Article 82). Hence, the Community's supreme organ is the OAU's Assembly of heads of state and government, which shall be responsible for implementing the objectives of the AEC (Article 8), whereas it is the Council of Ministers of the OAU which shall be responsible for the functioning and development of the Community (Article 11). These two shall possess normative powers, which shall be exercised through decisions for the Assembly (Article 10) and regulations by the Council (Article 13); both will be binding on member states. The Economic and Social Commission (Article 15) and the General-Secretariat (Article 21) shall also be those of the OAU. The Abuja Treaty nevertheless provides for the creation of new organs as well, which will be exclusive to the Community. These are the Pan-African Parliament (Article 14), the functions of which are likely to be essentially consultative; and the Court of Justice, which will be competent to "decide on actions brought by a member state or the Assembly on grounds of the violation of the provisions of th[e] Treaty, or of a decision or a regulation or on grounds of lack of competence or abuse of powers by an organ, an authority or a Member State" and to give advisory opinions, at the request of the Assembly or the Council (Article 18).

---

[20] Text in 30 ILM (1991) 1245. For comments, see, *e.g.* Thompson, "Economic Integration Efforts in Africa: A Milestone—The Abuja Treaty", 5 RADIC (1993) 743; Mahiou, "La Communauté économique africaine", A.F.D.I. (1993) 798.

[21] For more on this, see *infra*.

[22] The fact that Art. 92, para. 1 of the Abuja Treaty gives the Community the capacity to "conclude co-operation agreement with third states" may thus only be understood as a recognition of the AEC's capacity to do so *on behalf* of the OAU, which would eventually be the entity bound by such agreements and ultimately responsible for their (non)execution. On the Community's legal personality issue, see also LUMU, De la nature de la Communauté économique africaine, 8 RADIC (1996) 51.

10–015   This step-by-step approach of African economic integration relies heavily on regional economic co-operation organisations—these shall be presented in greater depth in the second part of this Chapter—which are to lay the foundations of the continental Community. A strong emphasis is therefore put on the need for co-operation and co-ordination between these and the Community. The Abuja Treaty thus states that:

> "Member states undertake to promote the co-operation and harmonisation of the integration activities of regional economic communities of which they are members with the activities of the Community, *it being understood that the establishment of the latter is the final objective towards which the activities of existing and future regional economic communities shall be geared*".[23]

It obviously remains to be seen whether these various organisations shall, in due time, be willing to dissolve themselves in order to merge into this larger entity. Co-ordination problems already experienced at the regional level definitely raise serious questions in that respect.

B. ORGANISATIONS OF LIMITED COMPETENCE

(a) THE AFRICAN DEVELOPMENT BANK

10–016 The African Development Bank (ADB) was established in 1963 in order to finance economic and social development in African countries (Article 1).[24] It finances development projects in member states, promotes private and public investment in such projects and provides technical assistance to members for the study, preparation, financing and execution of these types of projects (Article 2). Its organs are the board of governors, which constitutes the organ of general competence empowered to issue general directives concerning the credit policy of the bank (Article 29); the board of directors—composed of nine members elected by the board of governors— which is responsible for the conduct of the general operations of the bank and may exercise all powers transferred to it by the governors (Article 32); and the president, who is responsible for the management of the Organisation (Article 37). As within most financial institutions, decisions are taken with "weighted" voting in the first two of these organs. The bank has 53 regional, and 24 non-regional nembers, to which its capital stock has been open for subscription since 1978 under certain conditions aiming at preserving the Organisation's African character. At the end of 1996, the Bank's subscribed capital was U.S. $ 22.83 billion.

10–017   The African Development Fund was created in 1973 by an agreement adopted by the bank's governors. It supplements the latter's action by providing interest-free loans to African countries which do not meet the

---

[23] This was reiterated in greater detail in a 1997 Protocol on the Relationship between the AEC and the Regional Economic Communities, text in 10 RADIC (1998).

[24] August 4, 1963, 510 U.N.T.S. 47. Website: http://www.afdb.org.

criteria set for contracting loans with the ADB. Its members are the same as the bank's, with which it also shares part of its institutional structure, the governors of the bank being *ex officio* governors of the fund, and the president of the bank acting in the same capacity for the fund. Its resources were replenished for the seventh time in 1996, the total subscriptions amounting to U.S. $12.58 billion at the end of that year.[25] The fund was aiming to offer financial assistance to 42 African countries over the 1996–1998 period.

(b) REGIONAL ECONOMIC ORGANISATIONS

In the absence, over a long period, of concrete initiative to promote **10–018** economic co-operation at the continental level, states in various parts of Africa have attempted to reach that goal by creating regional economic integration organisations. The first such attempts date back to the 1960s in some regions; these have been followed since the beginning of the 1990s by the creation of what may be termed "second-generation" regional economic organisations in all five of Africa's geographical regions (North, West, East, Centre and South). Those more recent organisations present strikingly similar features, both in their institutional structure (a general outline of which shall be given later) and in the economic conceptions underlying their foundations and orientations. African states indeed appear to a large extent to have turned their backs to the rhetoric of the "new international economic order", which they had vigorously promoted during the 1970s at the UN, and to have embraced more modern, liberal, economic dogmas. A strong emphasis is thus put on the vast majority of those organisations' constituent instruments on free trade, the abolition of tariff barriers, free movement of persons and capital and the creation of unified markets. The general objective is to ensure the inclusion of African states and sub-regions in the "global economy." These various organisations shall be briefly presented, region by region, the main emphasis being put on the most important of them. It is worth mentioning at that point that some of these follow the lines of older integration patterns, most of them colonial in origin.[26]

(a) North Africa

North Africa definitely emerges as the continent's region where the **10–019** "organisational frenzy", which characterises almost every other part of Africa, has been the most tame. A single organisation, the Arab Maghreb Union (AMU), was established there in 1989 by five states of the region.[27]

---

[25] See 100 RGDIP (1996) 786.

[26] For more on this, see *e.g.* Mahiou, pp. 38–39.

[27] February 17, 1989; French text in 94 RGDIP (1990); see also 99 R.G.D.I.P. (1995) 114. For comments, see Belaid, Le traité de Marrakech et la construction de l'Union du Maghreb arabe, *Mélanges Virally* 125; "El Kadiri, Reflexions sur le traité de Marrakech constituant l'Union du Maghreb Arabe, 95 RGDIP 71 (1991); Mckeon, "The Arab Maghreb Union: possibilities of Maghrebine political and economic unity, and enhanced trade in the world community", 10 DickJIL 263 (1992).

This constitutes the first move to promote economic co-operation through institutional means in the history of North Africa. It is probably amongst the least integrative of the organisations more recently established on the continent, and puts a strong emphasis on classical and traditional means of political co-operation. The AMU was established by treaty in 1989, although its origins date back to more informal arrangements in the early 1960s. Its membership comprises five North African countries (Algeria, Libya, Mauritania, Morocco and Tunisia). The main objectives of the Union are to strengthen ties between the member states and to liberalise movement of goods and services among them, including the adoption of a common policy in various fields, such as economy and culture (Articles 2 and 3). The 1989 Treaty provides for the possibility for other Arab and African countries to join the Union at a later stage. Under the auspices of the Union nearly 40 conventions have been adopted addressing economic, social, and cultural matters, although it is to be noted that the conventions only bind those members which have ratified them. The Union's supreme institutional organ is the Council of Heads of State, decisions of which are adopted only by unanimity. The Council meets annually. A Council of Foreign Affairs Ministers also meets regularly to prepare for the sessions of the Council of Heads of State, and a Committee of representatives of the member state follows the implementation of resolutions adopted by the Council of Heads of State. A Consultative Assembly, consisting of 30 representatives from each member state to advise the Council of Heads of State, and a Court of Justice, composed of two judges from each member state, have been set up in Algiers and Nouakchott respectively. The Union's Secretariat-General, is based in Rabat, Morocco.

(b) West Africa

10–020 By contrast, West African states have a much longer tradition of institutional co-operation. This region's main organisation is the Economic Community of West African States (ECOWAS). It was formally established in 1975,[29] but the Organisation's constituent Treaty was extensively revised in 1993.[30] Its principal objective is the creation of an economic and monetary union of the 16 member states.[31] Its action is supplemented by the Fund for Cooperation, Compensation and Development, which finances development projects in member states and compensates them for losses resulting from the application of the Treaty. ECOWAS has played an increasing political role since the beginning of the 1990's. In a reaction to the civil war that had erupted in Liberia, the Organisation established a

---

[29] There was an earlier interim agreement of May 4, 1967 (595 U.N.T.S. 287).
[30] July 24, 1993, text in 351 (1996) 674. Website: http://www.ecowas.int.
[31] On the relation between ECOWAS and AEC, see Art. 78 of the 1993 Treaty, and Ajulo, "Temporal Scope of ECOWAS and AEC Treaties: A Case for African Economic Integration", 8 RADIC (1996) 111.

military force, the ECOMOG (ECOWAS Cease-Fire Monitoring Group), that was sent to this country in August 1990 to help restore peace.[32] The force engaged in military activities, going far beyond traditional peace-keeping operations; hence the Organisation's intervention in Liberia raised serious questions of legality, since it had not been authorised by the UN Security Council, although this organ nevertheless gave it *a posteriori* approval some time later.[33] The ECOMOG has since then been involved in conflicts in two other member states: Sierra Leone and Guinea-Bissau.[34] This interest for regional security was consecrated in the 1993 Treaty (see Article 58), and a more institutionalised Mechanism for Conflict Prevention, Management, Resolution, Peace-Keeping and Security was established within the Organisation in 1998.[35] A Mediation and Security Council is thereby created, which is empowered to take decisions on issues of regional peace and security on behalf of the ECOWAS' supreme organ, and to "authorise all forms of interventions, including the decision to deploy political and military missions" (paras 17 and 18). ECOWAS thus emerges as the first African organisation endowing itself with a sophisticated and operational security mechanism. In such a context, the question of coordination with—or subordination to—universal and continental organisation appears more important than ever.

Even though the member states of ECOWAS have decided that it would **10–021** "ultimately be the sole economic community in the region" (Article 2, para. 1 of the 1993 Treaty), a number of them also participated in efforts to create the West African Economic and Monetary Union (UEMOA, as it is known under its French acronym) in 1994. This succeeded the West African Monetary Union (UMOA), originally established in 1973 with a quasi-identical membership. Its members are Guinea-Bissau and the region's French-speaking countries—formerly integrated in the Afrique occidentale française—which have for quite some time experienced a degree of uneasiness with the predominant role played in the region —and in ECOWAS— by Nigeria.[36] Linked to the Union are the Central Bank of West African States (BCEAO) and the West African Development Bank (BOAD). UEMOA's objectives are essentially the same as those of

---

[32] In order to justify its involvement in military actions, the organisation relied on the 1981 ECOWAS Protocol Relating to Mutual Assistance on Defence; see generally the introduction and official documents in Weller (Ed.), *Regional Peace-Keeping and International Enforcement : The Liberian Crisis*, Cambridge, 1994.

[33] See Resolution 788 (1992) of November 19, 1992; on the issue of legality, see *e.g.* Kufuor, "The Legality of the Intervention in the Liberian Civil War by the ECOWAS", 5 RADIC (1993) 525; Mindua, "Intervention armée de la CEDEAO au Liberia : illégalité ou avancée juridique?", 7 RADIC (1995) 257.

[34] See *e.g.* UNSC Resolutions 1132 (1997) of October 8, 1997 and 1233 (1999) of April 6, 1999.

[35] Text in 11 RADIC (1999) 148.

[36] See generally Ibriga, L'uenoa: "Une nouvelle approche de l'intégration économique régionale en Afrique de l'Ouest", 6 African Yearbook I.L. (1998) 23.

ECOWAS, and its development should be facilitated by the fact that its members are already using a common currency, the CFA Franc. Its institutional achitecture draws heavily on that of the European Community. UEMOA's creation nevertheless inevitably raises issues of duplication between organisations pursuing essentially identical aims within the same region, especially when one considers that intergovernmental organisations other than ECOWAS and UEMOA are still relatively active in the economic field in West Africa.[37]

(c) East Africa

10–022 The East African Community was first established by Kenya, Tanzania and Uganda in 1966.[38] It was intended to take over the common services previously operated by the East African Common Services Organisation.[39] It functioned until 1977, when it ceased its activities due to political differences between the member states. This organisation was revived in 1996 as the Commission for East African Cooperation (EAC) and aims at promoting closer economic co-operation among its members as well as enhancing regional stability. It has expressed the desire to cooperate with other regional economic organisations. The same three states are also members of the East African Development Bank which finances development projects and promotes investments in various fields of economic activity.

(d) Central Africa

10–023 The Central African Economic and Monetary Community (CEMAC), established in 1994,[40] aims at the monetary and economic integration of the six states which were members of the earlier Central African Economic and Customs Union (UDEAC).[41] As in the case of UEMOA in West Africa, this integration process should be made easier by the fact that CEMAC member states already share the same common currency, the CFA Franc. The Bank of Central African States (BEAC) should continue to play in important role in that respect.[42] As in West Africa, however, a degree of

---

[37] An example of these is the Council of the Entente, which manages the Mutual Aid and Loan Guarantee Fund; its members are Benin, Burkina Faso, Côte d'Ivoire, Niger and Togo, which are all members of both ECOWAS and UEMOA. On the question of duplication and competition, see *e.g.* Ibriga, 43–44; Mahiou, 138–139.

[38] Agreement of May 5, 1966; text in 5 ILM (1966) 633.

[39] For more on this, see Tandon and Mazrui, The East African Community as a Sub-Regional Grouping, in El-Ayouty (Ed.), *Africa and International Organisations,* The Hague, Nijhoff, 1974, 182.

[40] See Kobila and Sokeng, La Cemac: A la recherche d'une nouvelle dynamique de l'intégration en Afrique centrale, 6 African Yearbook I.L. (1998) 65.

[41] Signed in 1964, the UDEAC Treaty embraced the states of Cameroon, the Central African Republic, Chad, Congo (Brazzaville), Equatorial Guinea and Gabon; text in 4 ILM (1965) 699.

[42] This was orginally created by a monetary co-operation agreement of November 22, 1972.

redundancy between organisations can be observed in the region. Indeed, CEMAC's member states are also parties to the 1987 Treaty establishing the Central African States Economic Community (CEEAC), which pursues partly similar aims.[43]

(e) Southern Africa

The origins of economic co-operation among Southern African countries **10–024** can be traced back to the *apartheid* period in an attempt of the so-called "frontline" states to reduce the region's economic dependence on South Africa. The Southern African Development Coordination Conference (SADCC) was established in 1979 for that purpose. Taking into account the political changes that had occurred in South Africa, and willing to further their co-operation in the economic field, the states of the region decided in 1992 on the creation of a more formal co-operation structure, the Southern African Development Community (SADC),[44] which succeeded the SADCC.[45] South Africa became a member in 1994. While its main objectives—including the creation of a free trade area—are clearly of an economic nature, this organisation more recently has become concerned with more general political matters. Hence, a protocol on politics, defence and security in the Southern African development community was concluded in 1997, which includes provisions on the settlement of disputes and on the measures—encompassing "punitive measures" to be taken in last resort, in accordance with the UN charter—the organisation could take in order to achieve this aim.[46] The emphasis is therefore once again—as in the case of ECOWAS—put on the close relation between a region's overall stability and its prospects for economic development.

Finally, there is yet another organisation, the Common Market for **10–025** Eastern and Southern Africa (COMESA), which covers those last three regions. It was created in 1993 by the member states of the Preferential Trade Area for East and Southern Africa (PTA), which it succeeded.[47] With more than 20 members, COMESA is the largest of Africa's economic organisations. But here again, risks of duplication are present. Hence, two member states, which are also members of the SADC, suspended their membership of COMESA because they perceived their simultaneous

---

[43] On this, see Kamto, "La Communauté économique des Etats de l'Afrique centrale (CEEAC), une Communauté de plus?", A.F.D.I. (1987) 858.
[44] Treaty of August 11, 1992; text in 32 ILM (1993) 116.
[45] See Art. 44 of the 1992 Treaty.
[46] Text in 11 RADIC (1999) 197; see especially Art. 5.
[47] Treaty of November 5, 1993; text in 33 ILM (1994) 1067. See generally Gondwe, From PTA to COMESA: The Quest for Sub-Regional Economic Integration in Eastern and Southern Africa, 6 African Yearbook I.L. (1998) 3. For elements of comparison with the SADC, see Mwenda, "Legal Aspects of Regional Integration: COMESA and SADC on the Regulation of Foreign Investment in Southern and Eastern Africa", 9 RADIC (1997) 324.

participation to both organisations as incompatible; one of them, Lesotho, purely and simply withdrew from COMESA in 1997.

(c) INSTITUTIONAL STRUCTURE

10–026 As has been mentioned at the beginning of this section, the institutional structures of most of these (sub-) regional organisations are broadly similar. Most of the time they have a two-level "executive" power: the supreme organ comprises heads of state or government and is empowered to make the broad policy decisions,[48] while the second executive organ is often a council of ministers which has a more limited power of decision but which plays an important role in the implementation of the constituent treaty. In all cases, the institutional structure is completed by a Secretariat which is in charge of administrative matters and responsible for the daily management of the organisation. Several of the second-generation African economic organisations also have a judicial organ, which may pronounce on the legality of the institutional acts taken by the executive organs or of member states' behaviour; in addition, they may in some cases give advisory opinions on legal questions arising in the framework of the organisation.[49] This nevertheless remains to a large extent theoretical, since the majority of these courts or tribunals have not yet rendered any judgment or advisory opinion. Finally, in more exceptional cases, a parliamentary organ has been created or projected, the role of which is generally strictly consultative.[50]

(d) OTHER

10–027 Beside those main regional groupings, mention still needs to be made of the many organisations set up by states to manage in common shared natural resources, including rivers, lakes and marine spaces. These include the Senegal River Committee, the Niger River Commission, the Lake Chad Basin Commission, the Nile Water Commission, the Mano River Union and, more recently, the Lake Victoria Fisheries Organisation. These organisations tend to operate in close co-operation with the UN Economic Commission for Africa and most enjoy UNDP financial support.

*

10–028 The proliferation of intergovernmental organisations across the African continent is striking, but it also raises the question of their effectiveness and efficiency. The risk of overlap between the various organisations active in a

---

[48] The Authority in UEMOA, ECOWAS and COMESA, Summit Meeting in SADC, or Council of Heads of State in AMU.

[49] See, generally, Kamto, "Les cours de justice des communautés et des, organisations d'intégration économique africains," 6 African Yearbook I.L. (1998) 107. See also *infra*, Chap. 13.

[50] See for instance the 1994 Protocol for the establishment of a regional parliament within the framework of ECOWAS, the Parliamentary Forum created within SADC in 1997, AMU's Consultative Assembly or UEMOA's Interparliamentary Committee.

same region has already been emphasised and, as some examples have shown, is not merely theoretical. It may legitimately be asked whether the second-generation economic organisations will achieve better results than their predecessors. The problems experienced with the latter are well-known; they included political interference by some member states in these organisations' work, as well as significant difficulties in the implementation of the decisions taken in their framework due to the lack of political will on the part of member states. It is true that the institutional structure of the newer organisations described in this chapter is generally more elaborate, and that the constituent instruments provide for clear powers of decision by the executive organs they establish. It nevertheless remains to be seen whether member states will be willing to play the integration game to a greater extent than previously, with the sometimes very significant restrictions on the exercise of sovereign powers it implies. Beyond this, doubts have regularly been expressed as to the existence, in most of the continent's regions, of the prerequisites for economic integration; factors such as the weakness of trade and exchanges between the member states, the poor conditions of communications infrastructure and the low levels of foreign direct investment are among those which have been frequently cited in that respect.[51] Structural economic problems persist in Africa, which will likely not be met by the creation of economic co-operation organisations alone. This must probably be viewed as a reminder that as strong co-operation devices as they can be, international organisations to a large extent reflect and must build on the material realities to deliver their promise.

---

[51] See, *e.g.* Kobila and Sokeng, 102–103; Mahiou, 187.

Part II

THE FUNCTIONS OF INTERNATIONAL ORGANISATIONS

CHAPTER 11

"LEGISLATIVE" OR NORMATIVE FUNCTION

The capacity to adopt norms—be they mandatory or not—addressed to **11–001** their members is often listed among the constitutive elements of international organisations.[1] Many authors have thus emphasised that international organisations are constituted essentially to adopt norms in their fields of competence, and that it is to a significant extent through this process that they fulfil their objects.[2] It must also be noted, as far as the production of norms is concerned, that international organisations often constitute fora for the elaboration, negotiation, and ultimately adoption, of international conventions by member states. Although this process relates to norm-production under the auspices of, rather than by, international organisations, it will also be dealt with in the present chapter in view of the close proximity between procedures followed, in some organisations at least, for the adoption of institutional acts and treaties, respectively.

The use of the term "legislative" in the title of the present chapter must **11–002** be taken with a degree of caution, for two main reasons. The first is that only a small number of existing international organisations are endowed with the power to take decisions—or, in broader terms, institutional acts[3]— which are binding *per se* on their members or on other addressees in the "external sphere" (*i.e.* not regarding matters relating to the functioning of the organisation itself).[4] The constituent instruments of most organisations

---

[1] See *e.g.* Cahier, *Etudes des accords de siège conclus entre les organisations internationales et les Etats où elles résident* (Milan: Giuffrè) 1959, 25; Schermers and Blokker, *International Institutional Law* (3rd ed., The Hague: Nijhoff) 1995, 22, para. 33; David, *Droit des organisations internationales* (Brussels: P.U.B.), 1996–97, 16.

[2] Virally, "Sources of International Law: Unilateral Acts of International Organisations", in Bedjaoui (Ed.), *International Law: Achievements and Prospects* (Paris: UNESCO— Dordrecht: Nijhoff), 1991, 241; Economides, "Les actes institutionnels internationaux et les sources du droit international" 34 AFDI (1988) 132; Frowein, The Internal and External Effects of Resolutions by International Organisations, 49 Z.f.a.ö.r.u. (1989) 778.

[3] This wording will preferably be used thereafter, since it is more generic; it encompasses the various terminologies found in most constituent instruments (resolutions, recommendations, decisions, regulations, standards, directives, etc.) the meaning of which may vary from one organisation to another.

[4] Schermers and Blokker, *op. cit.*, para. 1200.

enable them to adopt recommendations—or non-binding institutional acts—only. The results of this activity are also addressed since it will be seen that such acts adopted by international organisations in the "external sphere" may also have legal effects, and can have significant political implications. The second reason for expressing reservations regarding the use of the term "legislative" in the present context is that any strict parallel between the production of norms by—or within the framework of— international organisations and the legislative process on the national level would be misleading. The institutional structure of most "universal" organisations generally includes a plenary organ, on which all members are represented, and an organ of limited composition, endowed with more specific responsibilities. It may be tempting to equate the former with national parliaments—and hence with the exercise of legislative power— and the latter with national governments, entrusted with executive functions. But far from being vested in the "parliamentary" organ, the power to "legislate"—at least when it comes to the adoption of institutional acts binding on members or on other addressees—lies in most international organisations with the "executive" organ. The situation is not significantly different in the few regional organisations—such as the Council of Europe, the European Community, WEU or ECOWAS, for instance—where the institutional structure comprises an "Assembly" composed of individuals, who will often be members of national parliaments, sitting in their own capacity. The powers of these assemblies are more limited than those of their national equivalents, since they are generally concerned with the adoption of non-binding institutional acts. There too, the "legislative" power is to a large extent in the hands of organs which tend to describe as "executive" organs. Parliamentary organs thus appear, in those organisations, merely as "projections" of a democratic ideal, since they are not truly vested with any significant norm-making power which would entail direct legal consequences for members of those organisations in the international or in their domestic legal orders, or for third persons.[5]

11–003 This shows that in the realm of international organisations the production of norms, mandatory or not, is the task of various types of organs, be they plenary (and composed of representatives of member states or of private individuals) or of limited composition. In order to better understand how international organisations fulfil their "legislative" or normative function in the sense indicated above, we address the procedural aspects of this process (A), the various types of normative acts adopted by or within international organisations and their respective legal effects (B), and finally the requirement of legality of such acts (C).

---

[5] See *e.g.*, Klebbes, "Les institutions parlementaires internationales", 92 RGDIP (1988) 819. The only—recent—exception in that respect is the European Parliament (see *infra*, B).

A. PROCEDURAL ASPECTS

Bibliography: Wolfrum, The Protection of Regional or Other Interests as Structural Element of the Decision-Making Process of International Organisations, 1 Max Planck Ybk UN Law (1997) 259.

In all international organisations, the adoption of normative acts is **11–004** governed by specific procedural rules. Compliance with such rules is an essential condition of the validity of these acts,[6] Procedural rules vary widely between organisations. They generally reflect the political balance existing within the organisation—or envisaged by its founders—at the time of its creation.[7] They may nevertheless be altered by subsequent practice, as certain examples indicate. One of the most significant trends in respect of procedure is the evolution from the requirement for unanimity in decision-making towards majority voting.

(a) THE DECLINE OF THE RULE OF UNANIMITY

The absolutist conception of state sovereignty which dominated for most of **11–005** the nineteenth century entailed as a consequence the general application of the rule of unanimity in the vast majority of international conferences held during that period. The application of majority voting was nevertheless considered acceptable for the adoption of agendas or certain other procedural questions. It was within the more technical public unions that majority rule came into general use and, significantly, especially in those concerned with technical or scientific matters and involving non-diplomatic representation. The UPU (1874) and the International Commission for Aerial Navigation (1919)[8] even exercised a certain legislative power by majority; the ITU, the Metric Union, the International Office of Public Health (1907) and the ILO also adopted majority voting, although they only had powers to act *ad referendum*, so that no member became bound by the majority decision. Bodies with administrative functions such as the Commission for Cape Spartel Lighthouse (1865), the Central Commission for the Navigation of the Rhine (1815), the Governing Commission under the Saar Statute (1919), the Permanent Sugar Commission (1902) and the Permanent Central Opium Board (1925) similarly acted on the basis of a majority vote. In the few cases where unanimity was preserved, notably the Union for the Protection of Industrial Property (1883), the Union for the Protection of Literary and Artistic Works (1886) and the International

---

[6] Validity also depends on the satisfaction of requirements relating to substance; see *infra*, paras 11–015 *et seq*.

[7] See *e.g.* Virally, *loc. cit.* 247.

[8] Established by the Paris Convention (11 L.N.T.S. 173), this body used a majority vote varying from three-quarters to simple majority according to the nature of the question, *i.e.* two-thirds for the budget adoption, three-quarters for amendment of the Annexes, simple majority for recommendations to members.

Institute of Agriculture (1905), the rigours of the unanimity rule were mitigated by the practice of abstention from voting, by the authorisation of "partial" agreement[9] and the technique of allowing states to enter reservations in respect of agreements or conventions concluded.[10]

11–006   In the political conferences progress was necessarily slower. The rules of procedure of the great conferences at The Hague in 1899 and 1907 required unanimity on all really important questions[11] and at the Paris Peace Conference of 1919 unanimity was preserved in respect of the states entitled to take decisions.[12] Similarly, the unanimity rule was generally preserved in the Covenant of the League of Nations (Article 5). However, within the Assembly, on certain matters a majority sufficed[13] and the express provisions of the Covenant (*e.g.* admission of new members, Article 1 (2); amendments, Article 26 (1); procedural questions, Article 5 (2); election of non-permanent members of the Council) were supplemented by practice; hence abstention developed as a matter of practice, as did the distinction between decisions and "*voeux*" (the latter requiring only a majority), and committees normally took decisions by a majority. The Council adhered more strictly to the unanimity rule, but there too exceptions did exist, as in the making of reports on disputes likely to lead to a rupture of the peace (Article 15(4)), and in the exclusion from the vote of any party to a dispute (Article 15(6)).

11–007   It is in the light of this that the UN Charter emerged as a fairly radical break with tradition, for there the majority vote becomes the rule. Unanimity has also virtually disappeared from the specialised agencies.[14] It remains in a few organisations of limited membership, as for example in the

---

[9] Art. 15 of the Industrial Property Convention; note that the same technique is used even today to avoid the restrictions of the unanimity rule in the Committee of Ministers of the Council of Europe (see *infra*).

[10] Art. 17 of the Convention of the Union for the Protection of Literary and Artistic Works.

[11] Committees could, however, make recommendations to the plenary by majority (see Riches, *Majority rule in international organisation* (1940) p. 287).

[12] Participating states were divided into three groups, of which only the first (USA, Britain, France, Italy and Spain) were entitled to attend all sessions: for the rules of procedure see (1919) 13 A.J.I.L. Supp. 109.

[13] For a full list of such matters see Riches, *op. cit.* pp. 20–29 and Stone, 14 B.Y.B.I.L. (1933) 18.

[14] In conferences convened under the auspices of an international organisation the general tendency is to adopt rules of procedure modeled on those of the organisation, but the nature of the conference may well be the determining factor; see statement by Yuen-li Liang on the UN practice, sometimes adopting simple majority, sometimes two-thirds, in (1959) 1 Yearbook of the I.L.C. 50. This was made in connection with the statement that the simple majority was the normal rule at international conferences drafting treaties in the Fitzmaurice Report on the Law of Treaties (A/CN.4/101), new Art. 6; for the discussion thereon see *ibid.* pp. 40–54. The abandonment of unanimity in codification conferences goes back to The Hague in 1930; it may well not be an unmitigated blessing since it may produce a text which a large minority may be unable to ratify, or can only ratify with reservations. See Johnson, "The Conclusions of International Conferences", 35 B.Y.B.I.L. (1959) 1.

Committee of Ministers of the Council of Europe (though not for all decisions),[15] the Council of the OECD, the Council of the European Community (but only in respect of a diminishing number of specific matters)[16] and the Council of the Arab League. Obviously, the smaller the membership the greater the justification, in principle, for the retention of the unanimity rule. The difficulties raised by the requirement of unanimity are evidenced by the development, within the Council of Europe—within two years of the adoption of the Statute—of the practice of partial agreements.[17] These allow members favouring a particular proposal to proceed with it without the participation of non-assenting members, thereby avoiding the paralysis resulting from the unanimity and the power of members to veto decisions. The enlargement of the organisation, since the beginning of the 1990s has made the use of such partial agreements even more necessary.[18]

The adoption of equality of voting and majority rule is not, however, **11–008** without its problems. In the General Assembly it has led to a tendency towards ignoring practical realities in respect of some of the resolutions adopted. The first United Nations Conference on Trade and Development (UNCTAD) in Geneva produced an imposing set of "principles,"[19] adopted by the overwhelming vote of the developing countries, which for their execution required the active assistance of developed countries but which were, by and large, unacceptable to them. In this connection it is of interest to note that General Assembly resolution 1995 (XIX), in providing a constitution for UNCTAD, maintained equality of voting and a two-thirds majority rule on matters of substance but, at the same time, established an elaborate system of conciliation which may be requested by groups of members before any vote on a substantive matter occurs. The conciliation committee's essential task is to produce proposals which have a realistic chance of true acceptance by the Conference (or Board)—"true" being used in the sense of support from members having the capacity to give effect to the proposals—and to avoid proposals which, whilst capable of securing the two-thirds majority, could never find such true acceptance.

---

[15] See Art. 20 of the Statute, 1 E.T.S. See also the change brought by the Statutory Resolution (93) 27 on majorities required for decisions of the Committee of Ministers, adopted on May 14, 1993. It should be noted, however, that the unanimity required is that "of the representatives casting a vote," provided there is a *majority* among "the representatives entitled to sit on the Committee."

[16] See for instance Arts 67, para. 1 (visas, asylum and immigration), 88, para. 2 (aids granted by states), 93 (tax provisions) or 100 (economic policy) of the treaty (37 ILM (1998) 56). It should be noted in that respect that, according to Art. 205, para. 3 of the Treaty, abstentions by members present or represented do not prevent the adoption by the Council of acts which require unanimity.

[17] Resolution on partial agreements, adopted by the Committee of Ministers in August 1951.

[18] See in that respect Resolution (93) 28 on partial and enlarged agreements, adopted by the Committee of Ministers on May 14, 1993.

[19] *UN Yearbook* (1964) 198–201.

This is symptomatic of a trend towards a search for "consensus" as opposed to reliance on the results of formal voting.[20] This trend developed in the UN system from the late 1960s onwards. Consensus is a technique of adoption of institutional acts by which the president of the organ concerned, after consultations, reports that there is a general agreement between the members on the proposal before them, and declares the act to be adopted.[21] It does not mean, however, that the act concerned benefits from unanimous approval. In fact, the enhanced political authority that might characterise decisions adopted by consensus may be somewhat equivocal: although there is no clear opposition to the norms adopted (otherwise, a vote would have been required), the actual extent of support among the members is not always apparent.[22] That said, some of the most significant resolutions of the United Nations General Assembly, such as resolution 2625 (XXV), have been adopted by consensus, and this has not prevented them from enjoying a very high degree of authority, both politically and legally. It must also be noted that decision-making by consensus was the general practice followed by the GATT from its inception. It has been continued—and institutionalised—by the WTO.[23] The practice may also be found in other organisations.[24] In a number of organisations, however, the consequences of the strict application of the majority rule has led to the implementation of other means for distributing voting power.

(b) VARIATIONS IN THE RULE OF EQUALITY OF VOTING POWER

11–009   Departures from the somewhat unrealistic rule of "one state-one vote" were made in two ways, and again it fell to the technical international public unions to pave a way for "political" organisations to follow with greater deliberation and less haste.

11–010   The first technique was to allow separate representation for some of the colonies or separate territorial units of a state; this introduced a system of plural voting. Organisations like the UPU, ITU, Metric Union, Inter-

---

[20] See Jenks, "Unanimity, the veto, weighted voting, special and simple majorities consensus as modes of decision in international organisation" in Cambridge Legal Essays (1965), 48. The conciliation technique, aiming at consensus, was adopted in the Rules of Procedure of the UN Law of the Sea Conference: A/CONF. 62/30/Rev. 2, Rule 37.

[21] See, generally, Cassan, "Le consensus dans la pratique des Nations Unies", AFDI (1974) 456–485.

[22] Virally, *loc. cit.* 250.

[23] Art. 9, para. 1 of the Agreement. It is being specified that "[t]he body concerned shall be deemed to have decided by consensus on a matter submitted for its consideration, if no Member, present at the meeting when the decision is taken, formally objects to the proposed decision" (n. 1 to Art. IX).

[24] See *e.g.* Art. 161, para. 8, d) of the United Nations Convention on the Law of the Sea regarding certain decisions to be taken by the Council of the International Sea-bed Authority and section 3, para. 2 of the annex to the 1994 Agreement relating to the implementation of Part XI of the Convention; Arts 9, para. 3 and 12, para. 2 of the 1993 Treaty establishing ECOWAS regarding decisions taken by the Authority and regulations adopted by the Council of Ministers, respectively.

national Institute of Agriculture, International Wine Office and International Office of Chemistry, amongst others, adopted this approach. Occasionally, as in the International Wireless Telegraph Union of 1906, a limit (in that case six) would be placed on the number of votes so acquired. In one sense the separate representation of the members of the British Commonwealth in the League of Nations, or the separate representation the Soviet republics of Byelorussia and Ukraine in the UN, may be regarded as a perpetuation of this technique. Nevertheless, it clearly becomes a matter of separate representation simpliciter, and not plural voting, when the separate entities act independently and not as additional votes automatically cast with the former parent state. Plural voting is still provided for in a specific case: that of international organisations which are members of other international organisations. Hence, Article IX (1) of the Agreement establishing the WTO provides that "[w]here the European Communities exercise their right of vote, they shall have a number of votes equal to the number of their member states which are members of the WTO". This is simply the consequence of the fact that member states of the Community are represented by the latter within WTO, and do not therefore cast their vote separately.[25]

The second approach was by weighting the votes of members to **11–011** represent their real interest, which could reflect political, economic or financial factors. Weighting has been defined as "a system which assigns to members of international organisations votes allocated on the basis of predetermined relevant criteria."[26] The crucial problem is, of course, to find acceptable criteria by which the weighting can be done. A simple solution, adopted at an early stage in the International Office of Public Health and in the International Institute of Agriculture and now continued in the financial agencies of the UN, is to weight the voting powers of a member according to its financial contribution. The system has the merit of linking power with financial responsibility. Within the present financial agencies of the UN the votes are weighted according to the share of a member in the operating capital (not the budget); for example, in the IBRD each member of the Board of Governors has 250 votes plus one additional vote for each share of stock held (par value $100,000).[27] A similar system was applied,

---

[25] It should be noted in that respect that even though the E.C. is a full-fledged member of the WTO, it is not entitled to a separate vote that would come in addition to those of the member states (see n. 2 to Art. IX of the Agreement: "The number of votes of the European Communities and their member states shall in no case exceed the number of member states of the European Communities").

[26] McIntyre, "Weighted voting in International Organisations", 8 International Organisation (1954) 484; see also Sohn, "Weighting of Votes in International Assemblies", Am. Pol. Sci. Review (1944) 1192, and "Multiple Representation in International Assemblies" 40 AJIL (1946) 71; Weinschel, "The Doctrine of Equality and its Recent Modifications" *ibid.* (1951) Vol. 45, 417.

[27] Art. 5(3); compare Art. 6(3) of the International Development Association (500 votes plus one additional vote for each £5,000 of subscription), Art. 12(5) of the IMF (same as IBRD), and Art. 4(3) of the IFC (250 votes plus one for each share of $1,000).

before their privatisation, in the International Telecommunications Satellite Organisation (INTELSAT) and in the International Maritime Satellite Organisation (INMARSAT), where the voting power of each governor or representative on the Council was determined by the investment share of the signatory (or group of signatories) he or she represented.[28] There are yet other approaches. On the Executive Board of the International Fund for Agricultural Development (IFAD), a bloc of votes is allocated to each region (OECD, OPEC, Developing Countries—600 votes each bloc) and then, within the region, the bloc vote is divided amongst the members of the bloc by a dual formula: a certain percentage of votes being divided equally, the remainder according to financial contribution. The system is very far removed from the traditional one state-one vote rule.

11–012   Another similar but simpler technique is seen in the commodity councils, such as the Wheat and Sugar Councils. For example, in the International Wheat Agreement of 1959 the exporting countries were assigned 1,000 votes in the Council, and the importing countries 1,000. The allocation of specific numbers of votes to particular countries was by reference to the guaranteed sales or purchases for the current year.

11–013   In some cases a specific number of votes is assigned to each participating member in the basic agreement establishing the organisation. This technique goes back to the Central Commission for the Navigation of the Rhine (1815) which allocated unequal votes for the purpose of electing the Chief Inspector. Current examples of such a clearly pre-determined distribution of votes include that of the Council in the European Community, where the votes are weighted amongst the member states, ranging from ten votes (for Germany, France, United Kingdom and Italy) to two (for Luxembourg).[29]

11–014   It is notable that, outside the financial organisations and IFAD, no specialised agency has adopted a weighted voting system of the kind illustrated above. Weighting is achieved indirectly in allocating only to certain members a right of representation in various organs, just as it is achieved indirectly in the Security Council by giving to the vote of the permanent members more effect (*i.e.* the veto) than the vote of other members. Otherwise the tendency has been to rely more on the requirement of specific majorities for certain decisions, in part because in many organisations the success of a resolution may depend more on the number of states supporting it than on the weight of votes that can be collected for it.[30] It is probably for this reason that, in some cases where weighted voting

---

[28] Art. 9 INTELSAT (1220 U.N.T.S. 21); Art. 14 INMARSAT (1143 U.N.T.S. 105).
[29] See Art. 205 of the Treaty.
[30] See the statement by the spokesman for the department of state in the Hearings of the Senate Financial Committee on the proposed ITO Charter: U.S. Congress (80th, 1st Sess.) Senate, Committee on finance, Hearings (1947), pp. 532–533.

does exist, as in the board of governors of the IBRD, a formal vote is rarely taken, and the preferred method is for the chairman to take the sense of the meeting. However, the inability to agree criteria for weighting accepted in a political organisation is probably the dominant reason.[31]

(c) MAJORITY REQUIREMENTS

Whether based on the "one member-one vote" principle or on more **11–015** sophisticated systems of weighed voting, the rule of majority voting may follow different patterns depending on the organisation or organ concerned. The two main approaches remain voting on the basis of simple majority, on the one hand, or qualified majority on the other. In many instances, constituent instruments provide for the use of simple *or* qualified majority voting by the same organ, depending on the type of question with which it is seised.

In many organs simple majority is the rule followed for the adoption of **11–016** decisions either on procedural matters[32] or on substantive questions deemed to be of lesser importance than others, in the field of this organ's competences.[33]

The requirements for a qualified majority may be expressed either in **11–017** terms of proportions or in absolute figures. Hence, in a large number of organisations, decisions on specific or "important" questions must be taken by a two-thirds majority of the members present and voting. This is the case, for example, in the UN General Assembly,[34] the General Conference of the ILO,[35] and of UNESCO,[36] the World Health Assembly,[37] the

---

[31] For the democratic, but politically unacceptable, formula which would base votes in the General Assembly on population figures, see Clark and Sohn, *World Peace through World Law* (1960), 2nd ed. revised, pp. 20–23, 25–31.

[32] See, *e.g.* Art. 27(2) of the UN Charter for the Security Council; Art. 159(7) of the UNCLOS and section 3, para. 3 of the Annex to the 1994 Agreement amending Part XI of the Convention, for the Assembly of the International Sea-bed Authority; Art. X, para. 1 of the OAU Charter for the Assembly; Art. 20(b) of the Statute of the Council of Europe for the Committee of Ministers.

[33] See *e.g.* Art. 18(3) of the UN Charter for the General Assembly, Art. 17(2) of the ILO Constitution for the General Conference.

[34] Art. 18(2) of the UN Charter. See also the requirements for decisions taken with a two-thirds majority in the General Assembly expressed in the Charter (Arts 108 and 109) or the Assembly's rules (Arts 19 and 81); for more on this see Lewin, Commentaire de l'article 18, in Cot and Pellet (Eds.), *La Charte des Nations Unies—Commentaire article par article* (2nd ed., Paris: Economica) (1991) 390.

[35] Arts 1(4) (admission of new members—this requires a two-thirds majority of government delegates within the overall 2/3 majority), 13(2)(c) (budgetary and financial matters) and 36 (amendments to the Constitution) of the Constitution.

[36] For instance Arts II(2) (admission of new members) or XIII, para. 2 (amendments of the Constitution) of the Constitution.

[37] Art. 60 of the Constitution enumerates "important questions" which command such a majority.

Conference of the FAO,[38] the Ministerial Conference of the WTO,[39] the Assembly of the International Seabed Authority,[40] the OAU Assembly,[41] and the Committee of Ministers in the Council of Europe.[42] Higher requirements (generally of three-fourths of the members present and voting) are sometimes formulated for decisions on particularly important questions.[43] Examples of the second formula (absolute figures) include Article 27(3) of the UN Charter, according to which decisions of the Security Council on non-procedural matters are to be made by an affirmative vote of nine members including the concurring votes of the permanent members. This requirement results in the power of any permanent member to prevent by its sole vote the taking of a decision which has the support of a majority of the Council, *i.e.* of nine members.

11–018   This power, the power of veto, has been the instrument whereby much of the efficacy of the Council was destroyed during most of the "cold war" period, since the permanent members have not hesitated to use the veto when they felt their vital interests were at stake.[44] Among other examples of qualified majority expressed in absolute figures, one may also mention the Council of the European Community, where the votes are weighted, and where decisions require 62 votes out of the total of 87 although, in the case of a decision where no proposal has been made by the Commission, at least ten members must vote in favour.[45] In the case of the Global Environment Facility, decision making is generally to be by consensus, but decisions requiring a formal vote of the Council are to be taken by a double weighted majority, that is, an affirmative vote representing both a 60 per cent

---

[38] For instance, Art. II(2) (admission of new members) or XIV(1) of the Constitution (approval of conventions and agreements concerning questions related to food and agriculture).

[39] Art. XII(2) (approval of the agreement on the terms of accession of new members) of the Agreement.

[40] Art. 159(8) of the United Nations Convention on the Law of the Sea.

[41] Art. X(1) of the Charter.

[02] Art. 20(c) of the Statute, (admission of new members, by a two-thirds majority of the representatives entitled to sit on the Committee) and (d) (adoption of budget, of rules of procedure, etc., by a two-thirds majority of the representatives casting a vote).

[43] See, *e.g.* decisions of the WTO Ministerial Conference on requests made by a member to waive an obligation imposed on that member by the WTO Agreement or any of the Multilateral Trade Agreements (Art. IX(3) of the Agreement) or, before this was modified by section 3(8) of the annex to the 1994 Agreement relating to the implementation of Part XI of the United Nations Convention on the Law of the Sea, various decisions to be taken by the Council of the International Sea-bed Authority (Art. 161(8)(c) of the Convention).

[44] Since 1945 the veto power of the permanent members has been used most extensively by the USSR (which has been succeeded by the Russian Federation), with 116 vetoes between 1945 and May 1997. The United States did not exercise its veto power at all before 1970 but since then has vetoed decisions of the Council over 70 times. The usage of the veto power by the other permanent members between 1945 and May 1997 was as follows: U.K. 30 times, France 18 times and China 4 times (Bailey and Dawns, *The Procedure of the UN Security Council* (1998), p. 239).

[45] Art. 205 of the E.C. Treaty.

majority of the total number of Participants and a 60 per cent majority of the total contributions (GEF Instrument, para. 25(c)).

Except in cases where the situation is clear-cut (as in the European **11–019** Community, where it is easy to determine whether a proposal has been made by the Commission or not), the determination of questions pertaining to one or another category (procedural/non-procedural; important/other, etc.), requiring that the vote be taken with the corresponding majority, has sometimes raised difficulties. This has generally not been the case in the UN General Assembly, principally because a non-exhaustive list of "important questions" can be found in Article 18 (2) of the Charter. Although new categories of important questions can be created by a simple majority (Article 18(3)), the Assembly has tended not to create categories but to decide specific cases on an ad hoc basis.[46] Thus, the request for an advisory opinion on South West Africa in 1950 was ruled to be "not important", but without creating a general rule for all requests for advisory opinions.[47] A "question" is treated as being the individual resolution and not the problem or issue that the resolution addresses. All in all, it can be said that the practice of the Assembly in relation to this aspect has not been wholly consistent, with identical or similar questions being accorded different procedural treatments from one session to another, often for purely political reasons.[48] In practice, it is the President of the Assembly (advised by the Organisation's Legal Counsel) who indicates, when a draft resolution dealing with questions not explicitly listed as important in Article 18 or in other relevant instruments is put to the vote, that a qualified majority appears to be necessary in that specific instance. This determination is usually not contested.[49] This informal practice has been used more frequently than the adoption of a formal decision, as required by Article 18(3). In the Security Council, on the other hand, there is no enumeration of the matters that fall into the "procedural" and "non-procedural" categories comparable to the enumeration of "important questions" in Article 18 of the charter. The Security Council is thus faced with the problem of determining into which category any particular decision falls, a problem

---

[46] Kerley, "Voting on Important Questions in the UN General Assembly", 53 AJIL (1959) 324.

[47] It can nevertheless be noted that the latest request from the Assembly for an advisory opinion has also been dealt with as a "non-important" question in spite of its subject-matter (the legality of the threat or use of nuclear weapons—see resolution 49/75 K, adopted in December 1994 by 78 votes in favour, 43 against and 38 abstentions).

[48] See the practice described by Wolfrum, Comment of Art. 18, in Simma (Ed.), *The Charter of the United Nations—A Commentary* (O.U.P.: Oxford) (1994) 323–324. One striking example in that respect is the case of the representation of China. While the General Assembly, at its sixteenth and twentieth to twenty-fourth sessions, voted that any proposal to change this representation was an "important question", this organ changed its view on the subject at its twenty-sixth session, where it decided by 59 votes in favour, 55 against and 15 abstentions, that this question had to be considered "non-important".

[49] See Lewin, *loc. cit.* 391.

often referred to as the "preliminary question." In practice certain matters have been well-established as procedural,[50] but, when a dispute arises, the permanent members have relied upon the statement of the four sponsoring powers at San Francisco,[51] which stated:

> "1. In the opinion of the Delegations of the Sponsoring Governments, the Draft Charter itself contains an indication of the application of the voting procedures to the various functions of the Council.
>
> 2. In this case, it will be unlikely that there will arise in the future any matters of great importance on which a decision will have to be made as to whether a procedural vote would apply. Should, however, such a matter arise, the decision regarding the preliminary question as to whether or not such a matter is procedural, must be taken by a vote of seven members of the Security Council, including the concurring votes of the permanent members."

11–020   The USSR and the USA have relied upon this second paragraph and insisted upon deciding the preliminary question by a non-procedural vote, using their veto to determine that the main issue was non-procedural. Then, in the subsequent vote on the main issue, the permanent member would cast a second veto, exercising what was in effect a "double-veto." This practice, if carried to its absurd conclusion, could mean that no matter could be considered as procedural against the wishes of a permanent member. Thus used, it would be contrary to the first paragraph of the statement quoted above which indicates that resort to a vote on the preliminary question should only be had when the Charter does not itself contain an indication of the nature of a given question. In fact the Charter does, in chapters IV, V, X and XI, employ the heading "Procedure" to various Articles and this, together with the application of accepted canons of treaty interpretation, including the use of analogy, ought to resolve a particular issue without the need to resort to a vote on the preliminary question. One means of avoiding a double-veto is for the President to rule that the matter is procedural; under rule 30 of the Rules of Procedure this ruling stands if nine members support it, and thus there is no place for a veto. The practice depends for its efficacy on the astuteness and fairness of the delegate who happens to sit in the presidential chair. It must be noted that an informal agreement has led to the practice of the double-veto not having been used since 1959.[52]

---

[50] For example, decisions relating to the agenda, adjournment of meetings, conduct of business, invitations to states to participate in the meetings, or postponement of the consideration of a question (for further details see Simma and Brunner, Comment of Art. 27, *in* Simma (Ed.), *op. cit.* 440–442, and Bailey and Davis, *The Procedure of the Security Council* (1998) 226.

[51] Repertory, Vol. 11, p. 104. This statement, to which France later adhered, was prepared in an answer to a questionnaire submitted to the sponsoring powers by the lesser powers and concerning the operation of the voting procedure.

[52] Simma and Brunner, *loc. cit.* 446.

A further problem is related to the computation of the required majority. **11–021**
Rules in many organisations require the establishment of a specific quorum
for decisions to be validly adopted by the organ concerned.[53] Once the
quorum is established, it is on the basis of the total number of present and
voting members that the respective majorities will be calculated, at least
when they are expressed in terms of proportion. When majorities are
expressed in absolute figures, one would expect their computation not to
raise any particular problems. Some precedents, however, show that even
with such seemingly unambiguous provisions, difficulties of interpretation
may arise. The UN Security Council is, once again, a case in point. While
Article 27(3) of the Charter requires "an affirmative vote of nine members
including the concurring votes of the permanent members" for a decision
to be adopted, in many instances permanent members of the Council have
chosen to abstain from voting rather than cast a negative vote which would
prevent the Council from taking a decision. This practice of abstention is
apparently at odds with the Charter. But even though it is clearly not
envisaged in Article 27(3) (which might easily have added the proviso
"present and voting"), the practice has been generally accepted and must
now be deemed to be a constitutionally valid interpretation of the notion of
"concurrence." This evolution has been acknowledged by the I.C.J. which,
in its advisory opinion in 1971 on Legal Consequences for states of the
continued presence of South Africa in Namibia, upheld the practice of
abstention by a permanent member as "not constituting a bar to the
adoption of resolutions," since it had been "generally accepted by members
of the United Nations" and constituted "a general practice of that
Organisation."[54]

The amendment brought to Article 27 in 1965, by bringing the number of **11–022**
members of the Council from 11 to 15—and the majority requested by
paras 2 and 3 of that provision from 7 to 9—even made it possible for a
resolution to be adopted on a non-procedural question with none of the
permanent members concurring.[55] As long as other procedural conditions
are met, it must be considered that a resolution adopted with one or several
members of the Council abstaining is legally binding on all member states
of the organisation, in the context of Chapter VII or of other provisions of
the charter on which the power of the Council to take binding decisions
may be based.[56] A more difficult question arises in the Security Council
where a decision is taken in the absence of a permanent member. Cases
have occurred where the Council has taken a decision on a procedural

---

[53] See generally Schermers, "The Quorum in Intergovernmental Organs", in *Fetschrift Seidl-Hohenveldern* (Cologne: Heymann) (1988) 527–535.

[54] I.C.J. Rep. 1971, p. 22, para. 22.

[55] This happened in 1973, when resolution 344 (1973) was adopted by ten votes in favour, France, U.K., U.S. and USSR abstaining and China not taking part to the vote.

[56] See also Simma and Brunner, *loc. cit.* 453.

matter in the absence of a permanent member without objection; it is only in non-procedural decisions, where "concurrence" is required, that the real difficulty has arisen. The most notable case was that of the decisions of June 25 and 27, 1950, determining a breach of the peace in Korea and recommending that member states take up arms to assist South Korea. The decisions were taken in the absence of the USSR, which denied their legality. Even though it has been argued that an absent permanent member could not be considered as "concurring" in the majority (contrary to an abstaining permanent member) and that the resulting decision could therefore not be viewed as valid, most authors are of the opinion that such a conclusion would lead to a paralysis of the Council and is not sustainable. Absence—or voluntary absence, at least—of a permanent member should be equated to an abstention, since "[w]hile the Charter recognises permanent members of the SC, it does not provide for a permanent veto in the SC."[57]

11–023   Finally, it must be noted that members of some organs may be excluded from the voting procedure for specific reasons. One of the best-known examples may be found, once again, in Article 27(3) of the UN Charter, which provides that, "in decisions under Chapter VI, and under paragraph 3 of Article 52, a party to a dispute shall abstain from voting" in the Security Council. This is a re-statement of the general principle of law, *nemo judex in sua causa*, albeit confined to "disputes" dealt with under the specified provisions. It would not extend to the question of determining the existence of a "threat to the peace, breach of the peace or act of aggression" under Article 39 of the Charter, even though there may be a complete "dispute" about this question. Hence, in this most vital question, there is no obligation to abstain, and a permanent member can use the veto to prevent a finding that it has itself (or any other state favoured by its support has) been responsible for one of the situations envisaged in Article 39.

11–024   Other reasons for excluding specific members from the decision-making process in particular organs may also be found. In many organisations those members in arrears with their contribution may be barred from voting in specific organs.[58] Contrary to the rule followed in the Security Council, the purpose of which is simply to ensure that the organ concerned takes an impartial decision, the latter type of exclusion from voting may be viewed as a form of sanction imposed on a member state for non-compliance with the organisation's rules.[59]

---

[57] *ibid.* 455.
[58] See *e.g.* Arts 19 of the UN Charter, 13(4) of the ILO Constitution and 8(b) of the UNESCO Constitution (in all cases, deprivation of the right to take part in votes held in the plenary organ, when amount of arrears exceeds two years' contributions).
[59] For more on this, see *infra*, Chap. 16, A(b).

While in the overwhelming majority of international organisations the **11–025** adoption of institutional acts does not require action by more than one organ, the treaty establishing the European Community, as revised in 1992 and 1997, provides for complex procedures which impose a requirement of joint action by several organs of the Community for the adoption of institutional acts in specified fields.[60] This "co-decision" procedure, involving the Commission, the Council and the Parliament (the latter being in a position to block the adoption of Community legislation in the relevant fields, if it does not agree with the proposals submitted by the "executive" organs) may be seen as a reflection of progress towards a "democratic ideal" in some organisations (the E.P. being composed of representatives directly elected by the population of member states), in what resembles more closely a "legislative" process as envisaged in most states. It is nevertheless exceptional, and must be viewed as the trademark of a highly integrated organisation.

Finally, it is to be noted that a few organisations allow for postal voting; **11–026** for example, the IMF (Article XII, 2(f)), IBRD (Article V, 2(e)), WMO (Article 5(b)).[61] Somewhat surprisingly, IMO, which in Article 57 uses the phrase "present and voting" and thus would seem to exclude such a technique, has since 1970 used postal voting in the Council on a trial basis.

B. Types of acts and legal effects

Bibliography: Anderson, "Law-Making Process in the UN System", 2 Max Planck Ybk UN Law (1998) 23; Johnson, "IAEA Treaty-Making Activities in 1997", 2 Max Planck Ybk UN Law (1998) 51.

A great variety of institutional acts are adopted by or within international **11–027** organisations which may be presented as the result of the exercise of their "legislative" or normative function. Their legal effects *vis-à-vis* other organs or members of the organisation, or other addressees, will vary significantly. In this respect, a fundamental distinction should be made at the outset between the function of international organisations as fora for the adoption of multilateral conventions, on the one hand (a), and the adoption of norms by the organisations themselves, on the other (b).

(a) INTERNATIONAL ORGANISATIONS AS FORA FOR THE ADOPTION OF MULTILATERAL CONVENTIONS

As described above, international organisations may to a certain extent be **11–028** considered as the successors to the international conferences periodically convened by states to deal with particular issues or solve specific problems

---

[60] See the procedures organised by Arts 251 and 252, the use of which is provided for *e.g.* in Arts 135 (Customs co-operation), 148 (European Social Fund), 153 (Consumer protection), or 175 (Environment) of the Treaty.

[61] In the case of WMO, this is however limited to situations where urgent action is required between sessions of the Congress.

which had arisen in international relations.[62] Many of these conferences led to the adoption of multilateral treaties, embodying the rules agreed upon by states during their meeting.[63] The institutionalisation of international relations, which led *inter alia* towards the creation of intergovernmental organisations on a permanent basis, did not bring an end to that practice. To the contrary, the constituent instruments of many organisations list among the functions of one or the other of the organs they have established the conclusion or approval of multilateral conventions aiming at regulating subject-matters in the fields of competences of these organisations. Hence, Article 62(3) of the UN Charter provides that the Economic and Social Council "may prepare draft conventions for submission to the General Assembly, with respect to matters falling within its competence." It is on the basis of drafts submitted by the ECOSOC that conventions such as the 1966 Covenants on Economic, Social and Cultural Rights, and on Civil and Political Rights, respectively, or the 1984 Convention against Torture have been adopted by the General Assembly. Other pillars of the contemporary international legal order, such as the 1961 Convention on Diplomatic Relations, the 1969 Convention on the Law of Treaties, the 1982 Convention on the Law of the Sea, the 1992 Climate Change Convention or the 1998 Statute of the International Criminal Court have likewise been adopted under the auspices of the United Nations (though not by the General Assembly as such). The same type of procedure is envisaged in the constitutions of most of the UN specialised agencies. For instance, Article XIV(1) of the FAO Constitution provides that:

"The Conference [plenary organ of the organisation] may, by a two-thirds majority of the votes cast and in conformity with rules adopted by the Conference, approve and submit to Member Nations conventions and agreements concerning questions relating to food and agriculture."[64]

11–029   Similar provisions may be found in the constituent instruments of some regional organisations. A classical example is the Council of Europe, Article 1 of the Statute of which provides that the organisation's aim "to achieve a greater unity between its members" "shall be pursued through the organs of the Council [. . .] by agreements and common action in economic, social, cultural, scientific, legal and administrative matters."[65] Many other examples could be given. The conclusion of multilateral conventions within

---

[62] See general introduction (Chap. 1).

[63] See, *e.g.*, among the best-known of these, the General Act of the Conference of Berlin, on the Congo (1885; 165 C.T.S. 483) or the Final Act of The Hague Peace Conference (1899).

[64] See also, *e.g.* Art. IV(4) of the UNESCO Constitution.

[65] Up to now, close to 200 conventions have been concluded under the auspices of the Council of Europe, among which the 1950 European Convention on Human Rights (for more details, see *supra*, Chap. 6).

the framework of intergovernmental organisations is undoubtedly one of the most important ways for states to "legislate" collectively on the international plane.[66]

These conventions are ordinary multilateral treaties, within the meaning **11–030** of the 1969 Vienna Convention,[67] and will be binding only on states which become parties to them according to the procedures set forth in the organisation's constituent instrument or in the conventions themselves.[68] It is not the organisation which "legislates" for its member states and thereby force any kind of "collective will" upon them, but simply the latter which take part in the process of *adopting* a convention within the framework of an organisation of which they are members—retaining a complete freedom of choice on the question of whether to become a *party* to that instrument later on. The process has been most aptly described as "not real law-making by international organisations but rather the preparation of inter-state law-making within an international organisation."[69] In most cases, therefore, the fact that a specific convention has been concluded under the auspices of an international organisation will not entail for the members any other obligation than those flowing from the participation in the adoption of multilateral conventions concluded in a different context. The rules of a few organisations nevertheless provide otherwise, in order to promote as high as possible a level of adherence to the—conventional—norms adopted within the framework of the organisation. It is particularly the case with the ILO, where an international labour convention, once adopted, is communicated to all members for ratification, not merely to those whose government delegates voted for the proposal. Thereupon, all members are bound to submit the Convention to the appropriate authorities within the state for

---

[66] A rapid survey of recently published multilateral treaties can only confirm this conclusion. Examples include the African Nuclear Weapon-Free Zone Treaty, concluded under the auspices of the OAU (June 21–23, 1995, 35 ILM (1996) 698); the Convention on Liability and Compensation for Damage in Connection with the Carriage of Hazardous and Noxious Substances by Sea, adopted under the auspices of the IMO (May 3, 1996, 35 ILM (1996) 1415); the Joint Convention on the Safety of Spent Fuel Management and on the Safety of Radioactive Waste Management, adopted under the auspices of the IAEA (September 5, 1997, 36 ILM (1997) 1431), the European Convention on Nationality, adopted under the auspices of the Council of Europe (November 6, 1997, 37 ILM (1998) 44) and the Inter-American Convention against the Illicit Manufacturing of and Trafficking in Firearms, Ammunition, Explosives and other Related Materials, concluded under the auspices of the OAS (November 14, 1997, 37 ILM (1998) 143).

[67] According to Art. 5, the Convention "applies to any treaty [. . .] adopted within an international organisation without prejudice to any relevant rules of the organisation".

[68] Note that while ratification of such conventions is very generally opened to members of the sponsoring organisation only, accession to the convention by non-members is sometimes specifically envisaged, upon invitation by the organisation's competent organ (see for instance Art. 32 of the UNESCO Convention for the Protection of the World Cultural and Natural Heritage of 1972; 1037 U.N.T.S. 151. This is also a classical feature of the conventions adopted under the auspices of the Council of Europe).

[69] Sommer, "Environmental Law-making by International Organisations", 56 Z.a.ö.r.v. (1996) 638.

the enactment of legislation or other action necessary to give the convention application within the state[70]; and this submission must be within one year or, when this is impossible owing to exceptional circumstances, within 18 months (Article 19(5)). This is not an obligation to ratify, but an obligation to submit to the appropriate authorities who can give consent to ratification. Moreover each member must inform the Director-General of the measures taken in pursuance of this obligation, and of which authorities are competent and of the action taken by them (*Id.*). When the competent or appropriate authorities give their consent to the Convention, the member state then communicates a formal "ratification" of the Convention to the Director-General and is then bound to take such action as is necessary to make the Convention effective. This process has features which distinguish it from the normal process associated with a multilateral treaty. First, the "parties" which draft the text are not entirely state representatives,[71] and it is not signed by these; to this extent "ratification" is an unfortunate term to use to describe the final act of acceptance, for it is not an act whereby the state ratifies the previous signature of its representatives. Secondly, whereas with the normal multilateral treaty a state which does not vote for or accept the text cannot be regarded as having any further obligations in respect of it, in the ILO all members are bound notwithstanding any negative vote to submit the Convention to their legislature or other competent authority for approval and consent. Thirdly, a state actually ratifying cannot in so doing make a reservation; since 1921 the doctrine has been firmly established that, because the adoption of the text of the Convention is the act of the entire General Conference consisting of delegates other than governmental delegates, it is not possible for a member state to ratify subject to a reservation which constitutes an alteration of the obligations as set out in the agreed text. Further consequences of the adoption of the Convention by a "tripartite" Conference are that the states parties to a Convention cannot agree *inter se* on an interpretation of the Convention; this, as we shall see, is governed by a fixed procedure.[72] Nor can the states parties to a Convention revise it by their own action *inter se*; the ILO Conventions contain clauses enabling this to be done by a revising Convention in which the Conference as a "tripartite" body expresses its will.[73] For the member ratifying a Convention there is a continuing process of supervision, through reports submitted

---

[70] Where power to implement rests with some body other than the legislature, the Convention should nevertheless also be submitted to the legislature for the purpose of informing public opinion; see Report of the Committee on the Application of Conventions and Recommendations, ILO 53rd Sess. 1969.

[71] On the "tripartite" character of delegations representing members the ILO, see *supra*, Chap. 3.

[72] See *infra*, Chap. 14.

[73] For further details, see Jenks, "Some characteristics of international labour conventions" 33 Can. B.R. (1935) 448–462; "The revision of international labour conventions" 14 B.Y.B.I.L. (1933) 43–64.

annually to the organisation and a "complaints procedure" which will be discussed later.[74] For the member not ratifying there is also a continuing process of inquiry in that, upon the request of the governing body, such a member must at intervals report the position of its law and practice in regard to the matters dealt with in the Conventions, showing the extent to which compliance in fact exists, and stating the difficulties which prevent or delay ratification. In federal states, where sovereign power is divided between the federal and the state authorities, the actual implementation of conventions may well require action by the component states jointly with the federal authorities, or even exclusively by them. The ILO Constitution, Article 19(7), therefore provides that in such cases the federal government is required to make arrangements for the reference of the conventions to the appropriate state, provincial or cantonal authorities within 18 months, to arrange for periodical consultations between the federal and state, provincial or cantonal authorities with a view to co-ordinating the action necessary to give the conventions effect; and then the further obligations apply of reporting to the organisation on steps taken, on which are the appropriate state, provincial or cantonal authorities, on the position in law and practice and on the extent of implementation, just as in the case of a unitary state. All of this—whether relating to federal states or not—is indeed an advance on normal treaty practice; its whole purpose is to maximise the ratifications secured by the ILO Conventions. This has however, up to now, remained exceptional, the conventional process followed in other international organisations not having strayed from the traditional interstate procedures in that field.

While the legal effects of treaties concluded within or under the auspices **11–031** of an international organisation for the member states which decide to become parties to these instruments are clearly determined, such is not always the case for other types of institutional, normative, acts adopted by organs of the organisations as such.

(b) INSTITUTIONAL ACTS ADOPTED BY INTERNATIONAL ORGANISATIONS

It is for a significant part through the adoption of institutional, normative **11–032** acts that international organisations fulfil their objects. These norms may aim at regulating the action of members in the international legal order, or in their domestic sphere of competence (national legal orders), but the primary objective of a large proportion of them is to ensure the functioning of the organisation itself, by providing for more detailed rules than those contained in the constitutent instrument or by implementing those rules.[75]

---

[74] See *infra*, Chap. 12.
[75] See, generally, Skubiszewski, Preliminary exposé on "The elaboration of general multilateral conventions and of non-contractual instruments having a normative function or objective— Resolutions of the General Assembly of the United Nations" 61 A.I.D.I. (1985) 30.

This "secondary legislation" will, together with the constituent instruments and with subsequent practice, constitute the internal law of the organisation.[76] Constituent instruments generally provide for specific powers in that respect. Under Article 17 of the UN Charter, for example, the General Assembly is to approve the budget of the organisation (para. 1) and to apportion the expenses of the UN among member states (para. 2).[77] The mandatory character of decisions taken by the Assembly in that respect has been emphasised by the I.C.J. in its 1962 Advisory Opinion on Certain Expenses of the UN, where the Court pointed out that the budget item under consideration was "an expense of the organisation and under Article 17(2), the General Assembly therefore *has authority* to apportion it."[78] Even when decisions limited to the internal sphere of the organisation are taken by an organ on the basis of implied—as opposed to express—powers, it may safely be argued that they have the same mandatory character for other organs and for members.[79] It must also be noted that specific instruments, such as headquarters agreements, give the organisation concerned the power to regulate certain activities—*e.g.* in the headquarters district—thereby extending their "legislative" authority to private individuals, under specific circumstances.[80] Once again, this is limited to the "internal sphere" of the organisation.

11–033   The approach is much more restrictive, however, when it comes to institutional acts aiming at producing effects outside the organisation's legal order. It is largely agreed in that respect that the power to adopt normative acts binding on members in the "external sphere" must be expressly stated in the organisation's constituent instruments and may not be implied.[81] As we shall see, such explicit empowerment is the exception rather than the rule, most international organisations—or most organs within those organisations—having been given recommendatory or consultative powers only (i). This does not mean, however, that institutional acts which should technically be considered as merely recommendatory will be devoid of all legal effects *vis-à-vis* member states in the external sphere; some of them may indeed become legally binding in other ways (ii).

---

[76] Schermers and Blokker, *op. cit.*, para. 1196; on the law applicable to international organisations, see *infra*, Chap. 14.

[77] The Assembly also has the power to take mandatory decisions in other fields, such as the adoption of its own rules of procedure (Art. 21) and the establishment of subsidiary organs (Art. 22).

[78] I.C.J. Rep. (1962) 169–170; emphasis added.

[79] See, *e.g.* the reasoning of the I.C.J. in its Advisory Opinion on the Effect of Awards of Compensation made by the UNAT, I.C.J. Rep. (1954), p. 56 *et seq*.

[80] Hence, the UNGA has adopted four regulations (in 1951, 1953 and 1986) applicable within the Organisation's headquarters in New York (for more details, see Szasz, "The United Nations Legislates to Limit its Liability", 81 AJIL (1987) 741–742).

[81] Schermers and Blokker, *op. cit.*, para. 1320; Skubiszewski, *loc. cit.* 35.

(i) Institutional acts binding in the "external sphere" by virtue of the constituent instruments

In a limited number of intergovernmental organisations, provision is made **11–034** for the adoption of institutional acts binding on member states outside the "internal legal sphere" of the organisation concerned. These acts will produce mandatory legal effects *vis-à-vis* their addressees in the international legal order, and/or in their domestic legal order. This is the case for the United Nations, for some specialised agencies, and also for a few regional organisations. The principal example is Article 25 of the UN Charter, which provides that "[t]he Members of the United Nations agree to carry out the decisions of the Security Council in accordance with the present Charter." The mandatory effect of decisions taken by the Security Council under Chapter VII of the Charter, when exercising its responsibilities for the maintenance of international peace and security, is therefore beyond doubt. But this formal test is not the only one to be applied (it would be misleading, since the Council may also confine itself to the adoption of mere recommendations—non-mandatory as such[82]—under Chapter VII). As the I.C.J. put it in its 1971 Advisory Opinion on Namibia:

> "[i]t has been contended that Article 25 of the Charter applies only to enforcement measures adopted under Chapter VII of the Charter. It is not possible to find in the Charter any support for this view. Article 25 is not confined to decisions in regard to enforcement action but applies to 'the decisions of the Security Council' adopted in accordance with the Charter."[83]

The Court further indicated the method which should be used to **11–035** determine whether a particular resolution of the SC should be treated as a "decision" or not:

> "The language of a resolution of the Security Council should be carefully analysed before a conclusion can be made as to its binding effect. In view of the powers under Article 25, the question whether they have been in fact exercised is to be determined in each case, having regard to the terms of the resolution to be interpreted, the discussions leading to it, the Charter provisions invoked and, in general, all circumstances that might assist in determining the legal consequences of the resolution of the Security Council."[84]

It is therefore accepted that resolutions adopted by the council by **11–036** application of Articles 34 or 94(2) of the Charter, for example, may be considered as "decisions" within the meaning of Article 25 and, as such, are

---

[82] On these, see *infra*, paras 11–042 *et seq.*
[83] I.C.J. Rep. (1971) 53, para. 113.
[84] *ibid.*, para. 114 (see also para. 115 for the conclusions reached by the Court *in casu*).

binding on member states.[85] Not only are decisions of the Security Council binding on member states, but the combined effect of Articles 25, and 103 of the Charter, gives them precedence over the obligations undertaken by member states under any other international agreement. This was confirmed by the I.C.J. in its 1992 Order in the Lockerbie case, where the Court had to consider, at the provisional measures stage, the legal effects of—disputed—resolution 748 (1992), adopted by the Security Council a few days earlier. The Court ruled that prima facie the obligation resulting for members from Article 25 extended to the decision contained in that resolution, and that "in accordance with Article 103 of the Charter, the obligations of the Parties in that respect prevail over their obligations under any other international agreement [. . .]."[86] This—provisional—conclusion will of course have to be reconsidered if the Court was to find, at the merits stage, that resolution 748 (1992) has not been adopted "in accordance with the Charter."[87]

11-037   The constituent instruments of some of the UN specialised agencies similarly provide for the power to adopt institutional acts binding on members, although in a less automatic or far-reaching fashion than in the UN itself. Hence, the World Health Assembly may adopt regulations on matters such as sanitary and quarantine procedures, nomenclatures for diseases and pharmaceutical standards, and so on. On adoption these become binding on all members unless they "opt out" by communicating to the organisation their rejection or reservations.[88] The Regulations also bind new members three months after their admission, subject to their right to reject them or enter reservations.[89] In ICAO, the council may adopt international standards which in general consist of specifications the uniform application of which is necessary for the safety or regularity of international air navigation to supplement the Convention itself in the form of annexes.[90] These annexes become effective within three months unless a majority of the members register their disapproval with the council. Members are bound to conform to the standards and must notify the council if they find it impossible to comply with them. A similar system of "contracting out", according to which the institutional act becomes binding on members unless these express their will not to be bound, is also applied

---

[85] See Delbrück, Comment of Art. 25, in Simma (ed.) *op. cit.* 412; see however the doubts raised by Suy, "Commentaire de l'article 25", in Cot and Pellet (eds.), *op. cit.* 475–476.

[86] Questions of Interpretation and Application of the 1971 Montreal Convention arising from the Aerial Incident at Lockerbie (*Libyan Arab Jamahiriya v. United Kingdom*), Order of April 14, 1992, I.C.J. Rep. (1992) 15, para. 39.

[87] For more on the issue of legality, see *infra*, paras 11–052 *et seq.*

[88] Art. 22 of the 1946 Constitution. Reservations are, under the International Sanitary Regulations adopted in 1951, not valid unless accepted by the Assembly, and Regulations do not enter into force for a state making a reservation until so accepted.

[89] Off. Rec. of WHO, No. 37, pp. 335–353.

[90] Arts 38, 54(1) and 90(a) of the 1944 Chicago Convention.

to "technical resolutions" adopted within WMO[91] and, outside the UN system, to the "recommendations" adopted within the North East Atlantic Fisheries Commission.[92] The meeting of the Parties to the 1987 Montreal Protocol may adopt adjustments and reductions to the ozone depleting potential of controlled substances listed in the annex to the protocol and to production or consumption levels of controlled substances by a two-thirds majority of parties present and voting and which represent 50 per cent of the total consumption of controlled substances, and these are binding on all parties without possibility of objection (1987 Montreal Protocol, Article 9(c) and (d)).

Categories of institutional acts are similarly given a binding effect in **11–038** some regional organisations. This is for instance the case in the Arab League (Article 7), the OECD (Article 5),[93] EFTA (Article 32(4)) or the Benelux (Article 19). In each of these organisations, however, the relevant acts are to be taken by an unanimous decision, and are therefore not very different, from a theoretical point of view, from multilateral conventions adopted within an organisation. The only regional organisation which may be singled out in that respect—since only a minority of institutional acts have to be taken by unanimous decision therein[94]—is the European Community.[95] It is also one of the very few organisations in which the measure of obligations flowing from different categories of institutional acts is determined with such a degree of precision. Article 249 of the revised E.C. Treaty provides that:

> "A regulation shall have general application. It shall be binding in its entirety and directly applicable in all member states.
>
> A directive shall be binding, as to the result to be achieved, upon each member state to which it is addressed, but shall leave to the national authorities the choice of form and methods.
>
> A decision shall be binding in its entirety upon those to whom it is addressed.
>
> Recommendations and opinions shall have no binding force".

Whereas regulations leave no choice to member states in terms of **11–039** implementation, directives are thus more flexible, and bind member states only in respect of the result to be achieved. While, as the ECJ put it, "[t]he

---

[91] Arts 8(b) and 9(d) of the 1947 Convention.

[92] Arts 8 and 9 of the Convention of January 24, 1959.

[93] According to Art. 6 of the OECD Treaty, however, the decisions are not binding on any member until it has complied with the requirements of its own constitutional procedure.

[94] See *supra*, paras 11–004 *et seq.*

[95] It may also be noted that some treaties establishing regional organisations in Africa provide for the power of certain organs to adopt institutional acts binding on members of those organisations (see for instance Arts 9 and 12 of the 1993 Treaty establishing ECOWAS). These regimes nevertheless do not seem, in most cases, to have come into force yet. The application of Arts 9 and 12 of the ECOWAS Treaty, for example, is conditional upon the adoption of a protocol which does not appear to have seen the light up to this day.

direct application of a regulation means that its entry into force and its application in favour or against those subject to it are independent of any measure of reception into national law",[96] the same cannot be said of directives and decisions which most generally require measures of implementations on the part of the state(s) concerned.[97] But regulations and directives also share certain characteristics. Hence, the general character of these two categories of instruments may be distinguished from that of decisions, which have been described as "the means by which the Community adopts individual administrative acts", or by which "Community law is applied in specific cases."[98] A common feature of all categories of institutional acts listed in Article 249 (save for recommendations) is the possibility that, as various provisions of the Rome Treaty itself, they may be considered as having a direct effect, thereby enabling private persons to invoke them before national courts. In that respect, the ECJ ruled in 1974 that if, by virtue of the provisions of Article 189 (the content of which is identical to that of present Article 249):

"regulations are directly applicable and, consequently, may by their very nature have direct effects, it does not follow from this that other categories of acts mentioned in that Article can never have similar effects. It would be incompatible with the binding effect attributed to a directive by Article 189 to exclude, in principle, the possibility that the obligation which it imposes may be invoked by those concerned. In particular, where the Community authorities have, by directive, imposed on member states the obligation of a particular course of conduct, the useful effect of such an act would be weakened if individuals were prevented from relying on it before their national courts [. . .]."[99]

11–040   This of course, does not mean that all Community "secondary legislation" should be deemed to have such effect *ipso facto*. As the court emphasised in its ruling, "[i]t is necessary to examine, in every case, whether the nature, general scheme and wording of the provision in question are capable of having direct effects on the relations between

---

[96] Case 34/73 *Variola v. Amministrazione Italiana delle Finanze* (1973) E.C.R. 990, para. 10. Note also that the principle of supremacy of Community law over domestic legal orders extends to regulations (see, *e.g.* Case 43/71, *Politi S.A.S. v. Italian Ministry of Finance* (1971) E.C.R. 1049, para. 9).

[97] For exceptions, such as in the case where the existence of general principles of constitutional or administrative law does not make it necessary to adopt further measures of implementation, see the case 29/84, *Commission v. Germany* (1985) E.C.R. 1661.

[98] Kapteyn and VerLoren van Themaat, *Introduction to the Law of the European Communities* (3rd ed., 1998) revised by L.W. Gormley (London-The Hague-Boston: Kluwer) 332.

[99] Case 41/74, *Van Duyn v. Home Office* (1974) E.C.R. 1347, para. 12. The court had previously given a ruling to the same effect regarding decisions (see Case 9/70, *Grad v. Finanzamt Traunstein* [1970] E.C.R. 825; [1975] C.M.L.R. 1, para. 5a).

member states and individuals."[1] These various features of "secondary" community law evidence, once again, the nature of the European Community as an entity far more integrated than most other intergovernmental organisations.

It should not be concluded from this, however, that the E.C. is the only **11–041** organisation the organs of which have been endowed with the power to adopt norms binding not only on member states but also, beyond these, on other categories of addressees—and more specifically on private persons. Recent practice shows that this has also been the case—although in much more exceptional circumstances—of the United Nations. This has been limited to specific situations, *i.e.* the provisional administration of a territory by the UN. Acting under Chapter VII of the Charter, the Security Council decided in October 1999 to establish the United Nations Transitional Administration in East Timor (UNTAET) and to empower it "to exercise all legislative and executive authority" within the territory.[2] Pursuant to this authority, a total of 13 regulations had been issued by the Transitional Administrator by March 2000, replacing or supplementing the body of national laws previously applicable in East Timor.[3] This example, and the one of the E.C., show that, in a limited number of cases at least, the use of the terms "legislative functions" to describe the norm-making activities of international organisations is not entirely inappropriate. These situations, where organs of intergovernmental organisations adopt norms which, like domestic legislation, will have a binding effect on private persons, nevertheless remain exceptional. And even though it is possible to find in constituent instruments provisions that empower specific organs to adopt institutional acts binding on member states, the majority of international organisations—or of organs of these organisations—have only been given the power to adopt institutional acts that, in themselves, will have to be considered as recommendatory in the "external sphere."

(ii) Legal effects in the "external sphere" of norms adopted in virtue of recommendatory powers

The primary objective of states, in establishing international organisations, **11–042** is to institutionalise their co-operation in different fields and, to that end, to establish structures for the co-ordination of their policies or for the execution of common projects or actions. Except in limited cases, such as those described in the previous section, the founders of intergovernmental organisations generally did not intend to give them "law-making" powers in

---

[1] *ibid.*

[2] Resolution 1272 (1999) of October 25, 1999, para. 1.

[3] See specifically Regulation No. 1999/1 on the Authority of the Transitional Administration in East Timor, adopted on November 27, 1999. The Regulations are available on the Internet (http://www.un.org/peace/etimor/untaetR/UntaetR.htm).

the international or domestic spheres. Nevertheless, most of the organs which had not been endowed with this power have been given the power to make recommendations to members of the organisation within their field of competence, in order to promote or help to achieve the organisation's objectives. This is the case, amongst others, for the UN General Assembly (Articles 10–14), or the "parliamentary" organ of various regional organisations.[4] And organs which have been endowed with the power to adopt institutional acts binding on members of the organisations may also confine themselves to the adoption of recommendations only.[5] It is appropriate to refer in this respect to the UN Security Council[6] or to the organs of those of the specialised agencies which are empowered to adopt institutional acts binding on the members of those organisations.[7]

11–043 Recommendations constitute a significant part of the institutional acts adopted by these organs[8] and by international organisations as a whole. As one author has put it, "[s]everal international organisations, though they do not possess the power to legislate for states, adopt resolutions in which they say what the law is or should be."[9] Whereas the political effect and significance of such acts should not be disregarded,[10] it is widely accepted that they cannot, as such, be considered as binding on the members of the

---

[4] See, *e.g.* Arts 22 and 23 of the Statute of the Council of Europe (Consultative Assembly) and the references to parliamentary organs established—or planned—in some African organisations (*supra*, Chap. 10).

[5] In many organisations, it is expressly provided that a different majority will be required for the adoption of binding and recommendatory acts, respectively, or that the adoption of binding acts will be by unanimous decision, a simple majority being sufficient for the adoption of recommendations.

[6] In its 1998 Judgment on the Preliminary Objections in the Lockerbie case (*Libyan Arab Jamahiriya v. United Kingdom*), for instance, the I.C.J. noted that resolution 731 (1992) of the Security Council "was a mere recommendation without binding effect", thereby emphasising the difference between "decisions" and "recommendations" in the practice of the Council (I.C.J. Rep. (1998) 26, para. 44).

[7] See *supra*, paras 11–034 *et seq.*, regarding the WHO, the ICAO or the WMO.

[8] One may note in that respect that the Security Council has adopted since 1998 a string of resolutions addressing various problems of special importance for Africa. These, as opposed to resolutions hitherto voted by the Council, are not aimed at a specific country and present significant similarities with resolutions adopted by the General Assembly on broad topics such as disarmament or international co-operation, for instance. They clearly constitute mere recommendations; see *e.g.* Resolutions 1208 (1998) on the situation of refugee camps in Africa, 1209 (1998) on illicit arms flows to and in Africa, 1261 (1999) on the protection of children and civilians in armed conflicts, 1269 (1999) on the responsibility of the Security Council in the maintenance of international peace and security or 1296 (2000) on the protection of children in armed conflicts.

[9] Skubiszewski, *loc. cit.* 30.

[10] Even though this depends largely on the context; see Virally, *loc. cit.* 255. On the possible political weight of recommendations, see also Schermers and Blokker, *op. cit.* para. 1226.

organisation concerned.[11] This is not to say, however, that they will produce no legal effects whatsoever outside the organisation's legal order. In some organisations at least, members are required to act on the recommendations adopted and to report on various measures of follow-up. Such requirements are formulated in the constitutions of several UN specialised agencies.

In the ILO, for instance, recommendations adopted by the Conference **11–044** are communicated to all members with a view to effect being given to them by legislation or otherwise. The members have the obligation to bring them before the competent authorities within the state and to inform the organisation of the steps taken and of action taken by the competent authorities (Article 19(6)).[12] Beyond this no further obligation rests on the members other than that of reporting the position in the law and practice of their countries and of any progress made in implementing the recommendation or any modifications found necessary. The FAO Constitution also contemplates the submission to members of recommendations adopted by the Conference; although there is no constitutional obligation to submit these to the appropriate authorities, there is an obligation to report to the organisation periodically on the action taken on the basis of these, and these reports are then considered by the Director-General and submitted to the Conference (Article 9). UNESCO adopts recommendations by a simple majority, and each member state is bound to submit these to its competent authorities[13] within one year (Article 4(4)); the member states are then bound to report periodically to the organisation on their laws, regulations and statistics and on the action taken with regard to recommendations (Article 8). Such provisions obviously require members of the organisations concerned to consider recommendations much more seriously than if they were instruments devoid of all legal significance.

Beyond this, there are various situations in which institutional acts which **11–045** are formally recommendatory nevertheless entail more cogent legal consequences for member states in the "external" sphere. The norms enunciated in a recommendation will indeed sometimes be binding on their addressees not, of course, because they are enshrined in an instrument

---

[11] See, *e.g.* Skubiszewski, *loc. cit.* 33; Detter, "The effect of resolutions of international organisations", in Makarczyk (ed.), *Theory of international law at the threshold of the 21st century: essays in honour of K. Skubiszewski* (The Hague: Kluwer) (1996) 389–390. See, however, the opposite views developed by some authors and exposed—but not approved—by Tunkin, "The role of resolutions of international organisations in creating norms of international law", in Butler (ed.), *International law and the international system* (Dordrecht:Nijhoff) (1987) 6.

[12] A similar obligation bears on UNESCO member states (see Art. 4, para. 4 of the Constitution).

[13] "Competent" means competent to legislate, not just to study; see UNESCO Memorandum in (1965) U.N.J.Y. 137.

which remains in essence optional, but rather in view of the fact that they may be linked to one or another "classical" source of international law. Unilateral acts of states, treaties and international customary law are of particular importance in that respect. Thus, it is beyond dispute that a state is to be considered as bound by the content of a recommendation if it "formally enters into the obligation *vis-à-vis* the organisation to implement such a resolution."[14] The example of the formal acceptance by various member states of the food standards adopted by the *Codex Alimentarius* Commission (a joint FAO-WHO body) is one amongst several which shows that this is not a theoretical hypothesis.[15] It has also been noted in that respect that for various reasons—including recognition of the need for co-operation in certain technical fields and the fact that the recommendatory norms are applied by a significant number of other states—recommendations adopted by international organisations are often applied on a voluntary basis by members of these organisations.[16] Indeed, as the practice of the IMF shows, necessity sometimes brings members to comply with institutional acts which are not binding *per se*. By 1971, the system of exchange rate stability which was fundamental to the Articles of Agreement and the Fund's code of conduct had been virtually destroyed and the Fund was forced to adapt to the new system of floating currencies. The Fund does not adopt conventions, like the ILO, and revision of the Articles was at that stage premature. So, in 1974, the Executive Directors adopted "guidelines," of an experimental character, to keep of currencies floating within manageable limits.[17] Although strictly not binding, these guidelines served as, in effect, regulations until formal amendment of Article IV of the Agreement was achieved in 1976.[18] And even under the amended Article IV, the need for flexibility dictated that the Executive Directors could adopt "principles"[19] for its implementation, these principles being in effect binding on the members. At least in those cases where a formal undertaking is made by members to comply with a recommendation, the application of the doctrine of estoppel leads to the conclusion that they are bound by the institutional act in question, regardless of its originally non-binding character. Whether, along the same line of reasoning, the vote cast by a member of an international organisation in favour of a recommendation adopted by one organ of that organisation may be considered as an

---

[14] Frowein, *loc. cit.* 784; see also *e.g.* Schermers, *International organisations—Resolutions*, EPIL, Vol. II (1995) 1335.

[15] The example is mentioned by Schermers and Blokker, *op. cit.*, para. 1231.

[16] *ibid.* para. 1229 *et seq.* (various concrete examples are given by the authors). See also Dominicé, "Valeur et autorité des actes des organisations internationales", in Dupuy (Ed.), *A Handbook on International Organisations*, 2nd ed. (Dordrecht/Boston/London: Nijhoff) (1998) 457.

[17] Decision No. 4232 (74/67), June 13, 1974.

[18] 15 ILM (1976) 499.

[19] IMF Executive Directors decision on Surveillance over Exchange Rate Policies, 6 IMF Survey (1977) 131.

expression of that member's will to adhere to the norms enunciated in the institutional act remains a matter of controversy. A number of authors argue that the voting pattern is an element which must not be taken into account when it comes to assessing the possibly binding effects of norms contained in a recommendation, considering that "by its vote the State does not conclude any form of contract with the organisation or with other States."[20] It seems, however, that the question is not so much one of "contract" than as of expression by a state of its approval—or rejection—of the norms contained in a recommendation as reflecting the existing state of the law in the field concerned, or possibly, the legal regime that that state would wish to be applicable in that field.[21] In other words, there appears to be no reason to exclude the possibility that the position taken by a member of an international organisation through its vote in favour of a recommendation could subsequently be opposed to that state as an expression of its legal position regarding the subject-matter dealt with in the institutional act—assuming, of course, that the latter has used normative, as opposed to purely recommendatory, terms.[22] Here again, it is the principle of non-contradiction which comes into play, in respect both of the individual members and of the organ concerned as such.[23] This approach finds support in the Nicaragua case, where the I.C.J. stated that:

> "[t]he effect of consent to the text of such resolutions [2625 (XXV), *in casu*] cannot be understood as merely that of a 'reiteration or elucidation' of the treaty commitments undertaken in the Charter. On the contrary, it may be understood as an acceptance of the validity of the rule or set of rules declared by the resolution by themselves."[24]

In the same judgment, the Court carefully reviewed the positions taken **11–046** by the United States in respect of various resolutions of the UN General Assembly, and relied on the unqualified approval of some of these acts by that state to establish its *opinio juris* in respect of the existence and scope of the rule of non-intervention in customary international law.[25] The position taken by a state upon the adoption of a recommendation by an organ of an intergovernmental organisation is therefore far from being devoid of significance when it comes to assess the possible legal effects of the norms contained in that institutional act for the state concerned.

---

[20] Detter, *loc. cit.* 391–392; see also *e.g.* Schermers and Blokker, *op. cit.*, para. 1225.
[21] See *e.g.* Frowein, *loc. cit.* 789. As Tunkin similarly expressed it, "[i]n voting for a resolution, States express their approval of certain rules of conduct embodied in the resolution" (*loc. cit.* 11).
[22] On this requirement, see *e.g.* Skubiszewski, *loc. cit.* 62; David, *op. cit.* 193 *et seq.*
[23] See in that sense the example of the 1984 ICAO resolution given by Frowein, *loc. cit.* 790.
[24] I.C.J. Rep. (1986) 100, para. 188.
[25] *ibid.* 107, para. 203. Interestingly, the Court refers in that respect not only to resolutions of the General Assembly but also to other institutional acts of a recommendatory character adopted within other international arrangements, such as the CSCE (*ibid.*, para. 204).

11–047   But apart from individual acceptance, there are also other grounds on which the norms enunciated in an institutional act of a recommendatory character may be considered as binding on the members of the organisation concerned. It is not unusual for organs of international organisations to adopt resolutions which aim at stating, restating, clarifying or supplementing the provisions of the constitutent instrument on particular activities or situations falling within the competence of the organisation. Several examples of such resolutions can be found in the practice of the UN General Assembly; among them, resolution 1514 (XV) on the Granting of Independence to Colonial Territories and Peoples, which gives a more concrete content to the principle of self-determination proclaimed in the UN Charter; or resolution 3314 (XXIX) on the definition of aggression, which clarifies to a certain extent the scope of the right to self-defence recognised by Article 51 of the Charter. This type of institutional acts may be considered as being in the nature of "subsequent practice in the application of the treaty which establishes the agreement of the parties regarding its interpretation", within the meaning of Article 31(3)(c) of the Vienna Convention on the Law of Treaties. They may clarify the sense of the relevant provisions of the constitutent instrument, and may be viewed as authentic interpretation thereof, which will be binding on all members of the organisation concerned.[26]

11–048   Last—but certainly not least—the norms enunciated in a recommendation may have a binding effect on members of the organisation concerned when they can be considered to be the expression of customary international law.[27] The most basic situation is that of institutional acts which reaffirm existing—and generally well-accepted—customary norms of international law.[28] These obviously do not lose their binding character by the mere fact of being enunciated in a non-mandatory instrument, and will therefore continue to oblige the members of the organisation. More significantly, recommendations may also be the catalyst for the emergence of international customs. This has been emphasised by the I.C.J., amongst others, in its 1996 Advisory Opinion on the Legality of the threat or use of nuclear weapons, where the court noted that:

11–049   "General Assembly resolutions, even if they are not binding, may sometimes have normative value. They can, in certain circumstances, provide evidence important for establishing the existence of a rule or the emergence of an *opinio juris*. To establish whether this is true of a

---

[26] See Frowein, *loc. cit.* 790; Virally, *loc. cit.* 259; Schermers and Blokker, *op. cit.*, para. 1255.
[27] See generally Economides, *loc. cit.* 144; Virally, *loc. cit.* 259; Schermers, *loc. cit.* 1334; Dominicé, *loc. cit.* 458.
[28] This has, for instance, very frequently been the case of resolutions or other instruments adopted within the framework of the CSCE/OSCE; see *e.g.* Sapiro, Changing the CSCE into the OSCE: Legal Aspects of a Political Transformation, (1995) AJIL 631–632.

given General Assembly resolution, it is necessary to look at its content and the conditions of its adoption; it is also necessary to see whether an *opinio juris* exists as to its normative character. Or a series of resolutions may show the gradual evolution of the *opinio juris* required for the establishment of a new rule."[29]

The Court found that those elements were not present in the case of the **11–050** resolutions taken by the General Assembly on nuclear weapons, because their wording was not always consistent—raising doubts as to their normative character—and because they had been adopted with a significant number of states voting against or abstaining.[30] In contrast to their approach in the Nicaragua case, the judges paid greater attention to the overall attitude of the members of the organisation in respect of the resolutions under scrutiny, and not to the position taken by specific states or groups of states. The reason for this lies most probably in the fact that the Court was called upon to give an advisory opinion and determine the present state of the law on the issue, and not to pronounce a judgment on the legality of the particular activities of a particular state. By contrast, the customary character of norms contained in a number of other resolutions adopted by the UN General Assembly has been recognised, sometimes almost instantly (as in the classical example of the various resolutions enunciating the first norms in the field of space law, thereby paving the way for the adoption of subsequent conventions),[31] sometimes over a longer period of time, through re-affirmations or references to the norms contained in the resolution as being mandatory (as in the case of the Universal Declaration of Human Rights).[32]

It appears therefore that there will be circumstances in which institu- **11–051** tional acts which are non-binding in themselves may nevertheless create legal obligations for members of the organisation by an organ of which they have been adopted. This can be explained by the fact that the norms contained in these acts are binding because they can be linked to other, "traditional" sources of international law such as unilateral undertakings or international customary law. It must be emphasised, however, that institu-

---

[29] I.C.J. Rep. (1996) 254–255, para. 70.

[30] *ibid.* paras 71–73.

[31] See Skubiszweski, *loc. cit.* 69–70; Dominicé, *loc. cit.* 458.

[32] In the case of the United States Diplomatic and Consular Staff in Tehran, the I.C.J. ruled that "[w]rongfully to deprive human beings of their freedom and to subject them to physical constraint in conditions of hardship is in itself manifestly incompatible with the principles of the Charter of the United Nations, as well as with the fundamental principles enunciated in the Universal Declaration of Human Rights", without making any reservation as to the fact that the Declaration was in itself a non-binding instrument, thereby recognising the customary status achieved by the norms it contained (I.C.J. Rep. (1980) 42, para. 91). The Court did not pay any attention, in that respect, to the fact that the UDHR had not been adopted by an unanimous decision of the states which composed the General Assembly at the time.

tional acts of international organisations, be they binding per se or by the operation of other sources, will produce legal effects for their addressees only if they meet specific requirements of legality, *i.e.* of conformity, in terms both of form and substance, with the rules of the organisation concerned.

c. Legality of Institutional Acts

Bibliography: Lauterpacht, "The Legal Effect of Illegal Acts of International Organisations", Cambridge Essays in International Law—Essays in Honour of Lord McNair (London: Stevens and sons) (1965) pp. 88–121; Kawashima, "Some Aspects of Illegal Acts of International Organisations", Osaka U. Law Rev. (1968) pp. 13–35; Kim, "La validité des résolutions de l'Assemblée générale des Nations UniesKim, "La validité des résolutions de l'Assemblée générale des Nations Unies"RGDIP (1971) pp. 92–104; Morgenstern, *Legality in International Organisations, B.Y.B.I.L.* (1976–77) pp. 241–257; Osieke, "The Validity of Ultra Vires Decisions of International Organisations", A.J.I.L. (1983) pp. 239–256; Sanjose Gil, Las consecuencias juridicas de los actos ultra vires de las organisaciones internationales, en particular la O.N.U., R.E.D.I. (1990) pp. 443–462; Doehring, "Unlawful Resolutions of the Security Council and their Legal Consequences", 1 Max Planck Ybk UN Law (1997) 91.

11–052   International organisations may only exercise those powers which have been granted to them by their members. These powers are limited to those which are necessary for the organisation to perform the functions which have been assigned to it.[33] These limitations apply to the exercise of "legislative" or normative powers by international organisations. Institutional acts adopted by international organs will only be valid—and produce legal effects—if they comply with the rules of the organisation, in terms both of form and of substance, since it is only within those limits that the members have conferred a measure of normative power to the organs they have established to ensure the functioning of the organisation.[34] The principle of legality applies equally to institutional acts which are designed to have legal consequences within the organisation[35] or in the international or domestic legal orders. The principle is also applicable to all international organisations, irrespective of whether or not any review or sanction

---

[33] See *e.g.* Indiv. Op. of Judge Gros appended to the I.C.J. Advisory Opinion on the Interpretation of the Agreement of March 25, 1951 Between the WHO and Egypt, I.C.J. Rep. (1980) 103; Franck, "The Powers of Appreciation: Who is the Ultimate Guardian of UN Legality?" AJIL (1992) 520.

[34] See generally Virally, *loc. cit.* 246.

[35] See, *e.g.* in that respect, in virtually all organisations, the disputes relating to the application of the rules regulating the international civil service; the cases involving issues of division of competences between institutions of the European Communities (*e.g.* Case 22/70, ERTA (*Commission v. Council*), (1971) E.C.R. 263; [1971] C.M.L.R. 335); cases before the I.C.J. involving the legality of acts internal to specialised agencies (Advisory Opinion on the Composition of IMCO Maritime Safety Committee, I.C.J. Rep. (1960) 150) or of organs of the UN itself (*e.g.* Advisory Opinion on Certain Expenses of the United Nations, *loc. cit.*).

mechanism has actually been created or referred to within those organisations.[36]

The formal validity of institutional acts is generally easy to establish. The **11–053** procedural conditions of adoption have to be met, whether they relate to voting majorities, resort to prior consultations with other organ(s), or statement of reasons, for instance.[37] Few problems have arisen in this regard in practice,[38] partly because the organs of review—where such organs exist—have consistently taken the view that minor breaches of procedural requirements do not put the institutional act's validity into question.[39] But mere compliance with procedural requirements is not sufficient when it comes to establishing the validity of an institutional act. As the I.C.J. put it in the 1996 Advisory Opinion on the Legality of the Use by a State of Nuclear Weapons in Armed Conflicts:

> "[t]he mere fact that a majority of States, in voting on a resolution, have complied with all the relevant rules of form cannot in itself suffice to remedy any fundamental defects, such as acting ultra vires, with which the resolution might be afflicted."[40]

The institutional act must also be in conformity with substantive rules of **11–054** the organisation. In that respect, the illegality of institutional acts may result from two main causes: a breach of substantive rules pertaining to the organisation's legal order (*i.e.* a decision of the European Commission entailing a breach of fundamental human rights),[41] or a lack of competence (*i.e.* a resolution by which the Conference of the FAO would authorise the members of the Organisation to use force under certain circumstances). Debates over the substantive legality of particular institutional acts have often led to confrontations of a highly political, rather than legal character. This has been particularly the case in organisations where no system of judicial review exists, and where such debates are usually not tempered by

---

[36] See *e.g.* Bedjaoui, Du contrôle de légalité des actes du Conseil de sécurité *in* Nouveaux itinéraires en droit—Mélanges François Rigaux (Brussels: Bruylant) (1993) 93; Amerasinghe, Principles of the Institutional Law of International Organisations (C.U.P.: Cambridge) (1996) 166. On judicial, and other forms of review, see *infra*, Chap. 13, general introduction.

[37] As far as E.C. law is concerned, see the various requirements enumerated in Schermers and Waelbroeck, *Judicial Protection in the European Communities* (5th ed. Deventer/Boston: Kluwer) (1992) pp. 201–215.

[38] See however, in the European Communities, the cases studied by Schermers and Waelbroeck (*ibid.*) and, in the UN, the challenge, on formal grounds, to the legality of Security Council Resolution 276 in the *Namibia* case (see *supra*, paras 11–004 *et seq.*).

[39] For the ECJ, see *e.g.* cases 32/64, Customs Duties on Silk (*Italy v. Commission*) [1965] E.C.R. 372; [1967] C.M.L.R. 207 and 218/78, Van Landewijck (FEDETAB), (1980) E.C.R. 3243; for the I.C.J., see the judgment on the Appeal relating to the Jurisdiction of the ICAO Council (*India v. Pakistan*), I.C.J. Rep. (1972) 69–70.

[40] 1996 I.C.J. Rep. 82, para. 29.

[41] For more details on these rules, see *infra*, Chap. 14.

the intervention of a more "objective" actor, such as an international tribunal.[42] The contradictory positions assumed over time by the same members of an international organisation in relation to questions which were in essence identical reflect this phenomena. In this respect, practice concerning the interpretation to be given to Article 2(7) of the UN Charter (and the ensuing positions taken as to the validity of various General Assembly resolutions dealing with internal situations in different states or territories) offers one of the most striking examples of how debates on issues of legality may become influenced by political considerations.[43] This does not mean that the requirement of Article 2(7) does not apply to organs entrusted with a more political mission, merely that compliance with it will sometimes be more difficult to assess. This was emphasised by the I.C.J. in its Advisory Opinion on the Conditions of Admission of a State to Membership in the United Nations, where the Court stated that:

"[t]he political character of an organ does not release it from the observance of the treaty provisions established by the Charter when they constitute limitations on its powers or criteria for its judgment."[44]

11–055   What is true of predominantly "political" organs may also be said of organs which have broader discretionary powers (*i.e.* which are not bound to act in specific situations, and which have a wide margin of appreciation as to the measures to enact).[45] In that respect, the Appeals Chamber of the International Criminal Tribunal for the former-Yugoslavia, called upon to pronounce upon the legality of the UN Security Council resolution establishing the Tribunal, found that the wide margin of discretion conferred upon the council by Article 39 of the Charter did not mean that its powers were unlimited:

"The Security Council is [. . .] subjected to certain constitutional limitations, however broad its powers under the constitution may be. Those powers cannot, in any case, go beyond the limits of the jurisdiction of the Organisation at large, not to mention other specific limitations or those which may derive from the internal division of power within the Organisation. In any case, neither the text nor the

---

[42] This is not to say, however, than debates on the legality of institutional acts in other, more institutionalised organisations such as the European Community, are never influenced by clearly political considerations. A good example (far from being isolated) of this phenomenon may be found in the Case 294/86, *Greece v. Council* [1988] E.C.R. 5323.

[43] See, *e.g.* over the particular situation of Southern Rhodesia, Gowlland-Debbas, *Collective Responses to Illegal Acts in International Law—United Nations Action in the Question of Southern Rhodesia* (Dordrecht: Nijhoff) (1990) 123 *et seq.*

[44] (1947–48) I.C.J. Rep. 64.

[45] See *e.g.* Morgenstern, "Legality in International Organisations", B.Y.B.I.L. (1976–77) 242.

spirit of the Charter conceives of the Security Council as *legibus solutus* (unbound by law)."[46]

The fact that all institutional acts have to comply with requirements of **11–056** substantive legality therefore appears beyond doubt.[47] There is still another factor, however, that has to be taken in consideration when it comes to assessing the legality of such acts, more particularly in respect of the extent of a given organ's powers. The competences of international organisations' organs are not delimited in an immutable way. The need to adapt to changing circumstances, and to make sure that organs will have the means necessary to enable the organisation to function effectively and reach its aims has led to the formulation of the doctrine of implied powers, according to which an organisation "must be deemed to have those powers which, though not expressly provided in the Charter, are conferred upon it by necessary implication as being necessary for the performance of its duties."[48] The power of a particular organ to adopt an institutional act in a given field falls to be assessed not only in the light of the written rules of the organisation, but also in the context of subsequent practice, which must be taken into account.[49] This may be one of the elements which have led the International Court of Justice to formulate a general presumption of competence of international organs, in the following terms:

> "when the Organisation takes action which warrants the assertion that it was appropriate for the fulfilment of one of the stated purposes of the United Nations, the presumption is that such an action is not *ultra vires* the Organisation."[50]

This presumption has subsequently been re-affirmed in broader terms by **11–057** the I.C.J., as well as the ECJ, and is deemed to apply more generally to institutional acts adopted in accordance with the rules of procedure.[51] The aim, clearly, is to achieve a reasonably high level of stability as possible in

---

[46] Case IT-94-1–AR 72, 105 I.L.R. 465, para. 28. See also Bernhardt, Ultra Vires Activities of International Organisations, in Makarczyck (Ed.), *op. cit.* 606; Doehring, Unlawful Resolutions of the Security Council and their Legal Consequences, 1 Max Planck Ybk UN Law (1997) 92 *et seq.*

[47] See also *e.g.* in that respect the 1996 Advisory Opinion on the Legality of the Use by a State of Nuclear Weapons in Armed Conflicts, *loc. cit.* 82, para. 27 and 28.

[48] I.C.J., Advisory Opinion on the Reparation for Injuries Suffered in the Service of the United Nations, I.C.J. Rep. (1949) 178. The Court quotes in that respect an earlier Opinion of the P.C.I.J. concerning the ILO (Opinion of July 23, 1926, Series B, No. 13, p. 18).

[49] See generally Bernhardt, *loc. cit.*, 602. This is not without limits, however. See in that respect the Conclusions of Advocate General Tesauro in case C-327/91 before the ECJ (*France v. Commission*, E.C.R. (1994) I-3658, para. 29).

[50] Advisory Opinion on Certain Expenses of the United Nations, *loc. cit.* p. 168.

[51] I.C.J., Advisory Opinion on Namibia, *loc. cit.*, p. 22, para. 20; C.J.E.C., cases 15/85, Consorzio cooperative d'Abruzzo, E.C.R. (1987) 1019–1021, C-137/92, *Commission v. BASF et al., ibid.* (1994) I-2616–2617.

international relations, by conferring the maximum degree of certainty to acts of intergovernmental organisations.[52] It should however be kept in mind that this is nothing more than a presumption, which may be put into question either on the international or—though in more limited ways—the national plane.[53]

---

[52] See *e.g.* Thierry, Les résolutions des organes internationaux dans la jurisprudence de la C.I.J., 167 R.C.A.DI. (1980–II) 423.
[53] See *infra*, the general introduction to Chapter 13.

CHAPTER 12

"EXECUTIVE" AND ADMINISTRATIVE FUNCTIONS

The effectiveness of international organisations would be considerably **12–001** limited if their powers did not go beyond the mere adoption of institutional acts. If the execution and implementation of these were left to members only, without any kind of assistance, supervision or sanction, the risk would be that the norms and decisions adopted by or within the organisations would often remain ineffective. In order to ensure the effectiveness of their actions, most international organisations have been given significant powers concerning the implementation of decisions taken or programs agreed upon by their organs. Historically, this may even be said to be the most important function of international organisations, since these were initially exclusively conceived as instruments that would enable member states to manage in common shared resources or interests—at that stage, the functions of "execution" and "administration" were clearly predominant to that of "legislation." This is particularly evidenced by the fact that the first intergovernmental organisations essentially took the form of "bureaux" or "secretariats," initially clearly dependent on the national administrations of member states, and only gradually gaining more autonomy.[1] This aspect of their functions has remained essential, and the institutional structure of all contemporary international organisations includes an administrative organ, or Secretariat, which plays a central role in the management of the organisation and of its activities (A). But apart from this more classical, administrative function, most international organisations have been entrusted with "executive" functions, that include overseeing the implementation of the acts of the organisation and the supervision of compliance with those acts by the members (B).

A. MANAGEMENT OF THE ORGANISATION—INTERNATIONAL ADMINISTRATION AND INTERNATIONAL CIVIL SERVICE PRINCIPLES

Bibliography: Akehurst, *The Law Governing Employment in International Organisations*, Cambridge, C.U.P., 1967; Amerasinghe, *The Law of the*

---

[1] See *e.g.* Schermers and Blokker, *International Institutional Law*, 3rd ed., para. 434.

International Civil Service—As Applied by International Administrative Tribunals, 2 vols., 2nd ed., Oxford, Clarendon, 1994; Bedjaoui, *Fonction publique internationale et influences nationales,* Paris, Pedone, 1958; Beigbeder, *Threats to the International Civil Service,* London, Pinter, 1988; Bettati, "Recrutement et carrière des fonctionnaires internationaux", 204 Recueil des Cours (1987–IV) 171–443; de Cooker (ed.), *International Administration: Law and Management Practices in International Organisations* (incl. supplements I-VI), The Hague, Kluwer, 1999; Jordan, "Law of the International Civil Service", in Joyner (ed.), *The United Nations and International Law,* C.U.P., 1997, 385–408; Meron, Status and Independence of the International Civil Servants, 167 Recueil des Cours (1980–II) 285–384; Pellet and Ruzie, *Les fonctionnaires internationaux,* Paris, P.U.F., 1993; S.F.D.I., Les agents internationaux, Paris, Pedone, 1985.

12–002 Secretariats constitute the backbone of international organisations.[2] In most organisations, there is a single, unified secretariat, which serves all organs but in some, such as the European Community, each institution has its own secretariat.[3] They are mainly entrusted with administrative functions. Some of these functions are common to all organisations (such as the day-to-day management of the organisation), while others vary in accordance with the organisation's missions and fields of competences (such as the function of depositary of treaties, for instance). Secretariats are placed under the authority of a chief administrator (Secretary- or Director-General, Executive Secretary, Managing Director, are just some of the designations used in constitutive instruments)[4], and are generally composed of various categories of staff the recruitment and status of which are governed by detailed rules.

(a) THE CHIEF ADMINISTRATIVE OFFICER

12–003 The head of the administration of international organisations is usually elected[5] or appointed[6] by one or several of the organisation's political organs. In a number of organisations, the chief administrative officer is also empowered, in parallel with his or her administrative responsibilities, with other, executive functions, such as the participation in the functioning of

---

[2] One could see a practical evidence of this, amongst others, in the fact that under the 1994 WTO Articles of Agreement the Secretariat is the only organ of the GATT 1947 which is, as such, to become an organ of the WTO (see Art. XVI, (2)).

[3] For more on this, see *e.g.* Schermers and Blokker, *op. cit.*, para. 435. Staff members of these various secretariats however share a common administrative status.

[4] Note that in autonomous international judicial institutions, such as the International Tribunal for the Law of the Sea, the function of chief administrative officer devolves upon the Registrar (see the ITLOS Staff Regulations, preambular paragraph on "Scope and purpose" and Regulation 1.2; Doc. ITLOS/18/Rev.1 of 1998).

[5] See Art. XII, section 4, (a) of the IMF Articles of Agreement for the IMF Managing Director; Art. 108 of the OAS Charter for the Secretary General.

[6] For the United Nations, see Art. 97 of the Charter; for the interpretation given to this provision in practice, see *supra,* Chap. 2. See also *e.g.* Art. 8 of the ILO Constitution, VI, 2 of the WTO Agreement, 10 of the OECD Convention, 36, b) of the Statute of the Council of Europe, XVI of the OAU Charter, 18, 1 of the ECOWAS Treaty.

executive organs.[7] At this point we shall deal with administrative functions only. Constituent instruments ascribe in rather general terms to the chief administrative officer the responsibility for the "efficient conduct"[8] of the "ordinary business"[9] of the organisation and for the appointment, organisation and dismissal of the members of the staff.[10]

More concretely, the discharge of the first aspect of these administrative **12–004** responsibilities means that the head of administration's primary duty is to ensure the efficient working of the meetings of the organs and committees, and also of such conferences as may be convened under the organisation's auspices.[11] In this connection the chief administrative officer will generally be responsible for drawing up a provisional agenda, notifying invited states and other bodies of the convening of the sessions and meetings, providing staff and facilities, and examining the credentials of representatives and reports thereon to the organ concerned. For special conferences the chief administrative officer may also submit proposals regarding methods of work and procedure, and provide draft agenda and rules of procedure. During the course of a meeting or conference the chief administrative officer, through the Secretariat's staff, may undertake studies, advise on matters of procedure, and assist in the drafting of documents, resolutions, and reports, as well as give legal and technical advice.

In certain organisations a sometimes significant part of the decisions of **12–005** organs and committees can include a request for the preparation of studies and reports. In such cases, it is again the chief administrative officer who often assumes responsibility for this work.[12] In the UN, the work actually requested is, however, only a small part of the informative work and study which the Secretariat undertakes as part of its normal work programme. This work supplies much of the essential data upon which the UN organs rely in reaching decisions; it is generally of a high standard although occasionally, in an understandable attempt to be impartial, it may lack positive opinions or proposals.[13] In financial matters the chief administrative officer assumes responsibility for the preparation of the annual budget

---

[7] For the United Nations, see *supra*, Chap. 2; see also Articles XII, section 4, a) of the IMF Articles of Agreement for the IMF Managing Director and Art. VI, (3) of the UNESCO Constitution for the Director General.

[8] See *e.g.* Art. 8, (1) of the ILO Constitution.

[9] See *e.g.* Art. XII, section 4, (b) of the IMF Articles of Agreement. Art. XVI of the OAU Charter refers to the direction of "the affairs of the Secretariat".

[10] See *e.g.* Arts XII, section 4, (b) of the IMF Articles of Agreement and VI, (3) of the WTO Agreement.

[11] See *e.g.* Arts 112 (d) of the OAS Charter and 19, (3)(f) of the ECOWAS Treaty for explicit provisions in that respect.

[12] See *e.g.* Arts 112, (d) of the OAS Charter and 19, (3) of the ECOWAS Treaty.

[13] The independent secretariat of UNCTAD, at least during the period of office of Prebisch as Secretary-General, has been somewhat exceptional in its advocacy of the policies and aims of the developing countries (see Gardner, "The UNCTAD" 22 Int. Org. (1968) 106).

in most organisations, which is then submitted to one of the organisation's political organs for approval.[14]

12–006 Constituent instruments frequently provide for the possibility of adopting multilateral conventions under the auspices of international organisations or within one of their organs.[15] The chief administrative officer of the organisation concerned is generally entrusted with specific functions in that respect. He or she may be designated as depositary of these instruments and may be required to perform corollary tasks (notification of signatures, accessions, and reservations to the states concerned. communication of copies to members of the organisations, etc).[16] The UN Secretariat has been given particularly onerous responsibilities in this regard, since Article 102 of the Charter requires members of the organisation to register with the Secretariat every international agreement they enter into, the Secretariat being also responsible for their publication.[17]

12–007 Another classical function of the chief administrative officer is the submission of periodical—often annual—reports on the work of the organisation.[18] These generally provide a comprehensive summary of the work undertaken and provide a valuable source of information. In some organisations, it is also used as a means of exercising the chief administrative officer's political powers, in so far as these reports contain suggestions and proposals relating to political questions.[19] The Secretariat will also take responsibility for the organisation's website which nowadays will often be the public face of the organisation.

12–008 In many organisations, the chief administrative officer is endowed with the authority to act as the organisation's legal representative.[20] This includes the negotiation and conclusion of agreements and contracts under

---

[14] See *e.g.* Arts 9, (5) of the WIPO Convention; VII (1) of the WTO Articles of Agreement, XXIII of the OAU Charter; 112 (c) of the OAS Charter; 20 (1) of the OECD Convention, 38, (c) of the Statute of the Council of Europe (note that litt. (e) of the same provision also opens the possibility to request from the Secretary-General an estimate of expenditures to which the implementation of recommendations presented would give rise). Note that the drafting of the budget is a task for political organs in some organisations. In the European Community, for instance, it devolves upon the Commission (Art. 272). For more on the finances and budgets of international organisations, see also *infra*, Chap. 17.

[15] For more on this, see *supra*, Chap. 11, paras 11–027 *et seq.*

[16] See *e.g.* Article 19, 5 of the ILO Constitution, Art. 112 (f) of the OAS Charter.

[17] See generally on this the comments of Art. 102 in Cot and Pellet (eds.), *La Charte des Nations Unies—Commentaire article par article*, 2nd ed., 1365 *et seq.* and in Simma (ed.), *The Charter of the United Nations—A Commentary*, 1103.

[18] See *e.g.* Arts 98 of the UN Charter, VI, 3, b) of the UNESCO Constitution, 9, 5 of the WIPO Convention, 112 (g) of the OAS Charter; (19) (3) (e) of the ECOWAS Treaty. Again, in the European Community, it is the Commission which publishes the annual report (Art. 212).

[19] This is generally the case in the UN, for instance.

[20] See *e.g.* Arts 109 of the OAS Charter; 9 (4) (b) of the WIPO Convention; 19 (1) of the ECOWAS Treaty. This power may be deemed as implicit in organisations the constitutive instrument of which does not contain any specific provision to that effect.

private law with private companies for supplies and services and, of course, of contracts of service with individuals who become staff members. This also extends, in some organisations at least, to the negotiation and conclusion of international agreements with states[21] and/or with other international organisations.[22] Hence, agreements between the UN and the specialised agencies are typically concluded by the heads of the respective organisations. These representational functions may also extend to the conduct of court proceedings on behalf of the organisation. The Secretary-General of the UN, and the Director-Generals of several specialised agencies have, through their representatives, made statements in the interest of their respective organisation before the I.C.J. on several occasions on which the issues raised affected their organisation.[23] The chief administrative officer usually also represents his or her organisation before national tribunals in matters affecting the organisation's property, or privileges and immunities, and before the Administrative Tribunal or equivalent judicial or quasi-judicial organs on staff matters.[24] Finally, where, in any judicial proceedings, the questions of immunity arises for an official, it is normally for the chief administrative officer to decide whether to waive or maintain the immunity. This may combine with the broader duty of the administrative head to ensure the protection of staff members and of other agents working for the organisation.[25] As the I.C.J. stated, in relation to the UN, in its 1999 Advisory Opinion on the Difference relating to Immunity from Legal Process of a Special Rapporteur of the Commission on Human Rights:

---

[21] See, for example, the UN-USA 1947 Headquarters Agreement. This also provides for consultation and negotiation on several matters between the Secretary-General and the U.S. Government after the agreement has come into force. As a general rule such agreements are concluded by him at the request of one of the UN organs, but in certain cases, notably in those which concern agreements on the privileges and immunities of the UN, the Secretary-General will act on his own initiative.

[22] Note however that under Art. 7 of the 1986 Vienna Convention on the Law of Treaties between States and International Organisations or between International Organisations, the chief administrative officer is not expressly designated as a person who has the authority to represent an international organisation for the purpose of expressing the consent of that organisation to be bound by a treaty. This provision nevertheless recognises that a person is to be considered as representing an international organisation if "it appears from the circumstances that it was the intention of the States and international organisations concerned to consider that person as representing the organisation for such purposes, in accordance with the rules of the organisation, without having to produce full powers." This may of course apply in priority to the chief administrative officer.

[23] This is of course limited to advisory proceedings, there being no possibility under the I.C.J. Statute of international organisations appearing as parties in contentious proceedings (see *infra*, Chap. 13). For the UN, see for example, Reparation for Injuries Suffered in the Service of the UN, I.C.J., Oral Statement, pp. 3–4; Reservations to the Convention on the Prevention and Punishment of the Crime of Genocide, I.C.J., Oral Statement (Extract), p. 20; Applicability of Article VI, section 22, of the Convention on the Privileges and Immunities of the United Nations, I.C.J. Rep. (1989) 179, para. 8. For the WHO, see Legality of the Use by a State of Nuclear Weapons in Armed Conflict, I.C.J. Rep. (1996) 69, para. 9.

[24] See *infra*, Chap. 13.

[25] On the concept of functional protection, see *infra*, paras 12-027 *et seq*.

> "the Secretary-General, as the chief administrative officer of the Organisation, has the primary responsibility to safeguard the interests of the Organisation; to that end, it is up to him to assess whether its agents acted within the scope of their functions and, where he so concludes, to protect these agents, including experts on mission, by asserting their immunity."[26]

12–009 In the United Nations, because of the complexity of the UN system, another important duty of the Secretary-General is to secure adequate co-ordination and integration of the work programmes of the various branches of the Secretariat and of the specialised agencies and other intergovernmental organisations.[27] This need for co-ordination has been particularly evident in the economic and social fields. Generally, it covers problems such as the elimination of duplication of work, fixing responsibility for and priority of projects, preparation of budgets, allocation of staff, scheduling of meetings and conferences, and the dissemination of information. It is true that, in relation to the specialised agencies, the primary responsibility lies with the General Assembly and the Economic and Social Council.[28] However, under the agreements with the specialised agencies, specific powers have been assigned to the Secretary-General and, in addition, as Chairman of the Advisory Committee on Co-ordination (ACC), he can consult with the heads of the specialised agencies in a practical way so as to co-ordinate policies and work programmes.[29]

(b) THE SECRETARIATS

12–010 The efficient functioning of international organisations is to a significant extent dependent on the quality of their Secretariats and in particular on their ability to be perceived as truly international—that is to say independent and impartial and not serving the particular interests of a member or of a group of members. Specific rules and procedures therefore aim at ensuring both selectivity and representativeness in the recruitment of the staff (1) and a particular emphasis has been put in a large number of constitutive instruments on the international character of the Secretariats and of the functions of their staff (2). In spite of these formal guarantees, however, it is a regrettable but regular feature that the independence of international secretariats has often come under assault, and has in some cases been significantly eroded.

---

[26] I.C.J. Rep. (1999), p. 87, para. 60.
[27] See also in that respect Art. 80 of the 1993 ECOWAS Treaty, which however remains more theoritical since the specialised institutions of the Community do not seem to have come into being yet. See also Art. 112, h of the OAS Charter, which lists among the functions of the organisation's Secretariat the co-operation with specialised agencies of the OAS (but does not evoke any function of coordination, however).
[28] See *supra*, Chap. 2.
[29] For more on this, see *e.g.* Dubouis, "Commentaire de l'article 101", in Cot and Pellet (eds.), *op. cit.*, 1354 *et seq.*

(1) Recruitment, appointment and conditions of service

It has often been emphasised that the intrinsic qualities of staff members **12–011** has a considerable impact on the quality of the international organisation itself, and of its action. Constituent instruments therefore very often insist on the need to recruit persons with presenting the highest level of qualification for the positions at stake. But at the same time, the international character of intergovernmental organisations requires that no member or group of members is unduly privileged so far as recruitment is concerned, and that a fair geographical distribution is achieved. Hence, Article 101 (3) of the UN Charter provides that:

> "The paramount consideration in the employment of the staff and in the determination of the conditions of service shall be the necessity of securing the highest standards of efficiency, competence and integrity. Due regard shall be paid to the importance of recruiting the staff on as wide a geographical basis as possible."[30]

Other instruments, such as the UNESCO Constitution, are even more explicit, when they state that:

> "[s]ubject to the paramount consideration of securing the highest standards of integrity, efficiency and technical competence, appointment to the staff shall be on as wide a geographical basis as possible."[31]

There are, therefore, two main principles guiding recruitment: the first is **12–012** that of the personal qualifications of the applicant, the second that of securing a balanced geographical distribution. This second principle is not *per se* inconsistent with the first and paramount principle but, in practice, it sometimes proves relatively more difficult to secure staff of appropriate qualifications from countries which do not have long-established academic institutions or civil services. This problem is, however, more often experienced in universal organisations than in regional ones, where the level of training is generally more uniform in the various member states.

Several organisations have established a specific system by which dif- **12–013** ferent factors are weighted in order to determine the number of positions— or more generally a range of positions- that each member state may expect

---

[30] See also *e.g.* Articles XII, section 4 of the IMF Articles of Agreement; VIII (3) of the FAO Constitution; 9 (7) of the WIPO Convention; 18 (5) of the ECOWAS Treaty, 4.2 of ITLOS Staff Regulations; 27 of E.C. Staff Regulations. See also the re-affirmation of the principle in ICAO Res. A14–6.

[31] Art. VI (4); see also in that respect Art. 120 of the OAS Charter. A slightly different formula is used in other organisations yet; hence, the Staff Regulations of the Council of Europe refer to the "need for posts to be distributed fairly among nationals of the member States" (Art. 12(2).

to see allotted to staff members who are nationals of that state. This is, for example, the case in the United Nations and in the European Community.[32] In the UN, a system of national quotas has gradually been implemented, which is determined for each member by a combination of the following factors: membership (accounting for 36 per cent), population (7 per cent) and contribution to the budget (57 per cent).[33] As has been observed, this is not in contradiction with the Charter in itself, but it does tend to amount to a requirement of nationality which may raise problems if the actual merits of the candidate are not commensurate to what is required by the position he or she occupies.[34] Naturally, not all posts are subject to the same principles. For example, recruitment of language staff, such as interpreters or translators, or of manual workers (who are mainly locally recruited) cannot be governed by exactly the same principles as the other staff.[35] Moreover, the more senior posts are generally distributed in accordance with an understanding which is of a primarily political character.[36]

12–014   It also is to be noted that some organisations have in recent years emphasised the need to ensure a greater gender balance in the recruitment and promotion of staff members,[37] and some more recent constituent instruments refer to appointment in a gender neutral way. This has particularly been the case within the United Nations system, where some progress has been made in that respect.[38]

12–015   The appointment of staff members is generally vested in the Chief Administrative Officer,[39] although in some organisations, in the case of certain special organs, this appointment is made by the head of the organ.[40] In several organisations it is provided that, so far as practicable, the selection of candidates will be made on a competitive basis.[41]

---

[32] For a detailed description of the system used in the E.C., see Bettati, "Recrutement et carrière des fonctionnaires internationaux", 204 Recueil des Cours (1987–IV) 334.

[33] See *e.g.* UNGA Resolutions 35/210 of December 17, 1980 and 41/206 of December 11, 1986.

[34] Dubouis, *loc. cit.* 1361.

[35] For the General Services personnel, see *e.g.* UN Staff Rule 104.5 and ILO Staff Regulation 4.3.

[36] During the Cold War, this essentially meant that a balanced representation of both "blocs" had to be achieved at the highest levels within universal organisations. This "political" character also means that recruitment for such functions amounts to designation on the basis of propositions put forward by a particular state (or group of states), rather than recruitment based on competitive examinations, etc.; see *e.g.* Dubouis, *loc. cit.* 1351.

[37] See generally Bettati, *loc. cit.* 344 *et seq.*

[38] See in particular UNGA Resolutions 47/216 of December 23, 1992 and 52/216 of December 22, 1997.

[39] See *supra*, paras 12–003 *et seq.*

[40] *i.e.* in the UN, UNHCR, UNRWA, UNCTAD, UNDP and UNEP.

[41] See *e.g.* UNESCO Staff Regulation 4.3.2, Article 29 of the EC Staff Regulations and Article 15 of Appendix II of the Council of Europe Staff Regulations. For the implementation of competitive examination in the UN, see Bettati, *loc. cit.* 292.

The nature of the employment relationship and the conditions of service **12–016** vary from one organisation to another, although some common features may sometimes be found, in particular in organisations having a closer relationship, such as the UN and the specialised agencies. Employment relationships are based on statute in some organisations (European Community and the OECD, for example), on contract in others (NATO, Council of Europe and OAS, for example), and on an intermediary conception in a third group, where a "qualified contractual theory [predominates], which postulates contractual elements and objective statutory elements" (the World Bank, for example).[42] Those differences may of course affect the creation, dissolution or tranformation of the employment relationship.[43]

There is, in most organisations, a hierarchy in rules which govern the **12–017** employment relationship. In the UN, for example, there are the staff regulations which are adopted by the Assembly itself, the staff rules promulgated by the Secretary-General to implement those regulations, and the administrative instructions, which are of a more transitory character.[44]

In most organisations, appointments are of different kinds, and the rights **12–018** of the appointee vary accordingly.

(i) Permanent appointments. These are intended for career service staff and imply tenure until retirement age.[45] They are generally preceded by a probationary period of up to five years in some organisations.[46] They are also sometimes subject to a periodical revision on grounds of efficiency, competence and integrity.[47] These appointments can usually be terminated for failure to conform to the standard of integrity required under most constituent instrument, or if facts anterior to the appointment come to light which, had they been known, would have precluded appointment.[48] In various organisations, a final ground of termination is where it "would be in the interest of the good administration of the organisation," but this

---

[42] See in general, Amerasinghe, *The Law of the International Civil Service,* 2nd ed., Oxford, Clarendon, 1994, Vol. I, 82 *et seq.* and 96 for the quotation.

[43] *ibid.,* 99.

[44] For more on this, see *e.g.* Gottelman, Comment of Article 101, in Simma (ed.), *op. cit.* 1078.

[45] See UN Staff Rule 104.13, (a).

[46] It is the case of WHO, for instance (Staff Rule 420). The probationary period is of 12 to 18 months in FAO (Staff Rule 302.4111) and OAS (Staff Rule 104.5, c); of 2 years in UNESCO (Staff Rule 104.7) and the African Development Bank (Staff Regulation 6.6); and indeterminate in the IAEA (Staff Rule 3.03.2, B, 1).

[47] See *e.g.* UN Staff Rule 104.13, (a); UNESCO Staff Rule 104.7, c); Inter-American Development Bank Staff Personnel Policy 311, (a); and IAEA Staff Rule 3.03.2, B, 3.

[48] See *e.g.* UN Staff Regulation 9.1 (a) and UNESCO Staff Regulation 9.1.1., (b), ITLOS Staff Regulation 9.1, (a), ii).

ground exists only when the action is not challenged by the staff member.[49]

(ii) Temporary appointments. These are of three kinds:

(a) indefinite, *i.e.* with no fixed expiration date. These are mainly in use in the UN and are designed for persons recruited for field or mission service.[50] They do not carry expectancy of conversion to any other type of appointment and can be terminated where such action would be in the interest of the organisation.[51]

(b) fixed-term, *i.e.* with an expiration date and for a limited period of time.[52] These are designed for persons entrusted with specific and often clearly delimited tasks, or for persons seconded from government service or universities.[53] A probationary period may also be attached to contracts of this category. They generally carry no expectations of renewal or permanency.[54] They can be terminated for the same reasons as permanent appointments.

(c) short-term, which are in essence similar with fixed-term contracts, but are designed to cover shorter periods (generally less than one year).[55]

(iii) In most organisations, locally recruited staff members who have already satisfactorily served under a probationary appointment are given an appointment for an indefinite period.[56] This, in the same manner as permanent appointments for officials, may last until

---

[49] See *e.g.* UN Staff Regulation 9.1 (a); UNESCO Staff Regulation 9.1.2; IAEA Staff Regulation 4.1, b, iv; FAO Staff Regulation 301.0911; IFAD Personnel Policy 3.10.4; ITLOS Staff Regulation 9.1, (a) in fine.

[50] See UN Staff Rule 104.12, (c).

[51] See *ibid.* and Regulation 9.1 (c) for the termination.

[52] Depending on the organisations, fixed-terms contracts are awarded for periods of a minimum of one year to a maximum of five; see *e.g.* UN Staff Rule 104.12, b); UNESCO Staff Rule 104.6; IAEA, Staff Rule 3.03.2, D; WHO Staff Rule 420.2, FAO Staff Rule 3.2.4112; IFAD Personnel Policy 3.1.1, a); OAS Staff Rule 104.5, b, ii).

[53] The main characteristic of secondment is the fact that the person on secondment retains his or her position with his or her usual employer, and works only temporarily for the institution to which he or she is seconded. Staff seconded to international organisations are very generally on secondment from governments. This may of course raise particular problems in terms of impartiality and independence; for more on this, see *infra*.

[54] *ibid.* It may however be recalled that the I.C.J. has noted, about fixed term contracts in UNESCO "that there has developed in this matter a body of practice to the effect that holders of fixed-term contracts, although not assimilated to holders of permanent or indeterminate contracts, have often been treated as entitled to be considered for continued employment consistently with the requirements and the general good of the organisation, in a manner transcending the strict wording of the contract." (Advisory Opinion on Judgments of the Administrative Tribunal of the ILO, (1956) I.C.J. Rep., 91).

[55] See *e.g.* UNESCO Staff Rule 104.8; IAEA Staff Rule 3.03.2, E; FAO Staff Rule 3.02.4113; OAS Staff Rule 104.5, b, iii).

[56] See *e.g.* UN Staff Rule 104.13, b). But note that UNRWA, which employs several thousands locally-recruited staff, has a separate system of area staff regulations and rules which are *sui generis*.

retirement. These contracts can generally be terminated for the same reasons as temporary indefinite appointments.

It should be noted that while permanent appointments have long been **12–019** considered preferable in many organisations,[57] in particular because they provided organisations with a more stable and experienced work force,[58] financial considerations have led to a freezing of recruitment in a number of organisations since the 1980s.[59] When recruitment has taken place, there has been a tendency towards a more general use of short-term contracts.[60]

In order to attract the most qualified candidates, international organisa- **12–020** tions may offer relatively high salaries. In the UN system, these are determined by application of the "Noblemaire Principle", according to which the level of renumeration is established by comparison with that of the highest paying national civil service.[61] A similar system is applied in other organisations. The basic remuneration is generally supplemented by various benefits. Whatever the category of contract held by the staff member, he or she will usually be entitled to benefits such as a children's allowance, language allowance, annual leave, termination indemnity and participation in a social security scheme comprising a pension fund, sick leave, compensation for death, illness, etc. Benefits may also include an educational grant for the official's children, periodical home leave, and a grant of "service benefit" on repatriation at the conclusion of service.[62]

In most organisations, the staff is organised in various categories, which **12–021** reflect the nature and importance of the functions. These are generally the directors and principal officers category (policy-making staff), the profes- sionals category (main body of internationally recruited staff), and the general services category (clerical and technical staff). Various grades

---

[57] Though not in all; see for instance IAEA Staff Regulation 3.03 according to which "[t]he Agency shall be guided by the principle that its permanent staff shall be kept to the minimum compatible with the efficient operation of the Agency."

[58] See *e.g.* in that respect the arguments exposed by Amerasinghe, "The individuals", in Dupuy (ed.), *Handbook on International Organisations*, 2nd ed., 1998, 340–341.

[59] On the limitations on recruitment, see *e.g.* Bettati, *loc. cit.* 335.

[60] For an example on the preference expressed for short-term recruitment, see *e.g.* ICAO Res. A14–6, para. 2 (three-year contracts).

[61] See *e.g.* Resolution 44/198 adopted by the UN General Assembly on December 21, 1989, para. I, B, 1). In the UN, the reference is the United States federal civil service. For a recent reaffirmation of the application of the principle in the UN system, see UNGA Resolution 53/209 of February 12, 1999.

[62] See *e.g.* UN Staff Regulations, Articles VI and VII; WHO Staff Rules 350 *et seq.* and Sections 7 and 8; UNESCO Staff Rules 103.12 *et seq.* and Chapter VI; IAEA Staff Rules 5.01.07 *et seq.*, OAS Staff Rules 103.6 *et seq.* and 107.1 *et seq.* IADB Personnel Policies, Chaps VI and VII.

correspond to those categories, within which there are a number of "steps" which represent the normal within-grade promotion, occurring annually.[63]

12–022　The breach of the staff rules and regulations, or of the employment contract by staff members can give rise to disciplinary action by the chief administrative officer.[64] Such action may include a written censure, suspension without pay, demotion or dismissal for misconduct and summary dismissal in case of serious misconduct.[65] It must be noted that the grounds for termination of a staff member's services will vary according to the type of contract held, and different grounds may call for different procedure on termination.[66]

12–023　International administrative tribunals have in any event made it clear that participation of international civil servants in a strike did not constitute a proper motive for the termination of employment, nor for the imposition of disciplinary sanctions.[67] In fact many international organisations (including the ILO, UNESCO, the EC, OECD, NATO, FAO and the UN) have experienced strikes and the right to strike is in general now recognised. Most organisations have also recognised the syndicates or trade unions representing staff for pay and other contractual bargaining purposes.[68]

12–024　The disciplinary action taken by the Chief Administrative Officer is in most organisations subject to various safeguards, including review by administrative organs on which staff members are represented[69] and, ultimately, by administrative tribunals or appeals boards which will pronounce on the legality of the measure taken.[70]

12–025　It is clear, however, that international organisations do not rely for their functioning on international civil servants only. In a number of organisations, the need has arisen to turn to other categories of agents for certain

---

[63] See *e.g.* UNESCO, Staff Rule 102.1; ILO, Staff Regulation 2.2; FAO Staff Rule 302.314; OAS Staff Rule 102.1; EC Staff Regulations; Art. 5, Council of Europe Staff Regulations; Art. 4, AfDB, Staff Regulation 4.2.

[64] See *e.g.* UN Staff Regulation 10.2; WHO Staff Regulations, Art. X; ILO Staff Regulation 12.1; ITLOS Staff Regulations, Art. X; AfDB Staff Regulations, Art. 10.2.

[65] See *e.g.* UNESCO Staff Rule 110.2; ICAO Staff Regulation 10.1; IFAD Personnel Policy 3.9, OAS Staff Rule 111.1; Council of Europe Staff Regulations, Art. 54; EC Staff Regulations, Art. 86.

[66] For example, with the permanent appointment in the UN, under Regulation 9.1 (a) "unsatisfactory service" is a ground which does not require from the Secretary-General a statement of the reasons for termination whereas failure to "meet the highest standards of integrity" does. To take another example, summary dismissal is only permissible for "serious misconduct" (Regulation 10.2), whereas "unsatisfactory conduct" calls for disciplinary measures, not summary dismissal.

[67] For more on this, see *e.g.* Meron, "Status and Independence of the International Civil Servants", 167 Recueil des Cours (1980–II) 351–353; Amerasinghe, *The Law of the International Civil Service, op. cit.*, vol. II, 393 *et seq.*

[68] See Pellet, "La grève des fonctionnaires internationaux" RGDIP (1975) 932–971.

[69] See *e.g.* UN Staff Rules, Chapters X and XI; UNESCO, Staff Rules 110.2–111.2; FAO Staff Regulations; Art. XI, ITLOS Staff Regulations; Art. XI, IADB Personnel Policy 326.

[70] For more on this, see *infra*, Chap. 13.

types of functions. As the I.C.J. put it in its Advisory Opinion on the Applicability of Article VI, section 22, of the Convention on the Privileges and Immunities of the United Nations:

> "In practice [. . .] the United Nations has had occasions to entrust missions—increasingly varied in nature—to persons not having the status of United Nations Officials. Such persons have been entrusted with mediation, with preparing reports, preparing studies, conducting investigations or finding and establishing facts. They have participated in certain peacekeeping forces, technical assistance work, and a multitude of other activities. In addition, many committees, commissions or similar bodies whose members serve, not as representatives of states, but in a personal capacity, have been set up within the organisation [. . .]."[71]

The same could be said—although generally for a narrower range of **12–026** functions—of many other international organisations. Agents have been widely defined as "any person who, whether a paid official or not, and whether permanently employed or not, has been charged by an organ of the organisation with carrying out, or helping to carry out, one of its functions —in short, any person through whom it acts."[72] Whereas all international civil servants are to be regarded as agents of the organisations for which they work, it is therefore clear that a number of persons performing functions for an international organisation do not enjoy the status of international civil servants.[73] Indeed, most of the elements of the regimes described hereabove (in terms of recruitment, remuneration, conditions and termination of service, etc.) do not apply to agents other than international civil servants.[74] The fact that their position is less institutionalised and that the staff regulations and rules do not apply to them does not mean however that agents other than international civil servants do not have particular duties and do not enjoy some rights *vis-à-vis* the organisation for which they perform specific tasks, as we shall see below.

(c) THE INTERNATIONAL CHARACTER OF THE SECRETARIATS

The single most important characteristic of an international civil service is **12–027** its international character. This constitutes a cornerstone underpinning the impartiality of the activities of international organisations. The Secretariat's international character is safeguarded in the constituent instruments of

---

[71] I.C.J. Rep. (1989), 194, para. 48.
[72] I.C.J. Advisory Opinion on the Reparation for Injuries Suffered in the Service of the United Nations, I.C.J. Rep. (1949) 177.
[73] On the differences between international civil servants and other categories of agents , see *e.g.* Bettati, *loc. cit.* 205 and 216 *et seq.*
[74] See *e.g.* ILO Staff Regulation 0.2, a) and IAEA Staff Rule 0.00.1.

most international organisations,[75] which enjoin the chief administrative officers and their staff to, in effect, acknowledge their primary allegiance to the organisation, and generally state the corresponding obligation of all members to respect this international character.[76] Those provisions are often supplemented by the staff regulations,[77] and by the oath taken by staff members of a number of organisations upon appointment.[78]

12–028   In a number of organisations, the constituent instrument or staff rules or regulations further protect this international character by regulating the extent to which staff members can undertake outside employment, be associated financially with outside concerns, make public statements, accept honours, gifts and awards, or engage in political activities (other than the normal civic right of voting) which would be inconsistent with their international status.[79] In most constituent instruments, or staff rules and regulations, those obligations bear on the international civil servants only. But the requirement of independence is undoubtedly also applicable to agents other than international civil servants. Their impartiality, when carrying out functions on behalf of the organisation, is no less important than that of civil servants. This international character is sometimes provided for, at least indirectly, in the instruments applicable to the activities of these other agents.[80] It is for instance the case of the agreements concluded by the United Nations with states which contribute to a peacekeeping force or of the force regulations. Such instruments generally emphasise that, while they remain in the service of their national state, members of the force become, during the period of their assignment to the force, international personnel under the authority of the United Nations.[81] In the same sense, the 1994 the Convention on the Safety of

---

[75] This was not the case, however, for the League of Nations Covenant, but the international character of the League's Secretariat has rapidly been emphasised by the first Secretary General (see LoN O.J., June 4, 1920, p. 137).

[76] See *e.g.* Articles 100 of the UN Charter; VI, 5 of the UNESCO Constitution; 9, paras 4 and 5 of the ILO Constitution; VIII, 2 of the FAO Constitution; XII, Section 4, c) of the IMF Articles of Agreement; 9, 8 of the WIPO Convention; VI, 4 of the WTO Agreement; 118 and 119 of the OAS Charter; 36, e) and f) of the Statute of the Council of Europe; XVIII, paras 1 and 2 of the OAU Charter; 20, paras 1 and 2 of the ECOWAS Treaty.

[77] See *e.g.* UN Staff Regulations 1.1 and 1.3, WHO Staff Regulations; Art. I, IAEA Staff Regulation 1.01; ITLOS Staff Regulations 1.1–1.3; AfDB Staff Regulations 3.1 and 3.2.

[78] See *e.g.* Article 36, e) of the Statute of the Council of Europe; UN Staff Regulation 1.9, WHO Staff Regulation 1.10; ILO Staff Regulation 1.4; FAO Staff Regulation 301.019; IAEA Staff Regulation 1.11; OAS Staff Rule 101.7; IADB Personnel Policy 321.

[79] See *e.g.* Article 36, d) of the Statute of the Council of Europe; UN Staff Regulations 1.4, 1.6 and 1.7; WHO Staff Regulations 1.7–1.8; FAO Staff Regulations 301.016–017; IAEA Staff Regulations 1.05, 1.08 and 1.09; ITLOS Staff Regulations 1.4–1.7; E.C. Staff Regulations, Art. 11 and 15; AfDB, Staff Regulations 3.7–3.8. For the practice in the UN, see generally *Repertory*, Vol. V, pp. 186–196.

[80] Note that this is expressly provided for in Art. 11 of the Conditions of employment of temporary staff in the E.C., for example.

[81] See *e.g.* Point 6 of the UNFICYP Regulations of April 25, 1964, doc. S/5575, reproduced in 555 U.N.T.S. 133.

United Nations and Associated Personnel provides that the United Nations and associated personnel (the—broad—definition of which is given in Article 1 of the Convention) must "refrain from any action or activity incompatible with the impartial and international nature of their duties."[82] The necessity to preserve the independence of all agents while they perform functions on behalf of the organisation is evidenced by the fact that organisations deem it appropriate to extend their functional protection to all categories of agents, and not to civil servants only.[83]

As the I.C.J. put it in the *Reparation* case:

> "[b]oth to ensure the efficient and independent performance of these missions [with which the organisation entrusts its agents] and to afford effective support to its agents, the Organisation must provide them with adequate support [. . .]. To ensure the independence of the agent and, consequently, the independent action of the Organisation itself, it is essential that in performing his duties he need not have to rely on any other protection than that of the Organisation [. . .]."[84]

Members of peacekeeping forces are similarly entitled to the legal protection of the organisation.[85]

It is, however, in respect of international civil servants that the most **12–029** significant encroachments on the principle of independence have been seen. It is within the United Nations that one of the most controversial issues has arisen. It grew out of the allegation made in 1952 by a United States Grand Jury and a subcommittee of the Senate that certain United States nationals, employed as staff members, had engaged in subversive activities directed against the United States Government. Over a score of those staff members called upon to testify before these bodies refused to answer any questions relating to their political activities, claiming their constitutional privilege against self-incrimination embodied in the Fifth Amendment of the U.S. Constitution.

The Secretary-General suspended the staff members concerned and **12–030** established a Commission of Jurists to advise him as to what disciplinary measures might be taken. Their opinion was that conviction of subversive activities, or a refusal to testify about such activities, amounted to "serious misconduct" and a "fundamental breach" of the contractual obligations of a staff member.[86] Moreover, the Commission of Jurists advised that the Secretary-General should dismiss staff members where he had "reasonable

---

[82] Art. 6 (1) (b) of the Convention adopted on December 9, 1994; text in 34 ILM (1995) 482.
[83] For staff members, see *e.g.*, Art. 5 of the OECD Staff Rules.
[84] *Loc. cit.* 183.
[85] See *e.g.* UNFICYP Regulations, *loc. cit.*, Pt 25.
[86] UN Doc. A/INF/51, December 5, 1952. Convenient text in 47 AJIL (1953) 97–117.

grounds for believing (the staff members) to be engaged or to have been engaged, or to be likely to be engaged in any subversive activities against the host country."[87]

12–031   In their subsequent actions none of the Secretaries-General have accepted this opinion in its entirety. The Secretaries-General have retained a right to determine for themselves whether the conviction was secured in a fair trial, and Mr. Hammarskjold has rejected the "likelihood" test. So far as the actual refusal to testify is concerned, Mr. Lie accepted the view that this constituted a ground for dismissal, but only where the staff member had been given an opportunity to explain his actions to the Secretary-General and that explanation had failed to remove the unfavourable implication of the refusal to testify. However, certain permanent staff members refused to take the opportunity of explaining their refusal to testify to the Secretary-General and appealed to the United Nations Administrative Tribunal on the issue of whether refusal to testify by claiming the privilege against self-incrimination amounted to "serious misconduct." The Tribunal disagreed with the Commission of Jurists and held that summary dismissal, as opposed to other disciplinary measures, was not permissible.[88] The Secretary-General was therefore obliged to reinstate these staff members or pay them damages; he chose to do the latter.

12–032   Certain conclusions may be drawn with regard to the experience gained in the treatment of this particular problem. They are, first, that there is no necessary contradiction between an "international" and a "national" loyalty; on the contrary, cases of a contradiction will be highly exceptional and should be met either by the assignment of the staff member to other work, or, when this is impossible, by his resignation. Secondly, the Secretary-General has the duty to satisfy himself that allegations against staff are well-founded and in fact reveal conduct incompatible with the status of an international civil servant; neither a conviction nor a refusal to testify constitute, *ipso facto*, adequate grounds for dismissal. Thirdly, governments possessing information tending to cast doubt on a person's qualifications for a post should submit that information at the time of recruitment and not after appointment. And, fourthly, the obligations of the staff member are the same whether he is a national of the host state or of any other member state.

12–033   Even though the "loyalty" cases constitute the most important single incident, they certainly do not represent the only occasion where the independence of the international civil service has been threatened. In his

---

[87] *ibid.* p. 97.
[88] Judgments of the UN Administrative Tribunal Nos 29–38 (AT/DEC/29–38).

or her quality of administrative head of the organisation, the chief administrative officer is responsible for appointing and promoting staff in the best interest of the organisation.[89] There are many situations, however, where member states have played a role in the selection of candidates to specific positions or tried to influence the decision of the chief administrative officer. In a number of cases, in particular in the UN system, the candidates eventually appointed have been designated by their government, and most of them could be considered as representatives of their state of origin.[90] This situation has been aggravated in some organisations by the use, on a large scale, of secondment of national civil servants to those organisations' Secretariats.[91] As has been pointed out,[92] the I.C.J., when it decided that the UN Administrative Tribunal had not committed any error of law in ruling, in the *Yakimetz* case, that the extension of employment based on secondment required the involvement of the three parties (the individual concerned, his or her national state and the organisation), confirmed that a staff member recruited under secondment is totally dependent on his or her government.[93] The independence of international civil servants has sometimes also been threatened in more indirect ways, for instance through actions undertaken by member states regarding the emoluments of staff members having their nationality.[94] In spite of their relatively high level, these were deemed insufficient by some states which decided to supplement them, with the stated purpose to keep the international civil service attractive to the best candidates. This was however regarded as contrary to Article 100 of the UN Charter. The breach is of course much more obvious in the case of states (mostly Eastern European, during the Cold War) which appropriated a significant portion of the salary of international civil servants who were their nationals.

Finally, the independence of agents of international organisations has **12–034** often been threatened by direct, physical pressure or attack on international civil servants or other categories of agents.[95] Such pressures are often

---

[89] See *supra*.

[90] See *e.g.* Bayard, "L'attitude des Etats d'Europe de l'Est à l'égard des Secrétariats des Nations Unies", RBDI (1984–85) 675 *et seq.*; Ruzié, "Commentaire de l'article 100", in Cot and Pellet (eds.), *op. cit.*, 1344 *et seq.* According to Bettati, 41.3% of the staff appointed to professional posts at the UN Secretariat in New York during the seventies had been "recommended" by their national government (*loc. cit.* 292).

[91] For more on the practice of secondment to the UN, see Schreuer, "Comment of Article 100", in Simma (ed.), *op. cit.* 1063–1064.

[92] Schreuer, *ibid.* 1064.

[93] Advisory Opinion of July 12, 1987, I.C.J. Rep. (1987) 18. The practice of secondment did not raise similar problems in all organisations, however; see in that respect Bowett, Tenure, Fixed-Term, Secondment from Governments: The UN Civil Service and the European Civil Service Compared, 14 N.Y.U.J. Int'l L. & Pol. (1981–82) 804–805.

[94] On the two situations detailed hereafter, see generally Meron, *loc. cit.* 323 *et seq.*

[95] See *e.g.*, for the UN, UNGA Resolution 47/72 of December 14, 1992 on the attacks against members of UN peacekeeping forces.

exerted by the authorities of the state of which the civil servant is a national, such as in the *Mazilu* case. Mr. Mazilu, a Special Rapporteur for the UN Sub-Commission on Prevention of Discrimination and Protection of Minorities, was prevented by the Romanian authorities from having contacts with the UN Human Rights Centre and, later on, from travelling to Geneva to present his report. This prompted the ECOSOC to request an Advisory Opinion on the "Applicability of Article VI, section 22, of the Convention on the Privileges and Immunities of the United Nations" to D. Mazilu's situation. The I.C.J. concluded that, being a Special Rapporteur of the Sub-Commission, Mr Mazilu had to be considered as an expert in mission within the meaning of that provision;[96] he was therefore entitled to enjoy immunity against all such interferences by his national authorities. It is to react to even more extreme situations that, in complement to the more traditional institution of functional protection,[97] the Convention on the Safety of United Nations and Associated Personnel has been adopted under the auspices of the UN in 1994.[98] This imposes on contracting states the general obligations not to submit UN and associated personnel to attacks or action preventing them from discharging their mandate (Articles 7, 1), to release any such personnel which would be captured or detained (Article 8), and to prevent the commission of various crimes against the protected persons (Article 11). It also imposes on states parties to take the necessary measures to establish their jurisdiction over those crimes and to prosecute or extradite their authors (Articles 10 and 13–15, respectively). It is difficult to assess the Convention's practical impact up to now. One may but note that it did not prevent the taking as hostages of several hundreds UN peacekeepers in Sierra Leone in May 2000, for instance.

B. IMPLEMENTATION OF THE ORGANISATION'S RULES AND OBLIGATIONS

Bibliography: Charpentier, "Le contrôle par les organisations internationales de l'exécution des obligations des Etats," 182 RDC 143–245 (1983); Van Dijk (ed.), *Supervisory Mechanism in International Economic Organisations* (1984); Chowdury, *Legal Framework of International Supervision* (1986); Seidl-Hohenveldern, "Failure of Controls in the 6th International Tin Agreement, in Blokker and Muller (eds.), *Towards More Effective Supervision by International Organisations*, Vol. 1, (1994) at 252–274; Schermers and Blokker (1995), paras 1390–1558; Valticos, "L'action des organisations internationales. Contrôle" in Dupuy (1998) 461–84.

12–035 In Part I of this book we have seen that international organisations are now involved in a broad range of activities at global and regional levels. Their constituent instruments and the institutional acts which they adopt establish

---

[96] *Loc. cit.*, p. 198.
[97] For more on this, see *supra*, Pt 1.
[98] *Loc. cit.* This Convention entered into force in 2000. For comments, see *e.g.* Bloom, Protecting Peacekeepers: the Convention on the Safety of UN and Associated Personnel, 89 AJIL (1995) 621 *et seq.*; Bourloyannis-Vrailas, The Convention on the Safety of UN and Associated Personnel, 44 I.C.L.Q. (1995) 560 *et seq.*

technical standards (for example, in relation to postal standards), promote minimum standards of behaviour (for example, in relation to the protection of human rights and the conservation of the environment), provide financial and other assistance (for example, through the multilateral development banks), promote conditions for economic development (for example, in relation to trade, competition and intellectual property rights), and seek to avoid conflict and promote the pacific resolution of disputes (for example, within the framework of the United Nations). International organisations now play a central role in establishing these standards and rules. However, it is not sufficient that the standards be put onto the international statute books; it is also necessary that those to whom they are addressed should implement them. The executive function of international organisations therefore extends to overseeing the implementation of the standards which they assist in promoting. International organisations increasingly play a role in ensuring implementation of and compliance with the standards and obligations which they are charged with developing and promoting. Supervising compliance with their rules has been described as "one of the main tasks of international organisations", and it is one which has received increasing attention in recent years.[99]

There are no general principles governing the supervisory powers of **12–036** international organisations. The approach of each organisation depends upon the powers granted to it by its constituent instrument as subsequently interpreted and applied in the practice of the organisation and the parties to it. Some organisations—such as the United Nations and the European Communities—have very extensive powers of supervision, whereas others are given virtually no supervisory role. And in some cases the supervisory function is given not to the organisation but to the members. In general terms, however, the supervisory powers of international organisations may be divided into the following types: (i) establishment and oversight of reporting requirements; (ii) collection of information on its own account; (iii) inspection of the activities of its members and certain third persons; and, (iv) where non-compliance has occurred or is thought likely to occur, enforcement through various means, including in relation to rights associated with membership, sanctions, and recourse to judicial or other processes.

(a) REPORTING REQUIREMENTS

The obligation to report or to notify certain information on a regular or **12–037** periodic basis is a consistent feature of international organisations. It is intended to provide the basic information necessary for establishing compliance with constitutional and other obligations. In some cases it is the

---

[99] Schermers and Blokker (1995), para. 1390.

international organisation itself which is required to report on its activities, as a way of ensuring greater accountability to its members on its activities: an early example is the 1949 International Tropical Tuna Commission, which must "submit annually to the government of each high contracting party a report on its investigations and findings, with appropriate recommendation."[1] The 1990 Articles of Agreement of the EBRD requires it to provide an annual report on the environmental impact of its activities.[2] And frequently one institutional organ, or even an international organisation, may be required to report to another: this approach is reflected in the work of the UN's Administrative Committee on Co-ordination, which receives reports from 25 UN system organisations with a view to promoting co-operation between these organisations.[3] Similarly, the UN Commission on Sustainable Development receives reports from all relevant organs, organisations, programmes and institutions of the UN system dealing with various issues of environment and development to enable it to monitor progress in implementation of Agenda 21.[4]

12–038   Within the United Nations, an extensive system of reporting is directed towards the General Assembly, which receives annual reports from the Secretary-General (on the work of the Organisation, required pursuant to Article 98 of the Charter), ECOSOC,[5] and the I.C.J. (not expressly required by the Charter or by the Statute of the Court). The General Assembly also receives reports from the subsidiary organs which it has established, ranging from treaty bodies such as the Committee on the Elimination of Racial Discrimination to other bodies such as the ILC. Until 1975 the General Assembly used to receive annual reports from the Trusteeship Council. Similar arrangements exist in relation to more specific areas, such as budgetary matters: the General Assembly's Advisory Committee on Administrative and Budgetary Questions (ACABQ) examines reports on the regular and peacekeeping budgets of the UN and the administrative budgets of the UN specialized agencies. These reporting systems are recognised as being of considerable importance for information, control and decision-making, but the growth in their number and questions as to their quality have posed considerable burdens on personnel and budget and raised questions about their effectiveness.[6]

12–039   Many international organisations rely on reporting requirements imposed upon their members to keep themselves informed on implementation by their members of their obligations. In some cases the reporting require-

---

[1] 80 UNTS 3, Art. I(2).
[2] Chap. 6, paras 6–058–6–059; Art. 35.
[3] In 1997 the UN Secretary General established an Office for Internal Agency Affairs to support the work of the ACC and facilitate the consultative process.
[4] UN G.A. res. 47/191 (1992).
[5] This flows from Art. 60 of the UN Charter, which provides that ECOSOC is to function under the authority of the General assembly.
[6] See Simma (ed.), *The Charter of the United Nations: A Commentary* (1994), 292.

ments is expressly provided for by the organisation's constituent instrument. A rather general provision may be found in the IAEA Statute, which commits each member to make available such information as would, in the judgment of the member, be helpful to the Agency (Article VIII.A), although there is a slightly more onerous obligation to make available to the Agency scientific information developed as a result of assistance received from the Agency (Article VIII.B). The reporting requirements under the FAO Constitution establish a three-tiered approach; first, members are required to "communicate regularly to the Director-General, on publication, the texts of laws and regulations pertaining to matters within the competence of the organisation which the Director-General considers useful for the purposes of the organisation" (Article XI(1)); secondly, under similar conditions they must communicate statistical, technical and other information (Article XI(2)); and thirdly, the FAO Conference, Council or Director-General may request the member to furnish "other information, reports or documentation pertaining to matters within the competence of the organisation, including reports on the action taken on the basis of resolutions or recommendations of the Conference" Article XI(3)).

A different approach is reflected in the Constitution of the WHO. This **12–040** requires each member to report annually on action taken with respect to organisation's recommendations as well as conventions, agreements and regulation (Article 62). The Constitution of the ILO requires members to report on the measures they have taken to bring labour conventions and recommendations before their relevant national authorities and the measures taken by those authorities (Article 19(5) and (6)), as well as to provide annual report on the measures taken to give effect to the provisions of labour conventions to which it is a party (Article 22). The rules under the ICAO convention are rather more precise: each state is required to notify immediately the ICAO of differences between its own practice and that established by the convention's international standards and procedures (Article 38), and each contracting state undertakes to ensure that its international airlines will file with the ICAO council reports on traffic and statistics on costs and financial matters (Article 67). Even beyond this, the ICAO's Air Navigation Commission advises the Council on the collection and communication of information necessary to advance air navigation (Article 57). The constituent instruments of some of the other specialised agencies, such as UNESCO contain variations of these two themes (Article 8).

The economic institutions impose quite onerous obligations upon their **12–041** members in respect of reporting requirements. The WTO's Trade Policy

Review Mechanism establishes a particularly detailed set of obligations.[7] Under the TRPM each member reports regularly to the Trade Policy Review Board (TPRB), describing its trade policies and practices on all aspects of trade policies covered by the Multilateral Trade Agreements in Annex 1 to the WTO Agreement and some Plurilateral Trade Agreements. The TRPB will review the trade policies and practices of members every two, four or six years, depending on their contributions to world trade, or even longer in the case of least-developed countries. Between reviews by the TPRB the members must provide brief reports when there are significant changes in their trade policies and an annual update of statistical information. The reports follow an agreed format, and the WTO secretariat provides technical assistance to developing country members on the preparation of the reports. The IMF requires its members to provide prompt notification of exchange arrangements (Art. IV (1)), and to furnish the Fund with "such information as it deems necessary for the activities" (Art. VIII (5)).

12–042   In other fields, in particular disarmament, human rights and the environment, the relevant treaty organisations have extensive reporting requirements. In the disarmament field, for example, parties to the Chemical Weapons Convention must, within 30 days of becoming a party, provide detailed information to the Organisation for the Prohibition of Chemical Weapons on chemical weapons in their possession (Article III(1)), information on their annual destruction programmes (Articles IV(6) and VII), and declarations on industrial usage not prohibited by the Convention.[8]

12–043   In the human rights field most of the treaties impose upon parties the obligation to submit reports on measures they have taken to give effect to the requirements of the particular instruments.[9] In practice it is far from clear how effective these reporting requirements are, since it is apparent that there exists a very significant backlog in state reports, with up to 80 per cent of parties overdue in providing their reports,[10] with the relevant bodies having few if any powers to address the tardiness. Beyond late reporting, it is clear also that the bodies charged with reviewing them are under-

---

[7] 1994 WTO Agreement, Annex 3. See Mavroidis, "Surveillance Schemes: The GATT's New Trade Policy Review Mechanism", 13 Michigan Journal of International Law 374–414 (1992); Qureshi, "The Trade Policy Review Mechanism," in *The World Trade Organisation: Implementing International Trade Norms* (1996).

[8] See the *OPCW Draft Declarations Handbook*, at http://www.opcw.nl.

[9] See *e.g.* Convention on the Rights of the Child, Art. 44(1); CERD, Art. 9; CEDAW, Art. 18; CAT, Art. 19; HRC, Art. 40.

[10] As at 1998 the number of parties overdue in their reporting requirements has been reported as: CERD: 124 out of 151 parties; ICCPR, 97 out of 138 parties; CEDAW, 134 out of 162 parties; CAT, 72 out of 110 parties; CRC, 124 out of 191 parties: Crawford, "The UN human rights treaty system: A system in crisis?", in Alston and Crawford (eds.), *The Future of UN Human Rights Treaty Monitoring* (2000), at p. 5.

resourced, which means that many of the reports which are submitted are subject to backlogs in examination.[11]

Many international environmental agreements also establish detailed **12–044** reporting requirements. The information to be reported will vary from agreement to agreement, but it includes information on catch data and scientific permits (1946 International Whaling Convention), the state of conservation of World Heritage Sites (1972 World Heritage convention), texts of relevant laws, orders, decrees and regulations (1973 MARPOL), and national inventories of greenhouse gas emissions (1992 Climate change Convention). The information is to be reported to the relevant treaty body, which is frequently empowered to review the report and make recommendations upon it. As with the human rights field, however, there are serious doubts as to the quality of much of the information reported, and many states are late in fulfilling their reporting obligations.[12]

In other cases, the reporting requirements arise under the terms of a **12–045** specific institutional act. E.C. Directives almost routinely require the member states to report to the European Commission on the measures taken to implement the terms of the Directive, and subsequently for the Commission to produce a report summarising experience of implementation.[13] Finally, in the context of the activities of international judicial bodies, there can be a requirement for parties to report on the measures they have taken to implement an order or judgment: the International Tribunal for the Law of the Sea, for example, has required parties to report back on the measures taken pursuant to a provisional measures order.[14]

(b) FACT-FINDING, INFORMATION COLLECTION AND SURVEILLANCE

Apart from reports formally submitted by members, international organisa- **12–046** tions obtain information concerning members' compliance with the rules and obligations of the organisation from a variety of sources, both internal

---

[11] For different views on the extent of the problems see Bayefsky, "Report of the UN Human Rights Treaties: Facing the Implementation Crisis', in Committee on International Human Rights Law and Practice, First Report of the Committee (ILA, 1996); Alston, "Beyond 'Them' and 'Us': Putting Treaty Body Reform into Perspective", in Alston and Crawford (eds.), *The Future of UN Human Rights Treaty Monitoring* (2000), at 501–25.

[12] See Sands, *Principles of International Environmental Law* (1995), 600–5; Bodansky, "The Role of Reporting in International Environmental Treaties: Lessons for Human Rights Supervision", in Alston and Crawford, *supra*., at 361–80. On inadequate reporting see U.S. General Accounting Office, 'International Environment: International Agreements are not well Monitored', Report No. GAO/RCED-92–43, January 1992.

[13] See *e.g.* article 15 of the Council Directive 1999/31/EC of April 26, 1999 on the landfill of waste [1999] O.J. L182, at 1.

[14] Southern Blue-Fin Tuna Cases (*New Zealand v. Japan, Australia v. Japan*), Order on provisional measures, August 27, 1999, 38 ILM 1624 (1999), Order 2.

and external. These powers may be express or implied. Some international organisations are expressly authorised to obtain information on their own initiative, without awaiting the provision of information directly from their members, whether through reports or otherwise. The UN Security Council, for example, may investigate any dispute or situation which might lead to international friction or give rise to a dispute (Article 34).[15] In fact, Article 34 has only been relied upon very rarely,[16] and most 'investigations' carried out under the auspices of the Security Council are not based directly on Article 34 powers, largely because they require unanimity amongst the permanent members. Other UN organs, such as the General Assembly and the office of the Secretary-General, obtain information on particular matter in exercise of implied powers.[17]

12–047   Pursuant to its obligation under Article 211 of the E.C. Treaty (*ex Article 155*), and equivalent provisions under EURATOM and the ECSC, the E.C. Commission collects information on the activities of the member states and even of private actors within the Community. And some of the treaty bodies, particularly in the field of human rights, disarmament and international trade, have become active on their own initiative in identifying violations of treaty commitments which require international attention.[18] The OPCW, the IAEA and the WTO, for example, are each endowed with considerable powers of information gathering and surveillance. And under Article IV(3) of its Articles of Agreement the IMF is required to exercise "firm surveillance" over its members exchange rate policies, and to adopt specific principles for the guidance of all members with respect to those policies. To that end each member is required to provide the fund with the information necessary for such surveillance, and, when requested by the fund, to consult with it on the member's exchange rate policies.

(c) INSPECTION

12–048 Inspection connotes an altogether more intrusive act: the organisation itself obtains information on a particular matter directly from the place where the facts in issue arose. Because of their intrusiveness, the powers of inspection of international organisations remain limited, and their exercise will often be contentious.

12–049   Several provisions of the UN Charter envisage inspection. Article 87 envisaged that the General Assembly and, under its authority, the Trusteeship Council, would provide for periodic visits to the trusts territories by

---

[15] Kerley, "The powers of investigation of the United Nations Security Council", 55 AJIL 902 (1961).
[16] Examples include matters concerning Greek frontier incidents (S.C. res. 15 (1946)) and the India-Pakistan question (S.C. res. 39 (1948)).
[17] See e.g. G.A. res. 46/59, "Declaration on Fact-finding by the United nations in the Field of the Maintenance of International peace and Security", 30 ILM 235 (1992); Berg, "The 1991 Declaration on Fact-finding by the United nations" 4 EJIL 107 (1993); Simma (Ed.), *The UN Charter* (1994), at p. 515.
[18] See Chap. 13, paras 13–062 *et seq.*

their mission. Decisions authorising UN peacekeeping operations[19] will often allow them to carry out on-site inspections in furtherance of their talks. And UN observer groups have been established to supervise the application and observation of cease-fires[20] and monitor the withdrawal of troops.[21] Also relevant in this regard is the role of UN sanctions committees called upon to monitor the implementation of economic sanctions.[22] A more recent phenomena has been the verification of electoral processes, in which international observers are appointed pursuant to General Assembly or Security Council resolutions with the task of observing and verifying the legitimacy of the various stages of the electoral process, and the compliance of the national electoral authorities with the electoral regulations.[23]

It is against this pattern of inspection practices that the UN Security **12–050** Council, in 1991, provided for the terms for the cease-fire between Iraq and the coalition of UN members co-operating with Kuwait to include far-reaching power of inspection. Resolution 687 (1991) required the elimination of Iraq's weapons of mass destruction and ballistic missiles and production facilities, and measures to ensure that the acquisition and production of prohibited items were not resumed. To give effect to these objectives the United Nations Special Commission (UNSCOM) was set up to implement the non-nuclear provisions of the resolution and to assist the IAEA in the nuclear areas.[24] The Commission's mandate included carrying out on-site inspections of Iraq's biological, chemical and missile capabilities; taking possession of all chemical and biological weapons; supervising the destruction by Iraq of all its ballistic missiles; and monitoring Iraq's compliance with its undertaking not to use, develop, construct or acquire any of the prohibited items. UNSCOM was also entrusted to designate for inspection any additional site necessary for ensuring the fulfilment of the mandates given to it and the IAEA. It is noteworthy that the legal basis on which these inspections were to be conducted was achieved through an exchange of letters involving the UN Secretary-General, UNSCOM and Iraq. As a legal matter the power of inspection was not imposed without Iraq's agreement, even if such agreement was obtained in circumstances in which Iraq's room for manoeuvre was severely restricted. For its part, Iraq

---

[19] See Chap. 2, paras 2–052 *et seq.*

[20] *e.g.* S.C. res. 50 (1948), establishing the UN Truce Supervision Organisation (Palestine).

[21] *e.g.* S.C. res. 826 (1988), establishing the UN Angola Verification Mission (UNAVEM) to monitor the withdrawal of Cuban troops from Angola.

[22] See *e.g.* the Committee established to monitor implementation of sanctions against Iraq, S.C. res. 661 (1990).

[23] Examples include Angola (UNAVEM II), Eritrea (UNOVER), Haiti (ONUVEH), Mozambique (UNOMOZ), Nicaragua (ONUVEN), South Africa (UNOMSA), and Liberia (UNOMIL). See Report of the Secretary-General, Enhancing the effectiveness of the principle of periodic and genuine elections, A/52/474, October 16, 1997.

[24] See S.C. res. 687 (1991), at paras 7–13.

undertook to provide to UNSCOM unrestricted freedom of entry and exit, unrestricted freedom of movement within Iraq, the right to unimpeded access to any site or facility for the purpose of the on-site inspection, the right to designate any site whatsoever for observation, inspection or other monitoring, and the right to take and analyse samples of any kind, including for off-site analysis.

12–051   In January 1998 Iraq announced that it was withdrawing its co-operation with the inspection team and denied access to the commission to eight "Presidential sites." In February 1998 the UN and Iraq agreed on the terms of a Memorandum of Understanding, which secured Iraq's reconfirmation of its acceptance of all relevant resolutions of the Security Council and its undertaking to cooperate fully with UNSCOM and the IAEA. The memorandum also provided for the establishment of special procedures which would apply to initial and subsequent entries for the performance of the tasks mandated at the eight "Presidential sites."[25] However, in October 1998 Iraq announced that it would cease all forms of interaction with UNSCOM and its Chairman and to halt all UNSCOM's activities inside Iraq.[26] The Security Council unanimously condemned Iraq's actions,[27] and notwithstanding Iraq's subsequent undertaking to comply with the resolution, in December 1998 UNSCOM withdrew its staff from Iraq on the basis that it was unable to guarantee their security. In December 1999 the UN Security Council established the United Nations Monitoring, Verification and Inspection Commission (UNMOVIC) to undertake the responsibilities of the former United Nations Special Commission (UNSCOM), which was charged with monitoring the elimination of weapons of mass destruction in Iraq. The new Commission took over UNSCOM's assets, liabilities and archives and was mandated to establish and operate a reinforced, ongoing monitoring and verification system, address unresolved disarmament issues and identify additional sites to be covered by the new monitoring system.[28] The whole episode indicates that even where far-reaching power of inspection are provided for, and supported by the Security Council, their actual exercise may prove to be difficult.

12–052   In some ways UNSCOM's power of inspection are inspired by those to be found within the IAEA system of inspection, known as the safeguards system and established pursuant to the 1968 Treaty on the Non-

---

[25] Endorsed by S.C. res. 1154 (1998).
[26] Amongst the concerns raised by Iraq was the "leaking" of information obtained in the course of inspection to the United States; irrespective of the merits of that view, the allegation reinforces the need to ensure that the intrusive character of inspections under the auspices of an international organisation such as the UN requires that they be carried out under strict conditions of impartiality on the part of the organisation.
[27] S.C. res 1205 (1998).
[28] S.C. res. 1284 (1999).

Proliferation of Nuclear Weapons.[29] Under agreements that states conclude with the IAEA, Agency inspectors visit nuclear facilities to verify records of that state, check IAEA-installed instruments and surveillance equipment, and confirm physical inventories of nuclear materials. The inspector prepares detailed reports to the state concerned and to the IAEA. Verification can take place only on the basis of an agreement with the state in which the inspection is to occur, and the NPT and their regional equivalents (the Tlatelolco and Rarotonga Treaties) require contracting states to conclude such agreements with the Agency. Other safeguards agreements are concluded to cover individual nuclear installations not subject to these non-proliferation treaties, and inspections may also be made pursuant to the IAEA Statute (Article 12). Safeguards agreements have also been worked out between the IAEA and the original five nuclear-weapon states, under which the latter may invite the Agency to apply safeguards to all or some of the peaceful nuclear installations in their territory.[30]

Under the safeguards provisions of the EURATOM Treaty the Commis- **12–053** sion is required to ensure that nuclear materials are not diverted from their intended uses and that obligations under agreements with third states or international organisations are complied with.[31] The Commission may send inspectors into the territories of members states, following consultation with the state concerned. If inspection is refused the Commission may obtain an order from the ECJ for compulsory inspection.[32] EURATOM has entered into an agreement with the IAEA to fuse the safeguards arrangements. Elsewhere in the Community legal order, the Commission has the power to carry out on site inspections pursuant to other policies, for example, in the field of competition law. E.C. Council Regulation 17 of 1962 allows the Commission "to undertake all necessary investigations into undertakings and associations of undertakings," including the right of its officials to enter any premises.[33] Moreover, no advance warning need be given.[34]

---

[29] 729 U.N.T.S. 161.

[30] In 1998, 2,507 safeguards inspections were performed at 897 facilities and other locations worldwide. At the end of 1998, 222 safeguards agreements were in force in 138 states (and Taiwan, China). This includes safeguards agreements which were in force with 126 states pursuant to the NPT. The greater part of the safeguards activities was in those states where safeguards were being applied pursuant to full scope safeguards agreements (INFCIRC/153 type). Safeguards were also being applied to facilities, equipment, and non-nuclear material under agreements covering individual facilities (INFCIRC/66 Rev.2 type).

[31] EURATOM Treaty, Arts 77—85. See also Commission Regulation 3227/76 (EURATOM) concerning the application of the provisions on Euratom safeguards (as amended).

[32] EURATOM Treaty, Art. 81.

[33] Council Regulation No. 17, First Regulation implementing Articles 85 and 86 of the Treaty, [1959-62] O.J. English Spec. Ed. 87, Art. 14.

[34] Case 136/79 *National Panasonic v. Commission* [1980] E.C.R. 2033; [1980] 3 C.M.L.R. 169.

12–055   Some of the organisations established by disarmament treaties also have powers of inspection, including the OPCW.[35] International judicial and quasi-judicial bodies are also, on occasion, granted the power to carry out on-site investigations. In the field of international criminal law, the prosecutor is empowered to investigate all facts and evidence relevant to assessing whether there is criminal responsibility under the statute of the International Criminal Court, and may conduct investigations on the territory of a state including, where authorised by a pre-trial chamber, without having secured the co-operation of the state concerned.[36] The ICTY and ICTR prosecutor is similarly empowered to conduct on-site investigations and may, as appropriate, seek the assistance of the state authorities concerned.[37] Other international courts are able to carry out site visits, but require the agreement of the state concerned.[38] Similarly, agreement of the state concerned is required when the World Bank Inspection Panel seeks to carry out an inspection in the territory of a country.[39] And agreement is also required in relation to inspection activities of the various human rights bodies.[40]

(d) ENFORCEMENT POWERS: SANCTIONS

Bibliography: Leben, *Les sanctions privatives de droits ou de qualité dans les organisations internationales specialisées* (1979); Dolzer, "Enforcement of international obligations through regional arrangements: structures and experience of the OAS", 47 ZAÖRV 113 (1987); Frowein, "Collective enforcement of international obligations" 47 ZAÖRV 67 (1987); Schachter, Compliance and enforcement in the UN system, 85 Proc. ASIL (1991) 428; A. & A.H. Chayes, *The New Sovereignty: Compliance with International Regulatory Arrangements* (1995); Tanzi, "Problems of enforcement of decisions of the I.C.J. and the law of the United Nations", 6 EJIL 539 (1995); Rosenzweig, UN sanctions: creating a more effective tool for the enforcemnt of international law, 48 Austrian J. of Pub. & Int Law 161 (1995); M. Doxey, *International sanctions in contemporary perspective* (2nd ed, 1996); Downs, "Enforcement and the evolution of international co-operation", 19 Mich JIL 319 (1998).

12–056   Although the supervisory role of international organisations remains, for the most part, limited to reviewing reports and a degree of fact-finding, in some limited instances international organisations have been granted more extensive powers of enforcement to protect their own rights and enforce the

---

[35] See 1993 Chemical Weapons Convention, Arts. IV, V and VI, and the Verification Annex.
[36] ICC Statute (1998), Art. 54(2).
[37] ICTY Statute (1993), Art. 18(2); ICTR Statute (1994), Art. 17(2).
[38] The I.C.J. carried out its first site visit in 1997, in the case Concerning the Gabcikovo/Nagymaros project, 1997 I.C.J. Reps 14, para. 10.
[39] Resolution IBRD 93–10, para. 21. Sensitivities associated with such inspections are reflected in the 1999 clarifications of the Resolution, which require that "the profile of panel activities in country, during the course of an investigation, should be kept as low as possible." (1999 Clarifications, April 20, 1999). The Clarifications state: "The Panel's methods of investigation should not create the impression that it is investigating the borrower's performance."
[40] See Chap. 13, paras 13–062 *et seq*.

obligations that others have towards them.[41] What is meant here by the term "enforcement" is the right of an international organisation to take measures, including coercive measures, to ensure the fulfilment of obligations owed to it by its members, as well as the less frequent recourse to measures against non-members.[42] Such measures may include judicial (or quasi-judicial) measures, measures affecting cultural and communication links, diplomatic and political measures, measures affecting economic and trade relations, and military measures.[43]

There are of course no general rules determining the powers of **12–057** enforcement available to each organisation. There is a matter determined by each organisation's respective constituent instrument, as well as subsequent practise. Within the UN and outside, the decision to embark on sanctions nevertheless presupposes two prior stages:

(i) the acquisition of evidence to prove a breach of obligation, whether under the organisation's constituent instrument or some other convention. Such evidence can be provided by reports,[44] by inspection,[45] by complaints or petitions.[46]

(ii) The determination by a political organ that a breach has occurred and that measures ought to be taken to bring the member into compliance.

Once such a determination has been made a number of different types of measures may be available, as the sections which follow illustrate.

Judicial measures

Judicial measures refer to the possibility for an international organisation **12–058** to refer a matter to an international court or tribunal, or to quasi-judicial body, with a view to obtaining a determination by that body that one or more members are failing to comply with obligations to, or arising in the framework of the activities of, the organisation. It represents an extension of the reference by one organ of an international organisation to another, political, organ, such as the right of the General Assembly to refer a dispute involving one of its members to the Security Council, as provided by

---

[41] See *Reparations for Injuries* Case, 1949 I.C.J. Reps, 174, where the I.C.J. determined that the UN had an 'undeniable right' to 'demand that its Members fulfil the obligations entered into by them in the interest of the good working of the organisation'.

[42] See Abi-Saab, "De la sanction en droit international", in *Theory of International Law at the Threshold of the 21st Century: Essays in Honour of Krzysztof Skubiszewski* (1996), 61, 70–7.

[43] This typology is drawn from Doxey, *International Sanctions in Contemporary Perspective* (2nd ed, 1996), 11 and 14–15.

[44] See *supra*.

[45] See *supra*.

[46] See Chap. 13.

Articles 11 and 12 of the Charter.[47] A distinction is to be drawn between, on the one hand, a request for an advisory opinion from an international court or tribunal, and bringing a claim against a member in contentious (or quasi-contentious) proceedings.

12–059   As described in detail in Chapter 13, with respect to advisory proceedings a number of international organisations are empowered to make requests for advisory opinions from the International Court of Justice.[48] Further, the International Tribunal for the Law of the Sea may also be able to render an advisory opinion to an international organisation related to the purposes of UNCLOS.[49] Some of the regional human rights courts can give advisory opinions on the interpretation of the treaties for which they have responsibility, including at the instigation of an international organisation,[50] and certain regional economic integration organisations can request advisory opinions from their respective courts.[51] In each case the opinion may be sought to obtain an authoritative determination by the organisation that a member is not complying with its obligations. Although the opinion will not be binding there will often be powerful political incentives encouraging the member to bring itself into compliance.

12–060   The involvement of international organisations in international contentious proceedings is a more recent, and less wide-ranging, phenomenon. Some international organisations may of course bring arbitration proceedings against one or more of their members, for example, pursuant to the provisions of a headquarters agreement, if it considers that the member is not acting consistently with the terms of the agreement.[52] But rather more frequent nowadays is recourse to an international court, a route first made possible in the European Communities, and subsequently followed by treaties establishing other regional economic organisations,[53] and now UNCLOS.

12–061   The supervision and enforcement powers of the European Commission, under the E.C., ECSC and EURATOM treaties, are the most far-reaching of any organ of an international organisation,[54] and the approach is influencing developments elsewhere. The three treaties establish an enforcement role which is unparalleled in any other international organisation.

---

[47] See Chap. 2.
[48] Chap. 13, paras 13–024.
[49] Chap. 13, paras 13–070.
[50] For example, the Council of Europe's Committee of Ministers may request an advisory opinion: *infra*, Chap. 13, para. 13–117.
[51] *e.g.* Council and Commission to the E.C., Chap. 13, para. 13–149; the Central American Court of Justice, *ibid.*, para. 13–154; and the COMESA Court of Justice, *ibid.*, para 13–156.
[52] See Chap. 15.
[53] See *e.g.* Chapter 13, para. 13–154; the COMESA Court of Justice, *ibid.*, para. 13–156; and the Court of Justice of the Andean Community, *ibid.*, para. 13–155.
[54] Chapter 6, paras 6–044 *et seq.*

This reflects the extent to which the member states have been willing to subject themselves to compulsory third party adjudication, and not only at the instigation of another state (as is traditional) or of an individual (as in the case of human rights), but rather at the instigation of an international organisation. Under the E.C. Treaty the Commission is charged with ensuring that its provisions and the measures taken by the institutions under the treaty "are applied" (E.C. Treaty, Article 211, ex Article 155). To that end the Commission receives and reviews reports submitted by member states, and for some matters, such as anti-trust, is endowed with significant powers of inspection. But the Commission also has the power to institute proceedings before the ECJ: Article 226 of the E.C. Treaty (*ex Article 169*) provides that:

> "If the Commission considers that a Member State has failed to fulfil an obligation under this Treaty it shall deliver a reasoned opinion on the matter after giving the State concerned the opportunity to submit its observations.
> If the State concerned does not comply with the opinion within the period laid down by the Commission, the latter may bring the matter before the Court of Justice."[55]

Once the case reached the ECJ that body's function was originally limited **12–062** to declaring whether or not the member state was in violation of a treaty obligation (E.C. Treaty, Article 228(1), *ex Article 171*). In 1992 the E.C. Treaty was amended to address the situation where a member state failed to comply with a judgment of the ECJ: if the member state fails to comply with the judgment within the time specified by the Commission then the Commission may bring the case back to the ECJ, specifying "the amount of the lump sum or penalty payment to be paid by the member State which it considers appropriate in the circumstances" (E.C. Treaty Article 228(2)). This marks a logical extension of the Commission's power to impose fines in relation to certain areas for which it has oversight responsibility, such as anti-trust, subject to judicial control by the ECJ of the level of the fines, taking into account principles of proportionality and equality of treatment.[56] In July 2000 the ECJ gave effect to this provision for the first time,

---

[55] Similar powers exist in relation to the ECSC (Art. 88) and EURATOM (Art. 141). See generally Hartley, *Foundations of Community Law* (4th ed, 1998, pp. 294–323). The Commission also has a "screening" role in relation to traditional inter-state dispute brought under Art. 227 of the E.C. Treaty (*ex Art. 170*): before a member state can bring an action against another member state for an alleged infringement of the E.C. Treaty it must bring the matter before the Commission, which must deliver a reasoned opinion on the matters in issue after having heard the views of the states concerned. Only after the Commission's opinion has been given, or if no such opinion is given within three months, can the member state concerned bring proceedings to the ECJ.

[56] See, *e.g.* cases 56/64 and 58/64 *Consten and Grundig v. Commission,* 1966 E.C.R. p. 429; case C-157/96, *National Farmers' Union and Others,* 1998 E.C.R. I-2211, para 39.

imposing a fine of 20,000 euros for each day from the date of the judgment for delay in complying with a 1992 ECJ judgment finding that Greece had failed to take the necessary measures concerning the disposal of toxic and dangerous wastes.[57]

12–063   A similar approach may be seen in the UNCLOS provisions governing resource activities on the deep sea-bed. The International Sea-Bed Authority may be a party to contentious proceedings before the 11 member Sea-Bed Dispute Chamber of the International Tribunal for the Law of the Sea. Aside from its role as a potential respondent,[58] UNCLOS envisages that the Authority shall have access to the Chamber, to bring claims against a state party to UNCLOS which is alleged to be in violation of Part XI of UNCLOS (as amended) or its Annexes or of the Authority's rules, regulations and procedures.[59] UNCLOS also envisages that the Authority may bring claims against a party to a contract with it concerning the interpretation or application of a contract or a plan of work or acts or omissions of a party to the contract relating to activities in the Area (Article 187(c)), and claims against a prospective contractor who has been sponsored by a state concerning the refusal of a contract or a legal issue arising in the negotiation of the contract (Article 187(d)). In such cases it is the Council which shall institute proceedings on behalf of the Authority in cases of non-compliance.[60]

12–064   The UN specialised agencies do not have the power to initiate contentious proceedings before an international court. However, one agency with a rather more sophisticated system (although not reaching the heights of the E.C. approach) is the ILO, particularly in relation to the conventions and other acts adopted under its auspices and accepted by members by means of ratification or otherwise.[61] It will be recalled that under the

---

[57] Case C-387/97, *Commission v. Greece*, Judgment of July 4, 2000 (U.K. intervened in support of the Commission). The detailed background is set out in the interesting opinion of Advocate General Colomer, September 28, 1999, who suggested to the Court a lower fine of 15,375 euros for each day of delay. The Court opted for a higher figure, and usefully indicated the basic criteria to be taken into account to ensure that penalty payments have coercive force and Community law is applied uniformly and effectively: "the duration of the infringement, its degree of seriousness and the ability of the Member State to pay. In applying those criteria, regard should be had in particular to the effects of failure to comply on private and public interests and to the urgency of getting the member state concerned to fulfil its obligation" (*id.*, at para. 92).

[58] See Chap. 13, para 13–075.

[59] UNCLOS, Art. 187(b)(I). See also ITLOS Statute, Art. 37, and ITLOS Rules, Arts 115–123. Proceedings in contentious cases involving the Authority are governed by the rules applicable to other contentious cases: ITLOS Rules, Art. 115.

[60] UNCLOS, Art. 162(2)(u).

[61] See Ivanov, "The International Labour Organisation: control over application of the conventions and recommendations on labour", in Butler (ed), *Control over Compliance with International Law* (1991), pp. 153–64; Nielsen, "The supervisory machinery of the ILO", 64 Nordic JIL 129 (1995).

Constitution all members are bound to report to the organisation on measures taken in respect of conventions or recommendations relevant to them;[62] the Constitution further provides for means of enforcing legal obligations assumed by parties to such conventions, including at the instigation of the organisation itself. Complaints of non-observance may be made against a member by any other ratifying member or by a delegate to the Conference or by the governing body itself, and these may be referred by the governing body under Article 26 of the Constitution to a Commission of Inquiry either directly or after prior communication to the government concerned. The Commission, an independent body, is empowered to ascertain the facts and to make recommendations in a report which is published. Each government must, within three months, inform the Director-General whether it accepts these recommendations or wishes to refer the complaint to the ICJ. The Court may affirm, vary or reverse any of the findings or recommendations of the Commission of Inquiry and its decision on the matter or complaint is final. In the event that a member fails to carry out the recommendations of the Commission, or the decision of the Court, the governing body "may recommend to the conference such actions as it may deem wise and expedient to secure compliance therewith" (Article 33). The ultimate sanction therefore rests with the conference, and in view of the fact that originally neither suspension nor expulsion were provided for in the constitution, this seemed a rather tame ending to what appears an impressive machinery of enforcement. In practice the procedure under Article 26 has been used sparingly, having been invoked on 26 occasions since the founding of the ILO, only on four occasions at the instigation of one government against another,[63] and just once by resolution of the conference as a whole.[64] The majority of these cases are brought by a delegate or delegates (almost always workers delegates) or unions from a particular country. The reasons for limited reliance on the procedure include the cost of establishing a Commission of Inquiry and the role played by the Committee of Experts on the application of Recommendations and Conventions, which was established in 1926 to examine reports submitted under Articles 19, 22 and 35 of the Constitution, and which has rendered the use of the "enforcement procedure" a course of last resort.

It should also be noted that there is a special procedure under Article 24 for **12–065** dealing with complaints by industrial associations of employers or workers. These are transmitted to the government concerned by the governing body for its observations and, if no reply is received or the reply is unsatisfactory, the governing body may publish the complaints and the reply, if any. The sanction is then a political one, both within and without the organisation.

---

[62] See *supra,* para. 12–040
[63] Ghana against Portugal (1961); Portugal against Liberia (1962); France against Panama (1976 and 1978); Tunisia against Libya (1986).
[64] In relation to Chile (1974).

12–066   There is also, since 1950, a special procedure for complaints of the infringement of trade union rights, which are referred to the ILO either directly or through the UN Economic and Social Council. These are submitted to an independent fact-finding and Conciliation Commission of nine persons, working in panels of three members, whose terms of reference are to examine complaints of infringement of trade union rights referred to it by the ILO governing body in respect of countries that have ratified the Conventions and those that have not, though in the latter case referral may not be made without the consent of the country concerned. Since its establishment it has examined just six cases,[65] a reflection no doubt of the need to obtain the consent of many of the governments concerned. When the issue of consent became apparent, early on, the governing body created a Committee on Freedom of Association in 1951,[66] with the function of determining whether a complaint ought to be examined by the governing body. This Committee may only receive complaints from organisations of workers or employers or governments, although there is no requirement that the state concerned is bound by any of the conventions in relation to freedom of association since all members are deemed, by virtue of their membership of the ILO, to have recognised the principle of freedom of association which the Committee early on determined to be reflective of customary law.

Cultural and communications measures

12–067 The cultural and communications measures which may be available to international organisations include the curtailment of cultural exchanges and suspension of scientific co-operation and ties in the fields of areas such as education and sports. The UN Security Council has adopted measures relating to communications: it has acted to limit the entry into or transit through the territories of members of certain individuals associated with a military junta and adult members of their families,[67] and it has taken measures banning international flights.[68]

Diplomatic and political measures

12–068 Members which are not acting in compliance with their obligations may find themselves under greater pressure as a result of diplomatic and political measures taken by international organisations. These may include

---

[65] Concerning Japan, Greece, Lesotho, Chile, the United States/Puerto Rico, and South Africa.

[66] This Committee has become a substitute, quasi-judicial hearing, avoiding the need for consent. It has received nearly 2000 complaints since its establishment. See also Procedures of the Fact-Finding and Conciliation Commission and the Committee on Freedom of Association for the Examination of Complaints alleging Violations of Freedom of Association, Doc. 1901, para. 34, Committee on Freedom of Association Digest of Decisions (1996).

[67] Sierra Leone, res. 1132 (1997).

[68] Iraq, res. 670 (1991); Libya, res. 748 (1992); Federal Republic of Yugoslavia, res. 757 (1992); Afghanistan, Taliban, res. 1267 (1999).

protest and censure by the organisation, the postponement or cancellation of visits and meetings, and the reduction of diplomatic representation. More far reaching, however, are the measures detailed in Chapter 16, namely the suspension of rights relating to the organisation (for example, in relation to voting,[69] representation,[70] rights and privileges of membership[71]) and expulsion from particular organs or the organisation as a whole.[72] Such measures are typically made available, in one form or another, in the constituent instruments of international organisations, or as a result of their interpretation through subsequent practice.

Economic measures

Beyond the military measures available principally to the Security Council, **12–069** the UN also has machinery for imposing trade and other economic sanctions against members (and occasionally non-members) whose actions "constitute a threat to, or a breach of, international peace and security".[73] Although the General Assembly may recommend sanctions,[74] only the Security Council has the authority to adopt legally binding sanctions, pursuant to its Chapter VII responsibilities for the maintenance of international peace and security.

The power to adopt sanctions finds its roots in the Covenant of the **12–070** League of Nations, which adopted them on at least one occasion, in 1935 against Italy.[75] Until the 1990s the Security Council adopted economic and other sanctions only very rarely.[76] Following the unilateral declaration of independence by Southern Rhodesia the Council adopted resolution 232, calling on all UN members to halt trade with Southern Rhodesia in certain commodities. Subsequently these measures were extended to cover all trade and relations in general, and remained in force until December 1979 when the measures were terminated by Security Council resolution 460. Measures

---

[69] Chap. 16, para. 16-018 *et seq*.

[70] *ibid.*

[71] *ibid.* A leading example is the power of the Fund to suspend the ability of a member to use special drawing rights if found to have violated certain obligations under the Fund Agreement: Art. XXIII(2).

[72] *ibid*., para. 16–034 *et seq*.

[73] Under Arts 39, *et seq.* of the UN Charter: see Chap. 2.

[74] Early examples include G.A. res. 39(I) recommending that the Government of Spain of General Franco should be prevented from participating in international organisations and meetings, and G.A. res. 500 (V) recommending that states apply an embargo on the shipment of certain commodities to areas under the control of communist China and North Korea.

[75] Recommendations were adopted by the Council and Assembly on October 7 and 9, 1935, and were due to come into effect on October 15, 1935. In view of subsequent political developments most states did not give effect to the recommendations and the sanctions were lifted on July 6, 1936.

[76] For a more detailed background see Reisman and Stevick, "The applicability of international law standards to the United Nations economic sanctions programmes," 9 EJIL 86 (1998), at 96–126.

taken against South Africa by the Security Council were rather more limited, never reaching the full scale of the boycott and severance of relations recommended by the General Assembly as from 1962. In 1977 by resolution 418 the Security Council resolved that all states "shall cease forthwith any provision to South Africa of arms and related material" as well as the provisions of all types of equipment for their manufacture; further sanctions on investments and the sale of krugerrands were hortatory in character.

12–071　The political changes taking place in Central and Eastern Europe in 1990 transformed the conditions under which the Security Council operated. Since then it has adopted binding economic and other sanctions more frequently and in respect of a broader range of targets. The sanctions are usually addressed to deal with situations of its members, but in the case of Yugoslavia (Serbia and Montenegro) they have been addressed to a situation involving a non-member. In each case a dedicated Sanctions Committee is established to oversee the management of the sanctions.[77] Over the past decade economic sanctions have been adopted prohibiting the delivery of arms and material,[78] petroleum and petroleum products,[79] and weapons and petroleum;[80] freezing certain funds and financial resources;[81] and adopting more comprehensive economic sanctions.[82] Whilst the effectiveness of these measures remains very much open to question and, in the case of those relating to Iraq and Haiti have raised concerns about their effects on impoverished people[83] (and even questions as to their continuing legality as a matter of general international law), there can be no doubt that the Security Council's role has become more important and closer to the aspirations of the UN's founding members.

12–072　Other international organisations have also adopted their own international sanctions,[84] although frequently these are taken pursuant to measures adopted by the UN Security Council. In 1972 the OAS members decided to suspend trade with Cuba in arms and military materiel, measures which formally remained in force until 1975. In 1979 the League

---

[77] In relation to the Iraq sanctions (1990) see Koskenniemi, "Le Comité des Sanctions," 1991 AFDI 119.

[78] See, *e.g.* Yugoslavia (res. 713 (1991) and 1160 (1998)); Somalia (res. 733 (1992)); Liberia (res. 788 (1992)); Rwanda (res. 918 (1994)).

[79] Cambodia, Khmer Rouge, res. 792 (1992).

[80] Angola, res. 864 (1993); Sierra Leone, res. 1132 (1987).

[81] Angola, UNITA, res. 1173 (1998); Afghanistan, Taliban, res. 1267 (1999).

[82] Iraq, res. 661 (1990); Libya, res. 748 (1992) and 883 (1993); Federal Republic of Yugoslavia, Serbia and Montenegro, res. 757 and 787 (1992), 820 (1993); Haiti, res. 841 (1993) and 917 (1994).

[83] See Reisman and Stevick, *supra.* n. 119.

[84] See Carreau, "Les moyens de pression économiques au regard du FMI, du GATT et de l'OCDE", 18 Rev.Bel. DI 20 (1984–5).

of Arab States applied penalties to Egypt after it signed the Egypt-Israel peace agreement. And the E.C. has long applied its own economic sanctions against third states. These were originally limited to the freezing of trade associations, as occurred in 1967 against Greece following a military coup, or coordinating the responses of its members as occurred for example in respect of Southern Rhodesia, the Iran hostages crisis and the Soviet invasion of Afghanistan.[85] The first sanctions adopted in its own name were those taken against the USSR following the Polish crisis, in 1982,[86] and again Argentina in 1982 following the invasion of the Falklands/Malvinas.[87] In both cases the measures prohibited the imports of goods, and were based on old Article 113 of the EEC Treaty, providing for common measures on commercial policy. These measures led to a spirited debate on the legality under Community and international law of economic sanctions adopted by an international economic integration organisation against third states.[88] Subsequent practise has evolved,[89] and in 1992 the E.C. Treaty was amended to provide express legal bases for sanctions: Article 60 of the E.C. Treaty (*ex Article 73g*) permits the Council to take necessary urgent measures on capital movements and on payments to third countries,[90] and Article 301 (*ex Article 228a*) permits the Council to take urgent measures to "interrupt or to reduce, in part or completely, economic relations with one or more third countries," provided that the measures are pursuant to a joint action or common position adopted under the Treaty on European Union. The E.U. does not have a system for imposing such sanctions against its own members, in the context of judicial scheme described below. However, in January 2000 the government's of 14 members of the E.U. adopted a "joint reaction" to the integration of the right wing Freedom Party into the Austrian Government, which downgraded official contacts with Austria, and provided that the members would provide no support for Austrian candidates seeking posts in international organisations, and limiting the extent of diplomatic contacts with Austrian officials. The measures taken pursuant to the "joint reaction," which were lifted in September 2000, did not purport to constitute an act of the E.U., but rather an act of the individual members.

In relation to trade sanctions it is also appropriate to refer to the system **12–073** established under WTO rules, which places considerable emphasis on compliance with and enforcement of decisions of its Panels and the

---

[85] See generally Verhoeven, Communautés européennes et sanctions internationales, 18 Rev.Bel. DI 79 (1984–85).

[86] Council Regulation 596/82, of March 15, 1982.

[87] Council Regulation 877/82 of April 16, 1992.

[88] See Verhoeven, supra. note 85 at 92, and the response of Ehlermann, at 96, *et seq.*

[89] Sturma, "La participation de la Communauté européenne à des 'sanctions' internationales", Rev. du Marché Commun, 1993, 250.

[90] This is without prejudice to the right of individual members to take unilateral measures for serious political reasons and on grounds of urgency.

Appellate Body.[91] The system in effect removes the right of an individual member to suspend WTO concessions or take other compensatory measures against another member in breach of its WTO obligations, putting in place a multilateral system for the authorisation of such measures only under the authority of the WTO, through its Dispute Settlement Body (DSB). The DSB establishes panels and adopts reports of panels and the Appellate Body, and then maintains surveillance of implementation of rulings and recommendations and authorises suspension of concessions and other obligations under WTO covered agreements.[92] Where a panel concludes that a measure taken by a member is inconsistent with a covered agreement it recommends the removal of the measure, or an alternative way of bringing it into conformity with the relevant agreement. The panel's report will then be adopted by the WTO's Dispute Settlement Body (DSB) within 60 days from its circulation to the parties to the dispute, unless the DSB has decided by way of consensus not to adopt the report or if an appeal has been lodged to the Appellate Body.[93] If an appeal is lodged the report of the Appellate Body will be adopted by the DSB unless it decides by consensus not to adopt it.[94] Upon adoption by the DSB the report of the panel or the Appellate Body becomes binding on the parties, who must comply promptly with its recommendations or rulings.[95] The DSB is charged with keeping the implementation of adopted recommendations or rulings "under surveillance."[96] If a non-implementing member fails to bring a measure into compliance within a reasonable period, it must enter into negotiations with the complaining party (or parties), with a view to agree upon acceptable compensation. If no agreement on compensation is reached within 20 days, the complaining party may seek the authorisation of the DSB for suspension of concessions or other obligations applicable *vis-à-vis* the non-complying member, until compliance is restored (DSU, Article 22(2) and (8)). The DSB must then act promptly to grant authorisation to suspend concessions or other obligations, unless the request is rejected by consensus.[97] The entire scheme militates strongly against unilateral determinations and establishes a central role for the DSB, as confirmed by a panel in a case brought by the E.C. against the United

---

[91] See *infra.* Chap. 13, paras 13–078 *et seq.*
[92] WTO Dispute Settlement Understanding, Art. 2(1).
[93] *ibid.,* Art. 16.
[94] *ibid.,* Art. 17(14).
[95] *ibid.,* Art. 21(1).
[96] *ibid.,* Art. 21(6).
[97] *ibid.* The DSU allows the non-implementing member to challenge the suspension by way of an arbitration procedure: Art. 21(7). Additionally, a new panel may be requested in non-compliance cases.

States, after the latter had unilaterally taken a retaliatory measure against the E.C. in respect of non-compliance with WTO obligations.[98]

Military measures

The military sanctions which are available to be imposed by the UN Security **12–074** Council against members or non-members who are threatening or breaching international peace and security are the most far-reaching enforcement measures available to international organisations.[99] These are described in Chapter 2. The Security Council has also on occasion delegated its powers under Chapter VII,[1] a recent example being its decision in 1997 to authorise ECOWAS to ensure strict implementation of sanctions relating to petroleum and arms and related material of all types.[2] NATO's intervention in Kosovo in 1999 occurred without the benefit of authorisation from the Security Council, but subsequently the Council adopted a resolution which amongst other points decided "on the deployment in Kosovo, under United Nations auspices, of [an] international security presence[. . .]", which presence would have "substantial North Atlantic Treaty Organisation participation" and which "must be deployed under unified command and control."[3] Beyond the role of the UN a limited number of regional organisations claim the authority to establish military forces in their own name, including the OAS,[4] the Warsaw Pact,[5] and the League of Arab States.[6] It may be recalled that regional organisations may not autonomously use force (other than for reasons of self-defence), and that such actions are subject to the conditions enunciated in Chapter VIII of the UN Charter.[7]

---

[98] United States—Import Measures on Certain Products from the European Communities, WT/DS165/R, July 17, 2000, para. 6.92 ("when an assessment of the WTO compatibility of a measure taken to comply with panel and Appellate Body recommendations (an "implementing measure") is necessary (because parties disagree), such determination can only be made through the WTO dispute settlement procedures. Pursuant to Article 23.2(a), members are obliged to have recourse exclusively to a WTO/DSU dispute settlement mechanism to obtain a "determination" that a measure is WTO inconsistent. We consider that the obligation to use the WTO multilateral dispute settlement mechanism (*i.e.* as opposed to unilateral or even regional mechanisms) to obtain any determination of WTO compatibility, is a fundamental obligation that finds application throughout the DSU").

[99] See Chap. 2, paras 2–044 *et seq.*

[1] See Sarooshi, The United nations and the Development of Collective Security: the Delegation by the security Council of its Chapter VII Powers (1999).

[2] S.C. res. 1132 (1997).

[3] S.C. res 1244 (1999), para. 5 and annex 2, point 4.

[4] See Chap. 7, paras 7–002 *et seq.* In 1965 the OAS dispatched a military force to the Dominican Republic: OAS resolution of 6 may 1965; see Fenwick, "The Dominican Republic: Intervention or Collective Self-Defence?" 60 AJIL 64 (1966); Ferguson, "The Dominican Case: Unilateral Intervention", 60 AJIL 809 (1966).

[5] See Chap. 6, para. 6–003. In 1968 military forces from several Pact members invaded Czechoslovakia: see 7 ILM 1265 (1968).

[6] See Chap. 9, paras 9–002 *et seq.* In 1976 the League created an Arab force to replace Syrian troops in Lebanon: see Feuer, "La force arabe de sécurité au Liban," 22 AFDI 51 (1976).

[7] See Chap. 5, paras 5–004 *et seq.*

CHAPTER 13

JUDICIAL AND QUASI-JUDICIAL FUNCTIONS

A. Introduction

Bibliography: Malinverni, "The Settlement of Disputes within International Organisations" in *International Law: Achievements and Prospects* (Bedjaoui (ed.), 1991); Janis, *International courts for the twenty-first century* (1992); United Nations, *Handbook on the Peaceful Settlement of Disputes* (1992); Parra, Canela and Porges, "New Trends in International Dispute Settlement" (1993) 86 Proc. Am. Soc. Int'l L. 2; Brus, *Third Party Dispute Settlement in an Interdependent World* (1995); Guillaume, "The Future of International Judicial Institutions" (1995) 44 ICLQ 848; Koufa (ed.), *International Justice* (1997); Evans (ed.), *Remedies in International Law: The Institutional Dilemma* (1998); Collier and Lowe, *The Settlement of Disputes in International Law: Institutions and Procedures* (1999); Sands, Mackenzie and Shany, *Manual of International courts and Tribunals* (1999); J. Merrills, *International Dispute Settlement* (3rd ed., 1999); Dahlitz (ed.), *Peaceful Resolution of Major International Disputes* (1999); Alford and Bekker, "International courts and Tribunals" (1999) 33 Int'l Lawyer 537; "The Proliferation of International Tribunals: Piecing Together the Puzzle", Special Issue, 31 N.Y.U. J. Int'l L. Politics 697–933.

An increasing range of international procedures and mechanisms are **13–001** available to assist in the resolution of international disputes involving states and other members of international society. Article 33 of the UN Charter identifies the traditional mechanisms, including negotiation, inquiry, mediation, conciliation, arbitration, judicial settlement, resort to regional agencies or arrangements or other peaceful means of the parties' own choice. These techniques can be divided into two broad categories: *diplomatic means* according to which the parties retain control over the dispute insofar as they may accept or reject a proposed settlement (negotiation, consultation, mediation, conciliation, inquiry); and *legal means* which result in legally binding decisions for the parties to the dispute (arbitration and judicial settlement). Recourse to regional arrangements and international organisations as mediators and conciliators provides something of a middle way: the legal consequences of any decision taken will depend on the treaty establishing the institution. As these techniques and distinctions have evolved, in particular over the past three decades, two discernible trends have emerged: first, there has been a move from political arrangements

337

towards the resolution of disputes by means of binding third party adjudication; and secondly, there has been a move from inter-state dispute settlement towards techniques involving non-state actors, including international institutions, individuals, associations and the private sector. Both trends have occurred in the context of the move from ad hoc arrangements to established institutional bodies, and a marked increase in the number of international courts and tribunals.

13–002   Many of the international courts and tribunals discussed in this chapter are themselves international institutions, established by treaty under international law; others are organs of international organisations and do not possess a legal personality of their own. They fulfil a range of different functions. Some provide mechanisms for the resolution of disputes between states, or between non-state actors and states; others are established to address issues arising between an organisation and its members; yet others provide for dispute resolution between the organisation (or its members) and third parties (including employees and other non-state actors). A limited number address all of these aspects, providing a forum for judicial review of the acts of the organisation.

(a) SETTLEMENT OF DISPUTES BETWEEN STATES

13–003   The original function of international courts and tribunals was to resolve disputes between states. This, of course, is the stated aim of the Permanent Court of Arbitration, whose 1899 Convention reflected a desire to obviate, as far as possible, recourse to force in relations between states, and committed the signatory Powers "to use their best efforts to ensure the pacific settlement of international disputes" (Article 1). Traditional inter-state dispute settlement is also the object, in respect of their contentious jurisdiction, of the P.C.I.J. and the I.C.J., as well as the primary function of many of the more recently established bodies—such as the International Tribunal for the Law of the Sea and the WTO Dispute Settlement Body—and amongst the tasks of some of the regional courts. Thus, the European court of Justice and the various regional human rights courts and bodies are able to address inter-state disputes. In practice they do so only rarely: the overwhelming majority of cases before these institutions involve non-state actors, in particular individuals, associations and organs of international organisations (such as, in the E.U. context, the European Commission and Parliament).

(b) SETTLEMENT OF DISPUTES BETWEEN STATES AND NON-STATE ACTORS

13–004   The emergence on the international plane of non-state actors—individuals, associations, corporations and international organisations—provided a new role for international Courts and tribunals. This role has a history. The original 1907 Central American Court of Justice envisaged that non-state

338

actors might have a degree of locus standi, although this possibility was never actually utilised (see *infra*.) After the Second World War a most significant change was engendered by the adoption, in 1948, of the Universal Declaration of Human Rights, which envisaged the establishment of rights on the international plane for individuals and other victims of human rights violations. The first permanent institution to provide for the possibility of individuals to bring proceedings against a state was the European Commission of Human Rights, established in 1950. Although individuals did not originally have the right to bring claims to the European Court of Human Rights, practice evolved to make this possible (see *infra*.); in 1998 the Commission was dispensed with altogether and victims given direct, formal rights of access to the new European Court of Human Rights. The model is one followed in other regions—in Africa and the Americas—and on the global plane in relation to human rights generally as well as in regard to torture, racial discrimination and, most recently, discrimination against women. Beyond the human rights field, a degree of international *locus standi* has also been established in the economic field: the International Centre for the Settlement of Investment Disputes (ICSID) provides the first institutional framework of potentially universal application within which foreign nationals investing abroad may seek to resolve disputes directly with the states in which their investment occurs.

(c) SETTLEMENT OF DISPUTES BETWEEN MEMBERS AND THE ORGANISATION

In considering the resolution of disputes between members and the **13–005** organisation it is appropriate to distinguish between organisations having a general co-ordination function, and those committed to regional integration. It is only in relation to the latter that the judicial function is well-developed. For the former, dispute resolution remains predominantly a matter for political as opposed to judicial processes: if a member considers that an organisation has acted unlawfully, it is likely that the matter will be raised within the political organs of the institution. As a member of an organisation a state has a dual role—it contributes to the adoption of acts, and it is at the same time an addressee of those acts. It is therefore not surprising that within the process of adoption the question of legality will arise, almost by way of a "preventive control" of legality. If the proposed act does not satisfy the conditions of validity in the eyes of the required majority of the members then it will not be adopted.[1] Naturally, and as recognised by the I.C.J. in *Legality of the Use by a State of Nuclear Weapons*

---

[1] See Osieke, "Ultra Vires Acts in International Organisations: The Experience of the ILO" (1976–7) B.Y.I.L. 279; Paolillo, "The International Arrangements for the International Seabed and Their Impact on the Evolution of International Organisations" (1984) V RCADI 278; Osieke, "Unconstitutional Acts in International Organisations: The Law and Practise of the ICAO" (1979) 28 ICLQ 23.

in Armed Conflict, this does not mean that subsequently the validity of the act of an international organisation will not be challenged by members who were unable to gain a majority to oppose the adoption of the act that they consider to be unlawful, or perhaps may not have been represented within the organ adopting the act (for example, the Security Council).[2]

13–006   In some organisations it is envisaged that it will be a matter for the organ adopting the act to resolve questions as to its legality. This solution is foreseen expressly in the constituent instruments of various international organisations, including the IMO (Article 55) and some of the financial institutions of the UN system, as well as various commodity organisations.[3] Moreover, even in the absence of specific provisions to this effect, the members of any international organisation have the right to challenge the illegality of an institutional act by these means.[4] As Judge Bustamente put it in his dissenting opinion in the *Certain Expenses* case, the absence of a specific system for the control of the legality of acts of an international organisation "in no way excludes the Organisation's function of dealing with complaints by its Members."[5] Recalling that it is the UN itself which retains the power to rectify or confirm its own acts, he stated that:

> "It cannot be maintained that the resolutions of any organ of the United Nations are not subject to review: that would amount to declaring the pointlessness of the Charter or its absolute subordination to the judgment—always fallible—of the organs."[6]

The right of members to challenge the validity of institutional acts appears to be a necessary counterweight to the absence of a formal organ of control.[7] Recourse to the organ or body which is the author of the contested act is a logical consequence of the recognised powers of organs of most international institutions playing a coordinating role. Such organs generally have an extensive power to interpret the limits of their powers under their constituent instrument. This principle has been clearly established in relation to the political organs of the UN, at the time of the San Francisco conference,[8] and confirmed by subsequent practice. However, recognising that the organ is in effect judge in its own cause, that practice

---

[2] See [1996] I.C.J. Rep. 66, 82.

[3] See, *e.g.* Art. VII of the Statute of the International Cotton Institute (1966), and Art. 22 of the Agreement on Wheat (1967).

[4] See Seyersted, "Settlement of Internal Disputes of Intergovernmental Organisations by Internal and External Courts" (1964) ZaöRV 7; Osieke, "The Validity of Ultra Vires Decisions of International Organisations" (1983) 77 AJIL 240.

[5] [1962] I.C.J. Rep. 304.

[6] *ibid.*

[7] See Pollard, "Conflict Resolution in Producers' Associations" (1982) 31 ICLQ 119, *et seq.*

[8] See Report of Committee IV/2, Doc. 933, IV/2/24 (2) of June 12, 1945, in UNCIO, Vol. XIII, 719.

does not preclude the possibility of recourse to other means—in particular judicial means—by member states which maintain a different view from the organ itself. Notwithstanding their limitations, this element of political control allows for some control to be exercised. The constituent instruments of some organisations do provide for rather more formalised means of non-judicial interpretation. Thus, for the IBRD, the IMF and the EBRD any question concerning the interpretation of the constituent instrument is submitted to a decision of the Executive Directors, in which interested member states may raise their arguments.[9] This approach is relatively frequently used, and produces a binding result (so long as the decision is not tainted by an error of law).[10] This precludes recourse to other mechanisms for review, such as the advisory opinion before the I.C.J.

The constituent instruments of international organisations only rarely **13–007** provide for specific procedures which would permit member states to challenge the legality of institutional acts before judicial bodies. Those procedures which do exist are within the framework of the UN, and comprise one of three approaches: advisory, contentious or arbitral. The principal advisory function—addressed further below—is that provided by Article 96 of the UN Charter, recognising the right of the General Assembly or the Security Council, and other authorised bodies, to seek advisory opinions from the I.C.J.

The possibility of recourse to contentious procedures before the I.C.J. to **13–008** address constitutional questions of the UN and the specialised agencies is based upon two separate bases. One is dependent upon the constituent instruments of certain specialised agencies, the other upon the general mechanisms for the judicial settlement of international disputes. The fact that Article 34 of the Statute of the I.C.J. only permits states to be parties to contentious proceedings before the court excludes the possibility of the direct participation of the UN or other international organisations in cases; the question of legality can therefore only be raised in the context of a case brought by a state. The constituent instrument of several specialised agencies provide that disputes between members relating to the interpretation or application of certain acts may be submitted to the I.C.J. These include the ILO (Article 37), WHO (Article 75), UNESCO (Article XIV) and the IAEA (Article XVII). It is therefore theoretically possible that a member of one of these organisations could bring to the I.C.J. a dispute with one or more other members concerning the legality of the organisation's acts. No such case has yet been brought. The reasons for this are

---

[9] See, *e.g.* Art. IX of the IBRD Agreement, and "Decisions of the Executive Directors under Article IX of the Articles of Agreement on Questions of Interpretation of the Articles of Agreement" (IBRD, 1991).
[10] See Mann, "The 'Interpretation' of the Constitutions of the International Financial Organisations" (1968–69) B.Y.I.L. 17.

unclear. It may be that the limited scope of these acts is such that they rarely touch the fundamental political or economic interests of the members. Further, the acts of these bodies are often of a recommendatory and non-binding character. Finally, states are generally reluctant to engage in international litigation to resolve these matters, preferring to follow political or diplomatic solutions. Other organisations have analogous provisions. Recourse to judicial settlement (I.C.J. or arbitration) is provided by Article 84 of the ICAO Statute, permitting any member to bring a dispute with another member. The procedure has been used just once, leading the I.C.J. to reject an appeal based challenging a decision of the ICAO Council.[11] By contrast, judicial review at the instigation of a member state of an act of an institution of the European Community is not so rare, as described below.

13–009   A third route is for a member of a UN organisation to challenge the validity of an act adopted by one of its organs in the context of contentious proceedings before the I.C.J. Such challenge might be made as a principal cause of a case or as an incidental argument. Recent practice before the I.C.J. illustrates the latter aspect. In its order indicating provisional measures in the *Aerial Incident over Lockerbie* the court did not exclude the possibility that, if necessary, it might pronounce itself on the legality of decisions of the Security Council.[12] The court did not deem it necessary to proceed to challenge the legality of the act in that case. It considered it sufficient, at the provisional measures stage, to note that Article 103 of the Charter subordinated any rights which Libya might have by virtues of the 1971 Montreal Convention to any obligations which it might have under the UN Charter. The various views expressed by the judges, whether in the majority or dissenting, on the question of the powers of the court in this area nevertheless suggest that the exercise of judicial control by the court is far from being excluded.[13] As Judge Elihu Lauterpacht put it in his Separate Opinion in the *Application under the Genocide Convention* (*Bosnia v. FRY*):

> "That is not to say that the Security Council can act free of all legal controls but only that the court's power of judicial review is limited. That the court has some power of this kind can hardly be doubted,

---

[11] Appeal concerning the competence of the ICAO Council (*India v. Pakistan*), [1972] I.C.J. Reps 46.

[12] [1992] I.C.J. Rep. 1 and 113.

[13] See especially the dissenting opinion of Judge Lachs, at 27. On this aspect see Franck, "The Powers of Appreciation: Who is the Ultimate Guardian of UN Legality?" (1992) 86 AJIL 521; Alvarez, "Judging the Security Council" (1996) 90 AJIL 21; separate opinion of Judge Lauterpacht in [1993] I.C.J. Rep. 439. Other authors take a more reserved approach: see, *e.g.* Reisman, "The Constitutional Crisis in the UN" (1993) 87 AJIL 92; Herdegen, "The Constitutionalization of the UN Security System" (1994) 27 Vanderbilt. J. Transnat'l L 138. And others are altogether opposed to recognising such a power: McWhinney, "The International Court as the Emerging Constitutional Court and the Co-ordinate UN Institutions" (1992) 30 Can. Y.I.L.. 261.

though there can be no less doubt that it does not embrace any right of the court to substitute its discretion for that of the Security Council in determining the existence of a threat to the peace, a breach of the peace or an act of aggression, or the political steps to be taken following such a determination. But the court, as the principal judicial organ of the United Nations is entitled, indeed bound, to ensure the rule of law within the United Nations system and, in cases properly brought before it, to insist on adherence by all United Nations organs to the rules governing their operation."[14]

Contentious proceedings are available before other international courts **13–010** to address the legality of acts of international organisations. The approach is particularly well established at the ECJ (see *infra*). Other regional courts established in the context of arrangements for regional economic integration have similar powers,[15] as does the Sea-Bed Disputes Chamber in relation to acts of the International Sea-Bed Authority (see Article 187 UNCLOS).

Finally, it should be noted that the constituent instruments of certain **13–011** organisations provide for recourse to arbitration to address differences concerning the interpretation or application of that instrument. Examples include the WMO (Article 29) and the ICAO (Article 84 provides for recourse to the I.C.J. or to an arbitral tribunal). These procedures have not been used.

(d) SETTLEMENT OF DISPUTES BETWEEN THE ORGANISATION OR ITS MEMBERS AND THIRD PARTIES, INCLUDING INDIVIDUALS

Beyond the resolution of disputes between an organisation and its mem- **13–012** bers, there is increasingly the possibility for the international adjudication of disputes between organisations and third persons, in particular employees (or other functionaries), non-members, individuals, associations and private corporations. Each may find occasion to challenge the legality of the acts of an international organisation. With regard to personnel, administrative tribunals have been established within a large number of international organisations. These arrangements, addressed below, allow for recourse to proceedings of an administrative character, although in some cases procedures before administrative tribunals are also judicial. The model of the administrative review has recently been extended, in the

---

[14] [1993] I.C.J. Rep. 325. See also Lauterpacht, "Judicial Review of Acts of International Organisations" in Boisson de Chazournes and Sands (eds), *International law, the International Court of Justice and Nuclear Weapons* (1999), pp. 92–102.
[15] See, *e.g.* the Court of Justice of the Andean Community, the Central American Court of Justice and the Court of Justice of the Common Market for Eastern and Southern Africa.

context of the multilateral development banks, to allow persons affected by acts of these organisations to challenge their compliance with internal rules. The establishment of the World Bank Inspection Panel in 1993, described below, has led to other such bodies being created.

13–013 International judicial proceedings against international organisations initiated at the instigation of affected third persons remains limited. There is limited access to the European court of Justice for persons "directly and individually concerned" (non-privileged applicants), to challenge acts of E.C. institutions directly at the ECJ, as well as a power to challenge the validity or interpretation of community acts by way of reference from proceedings before national courts (see *infra*). And private contractors may, under limited conditions, challenge before the Sea-Bed Disputes Chamber a refusal of the International Sea-Bed Authority to grant them a contract for exploitation (see *infra*). But generally there is little possibility for judicial or arbitral challenge by private third persons of acts of the UN and its specialised agencies. Where acts of international organisations directly affect the rights of private persons—for example economic sanctions imposed by the Security Council—there is the possibility of these being reviewed by national courts, where these issues are most likely to arise, although they have only rarely found to be in illegal.[16] In this regard it is to be noted that a draft resolution of the Institut de Droit International, to the effect that "national courts shall [should] decide with full independence and without being influenced by national interests, upon the existence and validity of a resolution of an international organ" did not find favour with the members of the Institut and was not adopted.[17] Similar arguments could be raised where a dispute reaches an arbitration tribunal or the ECJ. In this regard, it is to be noted that the establishment by the Security Council of international criminal tribunals for former Yugoslavia (in 1993) and for Rwanda (in 1994) has also led to certain developments in relation to the control of legality of acts of the UN (including the Security Council itself). In the *Tadic* case the ICTY was called upon to address the validity of Security Council resolution 827 (1993), by which the Council had established the Tribunal, to address the arguments concerning the illegality of the Tribunal and its lack of competence. The matter was not addressed at first instance. However, the Appeal Chamber addressed the point in detail, noting that without wishing to claim the power to exercise the functions of "a constitutional tribunal, reviewing the acts of the other organs of the UN," it nevertheless had an ""incidental" jurisdiction" to consider the legality of its creation by the Council "solely for the purpose of ascertaining

---

[16] See Schreuer, "The Relevance of UN Decisions in Domestic Litigation" (1978) 27 ICLQ 8, and the case-law cited; Alvarez, *supra*. n. 13, 12, and the examples cited at n. 69.

[17] 1993 Ann.I.D.I, Vol. 65–I, 393 (draft resolution); 1994 Ann I.D.I., Vol. 65–II, 318 (final resolution).

its own "primary" jurisdiction over the case before it".[18] The reasoning is similar to that of the I.C.J. in a number of earlier decisions upon which the Appeal Chamber relied. The Chamber concluded that resolution 827 was valid. It recognised, subject to clear limits, that any judicial body has the power to determine, even if only as an incidental matter, on the validity of an institutional act which lies at the heart of the litigation.

(e) CONCLUSION

It can be seen that the possibility to challenge the legality of acts of international institutions varies widely, by reference to the different categories of persons active in a given legal order, and their degree of integration. The existence, and the utilisation, of specific mechanisms to address legality is most often conditioned by the extent of the powers of the organisation *vis-à-vis* each of these actors. In general, the more extensive these powers and the more complex the legal order, the greater are the needs to assure a high degree of judicial control of the legality of acts of institutions, and the better developed the arrangements. Political and diplomatic procedures predominate in the more general institutions performing a co-ordinating and essentially political role, whereas judicial bodies emerge in the context of institutions charged with promoting economic or other technical "integration." Outside the European Community the tendencies towards the "judicialisation" of international institutional law remains limited, notwithstanding recent developments. The close connection between civil servants and their employer institution explains the relatively extensive degree of institutional development established to address employment disputes. By contrast, private third persons continue to have a marginal role; even where they are granted access to adjudicatory bodies, it is under strict and limited conditions.

13–014

B. HISTORICAL BACKGROUND: THE EMERGENCE OF ARBITRATION AND JUDICIAL SETTLEMENT

(a) NEGOTIATION, CONSULTATION, GOOD OFFICES, MEDIATION, CONCILIATION, INQUIRY

International institutions have traditionally played an important role in seeking to assist in the resolution of disputes between members by non-judicial (or non-contentious) means. Many serve as independent fora under the auspices of which negotiations or consultations may take place. Recent examples include efforts to resolve disputes in Cyprus and Moldova,[19] as well as the numerous peacekeeping missions of the United Nations. In the

13–015

---

[18] (1996) 35 ILM. 32, 40.
[19] In 1993 the CSCE/OSCE sent a mission to Moldova to assist with negotiations on the status of the disputed Dneister region and the withdrawal of Russian troops based in the area.

Gabcikovo/Nagymaros case the International Court recognised the useful role which might be played in conducting bilateral negotiations by having recourse to "assistance and expertise of a third party" such as the European Communities.[20] The institution may play a more formal (and pro-active) role where it provides good offices or mediation. In some cases this may be expressly provided for in the constituent instrument of an organisation where the parties voluntarily agree, for example in the case of the WTO Dispute Settlement Understanding (Article 5).[21] In other cases good offices may be tendered without express provision, as for example happened at the instigation of the UN Secretary-General in the dispute between Argentina and the United Kingdom over the Falklands/Malvinas in 1982.[22] In the case of mediation the third person—it may be a state, international organisation or individual—is involved as an active participant in the interchange of proposals between the parties to a dispute, and may even offer informal proposals. A recent example is the role played by the E.C. and the UN in the Yugoslav conflict, in the period 1991–95.[23]

13–016 Beyond these techniques, there exists also conciliation (which provides for the third person to assume a more formal role, investigating the details underlying the dispute and making formal (but non-binding) proposals for the resolution of disputes) and inquiry (in which the third person generally seeks to resolve a dispute over a question of fact). Both techniques and their analogues date back, at least, as far as the 1899 and 1907 Hague Conventions, and have become increasingly institutionalised in recent years as an alternative to the contentious, adversarial techniques of arbitration and judicial settlement. This is reflected in particular arrangements established in the fields of human rights (including various regional commissions), trade (including WTO and NAFTA panels), the environment (including the non-compliance arrangements under various environmental agreements), and review of acts of certain multilateral development banks (including the World Bank Inspection Panel). These arrangements are described in more detail below.

13–017 The Council of the League of Nations, and now the Security Council of the United Nations, are themselves good examples of permanent conciliation commissions; admittedly they have (or had) other functions, and in relation to conciliation the League Council's jurisdiction was limited to disputes likely to lead to a rupture and the Security Council's to those "likely to endanger international peace and security." The defect of the Security Council's practice with regard to conciliation has been the

---

[20] [1997] I.C.J. Rep. 7, 76.
[21] See Merrills, *International Dispute Settlement* (3rd. ed., 1998), pp. 202–4.
[22] *ibid.*, at 28–9.
[23] *ibid.*, 30.

relatively little use made of its fact-finding powers. Fact-finding is a necessary stage of the process of conciliation and yet, in practice, the Council has used its fact-finding powers under Article 34 far more in relation to "peace-keeping" than peaceful settlement.[24] The UN has in the past considered ways in which to improve its machinery for fact-finding.[25]

Conciliation is also well-developed in the political organs of other **13–018** organisations and bodies. The Councils of NATO, the Arab League, the OAU and the OAS have all assumed this role. The OAU has established a Commission of Mediation, Conciliation and Arbitration[26] but in addition to this the OAU has undertaken conciliation in many disputes, including the Algerian/Moroccan dispute, in the Congo, in Nigeria and in Sierra Leone. The OAS has the most highly-developed practice of all, of which a special feature has been the Inter-American Peace Committee which has undertaken both fact-finding and conciliation. And other bodies specifically charged with conciliation functions in a more particular context include the International Joint Commission established by Canada and the United States in 1909.[27] As a general observation, it might in the past have been true that the immediate future held better hope for improvement of peaceful settlement via political organs—whether of the UN or of regional organisations—than it did for improvement of the more strictly legal techniques. That view, however, has been superceded by developments in the past two decades pointing to a broader acceptance of legal means of dispute resolution. In this regard, a threshold seems to have been crossed in 1982, with the arrangements adopted by the 1982 UN Convention on the Law of the Sea, auguring a greater commitment to compulsory jurisdiction and, to a lesser extent, the binding authority of decisions.

(b) ARBITRATION

The distinction between arbitration and judicial settlement lies in the **13–019** nature of the adjudicating body and not in the nature of the procedures: both provide for the settlement of disputes over the legal rights of the parties, on the basis of established law (unless the parties agree otherwise) and resulting in an award binding on the parties. The ILC has defined arbitration as "the procedure for the settlement of disputes between states by a binding award on the basis of law and as the result of an undertaking

---

[24] *International Disputes: the Legal Aspects* (1972), paras 18, 19.
[25] Secretary-General's Report on Methods of Fact-Finding (A/5694) and see G.A. res. 2326 (XXII) (1967) which encourages states to utilize the fact-finding facilities of international organisations and asks the Secretary-General to establish a register of experts for this purpose. This is minimal progress. What is needed is a more effective machinery available for use by the S.C. and G.A., preferably with a right of access to any state's territory.
[26] See Elias, "The Commission of Mediation, Conciliation and Arbitration of the OAU" (1964) 41 B.Y.B.I.L. 336.
[27] 1909 Boundary Waters Treaty, especially Arts VIII and IX.

voluntarily accepted."[28] With arbitration the initial undertaking to arbitrate, whether in the form of an ad hoc agreement or of a pre-existing general arbitration treaty, is essentially a *pactum de contrahendo*, an imperfect obligation which becomes effective only when the further stage of agreeing on the setting up of a tribunal and its terms of reference is completed. Hence, as Johnson has said "the constitution of the tribunal is, on the whole, the fundamental problem of arbitration, because without a tribunal there can be no arbitration and the failure of this particular method of settling international disputes is a total failure."[29] The problems inherent in the task of settling the composition of the tribunal afresh, for each new arbitration, do not need to be spelt out.[30] Moreover, the ideal of a "neutral" arbitral body was far from being realised as a necessary part of impartial adjudication. The idea of facilitating the solution of these problems by providing for the constitution of a tribunal in advance of particular disputes was given partial expression for the first time in the Permanent court of Arbitration, established by the 1899 and 1907 Hague Conventions. It is further developed in the 1965 ICSID Convention, which envisages the use of Conciliation Commissions and Arbitral Tribunals constituted from a Panel of arbitrators: its novelty lies in the institutionalised promotion of arbitration for disputes between states and individuals (see *infra*).

Permanent Court of Arbitration

Bibliography: Janis (ed.), *International Courts for the 21st Century* (1992); Griffith, "La Cour Permante d'Arbitrage (the Permanent Court of Arbitration at The Hague)" (1995) 69 *Australian L.J.* 434; Shifman, "The Revitalisation of the Permanent court of Arbitration" (1995) 23 Int'l J. Legal Info. 284.

13–020 The Hague Conventions of 1899 and 1907 established the Permanent Court of Arbitration, which continues to function today.[31] It is neither permanent nor a court, consisting essentially of a "panel" of arbitrators. Nevertheless, its establishment marked an important moment as the first standing international adjudicatory body. Each party to the Conventions can appoint four individuals of recognised competence in international law. If states parties to a dispute agree to go to arbitration (for there was no question of the Hague Conventions imposing compulsory arbitration) they are able to utilize this "panel" to compose their tribunal. By Article 45 of the 1907 Convention the parties could by agreement choose any number of arbitra-

---

[28] Report of the ILC concerning the Work of its Tenth Session, 1958, GAOR, Thirteenth Session, Suppl. No. 9 (A/3859).

[29] Johnson, "The Constitution of an Arbitral Tribunal" (1953) 30 B.Y.I.L. 152.

[30] For background see the 4th edition of this book. See also Merrills, *International Dispute Settlement* (3rd ed., 1998), Chapter 5; Collier and Lowe, *The Settlement of Disputes in International Law* (1999), 31–9.

[31] Convention for the Pacific Settlement of International Disputes (The Hague, July 29, 1899); Convention for the Pacific Settlement of International Disputes (The Hague, October 18, 1907).

tors from the panel, but in default of agreement each party would appoint two arbitrators, of whom one only could be its national or chosen from amongst the persons selected by it as members of the panel. These arbitrators would then choose an umpire, or, where their votes were evenly divided, a third state selected by the parties would choose him. Each party would choose a different state and these two states would then choose the umpire, or, failing agreement, would draw lots from amongst members of the panel not being those members appointed by the parties or nationals of the powers.[32] Thus, in the last resort, a tribunal could be constituted, including an independent "odd" member. This constituted a significant advance on the pre-existing ad hoc arrangement, but fell far short of a permanent tribunal in the accepted national or modern international sense. The only permanent organ was the International Bureau, the PCA's registry, which had custody of the archives, acted as intermediary for communications relating to the court and dealt with administrative questions. The Bureau remains subject to control by the Permanent Council consisting of the diplomatic envoys of the contracting Powers accredited to The Hague. The Conventions of 1899 and 1907 had other useful features. They established rules on and facilities for good offices and mediation and international commissions of inquiry,[33] which have been recently updated to expand its potential jurisdiction.[34] In relation to arbitration the Conventions not only provided for the "panel" of arbitrators but set out a code of rules of procedure for adoption by tribunals if the parties failed to adopt rules themselves by agreement and even provided a special summary procedure for arbitration.[35] Another ambitious (but apparently never used) provision is Article 53 of the 1907 Convention, which allows the Permanent Court to settle the agreement if the parties agreed. But these scarcely affected the institutional weaknesses of the system established with the Permanent court of Arbitration.

The proposal in 1907 for a Court of Arbitral Justice, a truly permanent **13–021** court, failed because no agreement could be reached on the method of selecting the judges, each state wishing to ensure that it had a judge of its own nationality on the court. The process of arbitration, quite apart from the desirability of a permanent judicial tribunal, remained a useful process to which improvements could be made. No doubt there will always remain a category of disputes which the parties may prefer to refer to arbitration

---

[32] See Art. 24 1899 Convention, Art. 45 1907 Convention.
[33] For good offices and mediation see Arts 2–8 of the 1899 and 1907 Conventions and for international commissions of inquiry see Arts 9–14 of the 1899 Convention and Arts 9–36 of the 1907 Convention.
[34] See Permanent Court of Arbitration Optional Rules for Fact-Finding Commissions of Inquiry, effective December 15, 1997, text available at: http://www.pca-cpa.org/inquiryenglish.htm.
[35] See Art. 86–90 1907 Convention.

by an ad hoc body based essentially on their own choice rather than an international court. The establishment of the Permanent Court of International Justice in 1920 did not lead to the abolition of the PCA; and the General Act for the Pacific Settlement of International Disputes of 1928[36] dealt in detail with arbitration. And the continued usefulness and growing importance of the arbitral process is reflected in the development of various model rules of arbitration,[37] such the Model Rules on Arbitral Procedure adopted by the International Law Commission in 1958,[38] the rules established under the auspices of the International Chamber of Commerce,[39] the UNCITRAL Rules,[40] and the rules established under the auspices of other bodies including the ILO, the UPU, UNESCO, WIPO and the various commodity agreements.[41]

(c) JUDICIAL SETTLEMENT

13–022 The continuing value of arbitration did not affect the desirability of a permanent judicial tribunal. In 1907 it was the selection of judges which constituted the main hindrance to agreement on the establishment of such a tribunal. This problem was first solved with the Convention for an International Prize court, which was adopted in 1907 but which never entered into force. It would have been a permanent court hearing appeals from the prize decisions of national courts, with 15 judges appointed for six-year terms. Eight states would have had an automatic right to appoint a member, other states' appointees would have sat according to a scheme of rotation. The problem of election of judges appeared less problematic when the number of states participating in any arrangement decreased. Thus, in 1907 five Central American states established a Central American Court of Justice, with each state having its own judge on the court; this court functioned until 1918, and during its brief history decided 10 cases.[42] By this stage states were moving in principle towards a permanent judicial body,[43] subject in particular to finding an acceptable system for the election of judges without resorting to the need for every state to have a judge on the court. The difficulty of electing the judges in a way acceptable to states acutely conscious of their "sovereign equality" was only removed with the establishment of the League of Nations, for the successful Root-Phillimore

---

[36] See now the Revised General Act, adopted by the General Assembly on April 28, 1949, substituting references to the I.C.J. and the UN organs for those to the P.C.I.J. and organs of the League. (G.A. res. 286 (III)).

[37] *The Flame Rekindles, New Hopes for International Arbitration* (Special issue of LJIL (1993).

[38] A/3859; G.A. res. 1262(XIII).

[39] Rules of Arbitration of the International Chamber of Commerce, in force as of January 1, 1998, available at http://www.iccwbo.org/court/english/arbitration/rules.asp.

[40] G.A. res. 31/98 (1976).

[41] See Schermers, pp. 655–9.

[42] See Howard, *The Local and General Context of the Central American Court of Justice* (1981).

[43] Note the Permanent International Joint Commission of 1909 established by U.S. and Canada to solve boundary problems and invested with judicial and quasi-judicial powers.

plan was able to utilize the League's own organs in the election process. This led to the first standing court of potentially global competence—the P.C.I.J.—which was followed by the International Court of Justice. Since 1945 there has been a significant expansion in the number of such bodies, as described below. Straddling these formal courts are arrangements providing for the quasi-judicial resolution of other matters, in particular in the fields of human rights, environment and other social matters.

C. JUDICIAL INSTITUTIONS OF GLOBAL COMPETENCE

Judicial or quasi-judicial bodies for the resolution of international disputes **13–023** are now well-established at the global and regional levels. This section describes the institutions of global competence, that is to say involving or potentially involving the participation of all states. Other institutions of potentially global reach, such as the World Bank Inspection Panel, are addressed in the subsequent sections of this Chapter.

(a) THE INTERNATIONAL COURT OF JUSTICE[44]

Bibliography: Fachiri, *The Permanent Court of International Justice: Its Contribution, Procedure and Work* (1925); Hudson, *The Permanent Court of International Justice, 1920–1942* (1943); Lauterpacht, *The Development of International Law by the International Court* (1958); Rosenne, *The Law and Practise of the I.C.J.* (2 vols., 1965); Rosenne, *Procedure in the International Court: a Commentary on the 1978 Rules of the I.C.J.* (1983); Fitzmaurice, *The Law and Procedure of the International Court of Justice* (1986); Jimenez de Arechega, "The Work and Jurisprudence of the I.C.J." (1987) 58 B.Y.I.L. 1; Damrosch, *The I.C.J. at a Crossroads* (1987); Rosenne, *The World Court: What It Is and How It Works* (1989); Elias, *UN Charter and the World Court* (1989); Thirlway, "The Law and Procedure of the I.C.J.: 1960–1989" (1989) 60 B.Y.I.L. 1, (1990) 61 B.Y.I.L. 1, (1992) 62 B.Y.I.L. 1, (1992) 63 B.Y.I.L. 1, (1993) 64 B.Y.I.L. 1; Rosenne, *Documents on the I.C.J.: first bilingual edition* (1991); Renata, *The Compulsory Jurisdiction of the International Court of Justice* (1993); Eyffinger, *The International Court of Justice, 1946–1996* (1996); Muller *et al*, *The International Court of Justice: Its Future Role After 50 years* (1997); Bowett (ed.), *The International Court of Justice: Process, Practice and Procedure* (1997); Evans, *Remedies in International Law: The Institutional Dilemma* (1998); Oduntan, *The Law and Practice of the International court of Justice (1945–1996): a Critique of the Contentious and Advisory Jurisdictions* (1999); Boisson de Chazournes and Sands, *International Law, the International Court of Justice and Nuclear Weapons* (1999).

Background: the P.C.I.J.

The I.C.J. finds its roots in Article 14 of the Covenant of the League of **13–024** Nations, which placed upon the Council of the League the duty to "formulate and submit to the Members of the League for adoption plans

---

[44] We shall not here be concerned with the substantive law evolved by either the Permanent Court or the I.C.J.: as to this see Lauterpacht, *The Development of International Law by the International Court* (1958); Hambro, *The Case-law of the International Court* (2 vols., 1952–60); *Fontes Juris Gentium*, Series A, Section I, Vol.1 (1922–30), Vol. 3 (1931–34).

for the establishment of a Permanent court of International Justice." The P.C.I.J. was established in 1922 and functioned until 1946. During that period it dealt with 29 contentious cases and gave 27 advisory opinions. Issues associated with the functioning of the P.C.I.J.—including parties and jurisdiction — are considered below in relation to the discussion of the I.C.J., where any salient changes between the two statutes are pointed out. It is appropriate to describe the process for the selection of judges, since this broke an international deadlock and established procedures which continue to be relevant to this day.

13–025   The League Council appointed an advisory committee of jurists, within which the Root-Phillimore plan emerged to address the crucial question of the election of judges. The plan, as embodied in the Statute of the Court, involved two stages—nomination and election—with the first being entrusted to the "national groups" in the PCA, which provided existing, acceptable bodies to make nominations. A state which wished to become a party to the Statute of the Court, but was not a member of the PCA, was required to establish a national group on the same conditions as those prescribed in Article 44 of the 1907 Convention (Article 4). Before proceeding to nomination each national group was to consult its highest courts, law faculties and national academies devoted to the study of international law (Article 6). Each national group was permitted to nominate up to four persons, no more than two of whom were to be of the nationality of the group (Article 5 (2)). From the list of nominees thus secured the Assembly and Council of the League would "proceed independently of one another to elect the members of the court" (Article 8), of which there were to be 15.[45] Any nominee securing an absolute majority in both organs was considered elected. If places remained unfilled further meetings would be held to secure an absolute majority in both organs. If places still remained unfilled, a joint conference of the organs (three members only from each organ) would attempt to choose one name for each vacancy by an absolute majority, and would recommend such names to both organs. If the joint conference failed to secure the necessary majority to agree on a nominee, then the members of the court already elected would proceed to fill the vacancies from among those candidates who obtained votes in either the Assembly or the Council. In the event of an equality of votes, the eldest judge had a casting vote.

13–026   This was the solution that made possible the first standing court of potentially global competence. It remains the system of election for the present I.C.J., subject to modest changes. The references to the Assembly and Council of the League have been changed to refer to the UN General

---

[45] Originally 11, with four deputy judges. Alteration was effected by resolution of the Assembly in 1930, although formal amendment came only in 1936.

Assembly and Security Council and, in the voting on elections within the Security Council, there is a specific provision to exclude the veto (Article 10(2)). Moreover Article 13 of the I.C.J.'s Statute embodies a scheme for "staggering" elections, so that five judges are elected every three years to serve a nine-year term, and any judge is capable of re-election. The system of "staggering" is intended to ensure continuity on the court. The three-yearly election is distinct from the occasional elections to fill vacancies caused by death or resignation.

The new court

The P.C.I.J. was replaced by the I.C.J. in 1946. It is the "principal judicial **13–027** organ" of the United Nations. Its governing rules are the UN Charter (Chapter XIV, Articles 92–96), its own Statute,[46] and the Rules of Procedure adopted by the judges and amended from time to time.[47] The Court's function is two-fold: to assist in the resolution of disputes between states, and to provide advisory opinions to specified international organisations on certain legal questions. The Court has no express task of providing for judicial review of the acts of international organisations, although this function is implicit in its advisory capacity and may be also be utilised in its contentious function.

(a) Composition

The system of election has been described above in broad terms. The UN **13–028** Secretary-General draws up a list of candidates nominated by national groups, and from this list the Assembly and Security Council elect judges, each on the basis of an absolute majority. Two criteria govern election. The first, in Article 2 of the Statute, is personal to the judges: they are to be persons "of high moral character, who possess the qualifications required in their respective countries for appointment to the highest judicial offices, or are jurisconsults of recognised competence in international law". The second, in Article 9 of the Statute, is that the body of judges as a whole should represent "the main forms of civilization and . . . the principal legal systems of the world." In practice election of the judges is based upon a degree of "equitable geographical distribution" which characterises the composition of most UN organs or bodies of limited composition. Whereas, with the ad hoc tribunal, the "representative" character of the judges was all too prominent, the essential aim of both the P.C.I.J. and the I.C.J. has been to secure a body of independent judges. Article 2 therefore provides for election "regardless of their nationality;" in practice the permanent members of the Security Council have always had a judge of their nationality on the Court, although they have no entitlement to this practice.

---

[46] June 26, 1945, Annex to UN Charter, XV UNCIO 355.
[47] Rules of Court, July 1, 1978.

This occurs notwithstanding the fact that four of the five permanent members have not accepted the compulsory jurisdiction of the Court. Consistently with the intent to disregard nationality in the election, a judge is not debarred from sitting on a particular contentious case to which the state of his nationality is a party. Yet, perhaps inconsistently, Article 31 of the Statute entitles the other party who does not have a judge of its nationality on the Court to nominate a judge ad hoc; and, if neither party has a judge of its nationality on the court, the Statute entitles both parties to nominate judges ad hoc. The political desirability of allowing the ad hoc judge as an inducement to states to use the court is one thing; but it is scarcely consistent with the notion of the court as an independent body and it is not without significance that despite the fact that ad hoc judges have been appointed in many of the court's contentious cases, only very rarely has an ad hoc judge voted against his or her own state.[48]

13–029   The independence of the judges is presumed to be reinforced by their security of tenure; they are elected for nine years, there is no retiring age and dismissal can be brought about only by the unanimous decision of the other members of the Court (Article 18). Moreover, judges are forbidden from exercising "any political or administrative function or engag[ing] in any other occupation of a professional nature" (Article 16).[49] Article 17 excludes from a particular case any judge who has acted in that case as agent or counsel or in some other capacity, and on this basis judges do from time to time recuse themselves.[50] This attempt to ensure independence means that the judges must be adequately paid as judges. They are paid a pensionable, tax-free salary and even ad hoc judges are paid out of the funds of the court and not by the parties (as was the practice in ad hoc tribunals). On the other hand, the view has been expressed that the system of re-election might indeed compromise independence, since any decision of a judge might tend to affect the likelihood of states to vote for him or her in the election proceedings at the General Assembly.

Access to the court

(a) Contentious Cases

13–030 By Article 34(1) of the Statute "only states may be parties in cases before the Court." The states which can appear are from one of three categories. The first includes all 189 UN members who, under Article 93(1) of the UN

---

[48] See Weiss, "Judicial Independence and Impartiality: a Preliminary Inquiry" in L. Damrosch (ed.), *The International Court of Justice at a Crossroads* (1987), pp. 123–154.

[49] This has not prevented the Court from allowing judges to engage in other judicial activities, including sitting as party-appointed arbitrators in ICSID and other arbitrations.

[50] Most recently this rule has operated to exclude Judge Higgins from two cases: the U.K. case against Libya concerning Questions of Interpretation of the 1971 Montreal Convention arising from the Aerial Incident at Lockerbie and Slovakia's application for an additional judgment in the *Gabcikovo-Nagymaros Case*.

Charter, are *ipso facto* parties to the Statute of the Court. The second includes non-UN members who desire a permanent association with the Court, and, under Article 93(2) become parties to the Statute on conditions to be determined in each case by the General Assembly on the recommendation of the Security Council. These conditions, imposed on Switzerland in 1947 and Liechtenstein in 1950 and voluntarily assumed by Nauru in 1989, involved acceptance of the Statute, of the obligations of UN members under Article 94 of the Charter, and of an undertaking to contribute an equitable amount to the expenses of the Court. The third category includes non-UN members who wish to appear before the court as parties in a particular dispute or class of disputes but without becoming parties to the Statute. This is possible under Article 35(2) of the Statute. By a 1946 resolution the Security Council imposed the conditions that such states should undertake to comply with the decision of the Court and accept the obligations of Article 94 of the Charter; the Court itself fixes the amount due towards the expenses of the particular case. The salient difference between the second and third categories is that, whilst the second can participate fully in the scheme for compulsory jurisdiction under Article 36(2) (the "Optional Clause", see *infra*)—the third category can sign the Optional Clause but cannot rely on it as against states who are parties to the Statute (*i.e.* in the first or second categories) unless they specifically agree.

It thus appears that international organisations have no *locus standi* as **13–031** parties in a contentious case before the Court.[51] This limitation assumes increasing importance as various international organisations (in particular the European Union) assume legal rights and responsibilities as members of other international institutions. The limitation does not apply in other fora, for example the WTO Panel and Appellate Body system or ITLOS, before which the E.U. may appear as a party even in contentious cases. We shall deal with the rights of international organisations to present information to the I.C.J. and to request advisory opinions from the Court at a later stage.

(b) Advisory jurisdiction

Article 65 of the Statute provides that the Court may give an advisory **13–032** opinion on any legal question at the request of whatever body may be authorised by or in accordance with the Charter of the United Nations to make such a request.[52] The constitutional significance of this procedure for

---

[51] But see the argument by Weissberg, *The International Status of the UN* (1961), p.195, that the UN may be regarded as a "State" for the purposes of Art. 34; the present authors do not accept this view.

[52] Contrast Art. 14 of the League Covenant which referred to opinions requested by the Assembly or the Council "upon any dispute or question."

the organs of the United Nations and the other intergovernmental organisations so authorised is addressed later. Suffice to point out at this stage that individual states cannot request an advisory opinion. Their rights are limited to furnishing information under Article 66 of the Statute.

Jurisdiction of the Court

13–033 The jurisdiction of the Court rests on the consent of the parties. As Article 36 (1) states, it comprises "all cases which the parties refer to it." Thus, as in traditional arbitration, a form of compromise might be agreed upon where jurisdiction rests essentially on an ad hoc agreement (for a recent example see the Agreement of Slovakia and Hungary in 1993).[53] However, this is not the only means of expressing consent to the Court's jurisdiction, since no special form is required. In the Corfu Channel Case a letter to the Registrar written by the Albanian Deputy Minister for Foreign Affairs was considered to be a sufficient expression of consent by Albania.[54]

13–034 In the Bahrain/Qatar dispute the Court ruled that exchanges of letters between the King of Saudi Arabia and the Amir of Qatar together with a document entitled "Minutes" and signed by the Ministers for Foreign Affairs of Bahrain, Qatar and Saudi Arabia, were international agreements creating rights and obligations for the Parties, including an undertaking to submit to the court the dispute between them.[55] Moreover, since nothing in the Statute requires consent to be given by both parties before an application to the Court can be made, it is possible for a prorogated jurisdiction to exist. In such a case the Court is seized with a unilateral application to which the other party pleads on the merits, without contesting the jurisdiction; this is treated as an acceptance of the jurisdiction, rather like an estoppel by conduct.[56] Consent can thus be express or tacit, and can be deduced from one act or a series of successive acts.[57]

13–035 Consent can be given in advance: Article 36(1) continues with the phrase ". . . and all matters specially provided for in the Charter of the United Nations or in treaties and conventions in force." The Charter contains no provision for an agreed jurisdiction; the power of the Security Council to recommend to members that they refer their legal disputes to the court (Article 36 (3)) was not regarded by the majority of the judges in the *Corfu Channel* case as involving an obligation on the parties to do so.[58] There are, however, many "treaties or conventions in force" which provide for

---

[53] (1993) 32 ILM 1294.
[54] Preliminary Objection [1948] I.C.J. Rep. 28.
[55] [1994] I.C.J. Rep. 112 at para. 25.
[56] See the *Minorities Schools Case*, P.C.I.J. Ser. A, No. 15.
[57] As in the *Monetary Gold Case* [1954] I.C.J. Rep. 19 so far as the U.K., USA, France and Italy were concerned.
[58] [1949] I.C.J. Rep. 4.

reference to the Court.[59] A primary purpose of the 1928 General Act was to establish the jurisdiction of the Permanent Court by this means.[60] Some of the specialised agencies have in their constitutions a "compromissory clause" to cover disputes between member states which is in effect a conferment of jurisdiction.[61] And other treaties, such as the 1982 UNCLOS, envisage a role for the I.C.J. alongside that of other institutions. The I.C.J. publishes annually in its Yearbook references to compromissory clauses in treaties in force. Special provision is made in Article 37 for the succession by the I.C.J. to jurisdiction conferred by pre-1945 treaties on the P.C.I.J.[62]

Lastly, jurisdiction may be accepted under Article 36(2), the "Optional **13–036** Clause", which provides that:

> "States parties to the present statute may at any time declare that they recognise as compulsory ipso facto and without special agreement, in relation to any other State accepting the same obligation, the jurisdiction of the court in all legal disputes concerning:
>
> (a) the interpretation of a treaty;
> (b) any question of international law;
> (c) the existence of any fact which, if established, would constitute a breach of an international obligation;
> (d) the nature or extent of the reparation to be made for the breach of an international obligation."

This provision marked the extent to which states were, in 1946, prepared **13–037** to accept compulsory jurisdiction: it is compulsory once it is voluntarily accepted. There is no obligation to make a declaration under Article 36(2). Currently some 62 states have made declarations, including just one permanent member of the Security Council (the United Kingdom). These declarations may be made for "a certain time" (Article 36(3)) and are often limited to a period of years. The extent to which they effectively confer compulsory jurisdiction is limited by three principal factors. First, the declarations are effective only "in relation to any other state accepting the same obligation" and, under Article 36(3), may be made "on condition of reciprocity." Hence, the subject-matter of the dispute must fall within the terms of the acceptances of both parties; either can rely on a reservation

---

[59] See 1994–1995, I.C.J.Y.B. 49, p. 46 *et seq.* for a recent list of treaties which provide for reference to the court. Note the reluctance of the court to allow a party to argue that such a treaty is void or terminated and its obligation to submit to the jurisdiction therefore ended: *Fisheries Jurisdiction case*, Judgment of February 2, 1973.

[60] See *Nuclear Tests cases*, [1973] I.C.J. Rep. 99 and 135.

[61] See for example Art. 26 of the ILO Constitution.

[62] Hence in the *S.W. Africa Case* [1950] I.C.J. Rep. 133, the Court noted that Art. 7 of the Mandate was still in force and South Africa therefore under an obligation to accept the compulsory jurisdiction of the I.C.J.

made by the other and impose a limitation on jurisdiction *ratione materiae*. Secondly, both declarations must be currently valid so that either party may rely on the other's limitation *ratione temporis*.[63] It will suffice, however, if both parties' declarations are valid and subsisting at the time of the application; the Court will not become disseised because of the expiry of a declaration during the proceedings.[64] The better view is that, once the declaration is made for a fixed period, it cannot be unilaterally terminated prior to the conclusion of the period, for this would undermine the whole purpose of the Optional Clause. This view was confirmed by the Court in *Military and Paramilitary Activities*.[65] A practice is being followed by some states whereby they make declarations terminable upon notice; if used to prevent a particular dispute from reaching the court, such declarations would make nonsense of the acceptance of compulsory jurisdiction and may well make the whole acceptance of doubtful validity. The third, and common, limitation arises from the appending of reservations to the declaration; these may exclude from the acceptance of compulsory jurisdiction a particular dispute or whole classes of disputes. The validity and effect of reservations has been the subject of some litigation before the Court. In the *Norwegian Loans Case*[66] and the *Interhandel Case* (1959)[67] several judges thought them invalid. Judge Lauterpacht believed them to be so fundamentally invalid that they rendered the entire acceptance of the Optional Clause invalid.[68] Other judges believed the invalid reservation could be severed from the remaining, valid acceptance, and the Court's Order of June 22, 1973 in the *Nuclear Tests* Case gives some support to this view.[69] In the *Nicaragua* Case the Court declined to deal with the effect of the United States' multilateral treaty reservation at the jurisdiction/admissibility stage (the reservation provided that the court would not have jurisdiction for disputes arising under a multilateral treaty unless "all parties affected by the decision are also parties to the case before the court"); at the merits stage the Court accepted that this reservation would take "full effect" if El Salvador, Honduras or Costa Rica were found to be "affected", and since El Salvador was so affected the Court could not entertain those claims relating to treaties to which El Salvador was a party.[70] In *Fisheries Jurisdiction* (*Spain v. Canada*) the Court accepted the effectiveness of Canada's reservation with respect to "conservation and management measures," despite its apparent breadth, holding that the intention of the reserving state may be deduced not only from the text of

---

[63] See the *Electricity Company of Sofia Case*, P.C.I.J. Ser. AIB, Nos. 77, 79, 80, where Bulgaria as defendant relied on the Belgian limitation *ratione temporis*.

[64] *Nottebohm case* [1953] I.C.J. Rep. 111.

[65] [1984] I.C.J. Rep. 392, 421.

[66] [1957] I.C.J. Rep. 9.

[67] [1959] I.C.J. Rep. 6.

[68] Id., at p.101.

[69] *Nuclear Tests cases*, 1973 I.C.J. Rep. 99 and 135.

[70] [1986] I.C.J. Rep. 3, 38.

the relevant clause but also from its context and an examination of the evidence regarding the circumstances of its preparation and purposes intended to be served.[71]

Article 36(5) provides for succession by the I.C.J. to jurisdiction con- **13–038** ferred upon the P.C.I.J. by declarations under the old Article 36(2), just as Article 37 provides for succession to the "conventional jurisdiction." It is only necessary to point out that where a state did not become a party to the Statute of the I.C.J. until some time after that Statute came into force its declaration under the old Statute will have lapsed with the extinction of the P.C.I.J. and will therefore not be a declaration "still in force" to which Article 36(5) applies.[72] In *Nicaragua v. United States* the Court accepted that a declaration made by Nicaragua in 1929 fell within Articles 36(2) and (5) of the Statute, interpreting Article 36(5) to cover declarations which had not acquired binding force at the time of the I.C.J. coming into being but which could so at a later time. The Court based its finding on the need to maintain the greatest possible continuity between the I.C.J. and its predecessor Court and the conduct of states and international organisations in consistently recognising Nicaragua as a state which had accepted the compulsory jurisdiction of the Court.[73]

Apart from the jurisdiction over the main issue, the Court has an **13–039** incidental jurisdiction to deal with three matters, by way of interlocutory proceedings. The first is the "preliminary objection." Where a party disputes the Court's jurisdiction, this is dealt with by the Court as incidental to the merits and without prejudice to the decision on the merits.[74] The second is an application to intervene. Under Article 63 of the Statute there is a right to intervene for a state party to a treaty the construction of which is in issue in a case. All other applications to intervene are decided at the discretion of the Court under Article 62 of the Statute. The Court must be satisfied that the state has an interest of a legal nature which may be affected by the decision. Successful applications to intervene had been few: for example, Malta's application to intervene in the Libyan/Tunisian dispute in 1981 was rejected because Malta failed to meet that test.[75] More

---

[71] [1998] I.C.J. Rep. (para. 49) NB. The judgment is reproduced on the I.C.J.'s website, *http://www.icj-cij.org*, but is yet to be published in the I.C.J. Rep. series. See also Aerial Incident case (*Pakistan v. India*), where the Court gave effect to an Indian reservation excluding the Court's jurisdiction over "disputes with the government of any State which is or has been a Member of the Commonwealth of Nations": [2000] I.C.J. Rep.

[72] Aerial Incident of July 27, 1955 (Preliminary Objection), [1959] I.C.J. Rep.

[73] [1984] I.C.J. Rep. 392

[74] See, for example, Request for an Examination of the Situation, *New Zealand v. France*, [1995] I.C.J. Rep. 288.

[75] [1981] I.C.J. Rep. 3; similarly applications to intervene were rejected in the *Nuclear Test* cases [1973] I.C.J. Rep. 320 and 324, *Continental Shelf (Tunisia/Libyan Arab Jamahiriya)* [1981] I.C.J. Rep. 3, and *Request for an Examinaton of the Situation in Accordance with Paragraph 63 of the Court's Judgment (2nd Nuclear Tests* case); cf. the case concerning the Land, Island and Maritime Frontier Dispute (El Salvador/Honduras) [1990] I.C.J. Rep. 92, where Nicaragua was successful in its application to intervene as regards any decision of the court on the legal regime of the waters of the Gulf of Fonseca.

recently there is some evidence that the Court has been willing to adopt a more flexible attitude.[76] It remains an open question whether, in addition, there must be a jurisdictional link between the actual parties and the would-be intervener.

13–040   The third type of interlocutory proceeding is the application for an order of interim measures of protection under Article 41 of the Statute. Here the jurisprudence shows that the Court's decision will depend, on a large part, on two, interrelated factors. One is the likelihood that the Court has jurisdiction on the merits, the other is the degree of urgency and risk of irreparable damage if an order of protection is not made. There must be prima facie evidence of a good basis for jurisdiction, and there must be a risk of real damage to a state's interests which any eventual judgment will not repair.[77] In recent years the Court has shown a greater willingness to indicate provisional measures and has even, on one occasion, done so where the situation of urgency (the imminent carrying out of a sentence of death) led it to dispense with hearings or even the right of the respondent state to file any written arguments.[78] The question of the legal effect of provisional measures indicated by the I.C.J.—unlike measures prescribed by ITLOS they are not expressed to be legally binding—remains an open question.

13–041   In the past much thought and discussion has been given to the problem of encouraging the use of the Court and extending its jurisdiction.[79] At the time of writing, however, the Court is busier than ever, and attention has turned to examining ways of speeding up the Court's work and increasing its budget. In the first 20 years after 1945, the Court gave just 13 judgments and 12 advisory opinions. The extraordinary decision in the *South West Africa* Case[80] did not enhance the reputation of the Court or give the confidence necessary to encourage its use by the newly independent nations. However, in 1972 the Court amended its rules to encourage states to make greater use of its jurisdiction. The recourse to Chambers of the Court was facilitated by conceding to the parties considerable influence over the composition of ad hoc Chambers, and this has led states to agree to the establishment of Chambers in three cases since then (although none are currently pending). The procedures for both contentious and advisory proceedings have been accelerated, although the Court is now under

---

[76] See *Cameroon v. Nigeria*, [1998] I.C.J. Rep. 275.

[77] See *e.g.* Passage through the Great Belt (*Finland v. Denmark*), [1991] I.C.J. Rep. 12. See also Mendelson, (1972–73) B.Y.B.I.L. 46, 259; Goldsworthy, (1974) 68 A.J.I.L. 68, 258 and subsequently the Order of September 11, 1976 (the *Aegean* Case) and December 15, 1979 (the *Hostages* Case).

[78] Lagrand (*Germany v. United States*), [1999] I.C.J. Rep 28.

[79] See, *e.g.* Jenks, *The Prospects for International Adjudication* (1964), providing a comprehensive account of early endeavors.

[80] *Supra.* Chap. 2, paras 2–083 and 2–084.

renewed pressure to speed up its work,[81] and indeed is taking steps to achieve that object. Further amendments to the Court's Statute were last introduced in 1978. Whether these changes have contributed to an increased use of the Court is unclear, but the 1980s saw a greater willingness of states, in particular developing states, to have recourse to the Court, which now has a docket exceeding 20 contentious cases.

Applicable law

This is set out in Article 38 of the Statute and constitutes a well-known **13–042** statement of the primary sources of international law.[82] The reference in Article 38(1) to "judicial decisions" as "subsidiary means for the determination of rules of law" is worthy of note in that, despite Article 59 which prevents any rigid doctrine of *stare decisis* from developing, it enables the Court to utilise the advantage of its own permanence by looking to its own previous decisions as evidence of what the law is. It is, of course, not limited to looking at its own decisions, but a certain consistency of special respect for them can be discerned in its judgments.[83] What the Court has not done is refer to judgments of other international courts, no doubt bearing in mind its position as the "principal judicial organ of the United Nations." Whether this approach is tenable over the long term, given the increased specialisation of various areas of international law, remains unclear. The power to decide *ex aequo et bono*, as provided by Article 38(2) of the Statute and which rests on the special agreement of the parties, whilst of theoretical interest, ought perhaps not to detain us here, for it is a power which has so far never been entrusted to the Court.

The institutional role of the Court

(a) Its relationship to the UN

Whereas the P.C.I.J. was, by its Statute, completely independent of the **13–043** League Covenant, the I.C.J. Statute is an "integral part" of the Charter and the I.C.J. is itself the "principal judicial organ of the United Nations"

---

[81] See Bowett, *et al.*, "The International Court of Justice: Efficiency of Procedures and Working Methods" (1996) 45 ICLQ 1.

[82] Art. 38 provides:
   1. The Court, whose function is to decide in accordance with international law such disputes as are submitted to it, shall apply:
      a. international conventions, whether general or particular, establishing rules expressly recognised by the contesting states;
      b. international custom, as evidence of a general practice accepted as law;
      c. the general principles of law recognised by civilised nations;
      d. subject to the provisions of Article 59, judicial decisions and the teachings of the most highly qualified publicists of the various nations, as subsidiary means for the determination of rules of law.

[83] Although it is not unknown for the court to alter position within a reasonably short period of time: see, *e.g. Nicaragua* (1986) and *Oil Platforms* (1996) on Treaties of Friendship.

(Article 92). Membership of the UN gives automatic participation in the Statute (Article 93(1)), unlike the League. Like the League, however, judicial settlement by the Court forms an essential part of the general procedures for settlement envisaged in the constitution of the general political organisation, without giving to any organ of the latter the power to impose compulsory judicial settlement.

13–044 The General Assembly and Security Council have assumed the same role in the election process as did the Assembly and Council of the League, and the Security Council has assumed a similar role to the League Council in respect of the enforcement of decisions given by the court. This power of enforcement, which is in all legal systems essentially one for the executive branch of government to wield in the last resort, rather than the judicial branch itself, is relevant to the effectiveness of the process for judicial settlement.[84] Under the Covenant the Council was empowered to "propose what steps should be taken to give effect" to the decisions of the Court (Article 13(4)). Under the Charter, Article 94(2) provides:

> "If any party to a case fails to perform the obligations incumbent upon it under a judgment rendered by the court, the other party may have recourse to the Security Council, which may, if it deems necessary, make recommendations or decide upon measures to be taken to give effect to the judgment."

13–045 This permits—but does not compel—the use, in the last resort, of the enforcement measures of Chapter VII. The essentially political factors which tend to stultify Chapter VII have already been noted; in this particular connection one has to add the historic reluctance of the former Soviet Union to utilise the Court (although this may have changed to some extent with the acceptance of the jurisdiction of the court in 1988 in relation to certain human rights instruments), and the more recent reluctance of the United States, and probable opposition to any attempt to use Article 94 in the way in which it was intended. That said, for the most part states have complied with decisions of the Court; the refusal of Albania to pay damages awarded in the *Corfu Channel* Case and of Iceland to comply with the judgment in the *Fisheries Jurisdiction* Cases are the exceptions, to which must be added Iran's refusal to comply with the Court's order for the release of the U.S. hostages and, more recently, in relation to provisional measures, the refusal of the United States to give effect to provisional measures orders adopted by unanimity calling on it to take all steps necessary to halt the execution of "death row" prisoners pending the

---

[84] See generally Schachter, "Enforcement of International Judicial and Arbitral Decisions" (1960) 54 AJIL 1; Reisman, "The Role of Economic Agencies in the Enforcement of International Judgments and Awards" (1965) 19 Int. Orgs. 929.

outcome of the merits stage of proceedings.[85] It must be noted, nevertheless, that institutional enforcement remains unlikely and a successful litigant will be left with such measures of self-help as are consistent with its obligations under the Charter, especially Article 2(4).

In budgetary matters the I.C.J.'s links with the UN are as close as the **13–046** P.C.I.J.'s were with the League. Article 33 of the Statute provides for the expenses of the court to be borne by the UN "in such a manner as shall be decided by the General Assembly." The court's budget is a part of the overall UN budget. The estimates are prepared by the Registry in close co-operation with the Secretary-General, leaving the Registry administratively free in its use of the monies once allocated. For non-UN members who are parties to the statute, the Assembly fixes an annual, percentage contribution acting under Article 93(2) of the Charter; the court itself fixes the amount due towards its expenses from states appearing before it under Article 35 (3) of the Statute.

The relationship between the court and the UN is close. The court is, **13–047** however, the "judicial organ," so that the relationship has been one in which the judicial independence of the court is recognised. Hence the court, alone of the principal organs, does not itself submit annual reports on its activities which then form the basis of discussion, and possibly criticism, within the General Assembly. Fears that this close relationship might prejudice the independence and integrity of the court are largely misplaced for this is to ignore the highly political role which the court plays,[86] and the role it has played in the constitutional development of the UN and specialised agencies. It is to this "constitutional" role, effected principally through its advisory function, that we now turn.

(b) Advisory opinions

No international organisation has *locus standi* before the court as a party in **13–048** a contentious case; this results directly from the "only states" provision in Article 34(1). The only participation in such cases envisaged for international organisations is that of presenting information relevant to cases before the court[87]—which international organisations may do as of right

---

[85] Vienna Convention on Consular Relations (*Paraguay v. United States of America*), [1998] I.C.J. Rep. 248 and Lagrand (*Germany v. United States*), [1999] I.C.J. Rep. 28. Discussion of enforcement of the Court's order for provisional measures in the *Anglo-Iranian Oil Case*, or of the A. O. on S.W. Africa does not directly concern Art. 94, since no "judgment" had been given. Refusal of states like Iceland, France, United States and Iran to even appear before the Court to defend cases is as disturbing as refusal to comply with a judgment, although this tendency appears to have been reversed more recently.

[86] This is the central thesis of Rosenne, *The Law and Practice of the International Court of Justice* (3rd ed., 1997); no better book on the court as an institution has yet been written and the extent of the present writers' indebtedness to it is readily and gratefully expressed.

[87] It was requested by the Court in the Advisory Opinions on Reservations, UN Administrative Tribunal and ILO Administrative Tribunal cases, but has never been used in a contentious case.

under Article 34(2)—and of being notified "whenever the construction of the constituent instrument (of the particular organisation) . . . or of an international convention adopted thereunder is in question in a case before the court" (Article 34(3)). Conversely, the advisory jurisdiction of the Court is available to organisations but not to states. In contrast to a judgment in a contentious case, however, an advisory opinion has of itself no binding force; it cannot create a *res judicata* and there are no parties in the strict sense. It is, therefore, a "weaker" statement of the law than a judgment, in formal legal terms; its moral and political authority and effectiveness is another matter, and the judges themselves have spoken of "all the moral consequences which are inherent in the dignity of the organ delivering the opinion,"[88] or "the legal position as ascertained by the court."[89] And the Court itself will refer back to an advisory opinion to identify the content of a legal rule.[90]

13–049   The right to request an advisory opinion is an original right under Article 96(1) of the Charter for the General Assembly and the Security Council.[91] It is a derivative right (in the sense of being conferred by the Assembly under Article 96(2)) to ECOSOC, the Trusteeship Council and the Interim Committee (and previously the Committee on Applications for Review of UN Administrative Tribunal Judgments)—all organs of the UN—and all the specialised agencies except the UPU (which has no power to request advisory opinions). With the Assembly and Security Council the advisory opinion may be requested "on any legal question;" hence, on occasions, doubts have been expressed over whether a given question was "legal" or "political," on the view that political questions were outside the jurisdiction of the Assembly to request and of the Court to grant.[92] The Court is never under a duty to give an opinion upon request, so that it could well refuse on grounds of propriety. In fact the Court has only once refused to accede to a request, namely that of the WHO Assembly concerning the legality of the use of nuclear weapons, to which we will return shortly. That decision

---

[88] Judge Azevedo in the AO on the Peace Treaties [1950] I.C.J. Rep. 80.

[89] Judge Lauterpacht in the AO on the South West Africa Committee, [1956] I.C.J. Rep. 47.

[90] *e.g. Gabcikovo/Nagymaros Case*, [1997] I.C.J. Rep. 7, 41 (recalling the significance it attaches to respect for the environment as stated in *Legality of the Threat or Use of Nuclear Weapons*, [1996] I.C.J. Rep. 241–42).

[91] The vote by which such a request can be made is not entirely clear; the S.C. has never made such a request, and, whilst the Assembly has, it is to be noted that as early as 1949 the President of the Assembly ruled that it was a procedural matter, G.A.O.R. (IV) Plenary, p. 536.

[92] See the doubts of Krylov and Zoricic in the AO on Admissions, [1948] I.C.J. Rep., similar objections were made in the Assembly in connection with the request on the *Reservations* Case. An excellent discussion of the problem is to be found in Rosenne, *op. cit.* pp. 454–68. The Court rejected this argument against its giving an opinion on Certain Expenses of the UN on July 20, 1962, [1962] I.C.J. Rep. 155; in its opinion on the interpretation of the W.H.O./Egypt Agreement, [1980] I.C.J. Rep. 1; and again in its opinion in *Legality of the Threat or Use of Nuclear Weapons*, [1996] I.C.J. Rep. 226.

confirmed that a refusal to give an opinion will not be based on the ground that the question at issue is a "political" one: the distinction between "legal" and "political" questions has many meanings and can hardly be used as a jurisdictional criterion. A more proper response for the Court is that the jurisdiction to make the decision requested has been allocated elsewhere (for example, to the Security Council or General Assembly) and is not reviewable by the Court.[93] It might also be argued that it is equally for the requesting organ to exercise propriety and that to involve the Court in an opinion when the issue has given rise to substantial disputes between member states affecting their own obligations, or when the political opposition to an opinion is likely to be so severe that the opinion will not be accepted by all the members, only harms the reputation of the Court and aggravates the difficulties of finding an eventual solution to the disputes. The unhappy experience of the Advisory Opinion on Certain Expenses lends support to this view. Equally, however, if both the requesting organ and the Court are satisfied on the propriety of giving an opinion, it would be harmful to the Court's reputation if the court declines to consider the "political" antecedents and implications of the issue before it. An opinion based on purely legal reasoning and abstracted from the political context in which it has been requested is unlikely to serve any useful purpose.

With the specialised agencies a fairly standard clause, adopted first in the **13–050** relationship agreement with the ILO, is to be found limiting much more rigidly the scope of opinions to be requested; the clause is "on legal questions arising within the scope of its activities other than questions concerning the mutual relationships of the organisation and the United Nations or the specialised agencies."[94] There is, finally, the limitation now firmly established in the jurisprudence of the court that an advisory opinion will not be given when in effect it would be tantamount to giving a decision on a dispute between parties, one of whom refuses to participate in the proceedings.[95] However, the effect of this limitation has to be considered in the light of the Court's opinions in the *Peace Treaties* case[96] and the *Namibia* case.[97] In the former the Court emphasised that its opinions are given to the requesting organ, not to the states, that they are not legally binding, and that the principle in the *Eastern Carelia* case would not apply where the opinion related to a purely procedural matter and not the substantive issue involved. In the latter case the Court found that there was

---

[93] See Greig, "The Advisory Jurisdiction of the I.C.J. and the Settlement of Disputes Between States" (1966) 15 ICLQ 325 and Higgins, "Policy Considerations and the International Judicial Process" (1968) 17 ICLQ 58 for valuable discussion of this point.
[94] Relationship Agreement, Art. 11.
[95] *The Eastern Carelia* case, P.C.I.J. Ser. B, No. 5, an opinion requested by the Council of the League.
[96] [1950] I.C.J. Rep. 121
[97] [1971] I.C.J. Rep. paras 30–35.

no dispute pending between states (as it was bound to do following its decision in 1966 rejecting the *locus standi* of Ethiopia and Liberia) and the Eastern Carelia principle could not therefore apply. The phrase used by the Court—that "the reply of the Court, itself an 'organ of the United Nations,' represents its participation in the activities of the organisation, and, in principle, should not be refused"[98]—suggests that refusal will come very reluctantly.

13–051 However, since there are limits to the jurisdiction to give opinions, and to the power to request them, a "preliminary question" of jurisdictional competence can arise. In practice there is no separate stage of the "preliminary objection;" the jurisdictional question is treated as part and parcel of the main opinion. In the nuclear weapons advisory opinions the Court refused the request of some states to treat jurisdictional questions by way of preliminary procedure. Similarly, there is no question of ad hoc judges being appointed.

13–052 Before turning to the typical constitutional problems on which opinions have been sought it is necessary to distinguish the so-called "compulsory" opinions from the normal advisory opinions. Lacking direct access to the Court as parties, organisations have resorted to a device whereby disagreements with states can, by a prior agreement which provides both for recourse to an advisory opinion and for the acceptance of the opinion as binding, be referred to the Court. The General Convention on Privileges and Immunities of 1946 and the Headquarters Agreement between the UN and the USA of 1947 both use this device, the former having been invoked in two cases[99] and the latter in one.[1] Needless to say, the binding force of the opinion derives from the prior agreement and not from the opinion as such.

13–053 This apart, the normal advisory opinion has been used for four main purposes. First, it has been used as a means of securing an authoritative interpretation of the Charter provisions, or of the provisions of the constitutional documents of the specialised agencies: the *Admissions and Competence* cases[2], the *IMCO* case,[3] or the *Certain Expenses* case,[4] are obvious examples. It must be added, however, that these interpretations are

---

[98] [1950] I.C.J. Rep. 71.
[99] Differences relating to immunity from legal process of a Special Rapporteur of the Commission of Human Rights, Advisory Opinion, April 29, 1999, [1999] I.C.J. Rep. 62.; Applicability of Article VI, section 22 of the Convention on the Privileges and Immunities of the UN, [1989] I.C.J. Rep. 177.
[1] Applicability of the Obligation to Arbitrate under section 21 of the UN Headquarters Agreement of June 26, 1947, [1988] I.C.J. Rep. 12.
[2] [1948] I.C.J. Rep. 57; [1950] I.C.J. Rep. 4.
[3] [1960] I.C.J. Rep. 150.
[4] [1962] I.C.J. Rep. 151.

"authoritative" and not strictly binding. The Charter has no specific provision regarding settlement of disputes over interpretation—no "compromissory clause" so-called—nor has the court been entrusted with any formal power of judicial review over the legality of the actions of the organs of the UN at the request of a member state (other than the former recourse from the UN Administrative Tribunal dealt with below). Nevertheless, this procedure amounts to a *de facto* form of judicial review, in a manner frequently incidental to the questions at hand. This was the case in the 1971 Namibia Advisory Opinion, where the court had to consider the arguments put forward by certain members that the General Assembly had exceeded its powers in adopting resolution 2145 (XXI), putting an end to South Africa's mandate over South-West Africa, which also raised questions about the validity of contested resolutions of the Security Council. The Court indicated that it was subject to certain limits in this regard, stating that:

> "Undoubtedly the court does not possess powers of judicial review or appeal in respect of the decisions taken by the United Nations organs concerned. The question of the validity or conformity with the Charter of General Assembly resolution 2145 (XXI) or of related Security Council resolutions does not form the subject of the request for an advisory opinion."

This reticence had earlier been reflected in the Certain Expenses Case **13–054** (para. 168). Nevertheless, the Court was not indifferent to the question of the validity of acts of the institution: its judicial function imposes clear tasks in this regard and explains why it verified, in its 1971 Opinion, the conformity of Security Council resolution 276 (1970) with the objects and purposes of the Charter before stating its views on the legal consequences of the resolution.[5] A similar approach informed the Court—without apparent hesitation—in its consideration of the request for an advisory opinion by the WHO in the legality of the use of nuclear weapons. Before addressing the request the Court sought to satisfy itself as to the competence of the WHO on the subject. It concluded that the WHO had no such competence, and that the WHO had failed to give effect to the principle of "speciality." It accordingly refused to answer the request.[6]

Secondly, it has been used to secure guidance for various organs in the **13–055** carrying out of their functions; the *Peace Treaties*,[7] *Reservations*,[8] *Reparations*,[9] *South West Africa (Voting)*,[10] *UN Administrative Tribunal*,[11] *ILO*

---

[5] [1971] I.C.J. Rep. 16, at para. 115.
[6] [1997] I.C.J. Rep. 84 (para. 31).
[7] [1950] I.C.J. Rep. 22.
[8] [1951] I.C.J. Rep. 15.
[9] [1949] I.C.J. Rep. 174.
[10] [1955] I.C.J. Rep. 67.
[11] [1954] I.C.J. Rep. 47.

Administrative Tribunal (UNESCO)[12] and the *Namibia*[13] cases are all opinions of this kind, as are the cases concerning *Mazilu*[14] and *Cumaraswamy.*[15] It is particularly in relation to these two purposes that the Secretary-General fulfils a role of *amicus curiae*, presenting information both by way of written statements and documentation and/or oral argument through counsel to the Court.

13–056   Thirdly, on one occasion the advisory function has been used to address a substantive legal question which, although having implications for the functioning of the organ concerned, was not primarily so concerned. The 1996 opinion given to the UN General Assembly on the legality of the threat or use of nuclear weapons examined the provisions of the Charter relating to the threat or use of force, the customary and conventional international law applicable in situations of armed conflict and international humanitarian law, concluding that the threat or use of nuclear weapons would generally be contrary to the rules of international law applicable in armed conflict and, in particular, the rules of humanitarian law.[16]

13–057   Fourthly, the advisory function has in the past been used as a means of introducing a form of recourse from judgments of administrative tribunals, although this type of proceeding has now been dispensed with (see *infra*).

(b) INTERNATIONAL CENTRE FOR THE SETTLEMENT OF INVESTMENT DISPUTES (ICSID)

Bibliography: Broches, "The Convention on the Settlement of Investment Disputes, Some Observations on Jurisdiction" (1966) 5 CJTL 263; Southland, "The World Bank Convention on the Settlement of Investment Disputes" (1979) 28 ICLQ 367; Muchlinski, "Dispute Settlement under the Washington Convention on the Settlement of Investment Disputes" in Butler (ed.), *Control over Compliance with International Law* (1991), p.175; Broches, "Observations on the Finality of ICSID Awards" (1991) 6 For. Inv. LJ 321; Reisman, "Repairing ICSID's Control System, Some Comments on Aron Broches' "Observations" (1992) 7 For. Inv. LJ 196; Schreuer, "Commentary on the ICSID Convention" (1997) 12 ICSID Rev. 59. Website: http://www.worldbank.org/icsid.

See generally also ICSID Review; decisions of ICSID tribunals are only made public with the consent of the parties involved. Such decisions are available in ICSID Reports published by the Research Centre for International Law of the University of Cambridge.

13–057a This institution was established by the 1965 Convention, which was sponsored by the World Bank, within whose institutional framework it is

---

[12] [1956] I.C.J. Rep. 77.
[13] [1971] I.C.J. Rep. 16.
[14] [1989] I.C.J. Rep. 177.
[15] [1999] I.C.J. Rep. 200.
[16] [1996] I.C.J. Rep. 288.

located.[17] The essential aim of ICSID is to foster private foreign investment by providing a mechanism for settlement of investment disputes, but without elevating such disputes to an inter-state confrontation. This necessarily means that the private investor is directly a party to the dispute with a state, litigating on the international plane, an approach drawing upon the earlier practice indicated above. We address ICSID here because it goes beyond these earlier efforts by establishing an institutional framework— with potentially global competence—for reviewing certain acts of states in their treatment of foreign investors.

The Centre does not itself settle disputes. Part of the World Bank group, **13–058** it has a fairly minimal structure of an Administrative Council (a plenary body, under the Chairmanship of the President of the World Bank) and a secretariat, overseen by the Secretary-General. However, the Centre maintains separate panels of conciliators and arbitrators, nominated by the contracting parties, and the secretariat facilitates the conduct of the proceedings. Settlement is by the conciliators and arbitrators, acting in their individual capacity. Consent to arbitration or conciliation—which is the basis of ICSID jurisdiction—must be in writing. It can be expressed in a contract, or in a compromise concluded after a dispute has arisen, or in national legislation, or even in separate submissions to the centre. Once given consent cannot be withdrawn unilaterally (Article 25). It can, however, be subject to qualifications or "reservations," such as requiring the prior exhaustion of domestic remedies. The parties to the dispute will be the state party to the 1965 Convention (or a subdivision or agency designated by the state) and the private investor, who must be a national (or a deemed national) of another contracting state, whether an individual or a corporate entity (Article 25(2)). Jurisdiction is limited to legal disputes "arising directly out of an investment" between the parties. The Centre does not have competence to address, directly at least, disputes between private investors and international institutions.

The process of settlement is initiated by a request filed with the **13–059** Secretary-General, who registers it unless he finds it to be "manifestly outside the jurisdiction of the Centre" (Article 36(3)). The request indicates whether conciliation or arbitration is required; to date arbitration has been the preferred option. In either event, the parties select the Conciliation Commission or Arbitration Tribunal, and are not confined to choosing persons from the two panels maintained by the Centre. However, they must have an odd number, and Article 39 of the Convention imposes restrictions on the number of nationals that may be chosen. The failure of the parties to agree on the choice of conciliators or arbitrators does not

---

[17] In force in 1966; 72 575 U.N.T.S. 159. As of March 2000, 149 states have signed the Convention and 131 have deposited instruments of ratification.

produce an impasse: it is the Chairman of ICSID's Administrative Council who then makes the appointment. Once constituted, the Commission or Tribunal applies the Rules of the Centre, unless the parties have agreed on other rules. They are each a judge of their own competence, and are not bound by the Secretary-General's view on receivability in registering the request. Their functions are those traditionally associated with conciliation and arbitration.

13–060   The function of the Conciliation Commission is to clarify the issues and attempt to bring about an agreement. Its recommendations are not binding on the parties. By contrast, the Arbitration Tribunal produces a binding award, applying rules of law as may be agreed between the parties, or, in the absence of such agreement, the law of the contracting state and any applicable rules of international law. The award is enforceable in the territory of the contracting states as if it were a final judgment of a court of the state (Article 54). By way of appeal, annulment of the award can be sought on limited grounds.[18] The nullity hearing is before an ad hoc committee of three new persons, nominated from the panel by the Chairman (Article 52). Article 64 provides for reference to the I.C.J. of any dispute between contracting states regarding the interpretation or application of the Convention, but this would not allow the I.C.J. to be used to challenge the validity of an award, or the appeal to an ad hoc committee for nullification of an award.

13–061   There are signs that ICSID is gaining in international acceptance. There are currently over 130 parties to the 1965 Convention, and within the past five years there has been a large increase in the number of cases being brought to it. The mechanisms it provides have been made available in relation to other international agreements, such as the European Energy Charter[19] and the NAFTA,[20] and its approach may be followed elsewhere.

(c) HUMAN RIGHTS COMMITTEE (AND OTHER GLOBAL HUMAN RIGHTS BODIES)

Bibliography: Annual Report of the HRC to the General Assembly of the UN (UN Doc. Supp. 40); Selected Decisions under the Optional Protocol (1985 -); Official Records of the Human Rights Committee (UN, 1993 -); Yearbook of the Human Rights Committee (1986 -).

Brar, "The Practice and Procedures of the Human Rights Committee under the Optional Protocol of the International Covenant on Civil and Political Rights" (1983) 26 Indian Journal of International Law 506; Ghandi, "The

---

[18] The grounds are: improper constitution of the tribunal, excess of power, corruption, a serious departure from a fundamental rule of procedure, and failure to give reasons.
[19] [1994] O.J. L380/24.
[20] (1993) 32 ILM 605.

Human Rights Committee and the Right of Individual Petition" (1987) 57 BYIL 201; Bossuyt, *Guide to the 'Travaux Preparatoires' of the International Covenant on Civil and Political Rights* (1987); Opsahl, "The Human Rights Committee" in Alston (ed.), *The UN and Human Rights: A Critical Appraisal* (1992), p. 369; Nowak, *A Commentary on the U.N. Covenant on Civil and Political Rights* (1993); McGoldrick, *The Human Rights Committee* (1994). Website: http://www.unhcr.Ch/html/menu2/6/hrc.htm.

The Human Rights Committee ("HRC") is an independent expert body, **13–062** located at the UN, established to monitor compliance with the 1966 International Covenant on Civil and Political Rights ("1966 Covenant").[21] It is entrusted with powers of supervision over the implementation of the covenant, which has been ratified by over 140 states. Though not a fully-fledged UN organ, the HRC has strong links to the UN: it reports to the General Assembly of the UN, conducts its sessions in UN facilities, is financed by the UN budget and receives administrative services from the UN Secretariat. Responsibility for administration of the HRC lies with the Secretary-General of the UN. The HRC has three functions: first, it receives periodical reports from the state parties to the covenant on their compliance with its human rights standards; secondly, it issues observations and general comments on the covenant;[22] and thirdly, under an Optional Protocol to the Covenant it may receive communications from individuals and states alleging violation of human rights by parties to the Covenant.[23] It is this last—essentially quasi-judicial—procedure with which we are concerned: the HRC admits evidence, receives submissions and makes its views available to the parties. Unlike a court, however, its views are not binding upon the state parties. Currently some 90 states have accepted the right of individual petition, and the HRC has received over 800 individual complaints. The Committee considered the communication on the merits and issued its views on some 300 cases, finding a breach of the ICCPR in over 220 cases. The rest of the communications have been found inadmissible, were discontinued or are still pending before the HRC. In short, no inter-state communication has ever been lodged with the HRC.

Composition

The HRC comprises 18 independent experts, who are nominated and **13–063** elected by the state parties for a renewable period of four years, and should be persons of high moral character having recognized competence in the

---

[21] International Covenant on Civil and Political Rights, December 16, 1966, Art. 28, UN G.A. res. 2200 A (XXI), GAOR, 21st Sess., Supp. No. 16 (A/6316) 52, reprinted in UN Doc. A/CONF. 32/4 [hereinafter "ICCPR"].

[22] Compilation of General Comments and General Recommendations Adopted by Human Rights Treaty Bodies, UN Doc. HRI/GEN/1/Rev.1 (1994)[General Comments 1–23]; General Comment 24 (52), UN Doc. CCPR/C/21/Rev.1/Add.6 (1994); General Comment 25 (57), UN Doc. CCPR/C/21/Rev.1/Add.7 (1996); General Comment 26 (61), http://www1.umn.edu/ humanrts/gencomm/hrcom26.htm.

[23] ICCPR, Art. 40; Optional Protocol to the International Covenant on Civil and Political Rights, UN G.A. res. 2200 A (XXI); GAOR, 21st Sess., Supp. No. 16 (A/6316) 59; 93 states have accepted the jurisdiction of the HRC to receive individual communications and 45 states have authorised the HRC to receive inter-state complaints.

area of human rights. The composition reflects equitable geographical distribution and represent the variety of forms of civilization and legal systems. In practice most—but by no means all—the members have legal backgrounds. The Committee sits in Plenary (a quorum of 12 members is required), but has subsidiary bodies to which parts of its functions are delegated. Thus, the admissibility of individual communications may be determined by a working group of five members.

Jurisdiction

13–064 The HRC receives communications against state parties that have accepted the jurisdiction of the Committee. Under the ICCPR and Optional Protocol, a separate declaration is required for each of the two heads of jurisdiction of the HRC. Individual communications may be brought only by individuals who are subject to the jurisdiction of the state complained against (this can be a non-national) and claim to be victim of a human rights violation under the covenant.[24] Communications can address any failure to fulfil the obligations of the covenant (in the case of an inter-state communication)[25]; or any violation of the rights enumerated in the covenant (in the case of individual communication) (Optional Protocol, Article 1). By way of limitation, the Committee can generally deal with any communication only after available domestic remedies have been exhausted. Other temporal conditions govern the admissibility of complaints depending on whether the communication was lodged by a state or an individual. According to its Rules of Procedure, in cases involving individual communications, the HRC may, at any time during the proceedings, recommend interim measures to prevent irreparable damage to the alleged victim (Article 86), which are not formally binding.

Admissibility

13–065 Before examining the merits of any communication, the HRC will consider the admissibility of the complaint. In inter-state cases, the Committee must have determined that both involved states made appropriate declarations under Article 41 of the ICCPR; that the six months time limit from the date of the initial communication has expired; and that domestic remedies have been exhausted, as required by international law, or that their application is unreasonably prolonged. The full Committee (or a working group) must confirm that (a) the communication is not anonymous and emanates from an individual (or individuals) subject to the jurisdiction of a state party to

---

[24] Optional Protocol, Arts 1–2. See A Group of Associations for the Defense of the Rights of Disabled and Handicapped Persons in *Group of Associations for the Defence of the Rights of Disabled and Handicapped Persons in Italy v. Italy*, Comm. No. 163/1984, GAOR, 39th Sess., Supp. No. 40 at 198 (holding that an NGO can bring a communication only if the organisation itself was a victim of a human rights violation).

[25] ICCPR, Art. 41(1).

the Optional Protocol; (b) the individual in question has sufficiently substantiated that he or she has been a victim of a violation by that state party of a human right prescribed by the Covenant; (c) the communication is not incompatible with the provisions of the Covenant; (d) the same matter is not the subject of another pending international procedure of investigation or settlement and (e) the individual exhausted all available domestic remedies, or the application of these remedies is unreasonably prolonged.[26]

In inter-state cases the Committee would usually prepare a report within 12 **13–066** months of the initial communication to it. If a friendly settlement has been reached, the report would describe the facts and the solution reached. If no solution was agreed, the report would state the facts of the case and will have attached to it the written and oral submissions of the parties. The Committee may then appoint a Conciliation Committee, with the agreement of the parties, to continue to deal with the dispute.[27] In individual complaints the HRC publishes its views after considering the communication on the matter.[28] The Committee's decisions are taken by a majority of the members, although, generally speaking, HRC's decisions are taken in practice by way of consensus. Members of the HRC may append to the views of the Committee their individual opinions.

Other global human rights bodies

The Committee on Elimination of Racial Discrimination ("CERD Com- **13–067** mittee") was established by the 1965 International Convention on the Elimination of All Forms of Racial Discrimination ("CERD").[29] It has operated since 1969, with the task of monitoring compliance by the 151 state parties with the provisions of CERD. Its administrative needs are provided for by the Secretary-General of the UN, and it comprises 18 independent experts elected by the state parties for four-year terms. It examines periodic reports of the state parties on the implementation of CERD and submits its general suggestions and recommendations to the UN General Assembly.[30] The Committee may also address complaints presented against state parties to CERD by other states, and in some cases, individuals or groups of individuals.[31] The complaint procedure involves quasi-judicial investigation of allegations of non-compliance with the Convention, leading to the preparation of a non-binding report by the Committee. By Article 11(1) any state party to CERD may bring a

---

[26] Optional Protocol, Art. 5(2), Rules of Procedure, rule 90.
[27] ICCPR, Art. 42; Rules of Procedure, rule 77E.
[28] Optional Protocol, art. 5(4); Rules of Procedure, rule 94(2).
[29] International Convention for Elimination of All Forms of Discrimination, December 21, 1965, UN G.A. Res. 2106A (XX), GAOR, 12th Sess., Supp. No. 14 (A/6014) 47, UN Doc. A/CONF. 32/4.
[30] CERD, Art. 9.
[31] CERD, Art. 11, 14.

complaint against any other state party, which has allegedly failed to give effect to the provisions of the Convention. So far no cases have been submitted to the CERD Committee by one state against another. Since 1982 the CERD Committee has been authorised to receive communications from individuals and groups of individuals who claim to be victims of a violation of CERD by a state party, to which jurisdiction they are subject.[32] However, complaints can only be filed against states that have accepted the competence of the Committee to receive individual communications. To date, 25 states have made declarations of acceptance, and the Committee has received eight individual communications. Of these, two were declared inadmissible, and two others are still pending. In three cases the Committee found a violation of CERD.

13–068   The Committee against Torture was established under the 1984 Convention against Torture and other Cruel, Inhuman or Degrading Treatment of Punishment, to which over 100 states are now party.[33] The Committee, which receives administrative support from the UN, monitors compliance by parties of their obligations under the Convention. It comprises 10 independent experts elected by the state parties for renewable four-year terms. As with other bodies of this kind, it considers periodic reports submitted by the parties on the measures taken by them to implement the Convention, and issues general comments thereon. Its remaining competence is divided into three areas. The Committee may investigate situations in respect to which information on systematic practice of torture has been received from reliable sources (Article 20). Under this procedure it may initiate an inquiry which may include, with the consent of the state concerned, a visit to the territory of the state concerned and hearings of witnesses and other individuals. Interestingly, states opt out of (rather than into) Article 20 (to date, ten state parties maintain such declarations). The Committee can receive inter-state complaints (under Article 21) alleging non-compliance with the Convention by one of the 40 or so parties accepting the jurisdiction of the Committee to investigate such complaints. So far there have been no inter-state cases before the Committee, and by Article 22 it may receive communications from individuals subject to the jurisdiction of one of the 39 parties that have accepted the competence of the Committee to receive individual complaints. Investigations under each of these heads involves the exercise of quasi-judicial powers by the Committee and the formulation of findings in the form of a non-binding report. So far, the Committee has dealt with 111 individual communications. In 23 of these cases the Committee submitted its views on the merits

---

[32] CERD, Art. 14(1). The Committee became competent to review individual communications immediately after 10 states declared their acceptance of this power of the Committee.

[33] Convention against Torture and Other Cruel, Inhuman or Degrading Treatment or Punishment, Dec. 10, 1984, G.A. Res. 39/46. 39 UN GAOR Supp. (No. 51), UN Doc. A/39/51, at 197 (1984), (1984) 23 ILM 1027.

(finding violation in 10 cases); 25 cases were found inadmissible; 13 cases discontinued and 49 cases are still pending.

ILO Representation and complaints procedure

As described earlier one of the ILO's functions is the adoption of **13–069** international labour standards by way of conventions (open to ratification by the member states) and non-binding instruments (recommendations, resolutions, declarations). To ensure compliance by member states with ILO standards, a number of supervisory procedures are relied upon, pursuant to Articles 24 and 26, as addressed in Chapter 12.[34]

(d) INTERNATIONAL TRIBUNAL ON THE LAW OF THE SEA

Bibliography: Report of the Preparatory Commission under Paragraph 10 of Resolution I Containing Recommendations for Submission to the Meeting of States Parties to be Convened in Accordance with Annex VI, Article 4, of the Convention Regarding Practical Arrangements for the Establishment of the International Tribunal for the Law of the Sea, Volumes I to IV (United Nations, document LOS/PCN/152, 1995); Rules of the International Tribunal for the Law of the Sea, adopted on October 28, 1997 (doc. ITLOS/8). Guidelines concerning the preparation and presentation of cases before the International Tribunal for the Law of the Sea, issued on October 28, 1997 (doc. ITLOS/9); Resolution on the internal judicial practice of the International Tribunal for the Law of the Sea, adopted on October 31, 1997 (doc. ITLOS/10).

Adede, *The System for Settlement of Disputes under the UNCLOS* (1987); Nordquist (ed.), *United Nations Convention on the Law of the Sea, 1982: a Commentary* (1995); Oda, "Dispute Settlement Prospects in the Law of the Sea"(1995) 44 ICLQ 863; Rosenne, "Establishing the International Tribunal for the Law of the Sea" (1995) 89 A.J.I.L. 806; Charney, "The Implications of Expanding International Dispute Settlement Systems: The 1982 Convention on the Law of the Sea" (1996) 90 A.J.I.L. 69; Treves, "The Proceedings Concerning Prompt Release of Vessels and Crews before the International Tribunal for the Law of the Sea" (1996) 11 International Journal for Marine and Coastal Law 197; Boyle, "Dispute Settlement and the Law of the Sea Convention: Problems of Fragmentation and Jurisdiction" (1997) 46 I.C.L.Q. 37; Treves, "The Jurisdiction of the International Tribunal for the Law of the Sea" (1997) 37 Indian Journal of International Law 396. Website: http://www.un.org/Depts/los/ITLOS/ITLOSHOME.htm.

The International Tribunal for the Law of the Sea ("ITLOS") is a **13–070** permanent international judicial body, established by the 1982 UN Convention on the Law of the Sea ("UNCLOS"). It became operational in August 1996, and is based in Hamburg, Germany. It forms an integral part of the regime established under Part XV of UNCLOS for the peaceful settlement of disputes concerning the interpretation or application of the Convention, a regime notable for the fact that it establishes a system of compulsory

---

[34] Chap. 12, paras. 12–064.

adjudication with limited jurisdiction over certain intergovernmental organisations and non-state actors. The parties to UNCLOS may elect, upon ratification, one or more dispute settlement mechanism from the four procedures enumerated in Article 287 of UNCLOS: I.C.J., ITLOS, general arbitration or special arbitration. If two states have selected the same procedure, it will apply in disputes between them. In the absence of agreement over the adjudication forum, a dispute is to go to arbitration. To date one matter—involving separate cases brought by Australia and New Zealand against Japan—has been submitted to arbitration under UNCLOS.[35] A separate Sea-Bed Disputes Chamber (SBDC) has exclusive and compulsory jurisdiction over disputes with respect to activities in the sea-bed area (in relation to Part XI of UNCLOS).[36]

13–071   ITLOS will primarily exercise jurisdiction over disputes between states that have selected it under Article 287 (to date, 14 states have chosen ITLOS). Additionally, however, ITLOS has compulsory jurisdiction over all states parties to UNCLOS for other specified cases, as described below. It may also receive cases on the basis of international agreements other than UNCLOS, as occurred with the *M/V Saiga* case.

Institutional aspects

13–072 ITLOS is to decide cases in accordance with the substantive provisions of UNCLOS and other rules of international law not incompatible with the Convention.[37] Like the I.C.J., if the parties agree the Tribunal can decide a case *ex aequo et bono.*[38] The SBDC, as well as applying the Convention and rules of international law, will apply the rules, regulations and procedures of the International Seabed Authority and the terms of contracts concerning activities in the Area in matters relating to those contracts.[39]

Organisation

13–073 The Tribunal has 21 judges, elected by the parties to UNCLOS from among persons enjoying the highest reputation for fairness and integrity and of recognised competence in the field of the law of the sea. The representation of the principal legal systems of the world and equitable geographical distribution is to be maintained, and no two judges may be nationals of the same state. Unlike the I.C.J. the permanent members of

---

[35] By its decision of August 4, 2000 the Arbitral Tribunal ruled that it had no jurisdiction: 39 ILM (2000). See ITLOS provisional measures order available at http://www.pict-pcti.org. An earlier case, the *M/V Saiga* (*St. Vincent and the Grenadines v. Guinea*) would have gone to arbitration save that the two parties agreed to refer the matter to ITLOS following the provisional measures phase.

[36] UNCLOS, Art. 186. The Chamber comprises 11 judges, elected by the body of ITLOS judges.

[37] UNCLOS, Art. 293(1); ITLOS Statute, Art. 23.

[38] UNCLOS, Art. 293(2).

[39] ITLOS Statute, Art. 38.

the Security Council have no "entitlement" to any seats, and as a result (in the view of the authors) the composition is drawn from a broader and more representative category of countries than that of the I.C.J. Judges will normally be elected for a renewable nine-year term; however, the terms of most of the judges elected at the first round election are shorter, in order to allow for staggered replacement of judges.[40] Every party to a dispute before ITLOS (or an ITLOS Chamber) is entitled to have a judge of its nationality on the bench. If there is no such judge, the concerned party may appoint a judge ad hoc (not necessarily of its nationality). Judges ad hoc will participate in a case on equal footing to the other judges.

ITLOS will normally hear cases in plenary (a quorum of 11 judges is **13–074** required). However, the Tribunal may form special Chambers, composed of three or more judges, for dealing with particular categories of disputes.[41] The Tribunal has established a Chamber for Fisheries Disputes and a Chamber for Marine Environment Disputes, and a Summary Procedure Chamber.[42] The Tribunal's Sea-bed Disputes Chamber has exclusive jurisdiction over disputes relating to activities in the sea-bed area (in pursuance with Part XI of UNCLOS).[43] The Sea-bed Disputes Chamber consists of 11 judges, elected by the body of judges of ITLOS, who serve for three years and are eligible for re-election. Its composition also reflects the principal legal systems and equitable geographical distribution. At the request of all parties to any case, a special ad hoc Chamber of ITLOS can be formed to deal with that particular dispute. The Tribunal is served by a Registry based in Hamburg.

Jurisdiction

The jurisdiction extends primarily to state parties to UNCLOS.[44] Any two **13–075** state parties may agree ad hoc, or through general declarations of acceptance under Article 287, to refer to ITLOS any dispute over the interpretation or application of UNCLOS.[45] In addition, ITLOS enjoys compulsory jurisdiction over all state parties to UNCLOS in three areas. First, in cases involving requests for "prompt release" of vessels and crews, ITLOS will exercise jurisdiction over any two state parties, if the parties to the dispute fail to agree upon an alternative forum (Article 292). An application for prompt release of vessel can be made by the flag state of the

---

[40] ITLOS Statute, Art. 4(4), 5(1). Seven of the first 21 judges will serve a three-year term, the other seven judges will serve a six-year term, and only seven judges will serve a full nine-year term.

[41] ITLOS Statute Art. 15(1); ITLOS Rules, Art. 29. As far as possible, special Chambers should be comprised of judges having special expertise in the subject matter entrusted to the Chamber.

[42] ITLOS Statute, Art. 15(3); ITLOS Rules, Art. 28.

[43] UNCLOS, Art. 186; ITLOS Statute, Art. 14, 35.

[44] ITLOS Statute, Art. 20(1).

[45] UNCLOS, Art. 287(1), (4).

detained vessel, or on its behalf. Two such cases have now been brought. Secondly, in disputes, which are to be referred to an arbitration tribunal, ITLOS (or SBDC in sea-bed area cases referred to arbitration) will have compulsory jurisdiction to hear requests for provisional measures, if the parties fail to agree upon an alternative forum (Article 290(5)). Thirdly, the SBDC (or, at the request of both parties, an ad hoc ITLOS Chamber) exercises compulsory jurisdiction over sea-bed area related disputes between state-parties to UNCLOS.[46] ITLOS is also open to state and non-state entities, which are parties to agreements, other than UNCLOS (but related to the purposes of that Convention), which confer jurisdiction to the Tribunal.[47] The jurisdiction of the SBDC is wider and, unlike the I.C.J., extends also to private persons. Its jurisdiction includes disputes between: states parties to UNCLOS; between a state party and the International Sea-Bed Authority; between parties to a contract governing activities in the sea-bed area (states, the Authority, state enterprises, or natural or juridical persons sponsored by a state party) and between the authority and prospective contractors (which are state enterprises or natural or juridical persons sponsored by a state party) (Article 187).

13–076   ITLOS jurisdiction generally extends to all disputes concerning the interpretation and application of UNCLOS (Article 288). However, certain disputes involving the rights and obligations of coastal states are excluded, including disputes over exercise of rights on the part of a coastal state pertaining to marine scientific research in the exclusive economic zone or continental shelf, and fisheries disputes involving the sovereign rights of the coastal states over the living resources of the exclusive economic zone (Article 297). Parties may also, upon ratification of UNCLOS, submit a declaration excluding from compulsory adjudication certain other categories of disputes (involving marine delimitation, military and law-enforcement activities and measures taken by the Security Council), although disputes so exempted can be referred to compulsory conciliation (Articles 297 and 298). ITLOS may also render advisory opinions on legal questions in pursuance with an international agreement, related to the purposes of UNCLOS, which confers such jurisdiction to ITLOS. Since there has not yet been any practice under the provision its scope is unclear. However, unlike the I.C.J., its advisory jurisdiction is limited to specified organisations, and is drafted so as to leave open the possibility that two (or more) states could agree to refer a request for an advisory opinion. The SBDC may also render advisory opinions.

Preliminary proceedings

13–077 ITLOS and its SBDC have the power to prescribe provisional measures to preserve the respective rights of the parties to a case or prevent serious harm to the marine environment pending the final outcome of the claim

---

[46] UNCLOS, Art. 187(1), 188(1)(a), 288(2).
[47] UNCLOS, Art. 288(2); ITLOS Statute, Art. 21.

(Article 290(1)). The Tribunal (or Chamber) must be satisfied that it has prima facie jurisdiction over the dispute and that the measures requested are appropriate under the circumstances. As indicated above, ITLOS and the SBDC also have jurisdiction to issue provisional measures in cases that are to be referred to arbitration, pending the constitution of an arbitral tribunal.[48] Unlike the I.C.J., provisional measures ordered by ITLOS are expressed to be legally binding.[49] So far the tribunal has on two occasions ordered provisional measures, latterly with the far-reaching effect of bringing to a halt an experimental scientific fishing programme by Japan in relation to southern blue-fin tuna.[50]

(e) DISPUTE SETTLEMENT BODY OF THE WORLD TRADE ORGANISATION

Bibliography: Adopted GATT Panel Reports are found in GATT Basic Instruments and Selected Documents Series (BISD). WTO Panel and AB Reports can be found in the WTO website and in a commercial publication titled- *The International Trade Law Reports* (1996–).

Pescatore, Davey and Lowenfeld, *Handbook of GATT Dispute Settlement* (1991); Hudec, *Enforcing International Trade Law: The Evolution of the Modern GATT Legal System* (1993); Canal-Forgues, *L'institution de la conciliation dans le cadre du GATT* (1993); Petersmann, "The Dispute Settlement System of the World Trade Organisation and the Evolution of the GATT Dispute Settlement System since 1948" (1994) 31 C.M.L.R. 1157; Lowenfeld, "Remedies Along with Rights: Institutional Reform in the New GATT" (1994) 88 AJIL 477; Jackson, *The World Trading System: Law and Policy of International Economic Relations* (2nd ed., 1997), p.107; Pescatore (ed.), *Handbook of WTO/GATT Dispute Settlement* (1997); Petersmann (ed.), *International Trade Law and the GATT/WTO Dispute Settlement System* (1997); Cameron and Campbell (eds), *Dispute Resolution in the World Trade Organisation* (1998).

The 1994 WTO Agreement introduced as an Annex the *Understanding on* **13–078** *Rules and Procedures Governing the Settlement of Disputes* (DSU). The DSU is intended to prevent and resolve disputes arising under the WTO Agreement and related instruments. It replaces the arrangements which had emerged in the context of the GATT, principally a system of panels with the power to make non-binding recommendations. Under the prior system, the adoption of panel recommendations could be blocked by any single contracting party. One of the principal innovations of the new WTO system is that panel decisions (as well as those of the Appellate Body) will be adopted and become legally binding unless these is a consensus to the contrary. The new WTO system therefore constitutes a system of compulsory third party adjudication with binding effects for its 135 or so

---

[48] UNCLOS, Art. 290(5).
[49] UNCLOS, Art. 290(6).
[50] See *Supra* n. 35.

members. In this sense it has the most far-reaching and important jurisdiction of any of the global bodies. Its first four years of operation suggest that it will exercise significant influence in the development of international trade law, and incidentally as a model of international adjudication.

13–079   The DSU establishes a dispute settlement system comprised of three bodies—the Dispute Settlement Body (DSB), ad hoc panels and the Appellate Body (AB)—all based in Geneva. The DSB is a political body, comprising representatives of all WTO members. It administers the dispute settlement process: supervises consultations between disputing members; establishes adjudicative panels on request of a party to a dispute; adopts or rejects panel or Appellate Body recommendations relating to the resolution of the dispute; and maintains surveillance over the implementation of the recommendation. It also has the power to authorise trade sanctions in the face of non-compliance with adopted panel or Appellate Body recommendations.

13–080   The WTO system establishes a detailed "road map" for inter-governmental dispute settlement, characterised by its speed and relative procedural clarity. In the event of a dispute between members of the WTO over their respective trade-related obligations, one party may request the other to enter into consultations and notify the DSB of this request (DSU, Article 4). If the consultations fail, each party may propose that other traditional dispute settlement procedures (good offices, conciliation or mediation) be employed, with the possible assistance of the WTO Director-General. If this fails to settle the dispute, the DSB may be asked to establish an ad hoc panel. Once established, a panel will conduct hearings and issue a non-binding report on the merits of the case. The recommendations of a panel become binding only after they have been adopted by the DSB (adoption is automatic, unless there is a consensus against it in the DSB). Unlike the old GATT system, the panel report may be appealed on legal grounds to a permanent seven-member Appellate Body. The Appellate Body constitutes a significant event in international trade law, and a reflection of the move towards the "judicialisation" of institutional arrangements in this area. The appeal is heard before a three-member division of the Appellate Body, which may uphold, modify or reverse the legal findings of the Panel. The report of the Appellate Body is then adopted by the DSB and given binding force, unless the DSB decides unanimously otherwise.

13–081   In its first three years of operation since 1995, when the WTO was created, some 141 requests for consultation were initiated before the DSB, involving over 100 distinct disputes. This compares to the 196 cases brought before the GATT procedures in its 45 years of existence. In 21 of the WTO cases where a panel was established, the DSB adopted a Panel or subsequent AB report; 15 cases are pending before panels at present and some three more cases are on appeal before the AB. In some of the other cases, no motion to establish a panel has yet been filled. It should be emphasised that the WTO system of dispute resolution encourages settlement agreements, even after the initiation of legal proceedings. Hence, in 26 of the 105 disputes brought before the DSB, a settlement was reached and the cases discontinued. It should be noted that the DSU specifically preserves the right of the parties to a dispute to agree to resolve their differences in the way of arbitration within the WTO (Article 25).

Institutional aspects

The WTO dispute settlement system is governed principally by Articles III **13–082** and IV of the WTO Agreement and the DSU. Working procedures have been adopted for panel proceedings and for Appellate Body,[51] as well as Rules of Conduct.[52] The substantive law to be applied by the Panels and the Appellate Body is to be found in the GATT 1994,[53] and in the various multilateral and plurilateral side-agreements to the GATT (the Multilateral Agreement on Trade in Services, General Agreement on Trade in Services and Agreement on Trade-Related Aspects of Intellectual Property Rights, Agreement on Trade in Civil Aircraft, Agreement on Government Procurement, International Dairy Agreement, International Bovine Meat Agreement).[54] At the first occasion the Appellate Body stated that these trade rules are "not to be read in clinical isolation from public international law",[55] and it has subsequently had occasion to refer to rules of general international law.

Composition

Panels normally comprise three persons (Article 8). The WTO Secretariat **13–083** proposes the nomination of panel members, normally on the basis of a roster maintained by the Secretariat (this comprises names put forward by the members and approved by the DSB). No nationals of the disputing parties may serve as a panel member, unless the parties agree otherwise. If the parties cannot agree on the composition of the panel within 20 days from the date of the DSB's decision to establish a panel, the Director-General of the WTO appoints a panel, after consulting. All administrative services are provided to the panels by the WTO Secretariat, which provides panels with assistance on the legal, historical and procedural aspects of each case.

---

[51] Working Procedures for Appellate Review (as amended), WTO Doc. WT/AB/WP/3, February 28, 1997 ("AB Working Procedures").

[52] Rules of Conduct for the Understanding on Rules and Procedures Governing the Settlement of Disputes, WTO Doc. WT/DSB/RC/1, December 11, 1996, ("Rules of Conduct").

[53] General Agreement on Tariffs and Trade, Geneva, October 30, 1947, as revised on April 15, 1994, (1994)33 ILM 28.

[54] DSU, Appendix 1.

[55] Case AB-1996–1, *U.S—Standards for Reformulated and Conventional Gasoline, Report of the Appellate Body*, April 29, 1996, at p. 18, WTO Doc. WT/DS2/9.

13–084 In contrast to the ad hoc nature of panel membership, the Appellate Body is a standing forum comprising seven members. They are elected by the DSB for a once-renewable four-year period. The Body members are independent experts with recognised authority in international trade law, and their composition is to be representative of the membership in the WTO. The first members of the AB took office in December 1995.

Jurisdiction

13–085 The compulsory jurisdiction of the WTO system encompasses all members of the WTO, comprising states and the European Communities. Non-members (including private entities, individuals and non-contracting states) do not have a right of standing before the WTO dispute-settlement institutions. Provided that all other conditions for jurisdiction are fulfilled, a member does not have to demonstrate a special legal interest in order to establish *locus standi* before the panel.[56] The subject-matter jurisdiction of the WTO dispute settlement mechanism includes all disputes between states arising under the WTO, the General Agreement on Trade in Services (GATS), the Agreement on Trade-Related Aspects of Intellectual Property Rights (TRIPS) and other side agreements to the GATT, as enumerated in Appendix I to the DSU.[57] The substantive conditions for initiation of proceedings are governed by Article XXIII of the GATT (to which all pertinent agreements refer). A member of the WTO may present a claim, if it shows that: (i) a benefit accruing to it under a relevant agreement to which it is a party has been nullified or impaired, or (ii) that the attainment of the object of that agreement is being impeded. These conditions do not have to be fulfilled in cases involving legal differences over the rights and obligations of the parties under the WTO Agreement and DSU themselves. Time limitations are imposed: the WTO dispute settlement mechanism only has jurisdiction over proceedings initiated at the DSB after the entry into force of the WTO Agreement (January 1, 1995). A distinguishing feature of the WTO system is the emphasis placed on strict time limits. These determine when proceedings may be brought, the timetable for their conduct before a panel and the appellate body, and the timetable for compliance (DSU, Articles 4 and 5).

13–086 The panel and AB do not have authority to issue provisional measures. However, when an urgent situation presents itself, the DSU provides for an even shorter period of consultations (30 days instead of 60 days), and for

---

[56] *EC—Regime for the Importation, Sale and Distribution of Bananas*, September 9, 1997 (WT/DS27/AB/R)(adopted), WL 577784.

[57] DSU Appendix 1. The other side agreements enumerated are the Agreement on Trade in Goods, Agreement on Trade in Civil Aircraft, Agreement on Government Procurement, International Dairy Arrangement, Arrangement on Bovine Meat. The applicability of the understanding to all these agreements (except the Agreement on Trade in Goods) is dependent upon a decision taken by the signatory parties to each agreement.

accelerated procedures. The panel is instructed in urgent case, including cases pertaining to perishable goods, to aim and complete its work within three months from the date of its constitution (instead of six months in normal cases). The panel and appellate body proceedings have a written and oral phase. As an intergovernmental system, the GATT arrangements do not allow private lawyers to participate in panel proceedings. However, the appellate body has ruled that, in exercise of their sovereign rights, in proceedings before the appellate body members are free to choose representatives as they see appropriate.[58] In practice the panels have now begun to exercise their discretion in favour of such participation. Further, any member having a substantial interest in a case pending before the panel has the right to join the proceedings as a third-party intervenor, after serving a notification to that effect to the DSB.

Enforcement

A distinct feature of the WTO system is the emphasis on compliance and enforcement, as described earlier.[59]

(f) WAR CRIMES TRIBUNALS AND THE PROPOSED INTERNATIONAL CRIMINAL COURT

Bibliography: Shraga and Zacklin, "The International Criminal Tribunal for the Former Yugoslavia" (1994) 5 EJIL 360; Pellet, "Le Tribunal Criminel International pour l'ex-Yugoslavie: poudre aux yeux ou avancée décisive?" (1994) RGDIP 7; Sunga, "The Commission of Experts on Rwanda and the Creation of the International Criminal Tribunal for Rwanda" (1995) 16 Human Rights Law Journal 121; Cherif Bassiouni, *The Law of the International Criminal Tribunal for the Former Yugoslavia* (1996); Lee, "The Rwanda Tribunal" (1996) 9 Leiden Journal of International Law 37; Jones, *The Practice of the International Criminal Tribunals for the Former Yugoslavia and Rwanda* (1998).

Rosenstock, "The Proposal for an International Criminal Court, McLean Lecture on World Law" (1994) 54 University of Pittsburg Law Review 271; Scharf, "Getting Serious About an International Criminal Court" (1994) 6 Pace International Law Review 103; Cherif Bassiouni, "From Versailles to Rwanda in 75 Years: The Need to Establish a Permanent International Criminal Court" (1997) 10 Harvard Human Rights Yearbook 11; Crawford, "A Permanent International Criminal Court: A Proposal that Overcomes Past Objections", (1995) 89 AJIL 404; C. Hall, "The First Two Sessions of the U.N. Preparatory Committee on the Establishment of an International Criminal Court" (1997) 91 AJIL 177. Websites: http://www.un.org/icty; http://www.ictr.org; http://www.un.org/law/icc.

The Statute of the International Criminal Court (ICC) was adopted in Rome **13–087** in July 1998, marking a new phase in the international community's commitment to international justice through international adjudicatory means.[60] The

---

[58] Bananas, Report of the Appellate Body *supra*.
[59] See Chap. 12, paras. 12–073.
[60] Statute of the International Criminal Court, (1999) 37 ILM 999 [hereafter "ICC Statute"].

adoption of the Rome Statute marks the culmination of efforts dating back to the Second World War, and the ad hoc Nuremberg and Tokyo war crimes tribunals. Subsequently, the idea of a permanent international criminal tribunal has been promoted from a wide range of non-governmental and governmental sources, and was given added impetus by the establishment by the UN Security Council of the ad hoc Yugoslavia and Rwanda international criminal tribunals and the draft statute prepared in 1994 by the International Law Commission. Negotiations for the statute commenced shortly thereafter, at around the same time that the Yugoslav and Rwanda war crimes tribunals were established, and which were not without their influence.

ICTY

13–088　　The International Tribunal for the Prosecution of Persons Responsible for Serious Violations of International Humanitarian Law Committed in the Territory of the Former Yugoslavia since 1991 (International Criminal Tribunal for the Former Yugoslavia, hereinafter: "the Tribunal" or "ICTY") is seated in The Hague, The Netherlands. It is an ad hoc international criminal tribunal, established to prosecute persons responsible for serious violations of international humanitarian law committed in the territory of the former Socialist Federal Republic of Yugoslavia after January 1, 1991. The tribunal was established by Security Council resolution 827, acting under Chapter VII of the UN Charter, as an enforcement measure. It exercises a jurisdiction limited to crimes set out in Articles 2–5 of its Statute (principally breaches of international humanitarian law), the violation of which entails individual criminal responsibility. Its jurisdiction is concurrent with but primary over that of national courts. The Tribunal's competence is limited to (a) grave breaches of the Geneva Conventions of August 12, 1949; (b) violations of the laws or customs of war; (c) genocide and (d) crimes against humanity. By Article 6, the tribunal has jurisdiction over natural persons accused with serious violations of international humanitarian law committed in the territory of the former Yugoslavia since 1991. The tribunal has no jurisdiction over states, legal persons and organisations. Since the mandate of the tribunal is based on a Security Council decision all states (including all the former belligerents) are bound by it and obliged to comply with the requests and decisions of the tribunal. In case of non-compliance the President of the tribunal may refer the matter to the Security Council.

13–089　　The prosecution of cases before the tribunal is the responsibility of an independent prosecutor, who investigates all matters falling within the jurisdiction of the ICTY and pursues the cases before the tribunal. The cases are dealt with by the Trial Chambers, whose decisions may, on limited grounds, be appealed to an Appeals Chamber. As a subsidiary organ of the

Security Council, the expenses of the ICTY are provided for by the regular budget of the United Nations. The tribunal comprises 14 judges, three judges serving in each Trial Chamber and five judges in the Appeals Chamber. They are elected for a renewable four-year term by the UN General Assembly from a list of candidates prepared by the Security Council from the nominees of the states.

ICTR

The International Criminal Tribunal for Rwanda has its seat in Arusha, **13–090** Tanzania. The Office of the Prosecutor (which is shared with the International Criminal Tribunal for the former Yugoslavia) is located in The Hague, with a Deputy Prosecutor based in Kigali, Rwanda. Like the Yugoslav Tribunal the ICTR is an ad hoc international criminal tribunal with a specific mandate to prosecute persons responsible for genocide and other serious violations of international humanitarian law committed in the course of or in relation to the 1994 Rwandan civil war. It is the first international tribunal having competence over crimes committed in an internal armed conflict. The tribunal was established by Security Council resolution 955, also under Chapter VII of the UN Charter, and is, in many respects, modelled on the ICTY with which it maintains close institutional links. The *ex officio* investigation and prosecution of matters falling within the jurisdiction of the ICTR is the responsibility of the prosecutor, assisted by a deputy prosecutor. The cases are heard by the Trial Chambers, whose decisions—subject to restrictions—may be challenged before the Appeals Chamber. The Appeals Chamber of the Yugoslavia tribunal also serves as Appeals Chamber for the ICTR. The substantive law applied by the tribunal is set forth in Articles 2 to 4 of its statute, and includes the rules of international humanitarian law the violation of which entails individual criminal responsibility. The Tribunal's competence is limited to the prosecution of (a) genocide, (b) crimes against humanity and (c) violations of Article 3 common to the Geneva Conventions and of Additional Protocol II. The temporal scope of the jurisdiction of the tribunal extends to the period of January 1 to December 31, 1994. The jurisdiction of the ICTR covers the entire territory of Rwanda as well as the territory of the neighbouring states in so far as crimes were committed outside Rwanda by Rwandan citizens in connection with the conflict. The tribunal comprises of 14 judges, three judges serving in each Trial Chamber and five judges in the Appeals Chamber. The election of, and the professional criteria for, judges are identical to those applying to the Yugoslavia Tribunal.

ICC

The ICC will be a permanent and independent court, to be located in The **13–091** Hague, entrusted with criminal jurisdiction over persons accused of committing one or more of the four categories of crimes enumerated in the statute: genocide, crimes against humanity, war crimes and aggression. The activities of the court will be "complementary" to national courts: the ICC will exercise its jurisdiction only when national courts are unable or unwilling to bring to justice a person accused of the crimes defined under the statute (Articles 1 and 17). Once a case is before the court, all state parties to the statute must co-operate with the investigation and prosecution.[61] The structure of the court generally follows the precedents of the two ad hoc UN criminal tribunals—the International Criminal Tribunal for the Former Yugoslavia and the International Criminal Tribunal for Rwanda.

13–092 A singular feature of the ICC is its independence from the states which establish it. The prosecution of cases before the court will fall under the responsibility of an independent Office of the Prosecutor. According to Article 32 this will be a separate organ of the court, headed by a prosecutor elected by the state parties. The prosecutor will receive cases on referrals from the state parties to the statute or from the Security Council; he or she may also initiate investigation on the basis of information received from other sources (Article 13). The prosecutor will investigate the criminal allegations and prosecute all cases before the court, and will be responsible for the management and administration of his or her office.

13–093 The role of state parties will be limited, through an Assembly of State Parties, to supervising the work of the ICC, but they will not be involved in the day-to-day activities of the court. The Assembly will review the administration of the court, approve its budget, receive reports on its operation and may decide to introduce changes in the structure and procedure of the court (*e.g.*, alter the number of judges or amend the rules of procedure and evidence).[62] A bureau (comprising 20 members of the Assembly, representing the legal and geographical diversity of the state parties, elected for a period of three years) will assist the Assembly in performing its functions. The Assembly may create other subsidiary bodies, as necessary.

13–094 Although independent, the court is expected to have strong links to the UN, to be set out in an agreement which will be concluded between the UN and the court (Article 2). The statute provides that the UN will participate in the funding of the court, together with the state parties, especially in relation to expenses incurred in cases initiated through referral by the Security Council.

Institutional aspects

13–095 The principal text governing the establishment, structure, jurisdiction and procedure of the ICC is the statute.[63] The court will also follow the Rules of Procedure and Evidence, to be adopted by the Assembly (by a vote of two-

---

[61] ICC Statute, Art. 86.
[62] ICC Statute, Arts 36(2), 51(2), 112 (2), (4).
[63] ICC Statute, *supra* n. 1.

thirds)[64] and the Regulations of the court (governing the routine operation of the court), which will be adopted by the court (and enter into force if the majority of state parties does not raise an objection.[65] The substantive law to be applied by the ICC will be the statute and an additional instrument on Elements of Crimes (specifying the interpretation and application to be given to the crimes that fall under the court's jurisdiction), yet to be adopted.[66] Other sources of law to be applied will be applicable treaties and rules of customary international law;[67] general principles of law accepted by municipal systems, including the state which has jurisdiction over the crime (*e.g.*, law of the *situs*);[68] and, to some extent, previous case law of the ICC.[69] In any event, norms applied by the ICC must be in conformity with internationally recognised human rights standards and must be of a non-discriminatory nature.[70]

Organisation

The ICC will comprise 18 judges, nominated and elected by the state parties for a term of nine years.[71] Unlike other international courts that term will be non-renewable. Judges will be persons of high moral character, impartiality and integrity who possess the qualifications required for appointment to the highest judicial office in their own countries. The particular character of the court is reflected in the requirements of Article 36 as to the expertise of the judges: at least nine of the judges must have established competence and experience in criminal law, and at least five must have competence and relevant experience in international humanitarian law and human rights law. The judges will be nationals of state parties, and no two judges can be nationals of the same state. The composition of the entire bench is to reflect equitable geographical distribution and represent the different legal systems of the world. Indicating a more modern tone, the statute also provides that adequate gender representation must also be taken into account in electing the judges. The judges will elect a president and first and second vice presidents for a once renewable three-year term. **13–096**

The ICC will be composed of three divisions: a pre-trial division, a trial division and an appeals division.[72] The pre-trial and trial divisions will each comprise six judges or more, and the appeals division will comprise five **13–097**

---

[64] ICC Statute, Art. 51.

[65] ICC Statute, Art. 52.

[66] ICC Statute, Art. 9, 21(1)(a). To the extent that they raise substantive law issues, the court will also apply the Rules of Procedure and Evidence.

[67] ICC Statute, Art. 21(1)(b).

[68] ICC Statute, Art. 21(1)(c).

[69] ICC Statute, Art. 21(2).

[70] ICC Statute, Art. 21(3).

[71] ICC Statute, Art. 36(1),(6),(9). At the first election, one third of the judges will serve three years, another third will serve six years and the remainder will serve nine years. Judges who serve three years will be eligible for re-election to a full term.

[72] ICC Statute, Art. 34(b).

judges (including the president). The court will deal with cases in Chambers. The appeals division will constitute a single Chamber; the trial division will sit in three-judge Chambers; and cases brought before the pre-trial division will be heard by a single judge or a three-judge Chamber.[73] Decisions of the pre-trial and the trial chamber may be appealed to an appeals chamber. Appeals may be brought by the Prosecutor or the defendant and, in some cases, by others involved in the proceedings (*e.g.* a state party investigating the same case, representatives of the victim). The appeals chamber may affirm, amend or reverse the original decision, order a new trial or send the case back on remand to the trial chamber.[74] The Registry will have responsibility for the administration and provision of secretarial services to the ICC.[75]

Jurisdiction

13–098 All cases before the court are to be brought by the Prosecutor, at his or her discretion.[76] A situation in which one or more crimes have been committed will be referred to the attention of the Prosecutor by a state party to the statute or by the Security Council, acting under Chapter VII of the UN Charter.[76] The Prosecutor will be able to initiate a case *proprio motu*, on the basis of information he or she receives on crimes within the jurisdiction of the court.[78]

13–099 Article 12 of the statute addresses the jurisdiction of the ICC over persons. It will have jurisdiction over persons accused of a crime under the Statute if one of two conditions are satisfied: either the state on which territory the crime was committed (or aboard a ship or aircraft registered under its name) is a party to the statute or has agreed to the jurisdiction of the court, or the state of nationality of the accused is a party to the statute or has agreed to the jurisdiction of the court. Exceptionally, the general rule on personal jurisdiction does not apply in cases which have been referred to the Prosecutor by the Security Council, acting under Chapter VII of the UN Charter. In this situation, a case can be brought against any person, regardless of his or her nationality or the place in which the alleged crimes were committed.

13–100 As to subject matter, the court will have jurisdiction over four categories of crimes: genocide, crimes against humanity, war crimes and the crime of aggression (Article 5), and only in cases of sufficient gravity.[79] By way of a

---

[73] ICC Statute, Art. 39(2).
[74] ICC Statute, Art. 83(1)-(3).
[75] ICC Statute, Art. 43(1).
[76] ICC Statute, Art. 53.
[76] ICC Statute, Art. 53.
[78] ICC Statute, Arts 13(c), 15(1).
[79] ICC Statute, Art. 17(1)(d).

declaration, a state party can exclude the jurisdiction of the court over war crimes committed by its nationals or in its territory. However, such a declaration can have effect for no more than seven years from the date in which the statute enters into force for that state.[80] The ICC will not have retroactive jurisdiction. It will generally only be able to deal with crimes committed after the entry into force of the statute, and it will not have jurisdiction over crimes committed in the territory of a state party, or by a national of a state party if the crimes took place before the entry into force of the statute for that state.

Provision is made to permit the Security Council to suspend the ICC's **13–101** exercise of jurisdiction for 12 months. Such a request must made through a resolution adopted under Chapter VII of the UN Charter, which means that any single permanent member could veto such a decision. Requests for suspension may be renewed.[81]

The ICC will have uncharacteristically extensive powers for an inter- **13–102** national organisation. For example, a Pre-Trial Chamber may order the arrest of a person, acting upon an application by the Prosecutor (Article 58 (1)). The Prosecutor may request the Pre-Trial Chamber to order measures necessary to take advantage of a unique opportunity to take testimony or statement from a witness, or to examine, collect or test evidence, which might not be available at the time of the trial.[82]

Decisions of the Trial Chamber on the merits of a case will be taken by a **13–103** majority vote. The decision cannot exceed the facts and circumstances alleged in the charges.[83] If the accused is convicted, the court will also consider the sentence to be imposed upon him or her. When deciding the sentence, the court will consider *inter alia* the gravity of the crime and the individual circumstances of the convicted person (including time already served for the same crime).[84] In addition, the court may decide, if requested, or acting *proprio motu* in exceptional circumstances, to order reparations to be made to the victims of the crimes. Such a decision will be taken after hearing the convicted person, representatives of the victims and other interested persons and states. The reparations will be collected from the convicted person, or where appropriate, from a special Trust Fund maintained by the Assembly.[85] This provides for a wholly novel approach in the law of international institutions. An appeal over a decision of the Trial Chamber on the guilt or non-guilt of the accused person can be brought by

---

[80] ICC Statute, Art. 124.
[81] ICC Statute, Art. 16.
[82] ICC Statute, Art. 56(1).
[83] ICC Statute, Art. 74(2).
[84] ICC Statute, Art. 78(1)-(2).
[85] ICC Statute, Arts 75(1)-(3), 79.

the Prosecutor or the convicted person (or the Prosecutor acting on that person's behalf). The appeal must allege (i) procedural error; (ii) error of fact; (iii) error of law; or (iv) any other ground that affects the fairness or reliability of the proceedings or decision.[86] Appeals will also lie in relation to sentencing (if it is disproportionate to the crime), and in respect of an order for reparations (Articles 81 and 82).

Enforcement of sentences

13–104 Any sentence of imprisonment will be served in the territory of a state designated by the court, which has volunteered to accept sentenced persons. If no state is designated, the sentence will be carried out in The Netherlands. The court may, however, transfer a convicted prisoner to any state other than that originally or subsequently designated (or the host state). The state in which the sentence of imprisonment is to be carried out is bound by the decision of the court and cannot modify the sentence, nor extradite the convict to a third state that wishes to prosecute or punish him or her (but with the court's approval).[87] The conditions of imprisonment must conform to the relevant international standards and will be supervised by the court. Fines and forfeitures ordered by the court will be recognised and enforced in the territory of the state parties in accordance to their laws, and without prejudice to the rights of bona fide third parties. The property forfeited, or, where appropriate, the proceeds of its sale (or the sale of other property of the convicted person of comparable value) will be transferred to the court.[88] After a person is convicted or acquitted by the ICC, he or she may not be tried again for the same conduct before another court or before the ICC itself.[89]

D. REGIONAL COURTS

(a) INTRODUCTION

13–105 Following the establishment of the I.C.J. there was a concerted effort to create permanent judicial institutions operating at a regional level. This may be easier task than on a universal basis, not least because it facilitates the problem of selecting the judges. In fact, regional bodies pre-dated global institutions: as already noted, the Central American Court of Justice was established by the 1907 Washington Convention,[90] before the advent of the League made the P.C.I.J. possible.

13–106 Subsequent developments have been uneven across the regions. Europe has the most developed system, in terms of the number of bodies and the extent of participation. The main courts are European Court of Human

---

[86] ICC Statute, Art. 81(1).
[87] ICC Statute, Arts 105, 108.
[88] ICC Statute, Art. 109.
[89] ICC Statute, Art. 20(1)-(2).
[90] For text of Convention see (1908) AJIL Suppl. 231.

Rights, established under the auspices of the Council of Europe in 1950 and the European Court of Justice, established in the framework of the European Economic Community in 1957. Both are described in some detail below. But they are not alone. The Council of Europe Assembly's proposal of 1951 for the establishment of a European Court of Justice was never taken forward, but other bodies were established, including the Tribunal of International Composition in the Saar (1956), the Tribunal of the OECD Nuclear Energy Agency (1957), the WEU Tribunal (1957), the Benelux Court of Justice (1965), the European Tribunal on State Immunity (1972)[91] and, more recently, the EFTA Court of Justice (1994).[92] Political changes in Central and Eastern Europe and the eruption of the conflict in the Balkans spurned other European developments in the field of arbitration and conciliation, including the Arbitration Commission in the context of the European Conference for Peace in Yugoslavia (the "Badinter Commission"),[93] the OSCE Mechanism[94] and the proposal for a European Court for Conciliation and Arbitration.[95]

Apart from the 1907 court and its successor, the Americas and the **13–107** Caribbean have seen relatively fewer bodies established. In 1979 the Andean Pact established its own Court of Justice, to function within that Pact rather like the court of the European Communities.[96] In 1980 the OAS established an Inter-American court of Human Rights, described below. And in 1994 Canada, Mexico and the United States established a more sophisticated dispute settlement mechanism to address disputes under the NAFTA, which may expand regionally as more countries join, also described below. Currently a group of Caribbean states are in the process of establishing a Caribbean court of Justice, which would have jurisdiction as a court of criminal appeal to replace the Privy Council.

It may be noted that the Arab League has also promoted the study of the **13–108** question of establishing an Arab court of Justice, and a commission prepared a draft statute in 1950;[97] there, too, no further progress by the member states of the League is apparent. In 1978 the Organisation of Arab Petroleum Exporting Countries established a Judicial Tribunal, which came into operation in 1980.[98–99]And the organisation of the Islamic Conference has proposed the creation of an Islamic International court of Justice.

---

[91] (1972) 11 ILM 470.

[92] [1994] O.J. L 278.

[93] Pellet, (1991) 37 AFDI 329; (1992) 38 AFDI 220; (1993) 39 AFDI 286.

[94] Convention on Conciliation and Arbitration with the CSCE, Annex 2, Decision on Peaceful Settlement of Disputes, Conference of Security and Cooperation in Europe, Stockholm, Dec. 1992.

[95] See Condorelli, "En attendant la 'Cour de conciliation et d'arbitrage de la CSCE': quelques remarques sur le droit applicable, in Dominice (et al.), Etudes de droit international en l'honneur de Pierre Lalive (1993) p. 457.

[96] Id., Art. 1.

[97] Foda, The Projected Arab Court of Justice (1957).

[98–99] (1968) 7 ILM **968**, Schermers, 638; See Protocol Establishing the Judicial Tribunal of the Organisation of Arba Petroleum-Exporting Countries, concluded in Kuwait, May 9, 1978.

13–109   In Africa the OAU had introduced its own regional machinery for settlement of disputes in the form of the Commission of Mediation, Conciliation and Arbitration, but this did not function and was replaced in 1993 by a new mechanism.[1] Similarly, one has yet to see whether the tribunals established within the economic communities of West Africa (ECOWAS) and East Africa (ECEA), including the Common Market Tribunal of the East African Community (1967),[2] the court of Appeal for East Africa[3] and the more recent court of Justice of the Common Market for Eastern and Southern Africa (1993)[4] will function effectively.

(b) REGIONAL HUMAN RIGHTS COURTS AND OTHER BODIES

(i) European Court of Human Rights

Bibliography: van Dijk and van Hoof, *Theory and Practice of the European Convention on Human Rights* (2nd ed., 1990); Beddard, *Human Rights and Europe* (3rd ed., 1993); Zwart, *The Admissibility of Human Rights Petitions: the Case Law of the European Commission of Human Rights and the Human Rights Committee* (1994); Clements, *European Human Rights—Taking a Case under the Convention* (1994); Harris, O'Boyle and Warbrick, *Law of the European Convention on Human Rights* (1995); Jacobs and White, *The European Convention on Human Rights* (2nd ed., 1996). Website: http://www.cchr.coe.int.

13–110   The European Court of Human Rights is a permanent court entrusted with monitoring compliance of European states with their obligations under the European Convention on Human Rights. It was established in 1950, operates within the organisational framework of the Council of Europe, and is located in Strasbourg. It is wholly independent from, and should not be confused with, the European Court of Justice in Luxembourg. In November 1998 new arrangements for the Court came into effect, replacing the institutional structure first established in 1950.

13–111   The 1950 Convention for the Protection of Human Rights and Fundamental Freedoms (ECHR)[5] was concluded under the auspices of the Council of Europe and is considered to be one of its principal achievements. The ECHR contains an enumeration of rights and freedoms derived in part from the 1948 UN Universal Declaration of Human Rights. In contrast to the purely moral value of that Declaration (at that time at least),

---

[1] See Chap. 10, para. 10–013. See also Elias, "The Commission of Mediation, Conciliation and Arbitration of the OAU" (1964) 41 B.Y.B.I.L. 336
[2] Schermers 639 (inactive).
[3] Schermers 640 (inactive).
[4] (1994) 33 ILM 1067 (not yet in force), Schermers, 641.
[5] November 4, 1950, [1950] ETS 5; 213 U.N.T.S. 221, as amended by Protocol No. 11, May 11, 1994, [1994] ETS 155 "EHR Convention"].

the Convention establishes binding obligations (to which, admittedly, certain reservations are permitted). Article 1 of the Convention provides that the parties "shall secure to everyone within their jurisdiction the rights and freedoms defined in section I of this Convention". Hence, by way of a radical departure from the traditional refusal of international law to concern itself with the relations between a state and its own nationals,[6] the Convention and its Protocols govern the relations between a state and all persons within its jurisdiction so far as they fall within the scope of the Convention.[7] Since 1950 11 Protocols have been adopted, some dealing with substantive matters and others establishing further rights to be protected.[8] As at March 2000 there are 41 parties to the Convention. Some of the parties have expressly incorporated the Convention into their municipal law so that the rights secured to individuals thereby become directly enforceable as part of municipal law.[9] It is, however, with the machinery for the supervision and enforcement of this far-reaching obligation assumed by the parties that we are here immediately concerned.

From 1950 to 1998 that machinery consisted of two organs, a Commis- **13–112** sion and a Court. In 1994 a Protocol to the Convention was adopted which fused the two bodies into a single institution. Under the original system, a petition alleging violation of the Convention had to be brought before the Commission, which would examine the admissibility of the petition, attempt to find an amicable settlement and bring the matter, if necessary, to the Court on behalf of the complainant. The Court could also receive inter-state cases, but only after the Commission had dealt with the matter. Following the entry into force in November 1998 of the 11th Protocol to the Convention, the Commission was abolished (although it continues to address those matters which it had declared admissible prior to April 1998) and most of its functions transferred to the Court. As a result, claimants (whether state parties or individuals) now submit applications directly to the Court. Unlike the Court, the function of the Commission was essentially one of the conciliation; hence the fact that it sat in private.

---

[6] There have been occasional exceptions: e.g. the Minorities Treaties concluded after the First World War, or the recognition of "crimes against humanity" in Art. 6 of the Charter of the Nuremberg Tribunal, or the Genocide Convention of 1948.

[7] For a consideration of questions relating to the court's jurisdiction see *Loizidou v. Turkey* (1996) ECHR Reps VI.

[8] A list of the Protocols is maintained on the court's website, see http://www.coe.fr/eng/legaltxt/e-dh.html#conv-dh.

[9] F.R. of Germany, Belgium, Italy, Luxembourg, Netherlands, Greece and Turkey; but not Denmark, Ireland, Norway, Sweden or the U.K. (Greece was in the former category but in 1969 denounced the Convention and withdrew from the Council of Europe, rejoining in 1974). The Human Rights Act 1998 incorporates the Convention into English law with effect from October 2000.

13–113   The Court first became operational in September 1958. It deals with complaints by states parties and individuals concerning the protection of human rights. The principal text governing the operation of the Court is the ECHR, as amended by the 11th Protocol. The ECHR establishes the Court and determines its composition, jurisdiction and the general contours of its procedure, which are further elaborated in the Rules of Court adopted in November 1998.[10] In addition, an agreement has been concluded on the treatment to be accorded by states to persons participating in proceedings before the Court, designed to guarantee to such persons certain immunities and facilitate their access to the Court.[11] The substantive law applied by EHR Court is the rights and freedoms listed in section I of the EHR Convention and in Protocols 1, 4, 6 and 7 to the Convention. Since its establishment in 1950, the Court has dealt with over 1,000 petitions. More than 670 of these petitions were adjudicated on the merits, and in over 460 of these cases a violation of the Convention has been found.

Organisation

13–114 The Court is composed of judges, equal in number to the number of state parties to the Convention. At present there are 41 judges. They are persons of high moral character who possess qualifications required for appointment to a high judicial domestic office or are considered to be jurisconsultants of recognised competence. They are nominated by the parties and elected by the Parliamentary Assembly of the Council of Europe. The judges serve in their individual capacity for a renewable six-year period and must retire at 70 (prior to November 1998 appointment was for nine years). The quorum for plenary sessions of the Court is two-thirds of the judges. The Court hears cases in Committees of three judges (reviewing the admissibility of applications), in Chambers of seven judges or in the Grand Chamber (comprising 17 judges and three substitute judges). The plenary court determines the composition of the Grand Chamber, of the four or more sections, from which ad hoc seven-judge Chambers are formed for each case (with the other judges of the section sitting as substitutes), and the presidency of these sections ("Presidents of Chambers"). The sections are composed with due regard to geographical and gender balance and are to be representative of the different legal systems of the state parties. All Chambers include the judges elected in respect of the state party concerned. If no such judge is available, the state concerned may appoint an ad hoc judge meeting the qualifications for appointment to the Court.

13–115   Cases will normally be heard before a seven-judge Chamber. However, when a case raises a serious question affecting the interpretation of the Convention or Protocols, or one that might result in a judgment incon-

---

[10] Rules of Court, November 4, 1998.
[11] European Agreement relating to Persons Participating in Proceedings of the European Court of Human Rights, March 5, 1996, [1996] E.T.S. 161.

sistent with a previous judgment of the Court, the Chamber may relinquish its jurisdiction in favour of the Grand Chamber. The Grand Chamber can hear cases as a second instance at the request of a party to a case decided by a seven-judge Chamber. However, this will occur only in exceptional cases that raise a serious question affecting the interpretation of the Convention or Protocols, or a serious issue of general importance (EHR Convention, Article 43). The administration of the Court is carried out by its Registry.

Jurisdiction and access to the court

The Court provides for traditional inter-state dispute resolution, as well as **13–116** the rights of recourse by victims of violations. By Article 33, any state party may bring to the Court a case against any other state party which is alleged to have breached the provisions of the Convention or Protocols. Individuals, NGOs and groups of individuals, who claim to have been victims of a human rights violation[12] may also bring a case against the state party which has committed the alleged violation.[13] In inter-state cases, of which there have been very few, the Court may address any complaint alleging a breach by a state party of the provisions of the Convention and Protocols. In cases brought by private parties, the Court has jurisdiction to receive claims alleging violation of the rights enumerated in the Convention and Protocols.

The Court may render an advisory opinion on the interpretation of the **13–117** Convention and Protocols, at the request of the Committee of Ministers. However, opinions can only deal with procedural questions and may not deal with matters concerning the scope of the substantive rights and freedoms enumerated in the Convention and Protocols, or any other matter which may be raised in ordinary proceedings before the Court.

Proceedings on admissibility and other procedural matters

Article 35 sets out the grounds for inadmissibility of an application to the **13–118** Court. An application from a state or individual source will be inadmissible if it fails to exhaust domestic remedies in accordance with the rules of

---

[12] The EHR Court and Commission have construed the term "victim" narrowly. The court has held that an individual cannot bring an *actio popularis* against a law *in abstracto*. *Klass v. Germany*, (1978) 2 E.H.R.R. 214. In addition, the EHR Commission has declined on several occasions to regard organisations, bringing complaints on behalf of their members, specific persons or the general public, as victims under the Convention. *e.g.*, Church of *X v. U.K.*, App. No. 3798/68, (1969) 12 *Yearbook of the European Convention on Human Rights* 306.

[13] EHR Convention, Art. 34. Under the old system, complaints presented to the Commission by individuals could be brought to the court by the Commission, or an interested state party. Only individuals from state parties to Protocol 9 could forward the complaint to the court after it has been dealt with the Commission. Old EHR Convention, Art. 48; Protocol 9 to the European Convention for the Protection of Human Rights and Fundamental Freedoms, November 6, 1990, [1994] ETS 140 .

international law or is submitted more than six months from the date on which the final decision of the competent domestic authorities was adopted. In individual applications, the Court will also refuse to entertain cases if the application is anonymous; if it is substantially the same as one which has been examined by the Court or submitted to another international investigation or settlement procedure and contains no new relevant information; and if it is incompatible with the provisions of the Convention or Protocols, manifestly ill founded or an abuse of right.

13–119   The Court has the power to indicate interim measures at the request of a party, any other concerned person or acting *proprio motu*.[14] Provision is also made for third party intervention by any person concerned with the outcome of the case to participate in the proceedings as third party interveners (or *amicus curiae* of the Court), if the interest of the proper administration of justice supports such intervention.[15] NGOs and other interested natural or legal persons may submit information to the Court through this procedure.[16] Judgments of the Court (but not provisional measures orders) are legally binding, and will usually include separate or dissenting opinion.[17] The Court may award just satisfaction only if the domestic law of the state party fails to afford satisfaction to the injury suffered.

13–120   Broadly speaking the Convention can be considered to be a considerable success. The Court has handed down hundreds of judgments, and the previous Commission gave several thousand decisions. Many of these judgments and decisions have had far-reaching implications. The evidence suggests that for the most part compliance is not a problem, and that states bring into effect measures to give effect to judgments. There is clear evidence of the impact of this case-law upon the law and the judicial decisions of the parties.[18] There is also evidence of its effect on the world at large. Certain states, which are not parties to the Convention, such as Nigeria, Sierra Leone and Cyprus, have adapted the Convention's statement of human rights to form part of their own constitutions. And other regions have now followed suit and established their own regional arrangements.

---

[14] Rules of Court, rule 39(1).
[15] EHR Convention, Art. 36(2).
[16] *e.g.*, *Malone v. U.K.*, (1984) 7 E.H.R.R. 14.
[17] EHR Convention, Art. 45(2); Rules of Court, rule 74(2).
[18] See Drzemczewski, *European Human Rights Convention in Domestic Law: A Comparative Study* (1983).

European Social Charter collective complaints procedure

Monitoring compliance with the 1961 European Social Charter[19] is pri- **13–121** marily a matter for the Committee of Independent Experts (CIE), comprising nine experts, assisted by the Secretariat of the Council of Europe. In 1995 a new Protocol was concluded establishing a collective complaints procedure.[20] This permits the CIE to receive complaints alleging failure on the part of state parties to the Protocol to give effect to their obligations under the Social Charter or the 1988 Additional Protocol. Complaints may be filed by selected national or international employers and trade union organisations, as well as by selected NGOs. The Committee receives written pleadings from the complainant, the state complained against and third parties (other state parties and international labour NGOs with observer status before the Governmental Sub- Committee). The Committee prepares a report which is communicated to the Committee of Ministers and the Parliamentary Assembly of the Council of Europe. The Committee of Ministers of the Council of Europe may adopt recommendations concerning the findings of the report. In 1998 the first complaint was submitted to the CIE by the International Commission of Jurists, directed against the Portugal.

(ii) Inter-American Commission and Court of Human Rights

Bibliography: Judgments of the IAHR court are published in a *series Inter-American court of Human Rights Reports*. Reports of the Commission can be found in the annual reports of the Commission and in two commercial publications: the *Inter-American Yearbook on Human Rights* (1992–98) and *Buergenthal & Norris' Human Rights: The Inter-American System*.

Buergenthal, "The Inter-American Court of Human Rights" (1982) 76 AJIL 231; Shelton, "Improving Human Rights Protections: Recommendations for Enhancing the Effectiveness of the Inter-American Commission and Inter-American Court of Human Rights" (1988) 3 *Am. U. J. Int'l L. & Pol.* 323, 332; Buergenthal *et al.*, *Protecting Human Rights in the Americas: Selected Problems* (3d ed., 1990); Davidson, *The Inter-American Human Rights System* (1997); C. Grossman, "Proposals to Strengthen the Inter-American System of Human Rights" 32 German Y.B. Int'l L. 264, 274.

The Inter-American Commission on Human Rights was established in 1959 **13–122** under the Declaration of the Fifth Meeting of Consultation of the OAS.[21] As with the original European system, all human rights complaints against

---

[19] European Social Charter, October 18, 1961, 529 U.N.T.S. 89, ETS 35. A revised version of the Social Charter and amending Protocols entered into force on July 1, 1999. European Social Charter (Revised), May 3, 1996, ETS 163.

[20] Additional Protocol to the European Social Charter Providing for a System of Collective Complaints, November 9, [1995] E.T.S. 158, in force July 1998.

[21] Declaration at the 5th Meeting of Consultation, Santiago, Chile, August 12–18, 1959. Final Act, OAS Official Records, OEA/Ser. C/II.5, pp. 10–11.

any of the 25 member states to the Convention must first be brought before the Commission, which examines the admissibility of the complaint; investigates the allegations against the state party; attempts to find a friendly settlement; and, if necessary, prepares a report on the case.[22] The Court is the principal judicial body entrusted with monitoring the human rights practices of state parties to the 1969 American Convention on Human Rights, which was concluded under the organisational framework of the Organisation of American States ("OAS").[23] The Convention entered into force in 1978 and the court was officially inaugurated the following year in Costa Rica. The Commission may further pursue the matter and present a claim before the Court against a state party.[24] The Court hears cases brought against states that have accepted its jurisdiction. To date, 17 of the 25 state parties to the American Convention on Human Rights have declared their acceptance *ipso facto* of the compulsory jurisdiction of the Court, a notable exception being the United States. In its judgments the Court rules whether the defendant state has violated any of the human rights protected by the Convention.[25] To date the court has decided more than 25 cases. By contrast, since 1965 the Commission has dealt with more than 12,000 complaints.

13–123   The principal text governing the structure, role and powers of the Court are Chapter VIII of the American Convention on Human Rights, the Statute of the Inter-American Court, and the Rules of Procedure of the Court.[26] The Commission has its own statute and regulations. The substantive law applied by the court is found in Part I of the American Convention on Human Rights and in some of the provisions of the Protocols to the Convention.[27] Additionally, in exercising its advisory competence the Court may give opinions on the interpretation of other human rights treaties applicable in the territory of an OAS member state. The Commission may also review complaints involving the human rights practices of OAS member states that are not parties to the American Convention on Human Rights. In cases brought against such states, the Commission applies not

---

[22] American HR Convention, Arts 44–50.
[23] American Convention on Human Rights, November 22, 1969, OASTS 36; OAS Official Records OEA/Ser.L/V/II.23, doc. 21, rev. 6 (1979); reprinted in 9 ILM 673 (1970).
[24] American HR Convention, Art. 61.
[25] American HR Convention, Art. 63.
[26] Statute of the Inter-American Court on Human Rights, OAS Res. 448 (IX-O/79), OAS Official Records OEA/Ser. P/IX.0.2./80, Vol. 1, at 98; Rules of Procedure of the Inter-American Court on Human Rights, Annual Report of the Inter-American Court of Human Rights, 1991, OAS Doc. OEA/Ser.L/V/III.25 doc.7 at 18 (1992). The 1996 Rules of Procedure, which came into effect on January 1, 1997 replaced the previous version of the Rules that were adopted in 1992.
[27] Additional Protocol to the American Convention on Human Rights in the area of Economic, Social and Cultural Rights, November 7, 1988, Art. 8(a), (not yet in force), 13, 19(6), OAS Official Records OAS/Ser.L.V/II.92, doc. 31 rev. 3; Inter-American Convention on Forced Disappearance of Persons, June 9, 1994, (1994) 33 ILM 1529.

the Convention but the American Declaration of the Rights and Duties of Man, approved by all OAS member states.[28]

The Commission comprises seven members of high moral character and **13–124** recognised competence in the field of human rights. They are elected by the member states of the OAS for a term of four years, which is renewable once. The Commission sits in plenary (quorum of four members), although it may conduct some preparatory parts of its work in working groups of not more than three members. The Court comprises seven judges, who are nationals of different OAS states (not necessarily states which are parties to the Convention). They are elected by the state parties to the American Convention for a renewable six-year term. Judges should be jurists of the highest moral authority, of recognised competence in the area of human rights, and must have the required qualifications for service in the highest judicial office of their state of nationality (or in the state that proposed them as candidates). Following the traditional conventions, in the event that a state party to a case does not have a judge of its nationality on the bench, it may appoint an ad hoc judge. The court sits in plenary, with a quorum for deliberation of five judges. A case dealt with by the Commission may be brought by a dissatisfied state party to the Court for additional review. Decisions of the Court are final and binding.

Jurisdiction

Any person, group of persons or NGO (recognised under the laws of at **13–125** least one member state of the OAS) may submit a petition to the Commission alleging a violation of the American Convention by a state party (Article 44). Any state party may accept, by way of a declaration, the competence of the Commission to receive claims against it from another member state (Article 45). Such declarations may be unrestricted, or for limited period, or a specific case. In any event, only states that have also made declarations under Article 45(1) may bring communications to the Commission. Persons, groups of persons and NGOs may also present to the Commission communications against OAS member states not parties to the Convention, alleging violation of fundamental human rights.

The Court has jurisdiction over claims against states that have accepted **13–126** its jurisdiction, through a general declaration of acceptance *ipso facto* of jurisdiction (pursuant to Article 62(1) of the Convention) or through ad hoc declarations or a special agreement. Seventeen state parties to the

---

[28] American Declaration of the Rights and Duties of Man, adopted by the Ninth International Conference of American States (1948), reprinted in Basic Documents Pertaining to Human Rights in the Inter-American System, OEA/Ser.L.V/II.82 doc.6 rev.1 at 17 (1992). The Commission must give particular attention to Arts 1–4, 18, 25–26 of the Declaration. IACHR Statute, Art. 20(a).

Convention have made general declarations accepting the Court's jurisdiction, and only they and the Commission may bring a case before the Court. Where declarations of acceptance of jurisdiction under Article 62(1) require reciprocity, only states that also made a declaration under the same Article may present a claim against the respondent state. In cases brought to the Court by the Commission, a representative of the victim may participate in the discussion and assist the Commission, if the Court authorises a request by the Commission to that effect. In all cases, the representatives of the victim may participate in the reparation stage of the proceedings.

13–127 Both the Commission and Court are required to assess the admissibility of any complaint, and both may take provisional measures. The Court is authorised to order provisional measures in cases of extreme gravity and urgency, if such measures are necessary to avoid irreparable harm to persons.

13–128 The final decision of the Commission is in the form of a report including findings of fact and the conclusions of the Commission. At this stage, the report is not published. Where the dispute has not been brought before the court within three months from the issuance of the report, the Commission may prescribe a period of time for the responding state to comply with the conclusions of the report. If no adequate measures have been taken within that period of time, the Commission may decide to publish the report. In any case, the report of the Commission is not formally binding upon the state parties. In contrast, the final decision of the Court is in the form of a binding judgment adopted by a majority of the judges. If a violation of the Convention has been found, the Court will order the respondent state to take measures so that the injured party be ensured the enjoyment of the rights or freedoms which were violated. The Court may also indicate reparations for the injured party.

(iii) The African Commission and Court on Human and Peoples' Rights

Bibliography: The observations of the Commission are published in the *Review of the African Commission on Human & Peoples' Rights* (4 Vols.) and in the *Annual Activity Reports* (1987–).

Okere, "The Protection of Human Rights in Africa and the African Charter on Human and People's Rights: Comparative Analysis with the European and American Systems" (1984) 6 Hum. Rts. Q. 141; Amoah, "The African Charter on Human and People's Rights—An Effective Weapon for Human Rights?" (1992) 4 Afr. J. Int'l & Comp. L. 226; Ankumah, *The African Commission on Human and Peoples' Rights* 18–20 (1996); Murray, "Decisions by the African Commission on Individual Communications under the African Charter on Human and People's Rights" (1997) 46 ICLQ 412, 422–23; Umozurike, *The African Charter on Human and Peoples' Rights* (1997). Website: http://www.umn.edu/humanrts/africa/comision.html.

The African Commission was established under Article 30 of the 1981 **13–129** African Charter on Human and People's Rights[29] and began to function in November 1987. It has supervisory powers over all 51 state parties to the African Charter, its principal task being to promote and ensure respect for human rights in Africa. The Commission receives periodical reports from the state parties to the African Charter and may receive communications from state and non-state actors alleging violation of the human rights guaranteed by the African Charter. The procedure for handling communications involves investigation by the Commission of the factual claims of the parties and issuing recommendations on the merits, in the form of observations or a report. In cases brought by a person or entity other than a state party, an in-depth study (involving active investigation on the part of the Commission) can be undertaken only with the approval of the Assembly of Heads of State and Government of the OAU ("Assembly"). An in-depth study will also lead to the writing of a report. The observations or reports of the Commission are not binding upon the state parties.

Since its establishment, the Commission has received more than 200 **13–130** communications from individuals and NGOs, the merits of which had been considered in some 25 cases. No inter-state case involving state parties to the Charter has been brought before the Commission. In June 1998, the member states of the OAU adopted a Protocol on the Establishment of a Court of Human and People's Rights.[30] The Court, which is not yet operational, is generally modelled on the former European Court of Human Rights and the Inter-American Court of Human Rights.

The principal texts governing the African Commission are Part II of the **13–131** 1981 African Charter and its Rules of Procedure. The court will be governed by the protocol and its own Rules of Procedure, which have yet to be adopted by the court. The Commission may also draw inspiration from other sources of international human rights law, such as the Charters of the UN and the OAU, the Universal Declaration of Human Rights, and other instruments on human rights to which African states are parties (or members of UN specialised agencies that sponsored such instrument).[31] It may also to take into consideration other international conventions setting out norms recognised by OAS member states, African practices (which are in conformity with the international human rights standards), customs generally accepted as law, general principles of law recognised by African states and legal precedents and doctrine.[32] Under the protocol on the Court, the Court is to apply the Charter and any relevant human rights instruments adopted by the states concerned.[33]

---

[29] June 27, 1981, (1982) 21 ILM 58.
[30] For the text of the Draft Protocol see OAU Doc. OAU/LEG/MIN/AFCHPR/PROT.1 rev.2 (1997).
[31] African HR Charter, Art. 60.
[32] African HR Charter, Art. 61.
[33] Court Protocol, Art. 7.

Organisation

13–132 The Commission comprises 11 members who are nationals of different state parties to the Charter, elected by the OAU Assembly for a renewable period of six years. Members must be persons of the highest reputation, known for their high morality, integrity, impartiality and competence in the field of human and peoples' rights (preferably having legal experience). The members sit on the Commission in their private capacity. The Court will comprise 11 judges, who are to be nationals of different OAU states, elected by the Assembly upon nominations of the state parties to the protocol on the Court. The bench will be representative of the main different regions and legal traditions in Africa and, almost uniquely amongst bodies of this kind, be required to achieve adequate gender representation. The judges will serve a once renewable six-year term. The administrative requirements of the Commission are attended to by the Secretary General of the OAU, who provides the Commission with the necessary staff, means and services. The new Court, once established, will have its own registry and staff, headed by a Registrar.

Jurisdiction

13–133 By Articles 47, 49 and 55 of the African Charter the Commission may receive communications against state parties to the African Charter submitted by another state party or any other source. In the latter case, the Commission may consider the communication only if the majority of its members so decide. The Commission also has an advisory jurisdiction to interpret the provisions of the African Charter at the request of a state party, an OAU institution or an African organisation recognised by the OAU. And, on its own initiative, the Commission has adopted several resolutions aimed at clarifying unclear provisions of the Charter. The Court will have jurisdiction over cases brought by the Commission or by the state party that lodged a complaint to the Commission or by the state party against which the complaint has been lodged or by the state party whose citizen is a victim of human rights breaches or by any African intergovernmental organisation. The Court will also be able to receive cases brought by individuals or NGOs with observer status before the Commission, if the state against which the complaint is made has submitted a declaration under Article 34(6) of the protocol, recognising the competence of the Court to receive such claims. The court will have similar powers to the Commission to render advisory opinions, provided that the same matter is not being dealt with by the Commission.

Preliminary proceedings

13–134 Before reviewing the merits of a communication, the Commission must take a decision on admissibility.[34] The Commission may indicate whether interim measures are needed to avoid irreparable damage to the alleged

---

[34] African HR Charter, Art. 50, 56; Rules of Procedure, rule 118.

victim.[35] The court will be able to adopt provisional measures in cases of extreme gravity and urgency, if such measures are needed to avoid irreparable harm to persons.[36] Provision is also made for limited rights of access to third parties.[37]

In cases brought by states, if no amicable settlement has been reached, **13–135** the Commission will prepare a report within 12 months from the date it was seized by way of notification.[38] The report will include the decisions and conclusions of the Commission on the merits of the case.[39] In cases brought by other complainants, the Commission will normally prepare observations, made on the basis of the information submitted to it by the parties.[40] In cases where the Commission believes that the communication, alone or together with other communications, reveals a series of serious or massive human rights violations or a case of emergency, it may notify the Assembly accordingly.[41] The Assembly may then request the Commission to conduct an in-depth study of the situation. The factual findings of such a study, as well as the recommendations of the Commission, will be made in the form of a report.[42] Decisions of the Commission are not binding, and will remain confidential unless the Assembly decides to publish them.

(iv) The Commission of Mediation, Conciliation and Arbitration of the OAU[43]

Article III (4) of the Charter of the Organisation of African Unity **13–136** prescribes as one of the principles of the organisation, "peaceful settlement of disputes by negotiation, mediation, conciliation or arbitration." This principle is reaffirmed in Article XIX of the Charter which states that

> "Member States pledge to settle all disputes among themselves by peaceful means and to this end decide to establish a Commission of Mediation, Conciliation and Arbitration, the composition of which and conditions of service shall be defined by a separate Protocol to be approved by the Assembly of Heads of State and Government. The said Protocol shall be regarded as forming an integral part of the present Charter."

Under Article VII, the Commission is established as one of the principal institutions of the Organisation. The Protocol was eventually signed at Cairo in July 1964.

---

[35] Rules of Procedure, rule 111(1).
[36] Court Protocol, Art. 27(2).
[37] Court Protocol, Art. 5(2).
[38] African HR Charter, Art. 52; Rules of Procedure, rule 101(1).
[39] Rules of Procedure, rule 101(3).
[40] Rules of Procedure, rule 120.
[41] African HR Charter, Art. 58.
[42] African HR Charter, Art. 58(2); Rules of Procedure, art. 120(3).
[43] Elias, "The Commission of Mediation, Conciliation and Arbitration of the OAU" (1964) 41 B.Y.B.I.L. 336.

13–137   The Commission consists of 21 members elected by the Assembly of Heads of State and Government, who are persons with recognised professional qualifications and are elected for a term of five years and are eligible for re-election. The jurisdiction of the Commission is traditional, limited to disputes between states which are referred to it by the Assembly of Heads of State and Government, the Council of Ministers, or one or both parties to the dispute. Having regard to the fact that if one or more of the parties refuse to submit to the jurisdiction of the Commission the Bureau is to refer the matter to the Council of Ministers for consideration, it seems clear that jurisdiction is dependent on the consent of the party or parties concerned and that the Protocol does not establish a system of compulsory jurisdiction. Under Article XVIII, the parties involved in a dispute and all other member states undertake to extend to those conducting an investigation or inquiry, for the purpose of elucidating facts or circumstances relating to a matter in dispute, the fullest co-operation in the conduct of such investigation or inquiry. However, it is doubtful whether this confers a right of entry into a party's territory without specific consent. For the settlement of a dispute, the parties may agree to resort to any one of the modes of settlement: mediation, conciliation and arbitration. In practice the Commission appears to have been little used, and arbitration not at all. Disputes there have certainly been, but following a pattern already clear in the UN, the OAS and the Arab League, the member states have shown a marked preference for political settlement as opposed to the more formal, expert (and quasi-judicial) techniques available in the Commission. Thus, the Somali/Kenyan and Somali/Ethiopia disputes, the Algerian/Moroccan dispute (territorial disputes) the Ivory Coast/Guinea disputes (detention of diplomats) and Western Sahara dispute have been dealt with outside the Commission.

(c) THE COURT OF JUSTICE OF THE EUROPEAN COMMUNITIES

Bibliography: Report of Cases before the Court of Justice and Court of First Instance (E.C.R.); Common Market Law Reports (C.M.L.R.). Brown and Jacob, *The Court of Justice of the European Communities* (1989); Schermers and Waelbroeck, *Judicial Protection in the European Communities* (1992); Bermann, Goebel, Davey and Fox, *Cases and Materials on European Community Law* (1993); Lasok, *The European Court of Justice—Practice and Procedure* (2nd ed., 1994); Anderson, *References to the European Court* (1995); March Hunnings, *The European Courts* (1996); Barling and Brealey (eds.) *Practitioners' Handbook of EC Law*. (1998)

13–138   The European Court of Justice (ECJ) was established by Article 4 of the 1957 Rome Treaty establishing the European Economic Community. It assumed the functions of the Court of Justice of the ECSC (in existence since 1953) and has become a common court for the three European Communities: ECSC, the E.C. and Euratom.[44] The three treaties were

---

[44] See Chap. 6, paras 6–030 *et seq.* for a description of these organisations.

modified by the Convention relating to certain institutions common to the European Communities of 1957 so as to ensure an identity of the texts governing the organisation of the Court; its powers vary according to whether it is acting as the court of one or other of the three communities. The Court has been subject to further changes with the adoption of the 1986 Single European Act,[45] the 1992 Maastricht Treaty on European Union,[46] and the 1997 Treaty of Amsterdam.[47] Its Rules of Procedures have been amended most recently in 1997.[48] In 1988 the E.C. Council, acting under an amendment of the E.C. Treaty introduced by the 1986 Single European Act, established a Court of First Instance (CFI) with limited jurisdiction and a right of appeal on points of law to the ECJ.[49] In 1993, following amendments to the E.C. Treaty made by the 1992 Treaty on European Union, the competence of the CFI was extended, as described below.[50]

The ECJ's principal task is to ensure the uniform interpretation and **13–139** application of the law by all community members and institutions; to serve as a forum for the enforcement of E.C. law; and to settle disputes between the different actors in the community (*i.e.* member states, community institutions and, on occasion, private parties). The CFI and the ECJ are not separate institutions, but rather different parts of the same judicial body. Since its establishment, the ECJ has dealt with over 9,000 cases, with the number growing more or less each year (in 1997, for example, 445 new cases were submitted to the ECJ and 644 cases were submitted to the CFI). Specific norms governing the operation of the ECJ are to be found in the Statutes of the court and the Rules of Procedure of the Court of Justice of the European Communities.[51] These statutes also govern the CFI, although it has its own Rules of Procedure.[52] The ECJ applies law deriving from several sources. These are principally the constitutive treaties of the three communities (the most important of which is the E.C. Treaty) and secondary community legislation (regulations, directives and decisions). However, the Court also applies international treaties to which the community is a party, as well as general principles of community law (which are largely derived from the constitutive treaties and the member states' national legal systems).

---

[45] (1986) 25 ILM 503.
[26] (1992) 31 ILM 247.
[47] (1998) 37 ILM 56.
[48] See Consolidated Text [1999] O.J. C 65.
[49] EC Treaty, as amended by 1986 SEA, Art. 168a; and Decision 88/591 [1988] O.J. C 251/1.
[50] Decision 93/350/Euratom, ECSC, EEC [1993] O.J. L 144/21.
[51] Protocol on the Statute of the Court of Justice of the European Economic Community, April 17, 1957, 298 U.N.T.S. 147 [as amended by Council Decision 88/591, [1989] O.J. C 215/1]; Rules of Procedure of the Court of Justice of the European Communities, [1974] O.J. L 350/1, as revised in [1991] O.J. L176/7.
[52] Rules of Procedure of the Court of First Instance of the European Communities, [1990] O.J. C136/1, as revised in [1991] O.J. L136/1.

13–140   The ECJ is now composed of 15 judges (coming from the 15 member states), appointed for a renewable six-year term through common accord of all member states. Although the treaties do not require that each member state shall have a representative on the bench, this has been the practice. The judges are assisted by eight advocates-general (a ninth is appointed to serve only until October 2000), who are entrusted with presenting to the court objective legal opinions on pending cases. They meet the same service requirements as judges, and also serve a renewable six-year term. These officers represented something quite new to international tribunals; they have no connection with the parties and serve the Court exclusively but without taking part in the deliberations preceding judgment.[53] The CFI is also comprised of 15 judges, appointed by the common accord of all member states for a six-year term. CFI judges must meet similar service requirements to ECJ judges and advocates-general. Like their counterparts in the ECJ, the judges of the CFI elect a president for a three-year term. However, unlike the ECJ, the CFI does not employ advocates-general. The judges and advocates-general are wholly independent: they may not hold any political or administrative office or engage in any paid or unpaid professional activities, and they have extensive privileges and immunities, although less extensive than other international courts.[54] They also have security of tenure unless removed from office by the unanimous vote of their fellow-judges. A striking corollary to their independence is the total lack of any reference to their nationality, except in the negative sense that no party can invoke the nationality of a judge, or the absence of a judge of his own nationality, as a reason for changing the composition of the Court; the "national" or "ad hoc" judge is unknown in the ECJ and CFI.

13–141   The ECJ can sit in plenary sessions, or assign cases to Chambers of three, five or seven judges. The use of Chambers has developed steadily and today most cases are referred to a Chamber, unless they are considered to be particularly difficult or important. The CFI normally sits in Chambers of three or five judges. However, the cases may be referred to the plenary court (or in the alternative, transferred from a three-judge Chamber to a five-judge Chamber). The ECJ sits as a court of appeal over judgments of the CFI, but on points of law only.[55] The ECJ is assisted in the conduct of its business by a Registrar appointed by it for a six-year term. The CFI has its own registrar for its business, entrusted with similar responsibilities to the ECJ's registrar.

---

[53] See Donner, "The Court of Justice of the European Communities" (1961) I.C.L.Q. Supp. No. 1, 66.

[54] See Chap. 15, para. 15–084.

[55] E.C. Statute, Art. 51; Euratom Statute, Art. 53; ECSC Statute, Art. 51. An appeal must allege one of the following grounds: (i) lack of competence of the CFI; (ii) breach of procedure which adversely affected the interests of the appellant; or (iii) infringement of community law by the CFI.

Jurisdiction

It may properly be said that no international tribunal has ever been **13–142** equipped with so varied a jurisdictional competence as the ECJ, although others are now following in its path. The jurisdiction of the court is complex: it sits in three capacities (*i.e.* as the court of each of the three communities) and it comprises several different kinds of proceedings. The Court discharges its primary function of ensuring the rule of law in the interpretation and application of the treaties and any rules made for their execution in two ways: contentious and advisory. The contentious jurisdiction of the court comprises three principal categories of cases:

(a) claims brought against member-states, alleging non-compliance with E.C. law;

(b) claims brought against one or more of the community institutions; and

(c) requests for preliminary rulings referred to the court by domestic courts of the member states concerning questions of E.C. law. In these cases, the court is requested to apply community law to questions that arise in municipal proceedings.

The Court also has jurisdiction in respect of staff cases; inter-state **13–143** disputes concerning one of the Treaties, brought by special agreement;[56] contractual disputes involving the community as a party to a contract, on the basis of a compromissory clause;[57] interpretative rulings in pursuance with international treaties (including the European Economic Area Treaty); and appeals over decisions of intellectual property arbitration commissions established under Article 18 of the Euratom Treaty.

Claims against member states

Non-compliance claims intended to ensure compliance with community law **13–144** can be brought against a member state by one or more member states (in what is a classical "international" dispute settlement jurisdiction)[58] or— almost uniquely in international law—by the European Commission.[59] The

---

[56] E.C. Treaty, Art. 239 (*ex Art. 182*); Euratom Treaty 154. Under Article 89 of the ECSC Treaty such procedure may be initiated unilaterally by any of the two concerned states if it concerns the application of that treaty, and cannot be settled by an alternative procedure.

[57] E.C. Treaty, Art. 238 (*ex Art. 181*); ECSC Treaty, Art. 42; Euratom Treaty, Art. 153.

[58] E.C. Treaty, Art. 227 (*ex Art. 170*); ECSC Treaty, Art. 89; Eurotom Treaty 142. To date only one such claim has been submitted, Case 141/178 *France v. U.K.* [1979] E.C.R. 2923.

[59] E.C. Treaty, Art. 226 (*ex Art. 169*); ECSC Treaty, Art. 88; Euratom Treaty, Art. 141. See Chap. 12, paras 12–061 *et seq.*
In addition, under Article 237(a) of the E.C. Treaty (*ex Art. 180*), the Board of Directors of the European Central Bank (hereinafter ECB) may also present a claim against a member state for failure to comply with the Statute of the Bank. Furthermore, according to subsection (d) of the same Article, the Council of the European Central Bank is authorised to bring non-compliance cases directly against the national banks of the member states for their failure to comply with the Statute of the ECB and the E.C. Treaty. In these cases, the bank organs shall have the same powers as the E.C. Commission.

exclusive ground for presenting a non-compliance claim against a member state is failure to fulfil an obligation under the relevant treaties.[60]

Claims against community institutions

13–145 Under this head of jurisdiction the ECJ may review the legality of acts[61] and omissions of the E.C. Council, Commission, Parliament and the European Central Bank (ECB).[62] In appropriate cases, where the acts or omissions of the community have resulted in damage giving rise to non-contractual liability (*i.e.* tortious liability), financial compensation may be ordered.[63] Claims against community institutions can be brought by any member state or by a community institution, other than the institution complained against (*i.e.* Commission, Council, Parliament, the court of Auditors and the ECB).[64] In addition, the ECJ may be seised by a natural or legal person having a direct interest in the matter.[65] This last condition has been construed narrowly by the court (less so in cases involving non-contractual liability of the community).[66] It should be noted that indirect challenges against any community legislation may be brought in any case in which such act is at issue, by any party to the proceedings.[67] Although, normally, contractual liability will be enforced by the municipal courts of the members, the three treaties provide that the court will have jurisdiction where an arbitration clause specifically vests jurisdiction in the court, and whether the contract be concluded under public or private law.

13–146 The jurisdiction of the court under Articles 230 and 232 (for review of acts of community institutions) is strictly limited *ratione materiae, ratione personae*, and *ratione temporis*. In the EEC and Euratom all acts of the

---

[60] E.C. Treaty, Arts 226–7 (*ex Art. 169–70*); ECSC Treaty, Art. 88; Euratom Treaty, Arts 141–142.

[61] Acts (recommendations and opinions excluded) have been defined in the case law of the ECJ as "measures intended to have legal effects". Case 22/70, *Commission v. Council*, [1971] E.C.R. 263, 277.

[62] E.C. Treaty, Arts 230 and 232 (*ex Arts 173, 175*); ECSC Treaty, Arts 33, 35, 38; Euratom Treaty, Arts 146, 148. Similar powers of review exist in respect of measures taken by the principal organs of the European Investment Bank. E.C. Treaty, Art. 237(b)-(c) (*ex Art. 180(b)-(c)*. It should be noted that under the ECSC Treaty only acts of Council and Parliament, and not their omissions, are reviewable: ECSC Treaty, Art. 38.

[63] E.C. Treaty, Arts 235, 288 (*ex Arts 178, 215*); ECSC Treaty, Art. 40; Euratom Treaty, Arts 151, 188.

[64] There are, however, certain restrictions upon the right of institutions to bring claim. Parliament, the Court of Auditors and the ECB may challenge acts only for the purpose of protecting their prerogatives (but under the Euratom Treaty, the latter two bodies cannot present such a challenge altogether); and the ECB may bring omission claims only in areas falling under its competence. Furthermore, under the ECSC the only community organs that can bring a claim against community institutions are the Commission and Council.

[65] Under the ECSC the right of private challenge can only be exercised by directly affected undertakings and associations: ECSC Treaty, Art. 33.

[66] The court has construed the latter alternative as applicable only to people with particular attributes, which differentiate them from all others affected by the decision. Case 25/62 *Plaumann v. Commission*, [1963] E.C.R. 95, 107. See most recently Case 321/95 *Greenpeace v. Commission* [1998] E.C.R. I-1651; [1998] 3 C.M.L.R. 1.

[67] E.C. Treaty, Art. 241 (*ex Art. 184*); Euratom, Art. 156. No equivalent provision exists under the ECSC Treaty.

Commission or the Council which have legal effects are challengeable. This includes regulations, directives, decisions and other legally binding acts which may be *sui generis*,[68] but not recommendations and opinions which are without legal effect. Failure to act can be challenged, as well as positive action.[69] So far as the grounds of challenge are concerned, as against the Commission there are four: lack of competence; infringement of an essential procedural requirement; infringement of the E.C. Treaty or any rule relating to its application; or misuse of powers.[70] The second limitation concerns the entities which have *locus standi* to mount a challenge before the court. In principle the right to challenge is always available to the member states and the executive organs of each Community. That in itself goes far beyond traditional practice; the I.C.J., for example, has only limited power of judicial review over actions by organs of the UN, nor can the organs of the UN challenge each other's acts or the acts of member states before that court. However, the more remarkable feature in the E.U. system is the grant of a right, albeit limited, of challenge to private persons and entities. This is, in a sense, a logical step once the executive bodies are given supra-national powers so that they can by-pass the member states and address their regulations and decisions directly to their subjects; nevertheless, it is a step which demonstrates the degree to which integration in these communities has progressed. In the E.C. and Euratom the general phrase "any natural or legal person" is used;[71] in the ECSC an attempt is made to define more narrowly these potential appellants. The "enterprises or associations" must be "engaged in production in the field of coal and steel within the territories" (of member states) or "engaged in distribution other than sale to domestic consumers or to craft industries" (Article 80) or be "buyers" (Article 63(2)). In every case where a private entity is the applicant, it must show that it was directly and individually concerned by the decision or other act in question.[72] The third limitation refers to the imposition of time-limits within which the acts or decisions must be challenged. In general the ECSC Treaty stipulates a one-month period, whilst the E.C. and Euratom Treaties stipulate a two-month period. The periods are short, but necessarily so once one grasps the fact that the legal regimes established by the treaties are dynamic and cannot be subject to alteration long after the event by appeals against decisions taken.

---

[68] See *Re the European Road Transport Agreement* [1971] C.M.L.R. 335.
[69] ECSC, Art. 35; EC, Art. 232 (*ex Art. 175*); Euratom, Art. 148. On the application of Article 175 see *Holtz v. Council* [1974] E.C.R. 1.
[70] E.C. Treaty, Art. 230 (*ex Art. 173*).
[71] *ibid.*, 173; Euratom, Art. 146. The difficulties over Art. 173 have arisen not so much over decisions addressed to a person, but more over decisions addressed to a person other than the plaintiff but of "direct and individual concern" to the plaintiff: see *Société C.A.M. v. Commission* [1973] E.C.R. 1393.
[72] "Individual concern" has been narrowly construed; see *e.g. Stichting Greenpeace v. European Commission*, 1998 E.C.R. I-1651; [1998] C.M.L.R. 1.

409

Preliminary rulings

13–147 In so far as the treaties form an integral part of the municipal law of the member states,[73] and decisions of the executive organs have executory force within those states, the situation may well arise in which a municipal court is seised with a case which concerns the interpretation of the treaty, or the validity of acts by the organs of the Community; indeed, a defendant may well attempt to justify his conduct on the ground that he was implementing a decision addressed to him. Hence, some system had to be devised to enable the ECJ exclusively to decide certain questions arising before municipal tribunals, and to ensure uniformity of application of Community law. Accordingly the ECJ (but not the CFI) may receive requests for authoritative interpretation of Community law from the national courts of the member states (referred to as the "Article 177/234 procedure").[74] Such requests may be referred to the ECJ where a question involving the interpretation of Community law has arisen in proceedings before a national court; however, when the question arises before a national court of last instance, a preliminary ruling must be sought (unless the matter is subject to the "acte clair" doctrine).[75] Although, the request is formally filed in the ECJ by the requesting national court, the parties to the domestic proceedings are entitled to participate in the preliminary ruling proceedings before the ECJ. Similar procedures of reference of questions to the ECJ for binding interpretation were introduced by some of the international treaties mentioned above (*e.g.* the Brussels Judgment Conventions, the Rome Convention on Contractual Obligations and the EEA Agreement). Requests for preliminary rulings are to be brought when a question has arisen in domestic proceedings concerning one of the following issues: (a) interpretation of the treaties (*i.e.* primary legislation); (b) validity or interpretation of acts of community institutions (*i.e.* secondary legislation); or (c) interpretation of statutes of subsidiary bodies (where the statutes provide so).

Administrative tribunal (staff and pension cases)

13–148 Whereas in other international organisations special tribunals have had to be created to deal with appeals by staff members against decisions of the administration (since such individuals had no *locus standi* before the I.C.J.),

---

[73] The supremacy of community law over the national laws of the member states is beyond question, and this applies equally to subsequent national legislation: *Costa v. ENEL* [1964] E.C.R. 585; C.M.L.R. 4295.

[74] E.C. Treaty, Art. 234 (*ex Art. 177*); ECSC Treaty, Art. 41; Euratom Treaty, Art. 150. Once a request is submitted, domestic proceedings are enjoined until the preliminary ruling is issued, and upon their renewal, the domestic court is obliged to implement the ruling in the case pending before it.

[75] Case 283/31 *Cilfit v. Ministry of Health* [1982] E.C.R. 3415 (holding that where the correct application of Community law is so obvious as to leave no scope for any reasonable doubt as to the manner in which the question is to be resolved, there is no obligation for the domestic court of last instance to refer the case to the ECJ).

the three communities have had no hesitation in giving individuals access to the ECJ, which has functioned as an administrative tribunal. This jurisdiction rests, in the ECSC, on the rather general provisions concerning contractual and non-contractual liability of the community and, more specifically, on the Staff Regulations. In E.C. and Euratom, Articles 179 and 152 provide quite specifically for this jurisdiction. The nature of this administrative jurisdiction, which is now fulfilled by the CFI, is more fully described later in the section on Administrative Tribunals.

Advisory jurisdiction

The ECJ has two, limited heads of advisory competence, which are only **13–149** rarely invoked. First, it may review, at the request of the Council, Commission or a member state, the compatibility of international treaties concluded between the community and third parties with the treaties.[76] In one case in particular—concerning the competence of a proposed EEA court—the ECJ took the opportunity to indicate in the clearest terms that no other court could have a superior competence to it in regard to the authoritative interpretation and application of community law.[77] Secondly, the Court may give its opinion on the need for amendment of the ECSC treaty, upon the joint request of the Commission and the Council.[78] Curiously enough, the Court is not brought into the treaty-amending process of the EEC and Euratom.

Division of jurisdiction between the ECJ and the CFI

Since the establishment of the CFI in 1989 there has occurred a gradual **13–150** transfer of elements of the original jurisdiction of ECJ to the CFI. Decisions on referral of classes of cases to the CFI are taken by the Council, at the request of the ECJ, after consultation with the Commission and Parliament. At present, the CFI is entrusted with handling staff, coal and steel, competition and certain trademark cases.[79] Since 1994, all claims against community institutions brought by natural or legal persons are initially submitted to the CFI.[80] It is expected that the process will continue and eventually result in the referral of all contentious cases (except Article 177 cases) to the CFI.

Other matters

Like many other international courts the ECJ is authorised to render **13–151** interim measures of protection and suspend the operation of any measure adopted by a Community institution.[81] Such measures will only be granted

---

[76] E.C. Treaty, Art. 300 (*ex Art. 228*).
[77] Opinion 1/91, December 14, 1991 [1991] E.C.R. I-6079.
[78] ECSC Treaty, Art. 95.
[79] ECSC, EEC, Euratom Council Decision 88/591, [1988] O.J. L 319/1; E.C. Regulation 40/94, Art. 63, [1994] O.J. L 11/1.
[80] ECSC, EEC, Euratom Council Decision 93/350, [1993] O.J. L144/21; ECSC, EEC, Euratom Council Decision of March 7, 1994, [1994] O.J. L66/29.
[81] E.C. Treaty, Arts 242–3 (*ex Arts 185–186*); ECSC Treaty, Art. 39; Euratom Treaty, Arts 157–158; E.C. Statue, Art. 37; ECSC Statute, Art. 33; Euratom Statute, Art. 38.

if the circumstances giving rise to urgency and pleas of fact and law establishing a prima facie case.[82] Under the three ECJ statutes, member states and community institutions may intervene in all cases in support of the submissions of one of the parties to the case (except in inter-state cases brought under the ECSC Treaty, where only states may intervene).[83] Private parties may also intervene, but only in cases involving other private parties (except under the ECSC, where there is no such limitation) and if they can establish an interest in the results of the case.[84]

The judgments of the Court[85]

13–152 Against non-state entities and individuals the judgments of the court have executive force in each member state; the municipal authorities, upon the request of the successful party, simply verify the judgment and then enforce it through the ordinary municipal procedures for enforcement as if it were a judgment of their own courts. This is an advantage which most other international tribunals do not have in the actual enforcement of their judgments. The judgment of the Court is a single judgment and, contrary to usual practice in international tribunals, no separate or dissenting judgments are allowed. It is a final judgment, creating a *res judicata* (but not a binding precedent) which, when emanating from the ECJ, is not appealable. There is, however, procedure for the interpretation of a judgment and for the revision of a judgment upon the discovery of new facts "capable of exercising a decisive influence" provided a request for review is made within ten years from judgment.

(d) OTHER REGIONAL COURTS

13–153 The ECJ is no longer alone in establishing a broad jurisdiction over a wide range of economic and related matters. Regional courts or related procedures have begun to spring up in Africa and the Americas, and it can surely not be long before similar bodies emerge in Asia. In the Caribbean, the focus has been on the establishment of a regional court of criminal appeal, to replace the remaining colonial jurisdiction of the Privy Council.

Central American Court of Justice

13–154 In its present incarnation the Central American Court of Justice was established in 1991 and is the judicial branch of the Central American Integration System (SICA) (a framework for political cooperation and

---

[82] Rules of Procedure, Art. 83; CFI Rules of Procedure, Art. 104.
[83] E.C. Statute, Art. 37; ECSC Statute, Arts 34, 41; Euratom Statute, Art. 38. It should be noted that the ECSC Statute refers only to a general right of intervention of natural and legal persons and states, but this has generally been interpreted to encompass community institutions too.
[84] E.C. Statute, Art. 37; ECSC Statute, Art 34; Euratom Statute, Art. 38.
[85] Since this chapter has to combine brevity with concentration on the institutional aspects of the court, no references can be made to the body of substantive case-law being evolved by the court. This can, however, be consulted in the official Recueil de la Jurisprudence de la Cour de la Communauté Européenne.

economic integration between six Central American states, replacing the more loosely structured Organisation of Central American States).[86] In a loose sense the Court is the successor to the court originally established in 1907, which was innovative in not admitting reservations to its compulsory jurisdiction and in having a jurisdiction comprising not only disputes between states, but also cases brought against states by individuals having the nationality of one of the states members of the court. Five claims were made before the original Court before it received its quietus in 1918. The composition of the Court itself presented little difficulty, for each member state had a judge of its nationality on the Court, and these were paid regular salaries from the treasury of the Court. Judicial independence was marginal; in one instance a judge was dismissed from office during the tenure of his five-year term by the state appointing him. No regional court was instituted to replace it until the new Charter of the Organisation of Central American States (ODECA) came into force in 1965 and provided for a new Central American Court of Justice. But this was a much less ambitious venture, having no compulsory jurisdiction over inter-state disputes nor allowing rights of access for individuals. The current Court of Justice, which is located in Managua, Nicaragua, constitutes a return to origins, with competence in three types of cases: inter-state disputes, complaints against states (initiated by state parties, SICA organs and natural or legal persons), and complaints against SICA organs (initiated by a state party and, in limited cases, a natural or legal person). The Court also has competence over staff cases, in respect of constitutional controversies between the main branches of government of a state party, and an advisory competence (allowing it to provide advisory opinions, including by way of preliminary reference procedure similar to that of Article 177 of the E.C. Treaty). Each participating state (currently three) has one judge. To date the Court has received some 16 cases (including nine requests for advisory opinions).

Court of Justice of the Andean Community

The Court of Justice of the Andean Community was established in 1979 **13–155** and has its seat in Quito, Ecuador.[87] The Court comprises five judges. In 1996 the five parties concluded a Protocol Modifying the Treaty Creating the court which will significantly enhance the jurisdiction of the Court (some provisions related to the recent reform in the structure of the Community order are already applied on a temporary basis). The competence of the Court is generally modelled on that of the ECJ. Complaints

---

[86] Protocol of Tegucigalpa of Reforms to the Charter of the Organisation of the Central American States, December 13, 1991: (1995) 34 ILM 921.

[87] Treaty Creating the Court of Justice of the Cartagena Agreement, May 28, 1979, (1979) 17 ILM 1203 (unofficial translation). In 1996 a modifying protocol was concluded in Cochabamba, Bolivia. Modifying Protocol of the Treaty Creating the Court of Court of Justice of the Cartagena Agreement, May 28, 1996, http://www.comunidadandina.org/MODITRIB.HTM [hereinafter "Modifying Protocol"].

against member states may be brought by another member state for failure to comply with obligations under community law, or on the initiative of the General Secretariat. Once the Modifying Protocol comes into force any natural or legal person whose rights are affected by a breach of community law by a member state will also be able to bring a complaint. Complaints against community institutions can be brought by another institution, a member state (except in case of a challenge to the validity of a decision or agreement it previously subscribed to), and natural and legal persons whose rights or legitimate interests are affected by the challenged act or omission. The Court may also give preliminary interpretive opinions on reference to national courts, and can exercise jurisdiction in private disputes (where so agreed by contract) and in respect of labour disputes involving the staff of the Andean Integration System. The Court has decided seven cases brought against member states (two of which were brought by another member state) and 12 cases brought against community institutions. It has also rendered some 150 preliminary interpretative opinions.

COMESA

13–156 The COMESA Court of Justice supervises the interpretation and application of the treaty establishing the Common Market for Eastern and Southern Africa (COMESA) and currently encompassing 21 African states.[88] It comprises seven judges and is to be temporarily seated in Lusaka, Zambia. The jurisdiction of the COMESA court is generally similar to that of the ECJ. It will exercise jurisdiction over (a) claims brought against states (alleging violations of the COMESA Treaty or its provisions) at the instigation of the Secretary-General of COMESA and any person who resides in a COMESA member state (provided local remedies have been exhausted); (b) claims brought against the COMESA Council of Ministers (by a member state or a person residing in a COMESA member state, on grounds *ultra vires*, unlawfulness, infringement of the COMESA Treaty and related law, or misuse or abuse of power); (c) preliminary rulings referred by a national court or tribunal concerning the application or interpretation of the COMESA Treaty or the validity of secondary legislation (*i.e.* COMESA regulations, directives and decisions). The Court also has jurisdiction over cases referred to it by way of an arbitration clause or special agreement between the Common Market or one of its institution and a third-party; or between two or more member states, and over staff cases and claims presented by any person against the Common Market or its institutions due to official acts of COMESA staff (*e.g.* non-contractual liability). The Court may render advisory opinions at the request of the Authority, Council of Ministers or any member state, on any question of law arising from the COMESA Treaty and affecting the COMESA organisation.

---

[88] COMESA Treaty, Art. 19. Website: http://www.comesa.int.

NAFTA

Supervision over the implementation of NAFTA is primarily for the **13–157** NAFTA Free Trade Commission, assisted by the Secretariat.[89] Most disputes arising under NAFTA are to be assigned by the Commission to ad hoc dispute settlement panels, roughly modelled on the GATT/WTO dispute settlement panels.[90] Chapter 20 of the NAFTA Agreement addresses disputes between the state parties concerning: (i) the interpretation or application of the NAFTA Agreement; or (ii) allegations that the application of an actual or proposed measure taken by a party is inconsistent with its NAFTA obligations, or would cause impairment or nullification of certain benefits that the complaining party expects to attain under NAFTA.[91] Once a dispute has arisen the parties must first enter into consultations. If no solution is found within a specified period the complaining party may request to convene the Free Trade Commission, which will put its good offices at the disposal of the parties in order to facilitate a settlement. If the parties fail to reach agreement within an additional fixed period of time, any party can request the Commission to establish an ad hoc arbitration panel.[92] A panel comprises five independent experts. The procedure taken by the panels follows closely that of GATT/WTO arrangements. The panel issues a final report containing factual and legal findings, which is binding upon the parties.

Chapter 19 of NAFTA introduces a separate dispute settlement mecha- **13–158** nism for review of antidumping and countervailing duties adopted by the three member states. The central feature of this mechanism is the establishment of ad hoc binational panels to review domestic administrative determinations relating to antidumping and countervailing duties. A state party to NAFTA may request the establishment of a binational panel if: (1) another party has adopted a statutory amendment which is inconsistent with the GATT (or certain specified side-agreements) or the object and purpose of NAFTA,[93] or has the function and effect of overturning a binational panel decision (and is also inconsistent with the GATT and/or NAFTA), and (2) if a determination of a competent domestic authority on antidumping or countervailing duties is incompatible with the domestic law

---

[89] NAFTA, Arts 2001–2002.
[90] North American Free Trade Agreement, December 17, 1992, (1993) 32 ILM 289 and 605. NAFTA is in fact an extension of the 1988 U.S-Canada Free Trade Agreement, on which the provisions of NAFTA are based. Canada-United States Free Trade Agreement, January 2, 1988, (1988) 27 ILM 868.
[91] NAFTA, Art. 2004.
[92] NAFTA, Art. 2008. The normal period before establishment of a panel is 30 days from the date the Commission was first convened to discuss the dispute.
[93] NAFTA, Arts 1902.2(d), 1903.1 (a). Subsection 2(d)(ii) defines the purpose and object of NAFTA as: "to establish fair and predictable conditions for the progressive liberalisation of trade among the Parties to this Agreement, while maintaining effective and fair disciplines on unfair trade practices."

of the importing state, as would have been applied by a domestic court of review.[94] Binational panels comprise five independent and qualified experts, which are supposed to be normally selected from a roster of at least 75 persons.[95] Binational panels established to review administrative determinations are to apply the same standards of review that a domestic court would have applied.[96] A private litigant is to have the same procedural rights before a binational panel, as he or she would have had before a comparable domestic review tribunal.[97] The supervision over the mechanism of binational panels reviewing administrative determinations is assigned to two ad hoc bodies—the Extraordinary Challenge Committee, which may be requested to review the integrity of the mechanism, and a Special Committee which oversees state compliance in relation to the operation of the mechanism.

E. ADMINISTRATIVE TRIBUNALS

Bibliography: Abla, *Les conditions de recevabilité de la requête devant les tribunaux administratifs de l'ONU et de l'OIT* (1991); Akehurst, *The Law Governing Employment in International Organisations* (1967); Amerasinghe, *Documents on International Administrative Tribunals* (1989); Amerasinghe, *The Law of the International Civil Service—As Applied by International Administrative Tribunals* (2 vols., 2nd ed., 1994); Amerasinghe, "Supervision by Administrative Tribunals of Legislative Acts of International Organisations in Relation with their Staff" in *Essays in Honour of Schermers* (1994) p. 239; Amerasinghe, *Case-Law of the World Bank Administrative Tribunal*, (3 vols., 1989, 1993, 1998); Bastid: *Le Tribunal Administratif des Nations Unies*, (1970); de Cooker (ed.), *International Administration: Law and Management Practices in International Organisations (part V: Judicial Protection)* (1999); Gomula, "The International Court of Justice and Administrative Tribunals of International Organisations" (1991) 13 Michigan Journal of International Law 83; Jenks, *The Proper Law of International Organisations* (1962), Part II; Pellet, *Les voies de recours ouvertes aux fonctionnairesinternationaux* (1982); Szasz, "Adjudicating Staff Challenges to Legislative Decisions of International Organisations" in *Liber Amicorum Professor Seidl-Hohenveldern—In Honour of his 80th birthday* (1998) p. 699; Wolf, *Le tribunal administratif de l'OIT* (1970); SFDI, *Le contentieux de la fonction publique internationale* (1996).

13–159 THE creation of international civil services, or secretariats, whose members are bound to the organisation they serve by a contractual or statutory relationship, made it desirable to establish special tribunals competent to determine disputes arising from that relationship. This is all the more so,

---

[94] NAFTA, Art. 1904.2.
[95] NAFTA, Annex 1901.2. The parties may also select non-roster panel members, however, in this case, the other party has a right to disqualify up to four of non-roster candidates.
[96] NAFTA, Art. 1904.3.
[97] NAFTA, Arts 1904.5, 1904.7.

given the difficulties raised by addressing these issues in the national courts, and once the view had been accepted that the employees of international organisations acquired legal rights which ought to be protected by a system of administrative justice, on the continental pattern, and not left to the unfettered discretion of the executive as had been traditionally the practice in the Anglo-American systems. Direct submission of such disputes to the P.C.I.J., or later the I.C.J., was impossible in view of the fact that the parties were respectively, individuals on the one hand and international organisations on the other. Submission to municipal courts was inappropriate, for it conflicted with the general immunity from local jurisdiction claimed by the organisations.[98]

Moreover, the dispute generally involved a question of the internal, **13–160** administrative law of the organisation and not local law. Further, municipal courts were themselves generally reluctant to assume any jurisdiction over such disputes even when no agreement on immunities existed.[99] Hence, if the acquired rights of the staff members were to be protected by an impartial judicial body, special tribunals had to be created.

In the League of Nations a system of appeal to the Council was, in 1927, **13–161** replaced by a permanent administrative tribunal. This was used also by the ILO, and this tribunal continues today as the ILO Administrative Tribunal. The International Institute of Agriculture in Rome established a tribunal in 1932, after the Italian courts had declined jurisdiction over disputes between staff and the Institute.[1] The United Nations did not continue with the League's tribunal but, after considerable opposition to the idea of a tribunal, established its own tribunal in 1949 (UNAT).[2] As the I.C.J. subsequently put it, it would hardly have been:

"consistent with the expressed aim of the Charter to promote freedom and justice for individuals and with the constant preoccupation of the United Nations Organisation to promote this aim that it should afford no judicial or arbitral remedy to its own staff for the settlement of any disputes which may arise between it and them."[3]

---

[98] See *e.g. Eckhardt v. Eurocontrol*, Maastricht District Court, January 12, 1984, 94 I.L.R. 338 and *Cristiani v. Italian-Latin-American Institute*, Italian Court of Cassation, November 26, 1985, 87 I.L.R. 26.

[99] See Bastid, "Les tribunaux administratifs internationaux et leur jurisprudence" (1957) 11 R.d.C. 354–370.

[1] *Institut d'agriculture c. Profili*, Cour de Cassation, (1929–30) A.D., Case No. 254.

[2] The Statute was adopted by the General Assembly on November 24, 1949 (res. 351 A (IV)). It was amended in 1953, 1955, 1995 and 1997. The Statute, as amended, is reproduced in Doc. AT/11/Rev. 5.

[3] Advisory Opinion on the *Effect of Awards of Compensation Made by the United Nations Administrative Tribunal*, July 13, 1954, [1954] I.C.J. Rep. 57.

13–162   The Statute of the ILO Tribunal (ILOAT) was amended in 1949 to enable other international inter-governmental organisations to use the tribunal as their administrative tribunal[4]; today, WHO, UNESCO, ITU, WMO, FAO, IAEA, UPU, WTO, WIPO, IFAD, UNIDO, CERN (European Organisation for Nuclear Research), Eurocontrol and EFTA are among the organisations which have provided for access to ILOAT.[5] Similarly Article 13 (3) of the UN Tribunal's Statute enables the competence of that tribunal to be extended to any specialised agency. Most of these agencies, being European-based, have preferred to utilise the ILO Tribunal; thus far the IMO and the ICAO are the only UN specialised agencies to have chosen the UNAT to settle staff disputes. However, because of the common pensions scheme, most specialised agencies—and some other universal organisations which are not part of the UN system—have accepted the jurisdiction of the UN Tribunal for pensions disputes.[6] More recently, the UNAT's competence has been extended to the staff of the I.C.J. Registry,[7] and of the ITLOS Registry,[8] respectively.

13–163   Suggestions for merging the two administrative tribunals coexisting within the UN system have never been acted upon.[9] On the contrary, the creation of the World Bank Administrative Tribunal (WBAT) in 1980,[10] and of the International Monetary Fund Administrative Tribunal (IMFAT) in 1992[11] confirmed the fragmentation of the system in that respect. Since

---

[4] The Statute has been further amended in 1986, 1992 and 1998; see text at http://www.ilo.org/public/english/tribunal/stateng.htm.

[5] The complete list, which includes more than 30 organisations, is available at http://www.ilo.org/public/english/tribunal/orgs.htm. The ILO Tribunal (and its predecessor under the League) has also been used as a "panel" of arbitrators to form an arbitral body for staff disputes by the Institute for the Unification of Private Law, the International Institute for Intellectual Co-operation, the Nansen Office and the International Institute for Educational Cinema.

[6] See *e.g.* in that respect Art. 11, para. 3 of the Relationship Agreement concluded on March 14, 1997 between the International Sea-bed Authority and the United Nations; text annexed to UNGA Res A/52/27 of November 26, 1997.

[7] See Art. 13, para. 1 of the UNAT Statute, as amended by UNGA Resolution 52/166 of December 15, 1997. Prior to that extension, Art. 11 of the Staff Regulations for the I.C.J. Registry provided that one judge was elected by the court to hear staff appeals against decisions of the Registrar; if no proper solution could be found, the matter could be referred by either party to the whole Court for settlement ([1978–1979] I.C.J. Y.B. 127). Disputes between staff members and the Court's Registrar never seem to have actually reached that judicial stage.

[8] In the latter case, provided that the conciliation procedure established by the staff Regulations has failed (see Art. XI, g) of the Staff Regulations, doc. ITLOS/18/Rev. 1 of October 8, 1998).

[9] See especially the views expressed by Lachs ("The Judiciary and the International Civil Service" in *Law of Nations, Law of International Organisations, World's Economic Law—Liber Amicorum Seidl-Hohenveldern* (1988) pp. 301–313), and more generally Tavernier, "La fusion des tribunaux administratifs des Nations Unies et de l'OIT : nécessité ou utopie ?" (1979) 25 AFDI 442.

[10] The WBAT may hear staff disputes to which the IBRD, IDA or IFC are parties.

[11] Resolution 48–1 of the Fund's Board of Governors.

their creation, the ILO, UN and World Bank Administrative Tribunals have produced a very significant body of jurisprudence, which constitutes an important contribution to the law of the international civil service.[12]

Administrative tribunals have similarly been established within numerous **13–164** regional organisations such as the OAS,[13] the Arab League, the Council of Europe,[14] the African Development Bank,[15] the Inter-American Development Bank,[16] the Asian Development Bank,[17] SELA and the OECD.[18] In the European Communities, it is the Court of First Instance which, along with other competences, is entrusted with the settlement of staff disputes and thus acts—partly at least—as an administrative tribunal.[19]

In other organisations—such as ESA, NATO and the Agence de la **13–165** Francophonie—the same function is performed by an Appeal Board, established as a body of final resort and capable of giving judgments binding on staff member and organisation alike. Finally, organisations which do not make use of either the UN Administrative Tribunal or the ILO Administrative Tribunal or which have not established their own judicial machinery for settling such disputes generally rely on internal administrative procedures or ad hoc arbitration.

What is the character of these bodies? The judicial character of the UN **13–166** Administrative Tribunal has been affirmed by the I.C.J. in its 1954 Advisory Opinion, where the court concluded that the "examination of the relevant provisions of the statute shows that the tribunal is established, not as an advisory organ or a mere subordinate committee of the General Assembly, but as an independent and truly judicial body pronouncing final judgments without appeal within the limited field of its functions."[20]

The same could safely be said of the other administrative tribunals **13–167** mentioned above, their respective statute being drafted along lines very similar to that of the UNAT. The differences between the existing

---

[12] Up to now, more than 1900 cases have been submitted to the ILOAT, more than 900 to the UNAT, and more than 250 to the WBAT.
[13] Res. AG/RES. 35 (I-0/71) adopted by the General Assembly on April 22, 1971. Text reproduced in doc. OEA/Ser. R/I.1 of July 6, 1998.
[14] Statute of 1982, amended by Res. (94)11 of April 5, 1994.
[15] Statute adopted by the Board of Governors on July 6, 1997.
[16] Statute adopted by the Board of Executive Directors on April 29, 1981.
[17] Statute amended on December 22, 1994.
[18] The latter was established in December 1991 and replaced the OECD Appeals Board—which had itself succeeded to the OEEC Appeals Board.
[19] See Art. 236 of the E.C. Treaty, combined with Art. 3 of the Council Decision 88/591 of October 24, 1988, [1988] O.J. L319/1. This function was exercised by the Court of Justice prior to the creation of the Court of First Instance. The judgments rendered by the Court of First Instance in staff disputes can be appealed by either party before the Court of Justice (Art. 225, E.C. Treaty).
[20] *Loc. cit.*, p. 53.

administrative tribunals indeed appear minimal in comparison to the broad similarity of purpose and jurisdiction; they shall therefore be dealt with here on a comparative basis.

(a) COMPOSITION

13–168 Being international tribunals,[21] the administrative tribunals are composed of judges of different nationalities. Their number varies and they are elected for relatively short periods (two or three years generally[22]) by the political organs of the organisations concerned.[23] The judges are all independent of the organisations concerned and, in the UN, dismissal by the Assembly is conditional on the agreement of all the other members of the Tribunal (Article 3(5), Statute). They benefit from the privileges and immunities accorded to experts on missions and are paid a *per diem* rather than a salary in view of the irregularity of their sittings. Each tribunal is assisted by its own secretariat or registry, normally supplied by the organisation but controlled by the tribunal itself, and this functions continually in between the sittings of the tribunal which are called by the President of the Tribunal as business requires.

(b) PROCEDURE

13–169 The Tribunals sit with a quorum, holding their proceedings in public as a general rule but with discretion to hold private sessions.[24] The procedure is predominantly modelled on the French system and is based very much on the written briefs lodged by the parties; this first stage is followed by a second short, oral hearing, at which counsel for both parties can be heard and even witnesses produced, but this is largely by way of supplementing the original written brief or in order to answer supplementary questions posed by the tribunal itself. Generally there is a right of intervention for all persons having access to the tribunal and whose rights are likely to be affected by the judgment;[25] some tribunals' rules of procedure even allow for hearing representatives of the Staff Association.[26]

13–170 The applicant must in all cases show that he or she is appealing against a final decision of the administration which has caused him or her some injury;[27] this is confirmed as a rule of general application by the jurispru-

---

[21] See [1956] I.C.J. Rep. 97.

[22] The OAS Administrative Tribunal may be viewed as an exception in that respect, since its statute provides that the judges' term of office is six years (Art. III(3)).

[23] Note that the chairperson of the Administrative Tribunal of the Council of Europe is to be a member of the European Court of Human Rights (Rule 1 of the Rules of Procedure).

[24] See *e.g.* the Statutes of UNAT (Art. 8), WBAT (Art. IX) or OECDAT (Art. 10).

[25] In some cases, this includes institutions or organisations which may have an interest in defending the normative act contested by the applicant (see for instance the *Pasetti-Bombardella* case before the CJEC, case 20/68, (1969) E.C.R. 235).

[26] See *e.g.* UNAT, Rule 19(2); Council of Europe Administrative Tribunal, Art. 10(1) of the Statute.

[27] See, *e.g.* the staff regulations of the OECD (Art. 22), E.C. (Art. 90), Council of Europe (Art. 59), OAS (Art. 112(2)).

dence of the tribunals.[28] This requirement is consistent with the notion that each tribunal is normally the body of last resort, and this is further emphasised by the requirement that the applicant must first have exhausted all remedies within the organisation itself. In the UN tribunal, for example, prior recourse to the joint appeals body is a necessary pre-condition to the jurisdiction of the tribunal except when both applicant and the Secretary-General have agreed to dispense with it (Article 7(1)). The ILO has similar internal procedures which must be exhausted, OECD envisages appeal to the Secretary-General and CERN, which uses the ILO Tribunal, even provides for arbitration by a body constituted from within the organisation.[29] Secondly, the applicant must submit his request to the tribunal within a prescribed time, running from the date on which he or she was notified of the final decision against which he or she is appealing.[30]

(c) JURISDICTION

As with other international tribunals, the administrative tribunals have the **13–171** power to determine their own jurisdiction (*Kompetenz-Kompetenz*).[31] *Ratione personae*, the jurisdiction of the tribunals is largely confined to disputes between officials of the organisation and the organisations themselves. The rank of the official,[32] or the duration of his contract, is irrelevant, but he or she must normally be (or have been) an official in the technical sense; hence temporary experts or consultants, or locally recruited personnel such as gardeners, cleaners, etc., usually do not have a right to access to the tribunal,[33] for they do not enter into a contract which incorporates the Staff Rules and Regulations. These categories of person-

---

[28] See, for example, ILO Tribunal, Judgment No. 15 (*Leff*); UN Tribunal, Judgment No. 56 (*Aglion*). Note that Article 7 (2) of the UN Tribunal's Statute treats failure to act by the Secretary-General in accordance with the opinion of the Joint Appeals Board favourable to the applicant as equivalent to a "decision" by the Secretary-General so as to allow the Tribunal to receive the application.

[29] Statute of the ILOAT, Art. 7; see also *e.g.* WBAT, Art. II(2)(i), OASAT, Art. VI(1)(a); IADBAT, Art. II(2), a), AsDBAT, Art. II(3)(a). For a discussion of the *ratio* of the rule's applicability in this field, see WBAT, Judgment No. 51 (*Berg*).

[30] This is 90 days in the ILO, the UN (although the UN Tribunal has power to extend the period, Art. 7 (5)), the OECD (Art. 4, a), the Inter-American Development Bank. (Art. II(2)(b) and the Asian Development Bank (Art. II(3)(b)).

[31] This is stated explicitly in some statutes; see *e.g.* WBAT, Art. III, OASAT, Art. II, 5, Council of Europe AT, Art. 4, IMFAT, Art. IV, AfDBAT, Art. V(1)(b), AsDBAT, Art. III. See the affirmation by the I.C.J. of *Kompetenz-Kompetenz* as a general principle in the *Nottebohm* case (prelim. objection), [1953] I.C.J. Rep. 119–120.

[32] Hence a former Secretary-General of the League of Nations became an applicant in *Joseph Avenol v. Caisse des Pensions S.D.N.*, ILO Tribunal, Judgment No. 2 (1947). An existing Secretary-General would be an unlikely applicant, since he is normally the nominal defendant, but presumably he could contest a decision of the Organisation affecting him.

[33] But note that the jurisdiction of the OECD Administrative Tribunal has been specifically extended to experts and consultants and to auxiliary staff (Statute, Art. 1(a)). The distinction between an official and an expert is elaborated in the decision of the Court of Justice of the European Communities in the *Roemer* case (Case 26/68, Vol. XV, p. 145) and of the OECD Appeals Board in the *Rufo* case (dec. No. 41).

nel will have to rely for a remedy upon arbitration or recourse to local courts, provided the organisation waives immunity.[34] For the purpose of the determination of the UN Administrative Tribunal's jurisdiction, the UN officials include officials of agencies like the Office of the High Commissioner of Refugees, UNICEF, UNRWA, UNDP or UNEP. Whether the respondent is the Secretary-General of the UN or the agency will depend on the degree of autonomy of the agency; hence, in the case of UNRWA applications are against UNRWA itself and not the Secretary-General.[35] The jurisdiction of the tribunals is generally extended to successors in title to a deceased official.

13–172 The extent of the jurisdiction *ratione materiae* of the administrative tribunals is somewhat less easy to ascertain. Article 2 (1) of the UN Tribunal's Statute provides:

> "The Tribunal shall be competent to hear and pass judgment upon applications alleging non-observance of contracts of employment of staff members of the Secretariat of the United Nations or of the terms of appointment of such staff members. The words "contracts" and "terms of appointment" include all pertinent regulations and rules in force at the time of the alleged non-observance, including the staff regulations."[36]

13–173 The ILO Tribunal's Statute (Article 2) is more complex but not essentially different.[37] In the European Court the formulation is briefer and more general. Basically, however, the task of the tribunals is to adjudicate disputes arising from the contracts or the terms of employment.[38] The problems arising from this task are really twofold. The first, a problem common to administrative tribunals generally, even in municipal systems, is how far the tribunal is competent to question the exercise of administrative discretion. The second, a problem peculiar to international administrative tribunals, concerns the law to be applied to these disputes.

The line between matters properly within the jurisdiction of administrative tribunals and those matters in which interference with the discretion of the

---

[34] Bastid, *loc. cit.*, pp. 444–450.

[35] See *Hilpern v. UNRWA*, UNAT, Judgment No. 57.

[36] See also *e.g.* the Statutes of WBAT, Art. II, IADBAT, Art. II, OASAT, Art. II, 1 and OECD Staff Regulations, Art. 22(c).

[37] It should nevertheless be observed that the ILOAT has the exceptional—and rather unusual—competence to settle disputes relating to contracts concluded by the ILO with private parties (for procurement, services, etc.) (Statute, Art. II(4)).

[38] ILO Tribunal Judgment No. 66 (*Press*) indicates that it will nevertheless assume jurisdiction over the statutory rights of the official *vis-à-vis* the organisation even if no specific provision of the staff regulation, rules or contract can be invoked. It should also be noted that the jurisdiction *ratione materiae* of the administrative tribunals includes the power to adjudicate claims for the compensation of service-incurred damages (see *e.g.* ILOAT Statute, Art. II, 2).

administration[39] is improper is always difficult to draw. International administrative tribunals acknowledge that they have but a limited power to review decisions taken by the administration within the realm of its discretionary powers.[40] They have nevertheless clearly indicated that such discretion is not to be viewed as absolute, and that its mere invocation will not bar them from exercising their power of review.[41] As the WBAT put it in one of its early judgments:

> "[t]he final decision in [. . .] respect [of performance evaluation] rests with the Respondent as long as the exercise of discretion is not discriminatory, improperly motivated, based on error of fact or otherwise tainted by abuse of power."[42]

Indeed, in practice, international administrative tribunals have not hesitated to rescind administrative decisions taken in virtue of discretionary powers when the judges were satisfied that the motives put forward by the administrative organ were not the actual grounds on which the decision had been taken (*détournement de pouvoir*),[43] or when it appeared that procedural requirements had not been respected by the administration. Discretionary administrative decisions have been rescinded for, *inter alia*, the following reasons: **13–174**

- they had been taken on a discriminatory basis;[44]

- they entailed a violation of the principle of equity;[45]

- they carried sanctions which were out of proportion with the agent's misconduct;[46]

---

[39] A classical example of such a discretionary power is the decision by the administration to renew—or not—a contract.

[40] See *e.g.* UNAT, No. 690 (*Chileshe*), para. V.

[41] See *e.g.* UNAT, No. 847 (*Wyss*), para. V.

[42] No. 28 (*Gyamfi*), para. 28; see also *e.g.* WBAT, No. 145 (*Sjamsubahri*), para. 20. See also the formula used by the OECDAT : ". . .choices of this type fall within the Organisation's discretionary powers which the tribunal has no jurisdiction to review unless there is something to suggest a misuse of powers or a manifest error of judgment" (No. 33, *Calogeropoulos*, p. 4); the tribunal notes amongst others that the applicant had not suffered discriminatory treatment.

[43] On this notion, see Amerasinghe, *The Law of the International Civil Service* (2nd ed., Vol. I, 1994), p.277.

[44] See *e.g.* ILOAT, No. 1706 (*Broere-Moore No. 5*), para. 18; UNAT, No. 702 (*Beg*), para. VI.

[45] See *e.g.* UNAT, No. 765 (*Andersen-Bieler*).

[46] See *e.g.* UNAT, No. 755 (*Chen*), para. VII; WBAT, No. 142 (*Carew*), para. 45 and No. 143 (*Planthara*), para. 41.

- they were taken on grounds which the applicable rules were forbidding to take into account;[47]

- there had been a failure to ensure a due disciplinary process.

13–175   This power of review of administrative acts based on discretion is not limited to individual decisions; it has in some cases been extended to normative or "legislative" acts taken by the respondent organisation.[49] What is clear is that the limits on the administrative tribunals' power of review lies in the fact that they are not entitled to substitute their views of what is administratively convenient or desirable for that of the administrative organ whose decision is challenged.[50]

13–176   The second problem concerns the law to be applied by the tribunals. Recognising that it would be inappropriate to apply either municipal or international law as such, there has developed a body of "internal administrative law" in each of the organisations concerned. This generally comprises the terms of the particular contract in question and the relevant Staff Regulations, Staff Rules and Administrative Instructions. These last three sources are in a hierarchy to which the *ultra vires* doctrine applies, so that the regulations established by the "political" organ govern the legality of the rules promulgated by the "administrative" organ (Secretary- or Director-General in most cases) and both, in turn, govern the Administrative Instructions. These texts may also be supplemented, in certain circum-

---

[47] ILOAT, No. 17 (*Duberg*), No. 18 (*Leff*), No. 19 (*Wilcox*), No. 21 (*Bernstein*); No. 23 (*Pankey*). In these cases, the Tribunal considered that the decision by UNESCO Director-General not to renew the applicants' contract on the ground that they had refused to appear before a Loyalty Board set up by the American authorities in order to exclude members or supporters of communist organisations from the ranks of American national or international civil servants was unlawful. The ILOAT decided that the Director-General was thereby associating himself with the execution of the policy of a member state's government and disregarding the achievement of the exclusively international objectives which the authority he had been entrusted with was designed to serve (see especially *Duberg, loc. cit.*, p. 8). The tribunal's competence to issue such judgments has subsequently been put into question before the I.C.J., but the court refused to give an opinion on the ILOAT's power to review the decision which had been taken by the Director General in virtue of discretionary powers since this issue lay outside the scope of matters on which, under Article XII of the Tribunal's Statute, opinions could be requested (*Judgments of the Administrative Tribunal of the International Labour Organisation Upon Complaints Made Against the UNESCO*, October 23, 1956, [1956] I.C.J. Rep. 77, 99). See also, more recently, UNAT, No. 686 (*Rebizov*), para. II and V.

[48] UNAT, No. 744 (*Eren et al.*), para. XXIII; OECDAT, No. 29 (*Morin*).

[49] WBAT, No. 1 (*de Mérode*), para. 47; *in casu* the normative acts contested were amendments to the rules defining the rights and obligations of the staff. See also the Statute of IMFAT, which expressly provides for the possibility to challenge "the legality of a regulatory decision" (Art. VI, 2). See Art. II, 2, (b) of the Statute for a definition of "regulatory decisions" and, for a comment, Powers, "Reinventing the Wheel—The Establishment of the IMF Administrative Tribunal" in *International Administration : Law and Management Practices in International Organisations* (de Cooker (ed.), Vol. 10, 1999) pp.4–7.

[50] See UNAT, Judgments No. 21 (*Rubin*), No. 43 (*Levinson*), No. 48 (*Wang*); ILOAT, Judgments No. 65 (*Morse*), No. 32 (*Garcin*), No. 69 (*Kissaun*); CJEC, Cases 35/62 and 26/63.

stances, by the practice of the organisation concerned.[51] In the event of any lacuna, or as an aid to the construction of the relevant contractual provisions, the tribunals may make reference to other sources such as the UN Charter, the principles applied in municipal law or "general principles of law." None of these tribunals adopt the principle of *stare decisis*, so that no judgment ever becomes a binding precedent; however, as the body of case-law develops, the tribunals do develop a *"jurisprudence constante"* to which repeated reference is made in subsequent cases. References by international administrative tribunals to the jurisprudence of other such tribunals are not exceptional.[52] It is interesting to note that, in at least one case, this "contentious" jurisdiction is supplemented by the power to give advisory opinions at the request of a specific organ "on any question of law concerning the general administration" of the organisation concerned.[53]

(d) JUDGMENTS

The judgments of the Tribunals must be reasoned[54] and, except for the UN, **13–177** IMF and Asian Development Bank Tribunals which allow dissenting judgments, they are single majority judgments. When the judgment is against the organisation the normal order (and the primary remedy of the applicant) is one of annulment of the contested decision or a decree for specific performance of the obligation of the organisation towards the staff member.[55] In the more exceptional cases, such as that of the IMFAT, where the statute provides for the possibility to challenge the legality of a regulatory decision (*i.e.* the normative act on the basis of which individual decisions have been taken), the regulatory decision is similarly annuled by the tribunal if it reaches the conclusion that the application is well-founded.[56] An award of compensation does not follow as a matter of right, but may follow when annulment or specific performance "is not possible or advisable."[57] In the case of the UN Tribunal and the OECD Administrative Tribunal, it is clearly for the Secretary-General to decide whether or not to

---

[51] See *e.g.* WBAT, No. 1 (*de Mérode*), para. 23. This may of course raise the problem of ascertaining the very existence of the practice in question (see *e.g.* ILOAT, No. 1806 (*Gran Olsen*), para. 16–17).

[52] See the position of principle taken by the WBAT in the *de Mérode* case, *loc. cit.*, para. 28. See more generally C. Amerasinghe, *The Law of the International Civil Service* (2nd ed., Vol. I, 1994), p.196 *et seq.*

[53] Art. IV of the Statute of the African Development Bank Administrative Tribunal. Opinions may be requested by the Board of Governors.

[54] See *e.g.* the Statutes of ILOAT, Art. VI(2), UNAT, Art. 10(3), WBAT, Art. X(1), IMFAT, Art. XIII(3), OASAT, Art. VIII(3), OECDAT, Art. 12(a), Council of Europe AT, Art. 12(1), AfDBAT, Art. XII(2).

[55] See Art. 9 (1) of the UN Tribunal's Statute: "If the Tribunal finds that the application is well founded, it shall order the rescinding of the decision contested or the specific performance of the obligation invoked". See also *e.g.* the Statutes of ILOAT, Art. VIII, WBAT, Art. XII, IADBAT, Art. IX, AfDBAT, Art. XIII(1), OASAT, Art. VII.

[56] Art. XIV(3) of the Statute.

[57] Statute of the ILOAT, Art. IX; see also *e.g.* the Statute of the OECDAT, Art. 12(c).

take the action required by the annulment or decree of specific performance; only if, "in exceptional circumstances" (for the UN) or "cases" (for the OECD), the Secretary-General decides not to take such action does the amount of compensation fixed by the tribunal become due to the applicant as a kind of secondary remedy. Most statutes also fix the normal limit of compensation as the equivalent of two or three years' net base salary, but some give the tribunal power to fix a higher sum upon—exceptional— reasons being stated.[58] In cases where the administrative decision is not rescinded, Tribunals may nevertheless award compensation to the claimant if the judges consider that the action—or lack thereof—of the administrative organ, while not unlawful *per se*, has actually caused some degree of material or moral damage to the claimant. Finally, legal costs may also generally be awarded by the Tribunal against the organisation.[59]

13–178   While the bearing of international administrative tribunals' judgments *inter partes* (*i.e.* the claimant on the one hand and the administration on the other) is very clearly defined by their respective Statute, the legal effects of these decisions *vis-à-vis* "political" organs of the organisation have raised serious controversies, within the United Nations system at least.[60] In 1953 certain member states of the UN were willing to oppose the supplementary appropriations in the budget necessary to implement the awards of compensation pronounced by the UNAT in the "5th Amendment Cases."[61] The issue was referred by the Assembly to the I.C.J. for an advisory opinion. In its answers to the questions submitted by the General Assembly, the court stated that although the tribunal was a subsidiary organ created by the Assembly (and capable of suppression by the Assembly) this did not imply subordination of the judgments of the tribunal to subsequent decisions of the Assembly; on the contrary, the Assembly had established a judicial body capable of rendering judgments in the nature of a *res judicata*, which the Assembly was under a legal duty to accept and give effect to.[62] According to the court:

> "[a]s th[e Tribunal] final judgment has binding force on the United Nations Organisation as the juridical person responsible for the proper

---

[58] See *e.g.* the statutes of the UNAT, Art. 9(1), WBAT, Art. XII, IADBAT, Art. IX, OASAT, Art. VII.

[59] The power to award costs is expressly recognised in some Tribunals' Statute (see *e.g.*, OECDAT, Art. 13(a)), and has been assumed by others as inherent in their jurisdiction (in the cases of ILOAT and UNAT, for example). No costs are awarded against staff members; a requirement that the staff member deposits a sum as security for costs was deleted from the old LoNAT Statute in 1946.

[60] It may also be noted in that respect that in 1946 already the Assembly of the League of Nations had refused to give effect to the League Tribunal's judgment in *Mayras v. S.G. of the League* which purported to interpret the Assembly resolutions (erroneously in the view of the Assembly).

[61] These include UNAT judgments No. 30 to 38. The factual background of the claims is the same as the one described *supra*, n. 47, in the context of UNESCO.

[62] Advisory Opinion of July 13, 1954, *loc. cit.*

observance of the contract of service, that Organisation becomes legally bound to carry out the judgment and to pay the compensation awarded to the staff member."[63]

Because of the dissatisfaction of certain member states with this position **13–179** provision for a kind of appeals procedure to the I.C.J. was made under the UN Tribunal's Statute.[64] The mandatory effect of judgments *vis-à-vis* the organisation concerned has in any event been strongly emphasised in later instruments. Hence, Article 13(4) of the UNAT Statute, as amended in 1997, makes it clear that agreements concluded with other international organisations or entities participating in the common system of conditions of service to which the competence of the Tribunal is extended must:

"provide that the organisation or entity concerned shall be bound by the judgments of the tribunal and be responsible for the payment of any compensation awarded by the tribunal in respect of a staff member of that organisation or entity."[65]

The judgments' binding force does not, however, prevent the possibility **13–180** for application to be made subsequently to the tribunals for the interpretation of a judgment.[66] Application can also be made to most administrative tribunals for the revision of a judgment upon the discovery of some new fact of such a nature as to be a decisive factor.[67]

(e) REVIEW OF JUDGMENTS

To establish a procedure for the review of judgments is, of course, totally **13–181** different from establishing a procedure whereby the tribunal concerned can interpret or revise its own judgments; a review procedure presupposes review by some organ other than the tribunal giving the judgment, and to that extent means that the judgment of the tribunal is not a final judgment from which no appeal can be made.

Under the League of Nations, as is now the case in most administrative **13–182** tribunals, the judgments were final. In 1946, however, the Statute of the ILO Tribunal was re-drafted to include a new Article XII allowing for what is virtually a limited right of appeal by the governing body or Administra-

---

[63] *ibid.*, p. 53.
[64] See *infra*, para. 13–182.
[65] As amended by A/RES/52/166 of December 15, 1997.
[66] Here again, the power is either specific in some tribunals' statute (see *e.g.* IMFAT, Art. XVII, AfDBAT, Art. XII(3), OECDAT, Art. 12(b)) or assumed as inherent in their jurisdiction by others.
[67] See *e.g.* the Statutes of the UNAT, Art. 12; WBAT, Art. XIII; (1) IMFAT, Art. XVI; OASAT, Art. IX(1); OECDAT, Art. 12(b); AfDBAT, Art. XII(4); AsDBAT, Art. XI. The same power is assumed as inherent by the ILOAT.

tive Board of the Pensions Fund of the ILO by means of a request for an advisory opinion from the I.C.J., that advisory opinion being treated as binding.[68] In 1955, following the dissatisfaction of certain states with the UN Tribunal's judgments in 1953 in the "5th Amendment" cases (a dissatisfaction which was rendered that much keener by the I.C.J.'s opinion in 1954 that the judgments were binding on the Organisation),[69] the General Assembly amended the statute of the tribunal so as to make the judgments no longer "final and without appeal," but rather subject to a review procedure similar to that in the ILO.[70] The amended statute—in Article 11—thus gave the right to any member state, the Secretary-General or the individual claimant objecting to a judgment to request that an advisory opinion be sought from the I.C.J.; this was much wider than the ILO, which limits the right to the governing body or the Administrative Board of the Pension Fund. There was established a special Committee on Applications for Review of Administrative Tribunal Judgments, composed of 21 states, to receive the request and decide whether or not the opinion should be sought. The grounds upon which an opinion could be sought were wider than those in the ILO Statute. They were that the tribunal had "exceeded its jurisdiction or competence or . . . ha[d] failed to exercise jurisdiction vested in it, or ha[d] erred on a question of law relating to the provisions of the Charter of the United Nations, or ha[d] committed a fundamental error in procedure which ha[d] occasioned a failure of justice. . .". As in the review procedure of ILOAT judgments, the opinion was to be treated as binding.[71]

13–183   It is, of course, entirely a question of policy at which stage in a judicial hierarchy decisions are to be regarded as final, and there is perhaps little objection in principle to the Court assuming an appellate jurisdiction from administrative tribunals. A more controversial point is the interposition in this hierarchy of a political body which takes the decision[72] on whether an appeal shall be allowed, a decision clearly involving an appreciation of purely legal questions. In *Application for review of Judgment No. 158 of the UNAT*, the I.C.J. dismissed this objection by considering that:

---

[68] The Annex to the ILOAT Statute gives the same possibility to "the Executive Board of an international organisation" which has recognised the jurisdiction of the tribunal in accordance with Art. II, 5 of the statute. This provision made it possible for the UNESCO Executive Board to submit the aforementioned request for advisory opinion to the I.C.J. in 1955 (see *supra*, n. 47.

[69] See *supra*.

[70] As shall be seen, however, this provision was repealed in 1996.

[71] For more on this, see *supra*, n. 68.

[72] This was so with the UN Committee on Review. In the case of the ILO the governing body does not appear to act as a "screening body," but simply as the body formally competent to request the opinion. However, in *Jurado v. ILO*, ILOAT Judgment No. 83 it appears that the ILO Secretariat declined to accede to the complainant's request to the governing body that an advisory opinion be requested from the I.C.J. The complainant appealed the refusal and the Tribunal held it had no power to review the decisions of the governing body.

"there is no necessary incompatibility between the exercise of these functions by a political body and the requirements of the judicial process, inasmuch as these functions merely furnish a potential link between two procedures which are clearly judicial in nature."[73]

There is little doubt however that, in the case of the UN, the sponsors of **13–184** the amendment wished to place some form of political supervision over the Administrative Tribunal, and it is precisely the excessive weight of political considerations in the process, combined with its limited efficiency, that led the General Assembly to do away with the review procedure in 1996.[74] Very little use had in any event been made of Article 11, three applications for review only having been authorised by the Committee between 1955 and 1995.[75] At present therefore, UNAT judgments, as those of all international administrative tribunals except the ILOAT and OASAT,[76] are final and may not be appealed.

F. INSPECTION PANELS

Bibliography: Bradlow, "International Organisations and Private Complaints: The Case of the World Bank Inspection Panel" (1994) 34 Virginia J. Int'l L. 553; Shihata, *The World Bank Inspection Panel* (1994); Forget, "Le 'Panel d'Inspection' de la Banque Mondiale" (1996) 42 Annuaire Francais de Droit International 656; Bissel, "Recent Practice of the Inspection Panel of the World Bank" (1997) 91 AJIL 741; Hey, "The World Bank Inspection Panel: Towards Recognition of a New Legally Relevant Relationship in International Law," (1997) 2 Hofstra Law and Policy Symposium 61.

The model of the administrative tribunal to receive complaints by **13–185** employees has been extended to the establishment of "panels" entitled to receive administrative complaints from persons aggrieved by certain acts of multilateral lending institutions. The first such body to be established was the World Bank Inspection Panel, following complaints from individuals and NGOS concerning Bank-supported projects, particularly in relation to their impacts on indigenous peoples, the environment and resettlement activities. Largely as a result of NGO pressure, in September 1993 the IBRD and the IDA adopted resolutions[77] establishing an inspection panel

---

[73] [1973] I.C.J. Rep. 176, para. 25.

[74] Res. 50/54 of January 29, 1996; see also Thierry, "Note sur l'abrogation de l'article 11 du Statut du TANU" (1995) AFDI 442.

[75] *Application for review of Judgment No. 158 of the UNAT* (Fasla), *loc. cit.*, n. 73; *Application for review of Judgment No. 273 of the UNAT* (Mortished), [1982] I.C.J. Rep. 325; *Application for review of Judgment No. 333 of the UNAT* (Yakimetz), [1987] I.C.J. Rep. 18.

[76] Art. XII(1) of the OASAT Statute provides that "[j]udgments of the tribunal may be reviewed by an ad hoc Administrative tribunal Review Panel [. . .] only in instances where the Tribunal's judgment is alleged to be *ultra vires* because it exceeds the Tribunal's authority in relation to its jurisdiction, competence or procedures under this Statute" (see the following paragraphs of Article XII for a description of the procedure).

[77] Resolution of the Executive Directors No. 93/10, September 22, 1993.

providing innovative access to international administrative remedies for non-governmental actors (the panel does not address complaints relating to the IFC, whose direct relationship with the private sector raises other policy considerations as to the most appropriate design for a system of review). The panel became operational in late 1994, and is authorised to receive requests for inspection from persons claiming to be affected by a World Bank project. An affected party, or in limited cases its representatives, can request an inspection if it can:

> "demonstrate that its rights or interests have been or are likely to be directly affected by an action or omission of the Bank as a result of a failure of the Bank to follow its operational policies and procedures with respect to the design, appraisal and/or implementation of a project financed by the Bank . . . provided that in all cases such failure has had, or threatens to have, a material adverse effect."[78]

13–186 The Panel consists of three members and may make a recommendation to the Bank's Executive Directors as to whether a matter complained of should be investigated. If the Executive Directors decide to investigate the matter one or more members of the panel (the inspectors) will conduct an inspection and report to the panel, which will then submit its report to the Executive Directors on whether the Bank has complied with its relevant policies and procedures. This new review body represents a most important development in international institutional law. It creates for the first time within a multilateral development bank an administrative procedure to permit review of the institution's compliance with its internal law at the instigation of third parties other than employees. The well-developed practice of administrative tribunals, described above, addressing employment and contractual matters for bank staff is thereby extended into the fields of social and environmental review. It is to be noted that the panel is limited to reviewing compliance by the Bank with its own internal rules, and that it can only make recommendations to the Bank's Directors, and not adopt binding decisions. Since the panel was established it has received over a dozen claims, finding non-compliance by the Bank in several cases. It is important to note that the panel may not review acts of recipient governments, and there has been a degree of tension between the panel and those states, mostly developing, who consider its activities to amount to an unwarranted interference in the domestic affairs of the state, since indirectly at least a degree of review of the state's acts will take place. The Bank's Inspection Panel has been followed by the creation of similar panels

---

[78] *ibid.*, para. 12. "Operational policies and procedures" consist of the Bank's Operational Policies, Bank Procedures and Operational Directives, and similar documents issued before these series were started. They do not include Guidelines and Best Practices or similar documents or statements: *ibid.*

under the auspices of the Asian Development Bank,[79] the Inter-American Development Bank,[80] the African Development Bank,[81] and the Caribbean Development Bank.[82] The EBRD has not followed suit, and there apparently remains little, if any, prospect for international review of the acts of the European Investment Bank.

G. Non-Compliance Procedures

Bibliography: Trask, "Montreal Protocol Procedure: The Best Approach to Resolving International Environmental Disputes?" (1992) 80 Georgetown L.J. 1973; Lang, "Compliance-Control in Respect of the Montreal Protocol" (1995) 89 Proc. Am. Soc. Int'l L. 206; Greene, "The Operation and Effectiveness of the Montreal Protocol's Non-compliance Procedure" in Victor, Raustiala and Skolnikoff (eds.) *The Implementation and Effectiveness of International Environmental Commitment: Theory and Practice* (1998); Yoshida, "Soft Enforcement of Treaties: The Montreal Protocol's Non-compliance Procedure and the Functions of Internal International Institutions" (1999) 10 Colo. J. Int'l Envtl. L. & Pol'y 95; Weiss, "Understanding Compliance with International Environmental Agreements: The Baker's Dozen Myths" (1999) 32 U. Rich. L. Rev. 1555.

A number of treaty-based environmental institutions have established **13–187** subsidiary bodies to deal with non-compliance and disputes over non-compliance. These are in the nature of conciliation bodies, having a function analogous to the commissions operating in the field of human rights. The most noteworthy example is the non-compliance procedure established under the 1987 Montreal Protocol, including the Implementation Committee established by the Second Meeting of the Parties in 1990.[83] Under the non-compliance procedure any party which has reservations about another party's implementation of its obligations under the protocol may submit its concerns in writing to the secretariat, with corroborating information.[84] The secretariat will then determine, with the assistance of the party alleged to be in violation, whether it is unable to comply with its obligations under the protocol, and will transmit the original submission, its reply and other information to the Implementation Committee.[85] The functions of the Implementation Committee, which consists of ten parties (originally five) elected by the parties to the protocol on the basis of

---

[79] See http://www.adb.org/Work/Policies/Inspection.

[80] See http://www.iadb.org/cont/evo/evo-eng.htm. (Office of Evaluation and Oversight).

[81] See http://www.afdb.org/about/trib-home-eng.htm. (Administrative Tribunal).

[82] See the Bank's website: http://www.caribank.org.

[83] See *supra*. Chapter 12, and Decision II/5 (Non-compliance), Report of the Second meeting of the Parties to the Montreal Protocol, UNEP/OzL.Pro.2/3, June 29, 1990; see now Decision IV/5 and Annexes' IV and V, adopting the non-compliance procedure; Report of the Fourth Meeting of the Parties, UNEP/OzL.Pro.4/15, November 25, 1992, (1993)32 ILM 874.

[84] Annex IV, para. 1, *supra*.

[85] Paras 2 to 4.

equitable geographic distribution for two years, are to receive, consider and report on submissions made by any party concerning reservations regarding another party's implementation of its obligations under the protocol, and any information or observations forwarded by the secretariat in connection with the preparation of reports based on information submitted by the parties pursuant to their obligations under the protocol.[86] The Committee may, at the invitation of the party concerned, undertake information gathering in the territory of that party, and will also maintain an exchange of information with the Executive Committee of the Multilateral Fund related to the provisions of financial and technical co-operation to developing country parties.[87]

13–188   The Committee's function is to try to secure "an amicable resolution of the matter on the basis of respect for the provisions of the protocol" and report to the Meeting of the Parties, which may decide upon and call for steps to bring about full compliance with the protocol.[88] The parties have adopted an indicative list of measures that might be taken by a meeting of the parties in respect of non-compliance. Such steps can include cautions and suspension of rights and privileges under the protocol.[89] The report must not contain confidential information and is to be made available to any person upon request.[90] It is noteworthy that resort to the non-compliance procedure does not prejudice the dispute settlement provisions available under Article 11 of the 1985 Vienna Convention, including submission to conciliation, arbitration or the I.C.J.. Since its establishment the Implementation Committee has dealt with some nine cases. The approach is now being followed in other environmental governments, including the Climate Change Convention[91] and the UNECE Sulphur Dioxide Protocol.[92]

H. OTHER

(a) IRAN–U.S. CLAIMS TRIBUNAL

Bibliography: Mapp, *The Iran-United States Claims Tribunal: The First Ten Years, 1981–1991: An Assessment of the Tribunal's Jurisprudence and its Contribution to International Arbitration* (1993); Avanessian, *Iran-United States Claims Tribunal in Action* (1993); Aldrich, *The Jurisprudence of the Iran-United States Claims Tribunal* (1996); Lillich and Magraw, *The Iran-United States Claims Tribunal: Its Contribution to the Law of State Responsibility*

---

[86] Para. 7(a) and (b).
[87] Para. 7(d) and (e).
[88] Paras 8 and 9.
[89] Decision IV/5, Fourth Meeting of the Parties.
[90] Paras 15 and 16.
[91] (1992) 31 ILM 849.
[92] Oslo Protocol to the 1979 Convention on Long-Range Transboundary Air Pollution on Further Reduction of Sulphur Emissions, in force August 5, 1998, (1998) 37 ILM 505.

(1998); Brower, *The Iran-United States Claims Tribunal* (1998); Mohebi, *The International Law Character of the Iran-United States Claims Tribunal* (1999). Also see Iran-United States Claims Tribunal reports 1981/2.

The Iran-United States Claim Tribunal was created in 1981 as a mechanism **13–189** to resolve various legal disputes involving Iran and the U.S. and their nationals arising out of the 1979 Iranian revolution. The tribunals' jurisdiction derives from two declarations signed by the two countries, collectively known as the Algiers Accords.[93] The Accords provided for the release of the American hostages held in the Tehran embassy since February 1979, the unfreezing of Iranian assets located in the U.S. and the creation, by Iran, of a "Security Account" out of which U.S. claimants could be paid.

(i) Composition

Article III(1) of the Claims Settlement Declaration provides that the **13–190** tribunal shall consist of nine members or such other multiple of three as Iran and the U.S. may agree upon. Three members are appointed by each government, with the remaining three to be designated by agreement of those six, or, in the event of disagreement, by an appointing authority. The tribunal has traditionally consisted of three Iranians, three Americans and three independent country judges. Cases may be decided either by the full tribunal or by chambers of three judges, each with one Iranian, one American and one other judge. The chambers are composed by the President of the tribunal and have been the main mechanism by which claims have been decided. Decisions of the Tribunal members are to be taken by majority vote.

(ii) Claims

Article II of the Claims Settlement Declaration specifies the types of claims **13–191** over which the Tribunal has jurisdiction. These are:

1. Claims of nationals of either country against the government of the other that arise out of "debts, contracts . . . expropriations or other measures affecting property rights" outstanding on the date of the Claims Settlement Declaration (January 19, 1981);

2. Official claims arising out of contracts between the two governments for the purchase and sale of goods and services; and

3. Disputes regarding the performance or interpretation of the Algiers Accords.

---

[93] Declaration of the Government of the Democratic and Popular Republic of Algeria, (1981) 20 ILM 224 and Declaration of the Government of the Democratic and Popular Republic of Algeria concerning the Settlement of Claims by the Government of the United States of America and the Government of the Islamic Republic of Iran, (1981) 20 ILM 230.

The tribunal's conduct of claims is governed by the UNCITRAL rules (except as modified by the tribunal or the two countries). Claims were to be filed not later than one year after the entry into force of the accords, that is, January 19, 1981.

13–192   The respondent in each claim must be either the United States or Iran, or an agency or instrumentality controlled by such a government. Claimants must also establish their nationality in one of the two countries in order to be eligible to file a claim.

(b) UN COMPENSATION COMMISSION

Bibliography: Lillich (ed.), *The United Nations Compensation Commission: 13th Sokol Colloquium* (1995); Lillich and Brower, "Opinion Regarding the Jurisdiction and Powers of the United Nations Compensation Commission" (1997) 38 Virginia J. Int'l L. 25; O'Brien, "The Challenge of Verifying Corporate and Government Claims at the United Nations Compensation Commission" (1998) 31 Cornell Int'l L.J. 1; Frigessi di Rattalma and Treves, *The United Nations Compensation Commission: A Handbook* (1999); Gray, "The Choice between Restitution and Compensation" (1999) 10 EJIL 413.

13–193   Following the formal ceasefire between the Iraq and the Allied forces in March 1991, the Security Council adopted resolution 687 declaring Iraq's international responsibility for:

> "any damage and the depletion of national resources, or injury to foreign Governments, nationals and corporations, as a result of Iraq's unlawful invasion and occupation of Kuwait".

13–194   Section E of the Security Council's resolution made provision for a fund out of which compensation claims against Iraq could be paid. The Security Council requested the Secretary-General to develop and present to the Council his recommendations for setting up the fund and a commission to administer it. The Secretary-General proposed the creation of a Compensation Commission to take the form of a claims resolution facility to verify and value the expected claims and to administer the payment of compensation. The Commission was envisaged to operate, not as a court or arbitral tribunal as such, but more as a fact-finding commission. By S.C. Res. 692 (1991), the UN Compensation Commission was created as a subsidiary organ of the Security Council.

(i) The Fund

13–195   The Compensation Fund established by Resolution 692 was originally intended to be made up of 35 per cent of the value of Iraqi petroleum exports.[94] However, the Iraqis failed to take advantage of the arrangements

---

[94] S.C. Res. 705 (1991).

for oil sales contemplated by the Resolution and the Commission was forced to draw on funds from the UN Working Capital Fund to remain operative. With the eventual launch of the "oil-for-food" scheme[95] in December 1996, which allowed Iraq to sell oil in exchange for basic food and other supplies, the Commission began to receive 30 per cent of the value of Iraqi oil sales and to pay out on compensation claims.

(ii) Organs

The principal organ of the Commission is the Governing Council, which is **13–196** responsible for setting the policy of the institution, within the framework of the various Security Council resolutions. The Council thus establishes criteria for the admissibility of claims, the rules and procedures to be followed by the Commissioners in investigating claims, guidelines for the administration and financing of the Fund and the procedures for payment of compensation. The composition of the Council is the same as that of the Security Council. Decisions are to be made by a majority of the Council's members (with no option for exercise of a veto power), though decisions are generally taken by consensus.

The verification and evaluation of claims is carried out by the Commis- **13–197** sioners, who then make recommendations on compensation in reports to the Governing Council. The Commissioners are chosen for their integrity, experience and expertise in a range of fields including law, accounting, loss adjustment, assessment of environmental damage and engineering. They are internationally recognised jurists or professionals in their respective fields. As of December 1998 there were 54 Commissioners of 40 different nationalities. The Commissioners work in panels of three, with each panel reviewing a specific category or subcategory of claims. To date there have been 18 panels established, three of which have concluded their work.

Administrative, technical and legal support is provided to the Governing **13–198** Council and Commissioners by a Secretariat based in Geneva. The Secretariat, headed by the Executive Secretary is also responsible for the administration of the Fund.

(iii) Claims

Claims for compensation are filed by governments on their own behalf or **13–199** on behalf of their citizens or corporations. International organisations may also file claims on behalf of individuals in circumstances where it is not possible to have the individual's government file the claim. Some 100 governments have submitted around 2.6 million claims seeking compensation in the order of U.S. $300 billion. Claims are divided into six categories

---

[95] S.C. Res. 986 (1995).

by the Commission—A to F. Category A claims are those submitted on behalf of individuals who were forced to depart from Kuwait or Iraq between Iraq's invasion of Kuwait on August 2, 1990 and the formal ceasefire in March 1991. Category B claims are those submitted on behalf of individuals who suffered serious personal injury or lost a spouse, child or parent as a result of the invasion. Category C claims are those submitted on behalf of individuals for amounts not exceeding US$100,000. The claims cover 21 different varieties of loss including commercial losses. Category D claims are those submitted on behalf of individuals for amounts exceeding US$100,000. They are generally commercial in nature. Category E claims are claims submitted on behalf of corporations, private legal entities and public sector enterprises. The final category of claims, Category F, consists of claims filed by governments and international organisations for losses incurred in evacuating citizens and providing relief to citizens, as well as claims for damage to diplomatic premises or other government property and damage to the environment.[96]

13–200　The Commission established filing dates for all categories of claims that have now expired, with the exception of claims put forward on behalf of missing persons and claims for damage and losses resulting from land mine or ordnance explosions.

I. Conclusions

13–201　Since the first edition of this book in 1963, and even the last edition in 1982, there has been a significant transformation in the landscape of international institutions performing judicial and quasi-judicial functions. Whilst attention used to be focused on the International Court of Justice, it has now been joined by a wide array of other judicial bodies established at the regional and global levels. And whilst the I.C.J. may still claim to be *primus inter pares*, as the principal judicial organ of the United Nations, by a number of different standards its relatively diminished role is apparent. In terms of the number of cases it has a significantly smaller case-load; of a total annual expenditure of some U.S. $250 million on international courts and tribunals, it accounts for just $10 million: the ECJ counts for some $120 million, and the ICTY and ICTR between them have budgets of around $80 million. This provides some indication of the level of support which states are willing to make to various institutions.

13–202　The sharp increase in the number of international judicial institutions — coupled with the increase in their caseload—poses a number of fundamental questions that increasingly will require attention from the international

---

[96] For a discussion of the Commission's work in the area of assessment of environmental damage see Mackenzie and Khalastchi, "Liability and Compensation for Environmental Damage in the Context of the Work of the United Nations Compensation Commission" (1996) 5 RECIEL 281.

community. First, there is the question of the relationship between the various adjudicatory bodies, both the relationship of regional institutions to global bodies (including the I.C.J.) and between global bodies *inter se*. This point goes to the question of whether the international legal order — including the institutional order — comprises a system, a loose agglomeration, or simply a bric-a-brac. Certainly, the possibility cannot be excluded that "regional" systems of international law developing in the "jurisprudence" of regional courts might take a different direction from the global bodies. The notion of an "international law of the Americas" is by no means new, and, indeed, there is scope for some regional rules which can exist without detriment to the universality of the general rules of international law: the *uti possidetis* doctrine relating to sovereignty over territory in the former Spanish territories in the Americas is a case in point. It may also be recalled that in the *Asylum* case[97] Colombia had invoked "American international law" to support an alleged regional or local custom peculiar to Latin American states. The I.C.J. did not, significantly, reject out of hand the notion that there could be rules of law of this character, but rather regarded Colombia as having failed to discharge the burden of proving such a custom. Foda, in his book on the projected Arab court of Justice, devotes a special chapter to "Islamic International Law Principles," clearly suggesting that there is a body of international legal rules peculiar to that region.[98] The danger of serious rifts developing between general and regional international law would, of course, be lessened if there existed a system akin to the "preliminary reference" procedure linking the national courts of EC member states to the ECJ, but that does not appear to be an immediate prospect even if recently invoked by the President of the I.C.J. The same issue arises in connection with the relationship between different global bodies. For example, the ICTY has recently (in the *Tadic* case) taken a different approach to that of the I.C.J. (in the *Nicaragua* case) regarding the attribution to a state of conduct by a private person;[99] and in relation to the severability of reservations the Human Rights Committee might be considered to have taken a different approach from the I.C.J.[1]

A second issue is that overlapping (and potentially conflicting) jurisdictions might arise, *i.e.* one party might refer a matter to the I.C.J. and another might refer the same matter to another court, whether regional or global. One solution that has been suggested might be to equip the I.C.J. with powers to order the suspension of such regional proceedings when the matter falls within the jurisdiction of the I.C.J., or to compel the regional court to refer some special point by way of case stated.[2] This approach **13–203**

---

[97] [1950] I.C.J. Rep. 276.
[98] See generally Foda, *The Projected Arab Court of Justice* (1957).
[99] (1996) 35 ILM 32.
[1] See Redgwell, "Reservations to Treaties and Human Rights Committee General Comment No. 24(52)" (1997) 46 ICLQ 390.
[2] *ibid.* And see Foda, *op. cit.* pp. 205–211.

places the I.C.J. on a pedestal which states have, thus far at least, not been willing to create for it, and fails to take account of the lack of speed with which the I.C.J. usually operates, as well as the extent to which the composition of the court reflects a value system of the 1940s rather than more recent tendencies. Another approach is the one adopted, for example, by the European Convention on Human Rights (Article 62), the European court of Justice and ICSID not to go to the I.C.J. (or for that matter any other means of settlement) in cases arising out of the interpretation or application of the Convention establishing the regional court. Certainly the existence of regional courts could pose problems for both the regional and global courts.

13–204 A third point is related to the previous one: with the growth in the number of courts and tribunals a degree of forum shopping may now be available. This will increasingly focus attention on the attributes of particular bodies: do they have compulsory jurisdiction? What remedies are available to them? Who is entitled to have access to the court? Who may intervene, or file an amicus brief? How speedily does the court function? How much does it cost to use? These are questions which are familiar to domestic lawyers, particularly those engaged in transnational litigation; the fact that they may now be posed in the broader public international context indicates the growing maturity of international judicial institutions.

Part III

COMMON INSTITUTIONAL PROBLEMS

CHAPTER 14

THE LAW GOVERNING THE ACTIVITIES
OF INTERNATIONAL ORGANISATIONS

Bibliography: Wilfred Jenks, *The Proper Law of International Organisations*, 1962; Balladore-pallieri, "Le droit interne des organisations internationales" (1969–II) 127 RCADI 1; Morgenstern, *Legal problems of international organisations* (1986) 3–46 and 91–135; Sato, *Evolving constitutions of international organisations: a critical analysis of the interpretative framework of the constituent instruments of international organisations* (1996); Klein, *La responsabilité des organisations internationales dans les ordres juridiques internes et en droit des gens* (1998); Cahier, "L'ordre juridique interne des organisations internationales" in Dupuy (ed.), *Manuel sur les organisations internationales/A handbook on international organisations* (1988) 377; Schermers, "The legal bases of international organisations acts" in Dupuy (1998) 401.

International organisations are legal persons whose activities are gov- **14–001**
erned by law, including obligations under general rules of international law, under their constitutions, and under international agreements.[1] Their powers are derived directly from their constituent instruments as reflecting the intentions of their founders, and are subject to the limits of law. In general terms the sources of legal obligations establishing the parameters within which such activities may be lawfully carried out may be divided into two broad categories. The first category comprises the "rules of the organisation," sometimes referred to as the "internal law" of the organisation.[2] The 1986 Vienna Convention defines these rules to mean "in particular, the constituent instruments, decisions and resolutions adopted in accordance with them, and established practice of the organisation" (Article 2(1)(j)).[3] The second category—sometimes referred to as the "external law"—comprises those rules arising outside the organisation itself, of which there are two types: the rules of international law (in particular treaties and custom) and the rules of national law. The applicability of one or more of these sources of obligation will turn on the circumstances of each particular matter, with a dominant factor being the

---

[1] I.C.J. Advisory Opinion, Interpretation of the Agreement of 25 March 1951 between the WHO and Egypt (1980) I.C.J. Reps 73, 89–90.
[2] See Klein (1998), p. 19.
[3] See generally 1972 YILC Vol. II, p. 197–9; 1977 YILC, Vol II(2), p. 118; 1981 YILC Vol. II(2) 124.

question of whether the issue has arisen in terms of the organisation's relations with one or more of its own members, or with other subjects of international law (*i.e.* other international organisations or non-member states), or other third persons such as its employees or agents, or private third parties. In this chapter we address first the internal law of international organisations (A) and then obligations arising under "external" law (B).[4]

A. INTERNAL LAW OF THE ORGANISATION

(a) THE CONSTITUENT INSTRUMENT

14–002 The constituent instrument of an international organisation is almost always a treaty, although in some exceptional cases an international organisation may be created by act of one or more existing international organisations.[5] The constituent instrument will provide for the functions and objects of the organisation, and indicate how they are to be achieved. It will also provide for the framework against which secondary acts of the organisation may be adopted and its other practice developed, even if such practise sometimes departs from the original object of a particular provision of the constituent instrument. On occasion the constituent instrument might also indicate the relationship between the organisation and other rules of international law, as well as any applicable or relevant rules of national law.

14–003 As a treaty the constituent instrument will be governed by the rules reflected in the 1969 Vienna Convention on the Law of Treaties (as well as those of the 1986 Vienna Convention), which are expressly stated to apply "to any treaty which is the constituent instrument of an international organisation and to any treaty adopted within an international organisation without prejudice to any relevant rules of the organisation" (Article 5(3)). The last part of this provision indicates the primacy which is to be given to "any relevant rules of the organisation", whilst recognising that where the instrument is silent on such rules the 1969 Convention could play a decisive role. The rules of the 1969 Convention which are most relevant to the life of international institutions are generally recognised to reflect customary law.[6] In this way the law governing the activities of international institutions is subjected to the principles of the 1969 Vienna Convention, including in relation to such matters as the circumstances governing the conclusion of the treaty, reservations, the rules governing the relationship between the constituent instrument and other treaties, interpretation (see *infra*) and withdrawal and termination.

---

[4] Parts of this chapter are inspired by David, Cours sur les droits des organisations internationales, 1998, Université Libre de Bruxelles.

[5] *e.g.* the Global Environment Facility, *supra.* Chap. 4 at para. 4–030.

[6] Case Concerning the Gabcikovo-Nagymaros Project, 1997 I.C.J. Reps 7 at 38.

(1) Elaboration

The constituent instrument of an organisation is the subject of elaboration **14–004** and adoption much like any other treaty. Once two or more states have agreed on the need to create an international organisation, they will establish a negotiating process (which could be ad hoc or established under the auspices of an existing international organisation) which could be open-ended in time or established for a limited period. The period of negotiation will vary widely: the Articles of Agreement of the World Bank were negotiated and adopted in just three weeks, whereas the instruments establishing the International Sea-Bed Authority—the 1982 UNCLOS—took nearly 20 years to negotiate, and even then was subject to significant modifications before it entered into force.[7] Once the draft text has been adopted, which may sometimes occur at a Diplomatic Conference of the representatives of the negotiating states, the constituent instrument will enter into force in accordance with its provisions on entry into force. Some constituent instruments require certain named states to have ratified to bring it into force: the UN Charter, for example, came into force within four months of its signature, after ratification by the five permanent members and by a majority of the other signatory states (Article 110(2)). Other constituent instruments come into force upon a particular event: the Articles of Agreement of the IBRD came into force once instruments of ratification had been deposited by governments whose minimum subscriptions to the Bank comprised not less than 65 per cent of the required total subscriptions (Article XI(1)). And yet others come into force once a certain number of states have become parties: the OAS Charter came into force once two-thirds of the signatory states had deposited their instruments of ratification (Article 145).

(2) Reservations

Practise is mixed on the subject of reservations to the constituent **14–005** instruments of international organisations. Some instruments expressly prohibit reservations, for example those establishing the International Sea-Bed Authority and the World Trade Organisation.[8–9] Other instruments, such as the UN Charter, are silent. None appear to expressly permit reservation. In the absence of an express rule it will be the rules on reservations reflected in Articles 19 to 23 of the 1969 Vienna Convention which will determine the permissibility of a reservation, including, in particular, whether it is compatible with the objects and purposes of the treaty (Article 19(c)). The permissibility of reservations will generally only be an issue when the instrument is silent on the subject, although an

---

[7] See *supra*, Chap. 4.
[8–9] See 1982 UNCLOS, Art. 309; 1994 Agreement establishing the World Trade Organisation, Art. XVI (5).

express prohibition (or even authorisation under certain conditions)[10] does not exclude the possibility of issues arising, since states may enter reservations raising questions about their compatibility with such conditions. Occasionally states have entered reservations even where they were expressly prohibited. This happened, for example, when Switzerland and Luxembourg joined the League of Nations, with a view to protecting their status as neutral states.[11]

14–006   Related to the questions of reservation is that of declarations (or interpretative declarations): where a state introduces a declaration but does not describe it as a reservation, how will it be characterised? In practise the depositary of the constituent instrument will usually communicate the "declaration" to other parties or, in the case of an international institution, to the relevant organ.[12] In many cases the declaration will have an overtly political character, for example in relation to the refusal to recognise the state of Israel[13] or the sovereignty claimed by the United Kingdom over the Malvinas/Falkland Islands.[14] If, on the other hand, the declaration purports to be a reservation in disguise it will be subject to the relevant rules of the institution and the 1969 Vienna Convention.

14–007   Where a reservation has been entered the question arises as to who is to determine its effect: is it the states parties or the institution? Prior to the 1969 Vienna Convention this remained an open and sometimes controversial question, and practise was mixed. In the case of Switzerland's reservation to the League of Nations, to protect its neutrality, it was the Council of the League that recognised the particular circumstances of Switzerland's situation, taking into account Article 435 of the Treaty of Versailles.[15] When the United states entered a reservation to is membership of the WHO in 1948, to the effect that it reserved the right to withdraw under certain circumstances but where the WHO Constitution provided for no rule on withdrawal, the WHO Assembly unanimously decided to accept the reservation.[16] By contrast, when Yugoslavia entered a reservation to the ICAO agreement when it sought to join in 1954, the United States (as depositary) invited the members to take a decision on the basis of unanimity. France took the view that a majority vote was enough, but when eight states voted against the reservation Yugoslavia was not admitted (and did not join until 1960 when it sought to join without a reservation).[17]

---

[10] See, *e.g.* Asian Development Bank, Art. 56(2).
[11] See Hudson, "Membership in the League of Nations", 1924 AJIL 439–42.
[12] This is the practice, for example, of the UN Secretary-General: see Report of the UN Secretary General on the practice followed by depositaries on the subject of reservations, YILC, 1965, II, pp. 79 *et seq.*
[13] See, *e.g.* Iraq's declaration to the IDA.
[14] See Argentina's declaration under 1982 UNCLOS.
[15] See Hudson, "Membership in the League of Nations", 1924 AJIL, 439–40.
[16] See Schermers, Blokker, *op. cit.* (1995) 716.
[17] *ibid.*

Practise has largely been superseded by Article 20(3) of the 1969 Vienna **14–008** Convention, which provides that:

> "When a treaty is a constituent instrument of an international organisation and unless it otherwise provides, a reservation requires the acceptance of the competent organ of that organisation".

This provision makes clear that, subject to an express provision other- **14–009** wise, it is the organisation and not the individual states which decide on the admissibility of a reservation. The main question which will arise then becomes: which organ is competent to determine the admissibility of a reservation? Most constituent instruments do not address this question. It will therefore be the organ which is charged with deciding on the candidacy of a state wishing to join the organisation which will adjudge the reservation. Ultimately this may go to a plenary organ or, if one has been provided for, a judicial or other body charged with authoritative interpretation.[18]

(3) Interpretation

The interpretation of constituent instruments of international organisations **14–010** has been described as an operation of "proverbial unpredictability" calling for "the highest qualities of statesmanship and judicial and legal skills."[19] Constitutional texts, like any multilateral treaty, are clearly capable of giving rise to disputes concerning their interpretation.[20] Such disagreement can arise between members of the organisations, between the organisation and one or more members, or between the organisation and a third person (who could be a state, another intergovernmental organisation, or a natural or juridical person, including an employee). The two principal questions which arise are: which body is authorised to interpret definitively the constituent instrument, and what techniques of interpretation are to be applied?

As to the first question, the matter is sometimes addressed expressly by **14–011** the constituent instrument, but more often is not.[21] Where it is so addressed, the constituent instrument can provide for authoritative interpretation by non-judicial means (by the political or technical organs of an organisation) or by judicial means, or a combination of the two. In practise the vast majority of disputes concerning interpretation are settled by the political or technical organs, and authoritative interpretation by judicial organs remains the exception rather than the rule.

---

[18] See generally Imbert, *Les réserves aux traités multilateraux, Paris, 1979.*

[19] S. Rosenne, *Developments in the Law of Treaties 1945–1986* (1989) 233.

[20] See Hexner, "Interpretation by Public International Organisations of their Basic Instruments," (1959) 53 AJIL 341. A useful article but limited to the "financial" organisations. Also Mann, (1970) 43 B.Y.B.I.L. 1–19.

[21] See generally Sohn, "The UN System as Authoritative Interpreter of its Law", in Schachter and Joyner (eds), *United Nations Legal Order* (1995), 169–229.

14–012   With regards to the different approaches set forth in constituent instruments, an example of the mixed approach is provided by the Articles of Agreement of the IMF. Article XXIX(a) of which provides that "[a]ny question of interpretation of this Agreement arising between any member and the Fund or between any members of the Fund shall be submitted to the Executive Board for its decision." Where the Executive Board has given its decision, within three months any member may require that the question be referred to the Board of Governors "whose decision shall be final" (Article XXIX(b)). The Board will be assisted by a Committee on Interpretation, as established by the Board of Governors.

14–013   In contrast, where the disagreement arises between the Fund and a member which has withdrawn or between any member during liquidation of the Fund, that disagreement will be submitted to arbitration by a tribunal of three members (Article XXIX(c)).

14–014   The UN Charter contains no specific compromissory clause providing for the judicial settlement of disputes with regard to the interpretation of the Charter; having noted the absence from the Charter of any procedure enabling the I.C.J. to determine the validity of acts of the organs, the I.C.J. has itself concluded that each organ must, in the first place at least, determine its own jurisdiction and the presumption of validity would apply to such determination.[22] Such clauses are common in the constituent instruments of the specialised agencies. By way of example, the ITU and the UPU contemplate, in their constitutions, only this first class of disputes. The ITU, in Article 28, contemplates the solution of disputes relating to interpretation through ordinary diplomatic channels or by reference to existing treaties between the members concerned for pacific settlement of disputes; failing that, recourse may (not must) be had to arbitration in accordance with a procedure set forth in Annex 3. The UPU provides directly for arbitration in Article 32 (although this clearly does not exclude political or diplomatic settlement) and, in stating that a disagreement "shall be settled by arbitration," would seem to envisage compulsory arbitration. However, since the ITU (but not the UPU) is authorised by the General Assembly of the UN to request advisory opinions from the I.C.J., it also possesses this means of settling any dispute as to interpretation to which the organisation itself is a "party," although not in binding form.

14–015   Most of the specialised agencies contemplate the settlement of disputes on interpretation by negotiation within the political organs of the organisation, although often subject to a right of appeal to an outside body. In some cases such as the IAEA (Article 17A) or the WHO (Article 75), reference is made to settlement by negotiation without specifying any particular

---

[22] See AO of July 20, 1962, on Certain Expenses of the UN, (1962) I.C.J. Reps 168.

organ. In other cases, the organ is specified, as in the case of the Conference of the FAO (Article XVII). It is the Council, the organ of 27 states, with its own Rules for the Settlement of Differences, which plays an important role as to disputes settlement in the case of ICAO (Article 84).[23] The IMO is slightly different; whilst the Assembly is named as the organ to settle disputes arising from the interpretation or application of the Convention, there is a special clause providing that "Nothing in this Article shall preclude the Council or the Maritime Safety Committee from settling such question or dispute that may arise during the exercise of their functions" (Article 65). As noted earlier, in this institution the plenary organ is not given as much power *vis-à-vis* the organs of limited composition as in other institutions. A second feature of the IMO is that legal questions not so settled may be referred for an advisory opinion to the I.C.J. (Article 66); however, there is no express provision by way of a compromissory clause to give the I.C.J. contentious jurisdiction between the member states as there is in other organisations. Reference has already been made to the IMO's use of the power to request an advisory opinion in order to determine the proper composition of the Maritime Safety Committee.[24] From these different organs appeal may lie to the I.C.J.[25]

Other institutions do not specifically mention the powers of their own **14–016** organs to interpret the convention in the event of a dispute, but provide that such disputes shall be referred directly to arbitration, as in the case of the UPU (Article 32) and WMO (Article 29), or to the I.C.J. or a tribunal specially appointed, as in the ILO (Article 37) or UNESCO (Article XIV).[26] It cannot seriously be contended that this excludes the organs of the organisation from attempting to settle points of interpretation; indeed, if, through an organ, the question can be settled there will be no dispute remaining to be submitted to the outside body. Moreover, in general it will often be better for such disputes to be settled internally. However, the ultimate recourse is to these judicial bodies, if needs be.

It must finally be observed that all the specialised agencies bar the UPU **14–017** have been authorised by the UN General Assembly to request advisory opinions from the I.C.J. This, as we have mentioned in Chapter 13, is the only way in which the organisation as such can appeal to the court for an interpretation of its constitution. The disadvantage is that the advisory

---

[23] See Appeal relating to the Jurisdiction of the ICAO Council (*India v. Pakistan*) (1972) I.C.J. Rep. 46. And note that the ICAO Council may also hear complaints under the numerous bilateral Air Transport Agreements.

[24] See *supra*, Chap. 13, para. 13–053.

[25] See *supra*, Chap. 13, paras 13–049 and 13–050.

[26] Hence the reference, under Art. 14(2), to an ad hoc tribunal of the question whether members of the Executive Board who cease to be members of the delegation of their state are eligible for re-election: the UNESCO (Constitution) Case, (1949) A.D., case 113.

opinion is not, *per se*, binding; to get a binding decision the organisation would have to have power to submit the dispute to some other arbitral body. The desirability of constant reference to the court is questionable, and it may be noted that the General Assembly always excludes from its grant power to request an advisory opinion on questions affecting the relationships of the specialised agencies *inter se*, or with the UN itself.

14–018   Beyond the UN and the specialised agencies practise varies. At the OAU it is provided that the Charter is to be interpreted by the Conference of Heads of State and Government, by way of "decision" (Article 27). At the E.C. it is the ECJ which is charged with resolving disputes between member states (Article 227), between the Commission and member states (Article 226), and between certain community institutions or community institutions and member states or third persons having a sufficient legal interest (Articles 230 and 232). Within the Law of the Sea Convention institutions, interpretative differences relating to the International Sea-Bed Authority may go to the Sea-Bed Disputes Chamber of ITLOS (1982 UNCLOS, Article 187(a)). Additionally, the ITLOS Rules provide for advisory opinions to be given "on a legal question if an international agreement related to the purposes of the Convention specifically provides for the submission to the Tribunal of a request for such an opinion."[27] This provision might be utilised, for example, by a body such as the International Whaling Commission, assuming that ITLOS concluded that the relevant conditions of Rule 138 were found to apply in respect of the 1946 Convention. But in the absence of these hithertoforth speculative routes, interpretation will take place by the organs of the institution or by its members.

14–019   In contrast to these arrangements, the constituent instruments of yet other institutions—such as the OECD, NATO, the Council of Europe and the League of Arab States—make no provision for a specific rule or procedure expressed to deal with the interpretation of the constituent instrument, whether by judicial or non-judicial means.

14–020   Turning to the second question, what is the effect of the process of interpretation? Where one member unilaterally interprets the constituent instrument, such interpretation will only be opposable against another member where it has so consented, or where there has been an informal agreement or principles of estoppel[28] or acquiescence apply. In the absence

---

[27] Rules, Art. 138(1).
[28] This may be seen as implicit in the I.C.J.'s conclusions in the *Certain Expenses* case in relation to the concurrence by France and the USSR in the vote on General Assembly resolution 1001 (ES-1), which was adopted "without a dissenting vote": 1962 I.C.J. Reps, p. 151 at 171. See also Namibia, Advisory Opinion of June 11, 1971, 1971 I.C.J. Reps, pp. 36–7; and Advisory Opinion of July 11, 1950, I.C.J. Reps 1950, p. 142.

of a mechanism for regulating conflict, where two such interpretations are in conflict neither one will formally prevail against the other. Where the interpretation emanates from the organ, rather from one or more of the members, the interpretation must be deemed to bind the organ which has adopted it and, if it has the necessary competences, the institution as a whole. In the *Ambatielos* Case the International Court of Justice found that a declaration by the parties to a 1926 Treaty of Commerce and Navigation was "in the nature of an interpretation clause and, as such, should be regarded as an integral part of the treaty, even if this was not stated in terms."[29] Similarly, the practise of an organ which attracts general support may constitute an interpretative act of a constituent instrument: this has been considered to be the case, for example, for practise demonstrating that the abstention of a permanent member in a vote of the Security Council will not be considered as precluding the adoption of a resolution by the Security Council under the conditions envisaged by Article 27(3) of the UN Charter.[30]

With regard to the techniques of interpretation, the I.C.J. has confirmed, **14–021** when it has been called upon to interpret the UN Charter, that "it has followed the principles and rules applicable in general to an interpretation of treaties, since it has recognised that the Charter is a multi-lateral treaty, albeit a treaty having certain special characteristics."[31] This approach has been confirmed by the 1969 Vienna Convention, the provisions of which apply without prejudice to any relevant rules of the organisation, including in relation to interpretation (Article 5). There is some authority for the proposition that a treaty of a constitutional character should be subject to different rules of interpretation to allow for the "intrinsically evolutionary nature of a constitution."[32] Subject to this perspective, and the comments set out below which address the practise of various international courts in relation to the interpretation of constituent instruments, the matter is generally governed by Articles 31 and 32 of the 1969 Vienna Convention. Article 31 establishes the primary rule that a treaty is to be interpreted "in good faith in accordance with the ordinary meaning to be given to the terms of the treaty in their context and in the light of its object and purpose." A person seeking to rely on a special meaning for the terms of the treaty, as opposed to the ordinary meaning, will have to prove that special meaning.[33] The context of a treaty includes the whole of its text, the preamble and annexes. Any agreement made between all the parties in connection with the conclusion of the treaty and any instrument made by

---

[29] 1952 I.C.J. Reps 28, at 44.
[30] See Chap. 11, para. 11–021.
[31] *Certain Expenses Case,* 1962 I.C.J. Reps at 157.
[32] See Jennings and Watts (eds), *Oppenheim's International law,* 9th ed., 1992, at 1268 (citing *Rights of US Nationals in Morocco,* 1952 I.C.J. Reps 176, 211).
[33] *Legal Status of Eastern Greenland Case,* P.C.I.J. (1933) Ser. A/B No. 53, 49.

one or more parties relating to the conclusion of the treaty and accepted by the other parties as such are included in the understanding of the treaty's context (Article 31(2)). Finally, apart from the context, Article 31(3) of the Vienna Convention provides that account is also to be taken of certain factors which are extrinsic to the treaty: subsequent agreement between the parties regarding the interpretation or application of the treaty; subsequent practise in application of the treaty which establishes the agreement of the parties regarding its interpretation;[34] and any relevant rules of international law applicable in the relations between the parties.[35]

14–022   If the application of the approach laid down by Article 31 produces a result which is not clear or which is ambiguous, Article 32 allows recourse to be had to supplementary means of interpretation, which may also be used to confirm a meaning already established. The principal supplementary means are the *travaux preparatoires* of a treaty,[36] including the minutes of formal negotiations, reports of session, and prior drafts of a text. Other supplementary means include the application of certain principles of interpretation, such as *in dubio mitius*,[37] and *expressio unius est exclusio alterius*.[38]

14–023   It is not possible here to review the totality of interpretative techniques of the organs of international organisations, and in particular the approach of the various international judicial and quasi-judicial bodies. Nevertheless by way of summary, it is clear that the case law of some of these international courts and tribunals, in particular the I.C.J. and the ECJ, indicates a tendency towards seeking to ensure that the approach to interpretation which is relied upon will assure the effectiveness of the organisation. This requires careful consideration of the objects and purposes of the organisation, by reference to what has been referred to as a "teleological approach."[39] It is reflected, for example, in the approach of the I.C.J. in the *Reparations* case, giving effect to a principle of implied

---

[34] See, *e.g.* the *Namibia Case*, 1971 I.C.J. Reps, p. 22: "the proceedings of the Security Council extending over a long period supply abundant evidence that presidential rulings and the positions taken by the members of the Council, in particular its permanent members, have consistently and uniformly interpreted the practise of voluntary abstention by a permanent member as not constituting a bar to the adoption of resolutions.[. . .] This procedure followed by the Security Council . . . [h]as been generally accepted by Members of the United Nations and evidences a general practise of that Organisation".

[35] On the interpretation of treaties by reference to customary international law see the *Reparations for Injuries Case*, 1949 I.C.J. Reps 174, 182.

[36] Resort to the travaux preparatoires is usually for the purposes of confirming an interpretation reached by other means: see the *IMCO* case, 1960 I.C.J. Reps 150, 160.

[37] The P.C.I.J. recognised the principle as meaning "if the wording of treaty provision is not clear, in choosing between several admissible interpretations, the one which involves the minimum of obligations for the parties should be adopted": Frontier between Turkey and Iraq (1925), Series B, No. 12, p. 25.

[38] Oppenheim (9th ed.), Vol. 1, p. 1279, describes it as an "essentially grammatical" rule.

[39] See Amerasinghe (1996) pp. 44–8.

powers deeming the UN to have powers conferred upon it "by necessary implication as being essential to the performance of its duties."[40] It is similarly reflected in the jurisprudence of the ECJ, for example its conclusion that the European Parliament had standing to challenge before the ECJ acts of the Council or the Commission which were necessary to "safeguard its prerogatives", notwithstanding the fact that the Treaty of Rome did not list the Parliament as one of the Community institutions having such power.[41] This looks to the object and purpose of the organisation, rather than adopt a literal (and therefore restrictive) approach to what the constituent instrument does or does not say. These cases indicate that where there exists a difference of views on interpretation relating to the extent of competences or powers of the organisation or its organs, and in the face of silence of the texts, one favourable towards a more extensive as opposed to a more minimal view, jurisprudence tends to favour a more extensive view taking into account the object pursued by the organisation rather than the text of its constituent instrument.

(4) Amendment, revision, etc.

The essentially dynamic character of a constitutional text, as opposed to the normal multilateral treaty, has led to a general recognition of the need for a specific clause envisaging revision or amendment of the text.[42] The procedures for revision are by no means uniform but may be appropriately discussed at this juncture. Before proceeding to a discussion of the three main types of amendment clause, two general observations may be made. First, whilst amendments are usually carried out by the established organs of the organisation, it is sometimes envisaged that a special "review conference" may be convened to deal with any comprehensive proposals for amendment: this is precisely what is envisaged in Article 109 of the Charter, in Article 18(B) of the IAEA Statute, and in Article 48 of the E.U. Treaty. An extreme contrast is afforded by the technique in the UPU whereby, in the intervals between the meetings of Congress, amendments may be proposed by members and agreement is obtained by circulation of the proposals by the Bureau.[43] **14–024**

The second general observation is that normally the amendment procedure involves two stages: the first is the vote of adoption within the organ or conference, the second is the depositing of ratifications by members. In some cases it will be observed that though unanimity is not required for the **14–025**

---

[40] 1949 I.C.J. Reps 174.
[41] Case C–70/88, *Parliament v. Council*, [1990] E.C.R. I–2041 (paras 23 and 27).
[42] Phillips, "Constitutional Revision in the specialised agencies" (1968) 62 AJIL 654; Zacklin, *The amendment of the constitutive instruments of the UN and Specialised Agencies* (1968).
[43] Arts 29 and 30. Amendments to the proposals circulated are, naturally enough, not admitted. For general discussion of amendment procedures see Schwelb, "The amending procedure of constitutions of international organisations" (1954) 31 B.Y.B.I.L. 49.

first, it is for the second in that ratification by all members is required for the entry into force of the amendment; hence one is dealing with a "consent" principle and not a "legislative" principle. At the other extreme only the first stage is required in that the amendment enters into force upon adoption by the organ itself, and there is no second stage:[44] the first stage may be either by majority vote or by unanimity, *i.e.* either the "legislative" or the "consent" principle.

The "consent" principle: the requirement of unanimity

14–026　As might be expected, the principle that amendments to the constitution require the consent of all the members is the older and more established principle. It was to be found in the League of Nations (Article 26)[45] and is still found in Article 94(a) of ICAO which specifies that an amendment adopted by a two-thirds vote of the Assembly (first stage) comes into force only when ratified by not less than two-thirds of the members (second stage) and then only "in respect of states which have ratified such amendment." The Council of Europe which, in Article 41, envisages amendments coming into force upon ratification by two-thirds of the members, does so on the condition that the first stage of adoption by the Committee of Ministers has been by unanimous vote; even under the alternative procedure for amendments to Articles 23–25, 38 and 39 (where only the first stage is required in that the amendments come into force, once adopted by the Committee and the Assembly, by certification by the Secretary-General) the unanimous vote of the Committee again ensures that all members agree to the amendment. Similarly in the E.C., where an action is necessary to attain the objectives of the Community but where the treaty has not provided the necessary powers, the requirement of unanimous consent is there (Article 308, *ex Article* 235).

The "legislative" principle: the possibility for decision-making by a majority

14–027　The contrasting principle is that which allows a majority of members to adopt an amendment to a constituent instrument which becomes binding on the dissenting minority. This is the principle adopted in the UN in that, under Article 108, after adoption by two-thirds of the Assembly and ratification by two-thirds of the members including all the permanent members of the Security Council, amendments of specific provisions enter into force for all members.[46] Article 109 of the UN Charter provides for a

---

[44] As in Art. 95 of ECSC; Art. 235 of EEC; Art. 41 of the Council of Europe; Art. 20 of FAO.

[45] A revision of Art. 26, allowing the Assembly to adopt amendments by a three-quarters majority vote, including the votes of all members of the Council, such amendments to come into force when ratified by a majority of the Assembly, including all the Council, never came into effect: it failed to do so because of the stringency of the old amendment clause.

[46] To date there have been three amendments of the UN Charter under this provision: 1965 (Arts 23, 27 and 61); 1968 (Art. 109); 1973 (Art. 61).

more general review of the Charter by a General Conference of the members, to be convened following a decision by two-thirds of the members of the General Assembly and nine members of the Security Council. Alterations to the Charter under this procedure take effect when ratified by two-thirds of the UN membership and all the permanent members of the Security Council. This provision has not yet produced amendments, although a Special Committee on the Charter of the UN and on the Strengthening of the Role of the Organisation (the Charter Committee) was established in 1975 to consider wide-ranging changes. WHO (Article 7), UNESCO (Article 13)[47] and the IAEA (Article 18) all envisage entry into force of amendments for all members even when adoption, or ratification where necessary, has been by only two-thirds of the members.

A combination of the two principles

A rational development has been that of differentiating between amend- **14–028** ments so as to govern the minor amendments by the "legislative" principle but the major amendments by the "consent" principle. To take the example of FAO, Article 20 distinguishes between amendments not involving new obligations for members which enter into force for all members upon adoption by two-thirds of the Conference, and other amendments which require the same adoption but followed by ratification by two-thirds and subject to the condition that amendments enter into force for each member ratifying and thereafter for each member on accepting the amendment. WMO (Article 28) is similar; and the Convention, the General Regulations and the Agreements of UPU differentiate by stating the articles requiring unanimity and providing for a two-thirds or even a simple majority in other defined cases. The IMF (Article 17) and the IBRD (Article 18) also distinguish between amendments requiring majority approval and those requiring unanimous approval. In the ECSC the consent principle, involving ratification by all members, is applied to normal amendments (Article 96), but a special procedure is envisaged under Article 95 for modifications arising out of "unforeseen difficulties" revealed in the experience with the treaty or due to profound changes in economic or technical conditions. This special procedure envisages proposal of the amendments by ten-twelfths[48] of the Council and Commission jointly and approval by three-quarters of the Assembly, including two-thirds of the total membership.[49] The amendments then enter into force for all.

---

[47] Here the second stage of "acceptance" is only necessary for amendments involving "fundamental alterations" to the Constitution or new obligations for members: other amendments enter into force upon adoption by two-thirds of the Conference.

[48] See Lennaerts and Van Nuffel, *Constitutional Law of the European Union* (1999) 263.

[49] A reference to the Court intervenes between the proposal and the adoption to ensure that, in fact and in law, the amendment is to deal with the "unforeseen difficulties" referred to in the article.

The problem of the members declining to accept an amendment

14–029 The refusal of a member to accept an amendment can occur either in the case where the "consent" principle is applied but, the requisite number having voted for an amendment, ratification is refused (as might happen under the League formula)[50] or, more commonly, where the "legislative" principle is applied and a member refuses to accept the will of the majority. The inconvenience of allowing a minority of members to continue their membership under conditions no longer obtaining for the majority needs no stress, and its solution lies, as we have seen, either in having a withdrawal clause which allows the member to withdraw or, to deal with the recalcitrant member, an expulsion clause. As we shall see,[51] considering the generality of the problem, these clauses are found relatively infrequently and this suggests that a good deal of faith is placed in the powers of political persuasion as opposed to clear-cut legal powers of terminating membership or political arrangements envisaging two-tier membership of a single organisation. In the case of the European Communities, the political realities were demonstrated in 1992 following a referendum in Denmark which refused to accept some of the amendments to the E.C. Treaty to be adopted pursuant to the Maastricht Treaty. Following changes to the Maastricht Treaty to accommodate Danish concerns in relation to citizenship, EMU, defence policy and justice and home affairs, a second Danish referendum was held in May 1993 which achieved the requisite majority vote of support and Denmark ratified the treaty.[52]

Variation as distinguished from amendment

14–030 Very exceptionally, authority is given to some organ to apply a principle or rule different from the one established in the constitutional text. There is no change of the text, so that the process is not formally one of amendment; yet a variation from the constitutional text is permitted. Examples can be seen in Articles V(7) and (9), and XXVI(2) of the IMF, where such power of variation is conferred on the Board of Governors or Executive Directors acting by special majorities.[53]

---

[50] Or under the Antarctica Treaty Organisation, Art. 12 (1), which provides for amendment by unanimous vote but compulsory withdrawal of a non-ratifying member: Peaslee, Vol. 1, p. 29.

[51] See *infra*, Chap. 16, paras 16–028 *et seq*.

[52] See European Council Decision, Conclusions of the Presidency: Denmark and the Treaty on European Union [1992] O.J. C348/1.

[53] See Gold, "The amendment and variation of their Charters by International Organisations" (1973)1 Revue Belge de D.l. 50.

(b) RELEVANT DECISIONS AND RESOLUTIONS OF THE ORGANISATION

Beyond the provisions set forth in an organisation's constituent instrument, **14–031** as may be subject to amendment from time to time, it is now well established that the rules of an organisation include relevant institutional acts. As described earlier[54] the constituent instrument of an international organisation will very often provide for one or more of its organs to adopt acts to give effect to the objects and purposes of the organisation. These acts can be normative or procedural, and range from formally binding acts (for example, Security Council resolutions, or regulations, directives and decisions of the European Communities) to those which are explicitly non-binding as such (for example, resolutions of the UN General Assembly). In addition, there will be other acts which are often not expressly provided for, for example, the Bulletin adopted by the Secretary-General of the United Nations,[55] whose normative status will not always be clear.

As we have seen, the legal consequences of any particular act falls to be **14–032** determined principally by reference to the constituent instrument of the organisation, but also by reference to obligations arising outside the organisation, including general international law. Beyond this, institutional acts can themselves establish obligations for the organisation which can place limits upon its actions. The institutional acts adopted by the organs of an organisation will themselves be subject to a hierarchy based on the powers of those different organs, and can themselves be part of the law applicable within the internal legal order of the organisation.[56] The validity of secondary acts has frequently been raised within international organisations: this is the case for institutional acts,[57] treaties concluded by the organisation with third parties, as well as the practice followed by organs of various international organisations. Issues arising with respect to the violation by an international organisation of obligations deriving from its internal law can usually be addressed by reference to the three categories of subjects addressed by the act: states (or international organisations), which are members, employees and agents, and private persons. By way of illustration, practise in two organisational settings may be referred to. The first is within the World Bank: in addressing claims from employees the Bank's Administrative Tribunal frequently invokes acts of the organisation to determine "the internal law of the bank", governing among other issues the "conditions of employment."[58] The second example is the E.C.: the

---

[54] See Chap. 11, paras 11–032 *et seq.*
[55] See Chap. 15, para. 15–098.
[56] See Klein (1998) p. 23, n. 38.
[57] See for example the *Certain Expenses* case (I.C.J. Reps, 1962, 151), the *Namibia* case (I.C.J. Reps, 1971, 14)), and *the Aerial Incident over Lockerbie* case (I.C.J. Reps, 1992, 1).
[58] *Decision in the matter of de Merode and al. v. the World Bank*, WBAT, July 5, 1981, [1981] WBAT Reports 11 at 13.

European Court of Justice frequently refers to regulations, directives or decisions to support the conclusion that the powers of an organ—the Commission or the Parliament—must be exercised in conformity with procedural, and sometimes even substantive, requirements imposed by the internal law of the organisation.[59]

(c) ESTABLISHED PRACTICE OF THE ORGANISATION

14–033 It is also broadly accepted that the established practise of the organisation, falling short of the adoption of formal acts of the kind described in the preceding section, may also form part of the rules of the organisation. In the *Namibia* case, the I.C.J. took the view that an established body of practice forms an integral part of the rules of the organisation: the example referred to here was the effect of abstention by permanent members of the Security Council in voting by that organ.[60] The ECJ has reached similar conclusions in relation to the practise of the Council, the Commission and the Parliament with the strict limit that such a practice "cannot derogate from the rules laid down in the treaty."[61] What is clear, however, is that each organisation must be considered in the context of its particular circumstances, and that practise must be "established" for it to amount to a rule for a particular organisation: practice which is uncertain or disputed will usually not be treated as "established."[62]

B. GENERAL INTERNATIONAL LAW (INCLUDING SECONDARY LEGISLATION OF OTHER INTERNATIONAL ORGANISATIONS)

14–034 As an international person an international organisation is subject to the rules of international law, including in particular conventional and customary rules. As the I.C.J. put it in an advisory opinion:

> "International organisations are subjects of international law and, as such, are bound by any obligations incumbent upon them under general rules of international law, under their constitutions or under international agreements to which they are parties."[63]

---

[59] Case T–194/94, *Carvel and Guardian Newspaper v. Council of the European Union* [1995] E.C.R. 11–2765, [1995] 3 C.M.L.R. 359.

[60] 1971 I.C.J. Reps, p. 22 (para. 22).

[61] See, *e.g.* Case 68/86 *United Kingdom v. Council* [1988] E.C.R. 855 (para. 24); Case 131/86 *United Kingdom v. Council* [1988] 905 (para. 29).

[62] But *cf.* the views of the I.L.C. Special Rapporteur to the effect that practises which have not been "established" may nevertheless constitute a relevant rule of the organisation in certain circumstances: YILC 1972 Vol. II, p. 198.

[63] Advisory Opinion on the Interpretation of the Agreement of March 25, 1951 between the WHO and Egypt, 1980 I.C.J. Reps, p. 73 at 89–90.

Similar conclusions have been reached by the ECJ, in respect of the **14–035** obligations of the E.C. arising under international law,[64] by the ICTY in respect of the law which it is bound to apply,[65] and by national courts.[66] The approach is also reflected in the practise of organisations, including Security Council resolutions,[67] and the rules of the ICTY concerning international arrest warrants,[68] as well as legal opinions of secretariats.[69]

With regard to international agreements, it is now well established that **14–036** international organisations may, in accordance with their constituent instruments, enter into treaty relationship with states (both members and non-members) and with other international organisations.[70] Treaties between states and international organisations are accepted for registration by the UN Secretariat under Article 102 of the UN Charter. In 1986, as a complement to the 1969 Convention, states adopted the Vienna Convention on the Law of Treaties between states and international organisations or between international organisations. The 1986 Convention was based upon draft Articles prepared by the ILC, following an exhaustive review of practise,[71] including in particular Headquarters Agreements and Peacekeeping Agreements (the latter regulating the conditions under which, for example, peacekeeping forces may be permitted to enter the territory of a state, or the conditions under which one state will make available to an international organisation (such as the UN) its forces). As certain international organisations become increasingly sophisticated in structure and function, the range of treaties to which they may become party is being extended. Thus, the European Community has entered into treaty obligations making it a member of the FAO and the WTO and, via the 1982 UN Convention on the Law of the Sea, of the International Sea-Bed Authority. These agreements establish institutional rights and obligations, as well as substantive rights and obligations for the E.C. Treaties such as this are

---

[64] See, *e.g.* Case C–162/96, *A. Racke*, E.C.R. 1998–I p. 3704.

[65] See *Simic et al.*, Case 95–9–P.T. July 27, 1999, para. 42.

[66] See *Nacci v. Bari Institute*, June 8, 1994, 114 ILR 544 (international organisations "are subject to the same rules of international law, with customary and treaty, that govern relations between states").

[67] *e.g.* Resolution 841 of June 16, 1993, concerning economic sanctions against Haiti, addressed to all international organisations as well as states.

[68] See Article 59bis of the ICTY Rules of Procedure, addressed to states as well as international bodies.

[69] For example, the UNIDO secretariat has determined that it "has to comply with decisions of the Security Council that are binding on all states, including UNIDO's member states, even if the resolution does not specifically address international organisations": Selected legal opinions, 1990 UNJY 313.

[70] See Chap. 15, paras 15–024 *et seq.*

[71] See 1982 YILC, ii, part 2, p. 17. On the 1986 Convention see Gaja, "A new Convention on Treaties between States and International Organisations or between International Organisations: a critical commentary" 58 B.Y.I.L. 256–69 (1987); Treves, "Innovations dans la technique de codification du droit international — La préparation de la Conférence de Vienne sur les traités passés par les organisations internationales" 32 AFDI 474–94 (1987).

governed by the ordinary rules of treaty law, and as such establish rights for, and impose obligations upon the international organisations which are party to them. Thus, the I.C.J. had little difficulty in concluding that the United States, as a party to the 1947 Headquarters Agreement between it and the UN, was under an obligation, in accordance with section 21 of that Agreement, to enter into arbitration for the settlement of the dispute between itself and the UN.[72] And the ECJ has frequently referred to the obligations of the Community arising under international agreements to which it is a party to give rise either to substantive causes of action (where the convention is intended to create rights and obligations directly enforceable in community law)[73] or to construe provisions of the constituent treaties or secondary legislation.[74]

14–037   With regard to rules of international law other than treaties, the I.C.J. has similarly recognised that international organisations are subject to the rules and principles of general international law. This is implicit in the approach taken in the *Reparation for Injuries* case, finding that an international organisation is "a subject of international law and capable of possessing international rights and duties,"[75] and also from more recent decisions of the Court.[76] What this means in practise is that the organisation should, in the conduct of its activities, be assumed to be subject to rules of customary international law, including any rules of *jus cogens*, which may be relevant to the conduct of its activities. In our view this would include, for example, rules of customary law relating to matters such as the protection of fundamental human rights, the protection of the environment, and the conduct of activities in maritime areas and in outer space. In relation to human rights one commentator has stated the position as follows:

> "The Universal Declaration and the International Covenants represent minimal standards for all people and all nations. Intergovernmental

---

[72] 1988 I.C.J. Reps, p. 12. See also Advisory Opinion on the Interpretation of the Agreement of March 25, 1951 between the WHO and Egypt, 1980 I.C.J. Reps, p. 73 ("a contractual legal regime was created between Egypt and the Organisation which remains the basis of their legal relations today": at 93).

[73] See, *e.g.* Case 104/81 *Hauptzollamt Mainz v. Kupferberg et cie.* [1982] E.C.R. 3641 (paras 8 *et seq.*); case T–115/94 *Opel Austria v. Council* [1997] E.C.R. II–39 (paras 100 *et seq.*). This approach had already been adopted by the Court *vis-à-vis* the GATT although the E.C. itself was never a member of it, but only "in so far as under the E.C. Treaty the Community has assumed the powers previously exercised by the members states in the area covered by the General Agreement". See case 21–24/72 *Third International Fruit Company Case* [1972] E.C.R. 1219 (paras 19 *et seq.*).

[74] See, *e.g.* Case 2/90 *Commission v. Belgium* [1992] E.C.R. I-4431 ff (para. 35).

[75] 1949 I.C.J. Reps 174 at 179.

[76] Advisory Opinion on the Interpretation of the Agreement of March 25, 1951 between the WHO and Egypt, 1980 I.C.J. Reps, p. 73, at 95.

organisations are inter-state institutions and they too are bound by the generally accepted standards of the world community."[77]

This view appears unimpeachable. We also consider that international **14–038** organisations, as subjects of international law, are bound by general principles of law recognised by civilized nations, that is to say principles common to national legal systems. These could include procedural rules and requirements, as well as principles such as proportionality, legitimate expectation, and equity. This has been long recognised in the legal order of the E.C. There is also no reason of policy why international organisations should not, like states, be bound by their own unilateral acts.[78–79] Thus, notwithstanding the fact that an international organisation is not a party to, say, a human rights treaty or an agreement for the protection of the environment, if the rule contained in an agreement is reflected in customary international law then it can, as such, bind an international organisation. It has been suggested, for example, that the World Bank is not subject to general international norms for the protection of fundamental human rights. In our view that conclusion is without merit, on legal or policy grounds, even if it may be the case that certain bodies charged with reviewing the legality of acts of the World Bank, such as its Inspection Panel, are not permitted to have recourse to such law in determining whether the Bank is acting in compliance with its obligations. Similar considerations apply in relation to other areas of international law, including the principles of state responsibility.[80] By way of recent example, the UN Secretary-General has recently promulgated a Bulletin stating that the fundamental principles and rules of international humanitarian law set out in the bulletin are applicable to UN forces conducting operations under UN Command and Control.[81] The Bulletin provides that in *Status of Forces Agreements* the UN shall undertake to ensure that forces conduct operations "with full respect for the principles and rules of general conventions applicable to the conduct of military personnel," and that the "obligation to respect the said principles and rules is applicable to [UN] forces even in the absence of a status-of-forces agreement" (section 3). In the European Community context the ECJ has frequently referred to provisions of the

---

[77] M. Cogen, "Human rights, prohibition of political activities and the lending policies of the World Bank and the International Monetary Fund", in S.R. Chowdury *et al.* (eds.), *The Right to Development in International Law* (1993), 387; but *cf.* E. Denters, IMF Conditionality in De Waart *et al.* (eds), International Law and Development (1988) 240 and 244.

[78–79] See *Nuclear Tests case (Australia v. France)* (1974) I.C.J. Reps, paras 42 *et seq.*

[80] See *infra*, Chap. 15, paras 15–088 *et seq.*

[81] UN Secretary-General's Bulletin on the Observance by UN Forces of International Humanitarian Law, August 6, 1999, 38 ILM 1656 (1999).

European Convention on Human Rights, to which the Community is not a party, to assist it in reaching its conclusions.[82]

(a) *THE PRACTICE OF OTHER INTERNATIONAL ORGANISATIONS*

14–039 A related issue concerns the question of whether one international organisation might in some way be bound by the acts of one or more others and whether there is, in the words of one commentator, an emerging "common law" of international organisations, which appears to refer to the fact that rules exist that are common to all international organisations (regarding, for example, personality, membership, withdrawal, etc.)?[83] This question arose, controversially, in the 1960s in the context of efforts by the UN General Assembly to bring to an end the colonial policies of Portugal and South Africa, raising the question of whether acts of the UN could bind or have effects upon the World Bank.[84] Similar issues have arisen in the context of the relationship between Security Council resolutions and the E.C. In addressing this issue it is appropriate to distinguish between the situation where the relevant organisations are linked by some special institutional relationship and where they are not.

14–040 In the first case, for example, when the E.C. became a member of the FAO like any other member it became bound by the obligations flowing from the FAO's constituent instrument and mandatory institutional acts of the organisation. Short of membership, organisations will often agree to enter into co-operation agreements, which establish certain links between the organisations. These generally do not establish detailed obligations, but they do sometimes specify the effect of acts of one organisation on the other. This is the case, for example, of agreements between the UN and specialized agencies and the IAEA, which typically envisage that the specialised agency will submit to its relevant organs any formal recommendation addressed to it by the UN and to then report on measures taken.[85] Similarly, specialised agencies will frequently undertake to co-operate with ECOSOC.[86] In general, however, the particular relations between the UN and different bodies will need to be considered separately.

14–041 In the absence of any formal institutional link the matter falls to be addressed according to general principles. Most organisations in fact are not formally linked, and a relationship of reciprocal independence pertains.

---

[82] See, *e.g.* Case 44/79, *Hauer v. Land Rheinland-Pfalz* [1979] E.C.R. 3727; [1980] 3 C.M.L.R. 42, referring to the right of property reflected in Art. 1 of the First protocol to the ECHR. See generally Spielmann, "Human Rights Case Law in the Strasbourg and Luxembourg Courts: Conflicts, Inconsistencies and Complementarities", in Alston (ed.), *The EU and Human Rights 1999* at pp. 757–80.

[83] Lauterpacht, "The development of the Law of International Organisations by the decisions of International Tribunals" (1976–IV) RCADI 396 *et seq.*

[84] See Report of the UN Secretary-General, Doc. A/6825, September 15, 1967, in 1967 U.N.J.Y. 120–47.

[85] See, *e.g.* Art. IV of the 1951 Agreement between the UN and the WMO, 123 U.N.T.S. 249.

[86] See, *e.g.* Art. VI of the 1946 Agreement between the UN and the ILO, 1 U.N.T.S. 183.

That independence does not, however, mean that there will be no interconnection. Thus, it is possible that all the members states of one organisation are also members of another organisation: in this connection it is difficult to imagine that the E.C. could entirely ignore acts of the UN General Assembly or Security Council. This feature is particularly visible in the practice of administrative tribunals who openly refer to the practice and jurisprudence of other organisations.[87]

C. NATIONAL LAW

Beyond their internal law and obligations under international law, inter- **14–042** national organisations are also by necessity in connection with the national law of one or more states. This will be because they are located within the territory of a state, whether a member of not, or because the conduct of some of their activities which seek to give effect to their objects and purposes—examples might include making loans and grants, purchasing commodities, or engaging in peacekeeping operations—will necessarily have a close connection with national legal systems. Other activities of international organisations relate to everyday operations, for example, purchasing materials needed to run offices. Each of these activities brings them into contact with third persons and can subject them to one or more regimes of national law. An important distinction should be made between relations of a contractual nature and those of a non-contractual nature. Although the discussion that follows is principally related to the relations between international organisations and private persons, in certain circumstances national law could equally govern relations between two international organisations or between an international organisation and a state.

(a) CONTRACTUAL RELATIONS

The principle that contractual relations of an international organisation can **14–043** be governed by the national law applicable to the contract is largely accepted.[88] In some international organisations this is set out in implicit or express terms. For example, Article 288 (*ex Article 215(1)*) of the E.C. Treaty provides that "[t]he contractual liability of the Community shall be governed by the law applicable to the contract in question." The provision recognises that the community is not to be entitled to any special privileges or immunities, and that it is not envisaged that there will develop a community law of contract to which the community institutions will be subject.[89] Community contracts governed by national law will therefore be

---

[87] See, *e.g. Decision in the matter of de Merode et al. v. the World Bank,* WBAT, July 5, 1981, [1981] WBAT Reports at para. 28.

[88] See for example Monaco, 'Observations sur les contrats conclus par les organisations internationales', in Mélanges Modins, 1968, 93–94; Lysen, '*The non-contractual and contractual liability of the European Communities*', 1976, p. 155.

[89] See Hartley, *The Foundations of European Community Law,* 4th ed., 1998, at p. 442.

subject to rules of private international law, including possibly the harmonized rules for choice of law in contracts for cases before national courts.[90]

14–044   Indeed, for reasons of expediency most international organisations will subject most if not all of their contracts to one or more systems of national laws, and this practice has generally not created difficulties. The practise applies equally to organisations of universal membership (and certain UN specialised agencies) as to regional organisations. By way of example, most contracts of the UPU and some of those of the WHO are governed by Swiss law, whereas those of the ICAO are governed by the law of the province of Quebec.[91] For the OAS, the law of the District of Columbia governs contracts carried out at the seat of the organisation, whereas in the case of contracts performed in the territory of other members it is that local law which will govern. The E.C., Council of Europe, the OECD, the IBRD and the IMF take the same direction in systematically submitting contracts to national law. In other organisations the practise varies by reference to different types of contract: local contracts relating to the supply of gas, water and electricity to the organisation, as well as local rental arrangements, will be subject to the national law of the territory in which the service is provided.[92] In some instances national law governs contracts of employment concluded with local persons[93] and contracts of insurance.[94] Without controversy national law is also applied to real estate transactions in application of the *lex rei sitae* principle. For these types of contracts local law is appropriate because it is able to address the various issues which are likely to arise in relation to the performance of contractual obligations, and the local juridical system is the one which is most closely related to the conduct of these activities.

14–045   For other types of contract national law may be justified by the technical character of the subject matter of the contract. This is the case for loan agreements of the IBRD and the IMF, which are governed either by the law of the place of the loan, or by the law of the state on whose territory the private contracting banks are incorporated,[95] or by the law of the State of New York.[96] Similarly, contracts between the ITC and different English and foreign banks and with exchange dealers at the London Metal

---

[90] See 1980 Rome Convention on the Law Applicable to Contractual Obligations, [1980] O.J., C266.
[91] See Klein p. 173, n. 27.
[92] See Valticos, 1977 AIDI, 57–1, 59.
[93] See, *e.g.* C. Dominicé, 1984–4 Hague Academy, Vol. 187, p. 191.
[94] See Wilfred Jenks, *The Proper Law of International Organisations*, 1962, pp. 171–2.
[95] See Delaume, 'The Jurisdiction of Courts and International Loans', 1957 AJCL 208.
[96] See, *e.g.* Art. 11(a) of the loan agreement between the IMF and the Monetary Agency of Saudi Arabia, Decision no. 6843 (81/75), May 6, 1981, Annex B in "Selected Decisions of the IMF", Annex to 14th issue, Washington DC, April 30, 1989.

Exchange were governed by English law[97] or by New York law.[98] Another example may be found in the *Westland* case where a contract between the Arab Organisation for Industrialisation (AOI) and a private company named Westland Helicopters United was governed by Swiss law.[99] Reference to national law may also serve more limited objectives, for example to assist in interpreting the provisions of contractual provisions which are the subject of a case.[1]

The identification of the national law which is applicable to a contract of **14–046** an international organisation may be established by operation of an express contractual clause (clauses reflecting the will of the parties will tend to predominate over other factors),[2] alternatively (if the contract is silent) by operation of ordinary conflicts of laws rules. Additionally, the application of a national law may result from normative instruments of more general application, such as a headquarters agreement. Thus, Article 8(1) of the 1992 Headquarters Agreement between the OAS and the United States envisages the application of local laws of the United States—both state and federal— for disputes subject to section 1605(a)(2)–(6) of the Foreign and Sovereign Immunities Act of 1976, with commercial contractual disputes expressly envisaged.

The choice of national law to govern contracts of an international **14–047** organisation is not entirely without its inconvenient aspects, of which the most notable is the potential for subjecting an organisation to the legislative will of the state whose law is applicable. This risk should not, however, be over-stated since it has not much arisen in practise. The problem is less significant than for contracts between two states, where one party to a contract may have a direct interest in unilaterally modifying its terms by way of a unilateral act. States are less likely to engage in such acts to benefit the private persons who are normally the parties to private contracts with organisations. The willingness of organisations to submit their contracts to national legal systems (usually that of the state in which they are located) while conserving their independence with regard to other state legislatures,

---

[97] For the loan agreement see *Arab Banking Corporation v. ITC*, January 15, 1986, 77 ILR 4 (Art. 8 of the facility letter of September 24, 1985) and also *Standard Chartered Bank v. ITC*, April 17, 1986, *ibid.* 10 (Art. 7 of the facility letter of July 19, 1982). For the fourth contract see *Maclaine Watson and Co. Ltd v. ITC*, May 13, 1987, *ibid.*, 44.

[98] By virtue *inter alia* of the 38 contracts concluded by the ITC with Amalgamet Inc. between 1982 and 1985; see *ITC v. Amalgamet Inc.*, United States Supreme Court, January 25, 1988, 80 ILR 33 and 36.

[99] *Westland Helicopters Ltd and AOI*, I.C.C. Court of Arbitration, Case 3879/AS, March 25, 1985, 80 ILR 596 *et seq.*

[1] On this hypothesis see Mann, "The Proper Law of Contracts Concluded by International Persons" 1959 BYIL, 38, *et seq.*

[2] See the *Decision of Advocate General Slynn in European Commission v. CO.DE.MI*, making reference to the 1980 Rome Convention to confirm the principle of the pre-eminence of the will of the Parties in determining the law of the contract (Case 318/81, 1985 E.C.R. 3697).

indicates that the problem arises less in terms of principles (the submission of the organisation to another state and its law) than to purely practical considerations (mastery of the national legal system at issue by the advisors of the organisation, for example). This is confirmed in the practice of organisations, from which it is apparent that the risks suggested above are in reality largely offset by the advantages which are offered by recourse to national law in terms of juridical security.

14–048   No doubt it is these considerations which seem to have motivated the drafters of the E.C. Treaty towards contractual responsibility based on different premises from those which govern non-contractual liability (see *infra*). Rather than involve itself in the moving and uncertain landscape of the "general principles common to the law of the member states" which govern the E.C.'s non-contractual liability, there is a marked preference in favour of the well-established provisions of national laws being applicable to contractual relations of the E.C. The consequences of this choice—which applies also outside the E.C. context to other international organisations[3]— are reflected in the limited number of cases which have reached the ECJ in relation to the E.C.'s contractual liability. A similar experience is to be found in disputes concerning contractual agreements involving UN specialised agencies.[4]

(b) NON-CONTRACTUAL OBLIGATIONS

14–049   Outside the realm of contract, the activities of international organisations in the territory of states (and indeed beyond) can have the effect of causing damage or harm to third persons, including private persons. Classical examples include road traffic accidents involving an official car of the organisation. In cases such as this, the applicable national law will be determined not by the clauses of a contract but rather by principles of general law governing the non-contractual liability of international organisations. It is therefore necessary to determine what law will apply to such situations.

14–050   The general principle that an international organisation will be responsible for damage resulting from its activities in the territory of a state is not controversial and is by now well-established. This aspect is addressed in Chapter 15, but it may be useful here to briefly address the main approaches which are available, since non-contractual liability may arise or be established in different ways. In some cases non-contractual liability is provided for in the treaty establishing the organisation. Such is the case of

---

[3] See Klein, *La responsabilité des organisations internationales* (1998) 176–178.
[4] See for example the disputes between the WHO and the Companie Française d'Enterprise, which was subject to Swiss law in this case, and indeed had reference to Swiss law, arbitration of May 31, 1966, unpublished, referred to in J-P. Laugier, see Klein p. 179, n. 67.

Article 22 of Annex III of UNCLOS which states that the ISBA "shall have responsibility or liability for any damage arising out of wrongful acts in the exercise of its powers and functions (. . .)." It is also the case for the non-contractual liability of the E.C.: Article 288(2) (formerly 215(2)) provides that "the Community shall, in accordance with the general principles common to the laws of the member states, make good any damage caused by its institutions or by its servants in the performance of their duties."[5] In practise, the European Court of Justice has been slow to recognise such liability, having early on adopted a high threshold which a claimant would need to reach to bring a successful claim against a community institution. Although such an approach may have been understandable early on in the life of the community, it is less easily justifiable as the community becomes ever more engaged in the day-to-day activities.[6]

Non-contractual liability also finds expression in a number of agreements **14–051** between organisations and states.[7] Examples include Article 8(1) of the Agreement between the Netherlands and the "ESRO" on the creation and functioning of the European Centre of Space Technology.[8] But the principle of responsibility has been accepted even absent an express treaty provision. To take just one example, the UN accepted *a priori* the principle that it should repair damage caused to property by the UNEF arising from acts of negligence and where military necessity could not be invoked.[9]

Given that most international organisations have not adopted general **14–052** rules governing non-contractual liability, it is generally accepted that it will be the law of the state in which the damage is suffered that will apply. This approach is reflected in numerous treaties addressing various types of activities. It is governed by agreements covering the activities of permanent installations of the organisation.[10] Reservations made by some of these

---

[5] See also Euratom Treaty (Art. 188(2)).
[6] See, *e.g.* Case 238/78, *Ireks-Arkady GmbH v. Council and Commission of the European Communities*, 1979 E.C.R. 2955, para. 9 ("The finding that a legal situation resulting from the legislative measures of the community is unlawful is not sufficient to give rise to [liability under Article 215(2)]. [. . .] the community does not incur liability on account of a legislative measure which involves choices of economic policy unless a sufficiently serious breach of a superior rule of law for the protection of the individual has occurred. Taking into consideration the principles in the legal systems of the member states governing the liability of public authorities for damage caused to individuals by legislative measures . . . the community did not incur liability unless the institution concerned manifestly and gravely disregarded the limits on the exercise of its powers.")
[7] See Chap. 15.
[8] Agreement between the Netherlands and ESRO on the creation and functioning of the European Center of Space Technology, U.N.T.S. Vol. 808, 145.
[9] See the study arising from the establishment and operation of UNEF, Report of the Secretary-General, UN Doc A/3943, October 9, 1958, para. 142.
[10] See for example Art. 6(1) of the Agreement between the IAEA and Austria relating to the Selbersdorf laboratories, Vienna, March 1, 1982, UNTS Vol. 1404, 129; Art. 8(1) of the Headquarters Agreement between the OAS and the United States, Washington, May 14, 1992.

instruments, relating to immunities of the organisation from the jurisdiction of national courts, serve to remind one of the limitations of the rule. The applicability of rules of national law also results sometimes in conventional provisions referring back to "general rules and principles of private international law".[11] In the current state of the subject, these rules designate the *lex loci delicti commisi* as the law applicable for the determination of non-contractual liabilities.

14–053 The application of national laws to the cases of non-contractual liability of international organisations is reflected in the practice of organisations. Thus, the internal law of the state on whose territory UN peacekeeping operations take place will play an important role in disputes relating to such operations.[12] In the *Stairways* case, the arbitral *compromis* charged the arbitrators with the task of determining the non-contractual liability of the UN for damage to third persons in the course of UN operations in the Congo, by a plane rented by the organisation to a third company. The text of the rental agreement envisaged that the law applicable to this question would be that of the former Belgian Congo, which remained in force in the newly established Democratic Republic of Congo.[13] In a similar fashion, the Bureau of Legal Affairs of the UNRWA has taken the view that the quasi-delictual responsibility of the Agency for damage suffered by refugees in camps which it administered in Lebanon were governed by Lebanese law. Recourse was also made to the local laws of the Syrian civil code to determine the responsibility of the Agency for a fatal accident in which it was involved in Damascus. Similarly, it was national law which governed the responsibility of the OAS for damages caused following its intervention in Santa Dominica in 1965. Similar practical solutions arise in the practise of other organisations.[14]

14–054 The application of the *lex loci delicti commisi* to establish non-contractual liability is also recognised by many commentators.[15] The principle constitutes a logical consequence of the obligation of all international organisa-

---

[11] See, *e.g.* Art. 10.1 of the Protocol on the implementation of application of the Agreement between Burundi and the WHO relating to the Regional Bureau for Africa of the OMS in the Republic of Burundi, Geneva, October 1, 1980, 1201 UNTS 166.

[12] The UN legal service has referred to local law in an opinion relating to the responsibility of the UNDP for a road accident caused by one of its drivers. See *UNJY* 1991, p. 309, para. 9.

[13] By reason of Art. 2 of the Law of May 19, 1960: see *Stairways Ltd v. UN*, *UNJY*, 1969, pp. 245–6. According to the Bureau of Legal Affairs of the UN, however, the application of the law of Congo in this case resulted merely from the desire of the parties as expressed in the arbitral *compromis*, and did not reflect the application of traditional conflicts rules: see *UNJY*, 1976, 172.

[14] In relation to buildings occupied by the IAEA, see Rainer and Szasz, *The Law and Practices of the IAEA 1970–1980*, 1993, p. 657.

[15] See Jenks *op. cit.*, 212 *et seq.*; P-M. Dupuy, *loc. cit.*, 1386; Amerasinghe, *Principles of the Institutional Law of International Organisations,* 1996, 228. See also Friedman, "International Public Corporations," 1943 MLR 205; Mann, "International Corporations and National Law," 1967, B.Y.I.L. 164.

tions to respect the law in force in the territory of states in which they carry out their activities, in so far as these do not go against the privileges and immunities which are recognised in respect of it. On occasion there may be a genuine conflict between what the organisation is required to do by its internal law, and the requirements of the national law of the state in which it carries out that activity. For example, national legislation may prohibit the publication of information which the organisation is, as a result of its statutory obligations, entitled or required to publish. In such circumstances the requirements of national law prohibiting publication might be argued to be overridden by the international legal requirements of the organisation, so that the organisation could claim not to be responsible for any damages caused which national law characterised as defamatory; alternatively, the organisation might claim immunity from process before the national courts. Setting aside of national law and refusal of all responsibility by the organisation in such circumstances would arguably be justified by the necessity to ensure that the organisation is able to carry out its functions. This, of course, was the argument of the United Nations in the *Cumaraswamy* case.[16] Such considerations would not, however, easily be said to apply in relation to road accidents or a failure to maintain buildings. It is therefore only in exceptional cases such as this that local law might be considered as not serving as the basis for the non-contractual liability of the organisation.

In some circumstances the *lex loci* may not be appropriate, for example, **14–055** where national law is invoked to determine the responsibility of an international organisation it may be that general principles of law are more appropriate. In respect of the liability of UNEF, for example, Professor Bowett was circumspect in observing that "[n]ot least of the problems faced by a claims commission attempting to deal with civil claims against the United Nations is the absence of an agreed "proper law", for it is by no means clear that the *lex loci* will be applied or will it even be suitable."[17] UN practice in this area appears fluid, and the claims commissions which were established in the context of UNEF and ONUC operations do not appear to have had a great deal of practice. Moreover, such practice as there is often results in settlements the terms of which remain confidential. Here it is likely that there will often be recourse to "general principles of law," comprising rules derived from various national legal systems, although the precise content may vary. Recourse to similar principles arising in different national legal systems introduces a degree of flexibility, and avoids the need to strictly apply the *lex loci*, where different moral and

---

[16] Difference Relating to Immunity from Legal Process of a Special Rapporteur of the Commission on Human Rights, I.C.J. Advisory Opinion of April 29, 1999.

[17] See Bowett, *United Nations Forces—A Legal Study of the United Nations Practice*, 1964, pp. 150 and 244, respectively. See also Simmonds, *Legal Problems Arising from the UN Military Operations in the Congo*, 1968, 235.

political values may be at play. Moreover, there may be areas in which there may not presently exist general principles of law. Similar considerations will apply in other areas, for example, determining the level of financial reparation due to a person who has been harmed by the act of an international organisation. In this context, organisations will develop their own system of material norms, and there may well be an emerging relationship between the national law of one or more states and that of the international organisation.

14–056 Beyond local law and general principles the picture may be completed by referring to standards reflected in international conventions which establish regimes of non-contractual liability and which may govern activities in which international organisations are involved. Examples include civil liability regimes governing nuclear damage and oil pollution.[18] Regimes of this kind could be seen to establish general rules applicable also to the conduct of activities by international organisations.

---

[18] See, *e.g.* the 1963 IAEA Vienna Convention on Civil Liability for Nuclear Damage, U.N.T.S. Vol. 1063 at 265; the 1969 Brussels International Convention on Civil Liability for Oil Pollution Damage, U.N.T.S. Vol. 973 at 3; as amended by the 1976, 1984 and 1992 Protocols; as well as the 1972 Convention on International Responsibility for Damage Caused by Space Objects, U.N.T.S. Vol. 961 at 187.

CHAPTER 15

LEGAL PERSONALITY

Bibliography: Morawiecki, "Legal Regime of the International Organisations", P.Y.I.L. (1986) 71–101; Reinisch, *International Organisations before National Courts*, Cambridge, C.U.P., 2000; Weissberg, *The International Status of the United Nations*, 1961; The Practice of the United Nations, the Specialised Agencies and the International Atomic Energy Agency Concerning their Status, Privileges and Immunities—Study Prepared by the Secretariat, rep. in Y.I.L.C. (1967), Vol. II, 154–324 and (1985), Vol. II. Part 1, 145–210.

Legal personality is now generally considered to be the most important **15–001** constitutive element of international organisations.[1] It is above all the fact that they are endowed with a separate legal personality that distinguishes international organisations from other entities which are nothing more than organs common to two or more states, as were most of the nineteenth century international secretariats or bureaux. There has for a long time been controversy as to whether public international organisations could be regarded as possessing legal personality.[2] During the first half of the twentieth century, such personality had been claimed by writers for organisations like the International Commission for the Cape Spartel Lighthouse, the Bank for International Settlements, the Reparation Commission and the European Commission of the Danube, but was at the same time challenged before national courts for organisations as important as the League of Nations.[3] The debate was not limited to the pre-1945 period. It continued unabated until the late 1960s, fuelled by the assumption that international legal personality was the hallmark of sovereign powers. The recognition that there was no necessary link between international personality and sovereignty, on the one hand, and the appreciation of an increasing role for intergovernmental organisations in international affairs and relations, on the other, gradually resulted in a more general acceptance of the fact that international organisations possessed—or could possess—a

---

[1] See *supra*, Chap. 1.
[2] See the formidable bibliography on this question cited by Jenks, "The Legal Personality of International Organisations" 22 B.Y.B.I.L. (1945) 267.
[3] On one such episode, see Seidl-Hohenveldern and Rudolph, Comment of Art. 104, in Simma (ed.), *The Charter of the United Nations—A Commentary*, Oxford, O.U.P., 1994, 1126, para. 1.

separate legal personality with consequential effects in the international and domestic legal orders.[4]

15–002 The concept of legal personality and its implications are not always easy to grasp. This seems to be particularly true in relation to international organisations, given that they are "secondary subjects" of international law the creation of which flows from the will of other international legal persons (mostly states, but also, more recently, other international organisations).[5] We therefore begin by addressing the principle of legal personality, and its sources as far as international organisations are concerned (A). We then consider some of the most significant consequences of the attribution of legal personality to international organisations, and the essential elements of their legal capacity (B). We conclude by addressing specific issues linked to the evolution of organisations as "living" entities, particularly succession and dissolution, two situations which affect the legal personality of the organisations concerned (C).

A. THE PRINCIPLE

Bibliography: Rama Montaldo, "International Legal Personality and Implied Powers of International Organisations", 44 B.Y.B.I.L. (1970) 111–155; Pescatore, "Les relations extérieures des Communautés europénnes (Contribution à la doctrine de la personnalité des organisations internationales)", 103 R.CA.D.I. (1961–II) 1–244; Seidl-Hohenveldern, "The Legal Personality of International and Supranational Organisations", 21 Rev. Egypt. D.I. (1961) 35–72; Seyersted, "International Personality of Intergovernmental Organisations : Do Their Capacities Really Depend upon their Constitution?", 4 IJIL (1964) 1–74; Seyersted, "Is the International Personality of Intergovernmental Organisations Valid *vis-à-vis* Non-Members?", 4 IJIL (1964) 233–268.

15–004 In order to carry out their functions, international organisations generally perform legal activities in various legal orders.[6] In each of these orders the question of their legal personality will arise. It is for this reason that this issue will successively be examined here in the framework of international law (a) and of domestic legal orders (b).

(a) INTERNATIONAL LAW

(i) Origins

15–005 The explicit conferment of international legal personality on intergovernmental organisations has for a long time remained the exception rather than the rule. Hence, it was only in a bilateral instrument aiming at

---

[4] On this assertion, see generally Reinisch, *International Organisations before National Courts*, Cambridge, C.U.P., 2000.
[5] For more on this, see *infra*, Chap. 16.
[6] See *supra*, Chap. 14.

governing its status in the host country, and not in the Covenant, that the League of Nations was recognised as possessing "international personality and legal capacity."[7] Similarly, the UN Charter, apparently due to a wish to avoid any implication that the UN was a "super-state,"[8] only provides in Article 104 for the legal capacity of the organisation "in the territory of each of its member states."[9] The vast majority of treaties establishing international organisations concluded after the Second World War likewise limit the recognition of legal personality to the domestic sphere of member states.[10] The explicit attribution of international legal personality to inter-governmental organisations has, however, become much more frequent since then, including in constituent instruments.[11] Provisions to the same effect may be found in recent treaties establishing autonomous international judicial institutions.[12] This evolution reflects changes in the international society itself, which is increasingly open to the co-existence of various categories of subjects of international law.

But such explicit recognition, by conventional means, is not the only way **15–006** in which international legal personality has been conferred upon international organisations. As early as 1949, the I.C.J. ruled in its celebrated Advisory Opinion on the Reparation for Injuries suffered in the Service of the United Nations that the organisation was to be deemed to possess "a large measure of international personality."[13] Confronted with the question of whether the UN had the capacity to bring an international claim against a state, the court relied on various elements (such as the attribution of legal capacity, privileges and immunities in the territory of member states, and

---

[7] 7 OJLN (1926), Ann. 911a, 1422.

[8] Report to the President on the results of the San Francisco Conference, Dept. State Publication 2349, (1945) Conference Series 71, 157.

[9] For more on this, see *infra*, paras 15–017 *et seq.*

[10] See *e.g.* IAEA Statute, Art. XV, WIPO Convention, Art. 12(1) UNIDO Constitution, Art. 21, 1, OAS Charter, Art. 133. More recent examples include the OPCW (Art. VIII, section 48). This limitation is also clear in most conventions or protocols on privileges and immunities, and headquarters agreements (on these, see *infra*, b, I). The situation is more ambiguous in instruments which grant "full legal personality" to the organisation established thereby, but the reference in the same provisions to the exercise of capacities usually governed by national legislations (*i.e.* contract, acquire or sell property, institute legal proceedings) cannot but lead to the conclusion that such provisions are only concerned with personality in domestic law (see *e.g.* ILO Constitution, Art. 39, IMF, Art. 9, Section 2, MIGA Convention, Art. 1, b)).

[11] A classical, and for a long period almost unique, example was the 1951 Treaty establishing the ECSC (Art. 6), proclaiming the organisation's legal capacity in international relations. More recent examples include the 1976 Agreement establishing IFAD (Art. 10, section 1), the 1982 United Nations Convention on the law of the sea (for the International Seabed Authority; Art. 176), the 1993 Treaty establishing ECOWAS (Art. 88, 1), the 1994 COMESA Treaty (Art. 186, 1) and the 1994 Protocol on the MERCOSUR institutions (Art. 34).

[12] See in that respect the 1998 Statute of the International Criminal Court (Art. 4, 1).

[13] I.C.J. Rep. (1949) 179.

the capacity to conclude treaties) to reach the conclusion that the organisation possessed a juridical personality on the international plane, and was therefore capable of presenting such a claim. The judges observed that the members had entrusted the organisation with a variety of functions, the fulfilment of which would not have been possible if the UN had not been endowed with a legal personality of its own.[14] In the words of the Court:

> "the organisation was intended to exercise and enjoy, and is in fact exercising and enjoying, functions and rights which can only be explained on the basis of the possession of a large measure of international personality and the capacity to operate upon an international plane. It is at present the supreme type of international organisation, and it could not carry out the intentions of its founders if it was devoid of international personality. It must be acknowledged that its members, by entrusting certain functions to it, with the attendant duties and responsibilities, have clothed it with the competence required to enable those functions to be effectively discharged."[15]

15–007 The approach of the I.C.J. in the *Reparation* case is essentially inductive. The Court's reasoning is based on the observation of the conferment of specific legal capacities on the organisation as such and of particular functions which could not practically be carried out if the organisation did not possess juridical personality in the international sphere. It is also noteworthy that the judges took great care to link the attribution of such personality to the will of the member states—which is necessarily implied in this case. Even though the I.C.J. emphasised the characteristics of the UN as an organisation entrusted with particularly important responsibilities on the international plane, it is now widely accepted that the same reasoning may be adapted to any international organisation, the international legal personality of which has not been explicitly proclaimed in its constitutive— or other—instrument(s).[16] This is not to say, however, that all organisations will have the same juridical status and capacities in the international legal sphere.

(ii) Effects

15–008 The precise effects of the attribution of international legal personality to an intergovernmental organisation have not always been assessed very clearly in the literature. The main ambiguity flows from the fact that specific *capacities* have sometimes been inferred from the recognition of personality to a particular organisation. Hence, a certain logical difficulty must be

---

[14] *ibid.* 178.
[15] *ibid.* 179.
[16] See, *e.g.* Schermers and Blokker, *International Institutional Law*, 3rd ed., The Hague/Boston/London, Nijhoff, 1995, para. 1568.

noted in the reasoning of the I.C.J. in the *Reparations* case; although it is possible to refer to specific powers as indications of personality, the court also went on to stress that other powers (such as the power to bring an international claim) not specifically granted in the constituent treaty could be implied from the very fact of personality. The problem is, therefore, that one might be tempted to deduce, say, a general treaty-making power, from the very fact of personality, even though personality is itself deduced from a specific treaty-making power.[17] In other words, the reasoning is circular.

To avoid such a consequence, it should be clearly understood that legal **15–009** personality has no pre-determined content in international law.[18] Its attribution does not as such, authorise an international organisation to perform one or other specific categories of acts. By recognising in its 1949 Advisory Opinion that "[t]he subjects of law in any legal system are not necessarily identical in their nature or in the extent of their rights"[19] and that the conferment of international legal personality upon the UN does not mean "that its legal personality and rights and duties are the same as those of a state" or "a super-state",[20] the I.C.J. acknowledged that the concept of legal personality has no uniform content in international law. The same conclusion is reached by the International Law Commission, when it pithily observes that "all entities having treaty-making capacity necessarily (have) international personality. On the other hand it (does) not follow that all international persons (have) treaty-making capacity."[21] The attribution of international legal personality simply means that the entity upon which it is conferred is a subject of international law and that it is capable of possessing international rights and duties.[22] The precise scope of those rights and duties will vary according to what may reasonably be seen as necessary, in view of the purposes and functions of the organisation in question, to enable the latter to fulfil its tasks. Therefore the test is a functional one; reference to the functions and powers of the organisation exercised on the international plane, and not to the abstract notion of personality, will alone give guidance on what powers may properly be implied.

This difference between the attribution of personality, on the one hand, **15–010** and of specific capacities, on the other, emerges from the constitutive instruments of some organisations. In determining the legal status of the

---

[17] Parry, The Treaty-making Power of the UN, 26 B.Y.B.I.L. (1949) 108.
[18] See, *e.g.* in that sense Dupuy, Du caractère unitaire de la CEE dans ses relations extérieures, AFDI (1963) 780; Lauterpacht, The Development of the Law of International Organisations by Decisions of International Tribunals, 152 RCADI (1976–IV) 407; U.N.J.Y. (1975) 165, para. 5.
[19] *Loc. cit.* 178.
[20] *ibid.* 179.
[21] A/4169, p. 10, para. 8 (a). See also Parry, *loc. cit.* 147; Kasme, *La capacité de l'ONU de conclure des traités* (1960).
[22] See, *e.g.* Schermers and Blokker, *op. cit.* para. 1570.

International Sea-bed Authority, for instance, the 1982 UNCLOS both proclaims this organisation's international legal personality, and gives it "such legal capacity as may be necessary for the exercise of its functions and the fulfilment of its functions" (Article 176).[23] If the attribution of the international legal personality entailed in itself the capacity to perform any—or particular—type(s) of legal act, one may ask why the founders of that organisation have deemed it necessary to add a further provision on the extent of the legal capacity to be recognised to the organisation in question. The extent of such capacity therefore has to be determined on a case-by-case basis, in view of each organisation's functions and mission. These functions and powers are often described in very general terms, leaving considerable scope for their extension in practice.

15–011   A good example of such extension is provided by the 1971 Advisory Opinion on Namibia where the I.C.J. was concerned with Security Council resolutions which were not expressly covered by the wording of the provisions in Chapters VI and VII (such as the reference to the termination of the mandate or the continued presence of South Africa being illegal). The court took the view that the Council had, in addition to its specific powers, certain general powers under Article 24 (1).[24]

15–012   The attribution of implied powers as a result of a liberal interpretation of the purposes and functions of an organisation will have certain consequences. It means that the organisation is treated as a dynamic institution, evolving to meet changing needs and circumstances and, as time goes by, becoming further and further removed from the formal language of its constituent treaty.[25] In some cases the scope of such implied powers has been limited by the members of the organisation. By way of example, the 1994 Agreement on the Implementation of Part XI of the UNCLOS defines the powers of the International Sea-bed Authority in slightly more restrictive terms than it had originally done.[26] Section 1 of the Annex to the 1994 Agreement provides that:

> "The powers and functions of the Authority shall be those expressly conferred upon it by the Convention. The Authority shall have such incidental powers, consistent with the Convention, as are implicit in, and necessary for, the exercise of those powers and functions with respect to activities in the Area."[27]

---

[23] This provision was modified in 1994 (see *infra* for its amended version), but this does not affect the point.

[24] I.C.J. Rep. (1971) 52, para. 110.

[25] On the implications of such evolutions on the issue of the legality of institutional acts, see *supra*, Chap. 11, paras 11–052 *et seq.*

[26] For the initial formulation, see *supra*, para. 15–010.

[27] 33 ILM (1994) 1311.

The formulation reflects the concern of the member states to retain a **15–013** degree of control on the organisation they establish, seeking to prevent it from extending its powers beyond certain limits.

What is beyond debate is that in creating this "potential capacity",[28] the **15–014** attribution of international legal personality to an intergovernmental organisation establishes it as an entity legally distinct from its members. This is one of the elements emphasised by the I.C.J. in its 1949 Advisory Opinion, noting that "[p]ractice —in particular the conclusion of conventions to which the organisation is a party—has confirmed this character of the organisation, which occupies *a position in certain respects in detachment of its members* [. . .]."[29] This consequence of the attribution of legal personality has been repeatedly referred to by national and international tribunals in various circumstances. For example, the Swiss Supreme Court (*Tribunal fédéral*) ruled in the AOI case that "[t]he personality accorded to the AOI, as well as the autonomy conferred on it at the legal, financial and procedural level [. . .] are the obvious and unequivocal signs of the total legal independence of the organisation in relation to the founding states."[30] This "individualisation" of organisations resulting from the conferment upon them of an autonomous international legal personality has significant practical consequences, including on the question of the responsibility flowing from illegal acts performed by an organisation.[31]

(iii) Recognition

Whether it flows directly from the constituent instrument or other multi- **15–015** lateral agreements, or whether it arises by implication from such instruments, the international legal personality of international organisations is based upon the will of the founders. The international legal personality of an organisation is therefore always opposable to its members, since these are bound by the very instruments from which this personality flows. Whether non-members of an organisation are also under a duty to recognise the latter's personality is, on the other hand, not so clear.

In its 1949 Advisory Opinion, the I.C.J. held that:

> "fifty states, representing the vast majority of the members of the international community, had the power, in conformity with international law, to bring into being an entity possessing *objective* international personality, and not merely personality recognised by them alone [. . .]."[32]

---

[28] The expression is borrowed from Kasme, who speaks of a "capacité en puissance" (*op. cit.* 31).

[29] *ibid.*; emphasis added.

[30] Judgment of July 19, 1988, 80 ILR 658.

[31] See *infra*.

[32] *Loc. cit.* 185, emphasis added.

15–016   This factor justified, in the Court's opinion, the capacity of the UN to present an international claim against a state which, at the time, was not one of the organisation's members. It is far from clear, however, that this reasoning extends to all other international organisations, as it has generally been viewed as a statement of the political and factual importance of the UN, rather than as the formulation of a more general rule or principle of law.[33] A majority of commentators have observed that the concept of "objective" personality runs counter to the principle of the relativity of treaties. The constituent instrument of international organisations—almost always a treaty—is a *res inter alios acta* for non-members and, as such, may not bind them.[34] While the international legal personality of an international organisation imposes itself on its members, the same cannot be said for non-members. They are free to acknowledge such international juridical personality, either expressly or implicitly—for example by concluding a treaty with the organisation—, or to disregard it and to affirm their preference for the establishment of legal relations with the members exclusively.[35] While this issue remains theoretical in most cases,[36] non-members generally not having particular reasons for refusing to recognise the separate legal personality of an international organisation, it is important to keep in mind that they are under no obligation to do so, for example in—exceptional—situations where third states might take the view that a particular organisation is simply a front for its members, or that its creation springs from an attempt on the part of the members to evade some of their international obligations.

---

[33] See, *e.g.* Carroz and Probst, *Personnalité juridique internationale et capacité de conclure des traités de l'ONU et des institutions spécialisées*, Paris, Foulon, 1953, 54; Dupuy, "Le droit des relations entre les organisations internationales", 100 RCADI (1960–II) 556; Pescatore, "Les relations extérieures des Communautés europénnes (Contribution à la doctrine de la personnalité des organisations internationales)", 103 RCADI (1961–II) 70.

[34] See, *e.g.* Weissberg, *The International Status of the United Nations*, London/New York, Oceana/Stevens & Sons, 1961, 26; Bindschedler, "La délimitation des compétences des Nations Unies", 108 RCADI (1963–I) 402; Shihata, role of Law in Economic Development—The Legal Problems of International Public Ventures", Rev. Egypt. D.I. (1969) 124; Verhoeven, *La reconnaissance internationale dans la pratique contemporaine*, Paris, Pedone, 1975, 211; Seidl-Hohenveldern, *Corporations in and under International Law*, Cambridge, Grotius, 1987, 87.

[35] See, *e.g.* in that sense Seidl-Hohenveldern, *op. cit.* 88.

[36] Note that there have already been some situations where third states have refused to recognise an organisation's separate international personality in practice. One of the best-known precedents in that respect is the position taken for some time by the USSR and other Eastern European countries, which refused to enter into legal relations with the European Community. For an expression of this position, see the reservation formulated by the USSR upon ratification of the International Agreement on Natural Rubber of October 6, 1979 (1201 U.N.T.S. 396). On this question see also *e.g.* Boulouis, "Le droit des Communautés européennes dans ses rapports avec le droit international général", 235 RCADI (1992–IV) 56.

(b) DOMESTIC LAW

(i) Origins

The attribution of legal personality to international organisations in domes- **15–017** tic legal orders raised considerably less difficulties and concerns than in the international sphere. The vast majority of constituent instruments proclaim the power of international organisations to act as autonomous legal persons in national legal orders.[37] These have often been supplemented by more specific instruments, such as multilateral conventions or protocols specifying the legal status and detailing the privileges and immunities of one or more organisation(s), or bilateral treaties concluded between one organisation and its host state to further define the organisation's legal status in that country (headquarters agreement). Instruments providing for an organisation's personality in the domestic sphere usually specify that the organisation has the capacity to conclude contracts, acquire and dispose of movable and immovable property and to institute legal proceedings, these being viewed as essential to the proper functioning of any intergovernmental organisation. This list is by no means exhaustive, and the legal capacity of international organisations in domestic legal orders encompasses the power to perform any legal act or function that would prove to be necessary for the organisation to fulfil its mission.[38] More generally, it may safely be said that even in the absence of any explicit instrument or provision of that kind, any international organisation must be deemed to enjoy an independent legal personality in domestic legal orders, since this will almost always prove necessary to enable it to discharge its functions on a daily basis.

(ii) Recognition

By definition, the "national" legal personality of international organisations **15–018** is to produce effects in domestic legal orders. The process through which such personality is recognised and given effect in national orders varies according to a number of factors. A first distinction is to be drawn between members and non-members of the organisation. As far as members are concerned, the reasoning is essentially the same as for international legal personality. Being bound by the legal instruments—generally the constituent instrument—in which the organisation's legal personality is established, the member states are to grant it *ipso facto* recognition in their domestic legal order. This will not raise any difficulty in monist states, where the rules of international law binding on the state can be invoked directly before national tribunals.[39]

---

[37] See, *e.g.* the various conventions mentioned *supra*, n. 10.
[38] See, *e.g.* for the UN Seidl-Hohenveldern and Rudolph, *loc. cit.* 1128. This may be viewed as another application of the implied powers doctrine.
[39] See for instance the recognition of the legal personality of a UN subsidiary organ by a Dutch court, based on the attribution of juridical capacity in treaty provisions, in *UNRRA v. Daan*, 16 ILR 337.

15–019   In contrast, such a recognition will only be possible in dualist states if the international norm from which the "national" legal personality of a given intergovernmental organisation flows has been incorporated in that state's domestic legal order.[40] The most striking formulation of this principle can be found in the House of Lord's 1989 decision in the *ITC* case, finding that "[t]he ITC as a matter of English law owes its existence to the Order in Council. That is what created the ITC in domestic law [. . .]." [41] In the United Kingdom, the adoption of an Order in Council conferring upon international organisations to which that state becomes a member the "legal capacities of a body corporate,"[42] or the enactment of a specific piece of legislation in respect to a given organisation[43] are the two ways by which the juridical personality of international organisations is given effect in that country's legal order.

15–020   The situation is slightly different in non-member states, since these are under no obligation to give effect to a legal personality deriving from an international instrument to which they are not parties.[44] In the vast majority of cases, however, the legal personality of international organisations is recognised in national courts of non-member states by application of their conflict-of-laws rules, or of other principles, such as "comity". Courts therefore tend to apply to "foreign" international organisations the same principle as the one they would use when called upon to pronounce on the legal personality of foreign corporations, *i.e.* agree to give effect to a personality which has been recognised in that foreign body's legal order of origin. Since, unlike foreign companies, international organisations are not "incorporated" under the laws of a particular state, it is to the international norms proclaiming the organisation's legal personality that national courts ought logically to turn to give effect to this personality in a non-member's domestic legal order. As the Court of Arbitration of the International Chamber of Commerce put it in the first Westland decision:

> "[h]aving regard to the supranational character of the [Arab Organisation for Industrialisation], it is [. . .] impossible to attribute to it, *a*

---

[40] On the differences of approach of this question in monist and dualist states, respectively, see Reinisch, *op. cit.* 47 *et seq.*

[41] *J.H. Rayner v. Department of Trade*, October 26, 1989, 81 ILR 709 (per Lord Oliver of Aylmerton). This view led to some serious difficulties in later cases where the recognition of the legal personality of an international organisation of which the U.K. was not a member was at stake (see *infra*, n. 47).

[42] By virtue of the International Organisations Act 1968. Note that the same procedure may be followed in respect of organisations of which the U.K. is *not* a member, but which maintain or propose to maintain an establishment in the U.K.

[43] See for instance the Bretton Woods Agreements Act 1945 or the International Sugar Organisation Act 1973, the European Bank for Reconstruction and Development (Immunities and Privileges) Order 1991 (Art. 4, Statutory Instruments 1991, nr 757) or the World Trade Organisation (Privileges and Immunities) Order 1995 (Art. 4, Statutory Instruments 1995, nr 266).

[44] See, *e.g.* Reinisch, *op. cit.* 41 and 45–46.

posteriori, an 'applicable law' according to the rules of private international law, that it to say to submit this entity to the law of either the
place of its incorporation (which, *in casu*, does not exist), or the place
where the centre of its business activities lies, or the place of its
management, or any other place. This private law manner of approach
is excluded if the legal entity in question is created by states which
have wished to give it a supranational character, that it to say to
exempt it from being subject to any national law."[45]

The recognition of personality as deriving directly from international law **15–021**
is, however, treated with circumspection in some states. Hence, the House
of Lords took a very different path to recognise the legal personality of an
organisation to which the United Kingdom was not a party in basing this
recognition on comity and on the fact that the organisation concerned had
been "given legal personality and capacity by the law of the state wherein it
has its seat or permanent location."[46] Whatever reasoning is followed, in
most cases the recognition of an international organisation's "national"
legal personality in non-member states has not raised particular
difficulties.[47]

The effect of the conferment of "domestic" legal personality on a given **15–022**
organisation—once recognised in the national legal order concerned—is
the same as on the international plane; it will distinguish the organisation,
as an autonomous legal person, from its members, and enable it to function
independently from them.[48]

B. ASPECTS OF INTERNATIONAL ORGANISATIONS' LEGAL CAPACITY AND
CONSEQUENCES OF THE ATTRIBUTION OF A SEPARATE LEGAL PERSONALITY

We turn now to consider aspects of international organisations' legal **15–023**
capacity in international law (a) and in domestic legal orders (b), before
addressing the specific consequences of the attribution to organisations of a
separate legal personality on issues of liability and responsibility which may
arise in the international as well as in domestic legal orders (c).

---

[45] Interim Award of March 5, 1984 regarding jurisdiction, 80 ILR 611.
[46] *Arab Monetary Fund v. Hashim* (n. 3), February 21, 1991, by Lord Bridge of Harwich, 85
ILR 8–9.
[47] See, however, the decision by which the Court of Appeal of England refused to recognise
any legal personality and capacity to act before English courts to the Arab Monetary Fund
(*A.M.F. v. Hashim* (n. 3), April 30, 1990, 83 ILR 263–264, per Lord Donaldson of
Lymington). On the various cases before English tribunals where this issue arose, see
generally Marston, "The Origin of Personality of International Organisations in United
Kingdom Law", 40 I.C.L.Q. (1991), 403–424.
[48] For particular implications of this on issues of responsibility, see *infra*.

(a) INTERNATIONAL LAW

(i) Treaty-making power

Bibliography: Carroz and Probst, *Personnalité juridique internationale et capacité de conclure des traités de l'ONU et des institutions spécialisées*, Paris, Foulon, 1953; Chiu, *The Capacity of International Organisations to Conclude Treaties*, The Hague, Nijhoff, 1966; Geiser, *Les effets des accords conclus par des organisations internationales*, Bern, H. Lang, 1977; Sonnenfeld, "International Organisations as Parties to Treaties", P.Y.I.L. (1981–82) 177–200.

15–024   Treaties to which international organisations are a party, whether agreements between organisations, between states and international organisations, bilateral or multilateral, are now commonplace.[49] The adoption, in 1986, of the Vienna Convention on the Law of Treaties between States and International Organisations or between International Organisations is symptomatic of the importance of such instruments in contemporary international law and relations.[50] Whether or not any given international organisation has treaty-making power can only be determined by reference to the constitution or other rules of the organisation.[51] This is not to adopt the somewhat narrow view of Kelsen to the effect that such treaty-making power must be expressly given,[52] but rather to state that such power must be conferred expressly or by reasonable implication as a competence required to enable the organisation to discharge its functions effectively.[53]

15–025   This is clearly so in practice; if one looks at the UN Charter there are specific categories of treaties envisaged, for example, the relationship agreements between the UN and the specialised agencies under Articles 57 and 63,[54] the trusteeship agreements under Chapter XII,[55] agreements under Article 43 and the conventions concerning privileges and immunities referred to in Article 105(3).[56] Yet there are many agreements concluded by the UN which rest on no such specific grant of power. The succession treaties of 1946 by which the United Nations assumed assets and functions of the League of Nations,[57] the agreements on technical assistance and the Children's Fund (UNICEF) which implement Chapter IX of the Charter, and the agreements made between the Secretary-General and states

---

[49] It has been estimated that more than 10,000 treaties had been concluded by international organisations by 1973 (see Dupuy, L'application des règles du droit international général des traités aux accords conclus par les organisations internationales, 55 AIDI (1973) 227).

[50] Doc. A/CONF.129/15. Convenient text in 25 ILM (1986) 543.

[51] See the general recognition of this in Art. 6 of the 1986 Convention.

[52] *Law of the United Nations* (1950), p. 330; also Lukashuk, "An international organisation as a party to international treaties" (1960) Soviet Y.B.I.L. 144.

[53] See, *e.g.* Weissberg, *op. cit.* 37; Lauterpacht, *loc. cit.* 388–478.

[54] See *supra*, Chap. 3.

[55] See *supra*, Chap. 2.

[56] See *infra*, paras 15–054 *et seq.*

[57] See *infra*, paras 15–087 *et seq.*

contributing armed forces to peacekeeping operations, as well as those concluded with the state(s) on the territory of which those operations unfold (Status of Force Agreements, or SOFAs) are clear illustrations. The contrast between express and implied powers is not one found only in the UN Charter. In the Council of Europe, for example, whereas Article 40 of the Statute envisages agreements for the conferment of privileges and immunities, and a special agreement with the host country, nothing is said of agreements with other inter-governmental organisations, akin to the "relationship agreements" concluded by the UN. In fact many such agreements have been made pursuant to a resolution of the Committee of Ministers adopted in May 1951.[58]

This, however, does not mean that any international organisation may **15–026** conclude any kind of treaty with third parties. A clear limit to their power in that respect is that the subject-matter of the treaty must fall within the overall field of competences of the organisation. In particular, the exercise of an implied treaty-making power may well give rise to issues over its legality. These issues could relate to whether the treaty was *ultra vires* the organisation or the particular organ concluding the treaty. Theoretically it would be open to any organisation having the right to request an advisory opinion from the I.C.J. to get such an opinion on a draft treaty before the organisation formally bound itself to the treaty. This procedure has, however, never been used for that purpose. In the treaty establishing the European Community (although here the treaty-making power is express), Article 300(6) specifically provides for the reference of an "envisaged agreement" to the ECJ for an opinion on its compatibility with the constituent treaty; a negative opinion requires the revision of the treaty under Article 48 of the Treaty on European Union before the Community may proceed with the contemplated agreement. In the exercise of its jurisdiction under Article 300 (6) (*ex Article 228*), the Court has on several occasions ruled that treaties which the European Community was contemplating with third parties were not compatible with the founding treaties, or that the community lacked the powers to enter into an international agreement on a specific subject-matter.[59]

The identity of the organ(s) vested with the treaty-making power is **15–027** clearly a matter for the rules of the organisation. This is expressly provided for in some cases. For the UN, for example, the conclusion of relationship agreements with the specialised agencies devolves upon the ECOSOC (Article 63). The pre-eminent role played in many organisations by the

---

[58] The text of the Resolution can be consulted on the Council of Europe's website (http://www.coe.fr/eng/legaltxt/1e.htm).

[59] See, *e.g.* Opinions 1–76, Rep. (1977) 741, 1–91, Rep. (1991) I-6079, 2–94, Rep. (1996) I-1763.

chief administrative officer in the conclusion of treaties with third parties has been emphasised earlier.[60] A more complex procedure is provided for in some organisations, such as the European Community. There, it is the Commission, after authorisation by the Council, which conducts the negotiations which are to lead to the conclusion of an agreement with a third party (Article 300(1) of the treaty). The conclusion of the agreement, on the other hand, falls to the Council, after having consulted the European Parliament or, in specific cases, obtained its assent.[61] This is akin to the parliamentary approval often required in municipal constitutions as a pre-condition to ratification of a treaty by the executive. When constituent instruments do not contain any provision governing the conclusion of agreements with third parties, the identification of the competent organ will have to be made on the basis of each organisation's practice. It is clear that, irrespective of the particular organ which concluded the agreement, it is the organisation itself which will be bound by the instrument, since it is the only entity which is vested with legal personality on the international plane (as opposed to the particular organs).[62] As the ECJ put it in respect of the legal effects of a treaty concluded by the Commission with a third state:

> "it is the Community alone, having legal personality pursuant to Article 210 of the Treaty, which has the capacity to bind itself by concluding agreements with a non-member country or an international organisation. There is no doubt, therefore, that the Agreement is binding on the European Communities."[63]

15–028   Ultimately, it is therefore always the organisation as such which is bound by the agreement concluded by any of its organ(s).[64] It is equally clear that the organisation alone is bound by the treaties to which it becomes a party. Such treaties are not directly binding on members of the organisation, and nor are they enforceable against them.[65] This is a direct consequence of the

---

[60] See *supra*, Chap. 12, paras 12–002 *et seq.*

[61] The agreements the conclusion of which is subject to the parliament's assent include association agreements and agreements establishing a specific institutional framework by organising co-operation procedures or having important budgetary implications for the Community (Art. 300(3)).

[62] See generally Geiser, *Les effets des accords conclus par les organisations internationales*, Berne, Lang, 1977, 108. For the specific example of UNRWA, see Salmon, "L'UNRWA— Un exemple de décentralisation internationale par service", Mélanges Rolin, Paris, Pedone, 1964, 342; for that of the UNEF and ONUC, see Seyersted, "United Nations Forces : Some Legal Problems", 37 B.Y.B.I.L. (1961) 412–413.

[63] Case C–327/91, *France v. Commission*, Rep. (1994) I–3674, paras 24–25.

[64] It should be noted that this will usually be the case even if the organ has exceeded its own competences, as defined by the rules of the organisations, in situations where the conclusion of the treaty is *ultra vires* the organ, but *intra vires* the organisation as a whole. Art. 46(2) of the 1986 Vienna Convention provides that "[a]n international organisation may not invoke the fact that its consent to be bound by a treaty has been expressed in violation of the rules of the organisation regarding competence to conclude treaties as invalidating its consent unless that violation was manifest and concerned a rule of fundamental importance."

[65] See generally Klein, *La responsabilité des organisations internationales*, Brussels, Bruylant, 1998, 439 *et seq.*

fact that international organisations are generally endowed with a separate legal personality. The situation is different only when the rules of the organisation or the agreement itself provide otherwise—which is exceptional[66]—or, obviously, when the members are themselves parties to the agreement alongside the organisation. The latter hypothesis, is however, rather uncommon, and is essentially a feature of the practice of the European Community. Therefore, the fact that the subject-matter of some proposed treaties fell partly within the organisation's field of competences and partly within that of the member states has led to the development of "mixed agreements," concluded jointly by the Community and its member states, on the one side, and by one or more third state(s) on the other.[67] This technique has been used on several occasions for the accession to multilateral treaties. Some of these require that in such cases, the division of competences between the organisation and its member states in the area covered by the treaty should be specified in the instrument of formal confirmation or of accession so as to make easier the assessment of the responsibilities bearing, respectively, on the organisation and on its members in respect of the performance of the treaty.[68]

It may be observed that the notion of a treaty-making power implies **15–029** participation in the treaty as a party; as such it should be sharply distinguished from the function of a quasi-legislative character possessed by

---

[66] Art. 300(7) (*ex Art.* 228(7)) of the E.C. Treaty, which provides that "[a]greements concluded under the conditions set out in that Art. shall be binding on the institutions of the community and on member states" has sometimes been considered as constituting such an exception (see *e.g.* in that respect Van Houtte, International Law and Community Treaty-making Power, Northwestern J.I.L. & Bus. (1981) 633 and Rideau, Commentaire de l'article 228, in Constantinesco, Kovar, Jacque and Simon (eds.), Traité instituant la CEE—Commentaire article par article, Paris, Economica, 1992, 1455). This is probably not the case, however, since this provision is generally interpreted as having an "internal" effect only, in the sense that it emphasises the fact that the inclusion in the Community's legal order of international agreements concluded by that organisation entails certain obligations for member states *within the organisation's legal order* (such as providing assistance to Community institutions when this is required for the execution of the agreement, for example). See, *e.g.* Louis and Bruckner, Relations extérieures, in Megret (ed.), *Le droit de la CEE*, vol. 12, Brussels, Ed. De l'Université, 1980, 18 and 62; Roucounas, "Engagements parallèles et contradictoires", 206 RCADI (1987–VI) 275; Sonnenfeld, "International Organisations as Parties to Treaties", PYIL (1981–82) 197–198; Tomuschat, "Liability for Mixed Agreements", in Schermers and O'Keefe (eds.), *Mixed Agreements*, Deventer, Kluwer, 1983, 129; Hartwig, *Die Haftung der Mitgliedstaaten fur internationale Organisationen*, Berlin/Heidelberg, Springer, 1993, 165.

[67] See generally Schermers and O'Keefe (eds.), *Mixed Agreements*, Deventer, Kluwer, 1983. On the origin of this practice, which does not have any basis in the Rome Treaty, see *e.g.* Cremona, The Doctrine of Exclusivity and the Position of Mixed Agreements in the External Relations of the European Community, *Oxford Journal of Legal Studies* (1982) 411–412.

[68] See for instance Art. 5(1) of Annex IX of the 1982 UNCLOS. See also Art. 6 on issues of responsibility. Similar clauses may be found in other instruments such as the 1991 Convention on Environmental Impact Assessment in a Transboundary Context (Art. 17(5) (30 ILM (1991) 802); the 1992 Convention on the Transboundary Effects of Industrial Accidents (Art. 29, (4) (31 ILM (1992) 1333); the 1994 Convention on Nuclear Safety (Art. 30, (4)(iii) (33 ILM (1994) 1518).

many organisations by which the organisation becomes the sponsor or the deliberative or negotiating forum of a treaty between states.[69] The distinction cannot always be drawn with ease. Whilst the I.C.J. clearly took the view that the UN was a party to the 1946 Convention on Privileges and Immunities, as did the Secretariat in registering the instrument *ex officio*, the matter is not entirely free from doubt since there are no signatories (the Convention was approved by the Assembly and acceded to by member states) and Article 105(3) suggests that it was for the Assembly to "propose conventions to the members," a phrase which on one construction could exclude actual participation as a party.[70] Similarly, the participation by the United Nations in the trusteeship agreements as a party in its own right is not entirely clear.[71]

15–030 In practical terms, the vast majority of treaties to which international organisations are parties are bilateral agreements, the purpose of which is to define the organisation's activities and legal status, or to provide for cooperation with states or other organisations. More recently, and in a much more limited way, international organisations have become parties to multilateral "law-making" treaties. An increasing number of multilateral conventions is now open to the participation of intergovernmental organisations.[72] In many cases, however, this is limited to "economic integration organisations," the European Community invariably being the only organisation to so participate. This phenomenon remains much more marginal as far as other organisations are concerned, the 1986 Vienna Convention constituting a notable exception in that respect.[73] This indicates that international law-making, through conventional instruments at least, continues to a very large extent to be the prerogative of states.[74]

(ii) Other powers

15–031 As explained above, the actual scope of legal capacities conferred upon organisations may vary from one organisation to another, according to each organisation's functions and mission. While the capacity to conclude

---

[69] On this, see *supra*, Chap. 11, paras 11–034 *et seq.*

[70] See Parry, "The Treaty-making Power of the UN", 26 B.Y.B.I.L. (1949) 142–145 and Weissberg, *op. cit.* 62–63.

[71] See Kelsen, *op. cit.*, pp. 586, 608, 609; Parry, "The Legal Nature of the Trusteeship Agreements" 27 B.Y.B.I.L. (1950) 185; Schachter, 25 B.Y.B.I.L. (1948) 130–131, Toussaint, *The Trusteeship System of the UN* (1956), p. 78.

[72] See, *e.g.* the examples mentioned above, n. 68. A number of these instruments are treaties establishing international organisations, on which see *infra*, Chap. 16, paras 16–002 *et seq.*

[73] It is only recently, however, and in limited numbers, that international organisations have become parties to this instrument (formal confirmation by the UN on December 21, 1998 and by the IMO on February 14, 2000; accession by the IOPCW on June 2, 2000). Signatories of the Convention include the FAO, the ICAO, the ILO, the ITU, UNESCO, the WHO, the WMO and the Council of Europe.

[74] It is symptomatic that ratifications or accessions by states are the only ones to be taken into account for the entry into force of the 1986 Vienna Convention, even though this instrument is equally open to international organisations (see Art. 85(1) of the Convention).

treaties is recognised for the vast majority of international organisations to enable them to achieve their objectives, the legal capacity of an organisation such as the United Nations extends far beyond, since this proved necessary for the fulfilment by this organisation of its wide-ranging aims. The first, and most obvious, example is the power to maintain an international force under a United Nations command utilising a United Nations flag.[75] Dozens of peacekeeping and peace enforcement operations have thus been established by the organisations since the 1950s.[76]

As a second example one might take the capacity to exercise jurisdiction **15–032** over territory; this is clearly anticipated in Article 81 of the Charter and was contemplated as a solution to the Trieste and Jerusalem problems;[77] it became an accomplished fact when the UN took over the interim administration of Western New Guinea pending the formal transfer to Indonesia on 1 May 1963.[78] Transitional administrations of the UN have since then been established in Cambodia (UNTAC, 1992–1993),[79] Eastern Slavonia, in Croatia (UNTAES, 1996–1998),[80] Kosovo (UNMIK, since 1999)[81] and East Timor (UNTAET, since 1999).[82] This capacity is also implicit in the General Assembly's establishment of the UN Council for Namibia in resolution 2248 (S-V) of May 1967 that the Assembly has power to administer territory. These are just examples of far-reaching powers and capacities, obviously not shared by all international organisations.[83]

(b) DOMESTIC LAW

(i) Contracts, *Jus Standi*

It has been seen that instruments attributing legal personality to inter- **15–033** national organisations in domestic legal orders generally grant them the capacity to enter into contracts, to acquire and dispose of movable or immovable property and to initiate legal proceedings. These various capacities are widely used by organisations throughout the world on a daily basis and do not raise particular questions. They are, however, not the only ones granted to international organisations in domestic legal orders. Others

---

[75] See generally Seyersted, *Some Legal Problems* . . ., *loc. cit.* 435 *et seq.*; Bowett, *U.N. Forces* (1964), Chap. 8.

[76] For more on these, see *supra*, Chap. 2.

[77] See, *e.g.* UNGA Res. 181 (II).

[78] Agreement between Netherlands and Indonesia of August 15, 1962 (Doc. A/5170 and Coor. I and Add. I).

[79] S.C. res. 745 (1992) of February 28, 1992.

[80] S.C. res. 1037 of January 15, 1996.

[81] S.C. res. 1244 of July 10, 1999.

[82] S.C. res. 1272 of October 25, 1999.

[83] Note, however, for example, that Art. 93 of the 1982 UNCLOS recognises the possibility for the UN, specialised agencies and the IAEA to use ships flying those organisations' flags. On the capacity of international organisations to bring international claims, see *infra* paras 15–109 *et seq.*

include, for instance, the capacity to issue official identity or travel documents, to run a specific system of registration for vehicles, or to adopt rules aimed at governing activities taking place in the organisation's headquarters district. In contrast with the three capacities mentioned above, these are obviously not legal capacities akin to those usually exercised by private persons; they are, on the contrary, an expression of the fact that international organisations enjoy, in national legal systems, a privileged legal regime which, once again, finds its basis in the need to ensure that organisations have at their disposal all the legal means necessary for their daily functioning and the fulfilment of their functions. It is therefore to the study of privileges and immunities enjoyed by international organisations that the bulk of this section is dedicated.

(ii) Privileges and Immunities

15–034   Bibliography: Ahluwalia, *The Legal Status, Privileges and Immunities of the Specialized Agencies of the United Nations and Certain Other International Organisations*, The Hague, Nijhoff, 1964; Bekker, *The Legal Position of Intergovernmental Organisations—A Functional Necessity Analysis of their Legal Status and Immunities*, Dordrecht/Boston/London, Nijhoff, 1994; Cully, "Jurisdictional Immunities of Intergovernmental Organisations", 91 Yale L.J. (1982) 1167–1195; de Bellis, *L'immunità delle organizzazioni internazionali dalla giurisdizione,* Bari, 1992; Dominicé, "L'immunité de juridiction et d'exécution des organisations internationales", 187 R.C.A.D.I. (1984–IV) 145–238; Duffar, *Contribution à l'étude des privilèges et immunités des organisations internationales,* Paris, L.G.D.J., 1982; Jenks, *International Immunities,* London/New York, Stevens & Sons/Oceana, 1961; Muller, *International Organisations and their Host States,* The Hague/London/Boston, Nijhoff, 1995.

15–035   The advent of the international organisation as an international person and the attribution to it of functions often analogous to those of sovereign states which, for their effective exercise, require the concession of privileges and immunities from states, has led to a considerable body of law concerned with the privileges and immunities of international organisations, their premises, their staff, and members' representatives to these organisations. The analogy of diplomatic privileges and immunities immediately suggests itself as a basis for this development, and to some extent this analogy has been accepted. However, certain major differences exist between diplomatic immunities and those of international organisations. First, privileges and immunities may well be most important in the case of relations between an official of an organisation and his own national state, whereas a national of the receiving state is, for the purposes of diplomatic immunity, accepted as a member of a foreign mission only by express consent and with a minimum of privileges and immunity in respect of official acts only.[84] Moreover, members of diplomatic missions generally

---

[84] Arts 8(2) and 38(1) of the 1961 Vienna Convention on Diplomatic Relations (500 U.N.T.S. 95).

do not enjoy any privilege or immunity *vis-à-vis* the sending state. Secondly, whereas the diplomat who is immune from the jurisdiction of the receiving state is under the general jurisdiction of his own sending state, no comparable jurisdiction exists where an official of an international organisation is concerned. And, thirdly, whereas observance of diplomatic privileges and immunities is ensured through the operation of the principle of reciprocity, an international organisation has no such effective sanction. These differences, coupled with a trend towards the diminution of privileges and immunities generally, have been reflected in the greater emphasis placed upon the functional basis for the privileges and immunities of international organisations.[85]

The sources of privileges and immunities of international organisations **15–036** are diverse, ranging from constituent instruments to domestic legislations. Hence, most treaties establishing international organisations contain a basic clause providing in general terms, along the lines of Article 105 of the UN Charter, that:

> "(1) The organisation shall enjoy in the territory of each of its members such privileges and immunities as are necessary for the fulfilment of its purposes.
> (2) Representatives of the members of the United Nations and officials of the organisation shall similarly enjoy such privileges and immunities as are necessary for the independent exercise of their functions in connection with the organisation."[86]

Constitutional texts generally do not deal in great detail with privileges **15–037** and immunities, although the provisions of the international financial institutions' constitutions, for instance, are far more detailed than those of the UN Charter or the constitutions of the other specialised agencies.[87] The general tendency has been to supplement the basic texts by a further instrument. The first to be concluded in the post Second World War period was the General Convention on the Privileges and Immunities of the United Nations, approved by the General Assembly on February 13, 1946, and now acceded to by close to 140 states.[88] A separate Convention on the Privileges and Immunities of the Specialised Agencies was similarly approved on November 21, 1947,[89] subject to variations for each specialised

---

[85] For more on this, and for concrete examples, see *infra*.

[86] See also *e.g.* Articles 40 of the ILO Constitution, 12 of the UNESCO Constitution, 10(2) of the IFAD Agreement, 21(1) of the UNIDO Constitution, XV of the IAEA Statute, 4(a) of the Council of Europe Statute, 133 and 134 of the OAS Charter.

[87] See Articles IX of the IMF Articles of Agreement, VII of the IBRD Articles of Agreement, VI of the IFC Articles of Agreement, VIII of the IDA Articles of Agreement and Articles 43 to 50 of the MIGA Convention.

[88] 1 U.N.T.S. 19.

[89] 33 U.N.T.S. 261. As of June 2000, 106 states were parties to that instrument. It should be noted that each state, when it becomes a party to the Convention, declares to which specialised agency or agencies it will apply the Convention. Application of the Convention to all specialised agencies constitutes the exception rather than the rule.

agency which are determined by the agency concerned and set out in a special annex.[90] These two conventions formed a model for later agreements made by other organisations such as the League of Arab States, the OECD, the Organisation of American States,[91] the Council of Europe[92] and, to a lesser extent, the European Communities.[93] The conclusion of similar agreements also followed the establishment of more recent international organisations.[94]

15–038   Whilst these agreements are of a multilateral character, it has often been found necessary to conclude a bilateral agreement with the host state in whose territory the headquarters or other offices of the organisations are maintained. The Headquarters Agreement between the UN and the USA,[95] the UN and Switzerland,[96] the Council of Europe and France,[97] the ILO and Mexico (in respect of its Field Office)[98] are but a few examples of this kind of agreement.[99] Special agreements, which provide for privileges and immunities for the organisation and its agents, are also frequently concluded by international organisations with states on the territory of which they undertake particular—generally temporary—activities, such as the provision of technical assistance or the establishment of peacekeeping operations.[1] In the latter case, the practice has developed for the UN to conclude systematically a so-called "Status of Force Agreement" (often referred to as "SOFA") with the host state, defining the legal status—including in terms of privileges and immunities—of the UN Force.[2]

---

[90] The regime of the 1947 Convention also applies to the WTO, in spite of the fact that this organisation is not a specialised agency (see Art. VIII (4) of the WTO Agreement).

[91] I Annals of the OAS (1949), Nr 3, 271.

[92] 250 U.N.T.S.12.

[93] The Protocol is annexed to the Merger Treaty of April 8, 1965.

[94] See for instance the 1998 Protocol on the Privileges and Immunities of the International Seabed Authority.

[95] 11 U.N.T.S. 11.

[96] 1 U.N.T.S. 163.

[97] 249 U.N.T.S. 207.

[98] 208 U.N.T.S. 225.

[99] See also e.g. the agreements between ILO and Switzerland (15 U.N.T.S. 377), FAO and Italy (1409 U.N.T.S., nr 23602), France and UNESCO (357 U.N.T.S. 3), Austria and IAEA (339 U.N.T.S. 111), United Kingdom and the International Tin Council (834 U.N.T.S. 287), Burundi and the WMO (Field Office; 1201 U.N.T.S. 164), Canada and ICAO (ICAO Doc. No. 9591).

[1] See for instance the Agreement between the UN and Kuwait concerning the legal status, privileges and immunities of the UN Iraq-Kuwait Observation Mission, April 15–May 20, 1992, U.N.J.Y. (1992) 71.

[2] See, e.g. the Agreements concluded with Egypt in 1957 on UNEF (260 U.N.T.S. 61), with Congo in 1961 regarding ONUC (414 U.N.T.S. 230), with Cyprus in 1964 regarding UNFICYP (492 U.N.T.S. 59), with South Africa in 1989 regarding UNTAG (Doc. S/20412/ Add. 1), and with Rwanda in 1993 on UNAMIR.

Clearly these agreements, whether multilateral or bilateral, impose legal **15–039** obligations on states under international law.[3] And since privileges and immunities will by their very nature need to produce their effects within the domestic legal order of member states, it is necessary for these to ensure that those rights and obligations are domestically enforceable. States have often implemented these obligations by passing municipal legislation. The International Organisations Immunities Act of December 29, 1945, in the United States, or the International Organisation (Privileges and Immunities) Act of July 12, 1950, in the United Kingdom are typical examples of such legislation.[4] In the United Kingdom, this legislation is supplemented by Orders in Council enacting the privileges and immunities granted to the particular organisations of which this country becomes a member.[5] Whatever view the municipal courts take, such legislation is not the source of the state's international obligations: that source remains the constituent texts and such supplementary agreements as may exist.[6]

One further general question remains, namely, whether in the absence of **15–040** a treaty obligation a state is under any duty to concede privileges and immunities to an international organisation. It is difficult to argue that all international organisations are to enjoy privileges and immunities by virtue of a rule of customary international law. The customary foundation of immunities seems to be generally accepted for the UN only, in view of the constant treaty practice of granting immunity to that organisation.[7] A more liberal view has been taken in a few countries, some governments and national courts considering that international organisations were entitled to jurisdictional immunity under customary international law.[8] It seems diffi-

---

[3] In its 1988 Advisory Opinion on the Applicability of the Obligation to Arbitrate under section 21 of the United Nations Headquarters Agreement of June 26, 1947, the I.C.J. observed that "[t]here is no question but that the Headquarters Agreement is a treaty in force binding the parties thereto" (I.C.J. Rep. (1988) 15, para. 7).

[4] For the most comprehensive collection of national legislation and international agreements concerned with the privileges and immunities of international organisations see *Hand book on the Legal Status, Privileges and Immunities of the United Nations* (1952) (ST/LEG/2), and *Legislative Texts and Treaty Provisions concerning the Legal Status, Privileges and Immunities of International Organisations*, UN. ST/LEG/SER. B/10 & 11. More recent examples of national legislation concerning the privileges and immunities of international organisations are published on a yearly basis in the *United Nations Juridical Yearbook* (see for instance the Malaysian International Organisations (Privileges and Immunities) Act 1992, U.N.J.Y. (1992) 9 *et seq.*

[5] See the examples mentioned *supra*, n. 43.

[6] For some practical consequences of this situation, see *infra*.

[7] See in particular the view taken by the UN Office of Legal Affairs, U.N.J.Y. (1976), 179, n. 56. See also *e.g.* Dominicé, L'immunité de juridiction et d'exécution des organisations internationales, 187 RCADI (1984–IV) 220.

[8] See in particular the opinion expressed by the Dutch government, as quoted by the Supreme Court of the Netherlands in the case *Iran-US CTR v. AS*, December 20, 1985 (94 ILR 327). This position was endorsed by the Court (*ibid.* 329). See also *e.g.* the judgment given by the Maastricht District Court in the case of *Eckhardt v. Eurocontrol* (No. 2), January 12, 1984, 94 ILR 338

cult, however, to regard such positions as representing the general opinion of states on this issue. This is not to say, however, that the conclusion of a formal agreement is the only means by which states may accept to grant privileges and immunities to a given international organisation. It could indeed be argued that once a state has consented to the presence of an organisation on its territory for a particular purpose it is bound, by the principle of good faith, to extend all such privileges and immunities as are necessary for the proper functioning of this organisation and the achievement of that purpose.[9]

15–041   What is clear in any event, is that states are under no duty to grant such privileges and immunities to particular organisations if they have not agreed to do so explicitly, or may not be deemed to have agreed to do so implicitly. There are numerous instances in which national courts have refused to decline jurisdiction in respect of a particular organisation, in the absence of any instrument providing for such immunity and binding on the state concerned. This was the case, for instance, for the International Tin Council, the constituent instrument of which provided for immunity from jurisdiction on the territory of the host state only.[10]

15–042   Turning from these general questions to specific aspects of immunities, it is convenient to deal separately with immunities attaching to the organisation as such, and immunities attaching to personnel.

(iii) Privileges and immunities attaching to the organisation

15–043   The main privileges and immunities attaching to the organisation as such are immunities from jurisdiction (a) and execution (b), the inviolability of premises and archives (c), currency and fiscal privileges (d) and freedom of communication (e).

(a) Immunity from jurisdiction

15–044   As a general rule, legal instruments defining international organisations' privileges and immunities provide for an absolute immunity of jurisdiction, i.e. protect the organisations concerned against any form of legal process, in all fields of activities. Section 2 of the 1946 Convention on the privileges and immunities of the UN is typical, providing that:

---

[9] Such a situation arose in the Congo when the UN placed a force in the territory of the Republic before it became a member of the organisation (see the Basic Agreements concluded on July 27, 1960, with the Congo (A/4800, p. 170); the Congo was not formally admitted to the UN until September 20, 1960).

[10] See Bank Bumiputra Malaysia BHD v. ITC, High Court of Malaysia, January 13, 1987, 80 ILR 29 and ITC v. Amalgamet Inc., United States Supreme Court, New York County, January 25, 1988, ibid. 35.

"the United Nations, its property and assets, wherever located and by whomsoever held, shall enjoy immunity from every form of legal process, except in so far as in any particular case it has expressly waived its immunity."

A substantially similar provision is found in the specialised agencies' **15–045** convention,[11] in the various headquarters agreements concluded by organisations belonging to the UN system with countries like Canada, France, Switzerland and Italy,[12] as well as in protocols on privileges and immunities of other organisations, outside the UN system.[13] The justification for this extensive immunity is primarily the view that it would be undesirable for courts of many different countries to determine, possibly in different senses, the legality of acts of the organisation. There may well be, in some countries, the further need to protect the organisation against prejudice in national courts, or frivolous actions by individuals.[14]

Notwithstanding the unambiguous wording of these instruments, a trend **15–046** has developed in some countries to apply to international organisations the same distinction as is now generally accepted for states, namely between acts *jure gestionis* (of a private law character) and acts *jure imperii* (typical of the exercise of sovereign power). This trend has been particularly obvious in the United States[15] and Italy,[16] and is supported by an increasing number of authors.[17] This may well lead to future changes in the law, but certainly does not excuse national tribunals from applying the relevant instruments as they now stand, and refuse to grant international organisations absolute immunity from jurisdiction when the texts so provide. Symptomatic in that respect are the serious tensions to which the position of national courts gave rise between the FAO and the Italian government,[18] and the fact that

---

[11] Section 4; see also *e.g.* Art. IX (3) of the IMF Arts of Agreement.

[12] But not in the UN/USA 1947 Headquarters Agreement.

[13] See, *e.g.* Art. 2 of the 1948 Protocol on the privileges and immunities of the OECD; Art. 3 of the 1949 General Agreement on privileges and immunities of the Council of Europe; Art. 5(1) of the 1997 Agreement on the privileges and immunities of the ITLOS (reproduced in ITLOS, Basic Texts, 1998, 83).

[14] See, *e.g.* Jenks, *International Immunities*, London/New York, Stevens & Sons/Oceana, 1961, 41–42; Bekker, *The Legal Position of Intergovernmental Organisations*, Dordrecht/Boston/London, Nijhoff, 1994, 98 *et seq.*

[15] This results from the fact that under the 1945 International Organisations Immunities Act organisations are granted the same immunities as states, these having been limited to acts *jure imperii* by the 1976 Foreign Sovereign Immunities Act (see Nash, Contemporary Practice of the United States Relating to International Law, 74 AJIL (1980) 918).

[16] See, *e.g. Branno v. Ministry of War*, June 14, 1954, 22 ILR 756; *Porru v. FAO*, June 25, 1969, summary in U.N.J.Y. (1969) 756; *Indpai v. FAO*, October 18, 1982, 87 ILR 5.

[17] See, *e.g.* Cully, "Jurisdictional Immunities of Intergovernmental Organisations", 91 Yale L.J. (1982) 1187 *et seq.*; Sadurska and Chinkin, "The Collapse of the International Tin Council: A Case of State Responsibility", Va.J.I.L. (1990) 853; Singer, "Jurisdictional Immunity of International Organisations: Human Rights and Functional Necessity Concerns", Va.J.I.L. (1995), 135 *et seq.*; Rainisch, *op. cit.* 393.

[18] For details, see Rainisch, *op. cit.* 131–133.

the Italian *Corte di Cassazione* reversed the previous trend by deciding in 1992 that FAO was entitled to a complete immunity from jurisdiction before domestic courts.[19]

15–047   There are, however, a number of organisations which are not protected by such a broad immunity from jurisdiction. The best-known exception in that respect is probably the provision found in the constituent instruments of the organisations belonging to the World Bank group, as well as in the constitution of most regional development banks, according to which:

> "[a]ctions may be brought against the [organisation] only in a court of competent jurisdiction in the territories of a member in which the [organisation] has an office, has appointed an agent for the purpose of accepting service or notice of process, or has issued or guaranteed securities."[20]

15–048   It should be noted that these provisions do not amount to a complete suppression of the immunity from jurisdiction. This departure from absolute immunity finds its justification in the fact that these organisations' lending operations made it desirable to allow suit by creditors and bondholders, in order to reinforce the latter's confidence.[21] This originally limited purpose seems however to have been relatively rapidly disregarded by judges before which private law claims have been brought against the organisations concerned. It has particularly been the case in the United States, where those provisions have been construed as a waiver of immunity against all types of private law claims, and not only against claims brought by bondholders.[22] Applying the distinction between acts *jure gestionis* and *jure imperii*, the American tribunals have nevertheless consistently ruled that claims brought against these organisations by staff members or former staff members were not concerned by this waiver of immunity —even interpreted broadly—because of their *jure imperii* character; these could therefore not be disposed of by national courts.[23] This exclusion has in any event been confirmed in the constituent instruments of international financial institutions established more recently.[24]

---

[19] *FAO v. Colagrossi*, May 19, 1992, 101 ILR 393.
[20] See the Articles of Agreement of the IBRD (Art. VII, section 3), the IFC (Art. VI, section 3), the IDA (Art. VIII, section 3), the MIGA (Art. 44). See also the constitutive instruments of the IADB (Art. IX, section 3), the East African Development Bank (Arts 44 and 45) and the EBRD (Art. 46).
[21] See Delaume, Jurisdiction of Courts and International Loans, A.J.Comp. L. (1957) 207.
[22] See, *e.g. Lutcher v. Inter-American Development Bank*, U.S. Court of Appeals, D.C. Circuit, 1967, 382 F.2d 454.
[23] See, *e.g. Mendaro v. World Bank*, September 27, 1983, 717 F.2d 618; *Chiriboga v. IBRD*, March 29, 1985, 616 F.Supp. 967; *Morgan v. IBRD*, September 18, 1990, 752 F.Supp. 492; *Atkinson v. IADB*, October 8, 1998, rep. in 38 ILM (1999) 91.
[24] See in particular Art. 44 of the MIGA Convention.

Limitations of the scope of immunity from jurisdiction are also found in **15–049** other organisations. Article 240 (formerly 183) of the treaty establishing the European Community provides:

> "Save where jurisdiction is conferred on the Court of Justice by this Treaty, disputes to which the community is a party shall not on that ground be excluded from the jurisdiction of the courts or tribunals of the member states."

This submission to domestic courts is actually more limited than it may **15–050** appear at first glance. It must be recalled that by virtue of Article 235 (formerly 178) of the treaty, "[t]he Court of Justice shall have jurisdiction in disputes relating to compensation for damage" caused by the Community or its agents, whereas Article 238 (formerly 181) provides that the ECJ.

> "shall have jurisdiction to give judgment pursuant to any arbitration clause contained in a contract concluded by or on behalf of the Community, whether that contract be governed by public or private law."

Disputes relating to a contract concluded by the European Community **15–051** and not containing an arbitration clause are therefore the only ones on which national courts may rule.[25]

The instruments governing the legal status of other organisations provide for exceptions to the latter's jurisdictional immunity in more specific cases, such as the inclusion in a contract of a clause by which the parties agree to defer to the jurisdiction of a national tribunal,[26] or more broadly, any dispute arising from contracts concluded by the organisation.[27] Exceptions to jurisdictional immunity are also sometimes provided in respect of tortious acts, either generally[28] or for certain categories (road traffic accidents being the most significant of these).[29]

---

[25] This situation proves to be relatively exceptional in practice, since arbitration clauses giving competence to the ECJ are now almost always inserted in the contracts to which the community is a party (see *e.g.* Vandersanden, Commentaire de l'article 218, in Megret (ed.) *op. cit.*, Vol. 15 (1987) 296–298).

[26] See, *e.g.* the 1971 Headquarters Agreement between Switzerland and the ITU, 793 U.N.T.S. 317.

[27] See, *e.g.* the Arts of Agreement of the Caribbean Development Bank (Art. 49), 712 U.N.T.S. 217, of the African Development Bank (Art. 52), 510 U.N.T.S. 3 and of the Asian Development Bank (Art. 50, 1), 571 U.N.T.S. 133.

[28] See, *e.g.* in that respect Art. 4(1)(c) and (d) of the 1991 Headquarters Agreement between the United Kingdom and the EBRD (Extracts in 62 B.Y.B.I.L. (1991) 583) and Art. 5(1)(d) and (e) of the 1996 Headquarters Agreement between the United Kingdom and the International Oil Pollution Compensation Fund (Extracts in 67 B.Y.B.I.L. (1996) 725).

[29] See, *e.g.* the 1972 Headquarters Agreement between France and the ACCT (Agence de la Francophonie) (Art. 16(a)), 961 U.N.T.S. 263; the 1976 Supplementary Agreement between Belgium and the UN on Privileges and Immunities, 1094 U.N.T.S. 11; the 1981 Agreement between Brasil and SELA (Art. XIX), 1292 U.N.T.S. 233.

15–052   Finally, it is of course always open to organisations to waive the immunity from jurisdiction they have been granted. As can be seen from section 2 of the Convention on the Privileges and Immunities of the UN, for example, this possibility is often expressly mentioned in the instruments providing for immunity.[30] These instruments generally require such waiver to be explicit. The scope of the waiver is clearly limited to the immunity from jurisdiction, and does not extend to the immunity from execution.[31] The authority to waive immunity normally rests with the administrative head of the organisation.

(b) Immunity from execution

15–053 The "immunity from any form of legal process" proclaimed in section 2 of the Convention on the Privileges and Immunities of the UN and similar instruments clearly extends to immunity from all measures of execution—of a judgment or an arbitral award, for instance—against the properties and assets of the organisations concerned.[32] This immunity from execution can of course be waived by the organisation to which it was granted, but this, again, must be explicit, and may never be implied from the fact that the organisation agreed to waive its jurisdictional immunity.[33] The constituent instruments of a number of organisations do provide exceptions to the principle of immunity from execution. It will come as no surprise that these are essentially the same organisations that envisaged jurisdictional immunity more narrowly. Hence, the Articles of Agreement of the organisations which constitute the World Bank group and of several regional development banks provide that:

> "[t]he property and assets of the [organisation] shall, wheresoever located and by whomsoever held, be immune from all forms of seizure, attachment or execution *before the delivery of a final judgment against the [organisation]*."[34]

15–054   Far from upholding an absolute immunity from execution, such provisions merely enunciate the conditions under which measures of execution can be carried out on the organisations' property and assets. A similar regime is instituted by Article 1 of the Protocol on the Privileges and Immunities of the European Community, according to which "the property and assets of the community may not be the subject of any administrative or legal measures of constraint without the authorisation of the Court of

---

[30] See also, for instance, Art. 2 of the Protocol on Privileges and Immunities of the OECD.
[31] See *infra*, paras 15–053 *et seq.*
[32] See generally Dominicé, *loc. cit.* 224–225.
[33] See, *e.g.* section 2 *in fine* of the Convention on the Privileges and Immunities of the UN and Art. 2 *in fine* of the Protocol on Privileges and Immunities of the OECD.
[34] References *supra*, n. 20; emphasis added.

Justice." It should however be observed that the immunity from execution is rarely invoked by international organisations in practice, and that they will almost invariably comply with judgments or awards given against them.[35]

(c) Inviolability of premises and archives

The inviolability of premises is a principle found in all the agreements.[36] **15–055** Practically this principle means that the authorities of the host state may not enter the premises, even for the purpose of effecting an arrest or serving a writ, without the consent of the administrative head of the organisation.[37] Moreover, since inviolability is to be secured against all persons, and not merely the authorities of the host state, it is usual to find in many headquarters agreements an undertaking by the host state to exercise due diligence in the protection of the premises.[38] Examples of breaches of the inviolability of international organisations' premises are rare. The most significant of these have occurred in respect of premises occupied by UN administrative services or military forces in the context of peacekeeping operations.[39]

The principle of inviolability necessarily raises problems once it is **15–056** accepted that an organisation is not sovereign over the territory occupied by its premises, but merely has control and authority, and that the organisation possesses no body of law to replace that of the host state in respect of civil or criminal offences committed within the premises. Admittedly some organisations may, in the same manner as the UN, have power to lay down regulations "operative within the headquarters district

---

[35] See generally on this Klein, *La responsabilité des organisations internationales*, Brussels, Bruylant, 1998, pp. 287–288.

[36] See, *e.g.* the Conventions or Protocols on Privileges and Immunities of the UN (sections 3 and 4), the specialised agencies (section 5), the OECD (Arts 3 and 4), the Council of Europe (Art. 4), the European Community (Art. 1), the ITLOS (Art. 3), the International Seabed Authority (Art. 4).

[37] See, *e.g.* section 9(a) of the 1947 UN/USA Headquarters Agreement. While retaining the same rule, some instruments prove more flexible in respect of the requirement of consent. The 1991 UK/EBRD Headquarters Agreement, for instance, provides in that respect that "[s]uch consent may be assumed in the case of fire or other disasters requiring prompt protective action." (Art. 6(2); see *e.g.* in the same sense Art. IX(1) *in fine* of the OAS/USA Headquarters Agreement of May 14, 1992; Art. 2 of the Arab League/Belgium Headquarters Agreement of November 16, 1995). The same provision also states that "[t]he Bank and the Government shall agree under what circumstances and in what manner any such [public] official may enter the Premises of the Bank without the prior consent of the Bank in connection with fire prevention, sanitary regulations or emergencies."

[38] See, *e.g.* section 16(a) of the 1947 UN/USA Headquarters Agreement; Art. IX(2) of the OAS/USA Headquarters Agreement; Art. 7(1) of the 1991 UK/EBRD Headquarters Agreement; Art. 2 of the Arab League/Belgium Headquarters Agreement.

[39] Hence, during the 1967 conflict in the Middle East, UNRWA, UNEF and UNTSO premises suffered attacks and other violations. Similarly premises occupied by UNOSOM and UNIFIL came under attack in 1993 and 1996, respectively.

for the purpose of establishing therein conditions in all respects necessary for the full execution of its functions."[40] In the case of the UN, such regulations override any inconsistent local law, but the only effective sanction for their breach is expulsion from the premises, carried out either by a Headquarters Guard Force, such as the organisation might possess, or by the local authorities who may be requested to enter for that purpose.[41] It is important, therefore, that the territory should remain under the law and the jurisdiction of the host state, and most headquarters agreements so provide.[42] A crime committed on the premises will therefore normally be appropriately dealt with by the local courts.[43] Indeed, some of the agreements specifically provide that the organisation is under a duty to prevent the headquarters district from becoming a refuge for persons avoiding arrest or the service of legal process.[44] Whether there is a right for the organisations to grant asylum in cases falling outside this particular duty must be regarded as an open question, for none of the agreements specifically recognise such a right. There is certainly a strong argument for the right of the organisation to afford asylum to its own officials against measures by the local authorities which are themselves a violation of the immunities of the organisation and of the official.[45]

15–057   The inviolability of archives and other official documents, for its part, is similarly affirmed in all agreements,[46] and also constitutes an important element in ensuring the good functioning of international organisations. Without it the confidential character of communications between states and the organisation, or between officials within the organisation, would be less secure. As a consequence of this principle, international organisations are under no duty to produce any official document or part of their archives in the context of litigations before national courts.[47] In one of its judgments relating to the *International Tin Council* case, however, the House of Lords ruled that the inviolability only applied to documents and archives which

---

[40] Section 8 of the 1947 UN/USA Headquarters Agreement. This "legislative" power may be—and has been—exercised for purposes other than security; for more on this, see *supra*, Chap. 11. A similar power is granted, *inter alia*, by Art. XII(1) of the OAS/USA Headquarters Agreement and Art. 6(1) of the 1991 U.K./EBRD Headquarters Agreement.

[41] See also *e.g.* in that respect Art. 7(2) of the 1991 U.K./EBRD Headquarters Agreement.

[42] See, *e.g.* section 7 of the 1947 UN/USA Headquarters Agreement.

[43] This was already the practice under the League of Nations. Hence, in 1928 the assailant of the representative of Hungary within the Palais des Nations in Geneva was arrested and tried by the Swiss courts.

[44] See, *e.g.* section 9(b) of the 1947 UN/USA Headquarters Agreement; Art. IX(3)(a) of the OAS/USA Headquarters Agreement; Art. 6(5) of the 1991 U.K./EBRD Headquarters Agreement.

[45] Jenks, *op. cit.* 51–52.

[46] See, *e.g.* the Conventions or Protocols on Privileges and Immunities of the UN (section 4), specialised agencies (section 6), the OECD (Art. 4), the Council of Europe (Art. 5), the European Community (Art. 2), the ITLOS (Art. 6), the IMF Arts of Agreement (Art. IX, section 5), the MIGA Convention (Art. 46(a)).

[47] Jenks, *The Proper Law of International Organisations*, 1962, 234.

remain in possession of the organisation, and not to those which have been communicated to third parties by an official of the organisation in the exercise of his or her functions.[48]

(d) Currency and fiscal privileges

Many organisations dispose of considerable funds, and, in view of the **15–058** geographical deployment of their activities, the mobility of such funds is often essential to the proper functioning of the organisation. Hence several instruments conferring privileges and immunities on international organisations recognise that these may "hold funds, gold or currency of any kind and operate accounts in any currency" and shall be free to "transfer [their] funds, gold or currency from one country to another . . . without being restricted by financial controls, regulations or moratoria of any kind."[49] The purchase of different currencies will not normally subject the organisation to the possibility of a prejudicial differential exchange rate, since these differential rates are inconsistent with the obligations of members of the International Monetary Fund, but some agreements between international organisations and states on the territory of which they operate nevertheless provide that the most favourable exchange rate should be available to the organisation.[50]

Exemption from direct taxation of the organisation, its assets, income or **15–059** property, is the general rule, but this does not extend to taxes which are in fact charges for public utility services enjoyed by the organisation.[51] An equally common privilege is the exemption from customs duties and import and export restrictions on articles required for official use and the publications of the organisation.[52] In contrast there is no right to exemption

---

[48] *Shearson Lehman v. Maclaine Watson (No 2)*, December 3, 1987, 77 ILR 154–158 (per Lord Bridge of Harwich).

[49] The terms are those of section 5 of the 1946 Convention on Privileges and Immunities of the UN, but similar formula may be found, *e.g.*, in Art. 5 of the Protocol on the Privileges and Immunities of the OECD or in Art. 5 of the Protocol on Privileges and Immunities of the International Sea-bed Authority. The freedom of assets from restriction is envisaged in a slightly different manner in the international financial institutions' constitutive instruments, which provide that "[t]o the extent necessary to carry out the operations provided for in this Agreement and subject to the provisions of this Agreement, all property and assets of the [organisation] shall be free from restrictions, regulations, controls and moratoria of any nature" (Articles of Agreement of the IBRD (Art. VII, section 6), the IMF (Art. IX, section 6), the IFC (Art. VI, section 6)).

[50] See, *e.g.* section 35 of the Agreement between the UN and Egypt over the status of UNEF (*loc. cit.*).

[51] See, *e.g.* the Conventions or Protocols on Privileges and Immunities of the UN (section 7(a)), specialised agencies (section 9), the OECD (Art. 6(a)), the Council of Europe (Art. 7(a)), the European Community (Art. 3), the ITLOS (Art. 9(1)), as well as Art. IX, section 9(a) of the IMF Arts of Agreement and Art. IX, section 9(a) of the IMF Articles of Agreement. By "direct" taxes is meant those taxes which ultimately fall upon the organisation for payment. The characterisation of the tax as "direct" or "indirect" in the particular state's municipal law is irrelevant: see U.N.J.Y. 1964, 220–221.

[52] See, *e.g.* the Conventions or Protocols on the Privileges and Immunities of the UN (section 7(b) and (c)), the OECD (Art. 6(b) and (c)), the Council of Europe (Art. 7(b) and (c)), ITLOS (Art. 9(2)).

from excise duties or sales taxes which are included in the price of property purchased; the Convention on Privileges and Immunities of the UN, for example, provides only that "members will, whenever possible, make appropriate administrative arrangements for the remission or return of the amount of duty or tax."[53]

(e) Freedom of communications

15–060   The freedom to communicate rests on three principles, all of which are embodied in the Conventions on Privileges and Immunities of the UN and of the specialised agencies as well as in several headquarters agreements: these are (i) the absence of censorship over official communications, (ii) the right to use codes, couriers and bags (equivalent to the "diplomatic bag" or "pouch"), and (iii) treatment for their communications by national administrations as favourable as that accorded to any government.[54] Several agreements concluded by the UN with states on the territory of which this organisation is established or operates also provide that it may establish and operate radio facilities.[55] It should be mentioned that the UN also has its own postal service (operated in the Headquarters District by the U.S. Post Office Department). Finally, it must still be noted that provision is sometimes made for organisations to use and register their own vehicles, aircrafts and even vessels.[56]

(iii) Immunities attaching to personnel

15–061 In addition to the privileges and immunities granted to international organisations as such, the various instruments which define their legal status also systematically provide for privileges and immunities attaching to individuals related to intergovernmental organisations. The purpose of this second category of privileges and immunities is not different from that of the former; in both cases, it is to enable organisations to function effectively and to fulfil their mission without being impeded in any way by the adverse action of states or of (groups of) private individuals. It is for this reason that the relevant legal instruments provide for privileges and immunities in

---

[53] Section 8. See also *e.g.* the Protocol on Privileges and Immunities of the OECD, Art. 7.

[54] Conventions or Protocols on Privileges and Immunities of the UN (sections 9 and 10), the specialised agencies (sections 11 and 12), the OECD (Art. 8), the Council of Europe (Art. 8), ITLOS (Art. 8). It is, curiously enough, on the principle of the "national treatment" of communications that difficulty has been encountered by the specialised agencies due to the opposition of the I.T.U. to this equality of treatment for specialised agencies—even though it has been conceded to the UN and its organs (see Jenks, *International Immunities, op. cit.* pp. 69–71).

[55] See, *e.g.* section 4 of the UN/USA. Headquarters Agreement; similar provisions were inserted in agreements with States where a UN Force was operating, such as Korea and Egypt. See also *e.g.* section 10 of the Agreement between the United Nations and the Supreme National Council of Cambodia on the status of UNTAC, of May 7, 1992 (U.N.J.Y. (1992) 53).

[56] See, *e.g.* sections 8 and 12 of the 1992 Agreement on the status of UNTAC.

favour not only of various categories of personnel employed by the organisations (b), but also of the representatives of members to the organisation (a).

(a) Representatives of members

The immunities and privileges accorded to this category are, not surprisingly, similar to those accorded to the traditional diplomatic agent, although rather greater emphasis is placed on the functional necessity for the privileges. Two main regimes may actually be distinguished in this respect, which are essentially at variance on the question of the scope of immunity from legal process. The most favourable one generally provides for the application to representatives of members of the "privileges, immunities and facilities normally enjoyed by diplomatic envoys of comparable rank."[57] Under the other, more restrictive, regime, immunity from legal process is granted only "in respect of words spoken or written and all acts done by them in their capacity as representatives," which is narrower than the general diplomatic immunity.[58] Other aspects of the legal status of members' representatives under the latter regime, on the other hand, are clearly in line with that of diplomats. Hence, by virtue of those instruments, representatives of members are to enjoy immunity from arrest, seizure of personal baggage, immigration restrictions or national service obligations, inviolability of papers and documents, the right of communication, and exemptions from customs duties (but only in respect of personal baggage as opposed to all imports for personal use).[59] Most instruments do however specify that this regime is not applicable as between a representative and the authorities of the state of which he or she is a national or is or has been the representative.[60]

15–062

---

[57] The language is that of the Protocol on Privileges and Immunities of the OECD (Art. 9). See also *e.g.* section 15 of the UN/USA Headquarters Agreement, and Art. 4 of the 1952 Protocol to the General Agreement on Privileges and Immunities of the Council of Europe (E.T.S. No 10—note that this regime is applicable to the Permanent Representatives only, and not to the other members of permanent missions).

[58] See, *e.g.* in that respect section 11, a) of the Convention on Privileges and Immunities of the UN, section 13 of the Convention on Privileges and Immunities of the specialised agencies, Art. IX, (8), (I) of the IMF Arts of Agreement; Art. 9 of the General Agreement on privileges and immunities of the Council of Europe, Art. 15, 2, a) of the UK/EBRD Headquarters Agreement and Art. 7, 1, a) of the Protocol on Privileges and Immunities of the International Sea-bed Authority. Note however that those instruments often stipulate that the immunity from legal process in respect of words spoken or written, and of other acts performed in the discharge of duties will continue to apply to the persons concerned even when they no longer exercise their official functions (see *e.g.* section 12 of the Convention on Privileges and Immunities of the UN).

[59] *ibid.* For a review of some of the early decisions of U.S. tribunals on immunities of representatives see Jenks, *International Immunities, op. cit.*, pp. 86–88.

[60] See, *e.g.* the Conventions on Privileges and Immunities of the UN (section 15) and of the specialised agencies (section 17), and the Protocol on Privileges and Immunities of the OECD (Art. 11).

15–063   An attempt has been made under the auspices of the United Nations to standardise the rules governing the legal regime of members' representatives. This resulted in the adoption, in 1975, of a comprehensive Convention on the Representation of States in their Relations with International Organisations of a universal character.[61] Its utility and effect have however proved fairly limited. The majority of states taking part in the diplomatic Conference drafting the Convention succeeded in securing privileges and immunities for missions of members to the headquarters of international organisations far more extensive than the host states were prepared to concede. As a consequence, the major host states did not ratify the Convention.[62] Some of its provisions are nevertheless considered to reflect customary law.[63]

15–064   It must be remembered that the representatives are not accredited to the host state, but rather to the organisation. As a rule, the host state therefore does not have to give its agreement to the designation of members' representatives. At the same time, it is obvious that it is upon the host state that the weight of the privileges and immunities granted to the representatives will ultimately bear. It is only logical therefore that its interests should also be taken into consideration when it comes to determining the categories of persons entitled to such privileges and immunities. It is for that reason that some instruments, such as the UN/USA Headquarters Agreement, provide that apart from the principal permanent representatives, the staff of any given mission have to be agreed upon between the host state, the chief administrative officer of the organisation concerned and the sending state.[64] This is similar to the "*agrément*" in diplomatic practice and in the case of the UN, once given, the names are placed in the "Bluebook" issued by the United States Mission to the UN. A further consequence of non-accreditation to the host states is the inapplicability of the remedy of declaring a representative *persona non grata*.[65] Some instruments deal with this by allowing expulsion for activities outside the representatives' official functions.[66] Yet another consequence is the fact that

---

[61] Text in U.N.J.Y. (1975) 87. See also Fennessy, The Vienna Convention on the Representation of States in their Relations with International Organisations of a Universal Characters. 70 AJIL (1976) 62–95.

[62] As of June 2000, 30 states only were parties to the 1975 Convention.

[63] See, *e.g.* in that sense the note by the WTO Secretariat on "International law and practice in respect of accreditation of representation to international organisations" (Doc. WT/GC/W/72 of December 4, 1997).

[64] Section 15 of the 1947 Agreement.

[65] Similarly, a host state cannot apply reciprocity to the treatment of such representatives, as it may to persons accredited to it: see the UN Secretariat opinion in (1967) 2 Y.B.I.L.C., 154, 177–8.

[66] See, *e.g.* the Convention on Privileges and Immunities of the specialised agencies and Art. 3 of the Agreement of March 20, 1975 between the USA and the OAS, relating to Privileges and Immunities (26 U.S.T. 1025). The United States relied on that provision to justify the expulsion of Nicaragua's permanent representative to OAS in 1988 (see Nash Leich, "Contemporary practice of the United States Relating to International Law", 82 AJIL (1988) 803, *et seq.*).

representatives may be received from governments not recognised by the host state. In the UN/U.S. Headquarters Agreement privileges and immunities are granted to such persons only within the Headquarters district, or in transit between the district and residences or offices, or whilst at such residence or office.[67] Other agreements stipulate more generally that immunities and privileges shall be granted irrespective of the relationship between sending state and host state.[68]

The presence of representatives of members on its territory also imposes **15–065** on the host state a special duty of protection. This has been reinforced by the 1973 UN Convention for the Prevention and Punishment of Crimes against Internationally Protected Persons (which also applies to officials of the organisation).[69] At the national level, several states have introduced legislation making assault, coercion or harassment of such persons a crime under municipal law.[70]

In the same manner as immunities granted to the organisations them- **15–066** selves, those enjoyed by the members' representatives may be waived. This is provided for in all the relevant instruments, which put a strong emphasis on the functional character of these immunities. The formulation of section 14 of the Convention on Privileges and Immunities of the UN remains one of the most exemplary in that respect:

> "Privileges and immunities are accorded to the representatives of members not for the personal benefits of the individuals themselves, but in order to safeguard the independent exercise of their functions in connection with the United Nations. Consequently a member not only has the right but is under a duty to waive the immunity of its representative in any case where in the opinion of the member the immunity would impede the course of justice, and it can be waived without prejudice to the purpose for which the immunity is accorded."[71]

It must still be noted that specific regimes have been established in **15–067** organisations in which delegations from members are not confined to governmental representatives. In the ILO the Employers' and Workers' delegates receive the same immunities and privileges as governmental

---

[67] On the right of access to headquarters of international organisations see Goy, "Le droit d'accès au siège des organisations internationales" 33 R.G.D.I.P. (1962) 357–370.
[68] See, *e.g.* Art. 15(4)(b) of the UK/EBRD Headquarters Agreement.
[69] Text in 13 ILM (1974) 41.
[70] See, *e.g.* the 1976 US Act: 18 U.S.C.A. s. 112.
[71] Similar provisions may be found *e.g.* in the Convention on Privileges and Immunities of the specialised agencies (section 16), the Protocol on Privileges and Immunities of the OECD (Art. 10) ; in the General Agreement on privileges and immunities of the Council of Europe (Art. 11) and the UK/EBRD Headquarters Agreement (Art. 19(2)).

representatives, save the right to use codes, couriers or sealed bags; waiver of immunities is by the governing body, rather than by the state of origin. In the parliamentary assemblies of the Council of Europe and the European Community the immunities are carefully defined and their functional basis is emphasised by their being modelled, not on diplomatic immunities, but more on parliamentary immunities in municipal law.[72]

15–068 The extension of privileges and immunities to representatives which do not possess a governmental affiliation is not limited to the abovementioned situations; it has also been recognised in favour of various categories of persons invited by an international organisation to take part in its work, whether on an occasional or on a more permanent basis. This is particularly the case for observers.[73] The latter's status, and the possibility for the host state to restrict their activity or their entry in its territory for security reasons, have given rise to serious controversies between the UN and the U.S. in the late 1980s. The first incident followed the adoption of the "Anti-Terrorist Act" by the U.S. Congress in December 1987, which was making unlawful the establishment or maintenance by the PLO of an office within the jurisdiction of the U.S.[74] This was deemed contrary to various provisions of the Headquarters Agreement by the UN, since the members of the PLO observer mission were, by virtue of UNGA Resolution 3237 (XXIX) invitees to the UN.[75] In spite of the fact that the I.C.J. unanimously concluded in its Advisory Opinion of April 26, 1988 that the U.S. was under the obligation to enter into arbitration for the settlement of the dispute to which this situation had given rise between itself and the U.S.,[76] it was eventually a local court which refused to grant the U.S. an injunction to force the closure of the mission, since this would have been contrary to the obligations imposed on the U.S. by the 1947 Headquarters Agreement.[77] The U.S. declined to appeal against this judgment.

15–069 The second incident, which took place against the same background was the refusal of the U.S. to deliver a visa to the PLO Chairman, Yasser Arafat, who had been invited to take part to the 43rd session of the UN

---

[72] See Arts 13–15 of the General Agreement on privileges and immunities of the Council of Europe, and 7–9 of the European Community Protocol.

[73] See generally Suy, "The Status of Observers in International Organisations", 160 RCADI (1978–II) 155 *et seq.*; Sybesma-Knol, *The Status of Observers in the United Nations*, Brussels (1981) 41–44.

[74] See, *e.g.* Fitschen, "Closing the PLO Observer Mission to the United Nations in New York: The Decision of the International Court of Justice and the US District Court, Southern District of New York", 31 G.Y.I.L. (1988) 595–620; Stern, "L'affaire du bureau de l'OLP devant les juridictions interne et internationale", 34 A.F.D.I. (1988) 165–194. The relevant extracts of the Act are appended to the Judgment of the US District Court, Southern District of New York of June 29, 1988 (rep. in 82 ILR 282 at 299).

[75] This view, initially expressed by the Secretary-General, was endorsed by the UNGA in Resolution 42/210B of December 17, 1987. The UN had previously made it clear that it regarded the Headquarters Agreement as applicable to the PLO Mission (see *e.g.* U.N.J.Y. (1979) 169–170 and (1980) 188).

[76] I.C.J. Rep. (1988) 35.

[77] 82 ILR 282 at 293.

General Assembly.[78] This refusal was stated to be motivated by security reasons, the U.S. authorities stating their opposition to the delivering of visas to persons linked to terrorist groups. Here again, the construction of section 11 of the Headquarters Agreement put forward by the U.S. Department of State to justify its position was strongly contested by the UN.[79] The only way out the deadlock to which this situation led proved to be the organisation of the part of the General Assembly's session dedicated to Palestine in Geneva in December 1988.[80]

(b) Officials of the organisation and other agents

(i) Officials. A number of privileges and immunities are also recognised in **15–070** favour of officials of international organisations. The main variation concerns the jurisdictional immunity, which varies according to the rank of the official. Hence, it is usual to find the chief administrative officer and his or her deputies or assistants accorded full diplomatic immunity,[81] whereas all other officials enjoy immunity from legal process only in respect of their official acts.[82] This raises the problem, to which there is no clear solution, of who decides the official or private character of a particular act. A municipal court could well accept as conclusive a statement by the organisation, or by the executive of the state in which the matter has arisen, or proceedings might be stayed whilst the matter went to arbitration. Certainly a conflict of view between the organisation and domestic courts is possible; in *Westchester County v. Ranollo* the City Court of New Rochelle convicted the Secretary-General's chauffeur of speeding despite a plea of immunity based on the fact that the accused was in the course of his duty, driving the

---

[78] See generally Reisman, "The Arafat Visa Affair: Exceeding the Bounds of Host State Discretion", 83 AJIL (1989) 519–527.

[79] Statement of the Legal Counsel concerning the Determination by the Secretary of State of the U.S. on the visa application of Mr. Y. Arafat (Doc. A/C.6/43/7 of November 29, 1988), endorsed by the General Assembly in its Res. 43/48 of November 30, 1988. The UN's view is shared by authors; see for instance Reisman, *loc. cit.* 526–527.

[80] See res. 43/48, para. 2.

[81] In some judicial institutions, this regime is applied to the Registrar (see *e.g.* Art. 14(1) of the 1997 Agreement on the privileges and immunities of the ITLOS and, for the situation of the European Court of Human Rights' Registrar, Art. 5(1) of the Sixth Protocol to the General Agreement on Privileges and Immunities of the Council of Europe (March 5, 1996, ETS No 162)).

[82] Conventions and Protocols on the Privileges and Immunities of the UN (sections 18 and 19), of the specialised agencies (section 21), of the OECD (Arts 14 and 15), of the Council of Europe (Arts 16 and 18), of the International Sea-bed Authority (Art. 8(2) and (3)). The same principle is followed in most headquarters agreements except for the UN/USA; the U.S. accession to the 1946 General Convention, in 1970, had the practical effect of filling this lacuna. Some instruments add that staff members "shall continue to be immune after completion of their functions as officials of the Organisation" (Protocol on the Privileges and Immunities of the OECD, Art. 14(a)).

Secretary-General.[83] The court suggested that it would require certification from the state department that immunity was in the public interest. For its part, the I.C.J. has recently insisted on the fact that it is for the UN Secretary-General to determine whether an official whose actions are disputed had committed those acts in the exercise of his or her functions.[84]

15–071   The determination of the official character of acts performed by staff members raises less difficulty in the European Community, where the ECJ has jurisdiction to entertain proceedings against the community or an official for official or personal fault.[85] Whenever the court comes to the conclusion that a given act has been performed by an official in the limits of her or his functions, the consequences of such ruling will be twofold. The first is that the organisation will have to bear responsibility *vis-à-vis* third persons which have suffered an injury as a result of the act in question. The second, which is a corollary to the first, is that the official concerned will be immune from all form of legal process before national courts in respect of the disputed act and of its consequences. There is therefore a clear and logical relation between the fact that the act is determined to partake to the exercise of official functions—and therefore justifies granting immunity, as provided for in the relevant instruments—on the one hand, and the corollary responsibility of the organisation—and not of the official individually—on the other. Conversely, any act which does not qualify as an act performed in the exercise of official functions will not be covered by immunity, and will result in the official's responsibility alone being brought into play before national tribunals, to the exclusion of the responsibility of the organisation. While this reasoning finds its origin in the particular circumstances of the European Community, it may undoubtedly be broadened to all international organisations.

15–072   It must be noted, however, that ECJ case-law on the subject is scarce, the Court having pronounced only once on such issues, in the *Sayag* case, where the judges took a rather narrow view of the concept of "official functions". They indeed limited these to "acts which, by their nature, represent a participation of the person entitled to the immunity in the performance of the tasks of the institution to which he belongs,"[86] and ruled that a road

---

[83] A.D. 1946, Case No. 77. *Contrast Curran v. City of New York*, Trygvie Lie *et al.*, 119 N.Y.L.Q., January 2, 1948, where the Court accepted the plea of immunity raised by the Organisation as defendant on a suit by a taxpayer to set aside grant of land and easements by the City to the Organisation; the Dept. of State did, however, "suggest" to the court that immunity be granted. In *U.S. v. Coplon and Grubitchev*, A.D. 1949, Case No. 102, no immunity was requested for a citizen of the USSR who was an official of the UN indicted for espionage; clearly, "official acts" could never include espionage.

[84] Advisory Opinion on the Difference Relating to Immunity from Legal Process of a Special Rapporteur of the Commission on Human Rights, I.C.J. Rep. (1999) 87, para. 60.

[85] Arts 235 and 288 of the treaty.

[86] Case 5–68, *Sayag v. J.P. Leduc*, July 11, 1968, Rep. (1968) 402.

traffic accident caused by a Community official who had used his personal car for an official mission could not be considered as an official act since:

> "driving a motor vehicle is not in the nature of an act performed in an official capacity save in the exceptional cases in which this activity cannot be carried out otherwise than under the authority of the community and by its own servants."[87]

This example shows that the determination of "official acts" or "functions" may lead to very different conclusions depending on the qualifying authority.

Exemption from taxation on salaries paid to officials is a further privilege **15–073** to be found in virtually all agreements on the privileges and immunities of international organisations.[88] The position generally taken by organisations is that this privilege entails the prohibition to sequester an official's salary, and to take it into account in calculating taxation on income from other sources.[89] Notable exceptions include the UN/USA Headquarters Agreement, which is completely silent on the point, and the agreements between IMO and the United Kingdom, for instance, in which the exemption is qualified. In these exceptional cases the exemption from taxation is denied to nationals of the host state,[90] and, in the case of the UN led to the adoption of the Staff Assessment Plan as a clumsy expedient for securing equality of treatment for officials. It must be remembered in that respect that exemption from taxation is not designed to create a privileged class, but simply to secure equality of salary treatment to officials, regardless of nationality, and to avoid the payment to individual member states of large sums by way of taxation on their nationals' salaries from funds contributed by the totality of the members for the general purposes of the organisation. Some agreements make the exemption from national taxation conditional upon the adoption of an internal tax within the organisation, for the latter's benefit.[91] Other "economic" privileges are those relating to the free importation of personal and household effects at the time of taking up an appointment, and privileges in respect of exchange facilities comparable to those enjoyed by diplomatic personnel of equivalent rank.[92]

---

[87] *ibid.*

[88] See, *e.g.* the Conventions and Protocols on the Privileges and Immunities of the UN (section 18(b)), of the specialised agencies (section 19(b)), of the OECD (Art. 14(b)), of the Council of Europe (Arts 16 and 18), of the European Community (Art. 13), of the ITLOS (Art. 11), of the International Seabed Authority (Art. 8(2)(c)).

[89] For the UN, see UNJY (1969) 239, 243. For a different solution as to the calculation of global taxation, see Art. 16(1) of the U.K./EBRD Headquarters Agreement.

[90] See also the reservations entered by Laos and the United States upon accession to the Convention on the Privileges and Immunities of the UN (text in Multilateral Treaties Deposited with the Secretary-General). Some states refuse this exemption to nationals residing on their territory (see *e.g.* the Canadian reservation to the same instrument).

[91] See, *e.g.* Art. 16(1) of the U.K./EBRD Headquarters Agreement.

[92] See in general the provisions listed *supra*.

15–074   Further discrimination against nationals is practised by some states in respect of the immunity from national service obligations, provided for in some instruments.[93] The justification for this immunity is less obvious, and, certainly in time of peace, it will cause relatively little diminution of essential personnel since the service is commonly undertaken at an early age, before recruitment into an international secretariat is likely to occur. Several instruments are therefore far less categorical, and confine this particular immunity to officials whose names have been agreed with their national state.[94] Other instruments contain no exemption from national service obligations.[95]

15–075   The refusal to grant nationals of the host state the privileges and immunities normally accorded to officials is not confined merely to the immunities from taxation on salaries and national service obligations. Canada, France and the United Kingdom, in relation to ICAO, UNESCO and IMO, respectively, deny jurisdictional immunity to the senior officials who are their nationals. Other states have maintained that "locally-recruited staff" are not covered by the protection of the 1946 Convention, a contention quite contrary to UNGA Resolution 76(1) which excluded solely those employees paid at hourly-rates.[96] Indeed, the discrimination against their own residents or nationals by states emerges as one of the most significant problems in relation to the immunities and privileges of officials; it implies a failure either to understand or accept the principle so clearly formulated by Jenks:

> "The purpose of international immunities is to protect (the organisations') international responsibilities and they require protection against the State of which the official is a national as fully as, and perhaps more fully than, against any other State."[97]

15–076   One last privilege—of dubious value—enjoyed by officials of organisations of the UN system (or closely related) and of some regional organisations (such as the European Community)[98] is the privilege of transit which the "laissez-passer" is designed to secure. The relevant instruments provide

---

[93] See, *e.g.* the Convention on the Privileges and Immunities of the UN (section 18(c)). See also in that respect the reservations by Mexico, Nepal, Korea, Thailand and the United States to the 1946 Convention.

[94] See, *e.g.* the Agreement on the Privileges and Immunities of the specialised agencies (section 20), of the Arab League (Art. 21) and of the International Sea-bed Authority (Art. 8(2)(c)). A similar approach is seen in the headquarters agreements between various organisations and Switzerland, France, Italy and Austria.

[95] See, *e.g.* the agreements on the privileges and immunities of OECD, the Council of Europe, the European Community and NATO.

[96] See UNJY (1965) 264–265.

[97] *International Immunities, op. cit.* 112.

[98] Art. 7 of the Protocol on Privileges and Immunities.

that it shall be recognised and accepted as a valid travel document by the authorities of members.[99] Although in a number of headquarters agreements (not the UN/USA) the states agree to treat the laissez-passer as equivalent to a passport, in the practice of some UN member states the document does not permit travel independently of national passports and visas. In such cases, the laissez-passer may only prove to be useful in securing the speedy issue of visas, or other special travel facilities.

Most instruments emphasise on the functional character of privileges and **15–077** immunities granted to officials employed by international organisations—in even more cogent terms than for the privileges of members' representatives. They reiterate the "right and duty" to waive such immunities in all cases where the immunity would impede the course of justice and can be waived without prejudicing the interests of the organisation.[1] The power to waive those immunities lies with the organisation's chief administrative officer and, where he or she is personally concerned, with one of the organisation's political organs.[2] Some instruments further provide on that question that:

> "[the organisation] shall co-operate at all times with the appropriate authorities of members to facilitate the proper administration of justice, secure the observance of police regulations and prevent the occurrence of any abuse in connection with the privileges, immunities mentioned [in the instrument]."[3]

Such provisions are clear reminders that the privileges and immunities **15–078** conferred upon international organisations' officials do not by any mean grant them a license to ignore the national legislation in force in the state within which they carry out their functions, and that the organisations concerned are under a positive duty to ensure that such legislation is complied with by their personnel. However, even in the event of serious breaches of domestic legislation committed by international officials in the course of their functions, it follows from the fact that those officials are not accredited to states (as diplomats are), that the principle of *persona non grata* is not applicable to them. The proper procedure is for the host state

---

[99] See in particular section 24 of the Convention on the Privileges and Immunities of the UN and, for more recent examples, Art. 21 of the 1997 Agreement on the privileges and immunities of the ITLOS and Art. 11(1) of the Protocol on the Privileges and Immunities of the International Sea-bed Authority.

[1] See, *e.g.* the Conventions and Protocols on the Privileges and Immunities of the UN (section 20), of the specialised agencies (section 22), of the OECD (Art. 16), of the European Community (Art. 18), of the International Sea-bed Authority (Art. 8(4)).

[2] *ibid.* In the UN, this competence belongs to the Security Council.

[3] See, *e.g.* the Conventions and Protocols on the Privileges and Immunities of the UN (section 21), of the specialised agencies (section 23), of the OECD (Art. 17), of the ITLOS (Art. 24), of the International Sea-bed Authority (Art. 8(5)).

to make its representations to the chief administrative officer who alone can decide whether they shall be withdrawn from the territory.[4]

15–079 (ii) **Other agents.** There are, as we have seen earlier, certain categories of persons employed by international organisations who are not "officials" in the accepted sense.[5] The fact that they contribute to the achievement of the organisation's purposes explains that various categories of those "other agents" are similarly granted privileges and immunities, albeit more limited than those of officials. We shall deal briefly hereafter with two of these categories which are of particular interest: experts and members of international armed forces.

15–080 Several instruments provide for such privileges and immunities for experts "as are necessary for the independent exercise of their functions during the period of their missions."[6] These privileges and immunities generally include the immunity from personal arrest and detention, and from any form of legal process in respect of words spoken and written and acts done in the course of the performance of their functions, as well as the inviolability for all papers and documents.[7] Those regimes differ from one organisation to the other, the main difficulty in providing for standard privileges and immunities being that the functions of experts vary enormously; those with quasi-judicial functions may well need different immunities from those with quasi-political functions. In the UN, members of the International Law Commission, the International Civil Service Commission, or the Human Rights Committee, for example, are considered as experts in mission and enjoy the immunities provided for in Section 22 of the 1946 Convention.[8] The I.C.J. also made it clear that the term "mission" is to be interpreted broadly, "Section 22 [being] applicable to every expert on mission, whether or not he travels," adding that experts enjoyed those privileges and immunities "in their relation with the States of which they are nationals or on the territory of which they reside."[9] The I.C.J. later took the view that, as it was the case for UN officials, it is for the UN Secretary-

---

[4] For the UN, see *UNJY* (1964) 262–263.

[5] See *supra*, Chap. 12, paras 12–002 *et seq*.

[6] The language is that of section 22 of the Convention on the Privileges and Immunities of the UN; see also *e.g.* Art. 18 of the OECD Protocol, Art. 15 of the ITLOS Agreement and Art. 9(1) of the International Sea-bed Authority Protocol.

[7] See Art. 18 of the OECD Protocol. The list is more exhaustive in the UN Convention (where it includes the right to use codes, facilities in respect of currency or exchange restrictions, and immunity in respect of their personal baggage) and in respect of the International Sea-bed Authority Protocol (which provides for the exemption from tax on salaries paid by the Authority, save in relations between the experts and the member of the organisation of which he or she is a national).

[8] See the I.C.J. Advisory Opinion on the Applicability of Art. VI, section 22, of the Convention on the Privileges and Immunities of the United Nations, I.C.J. Rep. (1989) 194, para. 48 *in fine*.

[9] *ibid.* 194, paras 50 and 51 *in fine*, respectively.

General to determine whether an expert whose actions are disputed had committed those acts in the exercise of its functions.[10] As for officials and representatives of members, the functional character of the privileges and immunities enjoyed by experts is clearly affirmed in all the relevant instruments.[11] Here too, it is for the chief administrative officer to waive the immunity when the conditions are met.[12]

The other category of agents of international organisations who enjoy **15–081** certain privileges and immunities is that of the members of international armed forces. Customary international law traditionally recognised a certain immunity from the supervisory jurisdiction of the host state for friendly forces stationed on its territory. This principle has been maintained in respect of armed forces placed by an international organisation in the territory of a state with its consent. The first truly international force was the United Nations Emergency Force, the operation of which was governed, in legal terms, by the first real status of forces agreement concluded by the UN with an host state (in that case, Egypt).[13] The terms of this agreement reveal the extent to which the experience with agreements such as the 1952 NATO Status of Forces Agreement[14] had been relied on in assessing the needs of an international armed force. The obligation to respect the local law is stressed, but total immunity from the local criminal jurisdiction is conceded (such jurisdiction rests exclusively with the states contributing the forces).[15] As for most other categories of international agents, immunity from civil jurisdiction lies only in respect of acts relating to official duties, and the certificate of the Commander of the Force is conclusive on the official or non-official character of an act. Other

---

[10] Advisory Opinion on the Difference Relating to Immunity from Legal Process, *loc. cit.* 87, para. 60.

[11] See, *e.g.* Section 23 of the Convention on the Privileges and Immunities of the UN, Art. 19 of the OECD Protocol, and Art. 9, 2 of the International Sea-bed Authority Protocol.

[12] *ibid.*

[13] Agreement of February 8, 1957, 260 U.N.T.S. 51. As explained earlier (*supra*, Chap. 2), the military forces which took part to the Korean War in the early 1950s cannot be considered as UN Forces from a strictly legal point of view. This conclusion finds confirmation in the fact that in Korea no single agreement was concluded, but rather a complex of bilateral agreements and arrangements, and even with Japan the agreement regarding the status of UN Forces (214 U.N.T.S. 51) was concluded by the governments of states contributing contingents, and not by the Organisation as such. There was an agreement between the UN and Korea, constituted by an exchange of letters of September 21, 1951, but this related to UN Civilian personnel, experts and representatives of members (ST.ILEG/SER/B110, p. 256); a similar agreement existed with Japan (*ibid.*, p. 266).

[14] 199 U.N.T.S. 67. This agreement is a multilateral treaty to which the member states only, and not the organisation as such are parties. It provides for the legal status of members of the armed forces of one the parties when they are stationed in or operate on the territory of another state party. The armed forces concerned by this agreement therefore cannot be considered as international armed forces within the meaning of the present section (for later developments concerning the NATO forces, see *infra*).

[15] See generally Art. 47 of the UN Model Status of Force Agreement (Annex to doc. A/45/594).

provisions cover an enormous range of matters—which are of interest for the Force itself, rather than its individual members—such as taxation, customs, communications of all kinds, public utility services, freedom of movement, uniform and arms, identification, use of flag and official markings, protection and immunity of property and assets, and settlement of disputes and claims. The status of force agreements concluded since then by the UN with host states have globally followed this model.[16] In this regard, the Statute of the ICC is of interest, since it provides in Article 27 (2) that "immunities [. . .] which may attach to the offical capacity of a person, whether under national or international law, shall not bar the court from exercising its jurisdiction over such a person." The effect of this provision, once it enters into force, will be to override the immunities described above in respect of members of international peacekeeping forces accused of having committed acts falling under the Court's jurisdiction.

15–082 **(iii) Holders of judicial offices.** Initially, once the need for immunities for persons holding international judicial office had been realised, the solution adopted was to confer diplomatic immunities and privileges. This was the solution in the Hague Conventions on the Pacific Settlement of Disputes of 1899 and 1907 for the Permanent Court of Arbitration, and was the solution of 1928 for the P.C.I.J. It is basically still the solution adopted for the I.C.J., both in its statute (Article 19) and in the 1946 agreement between the court and the Netherlands as host state,[17] although these diplomatic privileges are enjoyed only whilst engaged on the business of the court. In 1946, by resolution 90 (I), the General Assembly made certain recommendations to secure to the judges an extension of these diplomatic privileges to any country where they resided for the purpose of holding themselves permanently at the disposal of the court,[18] to secure transit facilities for the judges[19] and also to secure for agents, counsel and advocates before the court transit facilities and the immunities provided in the Convention on the Privileges and Immunities of the UN for representatives of members. Waiver of the immunities of a judge is a matter for the court; in the case of agents, counsel or advocates it is a matter for the state they represent. Taxation of salaries and allowances of judges is forbidden by Article 32(8) of the Statute of the I.C.J.,[20] although it is by no means

---

[16] The main differences between the 1957 Agreement and other SOFA's concluded later on—such as the agreement with the Republic of the Congo of November 27, 1961 (UN doc. S/5004) are the absence of the technique of incorporating the 1946 Convention on the Privileges and Immunities of the UN by reference (perhaps because the Congo was not a party thereto), the absence of any jurisdiction in the local courts (presumably because they were not functioning), a wider freedom of movement clause and a more detailed liaison clause. See generally Bowett, *U.N. Forces* (1964), Chap. 13.

[17] 8 U.N.T.S. 61.

[18] See in the same sense Art. 13(3) of the 1997 Agreement relating to ITLOS.

[19] See in the same sense Art. 13(2) of the 1997 Agreement relating to ITLOS.

[20] The judges themselves, in 1949, firmly rejected any suggestion that the Staff Assessment Plan of the UN should apply to them.

clear that all the parties to the Statute so provide in their municipal legislation.[21] The members of the International Tribunal of the Law of the Sea similarly enjoy diplomatic privileges and immunities when engaged on the business of the tribunal, and their salaries are exempt from taxation.[22] Agents and counsels, as well as witnesses are also granted various privileges and immunities during the course of their functions in relation with proceedings before the tribunal.[23] Diplomatic privileges and immunities are also applicable at all times to the judges of the European Court of Human Rights, the plenary Court alone having the competence to waive these.[24] The immunity from legal process in respects of all acts done by them in the discharge of their duties continues to be accorded even after the end of their functions.[25]

In contrast to these courts and tribunals, where diplomatic immunities **15–083** are broadly conferred, judges of other tribunals such as the Court of Justice of the European Communities have been accorded privileges and immunities based on a far more functional test, with the analogy being that of the privileges and immunities conferred on courts in municipal law. Hence immunity from legal process exists, and continues after the term of office expires in respect of words spoken or acts done in the course of their judicial duties. Waiver is by the court, and only the national courts with competence to judge members of the highest national judiciary may assume criminal jurisdiction over judges of the Court of the European Communities, whose immunity has thus been waived. Salaries are tax free. Privileges and immunities are accorded to counsel and advocates comparable to those enjoyed before municipal tribunals, and may be waived by the court.

In concluding this brief survey of the immunities and privileges accorded **15–084** to international organisations and to their agents it is appropriate to emphasise again the extent to which the functional test has been adopted; yet there still remains on the part of states a certain distrust of these immunities. This is very largely due to their failure to grasp the principle so well expounded by Jenks that:

---

[21] The U.K. legislation does so provide: S.R. & O. 1947 (No. 1772). Whether the immunity extends to pensions or not is an open question; in principle it should.

[22] Arts 10 and 18, 8 of the ITLOS Statute, respectively. See also Art. 13 of the 1997 Agreement on the privileges and immunities of the Tribunal.

[23] Arts 16 and 17, respectively, of the 1997 Agreement on the privileges and immunities of the ITLOS.

[24] Arts 1 and 4, respectively, of the Sixth Protocol to the General Agreement on privileges and immunities of the Council of Europe. See also *Zoernsch v. Waldock* [1964] 2 All E.R. 256, in which the Court of Appeal held that the defendant, formerly a member and president of the European Commission of Human Rights, was entitled to immunity since his name was included in the list established under section 2(1) of the International Organisations (Privileges and Immunities) Act 1950, and that his immunity had not come to an end because he had ceased to hold such office.

[25] *ibid.* Art. 3. See in the same sense Art. 13(7) of the 1997 Agreement relating to ITLOS.

"The proper measure of international immunities is what is necessary for the impartial, efficient and economical discharge of the functions of the organisation concerned, and in particular what contributes to the effective independence of the organisation from the individual control of its separate members exercised by means of their national law and executive authority as distinguished from their collective control exercised in a regular manner through the appropriate international organs."[26]

15–085 This statement undoubtedly remains accurate, and points to the need for a balance between the requirements of efficient and independent functioning of international organisations, on the one hand, and the necessity of justice being done, on the other. What should clearly be avoided is the development by organisations or their agents of what Jenks has termed "a psychology of privileges."[27] The fact that immunities are immunities of procedure only, which by no means prevent international organisations and their agents from complying with the law applicable to their activities, should never be overlooked. A clear distinction must be drawn in that respect between procedural and substantive aspects: the fact that international organisations and their agents may not be made subject to the jurisdiction of national courts under certain circumstances is not to be equated with their absence of responsibility whenever the rules governing their activities are breached. As the I.C.J. pointed it out in its 1999 Advisory Opinion:

"the question of immunity from legal process is distinct from the issue of compensation for any damages incurred as a result of acts performed by the United Nations or by its agents acting in their official capacity."[28]

Indeed, as it shall now be seen, the fact that international organisations may be held liable for the consequences of wrongful acts is widely accepted as a matter of principle.

(c) LIABILITY AND RESPONSIBILITY OF INTERNATIONAL ORGANISATIONS

Bibliography: Amerasinghe, "Liability to Third Parties of Member States of International Organizations — Practice, Principle and Judicial Precedent", 85 AJIL (1991) 259–280; Amrallah, "The International Responsibility of the United Nations for Activities Carried out by UN Peace-Keeping Forces", 32 Rev. Egypt. D.I. (1976) 57–82; Arsanjani, "Claims Against International

---

[26] *International Immunities, op. cit.* 167.
[27] *ibid.* 151.
[28] *Loc. cit.* 88–89, para. 66.

Organizations: Quis custodiet ipsos custodes", 7 Yale J. of World Public Order (1980–81) 131–176; Butkiewicz, "The Premises of International Responsibility of Intergovernmental Organizations", 11 PYIL (1981–82) 117–140; Cafari Panico, "The International Responsibility of the Host State for Damages to United Nations Agents, Il Politico", (1976) 112–138; Di Blase, "Sulla responsabilita internazionale per attivita de l'ONU", R.D.I. (1974) 250–280; Eagleton, "International Organizations and the Law of Responsibility", 76 R.C.A.D.I. (1950–I) 319–425; Hartwig, *Die Haftung der Mitgliedstaaten fur internationale Organisationen*, Berlin/Heidelberg, Springer, 1993; Higgins, "The Legal Consequences for Member States of the Non-Fulfilment by International Organizations of Their Obligations Towards Third Parties", 66 A.I.D.I. (1995–I) 249–469; Hirsch, *The Responsibility of International Organizations Towards Third Parties*, Dordrecht/Boston/London, Nijhoff, 1995; Klein, *La responsabilité des organisations internationales dans les ordres juridiques internes et en droit des gens*, Brussels, Bruylant, 1998; Meng, "Internationale Organisationen im volkerrechtlichen Deliktsrecht", 45 Z.f.a.ö.r.u. (1985) 324–357; Perez Gonzalez, "Les organisations internationales et le droit de la responsabilité", 92 RGDIP (1988) 63–102; Schermers, "Liability of International Organizations", 1 LJIL (1988) 3–14.

The fulfilment of their functions by international organisations may also **15–086** require that there be recognised the capacity to bring claims against other legal persons which have encroached upon their rights. Such capacity is widely recognised. As far as the situation in international law is concerned, the I.C.J. ruled in its 1949 Advisory Opinion that the UN has the "capacity to bring international claims when necessitated by the discharge of its functions" and to exercise the "functional protection" of its agents.[29] The UN, and other organisations, have since then developed a significant practice in that respect.[30] As has been seen earlier, the legal capacity conferred upon organisations in domestic legal orders by various international or national instruments generally includes the right to institute proceedings before domestic courts. The fact that international organisations may suffer the consequences of wrongful acts, and are entitled to bring claims against the author of such acts, whether in the international or in domestic legal orders, is thus well established.

The reverse situation, on the other hand, has proved more difficult to **15–087** manage, in some cases at least. From a theoretical point of view, the fact that international organisations may be held accountable for the consequences of their illegal or wrongful acts is widely accepted. Liability is thus generally presented as the logical corollary of the powers and rights conferred upon international organisations.[31] The principle is clearly recog-

---

[29] *Loc. cit.* 180 and 184, respectively.
[30] See generally Panico, *The International Responsibility of the Host State for Damages to United Nations Agents, Il Politico* (1976) pp. 112–138. More recent examples include the claim presented by the UN to Israel following the bombing by Israeli forces of a UNIFIL compound in Southern Lebanon in 1996.
[31] See, *e.g.* Mosler, Réflexions sur la personnalité juridique en droit international public, *Mélanges Henri Rolin*, Paris, Pedone (1964) 247; Reuter, *Sur quelques limites du droit des organisations internationales, Fetschrift für Rudolph Bindschedler*, Bern, Stämpfli (1980) 505; Ginther, "International Organizations—Responsibility", 5 EPIL (1983) 162; Conze, *Die völkerrechtliche Haftung der Europäischen Gemeinschaft*, Baden-Baden, Nomos (1987) 66.

nised by international organisations themselves. As the UN Secretary General put it, "[t]he international responsibility of the United Nations for the activities of United Nations forces is an attribute of its international legal personality and its capacity to bear international rights and obligations."[32] The same may of course be said in respect of any of the legal orders in the framework of which international organisations carry out their activities. It is clear indeed that responsibility may flow from a breach of the rules governing the activities of organisations and pertaining to their own legal order (i), to domestic legal orders (ii) and to international law (iii). As shall be seen, the rules governing the liability or responsibility regime within each of these legal systems are applicable to international organisations, as to any other subjects of the system concerned. There is, however, one particularly sensitive question, that of the degree of responsibility borne by member states of international organisations for the latter's illegal acts, which can only be approached, in all cases, by reference to international law. The confusion which this question leads to is reflected in decisions of national courts[33] and has led the Institute of International Law, in its 1995 resolution on the "Legal Consequences for member states of the non-fulfilment by International Organisations of their obligations toward third parties," to state that:

> "[w]hether States have concurrent or subsidiary liability for the fulfilment of such obligations due solely to their membership in an international organization is a matter of international law, whether a claim by a third party is made in an international court or tribunal or a national court."[34]

This last question will therefore be dealt with separately (iv).

(i) Internal law of the organisation

15–088 It has been seen earlier that illegal institutional acts of international organisations are to be considered as devoid of legal effects.[35] They may also, when they produce adverse consequences, make the organisation liable to compensate for the damages caused.[36] The internal law of a few

---

[32] Report on the "Administrative and budgetary aspects of the financing of the United Nations peacekeeping operations", doc. A/51/389, September 20, 1996, para. 6. See also the ruling of the European Court of Justice in *France v. Commission*, where the Court makes it clear that the non-performance of an international agreement by the Commission could make the Community liable at the international level (Case C-327/91, *France v. Commission*, Rep. (1994) I-3674, para. 25).

[33] For more on these, see *infra*.

[34] 66–II A.I.D.I. (1996) 447, Art. 4, a).

[35] See *supra*, Chap. 11, paras 11–052 *et seq*.

[36] See, *e.g.* Art. 233(1) of the E.C. Treaty and the statutes of most administrative tribunals that empower these to order compensation of the material damages that may result for officials from an illegal act addressed to them (for more on this, see *supra*, Chap. 13).

organisations extends this obligation to all damages caused by organs or agents in the course of their functions, thus covering the consequences of legislative or "executive" activities. The most developed of those systems is found in the European Community. Article 288 (2) (*ex Article 215*) of the Rome Treaty provides that:

> "[i]n the case of non-contractual liability, the community shall, in accordance with the general principles common to the laws of the member states, make good any damage caused by its institutions or by its servants in the performance of their duties."[37]

The creation of this regime of non-contractual liability finds its justifica- **15–089** tion in the desire to ensure that the transfer of powers by member states to the Community would not entail the withdrawal of the guarantees conferred upon private persons under national laws to be compensated for damages caused by national authorities in the exercise of their functions.[38] In spite of the reference, in Article 288, to "the general principles common to the laws of the member states," it is a true "system of community tort law" which has gradually been developed by the European Court of Justice.[39] This regime applies to the consequences of administrative or executive as well as—though under very restrictive conditions—legislative activities of the institutions.[40] The restrictive approach taken by the ECJ of the application of this provision—in order not to hinder the process of European integration—has meant that the community has only occasionally been found liable under Article 288.[41] A provision similar to Article 288 is to be found in the Euratom Treaty (Article 188 (2)).[42] Similarly, Article 22 of Annex III of the United Nations Convention on the Law of the Sea provides that the International Sea-Bed Authority "shall have responsibility

---

[37] According to para. 3 of that provision, it "shall apply under the same conditions to damage caused by the European Central Bank or by its servants in the performance of their duties."

[38] See in that respect the conclusions of Advocate General Roemer in joint cases 9 and 12/60, *Vloeberghs v. High Authority*, VII Rep. 449. See also Fines, *Etude de la responsabilité extra-contractuelle de la Communauté économique européenne*, Paris, L.G.D.J. (1990) 1 and 62.

[39] The expression has been coined by H.G. Schermers (in Schermers, Heukels and Mead (Eds.), *Non-contractual Liability of the European Communities*, Dordrecht/Boston/London, Nijhoff (1988)). The jurisdiction of the Court on matters of non-contractual liability is provided for in Art. 235 of the Treaty (see also *supra*, Chap. 13).

[40] The extension of this regime to legislative activities was first affirmed by the ECJ in the Schöppensted case (case 5/71, December 2, 1971, Rep. (1971) 975). The conditions under which the Community may be held liable for the consequences of legislative activities have been detailed by the Court, *e.g.* in the Amylum case (joint cases 116 and 124/77, December 5, 1979, Rep. (1979) 3497). See also, more recently, the Brasserie du Pêcheur S.A. case (March 5, 1996, Rep. (1996) I-1147, para. 45).

[41] Liability has been found in only four of the 69 cases brought before the court between its creation and 1992 (see Mancini, Il contributo della Corte de Giustizia allo sviluppo della democrazia nella Communità, Rivista di Diritto Europeo (1992) 723).

[42] See generally Hancher, *Issues of Non-contractual Liability under the Euratom Treaty*, in Schermers, Heukels and Mead (Eds.), *op. cit.* 55 *et seq.*

or liability for any damage arising out of wrongful acts in the exercise of its powers and functions [. . .]."[43] Finally, it may be noted that more cautious steps have been taken toward the creation of a regime for determining the legality of certain institutional acts under the internal law of several international financial institutions with the establishment, within these organisations, of inspection panels competent to examine claims of groups of individuals claiming to be adversly affected by projects carried out by these organisations in violation of their operational policies and guidelines.[44]

15–090 While these various—and rather exceptional—regimes are centered on the obligations of the organisations toward private persons, it is much more common to find internal rules providing for the liability of international organisations toward their own staff, for service-incurred damages.[45] These include damages resulting from work accidents, natural catastrophes, war operations, etc. In such cases, however, the organisation's liability is justified less by the illegal character of its acts than by the fact that it acts as "insurers" of the damages suffered by its agents in the exercise of their functions.

15–091 It follows that apart from this last situation, the cases in which the liability of international organisations finds its source in the latter's internal legal order are thus limited. Such liability much more often finds its roots in domestic law, or in general international law.

(ii) Domestic legal orders

15–092 Inasmuch as international organisations are to comply with the legislation in force in the countries on the territory of which they are carrying out their activities (with the notable exception of activities or transactions covered by specific privileges),[46] it is logical that breaches of domestic rules should entail the liability of the organisation in accordance with relevant domestic laws. Here again, it is the organisations' capacity to hold rights and obligations in those legal orders which engenders their responsibility for the consequences of unlawful acts. In practical terms, liability may arise either

---

[43] Text in 21 ILM (1982) 1339. There is no practice yet concerning this provision.

[44] On the fact that this may lead to the creation of specific regimes of non-contractual liability within these organisations, see *e.g.* Bradlow and Schlemmer-Schulte, "The World Bank's New Inspection Panel : A Constructive Step in the Transformation of the International Legal Order", Z.A.Ö.R.V. (1994) 395. The fact that these panels may not order compensation indicates that such mechanisms may not be considered as evidence of the creation of full-fledged liability regimes within the organisations concerned. For more on the functioning of inspection panels, see *supra*, Chap. 13, paras 13–078 *et seq.*

[45] See, *e.g.* Art. II, a) of Appendix D of the UN Staff Rules (Doc. ST/SGB/Staff Rules/ Appendix D/Rev. 1 (1966) and Amend. 1 (1976)); Appendix D of the IAEA Staff Rules.

[46] On the submission of international organisations to national laws, see *supra*, Chap. 14, paras 14–042 *et seq.* On privileges and immunities, see *supra*.

under contracts concluded by international organisations, and to which a national law is applicable[47] or in circumstances where tortious acts are attributable to an organisation irrespective of any contractual link. The fact that the contractual liability of international organisations is governed by the law applicable to the contract itself is undisputed.[48] Organisations may in such cases find themselves liable as a result of the non-performance, or wrongful performance of the contractual clauses, as would any party to such a contract.

The most striking examples of non-compliance by international organisa- **15–093** tions with contracts governed by national laws include the *Westland* and *International Tin Council* cases. In the first case, disagreements between the member states of the Arab Organisation for Industrialisation (AOI) led to the suspension of the organisation's activities, which in turn entailed the non-fulfilment of a large-scale joint-venture contract (governed by Swiss law) concluded with the British company Westland Helicopters. Westland initiated proceedings against the organisation and its members before the Court of Arbitration of the International Chamber of Commerce,[49] and, after several preliminary procedures before Swiss tribunals,[50] was ultimately awarded compensation in 1993.[51] In the second of these cases, it was the failure of the International Tin Council (ITC) to honour its commitments under a number of private law contracts that prompted creditors to institute proceedings before national courts in several countries. The ITC was a commodity organisation the mandate of which included the regulation of the international tin market.[52] To reach that aim, the organisation traded on the London Metal Exchange and the Tin Market in Malaysia. This involved the conclusion of a large quantity of contracts with brokers, but also with banks from which the ITC had borrowed the sums necessary to finance its trading activities. In 1985, a combination of factors—a drop in price, the constitution of a buffer stock exceeding by far the market's demand, poor management of the buffer stock, non-participation in the organisation of producer and consumer states accounting for a significant part of the world tin market—put the ITC in a situation in which it had inadequate funds, requiring it to suspend its operations.[53] The sums owed

---

[47] For more on this, see *supra* Chap. 14.

[48] See, *e.g.* Lysen, *The Non-contractual and Contractual Liability of the European Communities*, Stockholm, Almqvist and Wiksell (1976) 155; Butkiewicz, "The Premises of International Responsibility of Intergovernmental Organizations", PYIL (1981–82) 119.

[49] See the interim award regarding jurisdiction of 5 March 1984, 23 ILM (1984) 1071.

[50] Court of Justice of Geneva, October 23, 1987, 80 I.L.R. 622; Federal Supreme Court (First Civil Court), July 19, 1988, *ibid.* 652.

[51] Court of Arbitration of the International Chamber of Commerce, June 23, 1993 (unpublished).

[52] On commodities organisations, see *supra*, Chap. 4.

[53] See, *e.g.* McFadden, "The Collapse of Tin: Restructuring a Failed Commodity Agreement", 80 A.J.I.L. (1986) 811 *et seq.*

by the organisation to its unpaid creditors at that point totalled several hundred millions of pounds sterling. Numerous proceedings were instituted before arbitral tribunals as well as national courts (mostly in England, but also in the United States and in Malaysia), against both the organisation and all or some of its members. A final—though partial—settlement of most claims was reached in 1990.[54] In both cases, therefore, the central issue before the national courts was not so much the liability of the organisations concerned as a matter of principle (such liability not being challenged) but rather the possibility for creditors of an international organisation to hold its members liable for the non-fulfilment by the organisation of its obligations.[55]

15–094   The principle according to which international organisations may be liable under national law for damages resulting from their activities on the territory of a state is beyond dispute, and applies to contractual as well as to non-contractual damages (tortious liability).[56] In order to protect themselves against the consequences of their non-contractual liability, organisations generally conclude insurance contracts with private companies,[57] or, in the case of short-term activities (conferences, etc.), agreements with the host state providing for the transfer of liability (or, more exactly, of the consequences of such liability) to that state.[58] Whereas the implementation of the liability of international organisations before national courts may be limited by the jurisdictional immunity usually granted to organisations, this does not put into question the principle of liability. The obligation to compensate for damage inflicted results directly, unless other mechanisms have been put in place (insurance, transfer of liability to the host state, etc.). Various devices have been developed to ensure an impartial adjudication of questions of liability, and to accord a remedy to parties aggrieved by the acts or omissions of international organisations. Claims Commissions, arbitration clauses in contracts, and waivers of immunity all afford means

---

[54] £182.5 million were paid to the creditors, "in full discharge of their claims"; see Cheyne, International Tin Council, 39 ICLQ (1990) 945.

[55] As mentioned above, this last issue is dealt with below (*infra*, paras 15–100 *et seq*).

[56] It must be recalled, however, that tortious liability of international organisations is governed by national laws only when and to the extent that the organisations have not adopted specific rules to that effect within their internal legal order (as is, for instance, the case of the European Community; see *supra*, paras 15–088 *et seq.*).

[57] This is sometimes specifically required in headquarters agreements. See also *e.g.* resolution XIII.6 (E) of February 13, 1946, by which the UN General Assembly recommends that the drivers of all official vehicles of the organisation, and all staff members using vehicles be insured against third party risk.

[58] See *e.g.* Article XIII of the Agreement of January 29, 1992 between the United Nations and Colombia on the arrangements for the eighth session of UNCTAD, U.N.J.Y. (1992) 22; Article X of the November 2, 1992 Agreement between UNIDO and Cameroon regarding the arrangements for the fifth regular session of the General Conference of UNIDO, *ibid.* 116. A standard clause on the transfer of liability is to be found in all similar agreements concluded by the UN or specialised agencies with states on the territory of which meetings or conferences are held by those organisations.

whereby the responsibility of the organisation can be determined. Most instruments on privileges and immunities even make it a duty for organisations to provide alternative dispute resolution mechanisms in such cases. According to section 29 of the Convention on the Privileges and Immunities of the United Nations, for instance:

"The United Nations shall make provisions for appropriate modes of settlement of:
  (a) Disputes arising out of contracts or other disputes of a private law character to which the United Nations is a party;
  (b) Disputes involving any official of the United Nations who by reason of his official position enjoys such immunity, if immunity has not been waived by the Secretary-General."[59]

International organisations do not always comply with these obligations **15–095** in practice.[60] Such failures constitute a clear breach of their international obligations. In most cases, though, provisions are made in contracts or other agreements for such mechanisms, and these are regularly resorted to.

Likewise, in the vast majority of cases, international organisations comply **15–096** voluntarily with their obligation to provide compensation once their liability is established. Precedents such as the Westland and ITC cases show that it is not always so, and that it is sometimes only after lengthy judicial or arbitral proceedings that organisations finally comply with their obligations. Such situations, however, remain exceptional.

(iii) International law

Finally, it is clear that international organisations are responsible under **15–097** international law for breaches of international norms binding upon them. Though the International Law Commission has stated that its draft Articles on state responsibility are without prejudice of "any question that may arise in regard to the responsibility under international law of an international organisation, or of any State for the conduct of an international organisation,"[61] it is largely accepted that the rules governing the responsibility of states may apply equally to international organisations, with the necessary

---

[59] See also *e.g.* section 31 of the Convention on the Privileges and Immunities and Immunities of the specialised agencies. An identical or similar provision may be found in numerous headquarters agreement.

[60] See for instance the absence, in some of the contracts concluded by the ITC, of any clause providing for alternative dispute resolution, in spite of the inclusion in the headquarters agreement it had concluded with the U.K. of a provision similar to that of the UN Convention (see in particular *Standard Bank v. ITC*, High Court, Queen's Bench Division (Commercial Court), April 17, 1986, 77 ILR 8).

[61] Art. A of the Draft Arts provisionally adopted on second reading by the Drafting Committee, Doc. A/CN.4/L.569 of August 4, 1998.

modifications. As the UN Secretary-General put it, the international responsibility of the UN is:

> "a reflection of the principle of state responsibility—widely accepted to be applicable to international organisations—that damage caused in breach of an international obligation and which is attributable to the state (or to the organisation), entails the international responsibility of the state (or of the organisation) and its liability in compensation."[62]

15-098   The elements of state responsibility—breach of an international obligation and attribution of the wrongful act to the state—apply equally to the determination of an international organisation's responsibility. The fact that the international obligation breached must be in force for the organisation may sometimes raise difficulties, in view of the uncertainties surrounding the extent of an international organisation's obligations under international law.[63] What is clear is that organisations do not bear responsibility for acts which, even though harmful, do not constitute a breach of an international obligation. The practice of United Nations peacekeeping operations offers conclusive support for this proposition, since the UN has always refused—and rightly so—to acknowledge in that context any responsibility for damages resulting from "normal" war operations, *i.e.* military operations complying with the rules and principles of international humanitarian law.[64] Acts committed by any of their organs (in the formal and institutional sense), but also by any person or group on which they exercise a degree of control, be it informal, may be attributed to international organisations for international responsibility purposes. Breaches of international obligations by members of UN peacekeeping forces have been inevitably attributed to the organisation itself, rather than to the member states providing the contingent to which the peacekeepers concerned were attached.[65]

15-099   As may be clear, it is generally internationally wrongful acts committed in the context of peacekeeping operations that have up to now entailed the international responsibility of intergovernmental organisations. The United

---

[62] *loc. cit.*, para. 6.
[63] For more on the international norms binding upon international organisations, see *supra*, Chap. 14.
[64] See, *e.g.* Bowett, *United Nations Forces—A Legal Study of United Nations Practice*, London, (1964) 247; Salmon, "Les accords Spaak-U Thant du 20 février 1965", 11 A.F.D.I. (1965) 481. This principle is reaffirmed in the abovementioned 1996 report of the UN Secretary General (*loc. cit.*, para. 16). The exclusion of responsibility for the consequences of illegal acts justified on the ground of "military necessity" appears on the other hand much more debatable, in view of the constant refusal of the ILC to accept that "military necessity" may constitute a circumstance precluding wrongfulness, as far as states are concerned (see *e.g.* the comment of—then—Art. 33, Y.I.L.C. (1980), Vol. II, 2nd part, para. 28; this view is shared by special rapporteur Crawford in 1999, in his second report on state responsibility; Doc. A/CN.4/498/Add. 2, April 30, 1999, para. 280). There seems to be no reason why the situation of international organisations should be more favourable than that of states.
[65] See, *e.g.* Bowett, *op. cit.* 245; Seyersted, *United Nations Forces in the Law of Peace and War*, (1966) 119. For a recent reaffirmation, and more details on this issue, see the abovementioned UN Secretary General report, para. 17–19.

Nations Operation in the Congo (ONUC), during which extensive damages was caused to civilians of various nationalities by the UN forces in the early 1960s, undoubtedly constituted a most significant precedent. The UN has accepted responsibility for those acts, and compensated the victims; lump-sum agreements were concluded with the states concerned.[66] More recently, the responsibility of the UN—as well as of member states—in the Rwandan genocide of 1994 has also been brought to light, although maybe more from a political than a strictly legal point of view.[67] The international responsibility of NATO has similarly been evoked in relation with the bombing of Yugoslavia in 1999.[68] As the ONUC precedent shows, the international responsibility of international organisations may be implemented, as it would be against a state, through the use of diplomatic protection. Whether in this context, or in that of a direct action of the subject (state or other international organisation) injured, the responsibility of international organisations may be invoked by having resort to any of the classical mechanisms of international dispute settlement.[69] For the most part, the international responsibility of international organisations has remained minimal, at least as compared with cases of liability under their internal or domestic legal orders, which arise much more frequently.

(iv) A liability of states for the consequences of wrongful acts committed by international organisations of which they are members?

As indicated, the principle according to which international organisations **15–100** may be held liable or responsible for wrongful acts committed in the course of their activities is beyond dispute, in all legal orders (internal, national, international) within which such issues arise. The difficulties experienced on various occasions by creditors of international organisations in their attempts to recover the sums owed by organisations have sometimes led these creditors to try and establish not only the organisation's liability but also that of the member states. Arguments to that effect were developed in the *Westland* and *ITC* cases, where the creditors of the organisations attempted to establish a concurrent, or at least a subsidiary, liability of the

---

[66] See the agreements relating to the settlement of claims filed against the United Nations in the Congo concluded with Belgium (February 20, 1965, 535 U.N.T.S. 197), Switzerland (June 3, 1966, 564 U.N.T.S. 193), Greece (June 20, 1966, 565 U.N.T.S. 3), Luxembourg (December 28, 1966, 585 U.N.T.S. 147) and Italy (18 January 1967, 588 U.N.T.S. 197).

[67] See the report submitted to the UN authorities by the independent commission of inquiry on December 16, 1999, Doc. S/1999/1257.

[68] See, *e.g.* Egorov, "The Kosovo Crisis and the Law of Armed Conflicts", Int'l. Rev. of the Red Cross (2000) 183 *et seq.*; see also the contributions of Momtaz and Kovacs to that issue of the Review.

[69] As the I.C.J. put it in its 1949 Advisory Opinion, "[a]mong these methods may be mentioned protest, request for an enquiry, negotiation, and request for submission to an arbitral tribunal or to the court in so far as this may be authorized by the Statute" (*loc. cit.* 177).

members.[70] In both cases, however, the tribunals before which the issue was debated ruled that liability for the wrongful acts under consideration could be incurred by the organisation only, its separate legal personality making it impossible to hold the members liable for the organisation's acts. As Millett J. put it in *Maclaine Watson v. Dept of Trade*:

> "by conferring on the ITC the legal capacities of a body corporate, Parliament has granted it sufficient legal personality to enable it to incur liabilities on its own account which are not the liabilities of its members."[71]

15–101   More precisely, arguments based on representation or agency, control, or the absence of provisions excluding liability have all failed. According to the first of these arguments, the obligations of the International Tin Council were in fact incurred by its members, since the organisation was nothing more than the latter's agent.[72] This argument was dismissed by the English Court of Appeal judges, who ruled that:

> "the relationship between the member states and the ITC under the provisions of [the sixth International Tin Agreement] is not that of principals and agents but in the nature of a contract of association or membership similar to that which arises upon the formation of a company between the shareholders inter se and the legal entity which they have created by contract or association."[73]

15–102   The Court of Appeal added that the terms of the constituent instrument showed that "there was no intention on the part of the members to authorise the ITC as an agent in making the tin contracts or the loan contracts, and no intention on the part of the ITC to act as such."[74] This conclusion applies equally to other international organisations. The fact

---

[70] In its 1995 resolution the Institute of International Law defined concurrent liability as a "liability that allows third parties having a legal claim against an international organisation to bring their claim, at their choice, against either the organisation or its members", subsidiary liability being a "liability by which third parties having a legal claim against the international organisation will have a remedy against states members only if and when the organisation defaults" (Art. 2(b); *loc. cit.* 447).

[71] High Court, Chancery Division, May 13, 1987, 77 ILR 45; see also the decision of the House of Lords in *J.H. Rayner v. Dpt of Trade*, on the fact that the ITC "was invested with a legal personality distinct from its members, with the consequence that, when it entered into engagements, it and not the members was the contracting party" (*per* Lord Oliver of Aylmerton, October 26, 1989, 81 ILR 704).

[72] See in particular Court of Appeal, April 27, 1988, *Maclaine Watson & Co Ltd v. International Tin Council* (No. 2), 80 I.L.R. 110 ("constitutional agency", based on the constitutive instrument) and 115 ("factual agency", based on the contracts). See also Sadurska and Chinkin, "The Collapse of the International Tin Council: A Case of State Responsibility?", Va.J.I.L. (1990) 865.

[73] English Court of Appeals, *ibid.* 114 (Kerr L.J.).

[74] *ibid.* 178 (Gibson L.J.).

that such entities may act as their members' agents is not, however, to be entirely ruled out where it is based on clear evidence. [75]

The argument based on the control exercised by states on organisations **15–103** of which they are members was also unsuccessful. According to this reasoning, members of international organisations should be liable for the consequences of the organisation's wrongful acts since they are the subjects which, in fact, exercise control over the organisation's activities through their involvement in its functioning.[76] The autonomy of international organisations *vis-à-vis* their member states however will make it almost always impossible to assert such control upon the organisation. It is all in all rather exceptional that members would have at their disposal means—legal or others—enabling them to exercise a decisive influence on the organisation's behaviour. Hence, the Swiss Federal Tribunal concluded in the Westland case that:

> "the predominant role played by these [founding] states and the fact that the supreme authority of the AOI is a Higher Committee composed of ministers cannot undermine the independence and personality of the organisation."[77]

And Millett J. ruled in *Maclaine Watson v. Dpt of Trade* that:

> "[i]n the absence of actual authority [of a member state on the ITC], which must be distinctly alleged and proved, no such authority can be inferred from the fact of membership alone."[78]

Here again, a liability of members based on the control theory should not **15–104** be ruled out entirely, but such control would have to be clearly established, and cannot be deduced from the mere participation in the functioning of the organisation.

Finally, it was argued in the course of the ITC litigation that the absence, in the International Tin Agreement, of any provision excluding the liability of members for undertakings of the organisation should be construed as entailing the possibility that members could be liable for the organisation's default.[79] Provisions to that effect may indeed be found in a number of

---

[75] This possibility is recognised expressly in the Institute of International Law resolution (*loc. cit.*, Art. 5(c)(ii)). The resolution also contemplates the possibility that member states be held liable for acts of an international organisation whenever they have given their guarantee for the latter's commitments (Art. 5(c)(i) speaks in that respect of "undertakings by the state"). Such situations are however highly exceptional (see *e.g.* Klein, *La responsabilité des organisations internationales*, Brussels, Bruylant (1998) 504 *et seq.*).

[76] See, *e.g.* the conclusions reached by Nourse in *Maclaine Watson & Co Ltd v. International Tin Council* (No. 2), *loc. cit.* 144.

[77] July 19, 1988, 80 ILR 658.

[78] *Loc. cit.* 46.

[79] See, *e.g.* the arguments summarised by Gibson L.J. in *Maclaine Watson & Co Ltd v. International Tin Council* (No. 2), *loc. cit.* 173–174.

constituent instruments of international financial institutions or of commodity organisations.[80] The practice is however far from consistent, and was considered inconclusive by several English courts in the *ITC* case. In the Court of Appeal, the judges found themselves:

> "unable to accept that the practice shown in these treaties can fairly be regarded as recognition by the states concerned of a rule of international law that absence of a non-liability clause results in direct liability, whether primary or secondary, to creditors of the organisation in contrast to the obligation to provide funds to the organisation to meet its liabilities. Nothing is shown of any practice of states as to the acknowledgement or acceptance of direct liability by any states by reason of the absence of an exclusion clause."[81]

15–105   It is clear from these judicial precedents—the conclusions of which were confirmed by the Institute of International Law in its 1995 resolution—that the organisations themselves are the only subjects that may be held liable for the consequences of their wrongful acts, to the exclusion of their members.[82]

15–106   This conclusion does not prevent members of international organisations from incurring liability in some circumstances for the consequences of some of their acts which are performed with the organisations. Hence, members may be co-authors of illegal acts in parallel with the organisation, or lend their assistance to the commission of such acts by international organisations (complicity).[83] Moreover, members of international organisations are under an obligation of due diligence, which compels them to make sure that the transfer of competences to the organisation does not allow them to avoid their responsibilities under international law. This has been emphasised on several occasions by the European Commission and Court of Human Rights. As the Court put it in the *Matthews* case in 1999, the European Convention on Human Rights:

---

[80] See, *e.g.* Arts II, Section 6 and IV, Section 9 of the IBRD Arts of Agreement; Art. 6(5) of the Statute of the African Development Bank; Art. 6 of the Statute of the Common Fund for Commodities.

[81] *Maclaine Watson & Co Ltd v. International Tin Council* (No. 2), *loc. cit.* 174 (*per* Gibson L.J.); see also p. 108 (*per* Kerr L.J.) and p. 141 (*per* Nourse L.J.). See also the conclusion reached by Lord Oliver of Aylmerston in *J.H. Rayner v. Dpt of Trade, loc. cit.* 715. In the same sense, see Art. 6, b), i) of the Institute of International Law resolution (*loc. cit.*). Note however that the Institute has expressed the wish that the exclusive responsbility of organisations for their acts be made clear in all transactions with third parties (see Article 9(1) of the resolution). In the second part of its resolution, dedicated to "desirable developments", the Institute insisted on the fact that "[a] failure to take any [such] action should be taken as a relevant factor in considering the liability of the State members."

[82] Provided, of course, none of the abovementioned conditions is present (actual control, guarantee or agency).

[83] See, *e.g.* the abovementioned report on responsibilities in the Rwandan genocide of 1994, where the responsibility of the UN and of its members is evoked simultaneously.

"does not exclude the transfer of competences to international organisations provided that Convention rights continue to be 'secured'. Member States' responsibility therefore continues even after such a transfer."[84]

This led the court to conclude that "the United Kingdom is responsible **15–107** under Article 1 of the Convention for securing the rights guaranteed by Article 3 of Protocol No. 1 in Gibraltar *regardless of whether the elections were purely domestic or European.*"[85] In such cases, therefore, members of international organisations may be responsible not for the consequences of the latter's illegal acts, but for their own participation in that act, or for their failure to ensure that the powers they have transferred to an organisation have been exercised in conformity with their own international obligations.

Finally, it must be noted that although it is in principle the international **15–108** organisation which bears the consequences of its illegal acts, particularly in terms of reparation, its members are in most cases under an obligation to contribute to the supplementary financial expenses that compensation may entail.[86] This merely constitutes an extension of the members' obligation to contribute to the organisation's budget. It is true that the I.C.J. restricted the notion of "expenses of the United Nations" to those related to the purposes of the UN.[87] It may safely be said, however, that damages caused by international organisations to third parties usually occur in the course of activities related to these organisations' purposes. In that sense, "[i]t may be concluded that all expenses incurred as a result of the responsibility of an organisation are expenses of the organisation"[88] and, as such, must ultimately be borne by the members.[89] But here again, the matter is governed exclusively by the rules of the organisation concerned, and this "internal" obligation does not give third persons a direct cause of action against members.[90] One may note in this respect that ITC members, when they replenished the organisation's resources to enable it to settle the standing claims, took great care to insist on the fact that those payments

---

[84] February 18, 1999, Application 24833/94, para. 32.

[85] *ibid.*, para. 35; emphasis added.

[86] See generally R. Higgins' provisional report to the Institute of International Law, 66–I A.I.D.I. (1995) 415, para. 112.

[87] Advisory Opinion on Certain Expenses of the United Nations, July 20, 1962, Rep. (1962) 167.

[88] Amerasinghe, *Principles of the Institutional Law of International Organizations,* Cambridge, C.U.P. (1996) 314.

[89] See also Schermers, "Liability of International Organisations", LJIL (1988) 12.

[90] See generally the position taken by the House of Lords in *J.H. Rayner v. Dpt of Trade, loc. cit.* 682 (*per* Lord Templeman) and 684 (*per* Lord Griffith).

could not be considered as a discharge of any direct obligation owed by them to third parties.[91]

c. Dissolution of International Organisations and Problems of Succession

Bibliography: Chiu, "Succession in International Organisations", 14 ICLQ (1965) 83–120; Myers, *Succession Between International Organizations*, 1993; Ranjeva, *La succession d'organisations internationales en Afrique*, Paris, Pedone, 1978; Tanzi, "The Extinction of International Organizations: The Case of IBI, La Communità Internazionale" (1993) 731–757.

15–109 As "living" entities, international organisations may undergo significant changes. An organisation's existence may come to an end when its members decide that an organisation has completed its purpose or that the circumstances do not make it possible to keep it functioning. The organisation's dissolution may be accompanied by the transfer of all or part of its functions to an existing or to a new organisation. Cases of dissolution pure and simple (termination of the organisation without succession) include that of the East African Community in 1977,[92] the COMECON and the Warsaw Pact in 1991,[93] and the Intergovernmental Bureau for Informatics that same year.[94] Such situations are exceptional, since in most cases the functions of the organisation the existence of which is brought to an end are transferred to another organisation.

15–110 The dissolution of the predecessor organisation is in such instances followed, or accompanied, by a succession process described as the "transfer of functions and their ancillary rights and obligations from one organisation to the other."[95] Forms of succession are diverse:[96] the replacement of one organisation by another (as in the case of the replacement of the International Commission for Air Navigation by the International Civil Aviation Organisation, in 1944); the absorption of one organisation by another (as in the case of the absorption of the International Bureau of Education by UNESCO, in 1969); the merger of two pre-existing organisa-

---

[91] See, for example Amerasinghe, "Liability to Third Parties of Member States of International Organizations: Practice, Principles and Judicial Precedents", AJIL (1991) 269; Seidl-Hohenveldern, Failure of Controls in the Sixth International Tin Agreement, in *Towards More Effective Supervision by International Organizations—Essays in Honour of Henry G. Schermers*, Vol. I, Dordrecht/Boston/London, Nijhoff (1994) 267.

[92] Note however that this organisation was revived in 1996 as the Commission for East African Cooperation; see *supra*, Chap. 10.

[93] See *supra*, the introduction to Chap. 6.

[94] See Tanzi, *The Extinction of International Organizations: The Case of IBI, La Communità Internazionale* (1993) 731.

[95] Myers, *Succession Between International Organizations*, London/New-York, Kegan Paul Int'l (1993) 12.

[96] *ibid.* 16 *et seq.*

tions into a single entity (such as the merger of ESRO and ELDO into the European Space Agency in 1975);[97] the separation of a former organ of an organisation into a new organisation (as in the case of UNIDO, which became a full-fledged specialised agency in 1979, having been an organ of the UN for a dozen years);[98] and finally the transfer of specific functions by one organisation to another (such as the transfer of the social and cultural functions of the WEU to the Council of Europe in 1960).

Whether or not the constituent instrument provides for dissolution of an **15–111** international organisation's generally depends upon political factors: it is somewhat unlikely in the case of organisations like the UN, most specialised agencies, the European Community and other important regional organisations where permanence is the aim. Dissolution is, however, sensibly anticipated in the constitutions of the international financial institutions, for such institutions would inevitably face the problem of distributing their financial assets if they were to put an end to their activities. Hence, Article VI, section 5 of the IBRD Agreement contains detailed provisions providing for dissolution by a vote of the majority of the Governors, exercising a majority of the total voting power. The analogy with the winding-up of a company in municipal law is striking: payment of creditors and claims takes priority over distribution of assets, and the distribution is in proportion to the shareholding of each member.[99] The IMF Articles of Agreement contain a special Schedule K dealing with dissolution, or "liquidation" as it is called, and the constituent instruments of several regional development banks and of other organisations of the World Bank group also contain provisions on liquidation, modelled on the Bank's.[1]

By contrast, the dissolution of the League of Nations provides an **15–112** interesting case-study of termination of an international organisation whose constituent instrument was silent on the subject.[2] It was indeed in the absence of any constitutional provision for dissolution that the League Assembly, without convening the Council,[3] dissolved the League by its

---

[97] See *supra*, Chap. 6.
[98] See *supra*, Chap. 3.
[99] See paras to g).
[1] IFC, Art. V, section 5; IDA, Art. VII, section 5; MIGA, Art. 55; African Development Bank, Art. 45(7); IADB, Art. X, sections 2–4; EBRD, Art. 41(3).
[2] See generally Mackinnon Wood, "The Dissolution of the League of Nations" B.Y.B.I.L.(1946) 317; Myers, "Liquidation of the League of Nations' Functions", 42 AJIL (1948) 320.
[3] Prior to the dissolution, the Assembly had decided to "assume the functions falling within the competence of the Council," with the concurrence of all the members represented at the session (resolution of April 12, 1946).

resolution of April 18, 1946; all that survived was a Board of Liquidation, established for the sole purpose of liquidating the affairs of the League.[4]

15–113 With the League it was known, by 1946 that, in a political sense, the UN was its successor even though neither the Atlantic Charter nor the Dumbarton Oaks proposals referred to the League. So far as the transfer of functions was concerned, the Preparatory Commission of the UN, which had before it a report of the League's own Executive Committee, declined to accept the idea of a transfer of functions en bloc[5] and, instead, a review of the many functions was undertaken to ascertain those which it was considered desirable should pass to the UN or the specialised agencies. The review of "political" functions was undertaken by the General Assembly and the review of "technical and non-political" functions by ECOSOC; the acceptance of the transfer of any particular function was achieved by resolution of the Assembly.[6] In fact no political functions were assumed in the sense of a jurisdiction over political problems which had been before the League. With the Mandates system, as we have seen,[7] the transfer to the new Trusteeship system was a matter for the administering authority to decide; similarly with the bureaux in relationship with the League under Article 22 of the Covenant, a new agreement had to be negotiated with the UN. Where, under treaties, the League or related organisations had exercised administrative functions,[8] this transfer required consent of the parties to the treaties. The agreements on narcotic drugs, for example, had to be amended by a Protocol between the parties, substituting references to the UN and WHO for those to the League and the International Office of Public Hygiene.[9] The assumption of depositary functions in relation to treaties was more easily accomplished by a resolution of the General Assembly expressly stating the UN's willingness to assume these functions.[10] The transfer of the physical assets, including buildings, equipment, archives, libraries, etc., was provided for in the "Common Plan" prepared by the League of Nations Committee, and payment for them was made by the

---

[4] A similar, and perhaps even more questionable, method was adopted in relation to the P.C.I.J., dissolved by a resolution taken by the Assembly the same day; one might have expected this to have been done by the states parties to the statute, acting as such. For more on this, see Hudson, "The Succession of the International Court of Justice to the Permanent Court of International Justice", 51 AJIL (1957) 569–573.

[5] The USSR, having been expelled from the League, disliked this notion of almost automatic succession.

[6] See UNGA Resolution XIV (I) of February 12, 1946.

[7] See *supra*, Chap. 2.

[8] The League had published three publications on its functions under treaties: Powers and Duties attributed to the League of Nations by International Treaties (C.3, M.3, 1944, VI); List of Conventions with Indications of the Relevant Articles conferring Powers on the Organs of the League (C.100, M.100, 1945, VI); and The Committee of the League of Nations: Classified List and Essential Facts (C.99, M.99, 1945, V2).

[9] 12 U.N.T.S. 179.

[10] UNGA Resolution XII.7 (I) of February 10, 1946.

UN. All staff were discharged, although some were taken on under new contracts by the UN.[11]

In dissolving the P.C.I.J. care was taken to provide for the continuation **15–114** of acceptances of the Court's jurisdiction by including in the new Statute of the International Court of Justice Articles 36 (5) and 37. The judges' pension scheme was entrusted to the ILO. The ILO itself was carefully preserved; finances were transferred to it in the form of the Working Capital Fund and measures were taken by the League to vest in the ILO full ownership of its land and buildings and to preserve certain facilities for the use by it of the League's own buildings which were due to be transferred to the UN.[12]

The same kind of partial transfer as the one that occurred between the **15–115** League and the UN occurred in the case of the—partial—institutional succession between the GATT and the WTO.[13]

In contrast with the case of the League of Nations, the "reconstitution" **15–116** of OEEC into OECD in 1960[14] provides an example of succession where the personality of the old organisation was continued in the new.[15] Article 15 of the Convention establishing the OECD[16] provided in that respect:

"When this Convention comes into force the reconstitution of the organisation for European Economic Cooperation shall take effect, and its aims, organs, powers and name shall thereupon be as provided herein. The legal personality possessed by the Organisation for Euro-

---

[11] This seems a fairly normal procedure; in the transfer of UNRRA's functions and assets to the UN consequent upon its dissolution in 1948, the whole staff was taken over by the UN. The Agreement between UNRRA and the UN of September 27, 1948 (27 U.N.T.S. 350) is another useful case-study on succession: the treaty deals with settlement of claims, assignment of contracts, a very complicated accounting, and the usual problems of transfer of functions and physical assets. See also *e.g.*, regarding the succession of UNIDO to the UN, UNGA Res. 34/96 of December 13, 1979 and the Agreement of March 11, 1988 on the transfer of assets between the two organisations (1495 U.N.T.S. 375).

[12] See generally the Agreement of May 17, 1946 on the transfer of certain properties between the League of Nations and the ILO, 19 U.N.T.S. 188.

[13] See in particular Art. XVI (2) of the 1994 Agreement establishing the WTO ("To the extent practicable, the Secretariat of GATT 1947 shall become the Secretariat of the WTO [. . .]").

[14] See *supra*, Chap. 6. This course was necessitated, it is believed, by the constitutional position in the USA. It should be distinguished from the simpler course adopted when the Brussels Treaty Organisation became the Western European Union, of amending the earlier treaty and inviting new members to accede: see *2 European Yearbook*, documents relating to the revision and extension of the Brussels Treaty, pp. 313–340.

[15] In cases such as that of the League of Nations, the personality of the organisation is generally continued by a liquidation committee (or a similar structure) for the purposes of liquidation, until the liquidation process is completed (for a more recent example, see Tanzi, *loc. cit.* 736). During that period, the liquidation committee is the legal representative of the organisation.

[16] Convention of December 14, 1960, 888 U.N.T.S. 179.

pean Economic Cooperation shall continue in the Organisation, but decisions, recommendations and resolutions of the Organisation for European Economic Cooperation shall require approval of the Council to be effective after the coming into force of this Convention."

15–117   The method by which the reconstitution was to be effected was to establish a Preparatory Committee with power to review the acts of OEEC to decide which should be recommended for approval. Moreover, the members of the Council agreed in advance to accept these recommendations.[17] So far as the structure of the OEEC was concerned, the changes were not startling.[18] The review of functions and previous acts was done in the form of dividing them into four categories: the first included acts to be retained without any modification of substance, the second consisted of acts to be retained but with substantial modifications, the third of acts not to be retained but which embodied certain activities, principles or rules considered worthy of retention, and the fourth of acts that should lapse completely.[19]

15–118   Treaties and private-law contracts were continued,[20] although the contracts of employment with officials were terminated under the conditions governing notice, and the officials were recruited again as necessary with the specific proviso that the terms of service with OEEC were to count towards service with OECD.

15–119   Whether one organisation has been dissolved and replaced by a new legal entity depends upon the intention of the member states as reflected in the instruments effecting the constitutional change. For example, the changes to the constitution of the UPU as between 1874, 1878 and 1957 were simply amendments. By contrast, the ITU Convention of 1932, replacing the 1865 Convention, created a new legal entity which fused the personality of the old ITU with the former International Radiotelegraphic Union. Similarly, the commodity agreements, which are periodically restructured, are not regarded as having been intended by the parties to create a new organisation, but rather to perpetuate the original organisation, even though sometimes with transformed functions or powers.

15–120   These examples show that the legal framework and effects of succession of international organisations vary significantly from one precedent to another. However, certain principles would seem to emerge from practice and the law of treaties.

---

[17] Memorandum of Understanding on the Application of Art. 15 (reproduced in the "Bluebook," the publication of OEEC in 1960 entitled "The Organisation for Economic Cooperation and Development"). The USA and Canada entered into a much less binding commitment.

[18] See *supra*, Chap. 6.

[19] Part II of the Report of the Preparatory Commission, reproduced in the "Bluebook".

[20] Hahn, "Die Organisation fur wirtschaftliche Zusammenarbeit und Entwicklung", 22 Z.f.a.ö.r.u. (1962) 56.

(i) Even in the absence of specific provision(s) governing dissolution in **15–121** the constituent instrument of an organisation, there is "good evidence that there is a general principle of international institutional law that an organisation may be dissolved by the decision of its highest representative body."[21]

(ii) Succession may be characterised as conventional, in the sense that it **15–122** is based on agreement, which may be expressed in one or several instruments (resolution(s), treaty, etc.) or implied. The obligation of states individually to recognise the effectiveness of such a transfer similarly depends upon their consent.

(iii) The capacity of a successor organisation to accept a transfer of **15–123** functions may arise either from express or implied powers. Some constitutions contain express provisions (*e.g.* WMO Article 26(c), WHO Article 72, UNESCO Article XI (2)) but the UN acceptance of transfers of functions and assets from the League of Nations rested on implied powers. So did the General Assembly's succession to the supervisory functions under the Mandate for South West Africa.[22]

(iv) There is, as yet, no rule of "automatic" succession.[23]

(v) The form of transfer therefore should be such as to indicate consent and can therefore be expressed in either parallel resolutions of the two organisations or in amendment to or specific enactment in the constitutions of both organisations.

---

[21] Amerasinghe, *Principles of the Institutional Law of International Organisations*, Cambridge, C.U.P. (1996) 471. See also in the same sense the practice examined by Tanzi, *loc. cit.* 744–745. On voting requirements, see Amerasinghe, *ibid.* 470.

[22] See the *South West Africa* cases, I.C.J. Reps (1950) 128; (1952) 319.

[23] Fitzmaurice (29 B.Y.B.I.L. (1952) 8–10) and Myers (*op. cit.* 77) argue that the South West Africa Case supports the view that there can be automatic devolution. This view is refuted by Chiu (103–106) and Amerasinghe (*op. cit.* 480), arguing that implied consent could be established in that case.

CHAPTER 16

MEMBERSHIP AND REPRESENTATION OF MEMBERS

In this chapter we deal with two separate but related matters. The first **16–001** concerns the membership of international organisations, including issues such as the composition of and admission in organisations, as well as incidental matters that may affect membership (in particular suspension, and termination of membership of international organisations) (A). The second matter presupposes that the issue of membership has been clearly resolved and concerns the representation of members, and sometimes of other interests, in international organisations (B).

A. MEMBERSHIP

Bibliography: Morgenstern, *Legal Problems of International Organisations* (1986), pp. 46–86; Sato, *Evolving Constitutions of International Organisations* (1996), pp. 42–50; Schwartzenberger, *International Law—International Courts III—International Constitutional Law* (1976), pp. 30–35, 242–260; White, *International Non-governmental Organisations*, (1951), pp. 7–10; Schwebel, "Mini-States and a More Effective United Nations", 67 AJIL (1973) 108; Adam, "Micro-States and the United Nations", 2 ItYIL (1976).80; Gunther, "What happened to the United Nations Ministate Problem?", 71 AJIL 110 (1977); Osieke, "Admission to Membership in International Organisations: the Case of Namibia", 51 B.Y.I.L. 189 (1980); Qin, "GATT membership for Taiwan: an analysis in international law", 24 NYUJILP 1059 (1992); Mac-Donald, "The entry of new member states into the Council of Europe" 91 Proc. ASIL 523 (1997); Pasternack, "Succession, Secession and State Membership in the United Nations" 26 NYUJILP 623 (1994); Damrosch "GATT Membership in a Changing World Order: Taiwan, China and the former Soviet republics", Columbia Business Law Review (1992) pp. 19–38.

The membership of international organisations may vary widely, accord- **16–002** ing to a number of factors. Their geographical scope, their "political" or "technical" character and their level of integration are among the elements which determine the relative "openness" of organisations and the level of requirements for participation in each of them: admission to membership is generally conditional upon certain conditions being satisfied (a). Membership can also be affected by various kinds of events : in most organisations, it can be suspended when a member disregards its basic duties *vis-à-vis* the organisation (b), and of course it may be terminated under specific

533

circumstances, following either the organisation's initiative (expulsion) or that of the member (withdrawal) (c).

(a) ADMISSION

16–003 A broad distinction is to be drawn between "original" and "admitted" members of international organisations. The first category will normally include either those states or other entities[1] which were members of the organisation to which the new organisation is the successor, or those states or other entities which were invited to participate in the conference which drafted the constituent instrument of a new organisation. The signatories are generally given a period of time within which they may ratify or otherwise accept the convention and thus qualify as original members. The entities eligible for original membership are sometimes listed in an annex to the basic convention or agreement.[2]

16–004 The "admitted" members may well be of different types. In all international organisations, admission is conditional upon the satisfaction of specific requirements; in other words, organisations are never fully open in the sense that all states—or other entities—have a right to membership of an organisation. The first of these requirements regards the very nature of—potential—members. International organisations have for a long time been open to states only, and this remains the case for the majority of organisations: the United Nations and most specialised agencies, as well as regional organisations such as the Council of Europe, the European Community, EFTA, the OAS, the OAU or ECOWAS are illustrative in that respect.[3] It must however be noted that, even in such organisations, the requirement of statehood—which presupposes the political independence of the entities concerned[4]—has sometimes been interpreted liberally.[5] Hence, as a result of a political bargaining aimed at giving the USSR more voting power in the UN, the Soviet Republics of Byelorussia and Ukraine were admitted as full members of that organisation in spite of the fact that their actual status was that of federated republics within the USSR. Similarly, the relative dependence of "micro-states" upon their larger neighbours has never prevented the UN from accepting them in large numbers as full-fledged members.[6] Political factors have also led some

---

[1] For more on these, see *infra*.

[2] It is for instance the case in WMO, FAO, IFAD and MIGA.

[3] See also, among recent universal organisations, the Organisation for the Prohibition of Chemical Weapons (Art. 2).

[4] Some constitutions put a particular emphasis on that requirement : according to Art. IV of the OAU Charter, for instance, members of that organisation may only be "independent sovereign African States" (see also, *e.g.* Art. 8 of the OAS Charter).

[5] See, *e.g.* generally Cohen, "The Concept of Statehood in United Nations Practice," 109 University of Pennsylvania L.R. (1961) 1156–1161; Seyersted, "Federated and Other Partly Self-governing States and Mini-states in Foreign Affairs and International Organisations", 57 Nordic JIL (1988) 372–373.

[6] See, *e.g.* the recent admissions of Tonga (1999) and Tuvalu (2000) to the UN.

regional organisations the membership of which was theoretically open to states only to accept as members entities representing peoples whose right to self-determination was frustrated. This has been the case, for example, for the PLO, which was admitted as a full member of the Arab League and of some of its specialised agencies in 1976 as a true representative of Palestine, and of the Arab Sahrawi Democratic Republic which became a member of the OAU—after heated debates—in 1982.

Some constitutions are slightly more flexible regarding the statehood **16–005** criterion: the WMO, for instance, is open to "any territory or group of territories maintaining its own meteorological service,"[7] whereas the agreement establishing the WTO envisages accession by "separate customs territor[ies] possessing full autonomy in the conduct of [their] external commercial relations."[8]

The most significant evolution regarding membership is the gradual **16–006** opening of membership in international organisations to other international organisations. This was obviously prompted by the creation of the European Communities, to which the member states agreed to transfer the exercise of powers in various fields, thus making it necessary to authorise this organisa-tion's access to international organisations dealing with matters entering henceforth in the community's fields of competences.[9] The European Community has become a member of dozens of international organisations active in the field of fisheries,[10] trade[11] or commodities,[12] amongst others.[13] The constitution of the FAO was even amended in 1991 in order to make it possible for the E.C. to become a member of this organisation in its own right,[14] (Article II of the FAO Constitution) and the European Communities are expressly mentioned as original members of the WTO in the agreement establishing that organisation.[15] Most organisations open to other organisa-tions have, however, limited this possibility to "regional economic integration

---

[7] Art. 3(d) and (e). The application for membership must be presented by the state responsible for that territory's international relations.

[8] Art. XII(1).

[9] On various issues related to E.C.'s membership of other international organisations, see *e.g.* Dormoy (Ed.), *L'Union européenne et les organisations internationales*, Brussels, Bruylant (1997).

[10] Such as the North Atlantic Fisheries Organisation (NAFO).

[11] Such as the WTO.

[12] Such as the Natural Rubber Organisation or the ITC (before its dissolution).

[13] In 1995, the E.C. was a member of more than 60 international organisations (see Sack, "The European Community's Membership of International Organisations", C.M.L.R. (1995) 1239).

[14] Schowb, "L'amendement de l'acte constitutif de la FAO visant à permettre l'admission en qualité de membre d'organisations d'intégration économique régionale et la Communanté économique européenne", Rev.trim.dr.eur. (1993) 1.

[15] Art. XI (1). It is interesting to note, however, that accession to the WTO is restricted to states or "separate customs territory," thereby excluding membership of international organisations other than the E.C. (Art. XII (1)).

organisations.[16] Generally, a majority of members of the organisation applying for membership have to be members of the organisation applied to, and a declaration specifying the matters in respect of which competence has been transferred to the incumbent organisation must be submitted. Once the organisation is admitted, membership rights have to be exercised on an alternative basis with those of its members which are also members of the organisation acceded to.[17] More recently, some international organisations have been created by existing organisations exclusively.[18]

16–007   Finally, it may be noted that components of a federation have been admitted as full-fledged members in at least two international organisations.[19] These various developments show that international organisations remain in constant evolution and that their characterisation as exclusively "intergovernmental" or "interstate" entities is no longer warranted.

16–008   An alternative to full membership is provided for in some organisations, which permit certain entities not meeting the conditions for membership to become associate members. In several specialised agencies, "territories or groups of territories which are not responsible for the conduct of their international relations" may be admitted as associate members upon application by the state or other authority having responsibility for those relations[20]; those provisions sometimes also specifically anticipate a trusteeship territory administered by the UN as a possible candidate for associate membership.[21]

---

[16] FAO, Art. II (3). It is not always so; membership of the International Seabed Authority, for instance, is opened to all international organisations (UNCLOS, Art. 156 (2) combined with Art. 305 and Art. 1 of Annex IX; the only requirement is that members of the organisation applying for membership have transferred to it "competence over matters governed by this Convention").

[17] The various conditions are laid down in Art. II, (5) to (10) of the FAO Constitution.

[18] It is in particular the case of the Joint Vienna Institute; the members of this organisation are the OECD, the Bank for International Settlements, the IBRD, the IMF and the EBRD (see Rousseau, "Joint Vienna Institute"—Brèves remarques relatives à la création de l'Institut commun de Vienne, 99 R.G.D.I.P. (1995) 639 et seq.; see also the precedents listed by this author on p. 641). The fact that the institute is an international organisation possessing its own legal personality is unambiguously proclaimed in Art. I of its constitutive instrument; the parties to this agreement are listed in Art. XII (1) (see text in 33 I.L.M. (1994) 1505).

[19] The three Belgian regions are members of the International Commission for the Protection of the Meuse against Pollution, and of the International Commission for the Protection of the Escaut against Pollution, two international organisations established by the Agreements of April 26, 1994 concluded by the three Regions, France and the Netherlands (on the fact that these commissions qualify as international organisations, see e.g. d'Argent, L'évolution du statut juridique de la Meuse et de l'Escaut: Une mise en perspective des accords de Charleville-Mézières du avril 26, 1994, 30 R.B.D.I. (1997) 159).

[20] See, e.g. FAO, Art. II (11); UNESCO, Art. II (3); WHO, Art. 8; IMO, Art. 8.

[21] In the constitution of IMO, for instance (Art. 8).

Associate membership is also provided for in the constitution of some **16–009** regional organisations, such as the Council of Europe, for instance.[22] Not unnaturally, such associate membership does not confer quite the same rights as full membership. In the IMO, for instance, such members do not have the right to vote in the Council nor are they eligible for election to that body.[23] The WHO has regulated the rights and obligations of associate members by a resolution of the first Health Assembly which deprives them of a vote in the Assembly or main committees and of membership of the Executive Board.[24] In the Council of Europe, associate members are entitled to be represented in the Consultative Assembly only. Associate membership therefore appears as a useful device for associating with the work of the organisation entities other than sovereign states (in the case of universal organisations) or states which, for various reasons, do not (yet) meet the criteria for membership of an organisation in the activities of which they nevertheless have a particular interest.

Other requirements of membership vary considerably in relation to each **16–010** organisation's character, functions and mission. Unsurprisingly, the membership of regional organisations is almost always limited to states of the region.[25] In some instances, membership of various international organisations is linked, in the sense that states which are already members of a given organisation enjoy more favourable conditions of admission in one or more organisations related by particular institutional ties to the former institution. Hence, in most specialised agencies, states which are members of the United Nations are admitted as of right, simply by communicating a formal acceptance of the convention to the Secretary-General or Director-General of the organisation concerned, as in the ILO,[26] or to a government which exercises depository functions.[27] UNESCO,[28] WHO,[29] UPU,[30] IMO,[31]

---

[22] Art. 5 (a). West Germany and the Saar were associate members until West Germany became a full member in 1951 and the Saar became integrated into West Germany in 1955. Provisions are also made for association in the treaty establishing the E.C., but in a slightly different sense. There, association is exclusively aimed at "non-European countries and territories which have special relations with Denmark, France, the Netherlands and the U.K.", to which a specific regime applies in respect of trade, investments, custom duties, etc. (Arts 182 to 188 of the treaty). Associated countries and territories (which include for instance Greenland, French Polynesia, the Netherlands Antilles and the British Virgin Islands) do not enjoy a representation of their own in community institutions.

[23] Art. 9.

[24] Off. Rec. 13, 100, 337.

[25] See, *e.g.* Council of Europe (Art. 4), E.U. (Art. 49 of the Treaty on European Union), OAU (Art. IV), OAS (Art. 4).

[26] Art. 1 (3).

[27] With the ICAO, for example, the acceptance is to be addressed to the American Government (Art. 92).

[28] Art. II(1).

[29] Art. 4.

[30] Art. 11(1).

[31] Art. 5.

WMO,[32] WIPO,[33] IFAD,[34] UNIDO[35] and ITU[36] all have this membership link with the UN and the IBRD has a similar link with the IMF (and not with the UN),[37] just as the organisations of the World Bank Group have with the Bank.[38] Such linkage generally entails particular consequences in cases of suspension or termination of membership of the "parent" organisation.[39] In many organisations, admission is conditional on the fulfilment of conditions enunciated in the constituent instrument, and subject to the approval of one or several political organs, which pronounce on the satisfaction to these conditions in each case. In the United Nations, membership is open to all:

> "peace-loving states which accept the obligations contained in the [. . .] Charter and, in the judgment of the Organisation, are able and willing to carry out these obligations."[40]

16–011   In most organisations statehood alone will not be sufficient to justify membership, and other conditions will need to be satisfied. In the UN context the applicant for membership has to satisfy the organisation that it is "peace-loving," that it "accepts" the Charter obligations and that it is "able and willing" to carry them out (Article 4). The criteria are all capable of subjective appreciation by the existing member states in voting on an application for admission. However, the repeated failure of the Security Council in the first ten years of the UN's existence to admit many states was due more to the "Cold War", in which each side sought to keep out states politically sympathetic to the other, and the deadlock was only broken by the practise of admitting certain states "en bloc". The General Assembly frequently expressed its concern over the Security Council's failure to make favourable recommendations on admission and eventually requested an Advisory Opinion from the International Court of Justice on whether a state, in voting upon an application for admission to membership, was legally entitled to make its vote dependent on conditions other than those enumerated in Article 4(1). The Court advised that it was not and, in particular, that it was not entitled to make its affirmative vote subject to the condition that other states be admitted together with a particular state or states.[41] The Court stated:

---

[32] Art. 3(b).

[33] Art. 5(2)(i).

[34] Art. 3, section 1(a) (also for members of other specialised agencies or the IAEA).

[35] Art. 3(a).

[36] Art. 2(b).

[37] Art. II, section 1 of the Articles of Agreement. There is however no automaticity here, membership of the Bank being opened to members of the Fund "in accordance with such terms as may be prescribed by the Bank".

[38] IFC, Art. II, section 1; IDA, Art. II, section 1; MIGA, Art. 4. In IFC and IDA, there is a provision similar to Art. II, section 1 of the Bank's Articles of Agreement.

[39] For more on this, see *infra*.

[40] Art. 4(1); see also *e.g.* the similar formula used in Art. IV B of the IAEA Statute, Art. 4 of the Statute of the Council of Europe and Art. 6 of the OAS Charter.

[41] (1948) I.C.J. Reps, 65 (Advisory Opinion of May 28, 1948). As late as 1975, however, the USA was adamant in making its vote in the Security Council to admit the two Vietnams to membership dependent on the Council's willingness to admit South Korea.

"a member of the organisation cannot, while it recognises the conditions set forth in [Article 4 (1)] to be fulfilled by the State concerned, subject its affirmative vote to the additional condition that other States be admitted to membership in the United Nations together with that State."[42]

The practise of the Security Council showed no significant change, and **16–012** there was some indication of a will in the Assembly to "by-pass" the Council and proceed unilaterally to admit to membership. However, the Assembly requested a second Advisory Opinion on the legality of such a course, and the Court advised that the Assembly had no power to admit an applicant in the absence of a favourable recommendation from the Council. It is a reflection of the respect shown by some member states for the Court's opinions that it was not until 1955 that the impasse was broken and, as a result of a political compromise, 16 new members were admitted out of a proposed bloc of 18.

The role of political organs in the admission process is no less important **16–013** in other organisations. In the specialised agencies, the admission of members other than states which are already parties to the UN Charter has to be approved by the plenary organ, with a simple[43] or—generally— qualified majority.[44] In other organisations, the role of such organs is even more significant, since admission can only be envisaged following an invitation addressed by the main political organ to a state.[45] The organisation's initiative is decisive in such cases.

The admission process may sometimes prove complex. In many organisa- **16–014** tions dealing with matters possessing significant financial implications, the terms of accession are either determined by the organisation or agreed between the latter and the applicant state.[46] In highly integrated organisations such as the E.C., the conditions of admission are detailed in a usually lengthy agreement between the member states and the applicant state.[47]

Finally, it must be observed that changes affecting the existence of **16–015** member states in their very existence may entail particular consequences as far as their membership of international organisations is concerned. It is

---

[42] I.C.J. Rep. (1947–48) 65.

[43] Competence of the General Assembly for the Admission of a State to the United Nations (1950) I.C.J. Reps, 10 (Advisory Opinion of March 30, 1950).

[44] As in FAO, UNESCO, ILO and UNIDO, for instance.

[45] See for instance NATO (Art. 10); Council of Europe (Art. 4); OECD (Art. 16). Such decisions must in most cases be taken unanimously by the competent organ.

[46] See, *e.g.* the abovementioned provisions in the articles of agreement of the international financial institutions, and Art. 41 (1) of the Convention establishing EFTA; Art. 12 (1) *in fine* of the Agreement establishing WTO; Art. 194 (3) of the COMESA Treaty.

[47] These agreements and their annexes usually number several hundreds of pages; see for instance the 1994 admission agreement concluded with Austria, Finland, Norway and Sweden, approved in all these countries except Norway in 1995 (OJEC, August 29, 1994, C. 241).

particularly the case for situations of state succession. No specific problem arises when both pre-existing states merge into one, provided of course that one of them at least is a member of the organisation. Hence, when the German Democratic Republic was absorbed by Western Germany in 1990, Germany's membership of universal and regional organisations remained unaffected.[48]

16–016   The fragmentation of states, on the other hand, raises more complicated issues. The most simple situation is the emergence of a principal successor; hence, India remained a member of the UN when Pakistan seceded in 1947.[49] Such "automaticity" is less obvious when it is more difficult to identify the main successor state, in situations more akin to complete dissolution of the pre-existing state than to secession of a part of its territory. The existence of an agreement between the former components of the member state may of course make things relatively simple. The succession of Russia to the USSR is probably the most significant case in point in that respect. The former Soviet Republics indeed agreed in 1991 that Russia should be considered as the direct successor of the Soviet Union in all UN organs, including the Security Council of which Russia is since then a permanent member. This solution was readily accepted by third states.[50] In contrast, in the absence of such an agreement, the claims of one of the successor states to be the main successor has sometimes been strongly disputed, as the fate of the Federal Republic of Yugoslavia (Serbia and Montenegro) in the UN shows. While the other ex-Yugoslav republics were in the process of being admitted to the organisation, the Security Council noted in May 1992 that:

> "the claim by the Federal Republic of Yugoslavia (Serbia and Montenegro) to continue automatically the membership of the former Socialist Federal Republic of Yugoslavia in the United Nations has not been generally accepted,"[51]

and declared a few months later that it considered that:

> "the Federal Republic of Yugoslavia (Serbia and Montenegro) cannot continue automatically the membership of the former Socialist Federal Republic of Yugoslavia in the United Nations; and therefore recommends to the General Assembly that it decide that the Federal

---

[48] See also the situation of the United Arab Republic (composed of Egypt and Syria) in the early 1960s.

[49] So did Pakistan remain a member of the organisation after the secession of Bangladesh in 1971.

[50] For more on this, see Blum, "Russia Takes over the Soviet Union's Seat at the United Nations", 3 EJIL (1992) 354–361.

[51] Resolution 757 (1992) of May 30, 1992, 10th preambular paragraph.

Republic of Yugoslavia (Serbia and Montenegro) should apply for membership in the United Nations and that it shall not participate in the work of the General Assembly."[52]

This recommendation having been followed by the Assembly, the Federal **16–017** Republic of Yugoslavia (Serbia and Montenegro) had therefore no other solution than to apply for membership.[53] The specialised agencies have taken the same position.[54] The FRY has however maintained its claim, and the deadlock remained until, following the evolution of the political situation in Yugoslavia, it was admitted by the General Assembly in November 2000.[54a]

(b) SUSPENSION FROM THE PRIVILEGES OF MEMBERSHIP

In many international organisations, membership may be suspended as a **16–018** means of securing compliance by a member with its obligations. The circumstances in which such powers may be exercised vary considerably; and the extent of suspension may vary from loss of voting rights to loss of the right to attend meetings of one or more organs, or to have access to services provided by the organisation.[55] Suspension is frequently used as a sanction for non-fulfilment of financial obligations. Article 19 of the UN Charter thus provides for suspension in the sense of deprivation of a vote in the General Assembly when a member is in arrears with its budgetary contributions to an amount equal to the contributions due for the preceding two full years. The ILO and UNESCO similarly adopt two years,[56] whereas IMO allows only one year's grace[57] and ICAO refers only to "a reasonable period."[58] Other organisations extend the category of defaults for which suspension of voting rights may be imposed as a sanction, so that in WHO it applies "in other exceptional circumstances."[59] and WMO denies voting rights to a member who "otherwise fails in its obligations under the present Convention."[60] All in all, such provisions may be said to be of limited value, in particular in light of the fact that suspension is usually subject to review by one of the organisation's organs.[61] While this

---

[52] Resolution 777 (1992) of September 19, 1992, para. 1.
[53] See generally Blum, "UN Membership of the 'New' Yugoslavia: Continuity or Break?", 86 AJIL (1992) 830–833 and the Correspondents' "Agora" in 87 AJIL (1993) 240–251.
[54] See, *e.g.* Stern, *Le statut des Etats issus de l'ex-Yougoslavie à l'ONU*, Paris, Montchrestien (1996) 24–25.
[54a] See Res. A/55/23 of November 1, 2000.
[55] See *supra*, Chap. 12.
[56] Arts 13 (4) and 8 (b) respectively.
[57] Art. 56.
[58] Art. 62. See also for instance Art. 9 of the Statute of the Council of Europe, where no time limit is stated for the default of payment to induce sanction.
[59] Art. 7.
[60] Art. 31.
[61] In IMO, for instance, a defaulting member will be denied the right to vote "unless the Assembly, at its discretion, waives this provision".

may prevent too rigid an application of the rule in cases where the member concerned experiences serious financial difficulties which may amount to force majeure, it also potentially subjects the competent organ to political pressures, leading to inconsistent decisions in that respect. Highly symptomatic of such risks is, for instance, the fact that the UN General Assembly decided in 1968 to suspend the voting rights of Haiti and the Dominican Republic,[62] whereas it never took a similar decision *vis-à-vis* the Soviet Union (in the 1960s)[63] or the United States, in spite of their owing the Organisation sums considerably larger than the states previously suspended.[64]

16–019   Arrears in financial contributions are far from being the only motive for which international organisations may decide to suspend one of their members, and suspension may affect rights and privileges other than voting rights. Breaches of obligations owed to the organisation may, in many constituent instruments, lead to suspension; other causes include the fact that the member has been subjected to other specific measures or sanctions by the organisation. Article 5 of the UN Charter provides an example of the latter situation, since under this provision suspension will be a possible sanction against a member "against which preventive or enforcement action has been taken." The financial institutions and other international organisations also have a general power of suspension for breach of obligations towards the organisation generally.[65] The Council of Europe can suspend a member for having "seriously violated Article 3," this being the article enjoining acceptance of the rule of law and observance of human rights. Similarly, members of the E.C. and of the E.U. can be suspended in case of "serious and persistent breach" of principles mentioned in Article 6(1) of the Treaty on European Union, *i.e.* the "principles of liberty, democracy, respect for human rights and fundamental freedoms."[66] In the OAS, membership may be suspended when a member's "democratically constituted government has been overthrown by force."[67] The "linkage" of

---

[62] See doc. A/.7146 and the 1671 and 1672 Plen. Mtgs. of G.A., June 12, 1968.

[63] The fact that Art. 19 was not applied in 1965 over the arrears of peace-keeping contributions was due to the particular constitutional conflict over this vexed issue. To avoid a "confrontation" over this, the General Assembly operated during the 19th session by "consensus," avoiding any vote. Indeed, the USA and USSR, the main protagonists over the constitutional issue, joined in opposing Albania's attempt to force a vote. See Padelford, "Financing Peace-Keeping: Politics and Crisis" 19 Int. Orgs. (1965) 444. For more on this episode, see also Schricke, "Commentaire de l'article 19", in Cot and Pellet (Eds.), *La Charte des Nations Unies—Commentaire article par article* (1985) 402.

[64] On the present situation of the United States in that respect, see *infra*, Chap. 17.

[65] IMF, Art. XXIII, section 2 (suspension of the right to use special drawing rights) and Art. XXVI, section 2 (ineligibility to use the general resources of the Fund); IBRD, Art. VI, section 2; IFC, Art. V, section 2; IDA, Art. VII, section 2; MIGA, Art. 52; IFAD, Art. 9, section 2; IAEA, Art. XIX (B) (only for persistent violations).

[66] See Arts 7 of the Treaty on European Union and 309 of the Treaty establishing the European Community, respectively.

[67] Art. 9.

membership of organisations belonging to a same "system" also produces effects on suspension. In some specialised agencies, suspension from the exercise of the rights and privileges of membership of the UN automatically entails suspension from the same rights in the agency.[68]

Not only is there this broad distinction between organisations having **16–020** power to suspend members for non-fulfilment of financial obligations only, and those having wider powers, but it will also be seen that the effect of suspension varies considerably between organisations. In the UN, suspension under Article 19 of the Charter involves merely loss of vote in the General Assembly, whereas suspension under Article 5 involves loss of the "rights" and "privileges of membership" generally, therefore depriving a member of representation as well as vote in all organs.[69] The ILO confines the effect of suspension to loss of vote, but extends it to the Conference, the governing body, any committee or in the elections of members of the Governing Body.[70] WMO, IAEA and UNIDO Constitutions refer to the suspension of rights and privileges "as a member"[71] and the Council of Europe provision clearly covers loss of representation as well as loss of vote.[72] Article 309 of the treaty establishing the E.C. is rather imprecise and obviously gives the Council a wide margin of appreciation since it provides that suspension may concern "certain of the rights deriving from the application of this Treaty."[73]

Those organisations which provide services or more tangible advantages **16–021** have the more effective sanction in using suspension in that it may bring about suspension of these services and advantages. The WMO convention thus speaks of loss of voting privileges "and other services," and all the financial institutions have similarly comprehensive sanctions. The IMF is in a very strong position in being able to sanction any use of the resources contrary to the purposes of the Fund by either limiting the member's use of the Fund or even declaring it ineligible to use those resources.[74] Similarly

---

[68] See, *e.g.* UNESCO, Art. II (4) (upon request of the UN); ICAO, Art. 93 *bis*; UNIDO, Art. 5 (1) (automatically).

[69] See Leben, "Commentaire de l'article 5", in Cot and Pellet (Eds.) *op. cit.* 183. This provision has never been applied (on the alternative sanctions implemented against UN members in persistent breach of their obligations, see *ibid.* 187 *et seq.*

[70] Art. 13 (4). This suspension of privileges should be sharply distinguished from the refusal to approve the credentials of the delegates from a member state, such as occurred in 1958 and 1959 when the General Conference of the ILO rejected the credentials of government, employers' and workers' delegates from Hungary; see *infra*, paras 16–041 *et seq.*

[71] Arts 31 and 5 (1), respectively; see also Art. 9, section 2 (b) of the agreement establishing IFAD.

[72] In the OAS, it is the exercise of the right to participate in the work of all organs of the organisation which is suspended when Art. 9 is applied.

[73] Note also that this provision requires the Council, when it takes such a decision, to "take into account the possible consequences of such a suspension on the rights and obligations of natural and legal persons."

[74] Art. XXIII, section 2.

the IFC in Article V(2) has a quite general power of suspension from membership, the totality of rights and privileges, for a failure by a member to fulfil "any of its obligations to the Corporation." This suspension becomes a cessation of membership one year from the date of suspension unless the member is restored to its "good standing" by a decision of the governors. Article 6(2) of IBRD's Articles of Agreement is similar, and obviously formed the model for it. The extremely effective sanction in the hands of the financial agencies is all the more effective when it is recalled that the three organisations link suspension and cessation of membership, so that to lose the privileges of membership of the IFC and cessation of membership of the Fund, generally involves cessation of membership of the Bank. The same kind of extensive powers of sanction through suspension may also be found in the International Atomic Energy Agency which can enforce the observance of its provisions on safeguards by either suspending all privileges and rights of membership or by curtailing or suspending assistance provided by the Agency or even recalling materials and equipment provided.[75]

16–022 It is clearly desirable that suspension should follow, not as a matter of course upon the occurrence of some event, but rather as a result of the exercise of a discretion by a competent organ; that it should be permissive rather than mandatory, in other words. This is generally so; the apparent exceptions in Article 19 of the Charter, or 13 (4) of the ILO, are not true exceptions, for in both cases there is a proviso for waiver of the sanction when failure to pay financial contributions is "due to conditions beyond the control of the Member."[76] A truer exception is seen in those cases where suspension from one organisation brings about automatic suspension from another.

16–023 The procedure utilised for effecting suspension also varies. It is generally entrusted to the main plenary organ, although in Article 5 of the UN Charter, for example, the recommendation of the Security Council is a prior condition. Moreover, since suspension of a member is eminently a matter for the member states to decide, in organisations like the Council of Europe or the E.C., where the Assembly is not composed of state representatives, the decision is entrusted to the "executive" organ (Committee of Ministers and Council, respectively). The vote required varies, and, although normally a two-thirds majority is required, a simple majority suffices in ICAO and WHO, for example. Surprisingly enough, the requirement of prior notice to the offending member, and the affording to it of a

---

[75] Arts 19(B) and 12(A).

[76] Note however that the Secretary-General has for some time taken the view (opposed by the USSR) that the suspension is automatic unless (a) a challenge is made to the accuracy of the computation of the assessment or (b) the member state petitions the Assembly to use its discretion to waive the sanction (see docs. A/7111, A/7146).

chance to state its own case, are rarely found as essential parts of the procedure except in the financial institutions.

Particular problems may arise when initiatives are taken to suspend a **16–024** member in the absence of any provision authorising suspension in an organisation's constitutive instrument, or for motives others than that or those specified in the constituent. Such situations are not exceptional. Organisations like the ITU, the OAU or the OECD, for example, have no provisions for suspension, nor has UNESCO any independent power of suspension, since suspension occurs only as the automatic result of suspension from the UN. As set out above, in a number of organisations, provision is made for suspension only in the event of a member's failure to fulfil its financial obligations.

Between the 1960s and the 1980s, such situations led to acute controver- **16–025** sies in organisations in which an attempt was made to exclude South Africa from participation in meetings, although the constitutions of those organisations confined the power of exclusion, or suspension from participation, to very limited circumstances. The ILO,[77] WHO, UNESCO, ITU and UPU were among organisations which were presented with concerted moves of this kind.[78] An attempt to exclude South Africa from UNCTAD in 1968 was rejected by the General Assembly, and ICAO rejected a proposal to exclude South Africa in 1965. However, in 1975 WMO did suspend South Africa's membership on the grounds that the practice of apartheid was not conducive to the fulfilment of the objectives of WMO. There has thus been no consistent practice on this matter.

In the absence of a specific power of suspension serious doubts have **16–026** been expressed as to whether an organisation can exercise such a power against a member (hence the various "constitutional crises" referred to above). It seems however possible to argue that when there is a nexus between the motive for suspension and the rules and purposes of an organisation (the member's behaviour being in breach of the rules of the organisation), suspension of a member's rights and privileges may be invoked as a countermeasure, even in the absence of specific provisions on suspension in the constituent instrument.[79] In such a case, the wrongfulness

---

[77] South Africa withdrew from that organisation in 1964 following the sanctions of suspension threatened against it.

[78] In 1965 ITU resolved to exclude South Africa from Regional Conferences in Africa and all Plenipotentiary Conferences even though, in 1964, this had led to a major constitutional crisis in which the European members withdrew and the Conference adjourned sine die. The year 1966 saw a similar clash in UPU. In 1966 WHO suspended Portugal from participation in the Regional Committee for Africa and suspended technical assistance to Portugal in accordance with G.A. res. 2107 (X)C), para. 9. For the refusal of the IBRD to do so see *supra*, Chap. 3.

[79] Countermeasures have initially been envisaged by (then) special rapporteur R. Ago as covering all kinds of reactions to wrongful acts, and as including sanctions taken by international organisations against their members.

of the prima facie illegal act(s) of the international organisation which decides to suspend one its members' rights is precluded, since—and inasmuch as—it merely constitutes a reaction to prior wrongful acts attributable to that member. The conditions which countermeasures have to meet to be considered as legitimate should of course be respected, in particular proportionality between the initial wrongful act and the organisation's reaction.[80]

16–027 It may finally be noted that suspension does not free a member from its obligations but merely suspends the exercise of rights or privileges of one kind or another. This is explicitly specified in few constituent instruments only,[81] but must clearly be regarded as a principle of general application.

(c) TERMINATION OF MEMBERSHIP

16–028 Apart from the case of dissolution of the organisation,[82] termination of membership is likely to arise in three different ways: by withdrawal, as the voluntary act of the member (i); by expulsion, as a measure taken by the organisation against a member (ii); and by the loss of membership consequent upon a member's refusal to accept an amendment to the constitution of the organisation (iii).[83]

(i) Withdrawal

Bibliography: Singh, *Termination of Membership in International Organisations* (1958); Feinberg, "Unilateral withdrawal from an international organisation, 39 BYIL 189 (1963); Stein and Carreau, "Law and Peaceful Change in a Subsystem: "Withdrawal" of France for the North Atlantic Treaty Organisation", 62 AJIL 557 (1968); Alford, "The Prospective Withdrawal of the United States from the International Labor Organisation: Rationales and Implications", 17 Harv ILJ 623 (1976); Magliveras "The withdrawal from the League of Nations revisited", 10 Dickinson Journal Of International Law 25 (1991); Dock, "Le retrait des Etats membres des organisations internationales de la famille des Nations Unies", 40 AFDI (1994) 106.

16–029 A specific right of withdrawal is found in the constitutions of a large number of international organisations. It is amongst others the case in most

---

[80] For more on these conditions in the context of state responsibility, see Arts 49 and 50 of the ILC draft on state responsibility (as adopted in first reading by the Commission in 1996; doc. A/51/10, rep. in 37 ILM (1998) 440). The applicability of these conditions to countermeasures taken by international organisations is not disputed.

[81] See, *e.g.* Art. 9, section 2(b) of the agreement establishing IFAD, according to which "while under suspension, a Member shall not be entitled to exercise any rights under this Agreement, except the right of withdrawal, but shall remain subject to all of its obligations;" see also Art. 9(e) of the OAS Charter.

[82] On which see *supra*, Chap. 15, paras 15–109 *et seq.*

[83] See generally Singh, *Termination of Membership of International Organisations* (1958).

of the specialised agencies and in most regional organisations.[84] In contrast, there is no provision on withdrawal in the UN or WHO, or in the treaties establishing the E.U. and the E.C., for instance. There is considerable variation in the conditions attached to the right of withdrawal, when it is allowed. Whereas the financial institutions allow withdrawal simply upon submission of written notice, and allow this withdrawal to take effect immediately, other organisations impose clear limitations on withdrawal. In some cases it is not permitted during an initial period, so as to allow the organisation time to become established.[85] Sometimes a period is prescribed between the giving of notice to withdraw and the coming into effect of withdrawal, a kind of "cooling-off" period[86] to allow for reconsideration (and possibly a change of government) or even necessary budgetary readjustments.[87] A fourth condition sometimes attached to withdrawal is that outstanding obligations must be fulfilled before withdrawal is effective. In general the obligations specified are simply the financial obligations incurred as part of the budgetary commitment; thus Article 1(5) of ILO suspends effectiveness of withdrawal until financial obligations are fulfilled.[88]

When an organisation has working capital rather than a budget, as is the **16–030** case with the financial institutions, the settlement of accounts with a withdrawing member is even more complicated. To take the IBRD by way of example, under Article VI(4) the member remains liable for direct obligations to the bank and for contingent liabilities to the bank so long as its loans or guarantees remain outstanding; the member's shares are repurchased by the bank at their book value subject to the bank's right of set-off for amounts due under loans or guarantees. In some cases the fulfilment of obligations other than financial ones is specified. The ILO is a very special case in providing (in all likelihood *ex abundante cautela*) that withdrawal shall not affect the continued validity of obligations arising under any international labour convention to which the member withdrawing is a party (Article 1(5)). It is, of course, clear that even in the absence of such provision withdrawal could not in any event affect the obligations already incurred; these would still subsist, at least in the case of the

---

[84] See, *e.g.* IMF (Art. XXVI), IBRD (Art. VI), MIGA (Art. 51), ILO (Art. 1(5)), UNESCO (Art. II(6)), WIPO (Art. 18), FAO (Art. XIX), IFAD (Art. 9(1)), UNIDO (Art. 6), IMO (Art. 73), WMO (Art. 30), ITU (Art. 57), WTO (Art. XV), OECD (Art. 17), Council of Europe (Art. 7), OAS (Art. 143), OAU (Art. 31), ECOWAS (Art. 91).

[85] Such period may range from one year in the case of IMO (Art. 73) to 50 in that of ECSC (Art. 97).

[86] This period usually is of one (as in WMO, IMO, ITU and OECD, for instance) or two years (as in ILO and OAS, for instance). It is however of six months only in IFAD and WIPO, for instance.

[87] As in the Council of Europe, where withdrawal takes effect only "at the end of the financial year."

[88] Art. 1(3) of the League of Nations Covenant formulated the same limitation.

financial obligations. It is simply that a state might be more ready to pay if its effective withdrawal depended on settlement. States have availed themselves of such withdrawal clauses on several occasions: to mention a few examples, Greece withdrew from the Council of Europe in 1969, the United States from ILO in 1989 and from UNIDO in 1996,[89-90] the U.S., the United Kingdom and Singapore from UNESCO in 1984 and 1986, respectively.[91]

16–031   Considerable problems arise in the absence of any withdrawal clause. Prima facie a state must be deemed to be free to withdraw unless it has surrendered that right expressly or impliedly.[92] Therefore, in the absence of a withdrawal clause one is left with the problem of ascertaining what obligations the parties intended to assume in this respect. In the case of the UN Charter, which contains no withdrawal clause due to the desire of the parties to emphasise their aspirations to stability and permanence, it is nevertheless clear from the *travaux préparatoires* that the right to withdraw "in exceptional circumstances" (to use the phrase of the report of Committee I/2) was conceded.[93] The decision of Indonesia to "withdraw" from the UN (and also the specialised agencies) in January 1965 was eventually followed by a decision in September 1966 to "resume full co-operation" and the General Assembly concurred in the Secretary-General's view that Indonesia's absence was to be regarded as a cessation of co-operation, not withdrawal.[94] Again, in the absence of any provision, members have withdrawn from WHO and UNESCO,[95] although their subsequent re-entry makes it possible to regard this as a temporary rather than permanent decision.[96] In November 1983 the Council of Foreign Ministers of the European Communities decided to negotiate the terms of Greenland's withdrawal from the EEC and its transfer into an overseas country and

---

[89-90] See Nash, Contemporary Practice of the United States Relating to International Law, 91 AJIL (1997) 93.

[91] See U.N.J.Y. (1985) 91; on U.K.'s withdrawal, see also 57 B.Y.B.I.L. (1986) 523. The U.K. rejoined this Organisation in 1997.

[92] For the contrary argument see Feinburg, "Unilateral Withdrawal from an International Organisation" 39 B.Y.B.I.L. (1963) 215.

[93] UNCIO, Doc. 1178, I/2176(2), p. 5; see generally Kelsen, *Law of the UN.*, Chap. 7. The inability to accept an amendment was one of the situations listed by the Committee as a possible "exceptional circumstance" justifying withdrawal.

[94] The Secretary-General negotiated a financial settlement whereby Indonesia paid 10% of its usual assessment for 1965 and 25% for 1966. See Livingstone "Withdrawal from the UN", 14 ICLQ (1965) 637 and Blum, ibid. 16 ICLQ (1967) 522. Contrast the position in IMF and IBRD, both having an express withdrawal clause: Indonesia withdrew in 1965 and was formally re-admitted in 1967.

[95] There was no withdrawal clause in UNESCO's Constitution before 1954.

[96] Several states of the Soviet bloc "withdrew" from WHO between 1949 and 1955; Poland, Hungary and Czechoslovakia "withdrew" from UNESCO between 1952 and 1954. In both cases the organisations regarded these states simply as having temporarily ceased to participate and in fact a nominal budgetary contribution was exacted when they resumed participation to cover their years of absence.

territory (OCT). The transfer was completed on January 1, 1985, and came about as a response to a referendum held in Greenland in 1982 where the local government mandated a request to the Danish Government to negotiate the withdrawal of Greenland form the EEC. Although the EEC Treaty had no provision on withdrawal, and was widely considered not to permit it, the issue raised little legal debate at the time.[97]

Practice therefore appears rather inconclusive. Article 56(1) of the **16–032** Vienna Convention on the Law of Treaties provides some guidance in that respect; it states that:

> "A treaty which contains no provision regarding its termination and which does not provide for denunciation or withdrawal is not subject to denunciation or withdrawal unless:
> (a) It is established that the parties intended to admit the possibility of denunciation or withdrawal; or
> (b) A right of denunciation or withdrawal may be implied by the nature of the treaty."

This obviously leaves room for interpretation of the parties' intention or **16–033** of the treaty's nature. Such a determination is however not always beyond reach : a clear provision that a treaty such as a military alliance, creating an organisation, was to be of a fixed duration might for instance reflect unambiguously the intention of the parties and imply a surrender of the right to withdraw.[98] What is certainly clear is that mere silence on the question of withdrawal is not adequate to deprive a member of the right to withdraw.

(ii) Expulsion

The compulsory cessation of membership as a result of the decision of the **16–034** organisation is by no means generally envisaged in constitutions of international organisations. Article 6 of the UN Charter contemplates expulsion for persistent violation of the principles of the Charter, and so does Article 8 of the Statute of the Council of Europe for a "serious violation" of the fundamental principles of the organisation as set out in Articles 1 and 3. Of the specialised agencies, UNESCO (Article II(5)) and ICAO (Article 93*bis* (a)(1)) link expulsion from those organisations with expulsion from the

---

[97] See F. Weiss, "Greenland's withdrawal from the European Communities" *10 European Law Review* (1985), pp. 173–185.

[98] The proposed European Defence Community Treaty was silent on withdrawal and was expressed to be for 50 years; this probably prevented withdrawal. A provision similar to Art. 13 of the NATO Treaty allowing denunciation after 20 years must be regarded as an express provision preventing withdrawal during that period. But see *supra*, Chap. 6 on the French decision to withdraw from participation in certain activities of NATO without formally withdrawing from the organisation.

UN. The international financial institutions also contemplate expulsion in the sense that, in the organisations of the World Bank group, a suspension automatically ripens into expulsion after one year unless the Governors decide to restore the member to good standing,[99] and in the Fund a member which persists in its failure to observe its obligations can be "compelled to withdraw" (Article XXVI (2)). In those organisations, expulsion is always discretionary and never automatic.

16–035   In the absence of an expulsion clause it may be doubted whether, in general, an organisation has the power to expel a member. There is, however, the decision of the Meeting of Consultation of Ministers of Foreign Affairs of January 31, 1962 to exclude Cuba from participation in OAS,[1] a decision taken without specific constitutional power to expel. A number of the abstaining members, and Cuba itself, expressed misgivings over the legality of this step. Similar misgivings have been expressed over decisions within various of the specialised agencies, such as ITU and UPU, to exclude South Africa from participation in certain organs.[2] Of a similar kind was the decision by UNESCO to exclude Israel from the European Group in 1974. Because of doubts over the legality of this decision, France and the USA reduced their contributions to UNESCO, and in 1977 Israel was re-admitted to the European Group. In 1979 the UPU took the final step of expelling South Africa.[3] The member states of the European Community issued a joint declaration, claiming that this step was illegal, since the UPU constitution had no provision for expulsion: they therefore considered South Africa to be still a member and continued to treat her as such. Israel has also been excluded from membership of any one of five regional groupings of member of the UN, a situation which Sir Robert Jennings has described as "manifestly unlawful" and in breach of the letter and spirit of the UN Charter.[4]

16–036   Such reactions clearly support the view that, in the absence of an express constitutional power to expel, the general rule is that a member cannot be expelled. But, as it already was the case with suspension, it may on the other hand be argued that exclusion of a member in serious and persistent breach of its obligations towards the organisation could be considered as a legitimate countermeasure taken by that organisation.[5] It has even been

---

[99] IBRD and IFC, Art. VI (2); IDA, Art. VII, Section 2 (a); MIGA, Art. 52 (d). A similar regime is provided for in the Agreement establishing the IFAD (Art. 9, section 1 (a) in fine).

[1] Dept. State Bull., Vol. 46, No. 1182, 281.

[2] In 1969 the UPU Congress actually expelled the South African delegation from its 16th meeting: see (1969) U.N.J.Y. 118. An attempt to expel South Africa from the UN was vetoed in October 1974.

[3] See U.N.J.Y. (1979) 90.

[4] See opinion Regarding the Exclusion of Israel from the United Nations Regional Group System, November 4, 1999, available at http://www.mfa.gov.il.

[5] A measure of expulsion would of course have to meet the conditions set out in the ILC draft to be considered as a legitimate countermeasure (see *supra*, and n. 80).

written in that sense that expulsion, when used to protect the organisation (*i.e.* to maintain consistency within the organisation), should be "considered as an implied power of every organisation to enable it to defend itself against a situation which would prevent it from functioning."[6] Expulsion is also most likely justified when a member, having accepted by the constitution a procedure for amending the constitution without the consent of all the members, declines to recognise an amendment constitutionally effected. That being said, it may well be that expulsion and even suspension are of doubtful value, at least for a "political" organisation. The danger is, of course, that except when a member has decided advantages to lose by suspension or expulsion, as may be the case with the financial organisations, the suspension or expulsion simply removes the recalcitrant member from the very pressures of general opinion which, constantly in play within the organisation, are perhaps the best means of securing a return to fulfilment of obligations. The correct position was put by C.W. Jenks as far back as 1942 when, although writing with expulsion for non-payment of financial obligations in mind, he made this observation, which can equally be applied to suspension or expulsion in general:

> "International institutions are not clubs from which unpleasant and disagreeable members can be blackballed to the general advantage; they are an attempt to create machinery of government for a world where the unpleasant and the disagreeable cannot be assumed not to exist. Denationalisation is not normally regarded as an appropriate remedy when an individual fails to pay his income tax, and expulsion from an international institution is no more appropriate as a remedy when a Government defaults upon a payment due to the international fisc."[7]

(iii) Non-ratification of an amendment to a constitution

It is very rare to find specific provisions governing this matter. Article 26 of **16–037** the Covenant of the League of Nations did provide that amendments were to take effect when ratified by all members of the Council and a majority of the members of the Assembly, but that they should not bind dissenting members who "shall cease to be [members] of the League." Article 94 of ICAO provides that, in recommending the adoption of an amendment, the Assembly may provide that a member which has not ratified the amendments within a specified period shall cease to be a member.

There are, as we have seen in discussing amendments earlier,[8] broadly **16–038** two types of amendment procedures: those which adopt the "legislative" principle of allowing amendments by a majority, with binding effect on all

---

[6] Schermers and Blokker, *op. cit.,* para. 142.
[7] Jenks, "Financing of International Institutions" 38 T.G.S. (1943) 111.
[8] See *Supra*, Chap. 14, paras 14–002 *et seq.*

members, and those which make the amendment binding on individual members only with their consent. In the first category there is much to be said for providing expressly for compulsory withdrawal of the member, since it is declining to accept the will of the majority which it agreed in advance to accept; it may well be that, even without express provision, an organisation would be justified in expelling the member concerned in such circumstances. In the second category the dilemma is posed that the member has not agreed to be bound except with its consent, and yet in practice it is unwise to admit that any one member can either veto an amendment or remain a member under the terms of the old constitution whilst the majority continue under the amended constitution. In such a case withdrawal should be permitted, and probably compelled.[9]

16–039   This is essentially a problem facing the large, multipartite constitutions; in smaller organisations, such as the European Union, acceptance of amendments by all members is so essential to the well-being of the organisation that ratification by all members is made a pre-condition to the entry into force of the amendment.[10]

16–040   Whether it results from withdrawal, expulsion or refusal to accept an amendment to the organisation's constituent instrument, termination of membership of an international organisation in all cases entails legal and practical consequences. Hence, a member whose membership is terminated may not be represented as such within the organisation,[11] participate in the work of its organs, or use the services provided by the organisation, and it is only exceptionally that nationals of that (ex) member may be considered for recruitment by the organisation.[12]

B. REPRESENTATION

(a) REPRESENTATION OF MEMBERS

Bibliography: Briggs, "Chinese Representation in the United Nations", 6 Int. Org. 192 (1952); Higgins, *The Development of International Law through the Political Organs of the United nations* (1963); Ciobanu, "Credentials of Delegations and representation of members States at the United nations" 25 ICLQ 351 (1976); Erasmus, "The Rejection of credentials: A Proper Exercise

---

[9] IMCO, in adopting the constitutional amendments of 1964, resolved that members failing to accept them had to withdraw: A/ES. 11/Res. 69 and A IV/Res. 70.

[10] See Art. 48 of the Treaty on European Union.

[11] It may, however, obtain an observer status, as the U.S. and U.K. did with UNESCO after their withdrawal from that organisation. In UNESCO, the conditions under which observer status may be granted under such circumstances are specified in resolution 0.9 of 1985 (23rd session).

[12] For the situation in UNESCO, see para. 7 of the abovementioned resolution. On the financial consequences of withdrawal, see *e.g.* Dock, Le retrait des Etats membres des organisations internationales de la famille des Nations Unies, 40 A.F.D.I. (1994) 142–154.

of general assembly Powers or Suspension by Stealth", 7 SAYIL 40 (1981); Halberstam, "Excluding Israel from the General Assembly by a Rejection of its Credentials", 78 *AJIL* 179 (1984); Suttner, "Has South Africa been Illegally Excluded from the United nations General assembly", 17 CILSA 279 (1984); Flauss & Singer, "La vérification des pouvoirs à l'Assemblée générale des Nations Unies", 1985 AFDI 620.

The representation of the member of an international organisation **16–041** should be distinguished from the question of admission to membership; representation presupposes admission to the organisation and is concerned with the question of the persons to be recognised as being entitled to represent the member within the organs of the organisation.

Many organisations will provide for the number of representatives who **16–042** may serve on a delegation: for example each member state may have up to five representatives on its delegation at the United Nations General Assembly (Charter, Article 9(2)), whereas the IAEA allows one delegate per state at the General Conference (Statute, Article VB). Generally there is no qualitative restriction on who may serve as a representative, although some organisations require members of delegations to have particular qualifications. The classical example is the Conference of the ILO, at which each state has four representatives, two from government and one each representing employers and employees (Article 2(3)). Similarly, the WMO requires each member's delegation to include a representative of the Director of the national meteorological service (Article 7b), and the WHO requires that the three delegates at the World Health Assembly should be chosen from amongst the persons who are the most highly qualified in matters of health (Article 11).

Subject to requirements of this kind, a member of an organisation is free **16–043** in principle to nominate who it wishes to represent its interests before a particular organ of an international organisation. Occasionally, however, differences arise, as illustrated by a recent matter before a Dispute Settlement Panel established by the WTO Dispute Settlement Body. In a dispute between the United States and others against the European Union (in respect of the latter's banana import regime) a number of third states, including St. Lucia, intervened as third parties. At a Panel hearings in 1997 the Ambassador of St. Lucia appeared accompanied by advisors from the private sector, who were not nationals of St Lucia. The United States moved for the removal from the room of the two advisers, on the grounds that the dispute settlement procedure under the WTO system was an inter-governmental system in which non-state actors, in this case private lawyers, were not entitled to participate. That view was upheld by the WTO Panel. On appeal, the Appellate Body reversed, confirming that not-withstanding the intergovernmental character of the dispute settlement system, a member state was free, in accordance with customary international law and in the absence of express rules to the contrary, to nominate whoever it wished to represent its interests.[13]

16–044   Such restrictions as do exist on the composition of delegations do not, however, often raise legal issues or disputes. Where the issue of representation has been contentious is in the situation where two rival governments exist, both claiming to represent the state concerned, or when objection is taken to the circumstances in which a government has achieved power, or when one state succeeds another. Examples of these cases include China (until 1971), Germany, Hungary, the Russian Federation (after the dissolution of the USSR), Yugoslavia, and Afghanistan. Here the issue of the representation of a member will typically arise in the context of the examination of the credentials issued to a particular individual by the head of state or government or by a ministry of foreign affairs. Most organisations have a Credentials Committee: in the case of the General Assembly of the United Nations, for example, it comprises nine members appointed by the Assembly on the proposal of the President, who may determine the authority to represent a member in accordance with Rule 27 of the Rules of Procedure of the GA. It is in the case of disputed governments that the issue of representation usually arises, and often in the Credentials Committee.

16–045   The problem of representation in the case of competing governments is traditionally illustrated by the problems arising from the competing claims of the Nationalist Government and the Government of the People's Republic of China to represent China within the United Nations, between 1949 and 1971. In practice the question is dealt with under the rules of procedure of each organ of the United Nations, since it is not directly dealt with in the Charter. Hence, within the Security Council, representation was treated as a matter of credentials and under Rule 17—a representative to whom objection has been made continues to sit until the Council, by a simple majority vote, decides to expel him. Hence the Nationalist representative continued to sit until nine members were prepared to oppose him. Within the Assembly the vote on Chinese representation was initially regarded as procedural, but in 1962 was resolved to be an "important question" requiring a two-thirds majority for any change.[14]

---

[13] WTO, European Communities, regime applicable to the import, sale and distribution of bananas, September 9, 1997, WT/DS27/AB/R (97–3593); see also http://www.wto.org/wto/english/disputef/distabf.htm.

[14] (1962) UN Review, January, 38.

Various attempts have been made to discuss the substantive issues which **16–046** lie behind the question of representation which is generally treated as procedural. A memorandum of the UN Secretary-General in 1950[15] attempted to distinguish representation from the question of recognition by other member states and suggested that competing claims by two rival governments should be resolved according to a test of "effectiveness". In 1950 the General Assembly adopted resolution 396(V), in which it recommended that "whenever more than one authority claims to be the government entitled to represent a member state in the United Nations and this question becomes the subject of controversy in the United Nations, the question should be considered in the light of the purposes and principles of the Charter and the circumstances of each case." The resolution did not provide a great deal of assistance on difficult cases, including that of the People's Republic of China. Opposition to PRC representation was led by the United States but support for its position dwindled until, finally, on October 25, 1971 the General Assembly recognised the representatives of the People's Republic as "the only legitimate representative of China" and determined that the People's Republic is "one of the five permanent members of the Security Council."[16] The Assembly thus rejected any idea of Taiwan being given separate representation (although the question has not yet been finally resolved). As a result, the Assembly's own decision was quickly accepted and followed in the Security Council and various specialised agencies.[17] Whilst the Chinese problem has been the crucial one, it is by no means unique. Similar difficulties in circumstances of claims to representation by competing governments arose in relation to the representation of Congo in 1960, of Yemen in 1962 and of Kampuchea from 1970 to 1991,[18] as well as Zaire in 1993 and Afghanistan in 1999.

The issue of representation has also arisen where there are no competing **16–047** claimants, but rather where the legitimacy of a governmental authority was being challenged. This occurred in respect of Hungarian representation at the UN following the Soviet intervention of 1956: since the representatives of the new regime were the only feasible representatives they were allowed to sit but formal approval of their credentials was for a time withheld in the

---

[15] S/1466. In connection with the Chinese representation problem see Quincy Wright, "The Chinese Recognition Problem" (1955) 49 A.J.I.L. 320; O'Connell, "The status of Formosa and the Chinese Recognition Problem" *ibid.* (1956) Vol. 50, 405; Steiner "Communist China in the world community" (1961) 533 Int. Council.; Stone, Legal Controls of International Conflict (1959), pp. 238–242; Fitzmaurice, "Chinese representation in the UN" (1952) Y.B.W.A. 36.

[16] G.A. Res. 2758 (XXVI); see UNYB (1971), pp. 126–137.

[17] *UN Yearbook* (1971) 126–137. Although the PRC's acceptance into the other agendas was not immediate in all cases, depending on China's own wishes. For the arrangements with the IBRD in 1980 see (1981) 20 ILM 777.

[18] See, respectively, G.A. res. 1498 (XV), G.A. res. 1871 (XVII), and Warbrick, "Kampuchea: Representation and Recognition", 30 ICLQ 234–46 (1981).

UN by the Credentials Committee of the Assembly taking no decision regarding the credentials (but not opposing them). Other examples include the representation of Israel, Portugal and Chile, as well as South Africa. Prior to 1974, the view had been taken, both in the UN and in the specialised agencies, that failure to approve the credentials of South Africa (because of its refusal to comply with resolutions on Namibia) did not affect the rights and privileges of membership: that is to say, the non-approval of credentials, a procedural matter, could not be made an indirect way of achieving the same results as sanctions under Articles 5, or 6, or 19 of the United Nations Charter. In 1974, having failed to get adopted a resolution to expel South Africa from membership of the United Nations, the Afro-Asian bloc succeeded in having the General Assembly interpret, under the presidency of Mr Bouteflika, the non-approval of credentials as, in effect, suspending South Africa from any participation in the session. That action, which continued until the change of regime in South Africa in 1994, was considered by some commentators to be unconstitutional.[19]

16–048   Clearly the issue is not confined to the UN. Reference may be made to the independent action of the General Conference of the ILO in rejecting the credentials of Government, Employers' and Workers' delegates from Hungary in 1958 and 1959.[20] In 1981 the General Conference of the IAEA threatened Israel with suspension if it did not comply with a Security Council resolution condemning its attack on an Iraqi nuclear reactor and submitting its own nuclear installations to IAE control. The following year, in the absence of Israel' s having so complied, the IAEA General Conference voted by 43 votes to 27 against (with 16 abstentions) to suspend Israel. However, the majority was not sufficient for the resolution to take effect, so the conference moved to reject the credentials of the Israeli delegation, which it did on the basis of a simple majority vote.[21] The Credentials Committee by seven to six votes rejected the credentials of the Israeli delegation.

(b) REPRESENTATION OF OTHER INTERESTS

Bibliography: Suy, "The Status of Observers in International Organisations", 160 Rec. des Cours (1978–II) 75–179; Feuerle, "Informal consultations: a Mechanism in Security Council Decision-Making", 18 NYU JILP 267 (1985); "The accountability of international organisations to non-state ators", 92 Proc. ASIL 359 (1998); van Boven, "The Role of non-governmental organiza-

---

[19] See 4th edition of this book (1982) at p. 397. Also Simma (ed.), *The Charter of the United Nations* (1995), p. 225.

[20] On the procedure of the ILO (somewhat complicated because of the tripartite structure) see Jenks, *The International Protection of Trade Union Freedom* (1957), Chap. 4, and in March 1971 the OAU failed to agree when faced with rival delegations from Uganda.

[21] See Gross, "On the Degradation of the Constitutional Environment of the UN", v. 77 (July 1983) AJIL 569–88 (1983).

tions in international human rights standard-setting: a prerequisite of democracy", 20 Cal.WesternILJ 207 (1989/90); Novrot, "Legal consequences of globalisation: the status of non-governmental organisations under international law", 6 Ind.J.Glob.Leg.St. 579 (1999); Sladin, "Participatory development and NGOs: a look at the World Bank", 9 Trans.L.&Contem.Probs 175 (1999); Sands, "The International Lawyer and the Non-State Actor", in Wickremasinghe (ed), The International Lawyer as Practitioner (2000).

In the practice of many organisations, provision is made for the **16–049** representation of interests other than members. A distinction may be made between the representation of the interests of states (or groups of states) which are not members of the organisation, and the representation of non-state interests, including international organisations, national liberation movements, and non-governmental organisations (including the corporate sector).

With regard to the representation of non-member states, we have **16–050** considered forms of participation which are available to states which fall short of membership, such as associate membership.[22] States have been— and continue to be—the principal actors in the life of international organisations, but with the advent of the creation of international organisations numerous changes have occurred. We have already seen how it is possible for one international organisation to become a member of another, and how associate membership may also be available to international organisations. But in the modern world it has become evident that states and international organisations are not the only international actors: national liberation movements (such at the PLO), entities forming part of a federal state and non-state actors such as corporations, individuals and non-governmental organisations are now actively involved in international affairs including the activities of international organisations. Over time the representation of their interests in the activities of international organisations has been increasingly recognised and now features as regular part of the life of many organisations, including the United Nations.

Indeed, one of the most striking developments in international organisa- **16–051** tions has been the gradual breakdown of the monopoly once enjoyed by states in representation in international organisations. This has been achieved in various ways. First there has been the use of the device of "associate membership" to secure representation of non-state entities; the prime examples are the Council of Europe, OECD, UPU, WMO and ITU.[23] Whilst this is not confined to non-political organisations, so that one finds associate members contemplated in Article 5 of the Statute of the Council of Europe,[24] this category is unlikely to be of great appeal to

---

[22] See *supra.* para. 16–008.
[23] See *supra ibid.*.
[24] See *supra.* para. 16–009.

sovereign states in a political organisation, particularly since it usually carries diminished rights.

16–052   The granting of observer status is another way of allowing the representation of state and non-state interests. This status commonly allows a non-member or a non-state entity to submit documents or perhaps speak in debate, though without the right to vote or financial responsibilities and rights. However, in an organisation with membership confined to sovereign states, the matter is not without its controversies. A prime example is the decision of the United Nations General Assembly to extend an invitation—by resolution 3237 (XXIX)—to the Palestinian Liberation Organisation in 1974 to "participate in the sessions and the work of the General Assembly in the capacity of observer" and in its international conferences. This was challenged by some members, as was the Security Council's invitation to the PLO to participate in its debate on the Lebanese complaint of an Israeli air attack on Palestinian refugee camps in 1975.[25] The PLO has also been admitted as an observer to the ILO Conference which, in 1975, amended its Standing Orders to allow representation of liberation movements recognised by either the OAU or the Arab League. This route was also taken by the General Assembly in 1974.[26]

16–053   The potential for legal issues arising out of observer status is illustrated by subsequent developments concerning the PLO's observer mission at the United Nations, which had been established in 1974 through the maintenance of an office in New York City outside the United Nations Headquarters District. In May 1987 a Bill was introduced into the Senate of the United States, the purpose of which was "to make unlawful the establishment and maintenance within the United States of an office of the Palestine Liberation Organisation". The text of the Bill became an amendment to the "Foreign Relations Authorisation Act, Fiscal Years 1988 and 1989," from the terms of which it appeared that the United States Government would, if the Bill became law, seek to close the office of the PLO Observer Mission. On October 13, 1987 the Secretary-General wrote to the United States Permanent Representative to the United Nations that the proposed legislation ran counter to obligations arising from the Headquarters Agreement; the following day the PLO Observer brought the matter to the attention of the United Nations Committee on Relations with the host country. Subsequently a spokesman for the Secretary-General issued a statement to the effect that sections 11–13 of the Headquarters

---

[25] Much of the argument in the Security Council turned on the fact that Rules 37 and 39 of the Rules of Procedure did not cover or allow for such participation. Yet, if an organ is master of its own procedure that argument is trivial: the more fundamental point was whether the decision was contrary to the Charter's limitation of membership to states.

[26] G.A. res. 3280(XXIX) (1974) granted UN observer status automatically to African national liberation movements recognised by the OAU.

Agreement placed a treaty obligation on the United States to permit the personnel of the Mission to enter and remain in the United States in order to carry out their official functions. In December 1987 the Foreign Relations Authorisation Act Fiscal Years 1988–1989 became law. Following consultations the United Nations Secretary-General reached the view that the United States was not fully respecting the Headquarters Agreement and invoked the dispute settlement procedure set out in section 21 of the Agreement. The United Nations took the view that that the measures envisaged by Congress and eventually taken by the United States Administration would be incompatible with the Headquarters Agreement if applied to the PLO Mission, and their adoption gave rise to a dispute with regard to the interpretation and application of the Agreement. The United States had not disputed that certain of its provisions applied to the PLO Observer Mission, and taken a number of measures against the PLO Observer Mission which were regarded by the Secretary-General as contrary to the Agreement. The United States had stated that the measures in question had been taken "irrespective of any obligations the United States may have under the Agreement." By way of advisory opinion the court unanimously ruled that since the two positions were irreconcilable there existed a dispute between the United Nations and the United States concerning the application of the Headquarters Agreement and the United States was under an obligation, in accordance with section 21 of the Agreement, to enter into arbitration for the settlement of the dispute between itself and the United Nations.[27]

The PLO case indicated the legal issues that can arise in relation to the **16–054** rights of observer missions. There does not exist a general law on the functions and rights of observers. The 1975 Convention on the Representation of States in their Relations with International Organisations of a Universal Character reflects the view that permanent observer missions of states have the following functions:

"(a) ensuring the representation of the sending state and safeguarding its interests in relation to the organisation and maintaining liaison with it;

(b) ascertaining activities in the organisation and reporting thereon to the Government of the sending state;

(c) promoting co-operation with the organisation and negotiating with it."[28]

The rights of observers are rarely addressed by the constituent instru- **16–055** ment of an organisation, and consequently fall to be determined by the practise of the organisation or by adoption of particular rules. In general

---

[27] 1988 I.C.J. Reps, p. 33.
[28] 69 AJIL 730 (1975).

the rules governing observers recognise a right to participate in the work of the organisation, including particular organs, but without the right to vote in decision-making or, usually, to sponsor decisions or resolutions. Participation may include access to sessions of the organ, notification of meetings and sessions, the circulation of written statements and access to official documents and, on occasion, the right to make oral statements. In some cases there may be a possibility of observers receiving financial support to enable their participation.[29] Observer missions are also entitled to determine the composition of their delegations.[30] There is, moreover, the question of the entitlement of privileges and immunities of observer missions, a matter addressed by the 1975 Vienna Convention in its Article 30. The approach of the 1975 Convention has not met with widespread acceptance, indicating one of the reasons why none of the host states of the UN has yet ratified the 1975 Convention.[31] The approach taken in the United Nations, where each organ is subject to its own practise and rules, reflects the variety of possibilities.

16–056   The UN Charter is silent as to observer status in the General Assembly. Practise developed from Article 35(2) of the Charter, allowing non-member states to participate in debates of particular interest to them. Subsequently, non-member states gained observer status by communication with the Secretary-General, and today reference is made to observer status of states as having come to be regarded as "an institution of the unwritten constitutional law of the UN", even if in the case of divided states the grant of observer status has been subject to delays, for example in the case of the Democratic Republic of Vietnam (which had to wait 23 years after the Republic of Vietnam had become an observer) and the German Democratic Republic (which waited 20 years after the Federal Republic of Germany had been granted observer status).[32] Currently Switzerland and the Holy See have observer status at the United Nations. The General Assembly allows certain non-statal entities to participate as observers. A number of social and political as well as economic organisations, including groups of states, have been granted observer status at the United Nations pursuant to various General Assembly resolutions.[33] National Liberation movements have also been granted observer status, including the PLO (as described above) and the South West African People's Organisation (SWAPO).

---

[29] See *e.g.* G.A. res. 3280, *supra.* at para. 6.
[30] See G.A. res. 43/48 (1988), concerning the refusal by U.S. authorities to grant a visa to a member of the PLO delegation.
[31] Simma (ed). *The Charter of the United Nations,* (1995), p. 171.
[32] *ibid.*
[33] These include the OAS, the League of Arab states, the OAU, the E.C., the Organisation of the Islamic Conference, the Afro-Asian legal Consultative Committee, the Latin American Economic System, and the ACP.

In the Security Council the matter of observer status is governed by **16–057** Articles 31 and 32 of the Charter. The former provision permits participation without vote of United Nations members in the discussion of any question brought before the Council whenever the Council considers that "the interests of that member are specially affected." This provision is amplified by the Council's Rules of Procedure, including Rule 39 which allows the Council to invite other persons (including members of the secretariat) to participate in its deliberations if such persons could provide information or other assistance. Article 32 requires that members of the United Nations and states which are non-members be invited to participate without vote in discussions relating to a dispute under consideration by the Security Council to which it is a party. Where the entity which is a party to a dispute is not a state participation will be by application of Rule 39 rather than Article 32. In application of Articles 31 and 32 and the Rules of Procedure invitations to participate in meetings of the Council have been extended to a wide range of entities, including non-member states applying for admission to the United Nations, governments or other regimes which are in *de facto* control of a part of a state which is a member of the United Nations, and national liberation movements.

With regard to ECOSOC a clear distinction is drawn in the Charter of **16–058** the United Nations between participation without vote in the deliberations of the Council (observer status) and the arrangements for consultation. Under Articles 69 and 70, participation is provided for only in the case of states not members of ECOSOC and of specialised agencies. Article 71, applying to non-governmental organisations, provides for suitable arrangements for consultation. ECOSOC Resolution 1996/31 (which updated ECOSOC resolution 1296 (XLIV) of May 23, 1968) sought to introduce "coherence" into the rules on consultation as well as those governing participation of NGOs at UN conferences. The resolution provides for consultative relations with national, sub-regional, regional or international NGOs which are concerned with matters falling within the competence of ECOSOC and its subsidiary bodies and whose aims and purposes are in conformity with the spirit, purposes and principles of the Charter of the United Nations. In considering applications for consultative status, ECOSOC must ensure participation from all regions, and particularly from developing countries, to achieve a "just, balanced, effective and genuine involvement" of NGOs from all regions and areas of the world. In deciding on admission to consultative status the organisation must show that its work is of direct relevance to the aims and purposes of the United Nations and, in the case of national organisations, "after consultation with the member state concerned."

ECOSOC provides for three different types of arrangement: first, **16–059** "organisations in general consultative status," that are concerned with most of the activities of ECOSOC and can demonstrate substantive and sustained contributions to the achievement of the objectives of the United Nations; secondly, "organisations in special consultative status", which have a special competence in only a few of the fields of activity covered by ECOSOC; and thirdly, organisations included in a list (referred to as the Roster) that do not have general or special consultative status but that ECOSOC or the Secretary-General of the United Nations consider can make occasional and useful contributions. Consultative status brings with it certain rights: organisations in general and special consultative status may designate representatives to sit as observers at public meetings of ECOSOC and its subsidiary bodies, while those on the Roster may have representatives present at such meetings concerned with matters within their field of competence. Under certain conditions written statements may be submitted by organisations in general or special consultative status, and the former may also make an oral presentation and propose items for the provisional agenda of commissions, both subject to certain conditions. Resolution 1996/31 also makes provisions for suspension and withdrawal, and for the establishment of an ECOSOC Committee on Non-Governmental Organisations.

16–060 Outside the United Nations practise varies widely, with variations on the themes set out above. It should be noted that in many instances the international organisation concerned will have no rules, or no detailed rules, on the participation of entities as observers, including NGOs, raising the question of whether it can be said that common principles might have emerged. The IAEA is one organisation with no general rules on the rights of NGO observers. Its Standing Committee on Nuclear Liability nevertheless permitted three non-governmental organisations—Greenpeace International, UNIPEDE (representing certain electricity producers), and the European Association of Nuclear Insurers—to participate as observers at its sessions. At the beginning of each session the representative of one IAEA member would state his government's opposition to participation of Greenpeace, and its formal objection when, during one session, Greenpeace distributed certain documents to participants. In the absence of any rules establishing what observers were entitled to do the member concerned could not establish that any rules had been broken. The Standing Committee determined permissible practise on document distribution and made this a condition of participation by the observers. This practise was reflected in subsequent reports of the session of the Standing Committee, which stated that the participation of the non-governmental organisations was "on the basis of the understanding reached at the fourth session of the Committee."[34]

---

[34] Report of the Standing Committee on Nuclear Liability, 11th meeting, March 20–24, 1995, IAEA/SCNL/11/INF.5, April 24, 1995, para. 3.

In the context of this discussion it is also appropriate to mention the **16–061** tendency to establish organs in which non-state representatives may appear, either to the exclusion of state representatives or together with them.[35] The reasons for this may well vary. If one takes the secretariats of international organisations, the reason is to ensure the "international character" of the organ and immunise it from the political control of individual states.[36] With judicial organs or bodies such as the ILC the reason is to secure an independent body of individuals with expertise in particular areas who are capable of looking at legal or technical issues with a greater degree of impartiality, whilst recognising the need to represent the principal legal or socio-political systems of the world rather than those of specific states. Whether this ideal is in fact achieved by the systems of elections in the political organs of the United Nations and other organisations is another matter. In some organs the reason is to secure technical direction rather than political discretion; hence in the Commission of the European Communities[37] or the quasi-executive Boards under OECD,[38] the members, whilst appointed by governments, sit in their individual capacities as experts. Within the specialised agencies, as we have seen in examining the organs of limited composition[39] a compromise between traditional diplomatic representation and expert representation is sought by requiring the governments to appoint technically qualified representatives and requiring the organ to exercise its functions on behalf of the plenary organ rather than on behalf of the individual states which the members represent; this is the case with UNESCO, WHO, ITU, and to a lesser extent UPU and the multilateral development banks. In general, however, the use of experts is confined to subsidiary bodies acting in an advisory capacity in relation to the main political organs. Historically, the largely technical bodies comprising the economic and financial organisation of the League of Nations or administrative bodies like the Permanent Mandates Commission or the Permanent Central Opium Board or the International Commission of the Saar,[40] were the bodies in which the experts came into their own, often, significantly, voting by majority rather than the traditional unanimity of the political organs.[41]

---

[35] See Myers, "Representation in Public International Organs" (1914) 8 AJIL 81; Sereni, Organizzazione internazionale (1959), p. 282.

[36] Cross-refer to Chap. X.

[37] See *supra*, Chap. 6.

[38] See *supra*, Chap. 6.

[39] See *supra*, Chap. 3.

[40] Established by the Treaty of Versailles to govern the territory on behalf of the League, it consisted of one citizen of France, one Saar inhabitant (not French), and three persons of neither French nor German nationality, all five being appointed by the Council of the League.

[41] It may be recalled that many people regarded as retrogressive the decision at San Francisco to have the functional commissions of ECOSOC manned by government representatives rather than independent experts; see *supra*, Chap. 2, paras 2–061 *et seq.*

16–062   Within the UN the use of non-state representation, normally by experts, remains fairly restricted; the ILC is an example already mentioned, and others have been the UN Commission on the Racial Situation in the Union of South Africa, various Mixed Arbitration Commissions, the United Nations and other Administrative Tribunals and the Inspection Panel of the World Bank and other multinational development banks. A quite distinct reason from the desirability of expert direction or advice is the recognition that individuals may represent a set of interests, distinct from state interests, which ought to be represented in the organisation if the organisation in order to assist it in achieving its purpose. Hence the tripartite system of representation in the Conference and Governing Body of the ILO[42] is a recognition of the necessity to represent the interests of workers and employers separately from the representation of the state to which they may belong and which is represented by the governmental delegates. A significant, but only recent, elaboration of this approach is the parliamentary representation found in the Consultative Assembly of the Council of Europe[43] and, even more so, in the European Parliament[44]; in both cases the aim is to represent opinion in the national legislatures (or ultimately the opinion of the people, now that direct suffrage is achieved), as opposed to the opinion of the government of the state.

---

[42] See *supra,* Chap. 3, para. 3–050. Another example can be seen in the representation of private operating agencies by their own experts in the Consultative Committees of the ITU; *supra*, p. 000.

[43] See *supra,* Chap. 6, paras 6–012 *et seq.*

[44] See *supra,* Chap. 6, paras 6–049 *et seq.*

CHAPTER 17

FINANCIAL ASPECTS

Bibliography: Jenks, "Some Legal Aspects of the Financing of International Institutions" (1942) 28 TGS 87; Mangone and Srivastava, "Budgeting for the UN" (1958) 12 International Organisation, 473; Singer, *Financing International Organisations: The UN Budget Process* (1961); Stoessinger, *Financing the United Nations System* (1964); Nelson, "Current Development: International Law and US Withholding of Payments to International Organisations" (1986) 80 AJIL 973; Zoller, "The "Corporate Will" of the United Nations and the Rights of the Minority" (1987) 81 AJIL 610; Bovis, "Legal Aspects of the European Union's Public Finances: the Budget and the Communities Own Resources System" (1994) 28 Int'l Law. 743; Cardenas, "Financing the United Nations's Activities: A Matter of Commitment" (1995) U. Ill. L. Rev. 147; Wolfrum and Philipp, *United Nations: Law, Policies and Practice* (1995); Cardenas, "Comments and Remarks on the Papers presented by Francioni and Gerson", *The Role and Limits of Unilateralism in International Law: a United States-European Symposium*, University of Michigan, September 24–25, 1999; Williams, "A Billion Dollar Donation: Should the United Nations Look a Gift Horse in the Mouth" (1999) 27 Ga. J. Int'l & Comp. L. 425.

A. INTRODUCTION

In recent times, the financial aspects of international organisations have **17–001** assumed a central place in their overall affairs. The size of the budget of an international organisation, its means of assessment and the ability to obtain contributions from member states are all fundamental issues in an era when many international organisations face a precarious financial future. The importance of budgetary issues to the ongoing operation, and indeed, viability of modern international organisations is illustrated by the opening paragraph of the UN's "Facts about the United Nations" publication:[1]

> "The United Nations is today, more than ever, engaged in service to all the world's nations and peoples, but its ability to function is hampered by financial problems. Unless Member States pay their debts to the Organisation—over $2.6 billion is owed as of 31 May 1999—the UN will remain in a precarious financial situation."

---

[1] United Nations Department of Public Information—DPI/1753/Rev. 17—June 1999.

17–002   The proposed 2002–03 biennial budget of the UN for financing its core functions was approximately U.S. $2.5 billion.[2] As the organisation has previously pointed out,[3] this is about 4 per cent of New York City's annual budget and nearly a billion dollars less than the yearly cost of Tokyo's Fire Department. In contrast to the modest budget of the UN, the European Union had a budget for 1999 of some 97 billion Euros (approximately U.S. $104 billion). Other regional organisations have less substantial budgets. For its programme budget of January 1 to December 31, 2000, the OAS has approved a total appropriation of some U.S. $88 million, while the current annual budget for the OAU is around U.S. $30 million. Each of the UN specialised agencies has its own budget, with administrative expenses generally covered by funds derived from the UN regular budget. The current budgetary figures for the major UN specialised organisations are summarised in the table below.

Budgetary Figures for UN Specialised Agencies

Organisation	Budget
Food and Agriculture Organisation (FAO)	Biennial budget 1998–99 U.S. $650 million
United Nations Educational, Scientific and Cultural Organisation (UNESCO)	Biennial budget 1998–99 U.S. $544,367,000
International Civil Aviation Organisation (ICAO)	Budget for 1999 U.S. $51,126,000; 2000 $52,281,000; 2001 $53,657,000
World Intellectual Property Organisation (WIPO)	Biennial budget 1998–99 383 million Swiss Francs
International Labour Organisation (ILO)	Biennial budget 1998–99 U.S. $481,050,000
United Nations Industrial Development Organisation (UNIDO)	Biennial budget for 1998–99 U.S. $129.5 million
World Health Organisation (WHO)	Biennial budget for 1998–99 U.S. $842 million
International Telecommunications Union (ITU)	Biennial budget for 1998–99 302.6 million Swiss Francs
International Maritime Organisation (IMO)	Biennial budget for 1998–99 £36,612,000
World Meteorological Organisation (WMO)	Triennial budget for 1996–99 255 million Swiss Francs
Universal Postal Union (UPU)	Budget for 1999—35,451,300 Swiss Francs

[2] G.A. res. 55/233, Proposed Programme Budget outline for the Biennium 2002–03.
[3] *ibid.*, n.1.

In dealing with budgetary problems our main emphasis will necessarily, if **17–003** only for reasons of space, be placed on the UN: reference to other organisations will, however, be made by way of contrast where important differences exist.

B. STRUCTURE OF BUDGETS

There is a certain attraction in the idea of a common budget for the UN **17–004** and the entire family of specialised agencies. Certainly some degree of liaison between them and the UN on budgetary matters seems desirable. Hence, whilst in the constitutions of the IMF and the IBRD nothing is said on this score, the constitutions of other agencies reflect to a greater or lesser extent this idea of budgetary co-operation. The ILO envisages "such financial and budgetary arrangements with the UN as may appear appropriate" (Article 13 (1)); UNESCO anticipates that any agreement with the UN may "provide for the approval and financing of the budget of the Organisation by the General Assembly of the United Nations" (Article X). As has been seen, the agreements with the UN concluded by the various specialised agencies envisage varying degrees of budgetary co-operation, ranging from full budgetary integration to the mere submission of the budget to the General Assembly, the latter having the right to make recommendations to the specialised agency concerned, although even this is lacking in the agreements with the Fund and Bank which stress the "autonomy" of the agencies and contemplate the submission of copies of the budget for information purposes only.[4] At the present, therefore, there is no common budget and the agencies are virtually autonomous. There are, of course, practical difficulties in the way of a common budget; for example, membership is not uniform. The overriding obstacle is more likely to be the desire for independence of the agencies.

(a) COMPOSITION OF BUDGETS

The budget of an international organisation will normally include the **17–005** administrative costs of running the organisation (salaries of staff, printing, costs of conference services, etc.) and costs that result from a decision of policy that a particular activity be undertaken. Within the United Nations the relation between policy and cost is emphasised by the provisions in the Financial Regulations[5] which provide that no organ "shall take a decision involving expenditure unless it has before it a report from the Secretary-General on the administrative and financial implications of the proposal,"[6] and that, where the proposed expenditure cannot be made from existing

---

[4] See Chap. 3.
[5] Financial Regulations of the General Assembly (ST/SGB/Financial Regulations/1/Rev. 1).
[6] Financial Reg. 13.1.

funds, it shall not be incurred until the General Assembly has made the necessary appropriation.[7]

17–006 It will rarely be necessary to apportion the total cost of the activities of an organisation amongst the members, for most will have, on the credit side, a limited income from sales of publications or even of stamps. The European Community affords the prime example of an organisation with sources of income independent of the contributions of members.[8] This income is derived from agricultural and sugar levies, custom duties (the Common Customs Tariff duties and other duties established in respect of trade with non-member countries) and part of the value added tax (VAT). The VAT resource derives from application of a uniform rate (1 per cent in 1999) to the VAT base, determined in a uniform manner for all member states. Certain activities may be self-supporting, as for example when the UN raised funds for the clearance of the Suez Canal in 1956 by levying a tax on shipping through the Canal. Exceptionally an organisation may be entirely self-supporting, and even have to deal with the problem of allocation of net income. The IMF, IBRD and IFC are all operating agencies that derive an income from charges on transactions, income from certain short-term investments and, in the case of the IFC, more general investments.[9] They, therefore, have no need to resort to budgetary contributions from members, and the contributions of members to these organisations, in the form of quotas or shares, should be distinguished sharply from the budgetary contributions made by members in other organisations, for they are not used for the upkeep of the organisation itself, but rather form the backing for the financial operations of the organisation. The European Coal and Steel Community is self-financing by means of levies raised on community coal and steel products.

17–007 By and large, however, international organisations necessarily are also dependent on contributions from members for the financing of their activities. The problem therefore arises of how the net cost shall be divided

---

[7] Financial Reg. 13.2. There is an express exception for the case when the Secretary-General certifies that provision can be made under the head "unforeseen and extraordinary expenses." The Assembly's concern over the Organisation incurring large, unforeseen expenses as a result of decisions taken by the Security Council in order to maintain international peace and security can be seen in its resolutions in the 15th and 16th Sessions requiring a special session of the Assembly to be convened where more than $10 million is involved.

[8] Chap. 6, para. 6–052. One must distinguish loans from income: the loans will have to be serviced from income and serve only as a temporary means of acquiring capital; for example, see the Bond issues by the UN to the value of $200 m. (authorised by the G.A. in 1961 by Resol. 1739 (XVI) to relieve the pressure caused by defaults on contributions towards UNEF and ONUC) carrying 2% interest and repayable over 25 years. For a survey of such borrowing techniques see Salmon, *Le rôle des organisations internationales en matière de prêts et d'emprunts* (1958).

[9] For a list of organisations which have in the past derived an income from their activities see Jenks., "Some legal aspects of the financing of international institutions," 28 TGS (1942) 87 at p. 93 *et seq.*

between members, and it is at this stage that one appreciates how very far the principle of equality of states is from affording a workable solution to this problem.

(b) APPORTIONMENT OF EXPENSES

The ITU and UPU follow a system whereby a number of "classes" are **17–008** established, 22 in the case of ITU and 11 in UPU.[10] Each member or associate member is, according to the class in which it finds itself, obliged to pay so many "units" of the total budget. In the ITU the members, on joining, simply inform the Secretary-General of the class in which they wish to be included. A similar system of free choice of contribution class also prevails in the UPU.[11]

The more usual solution is to fix a percentage quota for each member, **17–009** most usually done by the plenary organ,[12] which is made subject to review in the light of fluctuations in the number of members or the relative prosperity of the members, as is the case under Article 17 (2) of the UN Charter. Revision of scales is, in practice, an annual task of the Committee on Contributions, even though the Assembly's rules of procedure[13] (Rule 161) contemplate revision only every three years. In general nothing is said of the criteria by which the plenary organ shall determine the respective quotas of the members. Within the UN the criterion adopted has been "capacity to pay,"[14] this being deduced from total national income, per capita income, and from evidence of economic dislocation due to war and ability to acquire foreign currency. The "capacity to pay" formula has proved controversial, with a number of countries, notably the United States, advocating a better structured and more equitable assessment system based on the principle of sovereign equality of states. U.S. opposition to the "capacity to pay" formula has led to continual attempts by that country to

---

[10] In the case of the ITU, the last two classes of 1/8 and 1/16 units are reserved for least developed countries; in the case of the UPU, the final class of 1/16 units is reserved for these countries.

[11] The 1974 Lausanne Congress abolished the power previously held by the Congress of the UPU to classify member states in the different contribution classes.

[12] It may be noted that, in the ILO, it is by a two-thirds vote of the government delegates that all budgetary questions are settled, hence the "tripartite" vote is ousted in view of the fact that it is the governments alone that assume the financial responsibilities. Organisations such as ICAO, IMO or WMO, for example, in which the plenary organ does not meet annually either have to vote a budget on a biennial or triennial basis or delegate to an executive organ the power to approve expenditures within limits imposed by the plenary organ.

[13] Rules of Procedure of the General Assembly, doc. A/520/Rev. 15.

[14] G.A. res. 14A(I) and Rule 160 of the G.A. Rules of Procedure. This is not the only feasible basis, of course. Contributions to the Pan-American Railway Congress were based on miles of railroad in operation in each country; population has provided the basis for the Inter-American Statistical Institute—equal apportionment was used in the Central Commission for Navigation on the Rhine and in OPEC.

lower its assessment. The original contribution determined for the U.S. was 39.89 per cent, which it was successful in lowering to 33.33 per cent in 1954. On the admission of Italy and Japan to the UN in 1955, the U.S. unsuccessfully insisted on lowering its contribution to 30 per cent, though, by the early 1970s, its contribution was down to 31.52 per cent. The "upper and lower limits on contributions" were introduced in 1972, with the Assembly accepting the principle that one-quarter of the budget should be the maximum that any one member should be required to pay.[15] The current share of the UN budget borne by the U.S. is thus 25 per cent.[16] Recently, in the Fifth Committee debate on the scale of assessments at the General Assembly's 52nd session, the U.S. sought to reduce its 25 per cent ceiling rate to 22 per cent in 1998 and to 20 per cent by the year 2000.[17] This attempt, however, met with a cool response from the General Assembly, which determined that lowering the ceiling rate of 25 per cent would be "unreasonable and contrary to the principle of equity."[18]

17–010   So far as a minimum contribution is concerned, this was originally established at 0.04 per cent. In 1974 this minimum share was lowered to 0.02 per cent.[19] A General Assembly resolution of 1978[20] further reduced the floor to provide for a minimum contribution of no less than 0.01 per cent. The Assembly has recently lowered this to 0.001 per cent.[21] The scale of assessments adopted for 1998, 1999 and 2000[22] allows 34 countries to contribute at the minimum assessment level in 1999.

17–011   In order to finance activities of the UN before member states have paid their assessed contributions, the General Assembly establishes a Working Capital Fund. This fund is financed through advance payments of the member states in accordance with the scale of assessment. Peacekeeping operations are financed through a separate system to the UN regular budget but are still apportioned amongst the member states. For the purpose of apportionment of these expenses, member states are divided into four groups, namely (a) permanent members of the Security Council, (b) specifically named economically developed member states that are not members of the Security Council, (c) economically less developed member

---

[15] G.A. res. 2961B(XXVII) of December 13, 1972.

[16] Despite U.S. attempts to lower its contribution it remains the largest contributor. The other principal contributors are Japan (19.984%); Germany (9.808%); France (6.540%); Italy (5.432%); the United Kingdom (5.090%); Canada (2.754%); and Spain (2.589%). Collectively they account for more than 77% of the regular UN budget.

[17] UN: Post of Deputy Secretary General, New Scale of Assessments, 98–99 Budget, Anti-Terrorist Bombings Convention, M2 Presswire, December 29, 1997.

[18] ibid.

[19] G.A. Res. 2961 (XXVII).

[20] G.A. Res. 31/95.

[21] G.A. Res. 52/215 Scale of Assessment for the Apportionment of the Expenses of the United Nations (1997).

[22] ibid.

states and (d) economically less developed member states that are specifi-cally named (mostly least developed countries). Group D pay 10 per cent of their regular budget share; Group C pay 20 per cent; those in Group B 100 per cent and those in Group A pay 100 per cent plus the amounts not otherwise apportioned. In 1998 the total cost of all UN peacekeeping operations was some U.S. $907 million. The assessed share of the U.S., which is the largest contributor, currently stands at around 31 per cent.[23]

It need not be assumed that all expenses of an organisation have to be **17–012** brought within one overall budget to be apportioned according to one set of scales. The ITU had to deal with the problem of financing the different levels of conferences (plenipotentiary, world and regional), the Council and the sectors; this became a problem because participation is not confined to members, but extends to private operating agencies and international organisations.[24] Hence the solution was adopted of requiring expenses incurred by the regional conferences to be borne by all the members of the region concerned in accordance with their unit classification and, where appropriate, on the same basis by any members of other regions who participated in such conferences.[25] Private entities and international organ-isations are also to share in defraying the expenses of a Plenipotentiary Conference, sector or world conference in which they participate unless they have been exempted by the Council, subject to reciprocity.[26] Such contributions are based on the free choice of a class of contribution by the entity or organisation.[27]

Within the United Nations certain programmes were set aside as "extra- **17–013** budgetary" programmes to which members would contribute voluntarily and not as part of their normal budgetary commitment: UNICEF, UNRWA, UNITAR, are cases in point. Some programmes were in part financed in this way: UNDP and the office of the UN High Commissioner for Refugees are examples.

The crucial financial issue that arose for the UN became, however, the **17–014** financing of the Emergency Force (UNEF) and the Operation in the Congo (ONUC). For UNEF a "special account" was opened, and for ONUC an

---

[23] United Nations Department of Public Information, Setting the Record Straight: Facts about the United Nations, DPI/1753/Rev. 17, June 1999.
[24] Art. 19 and 23 Convention of the International Telecommunication Union (as adopted by the Additional Plenipotentiary Conference (Geneva, 1992) and amended by the Plenipoten-tiary Conference (Kyoto, 1994)).
[25] Art. 28 Constitution of the International Telecommunication Union (as adopted by the Additional Plenipotentiary Conference (Geneva, 1992) and amended by the Plenipotentiary Conference (Kyoto, 1994)).
[26] Art. 33 Convention.
[27] Id. The lower contribution classes of 1/4, 1/8 and 1/16 units may not be selected. For sectors, the amount of the contribution payable towards the expenses of each sector concerned is set at 1/5 of the contributory unit of the members. The amount of the contribution payable per unit towards the expenses of a conference or assembly is set by dividing the total amount of the budget of the conference or assembly by the total number of units contributed by the members as their share of union expenses.

"ad hoc" account. In relation to UNEF the Assembly decided to apportion expenses "in accordance with the scale of assessments adopted by the General Assembly for contributions to the annual budget. . . ."[28] Whilst this did not attempt to account for the entire cost (for considerable voluntary subscriptions were also made) the pattern was clear, and it was this same pattern that was eventually adopted for ONUC.[29] It was implicit in this pattern (and had been contended by the Secretary-General all along) that the expenses of both operations were "expenses of the organisation" within the meaning of Article 17(2) of the Charter and for which, therefore, a legal obligation to pay existed. By the end of 1961 the UN faced a deficit of $150 million due to defaulting members. The reasons for refusal to pay varied;[30] some states opposed the legality of the operations, some the principle that the cost of the operations was a collective responsibility to be assumed on the normal basis for assessment. Finally the matter was referred to the I.C.J. by the General Assembly in the form of a request for an advisory opinion on whether the expenditures authorised by the successive resolutions of the General Assembly "constitute 'expenses of the organisation' within the meaning of Article 17(2) of the Charter of the United Nations."

17–015   The opinion of the Court of July 20, 1962, on Certain Expenses of the United Nations distinguished three possible questions:[31] first, the identification of what are "expenses of the organisation"; secondly, the question of apportionment; and, thirdly, the interpretation of the phrase "shall be borne by the members." The Court stressed that it was concerned with only the first of these questions. The Court rejected the distinction alleged by some states between "administrative" and "operational" budgets, just as it rejected the contention of the Soviet Union that financing of measures designed to maintain international peace and security was a matter for the Security Council and not the General Assembly. It then proceeded to examine whether the particular expenses incurred fell within the purposes of the United Nations, for it conceded that they would have to do so to qualify as "expenses of the organisation." Applying a presumption that the actions taken were *intra vires* (since it fell to each organ to determine, in the first place, its own jurisdiction), the Court found that the expenses of both UNEF and ONUC were "expenses of the organisation" within the meaning

---

[28] Res. 1089 (XI), December 21, 1956.
[29] Res. 1619 (XVI), April 21, 1961; however, by para. 7, Belgium was called on to make a "substantial" contribution, and by para. 8 the assessments of members whose normal assessments ranged from 0.04 to 0.25, or who received technical assistance under the expanded programme in 1960 were reduced by 80%; members receiving technical assistance and assessed normally above 1.26 were reduced by 50%.
[30] See the full analysis in the Report of the Working Group of Fifteen on the Examination of the Administration and Budgetary Procedure of the UN (A14971), November 15, 1961.
[31] (1962) I.C.J. Rep. 151. On the question of the division of powers between the Security Council and the General Assembly, with which the opinions dealt at length, see *ibid.*, p. 51.

of Article 17 (2) which, therefore, the Assembly had the right to apportion. The court did not advise that the method of apportionment must be the same as that for the regular budget.

(c) PROCEDURE FOR SETTING BUDGETS

The preparation of the budget estimates within the UN is the task of the **17–016** Under-Secretary for Administration and Management, the head of the Programme, Planning and Budgetary Board founded in 1982. The board sets up a medium term plan[32] and prepares the draft budget on the basis of proposals made by the departments. The draft is developed on the basis of a so-called "budget outline," prepared with the participation of the Advisory Committee on Administrative and Budgetary Questions (ACABQ)[33] and the Committee for Programme and Co-ordination (CPC),[34] and submitted to the General Assembly one year in advance of the draft budget.[35] The draft budget estimates will include the original estimates representing the cost of implementing decisions taken during the financial year to which the budget relates, revised budget estimates to cover new decisions, and supplementary estimates to cover "unforeseen or extraordinary expenses" arising after the budget has been voted.[36]

The estimates are reviewed successively by the ACABQ, the CPC, the **17–017** Fifth Committee of the Assembly, and finally by the Assembly. In one sense the Advisory Committee and the Fifth Committee duplicate each other's functions—the former has been called "little more than a Fifth Committee in microcosm"[37]—yet the smaller size of the former does enable it to spend more time on the budgetary problems than a plenary committee could manage. A critical question has always been how far the Advisory Committee and the Fifth Committee can, by reducing or eliminating an appropriation, interfere with or reverse a policy decision of another Main Committee or even the Assembly itself; in principle they should have no such power, and in the last resort the Assembly would be free to overrule and re-instate any items so affected. Clearly the final approval of the budget is, under Article 17 (1) of the Charter, a matter for the General Assembly, acting by a two-thirds majority vote.

Within the specialised agencies the preparation of the estimates is, **17–018** similarly, a task of necessity entrusted to the administrative head of the organisation. This is expressly recognised in the constitutions of the ILO,

---

[32] Medium term plans are drawn up for six years and are intended to translate legislative mandates into programmes.

[33] The Committee was established by G.A. res. 14(I) of February 13, 1946 and currently consists of 16 representatives of states (see G.A. res. 32/103 of December 14, 1977).

[34] The CPC was originally a subsidiary organ of ECOSOC; since 1976 it has been a subsidiary organ of both ECOSOC and the General Assembly.

[35] G.A. res. 41/213 Annex of December 19, 1986.

[36] The financial year begins on January 1 but most organisations now operate on a biennial budget cycle, although supplementary estimates are voted for one year at a time.

[37] Singer, *Financing International Organisations: the UN Budget Process* (1961), p. 176.

FAO, WHO and IMO. Even in organisations like ICAO, where it is said that the council submits the budget, in practice the preparation of the initial proposals must lie with the Secretary-General. The actual approval or acceptance of the budget is a different matter, and this, without exception, is a matter for the plenary organ. Where variation does occur is in the extent to which some organ of limited composition intervenes in the process. For example, whereas in the ILO and the FAO the Director-General submits directly to the plenary organ,[38] in WHO[39] and IMO[40] the executive head submits through the Executive Board and Council respectively. In IMO, where, as we have seen, the Council is given a strong position generally in relation to the Assembly, the former is expressly empowered to submit its comments and recommendations to the Assembly.

C. Control over Budgetary Expenditure

17–019 Administration of the budget of an international organisation is generally placed in the hands of the executive branch of the organisation, headed by its chief executive officer. In the absence of constitutional provisions, administration of the budget will largely be governed by the financial rules and regulations (or their equivalent) of the organisation.[41] Within the UN, implementation of the regular budget rests with the Under Secretary-General for Administration and Management. The Under Secretary-General has responsibility for ensuring that the expenses of the organisation remain within its framework of resource allocation. New programmes requiring funding may not be added or, existing programmes reformulated, without the consent of the General Assembly.

17–020 Within the UN, both internal and external auditing of the implementation of the budget takes place. The internal audit is carried out through a special audit service under the authority of the Secretary-General. The audit department is required to review and comment upon the regularity of all transactions, the conformity of obligations and expenditure with the appropriations, and the economic use of the UN's resources in general.[42] The external audit of the accounts of the UN, and its funds and programmes, is conducted by a Board of Auditors, composed of representatives from three member states, who are the Auditor-Generals of their respective states (or officials having an equivalent position).[43] Board

---

[38] Art. 13(2) and Art. XV111(1), respectively, of the ILO Constitution and the FAO Constitution.

[39] Art. 55 of the WHO Constitution.

[40] Art. 50 of the IMO Constitution.

[41] For the UN these are the Financial Regulations of the General Assembly (ST/SGB/Financial Regulations/1/Rev. 1) and the Financial Rules of the Secretary-General (ST/SGB/Financial Rules/1/Rev. 3, (1985)).

[42] Financial Regulation 10.1 and Financial Rule 11.12.

[43] The Board was established in 1946 by G.A. res. 74(I).

representatives are appointed for three-year terms on the recommendation of the Fifth Committee. The Board submits reports to the General Assembly either annually or biennially, depending on the financial periods of the respective organisations subject to audit. The report indicates expenditures not properly substantiated, any incidence of fraud, wasteful or improper expenditure, expenditure likely to commit the organisation to outlay further on a large scale, expenditure in excess of appropriations and not in accordance with the intention of the General Assembly and any defect in the general system governing the financial control of receipts and disbursements or of supplies and equipment. Reports, and the accounts of the organisation, are adopted by resolution of the General Assembly.

A question arises as to the scope, if any, for challenges to expenditures **17–021** authorised by the plenary body of the organisation. A similar issue has arisen in the European Community context, where budgetary authority is shared between the European Parliament and the Council. An annual budget is proposed by the Commission, which then has to be adopted by the Council and ultimately by the European Parliament, with the signature of the President of the European Parliament bringing the budget into effect. The Council has the final say on compulsory expenditure (essentially agricultural spending and costs arising from international agreements), whereas the parliament has the final say on all other expenditure (non-compulsory expenditure). Disputes between the parliament and the council over the distinction between compulsory and non-compulsory expenditure led to the parliament rejecting the 1980 budget, the 1983 supplementary and amending budget and the 1985 budget. In 1986 the parliament incorporated non-compulsory expenditure in the budget in excess of the amount fixed by the Commission, without obtaining the consent of the Council. The Council challenged the act of the president of the parliament declaring the budget for 1986 finally adopted and was successful in obtaining an annulment from the ECJ[44] The conflict between the parliament and the council over the budget has been much reduced in recent times as a result of an interinstitutional agreement[45] concluded in 1988 and renewed in 1993. The agreement sets a framework for determining the size of the budget and the spending ceilings for the main policy areas.

In the UN context, the issue of *ultra vires* expenditure was obliquely **17–022** raised in the *Expenses* case, where the I.C.J. found that the "expenses" of the organisation are the amounts paid out to defray the costs of carrying out the purposes of the organisation.[46] The implication from the I.C.J.'s

---

[44] Case 34/86 *Council v. Parliament* [1986] E.C.R. 2155.
[45] Interinstitutional Agreement of 1988, [1988] OJ L185/33.
[46] *Op. cit.,* n. 31 at p.158.

advisory opinion is that if expenditure is made for a purpose which not one of the purposes of the UN it is an *ultra vires* expense.[47] However, provided the expenditure is made in pursuance of an action within the scope of the organisation's functions, the fact that it is initiated or carried out by an organ acting beyond the scope it powers does not deprive the expenditure of its characterisation as an "expense" of the organisation.[48]

D. Legal Consequence of Failure to make Budgetary Contributions

17–023 At least until the dispute over UNEF and ONUC, the principle had generally been accepted that, once apportioned, the budgetary contribution became payable as a matter of legal obligation.[49] In the *Expenses* case the Court did not, strictly, deal with this question, although it instanced decisions under Article 17 as examples of decisions of the Assembly which have "dispositive force and effect,"[50] and referred to its previous opinion[51] that once obligations towards third parties are incurred by the Secretary-General, on the authority of the Security Council or General Assembly, the Assembly "has no alternative but to honour these engagements."[52] In his separate opinion Sir Gerald Fitzmaurice regarded the legal obligation as arising from the decision to take a given course of action, and not from the decision on apportionment: hence, in his view, the obligation arose from Article 25 when such decisions were taken by the Security Council. Even when action was undertaken on a mere recommendation of the General Assembly, then, for Sir Gerald, the obligation was equally imposed on all members, whether dissenting or not, for such was the essence of a majority vote.[53]

---

[47] In a separate opinion Judge Spender was of the view that acts amounting to *ultra vires* expenditure would include acts done by the Secretary-General that were outside the scope of his apparent authority, but not those which were within the scope of his apparent authority. *ibid.*, at p.183.

[48] *ibid.*, at p.168.

[49] For this reason the kind of provision that is found in Art. 33(3) of the ITU Convention, imposing an interest rate of 3% per annum during the first six months and 6% per annum from the beginning of the seventh month on amounts due from members is, whilst exceptional, perfectly logical. Once paid, the sums become the property of the organisation in question and do not remain the property of the contributor but are entrusted to the organisation for the achievement of its aims and purposes. Hence it should follow that any surplus is not, as a matter of right, returnable to contributing members; however, the League of Nations' financial regulations provided for such a return, and have been criticised on that account. Similarly, when withdrawal is permitted, it is frequently provided that this is subject to the fulfilment of any outstanding financial obligations of the member towards the organisation; there is no question of a right to a refund.

[50] *Op. cit.*, n. 31 at p. 163.

[51] *Effect of Awards of the UN Administrative Tribunal* (1954) I.C.J. Rep. 59.

[52] *Op. cit.*, n. 31 at p. 170.

[53] *ibid.*, at pp. 208, *et seq*. Note his qualifications where the resolution consists solely of the provision of finance, or when the functions are merely permissive and not mandatory.

Despite this, certain member states, which are not strictly bound by an **17–024** advisory opinion,[54-55] did not regard this opinion as imposing a legal obligation to pay the contributions, even though the Assembly "accepted" the opinion by resolution of December 19, 1962, by 76 votes to 17, with eight abstentions. The crucial test came in 1965 when the Secretary-General reported that 16 states, including France and the former USSR, were in arrears in an amount exceeding their assessed contributions for the preceding two years. As we have seen, following U.S. capitulation, the General Assembly declined to apply the sanction of deprivation of vote in the Assembly under Article 19 of the Charter.[56] More importantly than the U.S. capitulation, however, was the reservation which the U.S. attached to it, allowing itself the right to claim exemption from the principle of collective financial responsibility in the future, should it see overriding reasons.[57]

Up until the mid 1980s the U.S. had been a punctual remitter of its UN **17–025** dues but from that time onwards the largest contributor to the UN began a policy of selective withholdings of its assessed contribution. These withholdings were spurred by its own budget deficits and disapproval of the steeply rising costs of international organisations, as well as disagreement with the political programme content of a number of General Assembly resolutions. As a result of withholdings the UN estimates that the U.S. owed U.S. $1.6 billion as of May 31, 1999, $620 million for the regular budget and $1.02 billion for peacekeeping and international tribunals.[58] By the end of 1998 the U.S. had paid just enough to the UN to avoid the possibility of an Article 19 scenario arising. The U.S. had been warned that it needed to pay at least $300 million by the end of 1999 to avoid losing its voting rights in the General Assembly.[59]

The reluctance of the General Assembly to apply the Article 19 sanction **17–026** had raised the question of whether member states were under an unqualified obligation to pay assessed contributions, or whether there were circumstances in which assessed contributions could be legally withheld. Commentators have generally favoured the view that a legal right to withhold payment cannot be inferred from the reluctance on the part of member states to apply Article 19.[60] The numerous provisions on suspen-

---

[54-55] Chap. 13, para. 13–048.

[56] For more on Article 19 and similar provisions see Chap. 16, paras 16–018 *et seq.*

[57] The so-called "Goldberg Corollary" see UN Doc. A/5916/Add. 1 (1965).

[58] United Nations Department of Public Information, *Setting the Record Straight: the UN Financial Crisis*, DPI/1815/ Rev. 16, June 1999 (hereafter "UN Financial Crisis").

[59] FT Asia Intelligence Wire, "U.S. again told to pay dues to U.N.", The Hindu, October 29, 1999.

[60] Amerasinghe, *Principles of the Institutional Law of International Organisations* (1996), p. 316. For an alternate viewpoint, that withholding is justified to allow a member to protect itself against the tyranny of the majority, see Zoller, E., "The "Corporate Will" of the United Nations and the Rights of the Minority" (1987) 81 AJIL 610.

sion or even expulsion from membership as a sanction for non-payment of budgetary contributions[61] reinforce the view that the obligation to pay is a legal obligation. Although in recent years the General Assembly has applied the Article 19 sanction to a number of countries that have fallen more than two years behind in payment of their dues,[62] the sanction has never been applied to one of the major contributors. Nevertheless, the care with which the U.S. has avoided being more than two years in arrears may indicate that it is aware that the sanction could well be applied to major contributors for breach of obligation.[63]

E. Withholding of Assessed Contributions

17–027 Since the 1960s there has been a growing practice on the part of member states to withhold some or all of their assessed contributions to the UN.[64] At first these withholdings were selective, targeted to controversial peace-keeping operations or programmes that individual member states did not support. This reasoning underlay the U.S. withholdings in respect of the Law of the Sea Preparatory Commission,[65] programmes to protect the rights of Palestinian people[66] and the decision of the General Assembly to construct the headquarters of the Economic Commission for Africa in Addis Ababa, Ethiopia.[67]

17–028 In 1985 the U.S. instituted a more far-reaching withholding policy. Increasingly frustrated by the steeply rising UN budget and the fact that budget resolutions could be passed by votes of members who contributed only a small share of expenditure, the U.S. threatened to reduce its contribution to the UN budget by 5 per cent unless a system of weighted voting was adopted for budgetary questions.[68] While the Kassebaum-

---

[61] Chap 16, paras 16–034 *et seq.*

[62] See Williams, "A Billion Dollar Donation: Should the United Nations Look a Gift Horse in the Mouth?" (1999) 27 Ga. J. Int'l & Comp. L. 425. In 1999 two countries, Yugoslavia and Iraq, have already lost their voting rights owing $12.6 million and $9.1 million, respectively (Jane's Information Group Ltd, "America the deadbeat?", Foreign Report, October 14, 1999).

[63] Amerasinghe, *op. cit.,* n. 59.

[64] Specialised agencies of the UN have also been affected by budgetary withholdings. A particularly glaring case of budgetary result arose in 1970 when the U.S. stopped contributions to the ILO in an attempt to coerce the Director-General over his appointment of a Soviet Assistant D.G. See Schwebel, "The United States assaults the ILO" (1971) 65 A.J.I.L. 136, 137.

[65] See Statement of President Ronald W. Reagan, December 30, 1982, [1982] 2 PUB. PAPERS 162, reprinted in U.S. Mission to the United Nations, Press Release No. USUN 1–(83), January 3, 1983.

[66] 22 U.S.C. @ 287e note (1983 Supp.) (Pub. L. 98–164, sec. 114, 97 Stat. 1017, 1020, approved November 22, 1983).

[67] 22 U.S.C. @ 287e note (West Supp. 1986) (Pub. L. No. 99–93, sec. 114, 99 Stat. 405, 424, approved August 16, 1985).

[68] 22 U.S.C. @287e note (Supp. III 1985) known as the "Kassebaum-Solomon Amendment". See now US General Accounting Office, "United Nations: status of US contributions and arrears; Report to the Chairman of the Committee on International Relations, House of Representatives (1999, GAO/NSIAD-99-187).

Solomon Amendment was unsuccessful in forcing a change to the voting system within the UN, it did spur the General Assembly's acceptance of a package of reforms designed to rationalise UN spending and enhance consensus within the UN as far as budgetary questions are concerned.[69]

Other withholdings authorised by the U.S. Congress were non-specific **17–029** withholdings designed to address the U.S. budget deficit rather than to force policy change within the UN. In 1986 the Gramm-Rudman-Hollings Act[70] mandated a 4.3 per cent cut to almost all federal appropriations including those for international organisations. Withholding of assessed dues by its major contributors has brought the UN to the brink of financial crisis. To maintain liquidity the organisation has been forced to borrow periodically from peacekeeping funds. This has entailed the organisation being unable to reimburse promptly countries that provide troops and equipment for such operations. By the end of 1998 the UN owed 73 countries a total of $872 million for troops and equipment.[71]

Under the leadership of the current Secretary-General, Kofi Annan, **17–030** drastic savings measures have been implemented, especially in the area of personnel expenditure, to address concerns of members concerning budgetary inefficiencies and bureaucratic waste within the UN. The current biennial budget is a zero-growth plan that starts off with $100 million less in appropriations than for the 1994–95 biennium.[72] Despite this unprecedented reform process to address U.S. concerns about the financial accountability of the UN, the U.S. has continued to withhold assessed amounts from the UN. New attempts to influence the policy of the organisation through budgetary pressure have emerged with the U.S. House of Representatives seeking to condition the payment of 1999 dues on the basis that no U.S. funds are spent on family planning clinics offering abortions in other countries.[73] Indeed it may be to the advantage of major contributors, such as the U.S., to continue to keep the UN on the brink of financial disaster, allowing them to exercise a degree of control over the organisation that cannot be achieved through the multilateral forum of the General Assembly.[74]

---

[69] G.A. res. 41/213, 16 Dec. 1986. A central element of this package is that the 34 member CPC will be involved in the budget development process and is supposed to work on the basis of consensus.

[70] Balanced Budget and Emergency Deficit Control Act of 1985, Pub. L. No. 99–177, 99 Stat. 1037 (codified principally at 2 U.S.C. @ 901).

[71] UN Financial Crisis, *op. cit.*, n. 57.

[72] *ibid.*

[73] This is despite the Senate authorising immediate payment of an amount of $926 million to avert a loss of voting rights in the General Assembly. See Kenna, "Contrite U.S. Politicians Slam Non-Payment of UN Dues", The Toronto Star, November 4, 1999; "US Faces Loss of Voting Rights at UN General Assembly", The Bulletin's Frontrunner, October 28, 1999.

[74] See Cardenas, "Financing the United Nations's Activities: A Matter of Commitment" (1995) U. Ill. L. Rev. 147, who suggests that there may be a "power-game" pattern where major contributors "rescue" the UN from a financial crisis that they have precipitated with payments tied to policy goals.

17–031   The general view expressed by commentators is that withholding of an assessed contribution by a member state for any reason, let alone disagreement as a minority with the decisions of the UN, is illegal in light of the legal obligation of members to pay assessed dues to the UN.[75] Despite this, on a practical level, withholding policies of member states, and particularly those of the U.S., have achieved some degree of success in influencing decisions of the international body.[76] Galey[77] argues, however, that while withholding actions by states have contributed to changes in the rules and procedures of the UN, they have not brought about fundamental changes to the regime's norms and principles.

---

[75] Amerasinghe, *op. cit.,* 49; note, however, Zoller, *op. cit.,* n. 59 at 631–2 who argues that the power to withhold assessed dues is an inherent right of UN membership to keep the organisation from turning into a "super-state".

[76] Examples include reforms to the budget development process and reforms within the UN to increase accountability and bureaucratic waste. U.S. withholding of dues is also alleged to have been central in preventing the re-election of former Secretary-General Boutros-Boutros Ghali in 1996 (see Williams, *op. cit.,* n. 61).

[77] Galey, "Reforming the Regime for Financing the United Nations", (1988) 31 How. L.J. 543.

INDEX

(All references are to paragraph numbers)